HOW TO WRITE CORRECT ENGLISH

(APPLIED ENGLISH GRAMMAR)

Rajendra Prasad Sinha, MA
Ex-Chairman,
Bihar College Service Commission

Bharati Bhawan
PUBLISHERS & DISTRIBUTORS

Published by

BHARATI BHAWAN (Publishers & Distributors)

www.bharatibhawan.in email: editorial@bbpd.in

4271/3 Ansari Road, Daryaganj, NEW DELHI 110 002, Phone: 23286557
A-61 B/2 Sector 63, NOIDA 201 307, Phone: 4757400
Thakurbari Road, PATNA 800 003, Phone: 2670325
10 Raja Subodh Mallick Square, KOLKATA 700 013, Phone: 22250651
No. 98 Sirsi Circle, Mysore Road, BENGALURU 560 018, Phone: 26740560

First edition 1956
Twenty-first revised edition 1991
2023 print

How to Write Correct English (Anglo-Hindi)
Printed at Bharat Printers, Patna-800 004

PREFACE

The book has been designed to meet the requirements of the students who wish not only to score high marks in grammar but also to speak and write correct English; and correct English, in my opinion, is neither too loose a colloquial style which defies grammar nor too pure a grammar which refuses to recognise idioms established by usage. It is, on the contrary, a happy fusion of the two, for even dynamic neutrality or peaceful co-existence is not enough.

An attempt has, therefore, been made to find a golden mean between distilled purism and unbridled colloquialism. I should naturally hope that it would very well serve as a *utility reference book* in schools and colleges, and herein, I should plead, lies the justification for avoiding English as the medium of writing. To some, however, the very idea of English grammar in Hindi may appear to be audacious and even ridiculous. Call it what you will, but you shouldn't shut your eyes to the fact that to an average student a book in English, and that, too, on grammar, is a red rag to a bull. The result is that, in spite of a delicious flood of books, they get not even a drop to drink. What to do then? Do you propose to *make* them read books they can't understand? You can *make* one weep and even laugh but not sing, and is not reading a sort of singing to oneself? I can't say whether this book will be read without tears. It is for my readers to judge.

Summer, 1956 **R P Sinha**

TWENTY-FIRST EDITION

For this new edition the book has been thoroughly revised and enlarged in the light of new courses of studies of different Universities of India. New chapters on *Expansion, Non-finite Verbs, Time and Tense and Verbs: Voice* have been added and the chapter on *Analysis* has been recast to meet the requirements of students preparing for various university and competitive examinations. I am indebted to colleagues and friends for the wealth of suggestions.

May 1, 1991 **R P Sinha**

CONTENTS

❐

BOOKS CONSULTED

1. *Webster's New International Dictionary, Vols. I-IV*
2. *The Shorter Oxford English Dictionary, Vols. I-II*
3. *A Dictionary of Modern English Usage*—H W FOWLER
4. *King's English*—H W FOWLER
5. *Good English*—G H VALLINS
6. *Better English*—G H VALLINS
7. *A Higher English Grammar*—L TIPPING
8. *Senior Course in English Composition*—SOARES and MAZUMDAR
9. *English Idioms*—MCMORDIE
10. *English Grammar Series Bk. IV*—J C NESFIELD
11. *Modern English Grammar*—J C NESFIELD
12. *Errors in English Composition*—J C NESFIELD
13. *Aids To The Study and Composition of English*—J C NESFIELD
14. *Senior Course of English Composition*—J C NESFIELD
15. *Word Power*—NORMAN LEWIS
16. *Teach Yourself Grammar*—G S HUMPHREYS
17. *English Grammar*—G WHITAKER-WILSON
18. *How To Write English*—HUGH JARRETT
19. *Current English Usage*—F T WOOD
20. *College Composition*—H MARTIN
21. *A Manual of Advanced English*—BERNARD BLACKSTONE
22. *The English We Use*—R A CLOSE
23. *The Oxford English Course for Secondary School*—H B DRAKE
24. *A guide to Patterns and Usage in English*—A S HORNBY
25. *Living English Structure*—W S ALLEN
26. *Transformational Grammar And the Teacher of English*—OWEN THOMAS
27. *Introduction To Tagmemic Analysis*—WALTER A COOK

❒

It is necessary to know grammar, and it is better to write grammatically than not, but it is well to remember that grammar is common speech formulated. Usage is the only test.

— Somerset Maugham

Chapter I

TEST YOURSELF

I. *Correct or justify the following sentences.*

1. More books than one was bought.
2. There are no water in these rivers.
3. A greater part of the mangoes is rotten.
4. A number of boys and girls has come.
5. Fish and chips is ready now.
6. He as well as I am guilty.
7. There are still lots to do.
8. The jury was divided in their opinions.
9. What I need most are clothes and books.
10. The poet and scholar are dead.
11. Each of them have finished their work.
12. I am one of those who am of another opinion.
13. We each has a problem.
14. What proof is your tears?
15. Bread and butter are costly articles of food.
16. No boy and no girl have come.
17. She needs not write any more.
18. If I was he, I would not do it.
19. Neither of the roads are safe.
20. More than one boys were present there.
21. Our only guide were the stars.
22. Nothing but umbrellas are seen here.

II. *Match A with B, so as to make correct sentences.*

A	B
Nothing but trees	are seen.
He and I	is walking.
Each of them	have come.
Can you see what appears	to be boats?
A number of leaders	has arrived.
The eyes of this ant	is seen.
She as well as I	are singing.
Do you see what appear	to be a bird?

SYNTAX

Syntax का अर्थ होता है वाक्य-विचार। वाक्य पर विचार करते समय हमारा ध्यान सबसे पहले Subject और Verb पर जाता है। यहाँ एक बात ध्यान देने योग्य है। हिन्दी तथा उर्दू में क्रिया पर कभी तो कर्ता का प्रभाव पड़ता है और कभी कर्म का, पर कभी-कभी न तो कर्ता का प्रभाव पड़ता है और न कर्म का ही। अँगरेजी में क्रिया पर केवल कर्ता का प्रभाव पड़ता है, कर्म का नहीं। हिन्दी और अँगरेजी में यह एक महान अंतर है। हिन्दी और अँगरेजी में एक दूसरा अंतर भी है। हिन्दी की क्रिया के लिंग और वचन दोनों होते हैं, अर्थात क्रिया एकवचन या बहुवचन होती है और साथ ही पुँल्लिंग या स्त्रीलिंग भी। अँगरेजी की क्रिया एकवचन या बहुवचन तो अवश्य होती है, पर पुँल्लिंग या स्त्रीलिंग नहीं। इन अंतरों को ध्यान में रखकर हम यहाँ Subject और Verb से संबंधित कुछ नियमों पर विचार करें।

Agreement: Subject and Verb

S—S : P—P

वाक्य के Subject और Verb के बीच मेल (Agreement) का संबंध रहना आवश्यक है—

The Verb must agree with its Subject in Number and Person. —NESFIELD

इस नियम के अनुसार Verb का Number/Person वही होता है जो वाक्य के Subject का रहता है। इसलिए Singular Subject के साथ Singular Verb और Plural Subject के साथ Plural Verb आता है। वाक्य के Verb की कोई अपनी अलग हस्ती नहीं होती। वह सदा Subject पर निर्भर रहती है। इसलिए S—S और P—P सदा याद रखें।

S का अर्थ है Singular और P का Plural. इसलिए Singular Subject के साथ सदा Singular Verb का प्रयोग करें और Plural Subject के साथ Plural Verb का; जैसे—

1. Mohan writes.
2. Sita plays.
3. Karim dances.
4. Manju sings.

इन वाक्यों के Subjects (Mohan/Sita/Karim/Manju) Singular हैं। इसलिए यहाँ Singular Verbs (writes/plays/dances/sings) का प्रयोग हुआ है।

अब इन वाक्यों को देखें—

1. Boys write.
2. Girls play.
3. Actors dance.
4. Women sing.

इन वाक्यों के Verbs (write/play/dance/sing) Plural हैं। क्यों? इसलिए कि इनके Subjects (boys/girls/actors/women) Plural हैं। ये सभी वाक्य शुद्ध हैं, क्योंकि S—S : P—P को ध्यान में रखा गया है।

अब, इन वाक्यों को लें—

1. Players runs. 2. Women sings.

3. Mohan write. 4. Manju laugh.

यहाँ पहले दो वाक्यों के Subjects (players/women) Plural हैं, पर Verbs (runs/sings) Singular हैं। यहाँ P—P के बदले P—S हो गया है, अर्थात Plural Subjects के साथ Singular Verbs का प्रयोग कर दिया गया है। इसी प्रकार, तीसरे तथा चौथे वाक्यों में Singular Subjects (Mohan/Manju) के साथ Plural Verbs (write/laugh) का प्रयोग हो गया है, अर्थात S—S के बदले S—P हो गया है। इसलिए ये चारों वाक्य अशुद्ध हैं।

NOTE—यहाँ एक बात ध्यान देने योग्य है। जब Verb में s या es लग जाता है, तब वह Singular हो जाता है; जैसे—

Plural	Singular
write	writes
cry	cries

चूँकि Writes और cries में s/es लगा हुआ है, इसलिए ये Singular हैं। पर, write/cry में s/es लगा हुआ नहीं है, इसलिए ये Plural हैं। इसका अर्थ यह है कि writes/cries आदि का प्रयोग Singular Subjects के साथ होता है, पर write/cry आदि का Plural Subjects के साथ। यह नियम Noun के नियम का ठीक उलटा है। Noun में s/es लगाकर हम उसे Plural बनाते हैं, पर Verb में s/es लगाकर Singular.

Noun + s/es = Plural

Verb + s/es = Singular

Noun और Verb के इस रूप-परिवर्तन का सदा ध्यान रखें—

Nouns		Verbs	
Singular	**Plural**	**Plural**	**Singular**
book	books	go	goes
toy	toys	try	tries
bench	benches	laugh	laughs

....

EXERCISE

I. *Correct the following sentences.*

(1) Children is playing. (2) Why is these women laughing? (3) These leaves is green. (4) Teachers loves good students. (5) Stars shines at night. (6) The sun rise in the east. (7) Aeroplanes carries men and good. (8) All the students and teachers likes this book.

II. *Fill in the blanks with a subject from the box.*

Nights	Light	Bees	A child
Animals	Horses	A rose	Babies

1. ...... travels faster than sound.
2. ...... have no horns.
3. ...... are cooler than days.
4. ...... live on grass.
5. ...... give us honey.
6. ...... smells sweet.
7. ...... tries to rise but falls.
8. ...... cry for milk.

III. *Fill in the blanks with a verb give in brackets.*

1. These books ...... to me. (belong, belongs)
2. Why ...... these children crying? (is, are)
3. How many boys ...... there? (was, were)
4. His teeth ...... broken. (was, were)
5. These sheep ...... innocent. (is, are)

....

EXCEPTIONS
to
S—S : P—P Formula

इस नियम के तीन अपवाद हैं—

Exception I. *Dare not* and *need not*.

ये दो ऐसे Verbs हैं जो Singular Subject के साथ भी Plural Number में ही रहते हैं। इन वाक्यों को लें—

1. He need not go.
2. She dare not oppose me.

इन वाक्यों के Subjects (he/she) Singular हैं, पर Verbs (need/dare) Plural हैं, क्योंकि इनके आगे not लगा हुआ है। इस नियम पर प्रकाश डालते हुए कहा गया है—

The third person singular is 'need' and not 'needs' just as 'dare' is used for 'dares' provided it is followed by a negative—He need not *do any more work. He* dare not *leave the room.*

—J C Nesfield

NOTE—dare और need के संबंध में एक-दो और बातों का भी ध्यान रखें—

(i) जब इनके साथ not नहीं लगा रहता, अर्थात जब वाक्य affirmative रहता है, तब ये, सामान्य नियम के अनुसार, Singular Subject के साथ Singular रूप में और Plural Subject के साथ Plural रूप में रहते हैं; जैसे—

1. He needs.
2. They need.
3. He dares.
4. They dare.

(ii) जब वाक्य में Verb 'do' का प्रयोग होता है और not का स्थान dare/need के पहले रहता है, तब इनका प्रयोग, सामान्य नियमानुसार, Singular Subject के साथ Singular रूप में और Plural Subject के साथ Plural रूप में होता है; जैसे—

One **does not need to know** anything ... . —T S ELIOT

इस वाक्य में Verb 'do' का प्रयोग हुआ है और not का स्थान need के पहले है। इसलिए यहाँ Singular Subject (one) के साथ Singular Verb (does not need) आया है। यदि इस वाक्य में Verb 'do' का प्रयोग नहीं होता और not का स्थान need के बाद होता, तो यह वाक्य इस प्रकार का हो जाता—

One **need not know** anything ... .

Exception II. Subjunctive Mood of Verb: Supposition

Subject और Verb से संबंधित सामान्य नियम का दूसरा अपवाद यह है कि Subjunctive Mood रहने पर अर्थात वाक्य से कोरी कल्पना या असंभव शर्त (wish, condition, supposition) का भाव झलकने पर Singular Subject के लिए भी Plural Verb का प्रयोग होता है; जैसे—

1. *Life has now taken hold on him and tossed him into ... firmament, where he bursts into song as if* **he were** *combustible.* —D H LAWRENCE

2. If **it were** *so, poetry would cease to matter.* —F R LEAVIS

3. *The same fate would have overcome the pamphleteering of Defoe,* **were he** *not the author of* Robinson Crusoe *and* Moll Flanders; *or the pamphleteering of* Samuel Johnson, **were he** *not the hero of* Boswell. —T S ELIOT

इन सभी वाक्यों में Singular Subjects (He/It) के साथ Plural Verb (were) का प्रयोग हुआ है, जो शुद्ध है। क्यों? इसलिए कि इनसे शर्त या कल्पना का भाव झलकता है। कुछ और वाक्य लें—

1. I wish *I were* a king.
2. *Were he* a prince!
3. If *I were you,* I would do it.
4. I wish *it were* possible.
4. *Were she* a bird, she would fly to me.
6. He commanded as if *he were* my master

इन वाक्यों में भी Singular Subject के साथ Plural Verb (were) का प्रयोग शुद्ध है। क्यों? इसलिए कि इनसे ऐसी अभिलाषा (wish) या कल्पना (supposition) का भाव झलकता है जिसकी पूर्ति संभव नहीं। तो, इससे यह स्पष्ट हो जाता है कि असंभव शर्त या कोरी कल्पना के अर्थ में Rule of Agreement का Subject और Verb से संबंधित S—S : P—P का नियम भंग हो जाता है। कल्पनालोक में नियम का भंग होना स्वाभाविक है न!

Exception III. Subjunctive Mood of Verb: Wish

आशिष/इच्छा/अभिलाषा व्यक्त करने के लिए भी Singular Subject के साथ Plural Verb का प्रयोग होता है, जिसे Subjunctive Mood कहा जाता है। याद रखें कि केवल bless/live/save/help का ही ऐसा प्रयोग होता है, अन्य Verbs का नहीं; जैसाकि इन आचार्यों का मत है—

The Subjunctive form is almost dead in English, It survives in a few main sentences of **wish** *or* **desire** *like—God* **save** *the king.* —G H VALLINS: *Good English*

The Subjunctive Mood is in its death-throes and the best thing to do is to put it out of its misery as soon as possible. —SOMERSET MAUGHAM: *A Writer's Note-Book*

इन विचारों को ध्यान में रखकर Singular Subject के साथ भी bless/live/help/save (आशिष/इच्छा/अभिलाषा के अर्थ में) का प्रयोग Plural में करें; जैसे—

1. God *save* the king.
2. Lord *bless* you/*help* you.
3. Long *live* the king.
4. Long *live* our friendship.

. . . .

EXERCISE

Correct the following sentences.

(1) He needs not write more on this subject. (2) She dares not run away. (3) He need to work hard. (4) If I was you I would not agree to that foolish proposal. (5) If he was a bird, he would fly to his lady-love. (6) God saves the queen! (7) I would do it if I was he.

. . . .

तो इस प्रकार, इन अपवादों को छोड़कर, Rule of Agreement के अनुसार Subject के Number और Person पर Verb का Number और Person निर्भर रहता है। ऐसे ही Verb को Finite Verb कहा जाता है। Finite का अर्थ होता है सीमित (limited), इसलिए Finite Verb अपने Subject के द्वारा सदा सीमित रहता है। इसकी कोई अपनी अलग हस्ती नहीं होती। दूसरे शब्दों में, Finite Verb अपने Subject का सदा दास बनकर रहता है।

अब प्रश्न यह उठता है कि जब यह महत्त्वपूर्ण नियम इतना सरल है, तो फिर इसका उल्लंघन इतना क्यों होता है? इसके दो प्रमुख कारण हैं—

(क) कर्ता का पता नहीं लगना

(ख) कर्ता के वचन का पता ही नहीं चलना

इस रोग के ये दोनों ही कारण, वास्तव में, कीटाणु की तरह इतने सूक्ष्म और भयंकर होते हैं कि अच्छे लोग भी कभी-कभी इनके शिकार हो जाते हैं। इस समस्या की चर्चा महान आचार्यों के ही शब्दों में सुनें—

Verbs frequently change their forms and endings to make themselves agree with their nominatives. How necessary it is, then to know what is, and what is not, a nominative in a sentence! —COBBEIT: *A Grammar of the English Language*

..., and sometimes how difficult to determine its number and person!

—G H VALLINS: *Better English*

इन कठिनाइयों तथा उलझनों का ध्यान रखकर हम Subject और Verb से संबंधित नियमों की समीक्षा विस्तारपूर्वक करें और देखें कि भिन्न-भिन्न प्रकार के वाक्यों में Subject और Verb के बीच कैसा संबंध रहता है।

N + P + N and the Verb

Rule I. कुछ वाक्यों की बनावट इस प्रकार की होती है—
Noun + Preposition + Noun = (N + P + N); जैसे—

1. The merit *of* these books … .
2. The causes *of* war … .
3. The chairs *in* the corner *of* this room … .

ऐसे वाक्यों में Preposition के पहले आनेवाले Noun के Number और Person के अनुसार ही Verb का प्रयोग होता है। यदि वाक्य में एक से अधिक Preposition का प्रयोग हो (N + P + N + P + N + P + N + ...) तो सबसे पहले Preposition के पहले आनेवाले Noun के अनुसार Verb होता है; जैसे—

1. The *merit of* these books is well known.
2. The *cost of* production of consumer goods in all the countries is increasing.

यहाँ पहले वाक्य में एक Preposition (of) आया है और इसके पहले है एक Noun (merit), इसलिए यहाँ merit के अनुसार Singular Verb का प्रयोग हुआ है। दूसरे वाक्य में तीन Prepositions (of, of, in) आये हैं और सबसे पहले Preposition के पहले है एक Noun (cost), जिसके अनुसार Singular Verb (is) का प्रयोग हुआ है इन वाक्यों में books/goods के अनुसार Plural Verb का प्रयोग अशुद्ध होता। इसलिए ऐसे वाक्यों में Preposition के पहले आनेवाले Noun के अनुसार ही Verb का प्रयोग करें, Preposition के बाद आनेवाले Noun के अनुसार नहीं। ऐसा क्यों? इसलिए कि Preposition के बाद आनेवाला Noun कर्मकारक (Objective case) में रहता है, कर्ता कारक (Nominative case) में नहीं।

इस छोटे-से नियम को नहीं जानने से जो भूलें हो जाती हैं, उनके कुछ नमूने देखें—

1. The *details* of the incident *was* not known.
2. The *movement* of most animals *are* swift.
3. Military *help* from all the countries *were* received.
4. Your *views* on this subject *is* very old.
5. The *colour* of these pens *are* charming.

यहाँ पहले वाक्य में were का प्रयोग होना चाहिए, दूसरे में is का, तीसरे में was का और चौथे में are का तथा पाँचवें में is का।

....

EXERCISE

I. *Correct the following sentences.*

(1) The captain's comments in a newspaper on the preparation of the Test Matches for the present tour has been praised. (2) Economic co-operation between the two countries have increased. (3) The condolence messages received on the death of Pt Nehru speaks highly of his greatness. (4) The rule of this book is easy. (5) To these are added this.

(6) The smell of these flowers are very sweet. (7) The condition of people living in our villages are very bad.

II. *Fill in the blanks with a suitable Finite Verb.*

(1) The standard of answers ...... very low. (2) The standard of living of most of the people of the underdeveloped countries ...... not high. (3) Sweet ...... the uses of adversity. (4) My suggestions for improvement ...... accepted. (5) Too great a variety of studies ...... not very useful. (6) The cost of iron and cement ...... too high. (7) The colour and the smell of this flower ...... very pleasing.

....

Indefinite Number/Quantity + of + Noun

Rule II. कुछ वाक्यों की बनावट इस प्रकार की होती है—

Indefinite number + of + noun [*subject*]

Indefinite quantity + of + noun [*subject*]

1. a number of boys 2. a lot of books

2. a lot of poison 4. plenty of milk

ऐसे वाक्यों का कर्ता वह noun होता है, जो of के बाद (boys/books/poison/milk) आता है।

यह भी याद रखें कि indefinite number + of से अनिश्चित संख्या का बोध होता है और इसलिए of के बाद आनेवाला noun सदा Plural रहता है। पर indefinite quantity + of से अनिश्चित मात्रा/परिमाण का बोध होता है और इसलिए of के बाद आनेवाला noun सदा Singular रहता है। ऐसे वाक्यों के of का कोई अपना अलग अर्थ नहीं होता; जैसे—

a number of—बहुत all of—सब

a lot of—बहुत some of—थोड़ा

plenty of—बहुत heaps of—ढेर/बहुत

ऐसे वाक्यों का कर्ता वह noun होता है जो of के बाद आता है। इसलिए जब noun plural रहता है, तब verb हो जाता है plural और जब noun singular रहता है, तो verb हो जाता है singular, जैसे—

1. A number of *boys* have come. 2. A lot of *books* have been bought.

3. A lot of *milk* has been bought. 4. Plenty of *eggs* have been bought.

5. Plenty of *sugar* has been bought.

ऐसे वाक्यों में अनिश्चित संख्या (number) या मात्रा (quantity) बताने के लिए Noun/ Pronoun के पहले ये शब्द आते हैं—

a number of, a lot of, lots of, heaps of, plenty of, a quarter of, two-thirds of, three-fourths of, most of, some of, mass of, majority of, minority of, part of, per cent of, proportion of, all of, none of, both of, rest of, remainder of, a total of, half of, many of, much of, a handful of, a good deal of, a great deal of

इन वाक्यों को देखें—

1. *There* **are a large number** *of* **people** ... *who believe that all ills are fundamentally economic.* —T S ELIOT
2. *There* **were a number** *of such little* **reasons.** —ALDOUS HUXLEY
3. ... **a number** *of* **politicians were** *struggling to preserve the great traditions of republican Rome.* —H G WELLS
4. **A number** of **quotations are** added to show how common the abuse is ... . —H W FOWLER
5. **A large number** *of formal restrictons and ancient 'thou shalt nots' of academic grammar* **are** *now completely outmoded.* —NORMAN LEWIS
6. *Between them there* **is plenty** *of* **room** *for most talents to breathe freely.* —G B SHAW
7. *There* **are plenty** *of ecstatic* **instants** *which are valueless.* —I A RICHARDS
8. *A large* **proportion** *of these* **essays deal** *with ethical qualities.* —HUGH WALKER
9. *A large* **proportion** *of this northern* **army was** *British.* —H G WELLS
10. *A large* **part** *of the distinctive* **features** *of the mind* **are** *due to its being an instrument for communication.* —I A RICHARDS
11. *For some three or four hundred years a good* **part** *of* **Asia was** *under a kind of eclipse ... .* —JAWAHARLAL NEHRU
12. ... **most** *of human* **life has** *to disappear before he can do us a novel.* —E M FORSTER
13. *Most of* **those** *who use it* **are** *probably unaware that ... 'assets' is itself a singular.* —H W FOWLER
14. *The* **rest** *of the* **prose** *of the age* **is** *too voluminous.* —IFOR EVANS
15. *The* **majority** *of* **writers** *never* **pass** *that stage.* —EZRA POUND

इन सभी वाक्यों में of के बाद आनेवाले noun के अनुसार ही singular या plural Verb का प्रयोग किया गया है। कुछ और वाक्य लें—

1. A number of *boys are* absent.
2. A quarter of *it is* good.
3. A quarter of *them are* bad.
4. Two-thirds of the *site is* lovely.
5. Two-thirds of the *sites are* ugly.
6. The rest of the *book is* unfinished.
7. The rest of the *books are* unfinished.
8. Half *of the mango is* good.
9. Half of the *mangoes are* bad.
10. A part of the *mango is* rotten.
11. A part of the *mangoes are* rotten.
12. Lots of *men have* come.
13. Lots of *poison has* been prepared.
14. About 30 per cent of *votes have* been polled.
15. About 30 per cent of the *amount has* been spent.

इन वाक्यों में भी of के पहले Indefinite number/quantity का प्रयोग हुआ है। इसलिए of के बाद आनेवाले noun के अनुसार verb का प्रयोग हुआ है। आप भी इसी प्रकार वाक्य बनाएँ।

lots + infinitive

NOTE (a)—यदि 'lots' के बाद of के बदले Infinitive (to + verb) का प्रयोग हो, तो उसको (lots को) singular माना जाता है; क्योंकि Infinitive एक singular noun के बराबर होता है; जैसे—

1. There *is lots* to say. 2. There *is still lots* to do.

a number/the number

NOTE (b)—Number के पहले the या possessive adjectives (your, our या their) के आने पर verb सदा singular रहता है, क्योंकि वैसी अवस्था में वह (number) Indefinite Number का बोध नहीं कराता; जैसे—

1. **The number** *of potential poets born* **varies** ... *from age to age.*

—F R LEAVIS

2. **The number** *of persons interested in philosophy is always small.*

—T S ELIOT

इस प्रकार the number और a number में बहुत अंतर है। The number के साथ सदा Singular Verb का प्रयोग होता है, पर a number के साथ सदा Plural Verb का। क्यों? इसलिए कि the number का अर्थ होता है 'एक निश्चित संख्या' (figure). पर a number का अर्थ होता है 'बहुत' (many); जैसे—

1. A number of boys *have* come.—बहुत लड़के
2. The number of boys *is* increasing.—लड़कों की संख्या

यहाँ a number of boys का अर्थ है 'बहुत लड़के', पर the number of boys का अर्थ है, 'लड़कों की संख्या'। इन अर्थों का ध्यान रखकर ही इनके साथ verb का प्रयोग करें, नहीं तो भूल होने का खतरा पैदा हो सकता है।

NOTE (c)—यदि of के पहले the percentage (per cent नहीं) रहे, तो verb सदा singular होता है; जैसे—

1. The percentage of failures *is* small.
2. The percentage of good persons *is* very high.

....

EXERCISE

I. *Correct the following sentences.*

(1) The number of seats in all the colleges have been doubled. (2) A number of questions has been set. (3) Heaps of sand are lying on the bank. (4) The rest of what he said were

not heard. (5) Part of one of the lower galleries were occupied by musicians in the Elizabethan age. (6) Some of the original freshness of his works are still there. (7) Plenty of eggs is rotten. (8) There are still lots to decide.

Hints—(1) has; (2) have; (3) is; (4) was; (5) was; (6) is; (7) are; (8) is.

II. *Fill in the blanks with a suitable Finite Verb.*

1. There ...... a number of books in my library.
2. The number of fools in every society ...... large.
3. There ...... still lots to say on this point.
4. A greater part of the mangoes ...... rotten.
5. Two-thirds of the book ...... finished.
6. Most of his early youth ...... spent at home.

Hints—(1) are; (2) is; (3) is; (4) are; (5) is; (6) was

....

Singular Collective Nount + of + Noun

Rule III. कुछ वाक्यों की बनावट इस प्रकार की होती है—

Singular Collective Noun + of + Plural Noun

इन वाक्यों पर विचार करें—

1. *A team* of students has been selected.
2. *A set* of books has been bought.

ऐसे वाक्यों में Singular Verb का प्रयोग होना चाहिए। क्यों? इसलिए कि of के पहले Collective Noun के आ जाने से बहुत-सी वस्तुओं के एक समुदाय (collection) का बोध होता है और वह collection एकता (unity) का अर्थ सूचित करता है। ऐसे Plural Nouns एक सूत्र में बँधकर सिर्फ एक ही वस्तु (object) का बोध कराते हैं। जिन Plural Nouns से अनेकता (diversity) का बोध होता है, वे Collective Noun के द्वारा एकता (unity) प्राप्त कर लेते हैं। इसी एकता का अर्थ सूचित करने के लिए तो Plural Nouns को of से जोड़कर एक बना दिया जाता है न? यही कारण है कि ऐसे वाक्यों में Subject को Singular मानकर Singular Verb का प्रयोग किया जाता है।

इसलिए यदि of के पहले Singular Collective Nouns आएँ, तो Singular Verb का प्रयोग करें।

ध्यान दें कि ऐसे मुख्य Collective Nouns ये हैं—

a chain of, a garland of, a bouquet of, a set of, a series of, a team of, a batch of, a class of, a group of, a galaxy of, a bunch of, a band of, a herd of, a flock of

इन वाक्यों को देखें—

1. *Besides Hardy, Yeats and De La Mare, there* **was** *supposed to be a* **galaxy of** *Georgian poets.* —F R LEAVIS

2. *Then there* **is** *the* **central group of** *Georgian poets.* —F R LEAVIS

3. *On the other hand* **is** *a* **set of** *quite different factors.* —I R RICHARDS

4. *There* **is** *a large* **class of** *persons who regard any censure upon a great poet as a breach of peace ... .* —T S ELIOT

5. **A series of** *coincidences* **has** *permitted me to demonstrate the How To Read thesis in a medium nearer to poetry than painting is.* —EZRA POUND

कुछ और वाक्य लें—

1. A set of combs *has* been purchased.
2. A team of speakers *has* been selected.
3. A bunch of keys *is* lying there.

यहाँ Plural verbs का प्रयोग अनुचित होता।

. . . .

EXERCISE

I. *Match A with B to make correct sentences.*

A	B
A monkey	fly here and there.
There are	a set of books.
There is	a number of books.
Birds	jumps and runs.
The teeth of this baby	is lovely.
The colour of my dogs	are white.
Sweet is	the uses of adversity.
Sweet are	the milk of these cows.

II. *Fill in the blanks with a verb from the box.*

buy	sells	washes

1. He ...... clothes. 2. Sita ...... sweets. 3. We ...... books.

III. *Correct the following sentences.*

(1) A parcel of books have been received. (2) A basket of mangoes are lying there. (3) A chain of pearls have been prepared. (4) A band of musicians have been engaged. (5) A batch of delegates have been formed.

Hints—Use singular verbs in all the sentences.

. . . .

Collective Noun/Noun of Multitude and the Verb

Rule IV. जब वाक्य का Subject Collective Noun होता है और उसके बाद (of के द्वारा जुटा हुआ) कोई Plural Noun नहीं रहता, तब Verb के प्रयोग में एक कठिनाई सामने आ जाती है, क्योंकि वैसी अवस्था में उसे हम निस्सन्देह Singular या Plural नहीं मान सकते। ऐसा इसलिए होता है कि Collective Noun और Noun of Multitutde की सीमा निर्धारित नहीं है। आप ज़ानते हैं कि जब Collective Noun का प्रयोग Singular के अर्थ में होता है, तब उसे Collective Noun कहा जाता है, पर जब उसका प्रयोग Plural के अर्थ में हाता है, तब उसे Noun of Multitude के नाम से पुकारते हैं; जैसे—

government, board, staff, committee, company

अब समस्या यह खड़ी होती है कि किस अवस्था में इन्हें Collective Noun मानकर (अर्थात singular मानकर) Singular Verb का प्रयोग किया जाए और किस अवस्था में Noun of Multitude मानकर (अर्थात इन्हें plural मानकर) इनके साथ Plural Verb का प्रयोग किया जाए। नेसफिल्ड (Nesfield) साहब ने लिखा है—*The Jury were divided*, पर फाउलर (Fowler) साहब के मतानुसार *The Jury was divided* लिखना कहीं अच्छा होता।

जब इन महान आचार्यों के बीच इतना गहरा मतभेद है, तब साधारण लोगों का कहना ही क्या? वास्तव में, यह निर्णय करना कि किस अवस्था में इन्हें Singular और किस अवस्था में Plural माना जाए, कठिन है। इसलिए आप ऐसे संकट काल में एक सरल नियम की सहायता लें—आप अपने इच्छानुसार इन्हें Singular या Plural कोई एक मान लें और उस निश्चय पर दृढ़ होकर विश्वास के साथ Singular या Plural Verb तथा Pronoun का प्रयोग करें। इसका अर्थ यह है कि यदि आप इन्हें एक बार Singular मान लेते हैं, तो इनके साथ Singular Verb और Pronoun का प्रयोग आरंभ से अंत तक करें, पर यदि इन्हें आप Plural मानते हैं (क्योंकि आपकी ऐसी ही इ्च्छा है), तो इन्हें आरंभ से अंत तक Plural ही मानें। आप दोनों मजा एक साथ नहीं उठा सकते, अर्थात इन्हें आप एक बार Singular और दूसरी बार Plural नहीं मान सकते।

इन वाक्यों को देखें—

1. The Government *has* decided so in *its* own interest.
2. The Government *have* decided so in *their* own interest.

यहाँ पहले वाक्य में Government को Singular मानकर इसके लिए Singular Verb और Singular Pronoun का प्रयोग हुआ है। दूसरे वाक्य में Government को Plural मानकर इसके लिए Plural Verb और Plural Pronoun का प्रयोग किया गया है। इसलिए ये दोनों ही वाक्य शुद्ध हैं, पर ये हैं अशुद्ध—

1. The Government *has* decided so in *their* own interest.
2. The Government *have* decided so in *its* own interest.

यहाँ पहले वाक्य में Government को एक बार Singular मानकर इसके लिए Singular Verb का प्रयोग किया गया है, पर तुरंत ही लेखक ने इसे Plural मानकर इसके लिए Plural Pronoun (their) का प्रयोग कर दिया है। इससे यह स्पष्ट है कि लेखक के निर्णय में दृढ़ता और विश्वास की काफी कमी है। दूसरे वाक्य में भी ऐसा ही किया गया है। इसे पहले Plural माना गया है और फिर तुरंत Singular, तो Singular और Plural के बीच इस प्रकार असहाय होकर भटकना अनुचित है। इसलिए जब वाक्य में Collective Noun subject हो, तो आप एक बार यह दृढ़

निश्चय कर लें कि वह Singular है या Plural. यह आपकी इच्छा पर निर्भर है और इसमें शुद्ध और अशुद्ध प्रयोग का प्रश्न ही नहीं उठता। हाँ, एक बार जो निर्णय करें, उससे डिगें नहीं। इस संबंध में, आप इन मतों का ध्यान रखें—

Though Nouns of Multitude may be freely used with either a Singular or a Plural Verb, or be referred to by Pronouns of Singular or Plural meaning, they should not have both. —FOWLER: *King's English*

And again,

In general it may be said that while there is always a better and a worse in the matter, there is seldom a right and a wrong ... failure to abide by the choice when made and plunging about between 'it' and 'they', 'have' and 'has', 'its' and 'their', and the like, can only be called insult to the reader. —FOWLER: *MODERN ENGLISH USAGE*

The subject may be a collective noun, like congregation, council, federation, company, government, etc. In English usage the decision is left to the writer only; once having made it, he must stick to it .... But there is no rule. Usage changes: Sometimes the Singular is in fashion and sometimes the Plural. It is consistent respect for the decision that matters. —G H VALLINS: *Better English*

EXERCISE

I. *Correct the following sentences.*

(1) The committee are not unanimous in its opinions. (2) The Governing Body at its meeting today have decided to appoint a lecturer. (3) The Board has decided to elect their new members. (4) The public have cast its vote in favour of those who can help them in need. (5) The Teachers' Association has submitted a memorandum for the fulfilment of their demands. (6) The government has to do so in their own interest.

Hints—(1) are ... their or is ... its; (2) its ... has or their ... have; (3) has ... its or have ... their; (4) have ... their ... them or has ... its ... it; (5) has ... its or have ... their; (6) has ... it or have ... their

Weights and Measures and the Verb

Rule V. यदि वाक्य का Subject कोई ऐसा Noun हो जिससे निश्चित weights/measures/ amount/distance (नाप-तौल, परिमाण, रकम या दूरी) का बोध हो, तो Plural रहने पर भी ऐसे Subject के साथ Singular Verb का प्रयोग होता होता है। क्यों? इसलिए कि उससे एक निश्चित मात्रा या परिमाण (quantity) का बोध होता है, संख्या (number) का नहीं; जैसे—

1. *Ten miles is* a long way to walk.
2. *Five rupees is* equal to five hundred paise.

यहाँ पहले वाक्य का कर्ता miles है जो Plural है, पर इसके साथ Singular Verb (is) का प्रयोग हुआ है, क्योंकि यहाँ ten miles का अर्थ है—a distance of ten miles, जो एक स्थान की माप (measurement) बतलाता है। दूसरे वाक्य में rupees Plural है, पर इसके लिए Singular Verb (is) का प्रयोग हुआ है, क्योंकि इससे एक रकम (amount) का बोध होता है। इसी प्रकार ये वाक्य भी शुद्ध हैं—

1. Three *tons* of coal *is* enough for me.
2. Twenty *pounds is* a handsome amount.

यहाँ three tons से एक वस्तु की तौल (weight) का बोध होता है और twenty pounds से एक रकम (amount) का। इसलिए Plural रहने पर भी tons और pounds के लिए Singular Verb का प्रयोग हुआ है। ऐसा ही प्रयोग अच्छे लेखक करते हैं—

1. *Between 1630 and 1643* **£ 2,00,000** was spent in conveying 20,000 men, women and children to New England in 200 ships. —G M TREVELYAN
2. *Three thousand* **miles was** *a very long way* … —G M TREVELYAN

. . . .

EXERCISE

I. *Correct the following sentences.*

(1) Ten rupees were paid to him. (2) Sixty miles are a long distance. (3) There are five rupees in my pocket. (4) Three quintals of coal are my monthly requirement.

Hints—Use Singular Verbs in all the sentences.

II. *Fill in the blanks with a suitable Verb.*

(1) There …… ten rupees on the table. (2) Five kilos of rice …… purchased yesterday. (3) Ten miles …… not a long distance.

Hints—Use Singular Verbs in all the sentences.

. . . .

Names/Titles and the Verb

Rule VI. यदि वाक्य का Subject किसी व्यक्ति या देश का नाम (name) हो या किसी पुस्तक का शीर्षक (title), तो उसके लिए Singular Verb का प्रयोग होता है, क्योंकि उस Name या Title से केवल एक ही वस्तु का बोध होता है; जैसे—

1. The *United States of America is* a great country.
2. *Arabian Nights is* a popular book.
3. *Lamb's Tales From Shakespeare is* widely read.

इन सभी वाक्यों में Singular Verb का प्रयोग ही शुद्ध है, क्योंकि इनमें से प्रत्येक का Subject किसी देश या पुस्तक का नाम है। इनको पहचानने में कोई कठिनाई नहीं होती, क्योंकि ऐसी अवस्था में Names और Titles के सभी शब्द Capital Letters से शुरू होते हैं।

NOTE—आजकल खेलकूद (sports) की दुनिया में देश, प्रांत या क्षेत्र के नाम (name) भी Plural अर्थ में प्रयुक्त किये जाते हैं, जब उनसे एक Team का प्रयोग Noun of Multitude की भाँति Plural में होता है और इसलिए Plural Verb का प्रयोग होता है; जैसे—

1. *India have* lost by three wickets.
2. *Australia have* won.

इन वाक्यों में India/Australia के साथ Plural Verb का प्रयोग किया गया है जो शुद्ध है, क्योंकि यहाँ इनसे एक देश के नाम (name) का बोध नहीं होता, बल्कि एक Team का अर्थ सूचित होता है और इसलिए Noun of Multitude की भाँति Plural में प्रयुक्त होता है। ऐसी अवस्था में इनका प्रयोग Collective Noun के समान Singular अर्थ में करना जरा भद्दा लगता है।

EXERCISE

I. *Correct the following sentences.*

(1) *New Bearings* have been written by Leavis. (2) T S Eliot's *Selected Essays* are a standard book of criticism. (3) *Hard Times* by Dickens are worth reading. (4) *Aspects Of The Novel* have been written by Forster. (5) *Hard Times* are a great novel. (6) To Daffodils have been composed by Herrick. (7) Dickens have criticised utilitarian philosophy in *Hard Times.* (8) The United States of America are a big power.

Hints—Use Singular Verbs in all the sentences.

The Inseparables and Verb

Rule VII. कुछ Nouns ऐसे होते हैं जो सदा एक साथ जोड़े (pair) बनकर रहते हैं। उन्हें Inseparables (अभिन्न) कहा जाता है, क्योंकि उनका एक भाग दूसरे भाग से अलग नहीं होता। ये Nouns हैं—scissors, shears, trousers.

वाक्य में Subject की भाँति प्रयुक्त होने पर इनके साथ Plural Verb का प्रयोग होता है। इसका कारण यह है कि ये निस्सन्देह Plural हैं; पर यदि इनके पहले *a pair of* आए, तो Singular verb का प्रयोग होता है। क्यों? इसलिए कि वैसी अवस्था में इनके दोनों भागों से केवल एक वस्तु का बोध होता है; जैसे—

1. My *scissors* are sharp.
2. A *pair of scissors has* been purchased.
3. Your *trousers are* very loose.
4. A *pair of trousers has* been made for me.

NOTE—Whereabouts and Verb: Whereabouts के साथ singular या plural verb में से किसी का भी प्रयोग हो सकता है। पर singular verb का प्रयोग अधिक अच्छा माना जाता है; जैसे—Her whereabouts is/are still unknown.

The Hyphenated Expression

Rule VIII. कुछ वाक्यों में singular noun के बाद preposition आता है और उसके बाद उसी noun को दुहराया जाता है। शब्दों की ऐसी बनावट को Hyphenated Expression कहा जा सकता है; जैसे—row upon row; ship after ship.

ऐसे expressions के साथ Singular Verb का प्रयोग होता है—

1. *Ship after ship is* sailing by.
2. *One hour after another* (hour) *has* passed away.

Noun-equivalents and the Verb

Rule IX. यदि वाक्य का Subject कोई Noun-equivalent (Noun के समान प्रयुक्त होनेवाला infinitive/gerund/phrase/clause) हो, तो Verb Singular होता है; जैसे—

1. *To walk* is healthy.
2. *Walking* is a healthy exercise.
3. *How to do it is* a problem.
4. *That he is poor* is known to me.

यहाँ पहले वाक्य में 'to walk' एक Infinitive है, दूसरे में 'walking' एक Gerund, तीसरे में 'how to do it' एक Phrase और चौथे में 'that he is poor' एक Clause. ये सभी, Noun के समान, वाक्य के कर्ता हैं। इसलिए इनके साथ Singular Verb का प्रयोग हुआ है, जो शुद्ध है। यहाँ Plural Verb का प्रयोग अनुचित होता।

NOTE—यदि एक से अधिक clauses को and से जोड़ा जाए, तो verb होता है plural; जैसे—

Where she lives and what she does *are* not known to me [not, *is*]

The + Adjective and the Verb

Rule X. यदि adjective का प्रयोग noun की तरह हो और उससे बहुत-से व्यक्तियों या वस्तुओं का बोध हो, तो वाक्य का subject होने पर उसके साथ Plural Verb का प्रयोग होता है; जैसे—

1. *The rich are* happy.
2. *The poor are* unhappy.
3. *The honest are* poor.
4. *The virtuous are* blessed.
5. *The blind do* not *receive* light.
6. *The dumb do* not *speak.*

Rule XI (A). Many a/an, More than one

Many a/an + noun तथा more than one + noun के साथ सदा Singular Verb का प्रयोग होता है; जैसे–

1. Many a man *was* killed.
2. More than one boy *was* absent.

इस संबंध में इस मत का ध्यान रखें—

More than one, *though its sense is necessarily plural, is treated as a sort of compound of* **'one'**, *following its construction, and agrees with a singular noun and takes a singular verb—*

1. *More than one workman was* killed.

2. *More than one workman was killed, not 'workmen' or 'were'.*

—FOWLER: *Modern English Usage*

Rule XI (B). More + plural noun + than one

कुछ वाक्यों में more का प्रयोग होता है और उनकी बनावट इस प्रकार की रहती है—

more + plural noun + than one.

ऐसे वाक्यों में सदा Plural Verb का प्रयोग होता है; जैसे—

1. More books than one *have been* bought.

2. More boys than one *were* present.

ऐसे वाक्यों में more के बाद आनेवाले Plural Noun के अनुसार Plural Verb का प्रयोग होता है, one के अनुसार Singular Verb का नहीं।

....

EXERCISE

I. *Correct the following sentences.*

(1) More than one men were rewarded. (2) Many a books have been written. (3) More than one hours have passed. (4) Many a roses bloom and waste themselves in the desert air. (5) Many an ugly scenes were seen.

Hints—(1) man was; (2) book has; (3) hour has; (4) rose blooms and wastes itself; (5) scene was

....

Subject + Apposition and the Verb

Rule XII. यदि कर्ता के बाद Apposition का प्रयोग हो, तो Verb सदा Apposition पद के पहले आनेवाले Noun या Pronoun (कर्ता) के अनुसार होता है, Apposition पद के अनुसार नहीं; जैसे—

1. I, Rajendra Prasad, *am* a student. 2. *You*, boy, *are* very wicked.

यहाँ पहले में Rajendra Prasad और दूसरे में boy Apposition पद हैं, क्योंकि इनका प्रयोग I और You के अर्थ को स्पष्ट करने के लिए (इनकी व्याख्या के रूप में) हुआ है और इनको comma के बीच रखा गया है। इसलिए इन वाक्यों के Verbs Apposition पद के पहले आनेवाले Pronouns (I/you) के अनुसार हैं, Apposition पद (Rajendra Prasad और boy) के अनुसार नहीं। इन वाक्यों में am/are के बदले is का प्रयोग सर्वथा अनुचित होता।

NOTE—कर्ता (Subject) के बाद जो noun उस कर्ता की व्याख्या करने के लिए प्रयुक्त होता है उसे apposition (समानाधिकरण) कहा जाता है।

. . . .

EXERCISE

I. *Correct the following sentences.*

(1) I, Mohan, is a student of IA (2) You, the son of a rich man, is very lucky. (3) He, the only son of his old parents, are very dutiful. (4) I, the man you were looking for, is here. (5) You, my life-long companion, has been very helpful to me.

Hints—(1) am; (2) are; (3) is; (4) am; (5) have

. . . .

Distributive Pronouns and the Verb

Rule XIII. यदि वाक्य का Subject कोई Distributive Pronoun (each/everyone/either/neither) हो, तो Verb सदा Singular होता है; जैसे—

1. *Each* of them *has gone.*
2. *Neither* of the two view *is* good.

यहाँ Plural Verb का प्रयोग सर्वथा अनुचित होता। इस संबंध में इस नियम का ध्यान रखें—

Each *as subject is invariably singular, even when followed by 'of them', etc., e.g., Each of the wheels has three spokes.* —FOWLER: *Modern English Usage*

And again,

The use of plural verb after **Either,** *as in 'Either of these methods are successful' is a common grammatical blunder.* —FOWLER: *Modern English Usage*

इस छोटे नियम का उल्लंघन कर इन लेखकों ने कितनी भद्दी भूल की है—

1. *... but* **neither** *of them* **were** *able to enter it.* —S RICHARDSON
2. **Neither** *of these two* **were** *more than minor poets.* —LAWRENCE DURRELL
3. **Each** *of these two are a series of moral essays.* —OLIVER ELTON

इन वाक्यों को देखकर आप ऐसा न सोचें कि व्याकरण का यह नियम अब प्रयोग में नहीं है। आज भी सावधानी से लिखनेवाले लेखक इस नियम का पालन सम्मान के साथ करते हैं। अमेरिका में भी, जहाँ व्याकरण के बहुत-से पुराने नियम अब ध्वस्त हो चुके हैं, इसका पालन किया जाता है। नीचे देखिए अमेरिका के प्रसिद्ध व्याकरणाचार्य के वाक्यों को—

1. **Neither** *of Bile's sisters has much luck in snaring a husband.* —NORMAN LEWIS
2. **Is either** *of your sisters working?* —NORMAN LEWIS

NOTE—Plural noun/pronoun + each:

यदि each का प्रयोग plural noun या pronoun के बाद apposition की तरह हो, तो verb plural होता है; जैसे—

1. We each *wish* to rise. 2. They each *have* a problem.

इन वाक्यों के verbs (wish तथा have) plural हैं, क्योंकि each का प्रयोग plural pronouns (we तथा they) के बाद हुआ है। एक दूसरा उदाहरण भी लें—

The *wheels each have* twelve spokes.

यहाँ plural noun (wheels) के बाद each आया है। इसलिए यहाँ Plural Verb (have) का प्रयोग शुद्ध है।

....

EXERCISE

I. *Correct the following sentences.*

(1) Either of these methods are successful. (2) Neither of the faults were found out. (3) Neither of them were there. (4) Either of the roads are long. (5) Each of the students have to pay college tuition-fee every month. (6) Everyone of his sisters are unmarried. (7) They each has a book.

Hints—Use Singular Verbs in all the sentences except in (7).

II. *Fill in the blanks with a suitable Finite Verb.*

(1) Either of the two roads ...... bad. (2) Neither of the sisters ...... married. (3) Each of them ...... present. (4) Either of your sisters ...... working? (5) Everyone of them ...... a fool. (6) We each ...... a problem.

Hints—Use Singular Verbs in all the sentences except in (6).

....

Indefinite Pronouns and the Verb

Rule XIV. जब वाक्य का Subject कोई Indefinite Pronoun होता है, तब साधारणत: कोई कठिनाई नहीं होती है, क्योंकि वह निस्सन्देह Singular होता है या Plural; जैसे—one, everyone, anyone, no one, someone, nobody and somebody सदा Singular रहते हैं और इसलिए इनके साथ Singular Verb आता है।

इसी प्रकार, both, many, some और few Plural हैं। अत:, इनके साथ Plural Verb आता है; जैसे—

1. *Everyone knows* this. 2. *Many of* them *know* this.
3. *No one knows* this. 4. *Both* of them *know* this.
5. *Someone has* said so. 6. Some *have* said so.

हाँ, तीन ऐसे Indefinite Pronouns हैं जिनके प्रयोग में कुछ कठिनाई अवश्य होती है। ये हैं—None, Any, All, इसलिए इनपर विस्तारपूर्वक विचार करें।

The Number of NONE

None के साथ Singular Verb का प्रयोग हो या Plural का, इस संबंध इन मतों पर विचार करें—

None *is an abbreviated form of* **not one or no one** *and would, therefore, seem to be singular, but in its context it usually has a plural sense—'At the time of the collision several persons were in the tram-car, but none were injured.' Only a literary purist would write* **was** *and he would probably be influenced by Dryden's famous line—None but the brave deserves the fair. But in a mistaken devotion to grammar he would he sinning against usage.* —G H VALLINS: *Good English*

None *is more often used with the Verb in the Plural and has come to be regarded as the negative of 'any' (plural).* —L TIPPING: *A Higher English Grammar*

None *was originally used only as singular but it has also acquired a plural meaning—***None have** *gone away yet.* —NESFIELD: *Aids to Study English Composition*

It is a mistake to suppose that the pronoun **none** *is singular only and must at all costs be followed by Singular Verb;* The Oxford English Dictionary *explicitly states that plural construction is commoner.* —FOWLER: *Modern English Usage*

इन आचार्यों के कहने का अभिप्राय यह है कि अब आधुनिक अँगरेजी में None का प्रयोग Plural में हो चला है, जैसाकि ऊपर के उदाहरणों से स्पष्ट है—

1. *None were* injured. 2. *None have* gone away yet.

कुछ और वाक्य लें—

1. *He lived in the Victorian period ... unware of disharmonies because for him there* **were none.** —F R LEAVIS
2. *He looks anxiously to see whether there are any more. There* **are none.** —G B SHAW
3. **None** *of his translators* **have** *been able to catch the manner.* —*The Kenyon Review: Spring* 1955
4. **None** *of the military services* **get** *all they want, none* **are** *crippled.* —*The New York Times: Jan.* 20, 1957
5. ... **none** *of the minor characters* **are** *just decorative.* —E M FORSTER
6. ... *which stares and gapes at nature, or tremble at portents where* **none were** *intended.* —BASIL WILLEY

इन वाक्यों में none को plural मानकर इसके लिए Plural Verb का प्रयोग किया गया है। व्याकरणाचार्यों के मतानुसार भी ऐसा प्रयोग शुद्ध है। अब इन वाक्यों को देखें—

1. *I would suggest that none of the plays of Shakespeare* **has** *a meaning ...* —T S ELIOT

2. **None** *of the obvious complaints that were or might have been brought to bear upon the first Poems and Ballads* **holds** *good.* —T S ELIOT

3. **None** *of his works* **shows** *more clearly how wide and unexpected were the resources of his genius.* —IFOR EVANS

4. ... *which* **none** *of his imitators* **have** *approached.* —IFOR EVANS

यहाँ पहले दो वाक्यों में Singular Verb (has/holds) का प्रयोग किया गया है, क्योंकि Eliot साहब ने none को Singular माना है। तीसरे वाक्य में इसके लिए Ifor Evans साहब ने Singular Verb का प्रयोग किया है, पर इन्होंने चौथे वाक्य में Plural Verb का प्रयोग किया है। इससे यह स्पष्ट है कि none का प्रयोग आजकल दोनों ही प्रकार से हो रहा है। कोई इसे singular मानता है और कोई plural और कोई कभी singular और कभी plural. मेरे विचार में, व्याकरण और प्रयोग दोनों ही दृष्टियों से, सर्वोत्तम मार्ग यह है कि none के साथ आप Singular Verb का प्रयोग करें और none of + plural noun/pronoun के साथ Plural Verb का। यदि Eliot साहब ने ऊपर के अपने वाक्यों में Plural Verb का प्रयोग किया होता तो और अच्छा होता, पर यह कहना उचित नहीं कि इनके वाक्य अशुद्ध हैं। आप इतना ही कह सकते हैं कि ये वाक्य कुछ पुराने अवश्य लगते हैं।

The number of ANY

Any का प्रयोग singular और plural दोनों ही तरह से होता है; जैसे—

1. *Does any* of them know?
2. *Do any* of them know?
3. *Any* of these is long enough.
4. *Any of* these *are* long enough.

Any के साथ Verb के प्रयोग में कठिनाई नहीं होती, क्योंकि इसके साथ Verb Singular होता है और Plural भी, जैसाकि ऊपर के वाक्यों से स्पष्ट है।

The number of ALL

All का भी प्रयोग singular और plural दोनों ही तरह से होता है; जैसे—

1. *All is* well. 2. *All are* well.

ये दोनों वाक्य शुद्ध हैं। हाँ, इनके अर्थों में थोड़ा अंतर अवश्य है। पहले वाक्य में all से everything या whole (singular) का बोध होता है, पर दूसरे से all persons या things (plural) का। कुछ और वाक्य लें—

1. *All's* well that ends well. 2. *All* that glitters *is* not gold.

इन वाक्यों में All का प्रयोग everything के अर्थ में हुआ है और इसलिए Singular Verb का प्रयोग किया गया है। याद रखना चाहिए कि जब all का अर्थ all men या things हो तो plural Verb का प्रयोग होना चाहिए, पर जब all का अर्थ everything या whole हो, तब Singular Verb का। इसलिए All of us knows और All has gone away अशुद्ध वाक्य हैं, पर All is not yet lost बिलकुल शुद्ध।

Former/Latter/Following/Undersigned

Rule XV. Pronoun की भाँति इनका प्रयोग Noun के बदले होता है और इसलिए वाक्य में इनके साथ Verb Singular भी आ सकता है और Plural भी। यदि इनका प्रयोग केवल एक Singular Noun के बदले हो, तो Verb Singular होता है; पर यदि ये एक से अधिक Noun के बदले आएँ तो, Verb Plural होता है; जैसे—

1. *The great advantage of Dryden over Milton is that the* **former is** *always in control of his ascent ... the* **latter has** *created a perch from which he cannot afford to fall ... .* —T S ELIOT
2. *It is what makes Marvell a classic; classic in sense in which Gray and Collins are not; for the* **latter** *with all their accredited purity,* **are** *poor in shades of feeling.* —T S ELIOT

यहाँ पहले वाक्य में the former और the latter के लिए Singular Verb आया है। क्यों? क्योंकि ये दोनों ही Singular Noun के लिए प्रयुक्त हुए हैं—the former 'Dryden' के लिए और the latter 'Milton' के लिए। दूसरे वाक्य में the latter के लिए Plural Verb (are) का प्रयोग हुआ है, क्योंकि यहाँ यह Plural Nouns (Gray and Collins) के लिए आया है। इसलिए यहाँ are के बदले is का प्रयोग अशुद्ध होता।

यह नियम the following तथा the undersigned के साथ भी लागू होता है; जैसे—

1. *The* **following are** *the new rates.*
2. *The* **following is** *the weather-report.*
3. The **undersigned requests** the pleasure of your company tommorrow at 4 p.m. Mohan
4. The **undersigned request** the pleasure of your company tomorrow at 4 p.m.

Mohan
Radha

यहाँ पहले वाक्य में the following के साथ Plural Verb (are) का प्रयोग शुद्ध है, क्योंकि यहाँ यह Plural Noun (rates) के लिए आया है। दूसरे वाक्य में following के साथ Singular Verb (is) का प्रयोग हुआ है जो शुद्ध है, क्योंकि यहाँ यह Singular Noun (report) के लिए प्रयुक्त हुआ है। तीसरे और चौथे वाक्यों में भी इस नियम का पालन किया गया है।

NOTE—एक बात याद रखें कि former, latter, following तथा undersigned में s लगाकर इन्हें Plural बनाना भूल है। इसलिए following का followings और undersigned का undersigneds नहीं हो सकता।

. . . .

EXERCISE

I. *Correct the following sentences.*

(1) Both Keats and Shelly are good poets but the latter are not as great as the former.
(2) Shaw and Shakespeare are great dramatists, but the difference is that the former are

anti-romantic whereas the latter romantic. (3) The following are the market report. (4) The undersigneds request the pleasure of your company.

Hints—(1) the latter is; (2) the former is … the latter is; (3) is; (4) undersigned

. . . .

Subject + Verb 'to be' + Complement

Rule XVI. कुछ वाक्यों की बनावट इस प्रकार की होती है—

Subject + Verb 'to be' + Complement (noun/pronoun)

इन वाक्यों को लें—

1. It is he.
2. It is they.
3. It is I.
4. It is the boys who lost.
5. It is the girls who won.

यहाँ इन वाक्यों में 'it' Subject है और he/they/I/boys/girls complements (पूरक) हैं। ऐसे वाक्यों में Verb 'to be' का number Subject के अनुसार होता है, Complement के अनुसार नहीं।

Subject को पहचानने में कोई भी कठिनाई नहीं होती, क्योंकि Assertive Sentence में Verb 'to be' के पहले जो Noun या Pronoun रहता है वही Subject होता है और Verb 'to be' के बाद आनेवाला जो Noun या Pronoun होता है वह Complement, जैसाकि ऊपर के वाक्यों से स्पष्ट है। इसलिए दूसरे वाक्य में It is they को It are they कर देना अशुद्ध होगा। जो लोग It are they लिख मारते हैं, वे समझते हैं कि 'they' Subject है, पर वास्तव में यह तो है Complement और इसलिए इसका प्रभाव Verb पर पड़ ही नहीं सकता। कुछ और वाक्य लें—

1. The last *crop was* potatoes.
2. Our only *guide was* the stars.

इन वाक्यों में Singular Verb (was) का प्रयोग शुद्ध है, क्योंकि यह Singular Subject (crop/guide) के अनुसार प्रयुक्त हुआ है। यदि यहाँ potatoes/stars को Subject मान कर Plural Verb का प्रयोग किया जाता, तो वह अशुद्ध हो जाता। इस संबंध में इस नियम को याद रखें—

The noun that stands before the verb should be regarded as the subject and the verb adapted to it. —FOWLER: *King's English*

अच्छे लेखक इस नियम का पालन आदरपूर्वक करते हैं—

1. **What concerns criticism** *is not the avowed or unavowed* **motives** *of the artist … .* —I A RICHARDS
2. *Coleridge's supreme* **contributon** *to poetry* **was** *the three* **poems.** —C M BOWRA

NOTE (a)—एक बहुत पुराना पर प्रसिद्ध वाक्य है—

The wages of sin is death.

यहाँ Singular Verb (is) का प्रयोग हुआ है, यद्यपि Subject (wages) Plural है। आधुनिक प्रयोग के अनुसार यहाँ are होना चाहिए। लेखक ने शायद wages को Singular मानकर या death को Subject समझकर Singular Verb का प्रयोग किया है। आप ऐसा न करें और न इसके आधार पर कोई दूसरा वाक्य बनाएँ।

NOTE (b)—ऊपर कहा गया है कि Verb 'to be' के पहले आनेवाला Noun या Pronoun ही Subject होता है; पर Interrogative sentences में Verb 'to be' के बाद आनेवाला Noun या Pronoun ही Subject होता है, Verb 'to be' के पहले आनेवाला नहीं; जैसे—

What proof *are* these tears?

यहाँ are के बाद आनेवाला Noun (tears) Subject है, इसके पहले आनेवाला Noun (proof) नहीं, क्योंकि यह Interrogative sentence है। अतः, यहाँ Plural Verb का प्रयोग शुद्ध है। इसलिए, What armour is your *achievements* against death? में Plural Verb (are) का प्रयोग होना चाहिए, क्यों? इसलिए कि यहाँ Subject *achievements* है, armour नहीं।

....

EXERCISE

I. *Correct the following sentences.*

(1) The only difficulty are the fast changes brought about. (2) The most pompous monument of Egyptian greatness are the pyramids. (3) My great need are the clothes. (4) Man's only friend are his moral qualities. (5) What he requires are books and clothes. (6) The trouble with most men's family lives are their mothers-in-law. (7) What we need in the modern world are moral qualities. (8) I is he. (9) He am I. (10) You is he. (11) It are they.

Hints—Use Singular Verb in all the sentences from (1) to (7) but 'am' in (8), 'is' in (9), 'are' in (10) and 'is' in (11)

....

Relative Pronouns and the Verb: noun/pronoun + who/which/that

Rule XVII. यदि वाक्य का Subject कोई Relative Pronoun (who, which, that) हो तो Verb उसके Antecedent के अनुसार होता है। आप जानते हैं कि Antecedent उस Noun/Pronoun कहते हैं जो Relative Pronoun के पहले आता है, अर्थात जिसके लिए Relative Pronoun का प्रयोग होता है; जैसे—

1. The *man* who *is* here *is* my friend. 2. The *men* who *are* here *are* my friends.

यहाँ दोनों ही वाक्यों में Relative Pronoun 'who' है, पर पहले का Antecedent Singular Noun (man) है और दूसरे का Plural Noun (men)। इसलिए पहले वाक्य में Singular Verb का प्रयोग हुआ है और दूसरे वाक्य में Plural Verb का।

कुछ और वाक्य लें—

1. I am the *man* who *has* helped you.

2. It is *I* who *have* helped you.

3. The *pen* that *is* there *is* mine.

4. The *pens* that *are* here *are* mine.

पहले वाक्य में Singular Verb का प्रयोग हुआ है। क्यों? इसलिए कि Relative Pronoun (who) का Antecedent (man) Singular है। दूसरे वाक्य में Plural Verb (have) का प्रयोग हुआ है, क्योंकि यहाँ Relative Pronoun (who) का Antecedent (I) first person है, जिसके लिए Present Tense में Plural Verb (have) आता है। यहाँ पहले वाक्य में have और दूसरे वाक्य में has का प्रयोग अशुद्ध होता। तीसरे और चौथे वाक्यों में भी Antecedent (pen/pens) के अनुसार Verbs का प्रयोग हुआ है।

Caution: one of + plural noun/pronoun + who/which/that

जब वाक्य में *one of* का प्रयोग हो, तब of के बाद आनेवाले Noun/Pronoun को ही Antecedent मानें और उसके अनुसार Verb का प्रयोग करें, of के पहले आनेवाले one के अनुसार नहीं; जैसे—

She is one of *those* who *do* not accept this view.

यहाँ who का Antecedent 'those' है, 'one' नहीं और इसलिए Relative Pronoun (who) के लिए Plural Verb (do) का प्रयोग किया गया है। यहाँ Singular Verb का प्रयोग अशुद्ध होता। शायद असावधानी के कारण ही इन महान लेखकों ने इन वाक्यों में Singular Verb का प्रयोग किया है, जो उचित नहीं—

1. *This, it may be, is one of the first* **difficulties that faces** *us in a library.*
—VIRGINIA WOOLF

2. *It was this that was worrying Gide, or rather one of the* **things that was** *worrying him.*
—E M FORSTER

3. *One of the* **qualities that marks** *the romantic from the classical attitude derives from this difference in the feeling for time.* —DR A A MENDILOW

4. *I am not one of the desk-pounding* **types that likes** *to stick out his jaws.*
—*THE NEW YORK TIMES*: Jan. 20, 1957

इन वाक्यों में Plural Verbs (face/were/mark/like) का प्रयोग होना चाहिए, क्योंकि इन वाक्यों में Relative Pronouns के Antecedents हैं difficulties/things/qualities/types, जो Plural हैं।

देखिए सावधानी से लिखने पर वाक्य कैसे शुद्ध होते हैं—

1. *He (Dryden) remains one of those who have set standards for English verse ... .*
—T S ELIOT

2. *His (Andrew Long's) sonnet is one of the most interesting of the many* **documents that are** *to be found in the* **Oxford Book of English Verse.**
—F R LEAVIS

3. *But this is one of the hundred* **faults ... which do** *not matter.* —OLIVER ELTON

4. *Palpable is one of the* **words that are** *liable to clumsy treatment of this sort ... .*
—H W FOWLER

उपर्युक्त वाक्यों में Relative Pronouns (who/that/which/that) के लिए Plural Verbs का प्रयोग शुद्ध है, क्योंकि इनके Antecedents हैं those/documents/faults/words, जो Plural हैं। आप भी इसी प्रकार सावधानी से लिखें।

....

EXERCISE

I. *Correct the following sentences.*

(1) He is one of the best men that has ever lived. (2) I am the man who am to blame. (3) You are the boy who have beaten me. (4) It is you who has said so. (5) I am one of those who am of a different view. (6) He is one of those who has served this country heart and soul. (7) I am the man who have done it. (8) This is an epoch of one of the most singular discoveries that has ever been made. (9) It is I who is your best friend.

Hints—(1) have; (2) is; (3) has; (4) have; (5) are; (6) have; (7) has; (8) have; (9) am.

II. *Fill in the blanks with a suitable Finite Verb.*

(1) It is I who ...... responsible for this. (2) I am the man who ...... guilty. (3) This is one of the hundred facts which ...... so common. (4) I am the one who ...... to blame. (5) He is one of those men who ...... always finding fault. (6) You are the person who ...... really guilty.

Hints—(1) am; (2) is; (3) are; (4) is; (5) are; (6) is

III. *Fill in the blanks with a word from the box.*

has	have	those
one	that	are

(1) You are the man who ...... harmed me. (2) He is ...... of those who ...... helped me. (3) The pens ...... are here are mine. (4) I do not like ...... who ...... dishonest. (5) This is one of the faults that ...... led to his fall. (6) Each of us ...... said so. (7) Either of them ...... to do it. (8) A number of pens ...... black.

....

Subject + and + Subject and the Verb

Rule XVIII (A). जब दो या दो से अधिक Nouns या Pronouns को and से जोड़ा जाता है, तब Verb सदा Plural होता है; जैसे—

1. *Mohan* and *Sohan are* friends. 2. *Two* and *two make* four.

3. *She* and *I are* friends. 4. You and *he are* rich.

Rule XVIII (B). यदि and से संयुक्त Singular Nouns एक ही व्यक्ति या वस्तु का बोध कराएँ तो Verb Singular होता है। याद रखें—

Subject + Subject = one person;

The *magistrate* and *collector is* on tour.

यहाँ दो Singular Nouns (magistrate and collector) जो and से जोड़े गए हैं, एक ही व्यक्ति का बोध कराते हैं, दो का नहीं, क्योंकि सिर्फ पहले noun के साथ Article का प्रयोग किया गया है। यदि इन दोनों के साथ Article का प्रयोग हुआ होता, तो ये दो व्यक्तियों का बोध कराते और वैसी अवस्था में Plural माने जाते; जैसे—

The magistrate and *the* collector are on tour.

अब, इस वाक्य को लें—

The *poet* and *philosopher has* said so.

यहाँ Singular Verb (has) का प्रयोग शुद्ध है, क्योंकि यहाँ एक ही Noun के पहले Article आया है, इसलिए ऐसा मालूम होता है कि यहाँ एक ही व्यक्ति poet और philosopher—दोनों है। यदि यहाँ इन दोनों ही Nouns के पहले Article आ जाए, तो इससे मालूम होगा कि ये दो व्यक्ति हैं और इसलिए Verb Plural का प्रयोग इस प्रकार होगा—

The poet and *the* philosopher *have* said so.

NOTE—जब दो अंक (figures) and के संयुक्त रहते हैं और उनके बाद Verb आता है, तब वह Singular (is) हो सकता है या Plural (are) भी; जैसे—

1. *Two* and *two is* four. 2. *Two and two are* four.

जो ऐसे वाक्यों में Singular Verb का प्रयोग करते हैं, वे and से संयुक्त इन अंकों को एक mathematical concept मानते हैं और जो Plural Verb का प्रयोग करते हैं, वे इनको अलग-अलग मानते हैं। ये दोनों ही विचार तर्कपूर्ण हैं और इसलिए दोनों ही प्रयोगों को शुद्ध माना जाता है। इस संबंध में इस मत का ध्यान रखें—

Five and five is ten—right. But don't jump to the conclusion that 'Five and five are ten' is wrong—both verbs are equally acceptable in this or any similar construction.

—NORMAN LEWIS: *Word Power*

मेरी राय है कि ऐसे वाक्यों में Singular Verb (is) का प्रयोग करना चाहिए, क्योंकि mathematics के क्षेत्र में यही प्रयोग अधिकतर मिलता है।

1. *Two* plus (and) *two* is four. 2. *One* plus (and) *one* is two.

Parcel Subject

Rule XVIII (C). कुछ ऐसे Singular Nouns हैं जो and से संयुक्त रहते हैं और प्रयोग में बराबर एक साथ आते हैं, मानो एक Noun दूसरे का जोड़ा (pair) हो। इसलिए ऐसे Nouns को Parcel Subject भी कहा जाता है। ऐसे वाक्यों का Verb सदा Singular रहता है; जैसे—

1. *Bread* and *butter is* a rich food.
2. *Horse* and *carriage is* waiting at the gate.
3. *The crown* and *glory* of life *is* character.
4. *Pen* and *ink is* required for me.

इन सभी वाक्यों में दो-दो Nouns 'and' से जोड़े गये हैं, पर Verb है Singular, क्योंकि प्रयोग में and से संयुक्त ये Nouns बराबर जोड़े बनकर आते हैं और एक साथ मिलकर एक ही वस्तु का बोध कराते हैं।

NOTE—ऐसे वाक्यों में भी Plural Verbs का प्रयोग हो सकता है और होना भी चाहिए, जब ऐसे जोड़े Nouns से एक वस्तु का नहीं, वरन एक से अधिक का बोध होता है। ऐसी अवस्था में Verb के complement से यह पता चलता है कि ये Nouns मिलकर एक वस्तु का बोध कराते हैं या ये अलग-अलग कई वस्तुओं का बोध कराते हैं; जैसे—

Bread and water *are* the *necessaries* of life.

यहाँ 'necessaries' जो Plural Noun है, Verb का complement है। इसके Number से यह पता चलता है कि इस वाक्य में 'bread' और 'water' दो अलग-अलग वस्तुएँ हैं, दोनों मिलकर एक नहीं। यदि ये एक ही वस्तु का बोध कराते, तो complement Plural होता ही क्यों? अतः, इससे यह स्पष्ट है कि ऐसे वाक्यों में Plural Verb का प्रयोग होना चाहिए। अब इस वाक्य को लें—

Bread and water *is* the simplest *food.*

यहाँ Singular Verb (is) का प्रयोग शुद्ध है। क्यों? इसलिए कि Singular complement (food) यह बताता है कि bread और water दो अलग-अलग वस्तुएँ नहीं हैं, बल्कि ये दोनों मिलकर एक वस्तु (food) का बोध कराते हैं।

Each/Every/No + Subject

Rule XVIII (D). यदि Singular Nouns को and से जोड़ा जाए और उनमें से एक के पहले भी each/every/no का प्रयोग हो, तो Verb Singular होता है; जैसे—

1. *Each* man and *each* woman *is* of the same opinion.
2. *Every* Tom, Dick and Harry *wears* suit these days.
3. *Every* day and *every* night *brings* its own pleasures for us.
4. *No boy and no girl was* present there.

इन वाक्यों में Nouns को and से जोड़ा गया है, फिर भी Verbs Singular हैं, क्योंकि इन Nouns के पहले each/every/no का प्रयोग हुआ है। यहाँ Plural Verb का प्रयोग अनुचित होता। अब इन वाक्यों को देखें—

1. *Life ... is a long stretch full of variety, in which* **every hour** *and* **circumstance have their** *peculiar merit.* —VIRGINIA WOOLF
2. ... **every town** *and* **every village were** *so short of labour after the Black Death that high wages were given to immigrants.* —G M TREVELYAN

यहाँ नियमानुसार पहले वाक्य में has और its का प्रयोग होना चाहिए और दूसरे में was का। आप ऐसा न सोचें कि ऐसे वाक्यों में Plural Verb का प्रयोग अब शुद्ध माना जाता है, क्योंकि इनसे भी बड़े लेखकों ने इस नियम का पालन आदरपूर्वक किया है।

EXERCISE

I. *Correct the following sentences.*

(1) You and I am neighbours. (2) He and I is class friends. (3) The guide and guardian are dead. (4) The leader and scholar are to address this meeting today. (5) Ink and paper is necessary articles of daily use. (6) Rice and fish are my favourite dish. (7) Milk and honey is costly things. (8) The magistrate and collector were present there. (9) Every boy and every girl have attended this meeting. (10) No student and no teacher were present there.

Hints—(1) are; (2) are; (3) is; (4) is; (5) are; (6) is; (7) are; (8) was; (9) has; (10) was

II. *Fill in the blanks with suitable Finite Verbs.*

(1) Every thought and every feeling ...... not valuable. (2) The poet and the critic ...... of different opinions on this matter. (3) He and I ...... bosom friends. (4) Pen and paper ...... necessary articles for students. (5) Bread and butter ...... a rich food. (6) The poet and scholar ...... dead.

Hints—(1) is; (2) are; (3) are; (4) are; (5) is; (6) is

Rule XIX (A). कुछ वाक्यों के Subjects इन शब्दों के द्वारा जोड़े जाते हैं—

As well as, And not, With, Together with, Along with, In addition to, No less than, Rather than, More than, Like, Unlike, But, Except, Besides, Including, Excluding

ऐसे वाक्यों का Verb पहले Subject के अनुसार होता है; जैसे—

1. A robber with all his followers **was** arrested.
2. *His (Blake's)* **philosophy, like** *his visions ...* **was** *his own.* —T S ELIOT
3. *Solid* **qualities, like** *a good marriage settlement,* **endure.** —OLIVER ELTON
4. *This broken* **talk, with** *its exclamations, interruptions and changes of voice,* **is** *also found in Sterne.* —OLIVER ELTON
5. Dante, more than *any other poet,* **has** *succeeded in dealing with his philosophy ... .* —T S ELIOT

यहाँ पहले तथा दूसरे वाक्य में Singular Verb (was) का प्रयोग हुआ है और तीसरे में Plural Verb (endure) का, जो शुद्ध है। इसी प्रकार, चौथे और पाँचवें वाक्य में Singular Verb का प्रयोग शुद्ध है, क्योंकि with और more than के पहले Singular Noun (talk/Dante) का प्रयोग हुआ है। कुछ और वाक्य लें—

1. The *thief*, as well as his sons, *was* arrested.
2. The *thief*, and not his sons, *was* guilty.

3. *He*, rather than his victims, *was* really unhappy in the end.

4. *She*, no less than you, *is* responsible.

इन वाक्यों में as well, and not और rather than, no less than के पहले आनेवाले Noun या Pronoun के अनुसार Verb का प्रयोग हुआ है, इसलिए ये वाक्य शुद्ध हैं। इस साधारण नियम का उल्लंघन कर इन वाक्यों में भयंकर भूल की गई है—

1. **A taxi along with** *two passengers* **are** *traceless.*

2. *On the opening caremony* **were** *present a minister* **together with** *the District Magistrate.*

उपर्युक्त दोनों ही वाक्यों में Singular Verb का प्रयोग होना चाहिए, क्योंकि along with और together with के पहले क्रमशः taxi और minister आए हैं, जो Singular Nouns हैं।

not only ... but

Rule XIX (B). यदि दो Subjects को *not only ... but* के द्वारा जोड़ा जाए, तो Verb के number और person अंतिम Subject के अनुसार होते हैं; जैसे—

1. Not only India but all *countries are* in trouble.

2. Not only he but all his *friends were* arrested.

अगर यहाँ पहले वाक्य में India और दूसरे वाक्य में he के अनुसार Singular Verb का प्रयोग होता, तो ये वाक्य अशुद्ध हो जाते।

nothing but + noun

Rule XIX (C). ऐसे वाक्य में nothing but के बाद कोई Singular या Plural noun आता है, पर वाक्य का Verb सदा Singular होता है। इन वाक्यों को देखें—

1. Nothing but *snow is* seen.

2. Nothing but *trees is* seen.

यहाँ पहले वाक्य में nothing but के बाद एक Singular noun (snow) आया है और दूसरे में एक Plural noun (trees), पर दोनों वाक्यों का Verb Singular है। यहाँ दूसरे वाक्य में are का प्रयोग अशुद्ध होता, क्योंकि ऐसे वाक्यों का Subject होता है nothing जो सदा Singular रहता है। याद रखें कि ऐसे वाक्यों का Subject वह noun नहीं होता जो but के बाद आता है। इस नियम के अनुसार यह वाक्य अशुद्ध है—

Nothing but heads were seen.

Caution: as well as = so + auxiliary

1. He *as well as* I *likes* fish.

2. You *as well as* she *dance* well.

व्याकरण की दृष्टि से ये वाक्य शुद्ध तो अवश्य हैं, पर सुनने में बहुत ही भद्दे लगते हैं और बोलने में अस्वाभाविक। यही कारण है कि आधुनिक अँगरेजी में, और खासकर बोलचाल में, ऐसे

वाक्य विरले ही मिलते हैं। आप भी ऐसे वाक्य न लिखें तो अच्छा हो। ऐसे वाक्यों की बनावट को so + auxiliary के द्वारा इस प्रकार बदल दें—

1. He likes fish and so do I.
2. You dance well, and so does she.

अब, इस वाक्य को लें—

The thief as well as his sons was arrested.

इसे भी इस प्रकार बदला जा सकता है—

The thief was arrested, and so were his sons.

EXERCISE

I. *Correct the following sentences.*

(1) He as well as I are guilty. (2) The house with all its belongings, were sold away. (3) You, rather than your father, is to blame. (4) Ram, like all his companions, are a spoiled child. (5) No one except a few fortunate shareholders have reaped the harvest. (6) You as well as I am responsible for this action. (7) The ship with all its passengers were lost. (8) There are nothing but miseries in life. (9) Not only she but all her sisters has been married.

Hints—(1) is; (2) was; (3) are; (4) is; (5) has; (6) are; (7) was; (8) is; (9) have been

2. *Fill in the blanks with suitable Finite Verbs.*

(1) These houses with a garden in front ...... lovely. (2) He as well as I ...... present. (3) He more than his parents ...... responsible for his bad career. (4) Ram along with his friends ...... going to the college. (5) You, unlike your father ...... a miser. (6) The robber as well as his associates ...... arrested.

Hints—(1) are; (2) is or was; (3) is or was; (4) is or was; (5) are; (6) was

The Separators and the Verb

Rule XX (A). यदि or, nor, either ... or, neither ... nor के द्वारा दो या दो से अधिक Singular Nouns या Third Person के Singular Pronouns को अलग (separate) किया जाए, तो Verb Singular होता है; जैसे—

1. Neither *beauty* nor *duty is* an armour against death.
2. Either *rain* or *storm is* to come.
3. Neither *he* nor *she is* here.

इस नियम की अवहेलना अँगरेजी के कुछ प्रसिद्ध लेखकों ने की है—

1. *Neither search nor labour* **are** *necessary.* —Dr Johnson

2. *Neither painting nor fighting* **feed** *men.* —RUSKIN

3. *Parody or adaptation* **have** *enormous advantages to certain novelists.* —E M FORSTER

4. *A chance word or sigh* **are** *just as much evidence as a speech or a murder.* —E M FORSTER

5. *No young lady of Miss Austen's acquaintance waiting eagerly for the appearance of Scott's or Byron's next volume of verse, seems ever to have asked what* **Mr Thrope or Mr Ton Bertram were** *going to do to serve their country in times of danger.* —G M TREVELYAN

इन पाँचों वाक्यों में Singular Verb का प्रयोग होना चाहिए। आप इन महान लेखकों को देखकर ऐसा मत सोचें कि यह नियम अब टूट गया है। सच तो यह है कि सावधानी से लिखनेवाले आज के महान लेखक इस नियम का पालन कर रहे हैं, और ये लेखक तो निश्चय ही डॉ॰ जॉनसन और रस्किन आदि से बड़े हैं। इन वाक्यों को देखें—

1. *A reader or auditor* **is** *at liberty to remain passive.* —EZRA POUND
2. *The teacher or lecturer* **is** *a danger.* —EZRA POUND
3. *We say, in a vague way, that Shakespeare, or Dante, or Lucretius* **is** *a poet who thinks.* —T S ELIOT
4. *Neither the letter nor the writer* **was** *in any degree interesting.* —JANE AUSTEN

यहाँ महान लेखकों ने व्याकरण के नियमानुसार Singular Verb का प्रयोग किया है। आप भी इस नियम का पालन करें।

Rule XX (B). यदि Plural Nouns/Pronouns को or, nor, either ... or या neither ... nor के द्वारा अलग किया जाए, तो Verb Plural होता है; जैसे—

1. Neither *men* nor *women have* come.
2. Either *you* or *we have* to do it.
3. Neither *we* nor *they are* to blame.

Rule XX (C). यदि भिन्न-भिन्न Persons के Nouns/Pronouns को or, nor, either ...... or, neither ...... nor के द्वारा अलग किया जाए, तो वाक्य में पहले Second Person का Pronoun आता है, उसके बाद Third Person का और अंत में First Person का (2 3 1) और Verb अपने सबसे नजदीक आनेवाले Noun या Pronoun के अनुसार होता है; जैसे—

1. Either *he or I am* guilty.
2. Neither *you* nor *he is* guilty.
3. Neither *you* nor *I am* guilty.
4. *Is he* or *I* to blame?
5. *Are you* or *he* to blame?
6. *Are you* or *I* to blame?

इन वाक्यों में 2 3 1 फॉरमूला के अनुसार भिन्न-भिन्न प्रकार के Persons के Pronouns को रखा गया है और Verb अपने सबसे नजदीक आनेवाले के अनुसार।

Rule XX (D). यदि भिन्न-भिन्न Number के Nouns/Pronouns को or, nor, either ... or, neither ... nor के द्वारा अलग किया जाए, तो अंत में Plural (Noun या Pronoun) को रखा

जाता है और Verb अपने सबसे नजदीक आनेवाले Noun या Pronoun के अनुसार होता है; जैसे—

1. Neither the *son* nor his *parents are to* blame.

2. Either *he* or *they are* to blame.

3. Neither *she* nor *they are* to blame.

4. *Is he* or *they* to blame?

5. *Is the son* or *his parents* to blame?

इन वाक्यों में Plural Noun/Pronoun को अंत में रखा गया है और Verb अपने सबसे समीप आनेवाले के अनुसार प्रयुक्त है।

Caution—Rule XX (C) और **(D)** के संबंध में कुछ लोगों के मन में एक धारणा है जो मेरे विचार में ठीक नहीं। उनका मत है कि जब वाक्य में भिन्न-भिन्न Persons/Numbers के Nouns या Pronouns को or, nor, either ... or, neither ... nor के द्वारा अलग किया जाता है, तब अंत में आनेवाले Noun/Pronoun के अनुसार Verb होता है और वह Verb Plural होता है। देखिए उनलोगों के दिए हुए नियमों को—

When two or more nominatives in different numbers are joined by 'or' or 'nor' the Verb is in the **Plural :** *John or his friends are to blame.*

If one of the Subjects separated by 'or' or 'nor' happens to be plural, it should be placed nearest to the Verb which also should be Plural : Neither John nor his friends have come.

इस नियम के आधार पर क्या ये वाक्य अशुद्ध हैं?

1. *Is John* or his *friends* to blame?
2. *Has* neither *John* nor his *friends* come?

मेरे जानते ये वाक्य निस्सन्देह शुद्ध हैं। अपने मत की पुष्टि के लिए सबसे महान व्याकरणाचार्य का विचार आपके सामने है—

> *Give the verb the number of the alternative nearest it*—'**Mother** or **Children are** *to die.*', '**Is** *the* **child** *or the* **parents** to be blamed?' What should not be said is 'Mother or children **is** to die', '**Are** *the child or the parents to be blamed?* ......
>
> —FOWLER: *Modern English Usage*

इससे यह स्पष्ट है कि भिन्न-भिन्न numbers/persons के Nouns या Pronouns जब or, nor, either ... or या neither ... nor के द्वारा अलग किये जाते हैं, तब Verb अपने सबसे नजदीक आनेवाले Noun/Pronoun के अनुसार होता है। यह आवश्यक नहीं है कि Verb plural ही हो या अंत में आनेवाले Noun/Pronoun के अनुसार हो; जैसे—

1. *Were you or* he there? 2. *Were you* or I there?

इन दोनों ही वाक्यों में Verb के समीप you है और इसलिए इसके अनुसार were का प्रयोग हुआ है। यदि यहाँ अंत में आनेवाले he या I के अनुसार was का प्रयोग होता, तो वह अशुद्ध होता।

NOTE—Rule XX (C) और **(D)** के संबंध में व्याकरणाचार्यों के बीच कुछ मतभेद है। आप उनके विचार पर गौर करें—

When two Subjects are joined by 'or' or 'nor' the verb agrees in person with the Subject nearest to it—Either James or I am at the top of the class; Either you or James has done it. —NESFIELD

नेसफिल्ड साहब के मतानुसार जब दो Subjects को or या nor के द्वारा जोड़ा जाता है, तब Verb अपने सबसे समीप आनेवाले Subject के अनुसार होता है। उदाहरण देते हुए उन्होंने बताया है कि पहले वाक्य में First Person 'I' को either ... or से जोड़ने पर क्रिया 'I' के अनुसार हुई है क्योंकि यह Verb के नजदीक है। दूसरे वाक्य में क्रिया के समीप 'James' है और इसलिए क्रिया इसी के अनुसार 'has' है, 'you' के अनुसार नहीं। दूसरे लोगों ने भी यही कहा है कि यदि भिन्न-भिन्न numbers/persons के Subjects को either ... or या neither ... nor से जोड़ें, तो Verb अपने सबसे समीप आनेवाले Subject के अनुसार होता है।

अब एक दूसरे मत पर विचार करें—

In this construction the Number and Person of Verb must be common to both parts of the Subject. So both the parts of the Subject must be of the same Number and Person. When there is a clash between the Verb and one part of the Subject, the construction is better avoided. —G H VALLINS: *Good English*

इनका मत है कि वाक्य में यदि भिन्न-भिन्न Number और Person के कर्ता को either ... or या neither ... nor से जोड़ा जाए और क्रिया एक ही कर्ता के अनुसार हो, तो यह अशुद्ध है; जैसे—

Either he or I am wrong.

यहाँ am का प्रयोग I के साथ तो ठीक है, पर he के साथ am नहीं आता, is आता है। इस वाक्य में क्रिया और एक कर्ता के साथ मेल है, पर दूसरे कर्ता के साथ नहीं। इसलिए ऐसे वाक्य नहीं लिखें। फाउलर साहब ने भी यह कहा है कि बुद्धिमान लोग वाक्य की ऐसी बनावट को छोड़ देते हैं। इस विषय में नेसफिल्ड साहब का मत भी करीब-करीब यही है—

It would be better, however, to repeat the verb for each subject. The sentences would, then, be re-written as follows—Either James is at the top of the class or **I am;** *Either you have done it or James* **has.**

इस वाक्य को लें—Either James or I am at the top of the class. इस वाक्य की क्रिया (am) 'I' के साथ तो मेल खाती है, पर James के साथ नहीं।

इसलिए यदि वाक्य में भिन्न-भिन्न number/person के Subjects को either ... or या neither ... nor से जोड़ें, तो नेसफिल्ड साहब के बताये हुए नियम के अनुसार वाक्य की बनावट को थोड़ा-सा बदल दें; जैसे—

Neither you nor I am right = Neither you are right nor I (am).

यदि आप ऐसा कर सके तो अच्छा हो, पर यह कुछ कठिन अवश्य है। इसलिए आप चाहें तो ऊपर बताये गये Rule (C) तथा (D) के अनुसार ही चलें और जहाँ दो Nouns/Pronouns अलग-अलग person या number के हों वहाँ सबसे समीप आनेवाले Noun/Pronoun के अनुसार ही Verb का प्रयोग करें। यही नियम अधिक प्रचलित है। देखिए अमेरिका के प्रसिद्ध व्याकरणाचार्य

का वाक्य जिसमें उन्होंने इसी नियम को (अर्थात सबसे समीप आनेवाले Subject के अनुसार Verb के प्रयोग को) अपनाया है—

One or two of her features **are** *very attractive.* —NORMAN LEWIS

....

EXERCISE

I. *Correct the following sentences.*

(1) Neither chapter nor verse are given. (2) Either sugar or milk are required. (3) Neither a pen nor a pencil are there. (4) Either he or I is wrong. (5) Only one or two boys has come. (6) Neither his friends nor he is there. (7) Either his parents or he himself is to blame. (8) Are the child or his parents to blame? (9) Are he or they to blame? (10) Have John or his friends come? (11) Either Tom or Henry are coming here.

Hints—(1) is; (2) is; (3) is; (4) am; (5) have; (6) Neither he nor his friends are there; (7) Either he himself or his parents are to blame; (8) Is the child ...? (9) Is he ...? (10) Has John ...? (11) is

II. *Fill in the blanks with suitable Verbs.*

(1) Neither he nor his sisters ...... married. (2) Either you or I ...... to blame. (3) Neither he nor you ...... to go. (4) Either she or her friends ...... singing. (5) Neither he nor I ...... sorry for this. (6) ...... the son or his parents to blame? (7) ...... you or he to blame? (8) ...... neither he nor his friends come?

Hints—(1) are; (2) am; (3) are; (4) are; (5) am; (6) Is; (7) Are; (8) Has

III. *Match A with B to make correct sentences.*

A	B
Nothing but footprints	were found.
The poet and thinker	were present.
He and I	was absent.
Neither boats nor ships	was seen.
She no less than you	are responsible for this.
Not only he but all his sons	is really guilty.

....

Multiplication and the Verb

Rule XXI. गणितशास्त्र (mathematics) में गुणा (multiply) करने के संबंध में ऐसे वाक्य प्रयोग में आते हैं—

Six times four; twice two.

ऐसे वाक्यों में Verb Singular हो सकता है और Plural भी; जैसे—

1. Six *times* four *is* twenty-four.
2. Six *times* four *are* twenty-four.
3. *Twice* two *is* four.
4. *Twice* two *are* four.

जो ऐसे वाक्यों में Singular Verb का प्रयोग करते हैं वे मानते हैं कि ऐसी संख्या (जैसे six, two आदि) से केवल एक वस्तु (definite figure) का बोध होता है और जो Plural Verb का प्रयोग करते हैं वे समझते हैं कि ऐसी संख्या से अनेक वस्तुओं का बोध होता है। ये दोनों विचार तर्कयुक्त हैं और इसलिए इन दोनों को शुद्ध समझा जाता है। आपको जो अच्छा लगे वही करें, क्योंकि कोई दूसरा व्यक्ति इस समस्या का हल आपके लिए नहीं ढूँढ़ सकता—

> *That question each of us can answer, perhaps, for himself: but not one for other people, it is therefore equally correct to say—'Twice two* **is** *four, twice two* **are** *four'. Moreover, as the two are equally old, 'Four times six' was plural as long ago as 1380, and 'Ten times two was singular in 1425.*
>
> —FOWLER: *Modern English Usage*

ऐसे वाक्यों में Singular और Plural Verb दोनों ही शुद्ध समझे जाते हैं; पर मेरा विचार है कि ऐसे वाक्यों में Singular Verb का प्रयोग अधिक अच्छा मालूम पड़ता है, क्योंकि दैनिक जीवन में तथा गणितशास्त्र की पुस्तकों में भी ऐसा ही प्रयोग अधिकतर मिलता है। गणितशास्त्र के विद्यार्थी ऐसे वाक्यों में Plural Verb का प्रयोग कभी भी नहीं करते।

Quantity Words and the Verb

Rule XXII. Much/More/Little/Less हैं Adjective of Quantity जिनसे वस्तु की quantity (परिमाण) का बोध होता है। अतः, वाक्य में Subject की भाँति प्रयुक्त होने पर इनके साथ सदा Singular Verb का प्रयोग होता है; जैसे—

1. *Not much has* been done.
2. Much *more* remains to be done.
3. *Little has* been done so far.

....

EXERCISE

Correct the following sentences.

(1) Much remain to be done. (2) Much of the beauty and glory of life have disappeared. (3) Much of what he said have been criticised. (4) Little have been said on this point. (5) There are still much more to do. (6) Little have been said and much less have been done.

Hints—(1) remains; (2) has; (3) has; (4) has; (5) is; (6) Little has been said and much less has been done

....

As regards, As concerns and As follows

Rule XXIII. As follows/as concerns/as regards का प्रयोग plural में कभी भी नहीं होता। इनके अंत में s रहने पर भी ये सदा एक ही रूप में रहते हैं और वह है एकवचन रूप। इसलिए as follow/as concern/as regard लिखना अशुद्ध है। इन वाक्यों को लें—

1. The new *rates* are as *follows.*
2. The *description* is as *follows.*

पहले वाक्य में Plural 'rates' आया है और दूसरे में Singular 'description' पर दोनों ही वाक्यों में एकवचन as follows का प्रयोग हुआ है, क्योंकि इसके पहले it छिपा रहता है।

....

EXERCISE

Correct these sentences.

(1) The details are as follow. (2) His words were as follow. (3) The provisions of the Act are as follow.

....

There + Verb + Subject

Rule XXIV. There से आरंभ होनेवाले वाक्यों का Verb असली कर्ता (Subject) के अनुसार होता है, Preposition के बाद आनेवाले noun के अनुसार नहीं; जैसे—

1. There is a cup on the table. 2. There are cups on the table.
3. There is a match tommorow. 4. There are two matches tomorrow.
5. There is no food to eat. 6. There are books to read.

ऐसे वाक्यों का Subject वह noun/pronoun होता है जो preposition/adverb/infinitive के पहले आता है।

....

EXERCISE

Correct these sentences.

(1) There is books in the bag. (2) There is pens in the pocket. (3) There are water in these rivers. (4) There are sugar in sweets. (5) There is no temples in the town. (6) There is birds in the cage.

....

What/As/Than and the Verb
WHAT and the Verb

Rule XXV (A). What का प्रयोग एक Relative Pronoun की तरह होता है और इसका अर्थ होता है that which या those which, अर्थात यह singular होता है और plural भी। इसलिए

singular अर्थ में Singular Verb का प्रयोग होता है, पर plural अर्थ में Plural Verb का; जैसे—

1. Can you see *what appears* to be a *ship*?

2. Can you see *what appear* to be *ships*?

यहाँ पहले वाक्य में Plural Verb (appear) और दूसरे में Singular Verb (appears) का प्रयोग अशुद्ध होता।

As and the Verb

Rule XXV (B). वाक्यों में कभी-कभी As का प्रयोग होता है, पर इसके बाद subject छिपा हुआ रहता है। ऐसे वाक्यों में Singular या Plural Verb का प्रयोग वाक्य के अर्थ को ध्यान में रखकर करना चाहिए। इन वाक्यों को देखें—

1. There were not so many books *as were* needed.

2. There were not so many books *as was* expected.

यहाँ पहले वाक्य में as के बाद they छिपा हुआ है। इसलिए यहाँ were का प्रयोग हुआ है। पर दूसरे वाक्य में was का प्रयोग हुआ है, क्योंकि यहाँ as के बाद it छिपा हुआ है। इससे यह स्पष्ट है कि पहले वाक्य में as का अर्थ है 'जितने' पर दूसरे में 'जैसा कि'। इस अर्थ को ध्यान में रखकर ऐसे वाक्यों में, 'जितने' के अर्थ में, Plural Verb का प्रयोग होता है और 'जैसा कि' के अर्थ में Singular Verb का। एक-दो और वाक्य लें—

1. There were not so many deaths *as was* reported.

2. There were not so many horses *as were* asked for.

यहाँ पहले वाक्य में Plural Verb और दूसरे में Singular Verb का प्रयोग अनुचित होता। अब, इन वाक्यों को लें—

1. Speeches were made by a number of leaders, *as was* expected.

2. There were too many deaths, *as was feared.*

इन वाक्यों में as का अर्थ है **'और यह'** (and this) और as के पहले एक comma आया है। यह as पूरे वाक्य के लिए आया है। ऐसे वाक्यों में as के बाद Verb सदा Singular रहता है।

THAN and the Verb

Rule XXV (C). कुछ वाक्यों में, As के समान ही, than के बाद verb आता है, पर Subject छिपा हुआ रहता है। ऐसे वाक्यों में than के बाद Plural Verb आता है जब they या those छिपा रहता है, पर Singular Verb का प्रयोग होता है जब it छिपा रहता है। इन वाक्यों को देखें—

1. There were more deaths *than was* reported.

2. There were more pens *than were* needed.

यहाँ पहले वाक्य में than के बाद it छिपा हुआ है, पर दूसरे में they और इसलिए पहले वाक्य में Singular Verb (was) का प्रयोग हुआ है और दूसरे में Plural Verb (were) का।

EXERCISE

Correct the following sentences.

(1) I cannot see what appears to be camels. (2) There were more books than was required. (3) There were not as many chairs as was needed.

Hints—(1) appear; (2) were; (3) were

REVISION TEST 1

I. *Correct the following sentences.*

1. His knowledge of Indian languages are imperfect.
2. The export of tea and coffee and such other articles have been increasing.
3. One of the worst famines have taken place.
4. In him is centred the love and the ambition of his parents.
5. My friend and guide have come in time.
6. She and I was playing at the sea-shore.
7. Too great a variety of studies are likely to distract your mind.
8. Silver as well as gold have disappeared from the market.
9. Neither the minister nor his secretaries has agreed.
10. Are either of the candidates suitable?
11. Many a passengers were killed.
12. Milk and soda are a nice drink.
13. He is one of the richest boys that has ever met me.
14. The committee has arrived at this decision in their own interest.
15. Three parts of this work are still unfinished.
16. The results of investigation is awaited.
17. His means is extremely poor.
18. Either he or I are wrong.
19. Have neither of the boys passed?
20. The mother as well as her children are out.

Hints—1. is; 2. has; 3. has; 4. are; 5. has; 6. were; 7. is; 8. has; 9 have; 10. is; 11. passenger was; 12. is; 13 have; 14. has … its or have … their; 15. is; 16. are; 17. are; 18. am; 19. has; 20. is

REVISION TEST II

II. *Explain why the following sentences are correct or incorrect.*

1. The poet and scholar are dead.

2. It is one of the best books that has ever been written.
3. A large number of cattle is grazing there.
4. He, with his wife and children, has come.
5. Every man and every woman is useful.
6. The number of persons engaged are great.
7. Nothing but adventures are liked by me.
8. Neither of the sisters were selected.
9. The sum and substance are that he is guilty.
10. A variety of dishes have been served.
11. Each of us have separate work to do.
12. He is one of those who causes inconvenience to everybody.
13. Many a men run after wealth.
14. Either of the two boys have done this.
15. None have come yet.
16. More pens than one is red.
17. Much have been said so far.

REVISION TEST III

III. *Match each group of words in A with the right group of words in B.*

A	B
There are lots	to do.
Each of them	have reached.
The fruits of labour	is sweet.
To this	is added these.
Both of them	has left.
The smell of these flowers	are sweet.
A small number of books	is great.
A poet and thinker	are dead.
The number of books	are great.
A poet and a thinker	is dead.

REVISION TEST IV

IV. *Put a ring (o) around right words.*

1. A number of guests $\frac{\text{has}}{\text{have}}$ arrived.

2. Nothing but flowers $\dfrac{\text{is}}{\text{are}}$ seen everywhere.

3. Neither he nor I $\dfrac{\text{has}}{\text{have}}$ finished the work.

4. More books than one $\dfrac{\text{has}}{\text{have}}$ been bought.

5. The light of these lamps $\dfrac{\text{is}}{\text{are}}$ very bright.

6. Our only guide $\dfrac{\text{was}}{\text{were}}$ the stars.

7. Each boy and girl $\dfrac{\text{was}}{\text{were}}$ rewarded.

❐

A large number of formal restrictions and ancient 'thou shalt nots' of academic grammar are now completely outmoded. —NORMAN LEWIS

Chapter II

TEST YOURSELF

I. *Correct or justify the following sentences.*

1. My brother is a SI of police.
2. It is an humble attempt.
3. This is an historical work.
4. He is playing violin.
5. Will you have a coffee?
6. This poem is an eulogy.
7. I am a MA but he is a MSc.
8. This is a HMT watch.
9. This is a RTC bus.
10. I love the nature and the poetry.
11. There is a chicken in the menu.
12. The Everest is highest mountain.
13. He went home by a bus.
14. He came on the foot.
15. I have taken an action against him.
16. He was elected the president.
17. She came by a red car.
18. This is a his car.
19. He is a poet and a critic.
20. He goes to the church in time.
21. Have you read the every book?
22. I hit him on his head.
23. Turn to left/right.
24. He is going to theatre.
25. He will be back in a hour.
26. The dogs bark at the thieves.
27. The PM will be on air at 8 p.m.
28. Wheat is sold by kilo.
29. How well he plays violin?
30. I was invited to a dinner.
31. He plays the tennis well.

II. *Fill in the blanks with* **a, an** *or* **the.**

1. He is ...... MLA but she is ...... MP.
2. ...... water of this river is pure.
3. What ...... idea! What ...... fool!
4. ...... eyes of this baby are blue.
5. Which is ...... better of the two?
6. I read ...... Gita and ...... Bible everyday.
7. What ...... awful sight it is!
8. ...... FIR was lodged.
9. Don't make ...... noise.
10. He sent ...... SOS.

❐

ARTICLES

हिन्दी, उर्दू तथा अन्य कई भाषाओं में Article नाम की कोई चीज नहीं होती। अँगरेजी में भी Article की कोई आवश्यकता प्रतीत नहीं होती, क्योंकि Adjective से ही काम चल सकता था। पर अँगरेजी की यह अनावश्यकता इस भाषा की एक विशेषता है। इसलिए यहाँ हम इसके प्रयोग पर विचार करें।

The Use of a/an/the

Rule I. जब Singular Countable noun अनिश्चित रहता है, तब उसके पहले a/an अवश्य आता है। पर जब वह निश्चित रहता है, तब उसके पहले the का प्रयोग होता है—

> **(i) a/an + singular indefinite noun**
> **(ii) the + singular definite noun**

1. He is *a* boy. The boy is gentle.
2. This is *an* apple. The apple is sweet.

The Anaphoric Use of 'the'

Rule II. The का प्रयोग उस व्यक्ति या वस्तु के साथ होता है जिसकी चर्चा पहले हुई रहती है। इस प्रकार, the पीछे की ओर मुड़ता है, अर्थात पूर्वचर्चित noun की ओर देखता है और उसके साथ प्रयुक्त होकर उसे निश्चित (definite) बना देता है। इसी प्रयोग को Anaphoric Use कहा जाता है। ध्यान दें कि anaphora का अर्थ होता है—to carry back (पीछे की ओर जाना)।

इन वाक्यों को लें—

1. I have an apple. *The* apple is sweet.
2. He is a boy. *The* boy is gentle.

यहाँ पहले वाक्य में apple के साथ an आया है। पर दूसरे वाक्य में apple के साथ the का प्रयोग हुआ है। यहाँ the का Anaphoric Use है, क्योंकि the का प्रयोग पूर्वचर्चित noun (apple) के साथ हुआ है, अर्थात the पीछे की ओर मुड़कर उस noun के साथ आया है जिसकी चर्चा पहले ही हो चुकी है।

इस प्रकार जब countable noun की चर्चा पहली बार होती है, तब उसके पहले a/an आता है। पर जब उसकी चर्चा दूसरी बार फिर होती है तब उसके पहले the का प्रयोग होता है।

Generic And Specific Use of Articles

Generic Use

Rule III. कभी-कभी *a/an/the + singular noun* और *the + plural noun* से उस प्रकार के सभी व्यक्तियों या वस्तुओं का बोध होता है, अर्थात उससे पूरे वर्ग/जाति (whole class) का बोध होता है। Articles के ऐसे प्रयोग को Generic Use या Generalising Use कहा जाता है। इसलिए ऐसे a/an/the + noun का अर्थ होता है—*all + noun.* इन वाक्यों को लें—

1. A bird has wings. [a bird = all birds]
2. The bird has wings. [the bird = all birds]
3. An apple grows on a tree. [an apple = all apples]
4. The apple grows on a tree. [the apple = all apples]

इस प्रकार, Articles के Generic Use के कारण किसी Noun की संख्या में वृद्धि हो जाती है और इसके क्षेत्र में व्यापकता आ जाती है। क्यों? इसलिए कि ये Articles एक खास (particular) वस्तु को सामान्य (general) बना देते हैं और एक (one) से सब (all) का बोध होता है।

Specific Use

कभी-कभी a/an/the + singular noun से केवल एक खास (particular) व्यक्ति/वस्तु का बोध होता है, सबका नहीं। इसे Articles का Specific Use कहा जाता है। यह Generic Use का विपरीत प्रयोग है। क्यों? इसलिए कि Generic Use किसी Noun के क्षेत्र को बढ़ाता है, पर Specific Use उसके क्षेत्र को सीमित (limit) करता है। इसलिए इसे Limiting Use या Restrictive Use भी कहा जा सकता है। संक्षेप में, a/an/the + singular noun का अर्थ होता है—**one + noun.**

इन वाक्यों को देखें—

1. I have a dog. [a dog = one dog]
2. The dog is black. [the dog = one dog]
3. He is eating an apple. [an apple = one apple]
4. The apple is sour. [the apple = one apple]

a + consonant sound: an + vowel sound

Rule IV. जिस Singular Noun के पहले a/an का प्रयोग करना हो, उसे हिंदी में लिखें। यदि उसका पहला अक्षर (letter) हिंदी में व्यंजन (consonant) हो, तो उसके पहले a का प्रयोग करें। यदि उसका पहला letter हिंदी में स्वर (vowel) हो, तो an का प्रयोग करें; जैसे—

1. egg = एग। इसका पहला अक्षर (ए) स्वर (vowel) है, इसलिए इसके पहले an का प्रयोग होगा—an egg.
2. pen = पेन। इसका पहला अक्षर (प) व्यंजन है, इसलिए इसके पहले a का प्रयोग होना चाहिए—a pen.

इन्हें भी देखें—

a European (यू), an hour (आ), an MA (एम),

an FIR (एफ), an SDO (एस), a humble (ह) person

an MP (एम), an HMT watch (एच), an MLA (एम)

an RTC bus (आर), a unit (यू), a utensil (यू)

one-eyed a man (व), a one-year plan (व)

इन सभी उदाहरणों में Nouns को हिन्दी में लिखने पर उनके प्रथम अक्षर (letter) के अनुसार a/an का प्रयोग किया गया है, जो शुद्ध है।

अब इन वाक्यों को लें—

1. She is a LP School teacher.
2. Mr Jha is an university professor.
3. He is a honest worker.

यहाँ a के बदले an का प्रयोग होना चाहिए और an के बदले a का।

NOTE (a)— An with Vowel sounds

A का प्रयोग Consonant के पहले और An का Vowel के पहले क्यों होता है? केवल *A* से ही काम क्यों नहीं चलता? इसका कारण है उच्चारण की सुविधा। उच्चारण की दृष्टि से a + ass या a + umbrella (अर्थात vowel + vowel) थोड़ा कठिन होता है। पर a + nass या a + numbrella (अर्थात vowel + consonant) का उच्चारण सरल होता है। आप देखेंगे कि अँगरेज लोग an का पूरा उच्चारण नहीं करते। वे an (a + n) के n को अगले vowel में जोड़ते हैं और इस प्रकार वे शब्द consonant से आरंभ हो जाते हैं; जैसे—

an ass = a + nass, an + ant = nant,

an orange = a + norange, an elephant = a + nelephant.

आप भी इस उच्चारण का ध्यान रखें पर लेखन में an (a + n) को एक साथ मिलाकर रखें।

NOTE (b)—A/an with H sound

आधुनिक प्रयोग में hotel, historical तथा humble के पहले a का प्रयोग होता है, an का नहीं, क्योंकि इनका उच्चारण 'ओटल', 'इसटॉरिकल' और 'अम्बुल' के बदले क्रमशः 'होटल', 'हिस्टॉरिकल' और 'हम्बुल' हो गया है। इसलिए इन शब्दों के पहले अब an का प्रयोग पुराना समझा जाता है जैसाकि इन आचार्यों ने भी कहा है—

> ... **an** *was formerly used before an unaccented syllable beginning with h (an historical work), but now that the* **h** *in such words is pronounced the distinction has become pedantic, and 'a historical' should be said and written—similary* **an humble** *is now meaningless and undesirable.* —FOWLER: *Modern English Usage*

> *Anyone who says or writes 'an humble man' needs thoroughly shaking up and telling what century he lives in.* —C WHITAKER WILSON: *English Grammar*

वास्तव में, आधुनिक साहित्य में भी इन शब्दों के पहले अब a का ही प्रयोग होता है—

1. ... *but he is* **a humble** *man* .... —T S ELIOT

2. ... *being* **a humble** *engraver, he had no journalistic social career open to him.* —T S ELIOT

अब इस वाक्य को लें—

I therefore welcome this publication which is **an humble** tribute to his memory by the Ministry of Information and Broadcasting of the Government of India.

—DR RAJENDRA PRASAD: *Mahatma Gandhi*

आधुनिक प्रयोग (modern usage) के अनुसार यहाँ an का प्रयोग पुराना मालूम पड़ता है। इसलिए आप आधुनिक प्रयोग को अपना लें, तो अच्छा हो।

EXERCISE

I. *Correct these sentences.*

1. He is a NCC cadet.
2. This is a RTC bus.
3. He is an one-eyed man.
4. He is a SI of police.
5. This is a HMT watch.
6. It is an UNO resolution.
7. He is a Urdu poet.
8. He is an University student.

Hints—1. an; 2. an; 3. a; 4. an; 5. an; 6. a; 7. an; 8. a

a/an + adverb/adjective + noun

Rule V. यदि Noun के पहले adverb/adjective आए, तो a/an का प्रयोग अपने सबसे नजदीक आनेवाले शब्द के अनुसार होता है; जैसे—

1. This is *an* apple. This is *a red* apple.
2. He is *a* boy. He is *an honest* boy.
3. He is *an* honest boy. He is *a very* honest boy.

EXERCISE

II. *Correct these sentences.*

1. This is cup.
2. There is book in my bag.
3. This is ant.
4. There is glass in the hand.
5. I have horse.
6. Cat likes fish very much.
7. Cow is an useful animal.
8. He is a NCC officer.
9. There is egg in the nest.
10. This is a RTC bus.

11. He is an very honourable man.
12. This is an rotten egg.
13. He is an great artist.
14. This is an lovely inkpot.
15. This is a old house.
16. He is a exremely good boy.

III. *Fill in the blanks with a/an.*

1. This is ...... umbrella.
2. He is ...... honest man.
3. This is ...... owl.
4. This is ...... Indian game.
5. He is ...... European.
6. That is ...... English picture.
7. This is ...... good idea.
8. He is ...... great explorer.
9. This is ...... HE school.
10. That is ...... LP school.

....

a/an + more than one noun

Rule VI. जब एक से अधिक Noun या Adjective एक ही व्यक्ति या वस्तु का बोध कराएँ तब सिर्फ एक ही के पहले article का प्रयोग होता है, पर यदि अलग-अलग व्यक्तियों या वस्तुओं का बोध हो तो उनमें से प्रत्येक के पहले article का प्रयोग होना चाहिए; जैसे—

1. *a* red and blue pencil
2. *a* red and *a* blue pencil

poet and thinker

4. *a* poet and *a* thinker

यहाँ पहले उदाहरण में एक ही adjective के पहले article का प्रयोग हुआ है, क्योंकि ये दो adjectives ('red', 'blue') एक ही pencil के लिए प्रयुक्त हुए हैं। दूसरे उदाहरण में दोनों ही adjectives के पहले article का प्रयोग हुआ है, क्योंकि यहाँ दो पेंसिलों का बोध होता है—एक red और दूसरी blue. इसी प्रकार, तीसरे उदाहरण में एक ही noun के पहले article आया है, क्योंकि यहाँ poet और thinker एक ही व्यक्ति है। चौथे उदाहरण में एक व्यक्ति thinker है और दूसरा poet, इसलिए दोनों ही nouns के पहले article का प्रयोग हुआ है।

NOTE—यदि वाक्य में बहुत-से ऐसे nouns का प्रयोग करना हो जिनमें से किसी के पहले *a* और किसी के पहले an आना चाहिए तो उनमें से प्रत्येक के पहले उपयुक्त article का प्रयोग करना चाहिए; जैसे—

There are several things on this table—a book, a pen and an ink-pot.

पर यदि उन सभी Nouns से एक ही व्यक्ति या वस्तु का बोध कराना हो, तो सिर्फ पहले noun के साथ article का प्रयोग करना चाहिए, सबके पहले नहीं; जैसे—

1. *a* thinker and artist
2. *a* painter and philosopher

More uses of a/an [a/an + noun]

A/an का प्रयोग Singular Countable Noun के पहले इन अर्थों में होता है—

1. a/an = any [कोई के अर्थ में]

कोई (any) का अर्थ व्यक्त करने के लिए a/an का प्रयोग इस प्रकार होता है—

1. There was a king.
2. There was an *old* fox.

(2) a/an + noun [rate/weights/measures/speed]

दर, नाप-तौल, गतिसूचक शब्दों के पहले a/an इस प्रकार आता है—

1. Wheat sells at two rupees a *kilogram.*
2. He is driving at forty kilometres *an hour.*
3. He earns five rupees *a day.*
4. His salary is six hundred rupees a *month.*

(3) a/an + name of a person

जब किसी व्यक्ति (person) के संबंध में उसके नाम के अलावा कुछ और जानकारी नहीं रहती, तब उसके नाम के पहले a/an का प्रयोग होता है; जैसे—

A Mr Verma saw me yesterday.

(4) a/an + abstract noun

जब Abstract Noun का प्रयोग एक विशेष प्रकार के गुण (a kind of quality) के अर्थ में होता है, तब उसके पहले a/an आता है; जैसे—

1. She has received a good education.
2. He has a working knowledge of grammar.

(5) a/an + verb used as a noun

जब किसी verb का प्रयोग एक noun की तरह होता है, तब इसके पहले a/an आता है; जैसे—

1. He has gone for a walk.
2. May I go for a swim/a ride?
3. You should have a rest now.

(6) a/an + uncountable noun

जब uncountable noun का प्रयोग countable noun की तरह होता है तब उसके पहले a/an आता है; जैसे—

1. I have great love for her. —uncountable [प्यार/प्रेम]
   She is an old love of mine. —countable [प्रेमी/प्रेमिका]
2. This a lamb. —countable [भेड़]
   There is lamb in the menu. —uncountable [भेड़ का मांस]
3. He came here on time. —uncountable [समय]
   I had a bad time in Mumbai. —countable [परिस्थिति]
4. This room is full of smoke. —uncountable [धुआँ]
   Let's have a smoke now. —countable [सिगरेट]
5. I will buy a chicken tomorrow. —countable [मुरगी का बच्चा]
   I am fond of bread and chicken. —uncountable [मुरगा/मुरगी का मांस]
6. The angler has caught a big fish. —countable [जानवर]
   I am fond of fried fish. —uncountable [मछली का भोजन]

7. The sun gives us heat. —uncountable [गर्मी]
I did fairly well in a trial heat. —countable [प्रतियोगिता]
8. This window is made of glass. —uncountable [शीशा]
Give me a glass of water. —countable [बरतन]

(7) a/an in some phrases

to be in *a* hurry, to be in *a* temper, to have *a* pain/*a* headache/*a* fever, to have *a* mind to, have *an* eye to, to make *a* noise, to take *a* liking to, to take *a* fancy to, to have *a* liking/weakness/taste for, to run *a* temperature, to have *a* cold, to catch cold or *a* cold, to make *a* fire.

Uses of The [the + noun]

'The' का प्रयोग इस प्रकार होता है—

(1) Before names of ranges of mountains (पर्वतश्रेणी या शृंखलाबद्ध पहाड़); जैसे—

the Himalayas; *the* Alps; *the* Vindhyas.

ये plural हैं, क्योंकि इनमें शृंखला का बोध होता है और इसलिए the का प्रयोग हुआ है। जो पहाड़ एकवचन रूप में रहता है उसके पहले the का प्रयोग नहीं होता। इसलिए Everest/Mount Abu के पहले the नहीं आता।

(2) Before names of groups of islands; जैसे—

the East Indies; *the* Andamans; *the* West Indies.

बहुत-से ऐसे द्वीप हैं जो singular हैं और इसलिए उनके पहले the का प्रयोग नहीं होता; जैसे—Sicily, Java, Sumatra. ये सभी द्वीप Singular हैं। अतः, इनके पहले the का प्रयोग नहीं होना चाहिए।

(3) Before the names of rivers; जैसे—
the Ganga; *the* Danube; *the* Indus

(4) Before the names of gulfs, seas and oceans (खाड़ी, सागर तथा महासागर); जैसे—
the Gulf of Mexico; *the* Bay of Bengal; *the* Indian Ocean

(5) Before the names of great books; जैसे—
the Ramayan; *the* Mahabharat; *the* Bible; *the* Gita; *the* Koran

(6) Before the names of newspapers; जैसे—
the Indian Nation; *the* Leader; *the* Statesman

(7) Before the names of some planets or heavenly bodies; जैसे—
the sun; *the* moon; *the* sky; *the* earth

(8) Before the dates of a month; जैसे—
the 2nd of January; *the* 4th of March

(9) Before the ordinal numbers written in letters; जैसे—
the first; *the* second; *the* third; *the* sixth

NOTE—यदि ऐसी संख्या को Roman figures में लिखा जाए तो उसके साथ the का प्रयोग नहीं होता; जैसे—

Edward I, George III, George VI

(10) Before the Superlative Degree; जैसे—

the best boy; *the* most beautiful flower; *the* highest mountain

(11) Before adjectives used as nouns; जैसे—

the poor (poor men); *the* rich (rich men); *the* blessed

(12) Before the names of professions; जैसे—

the Bar; *the* Bench; *the* Press

the poet; *the* author/writer

(13) Before a singular countable noun representing the whole class; जैसे—

1. *The* cow is a useful animal.
2. *The* lion is the king of a forest.
3. *The* pen is mightier than the sword.
4. *The* rose is the sweetest of all flowers.

पर man तथा mankind के पहले किसी भी Article का प्रयोग नहीं होता।

(14) Before *office, cinema/theatre/picture/circus/station/bus-stop;* जैसे—

1. He is at *the* office.
2. I am going to *the* cinema/theatre.

(15) Before Common Nouns used as Abstract Nouns.

कभी-कभी Common Nouns का प्रयोग Abstract Nouns के समान होता है, क्योंकि इनसे किसी गुण का बोध होता है। ऐसी अवस्था में इनके पहले the का प्रयोग होता है; जैसे—

1. The *student* in me is still alive. 2. The *mother* in her is dead.

यहाँ student का अर्थ है student का गुण और mother का अर्थ है mother का गुण।

(16) Before Common Nouns in place of Possessive Adjectives

कभी-कभी Common Nouns के पहले Possessive Adjective नहीं आता। वैसी अवस्था में Possessive Adjective के बदले the का प्रयोग होता है; जैसे—

1. He caught her by *the* arm. 2. I hit him on *the* head.

2. He pulled the dog by *the* tail. 4. He hit her on *the* eye.

यहाँ by *her* arm के बदले by the arm आया है और on *his* head के बदले on the head. इसी प्रकार, by its tail के बदले by the tail का प्रयोग हुआ है और on her eye के बदले on the eye का।

(17) Before Common Nouns in the sense of *the same* (वही) ; जैसे—

1. This is the man *the* police wanted. 2. He is *the* leader of this place.

(18) Before Common Nouns used as apposition to Proper Nouns; जैसे—

Patna, *the* capital of Bihar; Gandhi, *the* fighter for freedom.

(19) Before names of musical instruments; जैसे—

He plays *the* tabla/*the* harmonium/*the* sitar/*the* violin.

(20) Before the names of historical places/buildings; जैसे—

The Taj Mahal; *The* Red Fort; *The* Golghar

(21) Before Proper Nouns qualified by adjectives; जैसे—

The late M Gandhi; *The* immortal Tulsi

(22) Before nouns showing *weights/measures/rate;* जैसे—

Silk is sold by *the* metre. Wheat is sold by *the* kilo.

Eggs are sold by *the* dozen. Wages are paid by *the* day.

(23) In some idioms; जैसे—

be in *the* air, be on *the* air, be in *the* right/wrong, be punctual to *the* minute/second, keep to *the* right/left, play *the* fool, speak to *the* point

(24) Before comparatives like these—

1. She is the wiser of *the* two. 2. The higher you go *the* colder it is.

(25) Before common nouns in the sense of **the same;** जैसे—

This is *the* book I was looking for.

(26) Before few/little + noun + adjective clause; जैसे—

I have lost *the* few pens I had.

She has spent *the* little money she had.

(27) Before noun + adjective clause; जैसे—

The gold he bought is not pure.

(28) Before definite objects/places; जैसे—

on *the* wall, on *the* earth, in *the* field, in *the* morning, in *the* evening

Omission of articles [zero article]

इन अवस्थाओं में **article** का प्रयोग नहीं होता है—

Rule I. Distributive adjective + noun

जब किसी noun के पहले distributive adjective (each/every/either/neither) का प्रयोग होता है तब उस noun के पहले Article नहीं आता है; जैसे—

1. He is a boy. I know each boy. [not, an each boy]
2. I have a dog. I love every dog. [not, an every dog]

Rule II. Possessive adjective + noun

जब किसी noun के पहले possessive adjective [my/our/your/his/her] आता है तब उस noun के पहले Article नहीं आता; जैसे—

1. This is a pen. This is my pen. [not, a my pen]
2. That is an egg. That is your egg. [not, an your egg]

Rule III. Numeral adjective + noun

जब किसी noun के पहले no/not any आता है तब उस noun के पहले Article का प्रयोग नहीं होता; जैसे—

1. He has a pen. He has no pen. [not, a no pen]
2. She has an apple. She has not any apple. [not, an any apple]

Rule IV. Proper noun + 's + noun

जब noun के पहले proper noun + 's आता है; तब उस noun के पहले Article नहीं आता है, जैसे—

1. This is a car. This is Mohan's car. [not, a, Mohan's car]
2. That is a ring. That is Sita's ring. [not, a Sita's ring]

NOTE—पर जब noun के पहले common noun + 's आता है, तब उस noun के पहले Article का प्रयोग होता है; जैसे—

1. This is a boy's hostel. [not, is boy's hostel]
2. That is a girl's frock. [not, is girl's frock.]

Rule V. Plural nouns and article

यदि Countable Noun plural हो तो Article का प्रयोग नहीं होता। Plural Nouns के पहले a/an का प्रयोग तो कभी हो ही नहीं सकता, the का भी प्रयोग नहीं होता है, यदि वह indefinite (अनिश्चित) हो—

1. Dogs bark. 2. Cows give us milk.

यहाँ dogs और cows से खास dogs/cows का बोध नहीं होता है, इसलिए ये वाक्य अशुद्ध हैं—

1. The dogs bark at night. 2. The cows give us milk.

NOTE—यदि किसी plural noun से निश्चित व्यक्ति या वस्तु का बोध हो, तो the का प्रयोग करना उचित है; जैसे—

1. The dogs of this place are black. 2. The cows of Ram give milk.

इन वाक्यों में dogs और cows से निश्चित dogs और cows का बोध होता है। इसलिए यहाँ the का प्रयोग शुद्ध है। आप देखेंगे कि साधारणतया जिन plural nouns के पहले the का प्रयोग होता है वे Preposition या Adjective clause के पहले आते हैं जो उन plural nouns को निश्चित बना देते है; जैसे—

1. Men are good. 2. The men of India are good.
3. Books are useful. 4. The books of Ram are useful.

यहाँ पहले और तीसरे वाक्य में men और books के पहले the का प्रयोग नहीं हुआ है। क्यों? इसलिए कि इनसे निश्चित व्यक्ति/वस्तु का बोध नहीं होता। पर दूसरे और चौथे वाक्यों में men तथा books के बाद of आया है जो इन्हें निश्चित बना देता है। इसलिए, इन वाक्यों में the का प्रयोग उचित है। अब, इन वाक्यों को लें—

1. The mangoes on my tree are not yet ripe.
2. The mangoes you gave me are not yet ripe.

यहाँ mangoes के पहले the का प्रयोग हुआ है। क्यों? इसलिए कि यह Preposition/ Adjective clause के पहले आया है।

Rule VI. Uncountable noun and article

Uncountable Nouns (Proper/Material/Abstract Noun) के पहले Article का प्रयोग नहीं होता; जैसे—

1. Shakespeare was a great poet.
2. We love beauty.
3. Coal is required in the kitchen.
4. I need milk.

NOTE (a)—Uncountable Nouns के पहले भी the का प्रयोग उचित है यदि ये Countable Nouns की भाँति प्रयुक्त किये जाएँ। ध्यान दें कि जब Uncountable Nouns के बाद कोई Preposition (in, of) आता है, तब ये निश्चित Countable हो जाते हैं और इसलिए इनके पहले the आता है; जैसे—

1. Kalidas is *the* Shakespeare of India.
2. *The* coal of Jharia is of good quality.
3. *The* prosperity of a country depends upon its citizens.
4. *The* beauty of Kashmir is praiseworthy.
5. *The* milk in the cup is meant for tea.

इन वाक्यों में Shakespeare, coal, prosperity, beauty और milk Uncountable Nouns हैं। फिर भी इनके पहले the का प्रयोग हुआ है, क्योंकि Common Nouns की भाँति ही इनका प्रयोग हुआ है। आप यह भी देखेंगे कि इन वाक्यों में ये सभी Nouns किसी Preposition के पहले आये हैं जो इन्हें निश्चित बना देते हैं। इसलिए यहाँ the का प्रयोग उचित है। याद रखें—

the + definite uncountables + preposition + noun.

Rule VII. Some Idioms/Phrases/Verbs and article

इन Idioms/Phrases में प्रयुक्त nouns के पहले Article का प्रयोग नहीं होता; जैसे—

1. to go to school/college/church/home/market/bed court/hospital/prison.
2. at home, at fault, at dawn, at night, at noon, at sight, at church, at school, at college, at hand, all day, all night.
3. day by day, side by side, face to face, hand to hand, hand in hand, part and parcel, from hand to mouth.
4. by road/land, by train/steamer, by sea/air/bus/ship.

लेकिन किसी खास या विशेष प्रकार की car/bus के पहले a का प्रयोग अवश्य होता है; जैसे—

She came in a big red car.

(v) for sale, for favour, four fear, for leave

(vi) in fact, in hand, in bed, in front of, in favour of, in debt, in trouble, in earnest, in jest, in prison

(vii) on demand, on sale, on earth, on foot

(viii) under consideration, under ground, under trial

1. The matter is under consideration.
2. He goes to school/college on time.

Rule VIII. Appoint/crown/elect/make के बाद आनेवाले Noun (complement) के पहले Article का प्रयोग नहीं होता; जैसे—

1. They elected him president.
2. He was appointed chairman.
3. He was crowned king.
4. They made him king.

Rule IX. द्रव्य/पदार्थ, भोजन तथा खेल-कूद के नामों के पहले Article का प्रयोग नहीं होता है; जैसे—

1. I play footbal/tennis/cricket.
2. When do you have lunch?
3. This house is made of brick/stone/glass/wood.
4. Breakfast is ready now.
5. He was invited to dinner/tea.
6. There is chicken/lamb in the menu. [मुरगा/भेड़ का मांस]
7. There is egg on his chin. [अंडे का अंश]

NOTE—जब meal/dinner से विशेष प्रकार के भोजन (special meal) का बोध होता है, या इसके पहले कोई Adjective आता है, तब इसके पहले Article का प्रयोग अवश्य होता है; जैसे—

1. Fifty guests were invited to *a dinner* given to welcome the new VC.
2. He gave me *a very good breakfast.*

Rule X. Kind of/sort of के बाद आनेवाले noun के पहले a/an का प्रयोग नहीं होता जब उससे 'भेद/प्रकार' का बोध हो; जैसे—

1. What kind of dress do you like?
2. I don't like this sort of man.

NOTE—जब kind of/sort of से **विशेष गुण/योग्यता** (quality/capacity) का बोध होता है, तब इसके बाद आनेवाले Noun के साथ a/an अवश्य आता है; जैसे—

1. What kind of an artist is he?
2. What sort of a book is this?

Rule XI. बीमारियों/पर्वों/ऋतुओं के नाम के पहले Article नहीं आता; जैसे—

1. She had an attack of cholera/fever/flu/pox.
2. All the friends are meeting at Christmas/Easter.
3. He goes to Simla in spring and stays at home in winter.

Rule XII. भाषाओं के नाम के पहले Article नहीं आता; जैसे—

1. He knows English/German/French.
2. He is learning Hindi these days.

Rule XIII. जब Collective Noun का प्रयोग सामान्य अर्थ में होता है, तब इसके पहले Article का प्रयोग नहीं होता; जैसे—

1. Society can't tolerate it. 2. Parliament meets next week.

Rule XIV. जब man/mankind का प्रयोग सामान्य अर्थ में होता है और इसका अर्थ होता है **मानवमात्र**; तब इसके पहले Article नहीं आता; जैसे—

1. Man is mortal. 2. Mankind is facing a great danger.

Rule XV. जब nouns का प्रयोग जोड़े (pair) में होता है, तब इनके पहले Article नहीं आता; जैसे—

father and son, husband and wife, brother and sister, arm in arm, hand to hand, from door to door, from village to village, face to face, neck to neck

Rule XVI. साधारणतः देशों के नाम के पहले Article नहीं आता, पर इन देशों के नाम के पहले the अवश्य आता है—

the USA, the USSR, the Sudan, the Netherlands

....

EXERCISE

Correct these sentences.

(1) At that time my memory was at the fault. (2) He came on the foot. (3) I left the school in 1941. (4) He sent the word that he would come. (5) Victoria, the Queen of England, was very kind-hearted. (6) Ram is in the bed these days. (7) I am not in the favour of this proposal. (8) He came here by the sea but went by the air. (9) He was elected a chairman. (10) He is learning the French. (11) He is moving from a village to a village. (12) They are a husband and a wife.

Hints—Don't use any article before fault, food, school, word, Queen, bed, favour, sea, air, chairman, French, village, husband, wife

REVISION EXERCISE

1. Use *a, an or some* where necessary.

1. ...... chair is made of ...... steel.
2. ...... table is made of ...... wood.
3. We get ...... milk from ...... cow.
4. We make ...... butter from ......milk.
5. I want ...... cup of ...... coffee.
6. I want ...... piece of ...... cloth.
7. This is ...... map of ...... Bihar.
8. I saw him ...... week ago.
9. He will leave in ...... hour.
10. That is ...... lovely island.
11. English is ...... easy language.

12. Give me …… food to eat.
13. …… dog has …… tail.
14. This door is made of …… glass.
15. I like …… fish and meat.
16. …… grass grows in …… field.
17. I don't like …… jam and cheese.
18. …… iron is …… hard metal.
19. I can't write …… poem without …… pen.
20. …… suit is made of …… wool or silk.
21. …… house is made of …… brick/stone.
22. I bought …… ink to write …… letter.
23. Give …… cup of milk with …… sugar.
24. I need …… sand and cement.
25. She bought …… tea and coffee.
26. …… honesty is …… good policy.

II. *Correct these sentences.*

1. Where there is will there is way.
2. While there is a life there is a hope.
3. What lovely sight it is!
4. What good idea it is?
5. What a good meat this is!
6. What a sweet music this is!
7. What a nonsense you talk!
8. What a lovely hair she has!
9. Put a lemon in your tea instead of milk.
10. There is a chicken in the menu.
11. He is at the college.
12. She goes to the church every day.
13. She has come by the train.
14. We elected him a monitor.
15. I have a lunch at 1 p.m.
16. There is an egg on her chair.
17. There is a lamb in the menu.

III. *Put a tick (✓) by the right words.*

1. I am fond of *music/a music.*
2. She is fond of *poetry/a poetry.*
3. I don't like a *jam/jam.*
4. He has bought *an ink/some ink.*
5. A knife is made of *steel/a steel.*
6. I want a *sugar/some sugar.*
7. I have *breakfast/a breakfast at* 7 a.m.
8. He has gone for *walk/a walk.*

Position of Articles

Rule I. Articles (a, an, the) का प्रयोग noun के पहले होता है; जैसे—

a book; *an* hour; *the* cow. [*article + noun*]

पर यदि noun के साथ adjective का प्रयोग करना हो, तो article को adjective के पहले रखना चाहिए, noun के पहले नहीं; जैसे—*a* good *book*. [*article + adjective + noun*]

यदि adjective के साथ adverb का भी प्रयोग करना हो, तो article को adverb के पहले रखना चाहिए, adjective के पहले नहीं; जैसे—*a* very good *book*. [*article + adverb + adjective + noun*]

Rule II. ऊपर के उदाहरणों से स्पष्ट है कि articles का स्थान adjectives के पहले रहता है, पर इनका (articles का) प्रयोग (many/such/what) के बाद होता है, पहले कभी भी नहीं; जैसे—

many a man; *many an* hour;

such a task; *such* a man;

what a book; *what a* place

Rule III. यदि किसी adjective के पहले as/how का प्रयोग हो, तो article का स्थान adjective के बाद आता है, पहले नहीं; जैसे—

as bad a man as he; as *good a* show as that;

how good a book; *how nice a* place

Rule IV. यदि किसी adjective के पहले so/too का प्रयोग हो तो article को adjective के पहले भी रख सकते हैं और बाद भी; जैसे—

1. so serious *an attempt* or *a* so serious *attempt*
2. *too* exact *an answer or a too* exact *answer*

यहाँ adjective (serious/exact) के पहले so/too का प्रयोग हुआ है। इसलिए article को adjective के पहले या बाद में रखना—दोनों ही शुद्ध हैं। हाँ, ऐसी अवस्था में यदि article को adjective के बाद रखा जाए तो और भी अच्छा हो, क्योंकि यह प्रयोग में अधिक है और सरल तथा स्वाभाविक भी मालूम पड़ता है।

EXERCISE

I. *Correct the following sentences.*

1. It is very lovely a place. 2. I cannot do a such difficult work. 3. How a lovely sight it is! 4. Ram is as a responsible man as Shyam. 5. A many man has come. 6. How a foolish plan it is!

Hints—(1) a very; (2) such as; (3) lovely a; (4) a man; (5) many a; (6) a plan

REVISION TEST 1

I. *Correct the following sentences.*

1. He is in the debt.
2. I sent him a word.

3. That is a his car.
4. The inner and outer walls are strong.
5. The secretary and accountant have been punished.
6. The honesty is a best policy.
7. Rich are dishonest.
8. Are you an university student?
9. Would you travel by a train?
10. Is it an hotel?
11. Himalayas lie to north of the India.
12. More you get more you want.
13. What sort of a book do you like the best?
14. How did this house catch the fire?
15. Is he in the jail/in the prison?

REVISION TEST II

Explain why the following sentences are correct or incorrect.

1. An ink is an useful article.
2. He is an African, not an European.
3. It is a fine poetry.
4. The man is mortal.
5. The love is a noble sentiment.
6. Ganges is in flood now.
7. Dead man tells no tales.
8. Friend in a need is friend indeed.
9. He is heir to the throne.
10. There is an ewe in the field.

REVISION TEST III

Match the words in A with the right words in B.

A	B
It is an	humble book.
It is a	LP school.
I like the	milk.
I like	Bible.
What a	idea!
What an	hotel!
I am at a	fault.
He is at	loss.

There are still certain minimum essentials of good English which the cultivated speaker carefully observes.

—Norman Lewis

❐

Chapter III

TEST YOURSELF

I. *Correct or justify the following sentences.*

1. Neither courses of action would be safe.
2. His either sons have passed with good marks.
3. As I have few money, I can give you ten rupees only.
4. Tell me if you have some doubt.
5. He didn't buy some sugar.
6. This is own house.
7. Which is worse: smoking, drinking or gambling?
8. The powerhouse of Chapra is bigger than Arrah.
9. I can run as fast if not faster than you.
10. He has read a few books he had.
11. This is the safest and intelligent way.
12. This book is more preferable than that.
13. The patient is comparatively better today.
14. Which is the best: meat or fish?
15. He is one of the best if not the best men.
16. Wordsworth, Keats, and Shelley are great poets but the latter is not so great as the former.
17. He is junior than me.
18. He is better than all boys.
19. Less trains are available now.
20. Who is the wisest than the two?
21. He has no any pen.
22. This book is most unique.
23. My all books were stolen away.

II. *Fill in the blanks with a word given in brackets.*

1. I have two pens and ...... pen is red. [each, every]
2. He is better than ...... in the class. [anybody, anybody else]
3. Who is the better ...... the two? [of, than]
4. She has ...... any book. [no, not]
5. I have ...... money. [no any, not any]
6. He is junior ...... me. [to, than]

7. How kind ...... you to help me! [of, for]
8. Could you take ...... of these mangoes? [some, any]
9. He has scarcely ...... food. [some, any]
10. There are ...... girls than boys in the class. [less, fewer]

❐

ADJECTIVES/DETERMINERS

Adjective के दो भेद होते हैं—

(i) Descriptives

(ii) Determinatives or Determiners

DESCRIPTIVE ADJECTIVES

Descriptive Adjectives किसी Noun के रूप-रंग, आकार-प्रकार, गुण-दोष आदि (colour/shape/size/quality) बताते हैं और उसका सामान्य वर्णन करते हैं। इस प्रकार, ऐसे Adjectives वर्णनात्मक (descriptive) होते हैं और ऐसे प्रश्नों का उत्तर देते हैं—**कैसा रूप/रंग/ आकार?**

Descriptive Adjectives का प्रयोग Noun के पहले होता है और Noun के बाद भी, अर्थात इनका Attributive use होता है और Predicative use भी; जैसे—

1. This is a **white cap.**—attributive use (adjective + noun)
2. This **cap is white.**—predicative use (verb + adjective)

Descriptive Adjectives के मुख्य भेद ये हैं—

(i) Adjectives of Quality—

red, white, long, full, round, ugly, beautiful, good, bad

(ii) Proper Adjectives—

Indian, Russian, Chinese, Japanese, British

(iii) Participle Adjectives—

इनकी रचना इस प्रकार होती है—

Present/Past Participle + noun

a drunken barber, a sunken ship, a running train

(iv) Preposition + Noun—

a chair in the corner, a book on the table

a boy with long hair

(v) Related to Adverbials—

कुछ adjectives की रचना adverbs से होती है और इसलिए इनका संबंध Adverbs से रहता है; जैसे—

an occasional reader = one who reads occasionally

past *students = students in the past*

a **former** *friend = a friend formerly*

a **hard** *worker = one who works hard*

a **big** *eater = one who eats much*

DETERMINERS/DETERMINATIVES

Determiners/Determinatives किसी noun की संख्या (number) या मात्रा (quantity) बताते हैं या किसी noun की ओर निश्चित रूप से संकेत (point out) करते हैं। इस प्रकार, ऐसे शब्द किसी noun के क्षेत्र को सीमित (limit/restrict) या **निर्धारित** (determine) करते हैं और ऐंसे प्रश्नों के उत्तर देते हैं— **कौन-सा? कितना?** Determinatives/Determiners की एक विशेषता यह है कि इनका प्रयोग noun के पहले होता है, noun के बाद नहीं; जैसे—

1. I have **a** cap.
2. I like **this** cap.
3. He hasn't **many** caps.
4. I have **a lot of** caps.

इस प्रकार, Determiner का प्रयोग होने पर यह सूचना मिलती है कि इसके बाद कोई-न-कोई noun अवश्य आएगा। इससे यह स्पष्ट है कि noun के बिना Determiner का प्रयोग हो ही नहीं सकता।

वाक्य में पहले Determinatives/Determiners का प्रयोग होता है और उसके बाद Descriptive Adjective का और अंत में Noun का; जैसे—

I have a red cap. [not, red a cap]

Determiners के मुख्य भेद ये हैं—

बहुत-से Determiners से मात्रा (quantity) या संख्या (number) का बोध होता है। ऐसे Determiners को Quantifiers (मात्रा/संख्या बतानेवाला शब्द) कहा जाता है।

I. Adjectives of Quantity [quantifiers expressing quantity]

इन शब्दों से मात्रा (quantity) का बोध होता है—

all, any, enough, little, less, much, more, most, some, no, a good deal of, a great deal of, a large amount of, a large quantity of, a lot of, lots of, plenty of, a piece of, a part of, a bottle/cup/glass/dish/plate/bowl of, a kilo/pound/ton/quintal of, a litre/metre of, a spoonful of, a loaf of, a pint of, a slice of, half of, a heap of, heaps of

इन वाक्यों को देखें—

1. He has drunk all the tea.
2. He hasn't any tea.
3. He has plenty of tea.
4. He has a lot of tea.
5. I have a cup/bottle of tea.
6. He has some tea.
7. He has little/a little tea.
8. He has no/enough tea.
9. I have a metre of silk.
10. He has a litre of petrol.
11. A part of the apple is rotten.
12. There is a heap of dust.

ऐसे Quantifiers के साथ सदा Singular Countable Noun का प्रयोग होता है।

II. Adjective of Number [quantifiers expressing number]

इन शब्दों से संख्या (number) का बोध होता है—

all, any, both, enough, each, every, either, neither, few, fewer, many, more, most, many a/an, several, some, no, one, two, etc., there, those, a lot of, lots of, plenty of, half of, a heap of, a number of, a large number of

इन वाक्यों को देखें—

1. I know all the boys. 2. I know both the boys.
3. I have some books. 4. I haven't any books.
5. I have no/enough books. 6. I have each/every book.
7. I have a lot of books. 8. I have plenty of books.
9. I have a heap of books. 10. I have read half of these books.

ऐसे Quantifiers के साथ सदा Countable Noun का प्रयोग होता है—एकवचन के साथ Singular Countable Noun और बहुवचन के साथ Plural Countable Noun; जैसे—

1. I haven't many books. 2. I have every book.

NOTE—कुछ Quantifiers से मात्रा (quantity) और संख्या (number) दोनों का बोध होता है; जैसे—

all, any, some, no, enough, more, most, a lot of, plenty of

इन वाक्यों को देखें—

Quantity	**Number**
1. He has drunk all the milk.	2. He has read all the books.
3. He has drunk some milk.	4. He has read some books.
5. He hasn't drunk any milk.	6. He hasn't read any books.
7. He has no milk.	8. He has no books.
9. He has a lot of milk.	10. He has a lot of books.
11. He has plenty of milk.	12. He has plenty of books.
13. He has enough milk.	14. He has enough books.
15. I want more milk.	16. I want more books.

III. Distributive Adjectives—

each, every, either, neither

IV. Demonstrative Adjectives—

this, that, these, those, such, same

V. Indefinite and Definite Articles—

a, an, the

VI. Possessive Adjectives—

my, our, your, his, her, their

VII. Interrogative Adjectives—

which, what, whose

VIII. Relative Adjectives—

which, what, whatever, whichever

IX. Exclamatory Adjectives—

what

X. Intensifying/Emphasising Adjectives—

own, same, very

XI. Limiters/Limiting Adjectives—

a certain/a particular + noun,

the only/the main/the same + noun

NOTE—Semantic Classification of Adjectives

Semantics का अर्थ होता है अर्थविज्ञान, जो शब्दों के अर्थ (meaning) का अध्ययन करता है, उनके रूप (form) का नहीं। इस दृष्टि से Adjectives के ये भेद किए जाते हैं—

(i) Stative Adjectives

Stative का अर्थ होता है—दृढ़, स्थिर, स्थायी। इसलिए ऐसे Adjectives से उन गुणों का बोध होता है जो किसी व्यक्ति/वस्तु में स्थिर या स्थायी रूप से रहते हैं; जैसे—

1. He is tall.
2. She is beautiful.
3. Iron is hard.
4. Milk is white.

(ii) Dynamic Adjectives

Dynamic का अर्थ होता है—सक्रिय, गतिशील, परिवर्तनात्मक। इसलिए ऐसे Adjectives से उन गुणों का बोध होता है जो सदा एक रूप में नहीं रहते, अर्थात उनमें परिवर्तन होता है या हो सकता है; जैसे—

1. He is ill.
2. She is poor.
3. He is funny.
4. She is talkative.
5. He is foolish.
6. She is greedy.

(iii) Gradable Adjectives

Grade का अर्थ होता है—क्रम, श्रेणी, मात्रा। इसलिए Gradable Adjectives श्रेणी या मात्रा (degree) हो सकती है; जैसे—

rich—richer—richest; poor—poorer—poorest.

यही कारण है कि ऐसे Adjectives की मात्रा बताने के लिए इनके साथ Adverb of Degree का प्रयोग हो सकता है; जैसे—

very/extremely + adjective

It is very/extremely hot.

(iv) Non-gradable Adjectives

Non-gradable का अर्थ होता है—जिसकी श्रेणी या मात्रा न हो सके। Non-gradable Adjectives की Degree (comparison) नहीं होती और इनके साथ very/extremely का प्रयोग नहीं होता। इस दृष्टि से ऐसे Adjectives को Degreeless Adjectives भी कहा जा सकता है; जैसे—

full, perfect, unique, round, square, excellent, Indian, American, Japanese, atomic, botanical, biological, chemical

(v) Inherent/Non-inherent Adjectives

Inherent का अर्थ होता है—निहित, जन्मजात, प्राकृतिक, स्वाभाविक। इसलिए Inherent Adjective से ऐसे गुण का बोध होता है जो किसी व्यक्ति/वस्तु में अपने प्राकृतिक या प्रत्यक्ष रूप में रहता है। इसलिए ऐसा Adjective किसी Noun का गुण सीधे रूप से (directly) व्यक्त करता है। पर Non-inherent Adjectives से ऐसे गुण का बोध होता है जो किसी व्यक्ति/वस्तु में स्वाभाविक रूप में वर्तमान नहीं रहता। इसलिए ऐसा Adjective किसी Noun में लाक्षणिक (figurative) रूप में रहता है, अर्थात उसका संबंध उस Noun के साथ घुमा-फिराकर स्थापित किया जाता है; जैसे—

a *tall* boy, a *red* car , a *big* fish.
a *wooden* leg, a *silken* blouse. } —Inherent

a *tall* talk, a *red*-letter day, a *big* man.
a *wooden* head, a *silken* voice/hair } —Non-inherent

ध्यान दें कि tallness/redness/bigness ऐसे गुण हैं जो boy/car/fish में स्वाभाविक या प्राकृतिक रूप में वर्तमान हैं, क्योंकि हम इन गुणों को इन व्यक्तियों/वस्तुओं में देख सकते हैं। पर, talk में tallness नहीं है, letter में redness नहीं है और man में bigness नहीं है। इसी प्रकार, leg में wood है और blouse में silk है, पर head में wood नहीं है और voice/hair में silk को देख नहीं सकते। इन उदाहरणों से यह स्पष्ट हो जाता है कि Inherent Adjectives किसी Noun में प्रत्यक्ष रूप में पाए जाते हैं और Non-inherent Adjectives अप्रत्यक्ष रूप में, अर्थात लाक्षणिक रूप में पाए जाते हैं। अब हम Adjective के प्रयोग पर विचार करें और इन नियमों का ध्यान रखें।

Rule I. Each, Every, Either and Neither

Each/Every/Either/Neither के साथ सदा singular noun का प्रयोग होता है—

1. Each *book* is good.
2. Every *book* is good.
3. Neither *book* is good.
4. Either *book* is good.

NOTE—यदि every के बाद कोई बहुवचन संख्यासूचक विशेषण (plural numeral adjective) आए, तो उस adjective के बाद plural noun आता है, singular नहीं [every + plural number + plural noun]; जैसे—

1. He takes water *every two hours.*
2. He comes to me *every five days.*

Rule II. Each and Every

Rule II (A). Each का प्रयोग सदा दो या दो से अधिक Countable Nouns के साथ होता है, पर every का प्रयोग दो से अधिक के साथ (अर्थात कम-से-कम तीन के साथ) होता है, केवल दो के साथ नहीं; जैसे—

1. The *two boys* had *each* a pen.
2. The *two babies* have *each* a toy.
3. The *ten boys* had *each* a pen.

इसलिए दो ही व्यक्ति या वस्तुओं का बोध हो, तो every का प्रयोग नहीं करना चाहिए। इस वाक्य को लें—

There are *two boys* here and *every boy* has a pen.

यहाँ every के बदले each का प्रयोग होना चाहिए।

ध्यान दें कि each/every का प्रयोग Uncountable Noun के साथ नहीं होता है। इसलिए ऐसे वाक्य न बनाएँ—

1. Every milk is white.
2. Each gold is yellow.

Emphatic Each

कुछ लोग each and every का प्रयोग करते हैं जो शुद्ध है। इसका प्रयोग each पर अधिक जोर देने के लिए ही किया जाता है, पर याद रखें कि यदि सिर्फ दो ही का बोध हो तो न every का प्रयोग होगा और न each and every का ही; क्योंकि इनसे दो से अधिक का बोध होता है। इसलिए यह वाक्य अशुद्ध है—

There are two boys here and each and every boy has a pen.

Rule II (B). Each of us/them—Each का प्रयोग pronoun की तरह भी किया जाता है, पर every का नहीं; अर्थात 'each' adjective और pronoun दोनों ही है, पर 'every' सिर्फ adjective है, इसलिए each के बाद of का प्रयोग होता है, पर every के बाद कभी नहीं; जैसे—

Each of them is doing his duty.

यहाँ each of them के बदले every of them का प्रयोग सर्वथा अनुचित होता। यदि every के साथ one को जोड़कर everyone बना दें, तो इसका प्रयोग Pronoun की तरह हो सकता है और इसे of के पहले रख सकते हैं; जैसे—

Everyone of them is doing his duty.

Rule II (C). Either and Both

Either का अर्थ 'दो में से एक' होता है, और 'दोनों' भी। अप जानते हैं कि both का अर्थ भी 'दोनों' होता है, पर both और either के प्रयोग में एक अंतर है। Either का अर्थ 'दोनों' तब होता है, जब एक भाग दूसरे भाग का पूरक (complementary) होता है; जैसे—

either side, either end, either hand

इसलिए जिस चीज के स्वाभाविक रूप से दो भाग नहीं होते, उनके साथ दोनों के अर्थ में both का प्रयोग होना चाहिए, either का नहीं। इन वाक्यों को लें—

1. There were trees on either side of the road.
2. His either son passed with good marks.

यहाँ पहला वाक्य शुद्ध है, पर दूसरा अशुद्ध। क्यों? इसलिए कि दो लड़के स्वाभाविक रूप से एक-दूसरे के पूरक नहीं होते। इसलिए दूसरे वाक्य में both sons का प्रयोग होना चाहिए।

Rule III. Distributive Adjective and Article

Distributive Adjective के पहले article का प्रयोग नहीं होता। इसलिए इस प्रकार न लिखें—

1. The each book is good. 2. An every boy is good.

EXERCISE

Correct the following sentences.

(1) Every boys are reading their books. (2) I have only two pens but every pen writes well. (3) The medicine is given to a patient every three hour. (4) You have to take one tablet each four hours. (5) You should take neither sides. (6) Either roads will lead you there. (7) Every of us should do his work. (8) An every book is not equally useful. (9) The each book should be read carefully.

Hints—(1) Every boy is reading his book; (2) each; (3) hours; (4) every; (5) side; (6) road; (7) Everyone; (8) Every book; (9) Each book

Rule IV. Possessive Adjectives and Possessive Pronouns

Possessive Adjectives का प्रयोग सदा noun के पहले होता है [possessive adjective + noun]; जैसे—

1. This is my brother. 2. This is your book.

Possessive Pronouns का प्रयोग सदा verb के बाद होता है [verb + possessive pronoun]; जैसे—

1. This book is mine. 2. That pen is yours.

इसलिए Possessive Adjectives का प्रयोग verb के बाद और Possessive Pronoun का प्रयोग noun के पहले इस प्रकार न करें—

1. This is mine book. 2. This book is my.

NOTE (a)—Possessive Pronoun + Verb

कभी-कभी *possessive adjective* और *noun*—ये दोनों ही छिपे रहते हैं और इनके बदले possessive pronoun का प्रयोग होता है। वैसी अवस्था में possessive pronoun वाक्य के आरंभ में आता है और इसके बाद verb आता है [possessive pronoun + verb]; जैसे—

1. Mohan's pen is red. Mine is black. [mine = my pen]

2. My bag is big. Yours is small. [yours = your bag]

ध्यान दें कि ऐसी अवस्था में Possessive Pronoun verb के पहले आता है, verb के बाद नहीं।

NOTE (b)—Possession and Relation

Possessive Adjectives से possession (अधिकार) और relation (संबंध) दोनों का बोध होता है; जैसे—

1. This book is mine. 2. That bag is yours.

संबंध बताने के लिए Possessive Pronoun का प्रयोग इस प्रकार नहीं हो सकता—

1. This brother is mine. 2. This friend is yours.

हाँ, ऐसे वाक्यों में *noun + of + possessive pronoun* का प्रयोग इस प्रकार अवश्य हो सकता है—

1. He is a friend of mine. He is a cousin of yours.

NOTE (c)—His का प्रयोग noun के पहले हो सकता है और verb के बाद भी, क्योंकि यह Possessive Pronoun है और Possessive Adjective भी; जैसे—

1. This is his book. 2. The book is his.

NOTE (d)—Possessive Pronoun के spelling का सदा ध्यान रखें—

its (it's नहीं), ours (our's नहीं), yours (your's नहीं), hers/theirs (her's/their's नहीं)। वाक्य में It's का अर्थ होता है—It is, 'इसका' नहीं।

Rule V. Possessive Adjectives and Articles

Possessive Adjectives के रहने पर noun के साथ article का प्रयोग नहीं होता; जैसे—

1. This is his pen. 2. That is her ink-pot.

यहाँ pen और ink-pot के साथ a/an/the का प्रयोग नहीं हो सकता, इसलिए ये वाक्य अशुद्ध हैं—

1. That is *a* my book. 2. This is *the* his best shirt.

....

EXERCISE

Correct the following sentences.

(1) These are mine books not your's. (2) Our's wants are unlimited. (3) Her's hair is black. (4) Their's ideas are old. (5) It is a your house. (6) This is the mine best dress. (7) These things are our's.

Hints—(1) These books are mine, not yours; (2) Our; (3) Her; (4) Their; (5) It is your house; (6) This is my best dress; (7) ours

....

Rule VI. Demonstrative Adjectives and their Number

Demonstrative Adjectives के प्रयोग के संबंध में यह ध्यान रखना चाहिए कि Singular Adjective के साथ Singular Noun का और Plural Adjective के साथ Plural Noun का प्रयोग होता है—

this boy; *these* boys; *a certain* man;

certain men; *another* pen; *other* pens

NOTE—आप यह भी न भूलें कि a, an, a certain, one तथा another शुद्ध Singular हैं। अतः, इनके साथ सदा Singular Nouns का प्रयोग होता है। इसलिए ये वाक्य अशुद्ध हैं—

1. These are another books.

2. There are a certain boys.

इसी प्रकार, certain और other शुद्ध Plural हैं और इसलिए इनके साथ सदा Plural Nouns का ही प्रयोग होना चाहिए; जैसे—

certain boys; *other* boys

कुछ ऐसे Indifinite Demonstrative Adjectives भी हैं, जो Singular और Plural दोनों ही होते हैं—

any, such, some, any other

इसलिए इनके साथ Singular या Plural noun का प्रयोग करना अपनी इच्छा पर निर्भर है; जैसे—

any country; *any* countries

Definite Demonstrative Adjectives में this और that singular हैं, पर these और those plural. अतः, इनके साथ भी noun का प्रयोग इनके वचन पर निर्भर रहता है। Such, the same तथा the other का प्रयोग Singular और Plural दोनों ही वचनों में होता है; जैसे—

the other *man*; the other *men*

Demonstrative Adjectives की चर्चा यहाँ विस्तारपूर्वक इसलिए की गई है कि आप इनके number का ध्यान रखें और singular के साथ singular noun का प्रयोग करें और plural के साथ plural noun का।

अब, इन वाक्यों को देखें जिनमें इस नियम का उल्लंघन किया गया है—

1. I like *these sort* of men.

2. I do not like *those kind* of men.

यहाँ these/those के साथ Singular Noun (sort/kind) का प्रयोग कर दिया गया है। इनके शुद्ध रूप ये होंगे—

1. I like *this sort* of men. 2. I do not like *that kind* of men.

कुछ लोग समझते हैं कि these kind और those sort लिखना शुद्ध है; पर वास्तव में यह प्रयोग बोलचाल तक ही सीमित है। इस संबंध में आप इस विचार का ध्यान रखें—

*The irregular uses—***those kind of** *and* **these sort of** *are easy to avoid when they are worth avoiding, that is, in print, and easy to forgive when they deserve forgiveness, that is, in hasty talk.* —FOWLER: *Modern English Usage*

इसलिए आप those kind या those sort आदि का प्रयोग न करें, अर्थात these और those के बाद आनेवाले Noun (kind, sort आदि) को Plural Number में रखें। अब इस वाक्य को देखें—

But I hope soon to put an end to **those sort** *of obligations.* —SAMUEL RICHARDSON

यहाँ those sort के बदले those sorts या that sort का प्रयोग होना चाहिए।

Rule VII. Another, Other and Any other

Another का प्रयोग singular noun के साथ और other का plural noun के साथ affirmative sentence में होता है, पर any other का प्रयोग singular और plural दोनों ही वचनों के nouns के साथ negative sentence में होता है; जैसे—

1. I have read *another* book. 2. I have read *other* books.

3. I have not read *any other* book or books.

अब इन वाक्यों को देखें—

1. I have read *any other* book. 2. I have not read *another* book.

यहाँ पहले वाक्य में another का प्रयोग होना चाहिए और दूसरे में any other का, क्योंकि पहला वाक्य affirmative है और दूसरा negative.

. . . .

EXERCISE

Correct the following sentences.

(1) I do not read these kind of books. (2) I do not like those sort of men. (3) There was certain man whose name I do not remember. (4) They are another men. (5) This is other pen. (6) I have met any other person this evening. (7) I have not used another pen today. (8) What does other teacher suggest?

Hints—(1) those kinds, or that kind; (2) those sorts, or that sort; (3) a certain; (4) other; (5) another; (6) another; (7) any other; (8) another

. . . .

Rule VIII. Many and Several

Many और Several के बाद सदा Plural Countable Nouns का प्रयोग होता है; जैसे—

many men; several men

इससे यह स्पष्ट है कि इनके साथ Singular Uncountable Nouns का प्रयोग नहीं हो सकता, क्योंकि इनका plural होता ही नहीं। इसलिए ये वाक्य अशुद्ध हैं—

1. He has many money. 2. You have many gold and silver.

. . . .

EXERCISE

Correct the following sentences.

(1) Ram has much pens and pencils. (2) He feels much difficulties. (3) He has observed many uncommon phenomenon. (4) I have faced much troubles. (5) The poet says that in life there are much cares and anxieties.

Hints—(1) many; (2) much difficulty or many difficulties; (3) phenomena; (4) much trouble or many troubles; (5) many

. . . .

Rule IX. Emphasing/Emphatic Adjectives

Rule IX (A). Possessive adjective + own/very own + noun

जब possessive adjective के बाद own आता है, तब वह emphatic बन जाता है; जैसे—

1. This is my own house. 2. That is her own car.
2. I want to have this car for my very own.

इसलिए केवल own + noun का प्रयोग इस प्रकार न करें—

1. This is own house. 2. That is own car.

Rule IX (B). Very/the same + noun

जब noun के पहले very/the same का प्रयोग होता है तब वह एक emphatic adjective का कार्य करता है; जैसे—

1. This the very book I want. 2. This is same book I want.

ऐसे वाक्यों में very/same के पहले the का प्रयोग अवश्य होता है।

Rule X. The Ordinals and Noun

Rule X (A). जिन Definite Numeral Adjectives से serial order का बोध होता है, उन्हें Ordinals कहते हैं, जैसे—first, second, third. इसके पहले the का प्रयोग होता है और बाद में Singular Noun का; जैसे—

the second class; the third period, the fourth dimension

यहाँ classes/periods/dimensions का प्रयोग अशुद्ध होता।

Rule X (B). Ordinals, Cardinals and Noun

यदि and से संयुक्त सभी Ordinals के लिए एक ही noun का प्रयोग हो और सिर्फ पहले Ordinal के पहले the आए तो वह Noun Plural Number में रहता है, पर यदि सभी Ordinals के पहले the का प्रयोग हो तो वह Noun Singular Number में रहता है; जैसे—

1. I have read the literature of *the* seventeenth and eighteenth *centuries.*
2. I have read the literature of *the* seventeenth and *the* eighteenth *century.*

यदि पहले वाक्य में century और दूसरे में centuries का प्रयोग कर दिया जाए तो यह अशुद्ध समझा जाएगा। ऐसे वाक्यों में थोड़ी-सी भी असावधानी के कारण भूल हो जाती है—

... let us merely remind ourselves of two relevant forces—the scientific movement of **the** *sixteenth and* **the** *seventeeth* **centuries.** —BASIL WILLEY

अब देखिए, सावधानी से लिखने पर इसका शुद्ध प्रयोग—

1. *... and the part of it that he has most enjoyed is the literature of the great ages,* **the** *sixteenth and seventeenth centuries.* —T S ELIOT
2. *... . Secondly, how did the religious conflict of* **the** *sixteenth and seventeenth* **centuries** *leap up to the growth of natural religion in our period?* —BASIL WILLEY

....

EXERCISE

Correct the following sentences.

(1) He has read the first and second chapter of this book. (2) He has read the first and the second chapters of this book. (3) G B Shaw lived through two centuries—the 19th and the 20th.

Hints—(1) chapters, (2) chapter, (3) the 19th and 20th

....

Rule XI. Few, A Few and The Few

Rule XI (A). इसके साथ सदा Plural Noun का प्रयोग होता है। इसलिए यह Noun वैसा होता है जिसका Plural हो सके (अर्थात Countable Noun का); जैसे—

1. He has *few pens.* 2. He has *a few pens.*

इन दोनों वाक्यों में Plural Noun का प्रयोग हुआ है, जो शुद्ध है। यदि यहाँ Uncountable या Singular Noun का प्रयोग हुआ होता, तो वाक्य अशुद्ध हो जाते; जैसे—

1. He has *few* rice. 2. He has a *few* money.

NOTE—Few and Little

Few और little, a few और a little तथा the few और the little के अर्थ में अंतर नहीं है, क्योंकि इनसे क्रमशः 'कुछ नहीं', 'कुछ' तथा 'जो कुछ थोड़ा' का बोध होता है, पर व्याकरण की दृष्टि से इनमें अंतर यह है कि few/a few/the few के साथ सदा Plural Countable Noun का प्रयोग होता है, पर little/a little/the little के साथ सदा Singular Uncountable Noun का; जैसे—

1. He has *little rice.* 2. He has *a little* money.

इसलिए few के साथ singular noun का प्रयोग और little के साथ plural noun का प्रयोग भयंकर भूल है। इस वाक्य को देखें—

I have *less* friends and *fewer* milk than Shyam.

यहाँ less के बदले fewer का और fewer के बदले less का प्रयोग होना चाहिए।

Rule XI (B). Few का अर्थ होता है 'कुछ नहीं', a few का 'कुछ' और the few का 'जो कुछ थोड़ा'। इससे यह स्पष्ट है कि जहाँ 'कुछ' अर्थ का बोध कराना हो वहाँ a few का प्रयोग होना चाहिए और जहाँ 'कुछ भी नहीं' का बोध हो वहाँ few का प्रयोग होना चाहिए। असावधानी से few के बदले a few या a few के बदले few का प्रयोग हो जाए, तो वह केवल व्याकरण की दृष्टि से ही नहीं, वरन अर्थ की दृष्टि से भी अशुद्ध समझा जाएगा; जैसे—

Ram has few books and so he can give me only two.

यहाँ few books से पता चलता है कि राम के पास कुछ भी (एक भी) किताब नहीं है। तो फिर, वह किताबें देगा कैसे? इसलिए, अर्थ की दृष्टि में रखते हुए, यहाँ a few का प्रयोग होना चाहिए।

EXERCISE

Correct the following sentences.

(1) He has few money. (2) She has few love for her husband. (3) I have purchased a few rice today. (4) I have few cows that give me five kilograms of milk. (5) I had few coins with me and so I gave only ten paise to the beggar. (6) I have few books which I have read very thoroughly. (7) He has a little pens. (8) She has a little rupees. (9) My cow does not give me fewer milk than yours. (10) He saw me few months after he had returned from England.

Hints—(1) little; (2) little; (3) a little; (4) a few; (5) a few; (6) a few; (7) a few; (8) a few; (9) less; (10) a few

Rule XII. Many, Many a/an + Noun

Many/a good many/a great many के साथ Noun सदा Plural रहता है, पर many a तथा many an के बाद सदा Singular; जैसे—

1. There are not *many men* there.
2. A *great (good) many men* have come.
3. *Many a man* has assembled.
4. *Many an ink-pot* has been bought.

EXERCISE

Correct the following sentences.

(1) Many a soldiers have attended the parade. (2) A great many flower was offered to him. (3) A good many poem is bad. (4) Many an HE Schools have been started this year. (5) Many an hours have passed away. (6) Many a men run after name and fame.

Hints—(1) soldier has; (2) flower were; (3) poems are; (4) school has; (5) hour has; (6) man runs

Rule XIII. Definite Numerals and Of

कुछ ऐसे Definite Numeral Adjectives हैं (a dozen/a hundred/a thousand/a million) जिनके बाद of का प्रयोग नहीं होता। उनके बाद केवल noun आता है; जैसे—

a dozen pens, a hundred rupees, a thousand rupees, a million rupees

NOTE—पर *a lakh/a couple/a pair/a score/a gross* के बाद of अवश्य आता है, जैसे—

a lakh of men, *a pair of* shoes, *a couple of* hours

यदि यहाँ of का प्रयोग नहीं होता, तो वह अशुद्ध समझा जाता। यहाँ एक बात का ध्यान अवश्य रखें। यदि Definite Numerals के पहले a नहीं रहे और उन्हें Plural बना दिया जाए, तो उनसे अनिश्चित संख्या का बोध होता है; जैसे—dozens, hundreds, thousands आदि। जब ऐसी अनिश्चित संख्या के बाद noun आता है, तो इनके साथ of का प्रयोग अवश्य होता है—

definite plural numerals + of + noun

1. He has dozens of pens.
2. A king had hundreds of servants.
3. Thousands of men and women assembled there.

इन वाक्यों से यह भी स्पष्ट हो जाता है कि of नहीं रहने पर ऐसी अनिश्चित संख्या के बाद noun का प्रयोग नहीं हो सकता। इसलिए इस प्रकार न लिखें—

1. He has thousands rupees.
2. I have dozens books.

हाँ, यदि of + noun का प्रयोग न हो, तो ऐसी अनिश्चित संख्या का प्रयोग noun की तरह इस प्रकार हो सकता है—

Thousands heard him with attention.

....

EXERCISE

Correct the following sentences.

(1) I have dozens pens. (2) You have a thousand of rupees. (3) I have seen a lakh men today. (4) The Government have spent a million of rupees over this project.

Hints—(1) dozens of pens; (2) thousand rupees; (3) lakh of; (4) million rupees

....

Rule XIV. Much + Noun

Much से परिमाण (how much) का बोध होता है, इसलिए इसके साथ Singular Uncountable Noun का प्रयोग होता है। इससे यह भी स्पष्ट है कि much के साथ plural noun का प्रयोग नहीं हो सकता; जैसे—

not much water; not much milk

अब इन वाक्यों को देखें—

1. I don't feel *much* difficulties these days.
2. He does not have *much* cares and anxieties.

इन वाक्यों में much के साथ plural nouns का प्रयोग हुआ है, जो अशुद्ध है। यहाँ much के बदले many का प्रयोग होना चाहिए, या plural nouns के बदले singular nouns का।

EXERCISE

Correct the following sentences.

(1) She has not much golds and silvers. (2) You have not much cows and horses. (3) She has not much books and pens. (4) He has not passed through much sorrows and sufferings.

Hints—(1) gold and silver; (2) many; (3) many; (4) many

Rule XV. All/Most/Some + Noun

जब all/most/some का प्रयोग Adjective of Quantity (परिमाणवाचक) की भाँति होता है, तब इनके साथ Singular Noun आता है, पर जब इनका प्रयोग Adjective of Number (संख्यावाचक) की भाँति होता है, तब इनके साथ Plural Noun आता है; जैसे—

1. Not *all* his *poetry* is good.
2. *Some* of his *poetry* is good.
3. *All men* are mortal.
4. *Some men* are foolish.
5. *Most* of his *money* was wasted.
6. *Most* of the *boys* are poor.

ऐसा प्रयोग मान्य है—

1. ...... *where* **all vision** *is lost and* **all memory** *dies out.* —D H LAWRENCE
2. ...... *they chose rather to bear* **all hardship** *than to make away with themselves.* —JOHN BUNYAN

Rule XVI. Much/Many + Subject/object

Rule XVI (A). Much/Many का प्रयोग साधारणतया negative और interrogative sentences में होता है; जैसे—

1. I haven't *much* money. 2. I haven't *many* friends.

3. Have you *much* money. 4. Have you *many* friends?

Rule XVI (B). Affirmative sentences में Much/Many का प्रयोग subject के साथ तो होता है, पर Object के साथ नहीं। Affirmative sentences में Object के साथ Much/Many के बदले निम्नलिखित का प्रयोग होता है—

lots of/a lot of/plenty of/a good deal of/a large number of/a large quantity of/a large amount of

इन वाक्यों पर विचार करें—

1. *Many* men came. 2. *Much milk* was wasted.

इन वाक्यों में men और milk Subjects हैं। इसलिए इनके साथ many/much का प्रयोग उचित है, पर यदि men और milk को Object बना दिया जाए, तो इनके साथ much/many का प्रयोग नहीं होगा। इसलिए ये वाक्य अशुद्ध हैं—

1. I know many men. 2. I bought much milk.

इनके शुद्ध रूप ये होंगे—

1. I know a lot of men. 2. I bought plenty of milk.

Rule XVI (C). Affirmative sentences रहने पर भी much/many का प्रयोग Subject और Object दोनों के साथ होता है, जब much/many के साथ *as/how/too* लगा रहता है; जैसे—

1. I do not like *too much* of fish.
2. I do not like *too many* friends.
3. I don't know *how many* mangoes he will buy.
4. You may take *as much as* you like.
5. You may have *as many* pens *as* you like.

Much और Many के संबंध में जो कुछ कहा गया है उसका आधार यह नियम है—

There is a tendency for *much* and *many*, when not modified by *how* or *too*, to occur in Negative and Interrogative sentences and not normally in purely Affirmative sentences. In Affirmative sentences such compound determinatives as *a lot (of), a large number (quantity, amount) of,* and *plenty of* are preferred.

—A S HORNEY: *Patterns and Usage in English*

. . . .

EXERCISE

Correct the following sentences.

(1) I have many books and paper. (2) You have much gold and houses. (3) He has purchased much milk and mangoes. (4) I have brought many cups and tea. (5) Shakespeare has written much poetry and plays.

Hints—(1) much paper; (2) many houses; (3) many mangoes; (4) much tea; (5) many plays

. . . .

Rule XVII. Some and Any

Rule XVII (A). Some का प्रयोग affirmative sentences में होता है, पर any का negative में, और hardly/scarcely/barely के साथ; जैसे—

1. He has *some* money. 2. He has *not any* money.
3. I have *some* food. 4. I have *not any* food.
5. He has *hardly any* food. 6. Thee are *scarcely any* good books here.

Rule XVII (B). वाक्य में if या अन्य संदेहसूचक शब्द (expression of doubt) के साथ any का प्रयोग होता है, some का नहीं; जैसे—

1. Tell me if you have *any* doubt.
2. I wonder whether there is *any* money left.

इस दृष्टि से ये वाक्य अशुद्ध हैं—

1. He has *not some* bread.
2. I want to know if you have *some* doubts.

यहाँ some के बदले any क प्रयोग करना चाहिए।

NOTE—Not any/No any—जब any का प्रयोग negative sentence में होता है, तब any के पहले not आता है, no नहीं। No any का प्रयोग नहीं हो सकता, क्योंकि No adjective है और Any भी। फिर adjective किसी adjective का गुण कैसे बतला सकता है? Not है adverb जो adjective 'any' का गुण बतला सकता है; जैसे—

1. I have *not any money.*

यहाँ not any के बदले *no any* का प्रयोग अशुद्ध होता।

Rule XVII (C). यदि वाक्य Interrogative हो, तो some और any के प्रयोग में कोई अंतर नहीं माना जाता पर यदि Interrogative sentence से प्रार्थना/निमंत्रण का बोध हो, तो some का प्रयोग होता है; जैसे—

1. Have you any/some food?—प्रश्न
2. Could you give me some food?—प्रार्थना

EXERCISE

I. ***Fill in the blanks with an adjective from the box.***

some	**any**

1. There isn't ...... milk here.
2. Please give me ...... water.
3. There are ...... pictures in this book.
4. She has ...... books and pens.
5. She asks for ...... money but I can't find ....

II. *Make the following sentences (a) negative, (b) interrogative.*

1. He has some books.
2. She bought some cows.
3. There is some information.

Rule XVIII. Little, A little and The little

Rule XVIII (A). Little का अर्थ होता है 'कुछ नहीं', a little का 'कुछ' (थोड़ा) और the little का 'जो कुछ थोड़ा'। इस अर्थ को ध्यान में रखकर इनका प्रयोग करना चाहिए, क्योंकि 'कुछ नहीं' के अर्थ में a little के प्रयोग से और 'कुछ' के अर्थ में little के प्रयोग से काफी गड़बड़ी पैदा हो जाती है; जैसे—

As I have little rice, I can give you only two kilograms.

यहाँ प्रश्न यह उठता है कि जब मुझे little rice (कुछ भी चावल नहीं) है, तो फिर दो किलोग्राम कैसे दिया जाएगा? अतः यहाँ a little का प्रयोग होना चाहिए, little का नहीं।

Rule XVIII (B). Little, a little और the little के संबंध में एक और बात याद रखें कि 'कुछ' के अर्थ में इनके साथ सिर्फ Singular Uncountable Noun का ही प्रयोग हो सकता है, क्योंकि ये शुद्ध परिमाणवाचक विशेषण हैं। जिस प्रकार few के साथ uncountable noun का प्रयोग नहीं हो सकता, उसी प्रकार little के साथ countable noun का प्रयोग नहीं होता। इसलिए ये वाक्य अशुद्ध हैं—

1. I have *few* money. 2. I have *little* books.

यहाँ few के बदले little का और little के बदले few का प्रयोग होना चाहिए।

Rule XVIII (C). The few/The little

The few और The little के बाद एक adjective clause आता है, पर few, a few, little और a little के बाद नहीं; जैसे—

1. He spent *the little* money *he had.* 2. He has read *the few* books *he had.*

इन वाक्यों के अधार पर आप ऐसे वाक्य न बनाएँ—

1. He lost little/a little money *he had.*

2. He has read few/a few books *he had.*

Rule XIX. No/None and the Noun

Noun के पहले no आता है, none नहीं; जैसे—

1. I have no money [not, none money]

2. I have *no* bread. [not, none bread]

EXERCISE

Correct the following sentences.

(1) I have no any book. (2) I have not some money. (3) He has any books. (4) I have little rice and so I shall give you ten kilograms. (5) He has spent a little money he had. (6) You have none books. (7) You have a little books. (8) There were not less than twenty persons. (9) I did not know his whereabouts and so had little difficulty in finding him out. (10) He is too busy to attend to some work. (11) He did not buy some pens.

Hints—(1) no book or not any book; (2) any money or have some money; (3) some; (4) a little; (5) the little; (6) no; (7) a few; (8) fewer than; (9) a little; (10) any work; (11) any pens

Position of Adjecties

Adjective का प्रयोग दो प्रकार से होता है। जब हम Adjective को Noun के पहले रखते हैं, तब उसे Attributive use कहते हैं और जब उसे Verb के बाद रखते हैं, तब Predicative use; जैसे—

1. This is a *useful book*. 2. This *book is useful.*

Adjective का प्रयोग Attributive हो या Predicative, इस संबंध में एक-दो बातों का ध्यान रखें—

Rule I. Qualitative and Proper Adjectives

Proper Adjective तथा Adjective of Quality का प्रयोग दोनों ही तरह से होता है—Attributive की तरह और Predicative की तरह भी; जैसे—

1. This *game is Indian.* 2. This is an *Indian game.*

3. He is a *brave boy.* 4. The *boy is brave.*

बहुत-से adjectives का प्रयोग दोनों तरह से होता है, पर कुछ adjectives ऐसे भी हैं जिनका केवल Predicative use ही होता है, Attributive नहीं। ये adjectives हैं—

asleep, awake, afraid, ashamed, alike

alone, alive ill (unwell के अर्थ में); जैसे—

1. The baby is asleep. 2. The boy is awake.

3. The girl is alone. 4. The man is alive.

5. I have no ill will. 6. He is afraid of me.

इन्हें इस प्रकार नहीं लिखा जा सकता—

1. There is an asleep baby or an awake boy.

2. There is an alone girl or an alive man.

NOTE (a)—याद रखें कि 'ill' का attributive प्रयोग हो सकता है, पर उस अवस्था में ill का अर्थ हो जाता है 'बुरा' (bad), 'बीमार' (unwell) नहीं; जैसे—

I have no *ill will* against anybody.

Rule II. Indefinite Pronouns and Adjective

Adjective का प्रयोग Indefinite Pronouns (something, nothing, anything, somebody, anybody, nobody, no one) के बाद होता है; जैसे–

1. Tell me something *new.* 2. I have nothing *useful* to do.

Rule III. More than one Adjective

यदि एक ही साथ बहुत-से adjectives का प्रयोग एक ही noun के लिए करना हो, या ये adjectives काफी लंबे हों, तो उन्हें noun के बाद रखना अच्छा होता है; जैसे—

1. A *man, young, strong,* and *intelligent* …..

2. God is the Maker of all *things—visible* and *invisible, animate* and *inanimate.*

इसी प्रकार, जब कोई adjective पदवी (title) के लिए प्रयुक्त होता है, तब वह noun के बाद आता है; जैसे—

1. *Alexander the Great; Queen Victoria* the *Good*

2. Yudhisthir the *Just; Louis* the *Pious*

3. *Pitt* the *Younger; Cato* the *Elder*

Rule IV. Phrases and Adjective

कुछ प्रचलित phrases में adjective को noun के बाद रखा जाता है; जैसे—

the body *politic*; heir *apparent*; governor-*general*;

the sum *total*; a god *incarnate*; president *elect*.

Rule V. Ordinals and Cardinals

यदि किसी noun के पहले Cardinal तथा Ordinal—दोनों ही प्रकार के adjectives आएँ, तो वाक्य में पहले Ordinal को रखना चाहिए और उसके बाद Cardinal को; जैसे—

I have read the *first two* chapters of this book.

यहाँ पहले Ordinal (first) आया है और उसके बाद Cardinal (two). इसलिए आप ऐसे वाक्य न बनाएँ—

I have read the two first chapters.

Rule VI. Numeral and Possessive adjectives

यदि Numeral Adjectives और Possessive Adjectives और Possessive Adjectives (my, your, his, her, its, their) दोनों ही का प्रयोग किसी noun के पहले करना हो, तो पहले Numeral Adjective को रखें और उसके बाद Possessive Adjective को; जैसे—

1. *All my* books are missing.
2. *All his* friends are rich.

यहाँ Nouns के पहले दो Adjectives आए हैं—Numeral और Possessive, इसलिए पहले Numeral Adjective आया है और बाद में Possessive. पहले Possessive Adjective और उसके बाद Numeral को रखकर ऐसे वाक्य न बनाएँ—

1. My all pens are good.
2. Her all books are good.

NOTE—वाक्य में the/this/that का स्थान Numeral Adjective के बाद रहता है; जैसे— all the books, all this, both the boys; इसलिए this all, the all, the both का प्रयोग सर्वथा अनुचित है। अतः, ऐसे ऐसे वाक्य न बनाएँ—

1. The all friends are false.
2. The both girls are tall.

. . . .

EXERCISE.

Correct the following sentences.

(1) My all friends came. (2) His all books are missing. (3) My both pens are good. (4) Your some teeth have fallen. (5) His many teeth have fallen. (6) My a few books are lost. (7) These all men are bad.

Hints—(1) All my; (2) All his; (3) Both my; (4) Some of your; (5) Many of his; (6) A few of my; (7) All these

Correct the following sentences.

(1) He has read the four first books of the Paradise Lost. (2) The two first boys were rewarded. (3) The five first competitors got gold medals and three last silver ones. (4) The three first candidates have been selected for appointment.

Hints—(1) first four; (2) first two; (3) first five … last three; (4) first three

. . . .

Rule VII. Adjective + Infinitive

कभी-कभी adjective के बाद infinitive इस प्रकार आता है—

1. He was *kind enough to help* me.
2. It is *foolish to say so.*

ऐसे adjectives को प्रधानता देने (या उसपर जोर देने) के लिए वाक्य की बनावट इस प्रकार की हो जाती है—

It + is/was + adjective + of + noun/pronoun + infinitive; जैसे—

1. It was *kind of him to help* me.
2. It is *foolish of him to say* so.

ऐसे अर्थ में Exclamatory Sentences में वाक्य की बनावट इस प्रकार की हो जाती है—

How + adjective + of + noun/pronoun + infinitive; जैसे—

1. *How kind of him to help* me!
2. *How foolish of him to say* so!

Degree of Adjectives

किसी व्यक्ति या वस्तु में कोई गुण कितनी मात्रा (Degree) में है इसकी छानबीन को ही Degree of Comparison कहते हैं। यह मात्रा निम्नांकित तीन प्रकार की होती है—

(A) Positive, (B) Comparative, and (C) Superlative

Positive Degree

यदि adjective के मूल रूप का प्रयोग हो, तो उसे Positive Degree कहते हैं; जैसे—

1. He is a *good* boy. 2. This is a *nice* book.

Positive Degree में व्यक्तियों/वस्तुओं के गुणों की तुलना नहीं की जाती और यदि तुलना होती भी है तो उनके बीच समानता दिखलायी जाती है, गुणों का अधिक या कम होना (असमानता) नहीं। ऐसे वाक्यों की बनावट होती है—

(i) subject + verb + adjective

(ii) subject + verb + as + adjective + as

1. He is clever. 2. He is as clever as she.

Comparative Degree

जब एक ही प्रकार के दो व्यक्तियों या वस्तुओं की तुलना की जाती है ओर यह बताया जाता है कि गुण की मात्रा एक में दूसरे की अपेक्षा अधिक है, तब उसे Comparative Degree कहा जाता है; जैसे—

1. Mary is taller than Dolly.
2. Karim is richer than Rahim.

Superlative Degree

जब एक ही प्रकार के तीन या तीन से अधिक व्यक्तियों या वस्तुओं की तुलना की जाती है और यह बताया जाता है कि गुण की मात्रा एक में सबसे अधिक है, तब उसे Superlative Degree कहते हैं; जैसे—

1. Mary is the tallest of all girls.
2. Karim is the richest man in this village.

NOTE—signs/markers of comparatives/superlatives

Comparative Degree का चिह्न (sign/marker) है r/er और Superlative Degree का st/est.

एक syllable के adjective में r/er जोड़कर comparative बनाई जाती है और st/est जोड़कर superlative की रचना की जाती है; जैसे—

Positive	**Comparative**	**Superlative**
tall	taller	tallest
great	greater	greatest
sweet	sweeter	sweetest
brave	braver	bravest
wise	wiser	wisest
easy	easier	easiest
happy	happier	happiest

कुछ adjectives की comparative और superlative degree अनियमित रूप से बनाई जाती है, जैसे—

good	better	best
bad	worse	worst
little	less	least
much	more	most
many	more	most

दो या दो से अधिक syllables के adjectives के पहले more के प्रयोग से comparative का बोध होता है और most से superlative का—

useful	more useful	most useful
beautiful	more beautiful	most beautiful
difficult	more difficult	most difficult
important	more important	most important

Constructions with Comparisons

Rule I. Comparison of Equality

जब दो व्यक्तियों, वस्तुओं या गुणों की तुलना की जाती है और उनके बीच समानता (quality) दिखलाई जाती है, तब **as + adjective + as** का प्रयोग इस प्रकार किया जाता है—

1. This boy is as tall as that. 2. My pen is as cheap as yours.

Rule II. Comparison of Inequality

जब दो व्यक्तियों, वस्तुओं या गुणों की तुलना की जाती है और उनके बीच असमानता (inequality) दिखलाई जाती है, अर्थात जब तुलना negative होती है, तब **not as** या **not so + adjective + as** का प्रयोग इस प्रकार होता है—

1. This boy is not as tall as that. 2. My pen is not so cheap as that.

less + adjective + than

NOTE (a)—इस प्रकार के वाक्यों में less + positive degree + than का भी प्रयोग हो सकता है—

1. This boy is less tall than that.

पर आधुनिक अँगरेजी में *less + positive degree + than* का प्रयोग विरले ही होता है। इसलिए ऐसे वाक्यों में *not so + positive degree + as* का प्रयोग करें तो अच्छा होगा, जैसे—

This boy is not so tall as that.

that + adjective/so + adjective

NOTE (b)—आजकल positive degree में *not all that + adjective* का प्रयोग इस प्रकार हो रहा है—

1. It is not all that dear. 2. It is not all that high.

पर तुलना करते समय *not all + that* के बदले not so ... as का प्रयोग करना चाहिए—

It is *not so* high *as* that.

Than and the case of pronouns

NOTE (c)—वाक्य में transitive verb रहने पर than के बाद आनेवाला pronoun रहता है nominative case या objective case में। ऐसे pronouns का case निर्भर करता है वाक्य के अर्थ पर, जैसे—

1. I like you more than he. [that is, more than he likes you]
2. I like you more than him. [that is, more than I like him]

पर intransitive verb रहने पर than के बाद आनेवाला pronoun, शुद्ध व्याकरण की दृष्टि से रहता है nominative case में, जैसे—

1. He is taller than she. 2. She is richer than he.

आजकल बातचीत की भाषा में ऐसे वाक्यों में than के बाद objective case का भी प्रयोग शुद्ध माना जाता है, जैसे—

He is better than **me.**

Rule III (A). Comparison of Actions [verbs]

दो कार्यों (actions) की तुलना इस प्रकार की जाती है—

1. Talking is as easy as playing.
2. Running is not as easy as walking.
3. Cooking is not as easy as eating.
4. It is as easy to talk as play.
5. It is not as easy to run as walk.
6. It is not as easy to cook as eat.

ऐसे वाक्यों में पहले infinitive का to चिह्न प्रकट रहता है, पर दूसरे infinitive का to चिह्न छिपा रहता है—

to talk as play [not, to play]

Rule III (B). Comparison of Actions [verb]

दो कार्यों के बीच तुलना इस प्रकार भी की जाती है—

(i) Subject + prefer + verb + ing + to + verb + ing [gerund]

(ii) Subject + prefer + infinitive + rather + than + infinitive [without to]

(iii) Subject + had better + infinitive [without to] + than + infinitive [without to]

(iv) Subject + had rather + infinitive [without to] + than + infinitive [without to]

(v) Subject + had sooner + infinitive [without to] + than + infinitive [without to]

(vi) Subject + would sooner/would rather + infinitive [without to] + than + infinitive [without to]

(vii) Subject + had as soon + infinitive [without to] + as + infinitive [without to]

1. I prefer walking to swimming.
2. I prefer to walk rather than swim.
3. He would prefer dying to begging.
4. He would prefer to die rather than beg.
5. He had better die than beg.
6. He had rather die than beg.
7. He had sooner die than beg.
8. He would sooner die than beg.

9. He would as soon die as beg.

10. He would rather die than beg.

Rule IV (A). Comparison of Qualities

दो व्यक्तियों/वस्तुओं के गुण की तुलना करने के लिए comparative degree + than का प्रयोग होता है; जैसे—

1. Radha is taller than Mohan. 2. This book is better than that.

Rule IV (B). Comparison of Qualities

यदि एक ही व्यक्ति या वस्तु के दो गुणों (qualities) की तुलना की जाए, तो उस adjective के पहले सदा more/less का प्रयोग होता है और than के बाद आनेवाला adjective सदा positive degree में रहता है; जैसे—

1. Mohan is *more brave* than good.
2. Ram is *more* good than intelligent.

यहाँ पहले वाक्य में एक ही व्यक्ति (Mohan) के दो गुणों (brave/good) की तुलना की गई है। इसलिए एक syllable के विशेषण रहने पर भी brave/good के पहले more का प्रयोग हुआ है। यहाँ more good के बदले better और more brave के बदले braver का प्रयोग नहीं होना चाहिए।

अब इन वाक्यों को लें—

1. You are *wiser* than good. 2. The book is *better* than cheap.

यहाँ wiser के बदले more wise तथा better के बदले more good का प्रयोग होना चाहिए।

Rule V. Comparison of Number/Quantity

संख्या (number) और मात्रा (quantity) की तुलना इस प्रकार की जाती है—

subject + verb + fewer/less + noun + than + noun.

इन वाक्यों को लें—

1. She has fewer rings than chains.
2. He has fewer bags than books.
3. I have less salt than sugar.
4. He has less gold than silver.

ध्यान दें कि fewer के साथ Plural Countable Noun आता है, पर less के साथ Singular Uncountable Noun. इसलिए इस प्रकार के वाक्य न बनाएँ—

1. I bought fewer butter than milk.
2. She bought less pens than pencils.

Rule VI. Comparison of Weights and Measures

Weight (तौल) की तुलना इस प्रकार करनी चाहिए—

... times + as + positive degree + as ...,

This box is five times as heavy as that.

कुछ लोग ऐसी अवस्था में इस प्रकार तुलना करते हैं—

... times + comparative degree + than; जैसे—

This box is five times heavier than that.

यह वाक्य अशुद्ध है। ऐसे वाक्यों में आप as ... as के द्वारा ही तुलना करें।

NOTE—यदि वाक्य में निश्चित amount या quantity रहे, तो तुलना इस प्रकार की जाती है—

... comparative degree ... + ... than ...

1. This is five pounds heavier than that.
2. This shirt is three shillings dearer than that.

....

EXERCISE

Correct the following sentences.

(1) Ram is stronger than brave. (2) The book is cheaper than better. (3) You are stronger than wiser. (4) This flower is redder than whiter. (5) He is bolder than wiser. (6) This house is finer than stronger.

Hints—(1) more strong than brave; (2) more cheap than good; (3) more strong than wise; (4) more red than white; (5) more bold than wise; (6) more fine than strong

....

Rule VII. Comparative-cum-Superlative

यदि हम दो व्यक्तियों/वस्तुओं के बीच तुलना करने के बदले एक ही व्यक्ति/वस्तु की तुलना उस वर्ग के सभी (all) व्यक्तियों या वस्तुओं के साथ करें (जैसा Superlative Degree में किया जाता है) तो than के बाद आनेवाले Noun/Pronoun के साथ other/else का प्रयोग होना चाहिए; जैसे—

1. Ram is better than *all other* students.
2. I like it better than *any other* book.
3. You are better than *anybody else* in the class.

यहाँ पहले वाक्य में Ram की तुलना सभी लड़कों से की गई है। यहाँ सिर्फ दो ही व्यक्तियों की तुलना नहीं की गई है। इसलिए all के बाद other का प्रयोग आवश्यक है। इसी प्रकार, दूसरे वाक्य में भी any के बाद other का प्रयोग हुआ है, क्योंकि यहाँ it की तुलना सभी किताबों के साथ हुई है, सिर्फ एक ही किताब से नहीं। तीसरे वाक्य में you की तुलना सभी (anybody) से हुई है। अतः, यहाँ else का प्रयोग हुआ है। यदि आप ऐसे वाक्यों में than के बाद आनेवाले all, anybody, anyone, everybody आदि के साथ other/else का प्रयोग नहीं करेंगे, तो वाक्य अशुद्ध समझे जाएँगे; जैसे—

1. Ram is better than *all* students.
2. I like it better than *any* book.
3. You are better than *anybody* in the class.

यहाँ all/any के बाद other का और anybody के बाद else का प्रयोग होना आवश्यक है।

NOTE—याद रखें कि than के बाद Noun रहने पर other का प्रयोग होता है, पर Pronoun रहने पर else का; जैसे—

all other books, any other man, anyone else,

everybody else, anybody else.

अब इन वाक्यों को देखें—

1. *There is another ego according to whose action the individual is recognizable, which needs a* **deeper** *sense than* **any** *we have been used to exercise.* —D H LAWRENCE
2. *The world of our daily life is* **more man made** *than at* **any** *previous epoch.* —BERTRAND RUSSELL
3. *Yet Marx is a strong force in the world,* **stronger** *than* **any** *we had in the past.* —*The Modern Review*, Feb. 1957

इन वाक्यों में any के बाद other का प्रयोग होना चाहिए। याद रखें कि सतर्कता से लिखनेवाले ऐसी गलती नहीं करते—

Milton handled blank verse in a way which no one has even approached ... and in so doing he did **more** *than* **anyone** *or* **anything else** *to make it impossible for the drama.* —T S ELIOT

. . . .

EXERCISE

Correct the following sentences.

(1) He is wiser than anybody in the town. (2) You are taller than all students of your class. (3) I like him better than any man. (4) He is more intelligent than any student of his class. (5) This book is better than any on the subject.

Hints—(1) anybody else; (2) all other; (3) any other; (4) any other; (5) any other

. . . .

Rule VIII. 'Preferable' and Comparative Degree

Preferable एक ऐसा Adjective है जिसके पहले, Latin comparative की भाँति, more/less का और बाद में than का प्रयोग नहीं होता। इसके साथ than के बदले सदा to का प्रयोग होता है; जैसे—

1. This is preferable *to* that.
2. Milk is preferable *to* meat.

इसलिए ऐसे-ऐसे वाक्य न लिखें—

1. This is preferable *than* that.
2. Milk is *more* preferable to meat.

. . . .

EXERCISE

Correct the following sentences.

(1) This book is more preferable than that. (2) That plan is more preferable than this. (3) Milk is preferable than egg.

Hints—(1) is preferable to that; (2) is preferable to this; (3) is preferable to egg

. . . .

Rule IX. 'Comparatively' and Comparative Degree

यदि किसी Adjective या Adverb के पहले *Comparatively* शब्द का प्रयोग हो, तो वह adjective/adverb Positive Degree में रहता है, Comparative में नहीं; जैसे—

I am *comparatively well* today.

यदि हम यहाँ comparatively better लिखें तो वह अशुद्ध होगा। यदि Adjective या Adverb को Comparative Degree में रखना ही हो तो Comparatively शब्द का प्रयोग उस Adjective या Adverb के पहले न करें; जैसे—

I am better today.

इसलिए comparatively well लिखें या सिर्फ better, पर दोनों नहीं, क्योंकि अच्छे लेखक इन दोनों की खिचड़ी कभी नहीं पकाते—

1. *It was, of course,* **comparatively easy** *for Burke to accept the English Constitution as part of the order of nature.* —BASIL WILLEY
2. *This is* **comparatively easy.** —CHRISTOPHER CAUDWELL

इन वाक्यों में comparatively easy का प्रयोग शुद्ध है। यहाँ easy को easier कर देने से वाक्य अशुद्ध हो जाता। अब इस वाक्य को देखें—

... that an advance against Government securities now becomes comparatively **higher** *or* **costlier.** —*The Eastern Economist,* Feb. 8, 1957

इस वाक्य में higher के बदले high और costlier के बदले costly का प्रयोग होना चाहिए।

. . . .

EXERCISE

Correct the following sentences.

(1) How are you? I am comparatively better today. (2) This method is comparatively easier and safer. (3) That plan is comparatively cheaper.

Hints—(1) I am better ... or comparatively well; (2) is easier and safer or comparatively easy and safe; (3) is cheaper or comparatively cheap

. . . .

Rule X. the + comparative degree + of the two

यदि Comparative Degree के पहले the आए तो उसके बाद सदा *of the two* आता है। ऐसे वाक्यों की बनावट इस प्रकार की होती है—

... *the + comparative + of the two;* जैसे—

1. This boy is *the* better *of the two*. 2. He is *the* wiser *of the two*.

ऐसे वाक्यों में of के बदले than और two के बदले three, four आदि का प्रयोग भयंकर भूल है। इसलिए ये वाक्य अशुद्ध हैं—

1. This boy is *the* cleverer *than the two*.
2. This boy is *the* cleverer *of the three*.
3. This boy is *the* cleverer *than the three*.

....

EXERCISE

Correct the following sentences.

(1) You are the stronger of the three. (2) He is the wiser than the two. (3) This is the finer than the three. (4) This plan is the better than all.

Hints—(1) strongest of the three; (2) wiser of; (3) finest of the three; (4) better of the two or best of all

....

Rule XI. Parallel increase or decrease/Gradual increase

कुछ वाक्यों से Parallel increase का बोध होता है, अर्थात उनसे यह बोध होता है कि जब कोई गुण एक ओर बढ़ता है, तो वह उसी अनुपात में दूसरी ओर भी बढ़ता है। ऐसे वाक्यों की बनावट इस प्रकार की होती है—

the + comparative ... the + comparative; जैसे—

1. *The bigger* a house is, *the richer* its owner grows.
2. *The richer* a man is, *the more greedy* he becomes.

कुछ वाक्यों से Gradual increase का बोध होता है, अर्थात उनसे यह बोध होता है कि गुण की मात्रा बढ़ती ही जाती है। ऐसे वाक्यों की बनावट इस प्रकार की होती है—

... + *comparative + and + comparative;* जैसे—

1. He is getting *worse and worse*.
2. The weather is getting *hotter and hotter*.

Rule XII. Latin Comparatives

कुछ ऐसे Adjectives हैं जो Latin से आये हैं। इन्हें Latin comparatives कहा जाता है—senior, junior, prior, posterior, superior, inferior तथा anterior.

इनके पहले more या less का प्रयोग नहीं होता; इनके बाद to का प्रयोग होता है, than का नहीं; जैसे—

1. I am *senior to* him. 2. He is *junior to* me.

अतः आप ऐसे वाक्य न लिखें—

1. He *is more* superior *than* me.

2. You are *more* junior *than* him.

इनके शुद्ध रूप ये होंगे—

1. He is *superior to* me 2. You are *junior to* him.

NOTE—कुछ ऐसे भी Latin comparatives होते हैं जो अब Comparative Degree में व्यवहृत नहीं किये जाते। इनका प्रयोग अब केवल Positive Degree में साधारण विश्लेषण की ही भाँति होता है। इसलिए इनके बाद to का प्रयोग नहीं होना चाहिए; जैसे—

1. It is a *major* operation. 2. It is of *minor* importance.

3. I have no *ulterior* motive in doing this work.

उपर्युक्त वाक्यों में major, minor तथा ulterior का प्रयोग Positive Degree में हुआ है, Comparative में नहीं। इसलिए यहाँ to के प्रयोग करने का प्रश्न ही नहीं उठ सकता। वास्तव में, इनका प्रयोग Noun की तरह भी होने लगता है; जैसे—

1. He is a minor. 2. You are a major.

कहने का तात्पर्य यह है कि major और minor का प्रयोग, senior और junior की तरह, Comparative Degree में कभी न करें। इसलिए ये वाक्य अशुद्ध हैं—

1. He is major *to* me. 2. You are minor *to* him.

....

EXERCISE

Correct the following sentences.

(1) Your position is superior than his. (2) Shakespeare's plays are more superior than Shaw's. (3) You are more junior than me. (4) I am more senior than him. (5) My status is more superior than yours.

Hints—(1) superior to; (2) are superior to; (3) are junior to; (4) am senior to; (5) is superior to

....

Rule XIII. As/Than and Comparative Degree

यदि वाक्य में तुलना करने के लिए as और than—दोनों ही का प्रयोग हो, तो as के बाद आनेवाले Adjective/Adverb के बाद एक और as का प्रयोग करें (as ... as), सिर्फ एक ही as का नहीं; जैसे—

I can work *as fast as,* if not faster than you.

यहाँ as के बाद फिर as का प्रयोग किया गया है, क्योंकि वाक्य में than आ गया है। ऐसे वाक्यों में यदि हम एक ही as से काम चला लेना चाहें तो वह अशुद्ध होगा; जैसे—

I can work as fast, if not faster than you.

इन्हें भी देखें—

1. I am as good, if not better than he.
2. Drinking is as bad, if not worse than smoking.
3. This book is as good, or even better than that.

इन वाक्यों में as ... as के बदले एक ही as का प्रयोग करके भयंकर भूल की गई है। इनके शुद्ध रूप ये होंगे—

1. I am *as* good *as*, if not better than he.
   Or, I am *as* good *as* he, if not better.
2. Drinking is *as* bad *as*, if not worse than smoking.
   Or, Drinking is *as* bad *as* smoking, if not worse.
3. This book is *as* good *as*, or even better than that.
   Or, This book is *as* good *as* that or even better.

. . . .

EXERCISE

Correct the following sentences.

(1) I can run as fast, if not faster than you. (2) He is as good, if not better than I. (3) It is as bad, if not worse than that. (4) Drinking is as bad, if not worse than gambling. (5) I am as strong or even stronger than he.

Hints—(1) as fast as; (2) as good as; (3) as bad as; (4) as bad as; (5) as strong as

. . . .

Rule XIV. Unequal Comparatives

जब दो व्यक्तियों या वस्तुओं के लिए Comparative Degree का प्रयोग हो, तब उन व्यक्तियों या वस्तुओं को स्पष्ट रूप से वाक्यों में रखना चाहिए। ऐसे वाक्यों में एक व्यक्ति या वस्तु को than के पहले रखा जाता है और दूसरे को than के बाद; जैसे—

The *climate* of Chapra is better than *that* (climate) of Patna.

यहाँ दो वस्तुओं की तुलना की गई है—Chapra का climate एवं Patna का climate और कहा गया है कि इन दोनों में Chapra का climate Patna के climate से अधिक अच्छा है। अब वाक्य की इस बनावट पर विचार करें—

The climate of Chapra is better than Patna.

यह अनुचित है। क्यों? इसलिए कि इससे ऐसा लगता है कि Chapra के climate की तुलना स्वयं Patna से (Patna के climate से नहीं) की गई है। इसका कोई अर्थ ही नहीं लग सकता। अब इस वाक्य को लें—

My shirt is better than *you*.

यहाँ लेखक shirt की तुलना करना चाहता है—my shirt और your shirt के बीच, पर your shirt के बदले यहाँ you का प्रयोग कर दिया गया है। इससे ऐसा मालूम पड़ता है कि एक

ओर shirt है और दूसरी ओर you. यह कुछ हास्यास्पद प्रतीत होता है, क्योंकि shirt और you की तुलना तो बहुत ही बेढंगी लगती है न! इसलिए इस वाक्य को इस प्रकार लिखना चाहिए—

My *shirt* is better than *yours* (your shirt).

ध्यान दें कि singular noun के छिप जाने पर *than that of* का प्रयोग होता है और plural noun के छिप जाने पर *than those of* आता है; जैसे—

1. The colour of his shirt is brighter *than that of* his coat. [not, *than his coat*]
2. The roads of Patna are wider *than those of* Munger. [not, *than Munger*]

Rule XV. Wrong Comparatives

दो से अधिक व्यक्तियों/वस्तुओं की तुलना करने पर comparative degree का प्रयोग नहीं करना चाहिए। क्यों? इसलिए कि इससे वाक्य में wrong comparative का दोष आ जाता है। अतः, ऐसे-ऐसे वाक्य न बनाएँ—

1. Which is better: milk, meat or fish?
2. Which is easier: Hindi, English or Sanskrit?

Rule XVI. Double Comparatives

वाक्य में more + comparative form का प्रयोग नहीं करना चाहिए। क्यों? इसलिए कि इससे double comparative का दोष आ जाता है। अतः, ऐसे-ऐसे वाक्य न बनाएँ—

1. He is more richer than she. 2. She is more fatter than he.

Rule XVII. Emphatic Comparatives

Comparative को जोरदार (emphatic) बनाने के लिए much/far/by far/far and away/still का प्रयोग किया जाता है, very का नहीं; जैसे—

1. He is much wiser than you.
2. This book is far better than that.
3. This book is better by far.
4. This book is still better.
5. This book is better still.

NOTE (a)—rather + comparative

Comparative के पहले rather का प्रयोग हो सकता है, पर fairly का नहीं; जैसे—

She is rather better today. [not, fairly better]

NOTE (b)—all + the + comparative

Much/so much (और भी) के अर्थ में comparative के पहले all + the का प्रयोग इस प्रकार होता है—

It is all the better = It is much better.

Rule XVIII. the + superlative + of/in/among

जब दो से अधिक व्यक्तियों या वस्तुओं की तुलना की जाती है तब वाक्य में the + superlative + of/in आता है; जैसे—

1. He is the wisest of all boys.
2. She is the tallest in her class.
3. This book is the best in the market.

ध्यान दें कि

NOTE—in/of/among

सामान्यतः superlative के साथ of आता है, पर जब स्थान (place) का बोध होता है तब of के बदले in का प्रयोग किया जाता है; जैसे—

1. He is the richest of all.
2. He is the richest in the town.

वाक्य में in/of के बदले among का प्रयोग one of (में से एक) के अर्थ में होता है जब superlative + plural noun का प्रयोग होता है; जैसे—

1. Patna is among the dirtiest towns in India.
2. Jamshedpur is among the cleanest towns in Jharkhand.

ऐसे वाक्यों में among के बदले of का प्रयोग नहीं होना चाहिए।

Rule XIX. Emphatic Superlative

Superlative degree को जोरदार (emphatic) बनाने के लिए इसके पहले much the/the very/by far the/out and out the का प्रयोग इस प्रकार होता है—

1. This is much the best book.
2. This is the very best book.
3. This is by far the best book.
4. This is out and out the best book.

Rule XX. Wrong Superlative

केवल दो व्यक्तियों/वस्तुओं की तुलना करने पर superlative का प्रयोग नहीं करना चाहिए, क्योंकि इससे wrong superlative का दोष आ जाता है। इसलिए ऐसे-ऐसे वाक्य न बनाएँ—

1. Which is the best of the two books?
2. Which is the cheapest—iron or gold?

Rule XXI. Double Superlative

वाक्य में most + superlative form का प्रयोग नहीं करना चाहिए, क्योंकि इससे double superlative का दोष हो जाता है। इसलिए ऐसे-ऐसे वाक्य न बनाएँ—

1. He is the most tallest of all.
2. This road is the most longest of all.

Rule XXII. Other and Superlative

Superlative के बाद other का प्रयोग नहीं करना चाहिए। इन वाक्यों को लें—

1. He is the tallest of all boys. [not, all other boys]
2. She is the richest of all girls. [not, all other girls]

Rule XXIII. one of + Superlative

one of के बाद adjective सामान्यतः superlative degree में रहता है; जैसे—

1. He is one of the greatest men.
2. She is one of the wisest girls.

Rule XXIV. the + Superlative

Superlative Degree के पहले the का प्रयोग अवश्य ही होना चाहिए; जैसे—

1. He is *the* best boy.
2. This is *the* most important question.

इसलिए ये वाक्य अशुद्ध हैं—

1. He is best boy.
2. This is most important question.

NOTE (a)—यदि Superlative Degree के पहले कोई Possessive Adjective (my, our, your, her) या Possessive Case (Noun + 's) आए तो Superlative के पहले the का प्रयोग नहीं हो सकता; जैसे—

1. It is my best dress. 2. It is Ram's best pen.

NOTE (b)—a + Superlative

कभी-कभी कुछ लोग a most का प्रयोग very के अर्थ में करते हैं। ऐसी हालत में adjective के पहले the का प्रयोग नहीं होता; जैसे—

It is a most interesting *story*.

ऐसे प्रयोग बहुत मिलते हैं, पर ये बातचीत की भाषा तक ही सीमित हैं। इसलिए most का प्रयोग very के अर्थ में न किया जाए, तो अच्छा हो। इस संबंध में इस मत का ध्यान रखें—

The use of **most**, *in the sense of* **very**, *is condemned by some grammarians, but it is very frequently heard and may be accepted in colloquial English, though, it is better excluded from writing.* —F T Wood: *Current English Usage*

इसलिए आप a + superlative degree के बदले a very + positive degree का प्रयोग करें या the + superlative degree का; जैसे—

1. This is a very good book. 2. This is the best book.

इसलिए इस प्रकार के वाक्य न बनाएँ—

1. This is a best book. 2. He is a worst boy.

Rule XXV. *Like best/like most; like better/like more*

ये दोनों ही प्रयोग शुद्ध हैं। इसलिए आप ऐसे वाक्य लिख सकते हैं—

1. Which of the books do you like best?
2. Which of the books do you like most?

हाँ, *like best* और *like most* में, अर्थ की दृष्टि से, कुछ अंतर अवश्य है। वाक्य में like best का प्रयोग तब होता है जब हम किसी व्यक्ति/वस्तु के खास गुणों से प्रभावित होते हैं, पर

like most से साधारण पसंद का भाव प्रकट होता है, इसके लिए कोई विशेष कारण की आवश्यकता नहीं होती। यही बात like better और like more के साथ भी लागू होती है; जैसे—

1. Which of the two stories do you like better?
2. Which of the two stories do you like more?

Rule XXVI. one of + Superlative + if not + Superlative

यदि वाक्य में *one of the* + superlative आए और उसके बाद *if not the* + superlative आए, तो one of the के बाद आनेवाले adjective के साथ एक plural noun का प्रयोग करना चाहिए और if not the के बाद आनेवाले adjective के साथ singular noun का; जैसे—

He is *one of* the richest *men*, if not the richest (*man*).

यहाँ one of the के बाद plural noun (men) का प्रयोग हुआ है और if not the के बाद singular noun का, जो शुद्ध है। यदि इस वाक्य को इस प्रकार कर दें—

He is one of the richest, if not the richest *men*.

तो यह अशुद्ध हो जाएगा, क्योंकि यहाँ one of the और if not the दोनों ही के लिए एक ही plural noun (men) का प्रयोग कर दिया गया है।

एक-दो और उदाहरण लें—

1. He is *one of* the strongest *men*, if not the strongest (*man*).
2. He is *one of* the tallest, if not the tallest *men*.

यहाँ पहला वाक्य शुद्ध है, क्योंकि यहाँ one of the के बाद plural noun आया है और if not the के बाद singular. दूसरा वाक्य अशुद्ध है, क्योंकि इन दोनों ही के लिए एक plural noun (men) का प्रयोग हुआ है। इस वाक्य की बनावट इस प्रकार की होनी चाहिए—

He is one of the tallest men, if not the tallest (*man*).

NOTE—ऐसे वाक्यों में if not the के बाद आनेवाला singular noun छिपा हुआ रहता है, क्योंकि ऐसा करने से वाक्य सरल और सुंदर मालूम पड़ता है।

. . . .

EXERCISE

Correct the following sentences.

(1) Socrates was one of the wisest if not the wisest men. (2) Aristotle has been one of the most learned if not the most learned men. (3) Mahatma Gandhi was one of the greatest if not the greatest thinkers. (4) Gautam Buddha was one of the greatest if not the greatest religious teachers. (5) This is one of the best if not the best book.

Hints—(1) one of the wisest men if not the wisest (man); (2) one of the most learned men if not the most learned (man); (3) one of the greatest thinkers if not the greatest (thinker); (4) one of the greatest religious teachers if not the greatest (religious teacher); (5) one of the best books if not the best (book)

. . . .

Rule XXVII. 'And' and the degree of adjectives

यदि बहुत-से adjectives को and से जोड़ा जाए, तो उन सबको एक ही degree में रहना चाहिए। यदि एक adjective Positive Degree में हो और दूसरा Comparative में, तो उन्हें जोड़ा नहीं जा सकता। अगर Comparative Degree का प्रयोग करना जरूरी हो तो उन सबको Comparative Degree में ही रखें। इसी प्रकार, यदि एक adjective Positive Degree में हो और दूसरा Superlative में तो उन्हें जोड़ा नहीं जा सकता। अगर adjective के साथ Superlative Degree का प्रयोग करना आवश्यक हो, तो उन सभी को Superlative Degree में रखें; जैसे—

1. Ram is *better* and *wiser* than Mohan.
2. You are *braver* and *stronger* than I.

इन वाक्यों में दो adjectives and से जोड़े गए हैं। इसलिए better और wiser तथा braver और stronger Comparative Degree में हैं। हम ऐसा नहीं लिख सकते—

1. Ram is *better* and *wise* than Mohan.
2. You are *braver* and *strong* than I.

पहले वाक्य में 'better' Comparative Degree में है, पर 'wise' Positive में। फिर दूसरे वाक्य में 'braver' Comparative Degree में है, पर 'strong' Positive में। यहाँ wise के बदले wiser तथा strong के बदले stronger का प्रयोग करें। Superlative Degree के Adjective के साथ भी यही नियम लागू होना चाहिए; जैसे—

1. He is the *bravest* and *strongest* man.
2. It is the *best* and *wisest* plan.

ये दोनों ही वाक्य शुद्ध हैं, क्योंकि and से जोड़े गए दोनों ही adjectives Superlative Degree में हैं।

अब इन वाक्यों को देखें—

1. He is the *bravest* and *strong* man.
2. It is the *best* and *wise* plan.
3. This is the *surest* and *intelligent* way.

यहाँ दोनों ही adjectives को Superlative Degree में रहना चाहिए जैसे—

This is the *surest* and *most intelligent* way.

....

EXERCISE

Correct the following sentences.

(1) I am bolder and brave than he. (2) This plan is better and easy than that. (3) This is the cheapest and safe course of action. (4) He is the wisest and brave man. (5) This house is finer and strong than that.

Hints—(1) braver; (2) easier; (3) safest; (4) bravest; (5) stronger

....

Rule XXVIII. Degreeless/Non-gradable Adjectives

कुछ ऐसे adjectives होते हैं जो सदा Positive Degree में ही रहते हैं। इनकी Comparative या Superlative Degree नहीं होती और Positive Degree में भी इनके साथ very/extremely या किसी अन्य Adverb का प्रयोग नहीं होता। इसलिए इन्हें non-gradable भी कहा जाता है। ये adjectives हैं—

absolute, perfect, complete, entire, full, whole, chief, extreme, unique, excellent, right, wrong, circular, annual, monthly, milky, blue, golden, lunar, solar, oblong, round, square, universal, impossible, dead, dumb, blind, matchless

NOTE—इस नियम के संबंध में इतना ही कहना है कि कुछ आधुनिक महान लेखकों ने अपनी शैली (style) को प्रभावशाली बनाने के लिए इस नियम में थोड़ा परिवर्तन किया है जो अनुचित नहीं। इसलिए आजकल fuller, fullest, more perfect, most perfect, most impossible, most universal इत्यादि का प्रयोग कुछ अच्छे लेखकों ने किया है। नीचे कुछ नमूने देखें—

1. *In the play of Shakespeare a musical design can be discovered in particular scenes, and in his* **more perfect** *plays as wholes.* —T S ELIOT
2. *Decorum is the* **most universal** *of all the rules.* —BASIL WILLEY
3. *But there are other things in Pilgrim's Progress besides the* **most perfect** *representation of Evangelical religion.* —G M TREVELYAN
4. *... and this* **fuller** *kind of criticism in what we desire.* —I A RICHARDS
5. *... but the play, the Shadow Waters, seems to me one of the most perfect expressions of the vague enchanted beauty of that school.* —I A RICHARDS

इन उदाहरणों से यह स्पष्ट है कि आजकल full और perfect की degree बनाई जाती है जो काफी लोकप्रिय है। हाँ, ऊपर दी गई सूची में जो अन्य Adjectives हैं, उनका प्रयोग Comparative या Superlative में प्रायः नहीं मिलता। इसलिए उनकी degree बनाने का प्रयत्न न करें, तो अच्छा हो।

Rule XXIX. Some Confusing Comparatives and Superlatives

अब हम कुछ ऐसे Adjectives पर विचार करें जिनके प्रयोग में कुछ कठिनाई होती है—

(i) *ELDER* and *ELDEST*: *OLDER* and *OLDEST*

Elder और eldest का प्रयोग एक ही परिवार के अधिक उम्रवाले लोगों के लिए होता है, पर older का अन्य लोगों या वस्तुओं के लिए होता है। याद रखें कि elder के बाद than का प्रयोग नहीं किया जाता, पर older के बाद than आता है; जैसे—

1. My *elder* brother loves me much.
2. My *eldest* brother is the head of the family.
3. My friend is *older* than I.
4. This is the *oldest* tree here.

इन वाक्यों में elder के बदले older और older के बदले elder का प्रयोग अशुद्ध होता।

(ii) *FARTHER* and *FURTHER*

Farther का अर्थ होता है 'अधिक दूर' (more distant) पर further का 'अतिरिक्त' (additional, in addition); जैसे—

1. Chapra is *farther* from Patna than Sonepur.
2. Has he anything *further* to say?
3. *Further* argument is not required.

यहाँ पहले वाक्य में farther का प्रयोग 'अधिक दूरी' के अर्थ में और दूसरे तथा तीसरे वाक्यों में further का प्रयोग 'अतिरिक्त' के अर्थ में हुआ है। इन नियमों का ध्यान रखें—

1. *A rough distincton is this:* **farther, farthest** *are applied to distance and nothing else;* **further, furthest,** *either to distance or to addition.*

—ERIC PATRIDGE

2. *... The most that should be said is perhaps that* **farther** *is not common except where distance is in question.*

—FOWLER

(iii) *NEAREST* and *NEXT*

Nearest का अर्थ होता है 'सबसे नजदीक' और इससे 'दूरी' (distance) का बोध होता है, पर next का अर्थ होता है 'इसके बाद' और इससे क्रम (order, position) का बोध होता है; जैसे—

1. What is the *nearest* market from your home?
2. He is my *nearest* relation.
3. What is your *nearest* railway station?
4. I sat *next* to my friend.
5. I am going by the *next* train.
6. We are *next* door neighbours.
7. Who comes *next*?

(iv) *LAST* and *LATEST*

Last 'first' का विपरीतार्थक है, पर latest 'earliest' का। इसलिए last से स्थान या क्रम (order) का बोध होता है, पर latest से समय (time) का; जैसे—

1. I am the *last* man to bear this insult. 2. What is the *latest* news about him?

EXERCISE

Correct the following sentences.

(1) This temple is elder than that. (2) He is my older brother. (3) You are the eldest man of this village. (4) Darbhanga is further from Patna than Chapra. (5) No farther discussion is allowed. (6) What is the latest day for fee-collection? (7) I was the first man to support this resolution but you were the latest. (8) Farther evidence was not available.

Hints—(1) older; (2) elder; (3) oldest; (4) farther; (5) further; (6) last; (7) last; (8) further

(v) *LATER* and *LATTER*

Later 'late' की Comparative Degree है, पर latter 'former' का विपरीतार्थक। इससे यह स्पष्ट है कि later से समय (time) का बोध होता है और latter से क्रम या स्थान (order) का; जैसे—

1. You came *later* than he.
2. Shakespeare and Milton are great poets but I prefer the former to the *latter*.

यहाँ पहले वाक्य में latter और दूसरे में later का प्रयोग अनुचित होता।

(vi) *FORMER* and *LATTER*

जब वाक्य में केवल दो व्यक्तियों या वस्तुओं की चर्चा होती है, तब पहले के लिए former का प्रयोग होता है और दूसरे के लिए latter का; जैसे—

Keats and Shelley are romantic poets but the *former* is greater than the *latter*.

इस वाक्य में दो व्यक्तियों (Keats/Shelley) की चर्चा हुई है। इसलिए पहले के लिए former और दूसरे के लिए latter आया है। यदि यहाँ दो से अधिक (तीन-चार) व्यक्तियों की चर्चा हुई होती, तो former और latter का प्रयोग नहीं होता। वैसी अवस्था में former के बदले first का और latter के बदले last का प्रयोग होता। आप इस नियम को ध्यान में रखें—

1. *The* **latter** *should not be used when more than a pair are in queston ... .*

—FOWLER

2. *When the reference is to one of three or more individuals, the* **First** *not the* **Former,** *should be used.*

—FOWLER

इस नियम के अनुसार यह वाक्य अशुद्ध है—

Wordsworth, Keats and Shelley are romantic poets, but the *former* is greater than the *latter*.

इस वाक्य में तीन व्यक्तियों का प्रसंग आ गया है। इसलिए यहाँ former के बदले first का और latter के बदले last का प्रयोग होना चाहिए।

(vii) *FIRST* and *LAST*

जब वाक्य में दो से अधिक व्यक्तियों या वस्तुओं की चर्चा हो, तो पहले के लिए first का और अंतिम के लिए last का प्रयोग होता है, former और latter का नहीं; जैसे—

Wordsworth, Keats and Shelley are romantic poets but the first is greater than the *last*.

यहाँ first के बदले former का और last के बदले latter का प्रयोग अनुचित होता, क्योंकि इस वाक्य में तीन व्यक्तियों की चर्चा हुई है, दो की नहीं। हाँ, यदि यहाँ दो ही व्यक्तियों की बात होती, तो former और latter का प्रयोग होता, first और last का नहीं। अब देखें इस वाक्य को—

There was a second triumvirate of Lepidus, Mark Antony and Octavius Caesar, the **latter** *the nephew of Julius Caesar.*

—H G WELLS

यहाँ latter के बदले last का प्रयोग होना चाहिए, क्योंकि वाक्य में तीन व्यक्तियों की चर्चा हुई है।

(viii) *FIRST* and *FOREMOST*

First का अर्थ होता है 'पहला' और इससे क्रम (order, position) का बोध होता है। Foremost का अर्थ होता है 'सबसे अधिक महत्त्वपूर्ण' (most eminent/important) और इससे श्रेणी (rank) का बोध होता है; जैसे—

1. He was the *first* man to tell me.
2. Who got the *first* prize?
3. Pandit Nehru was the foremost stateman of his time.

(ix) *FEWER, LESS* and *LESSER*

Fewer तथा Less का अर्थ होता है 'से कम'; पर इनमें कुछ अंतर भी है। Fewer से संख्या (number) का बोध होता है और Less से मात्रा/परिमाण (quantity) का। Lesser में double comparative है, जो प्रयोग के अनुसार शुद्ध माना जाता है और इसका अर्थ होता है 'less important/less serious' (कम महत्त्वपूर्ण)।

इन वाक्यों को देखें—

1. *Fewer* persons are seen today.
2. *Fewer* trains are available now.
3. He has *less* time these days.
4. I have *less* money today.
5. Which is the *lesser* of the two evils?
6. The *lesser* poets of the seventeenth century are not receiving attention.

NOTE—वाक्य में **definite numeral adjective + plural noun** रहने पर fewer के बदले less का प्रयोग होता है; जैसे—

1. There are now two persons *less* for work.
2. I have to pay five rupees *less* now.

इन वाक्यों में fewer का प्रयोग अनुचित होता।

EXERCISE

I. *Fill in the blanks with a suitable word given in brackets.*

1. Who came ......? [first, foremost]
2. Who is the ...... leader of your state? [first, foremost]
3. ...... cars are seen today. [Fewer, Less]
4. This cow gives ...... milk now. [Fewer, Less]
5. ...... opportunities are available now. [Fewer, Less]
6. He has to feed three ...... mouths now. [less, fewer]

II. *Correct the following sentences.*

(1) The Gita, the Quoran and the Bible are great books but the former is older than the latter. (2) The Indian civilization and the Greek civilization are very old but the first is older than the last. (3) Ram, Shyam and Mohan are good painters but the latter is a greater artist than the former. (4) Good English and Better English are very good books on Grammar but the last is not as good as the first. (5) He came latter than his father.

Hints—(1) first ... last; (2) former ... latter; (3) last ... first; (4) latter ... former; (5) later

REVISION TEST I

Correct the following sentences.

1. These roses smell sweetly.
2. These kind of things are bad.
3. Which is the best of these two?
4. Which is the least of these two evils?
5. Is he stronger than any man living?
6. Is he not the wisest of all other man?
7. Keats is superior than Shelley.
8. He has the sweetest voice than any other singer.
9. The population of China is greater than any country.
10. This is the most unkindest remark.
11. Nothing can be more cheaper than this.
12. Is he the wisest of all other man?
13. Is your scheme preferable than mine?
14. Not less than one hundred men were killed.
15. It is most unique.
16. He is elder than his sister.
17. I made no farther demand.
18. The three first chapters of that book are good.
19. We were glad to see our mutual friend.
20. There is still little hope of his recovery.
21. I will not buy some fish.
22. I haven't done nothing.
23. This is smaller than all.
24. Is he the oldest of the two brothers?
25. Knowledge is more preferable than power.
26. These sort of suit are still in fashion.

27. The two first pages are blank.
28. A deer is swifter than any animal.
29. He is more learned but not so responsible as his father.
30. You are as rich or even richer than I.
31. Neither roads are safe.
32. Which is the better of the three methods?
33. This bundle is three time heavier than that.
34. He is better than any man.
35. Of the three, meat, fish and milk, the latter is my favourite.

Hints—1. sweet; 2. things of this kind; 3. the better; 4. the lesser; 5. any other man; 6. all men; 7. superior to; 8. sweeter voice than that of any other singer; 9. than that of any other country; 10. the unkindest or the most unkind; 11. be cheaper than; 12. the wisest of all men or wiser than all other men; 13. to mine? 14. No fewer than; 15. is unique; 16. older than; 17. further; 18. the first three; 10. common friend; 20. a little; 21. any fish; 22. done anyting; 23. the smallest of all; 24. older of; 25. to; 26. the suit of this sort is, or this sort of suit is; 27. The first two; 28. than any other; 29. learned than; 30. as rich as; 31. road is; 32. the best; 33. three times as heavy as that; 34. any other, 35. the last is

REVISION TEST II

Explain why the following sentences are correct or incorrect.

1. He has not brought some bread.
2. He spent a little money he had.
3. Will you give me few rice?
4. Every of the two boys had a book.
5. Neither of the four pens will do.
6. This boy is the cleverer than the two.
7. He is a worst man.
8. Who is the greatest poet: Keats or Shelley?
9. He is the better of the three brothers.
10. He is the dullest of all other boys.
11. Gold is the most precious of all other metals.
12. He has the shortest memory of any other boy.
13. The population of Patna is greater than Chapra.
14. There was a hot blooded murder.
15. Knowledge is more preferable than power.
16. This the best and powerful engine.
17. Mumbai is one of the biggest if not the biggest cities in India.
18. That book is cheaper than better.
19. My friend is richer than me.

20. He is more senior to me by four years.
21. He is as rich or even richer than me.
22. I have finished a few books I had.
23. Who is the richest than the two?
24. Could you lend me few books for few days?
25. The grammar of Hindi is simpler than Sanskrit.

REVISION TEST III

Match each group of words in A with the right group of words in B.

A	B
Neither	roads are safe.
Both	book is bad.
Which is best	meat or milk?
Which is better	Hindi, Urdu or English?
I will not buy	some fish.
I will buy	any fish.
This is preferable	than that.
This is better	to that.

REVISION TEST IV

Fill in the blanks with words given in brackets.

1. Our head should be …… . [cool, cold]
2. Our heart should be …… . [warm, hot]
3. I like her …… nature. [womanish, womanly]
4. He is the …… of the two. [better, best]
5. My father is …… that I. [older, younger]
6. She is the wiser …… the two. [of, than]
7. This is preferable …… that. [than, to]
8. I had not …… rest today. [some, any]
9. She is the tallest …… all. [of, among]
10. I would prefer to die rather than …… . [beg, to beg]

❐

Chapter IV

TEST YOURSELF

I. *Correct or justify the following sentences.*

1. I am too glad to see you.
2. My son's health is too good.
3. He was enough kind to help me.
4. This story is much interesting.
5. He hasn't begun the work already.
6. This boy is much intelligent.
7. She doesn't sing and I, too, do not.
8. This shirt is not different from that.
9. I first saw you five years ago and remember you ever since.
10. I request you to kindly help me.
11. I don't like him very much.
12. He only died yesterday.
13. I am very surprised at the news.
14. I have passed the examination last year.
15. It is nothing else than pride.
16. He seldom or ever tells lies.
17. He will come back just now.
18. He asked me to not go home.
19. He got success because he worked hardly.
20. He is complaining always.
21. Do you go to home every day?
22. He was born in 1920 on Monday in the morning at 6 o'clock.
23. He will come here on last Sunday.
24. A pen is in her pocket.
25. A party is tomorrow morning.
26. It is not good repenting now.

II. *Fill in the blanks with words given in brackets.*

1. I am …… glad to see you. [too, very]
2. This book is …… useful. [much, very]
3. …… I am not ill. [no, yes]
4. It was five years ago …… he died. [since, that]

5. She looks ugly because she is …… tall. [rather, fairly]
6. He seldom …… wears a costly dress. [or ever, or never]
7. It is nothing else …… dishonestly. [but, than]
8. Tulsi Das was a …… good poet. [quite, very]
9. He came here …… . [last week, in the last week]

❒

ADVERBS

हिन्दी में Adverb को क्रियाविशेषण कहते हैं, पर Adverb और क्रियाविशेषण में एक अंतर है। हिन्दी में क्रियाविशेषण उन शब्दों को कहते हैं जो केवल क्रिया की विशेषता बतलाते हैं, पर अँगरेजी में Adverb उसे कहते हैं जो Verb के अतिरिक्त Adjective तथा अन्य Adverb की भी विशेषता बतलाता है। इस अंतर का ध्यान रखकर हम यहाँ कुछ Adverbs के प्रयोग पर विचार करें।

Rule I (A). Too + Adjective/Adverb [excess]

Too का अर्थ होता है 'उतना जितना नहीं होना चाहिए' (more than enough). आप too का प्रयोग very के अर्थ में न करें। क्यों? इसलिए कि very का अर्थ होता है 'बहुत'। यदि आप अपने मित्र को देखकर कहें—I am too glad to see you.—तो इसका अर्थ होगा—**मैं आपको देखकर इतना अधिक प्रसन्न हूँ जितना नहीं होना चाहिए।** इसी प्रकार, यदि आप कह उठें—My son's health is too good—तो इसका अर्थ होगा—**मेरे पुत्र का स्वास्थ्य इतना अच्छा है जितना नहीं होना चाहिए।** आप जानते हैं कि कोई भी व्यक्ति अपने मित्र या पुत्र के विषय में ऐसा सोच भी नहीं सकता। वास्तव में, इन वाक्यों में मित्र और पिता को too तथा very के प्रयोग का ज्ञान ही नहीं। यहाँ उन्होंने अज्ञानवश ही very के बदले too का प्रयोग कर अर्थ का अनर्थ कर दिया है। इसलिए यह न भूलें कि too से दोष का बोध होता है, गुण का नहीं, क्योंकि too से अतिशयता (excess) का भाव व्यक्त होता है। इसलिए इन वाक्यों में very का प्रयोग होना चाहिए, too का नहीं—

1. God is *too* merciful to me.
2. This house is *too* strong.
3. This flower is *too* beautiful.
4. I write *too* correctly.

अब, इन वाक्यों को देखें जिनमें too का प्रयोग शुद्ध है—

1. You are *too* weak in English.
2. It is *too* hot to go out.
3. It is *too* cold today.
4. The price of iron is *too* high.
5. It is *too* much for me.
6. The house is *too* small for me.

Rule I (B). Too + Infinite [cause]

कुछ वाक्यों में too के बाद infinitive आता है [too + infinitive] और यह कार्य नहीं होने का कारण (cause) बताता है। इन वाक्यों को देखें—

1. She is too poor to buy a car.
2. He is too weak to run fast.
3. He is too small to touch the ceiling.

इस अर्थ का ध्यान रखें और ऐसे-ऐसे अर्थहीन वाक्य न गढ़ें—

1. He is too rich to buy a new suit.
2. He is too strong to lift this box.

Rule I (C). Too/Neither/Not ... either/So + Auxiliary

Too का अर्थ 'भी' (also, in addition to) भी होता है। इस अर्थ में इसका प्रयोग Affirmative sentence में होता है और Negative sentence में *too* के बदले *neither* या *not ... either* का प्रयोग इस प्रकार होता है—

1. He lost his book and purse, too. [too = भी]
2. He does not sing and I do not sing either. [either = भी]
3. He does not sing and neither do I. [neither = भी]

NOTE (a)—जब दो Affirmative sentences में एक ही प्रकार का कार्य होता है तो वाक्य में too के बदले so + auxiliary verb का प्रयोग होता है और उसका अर्थ 'भी' होता है—

1. Ram sings well, Shyam sings well.
   = Ram sings well and *so does* Shyam.
2. Abdul lost his purse. Karim lost his purse.
   = Abdul lost his purse and *so did* Karim.
3. Sita is ill. Radha is ill.
   = Sita is ill, *so is* Radha.

NOTE (b)—कभी-कभी Noun/Pronoun/Verb के पहले even का प्रयोग होता है और इसका अर्थ 'भी' होता है। ऐसे वाक्यों से यह बोध होता है कि जो कार्य हुआ है या होनेवाला है वह आशा के विपरीत है; जैसे—

1. Even his father cheated him.
2. He didn't even speak.
3. She can't take even water.
4. She can't even stand.

....

EXERCISE

Correct the following sentences.

(1) I am too glad to meet you. (2) My son's health is too good. (3) This book is too good. (4) The weather is too fine. (5) God is too kind to me. (6) Peace is too good for mankind. (7) It is very hot to play football. (8) He didn't help and I, too, did not. (9) He is too rich to buy a bus.

Hints—(1) to (6) use 'very' instead of 'too'; (7) too hot; (8) He didn't help and neither did I; (9) too poor

....

Rule II. Adjective/Adverb + Enough [proper limit/cause]

यह Adverb of Quantity है। इससे परिणाम या मात्रा का बोध होता है और इसका अर्थ होता है—पूर्ण या उचित मात्रा में (proper limit or degree)। इसके प्रयोग के संबंध में एक और बात याद रखने योग्य है। आप देखेंगे कि यह जिस adjective/adverb का गुण बतलाता है उसके बाद आता है और कार्य होने का कारण (cause) बताता है—

adjective/adverb + enough; जैसे—

1. He was *kind enough* to help me.

2. The weather is *fair enough* for me.

इन दोनों ही वाक्यों में enough का प्रयोग Adjective (kind/fair) के बाद हुआ है। आप इस प्रकार नहीं लिख सकते—

1. He was *enough kind* to help me.

2. The weather is *enough fair* for me.

NOTE—याद रखें कि जब enough का प्रयोग Adjective की तरह होता है, तब यह Noun का गुण बतलाता है और इसलिए Noun के पहले आता है और बाद में भी; जैसे—

enough loaves; loaves enough

जब enough का प्रयोग Adverb की तरह होता है, तब यह सदा Adjective तथा Adverb के बाद आता है, पहले कभी नहीं; जैसे—

good enough, cold enough, bold enough, fast enough

....

EXERCISE

I. *Correct the following sentences.*

(1) He runs enough fast to win this race. (2) He is enough intelligent to do this work. (3) He has acted enough boldly to deserve praise. (4) He is enough rich to spend so much. (5) He was enough good to help me. (6) He is dull enough to understand me.

Hints—(1) fast enough; (2) intelligent enough; (3) boldly enough; (4) rich enough; (5) good enough; (6) wise enough

II. *Remake the following sentences, using 'too'.*

1. It's very hot. We can't go out.
2. That book is very difficult. I can't read that.
3. It's very dark. We can't see anything.

III. *Remake the following sentences, using 'enough + infinitive'.*

1. He is very clever. He understands well.
2. She has enough money. She can pay for this book.
3. You are tall. You can reach this picture.

....

Rule III. Little and A little

जब little या a little का प्रयोग Adverb के समान होता है, तब, Adjective की ही भाँति, little का अर्थ होता है 'कुछ भी नहीं' और a little का 'कुछ' या 'थोड़ा'। इस अर्थ का ध्यान रखकर ही इनका प्रयोग करना चाहिए, नहीं तो अर्थ का अनर्थ हो सकता है; जैसे—

Ram failed, and so he was *little* sorry.

'Little sorry' का अर्थ यह है कि राम को कुछ दुःख हुआ ही नहीं। क्या ऐसा हो सकता है? जब राम ने फेल किया तब क्या उसे कुछ भी दुःख नहीं हुआ? वास्तव में कहने का तात्पर्य यह था

कि राम को 'थोड़ा दुःख' हुआ। इसलिए यहाँ little sorry के बदले a little sorry का प्रयोग होना चाहिए। एक और वाक्य लें—

When Ram was banished, Dashrath was *little* unhappy.

'Little unhappy' से यह मालूम होता है कि दशरथ को कुछ भी दुःख नहीं हुआ, जो वास्तव में ठीक नहीं। अतः, यहाँ a little या very का प्रयोग होना चाहिए।

NOTE—The little का प्रयोग Adverb की भाँति नहीं होता। इसलिए आप ऐसे वाक्य न लिखें—

1. He was *the little* sorry. 2. You are *the little* ashamed.

EXERCISE

Correct the following sentences.

(1) When the dearest son died, the father was little sorry. (2) When a tiger appeared suddenly, we were little surprised. (3) When the traveller lost his way and wandered for days and nights, he felt little tired. (4) When he felt little hungry and thirsty, he cried for help.

Hints—(1) a little sorry; (2) a little surprised; (3) a little tired; (4) a little hungry

Rule IV. Much and Very

Rule IV (A). Much का प्रयोग Adjectives और Adverbs के पहले होता है, जब वे Comparative Degree में रहते हैं। इससे यह स्पष्ट है कि much का प्रयोग Positive Degree में नहीं हो सकता। Positive Degree के Adjectives तथा Adverbs के साथ very का प्रयोग होता है, much का नहीं; जैसे—

1. Ram is *much* better than Shyam.
2. You are *much* more intelligent than Mohan.
3. Ram is *very* good.
4. You are *very* intelligent.

इस नियम का इन वाक्यों में उल्लंघन किया गया है—

1. Ram is *much* intelligent.
2. You are *much* lucky.
3. She is *much* beautiful.
4. He is *very* worse than you.
5. You are *very* stronger than Mohan.
6. He explained the poem *much* clearly.

यहाँ very के बदले much और much के बदले very का प्रयोग होना आवश्यक है।

NOTE—जब Much का प्रयोग Comparative Degree के पहले हो, तब very का प्रयोग much के पहले (very much) हो सकता है; जैसे—

1. He is *very much* stronger than I.
2. You are *very much* better than he.

तो इस प्रकार, very stronger अशुद्ध है, पर very much stronger शुद्ध।

Rule IV (B). Much और Very का प्रयोग Superlative Degree के पहले होता है, पर दोनों में अंतर यह है कि much का प्रयोग the के पहले होता है, पर very का the के बाद; जैसे—

1. Ram is *much* the best boy in the village.
2. Ram is *the very* best boy in the village.

अतः, ये वाक्य अशुद्ध हैं—

1. You are *the much* strongest man.
2. He is *very the* strongest man.

Rule IV (C). Much और Very में एक और अंतर यह है कि 'much' Verb तथा Past Participle का गुण बतलाता है, पर 'very' Present Participle का; जैसे—

1. She talks *much* but does nothing.
2. She was *much* surprised.
3. Her talk was *very* interesting.
4. This news is *very* distressing.
5. I am *much* obliged to you.
6. This situation is *very* perplexing.

आप much और very का उलटा प्रयोग नहीं करें, अर्थात Present Participles के साथ much का और Past Participles के साथ very का। इसलिए ये वाक्य अशुद्ध हैं—

1. It is *much* interesting.
2. It is *much* distressing.
3. I am *very* surprised.
4. You are *very* ashamed.

NOTE (a)—much + past participle

कुछ phrases ऐसे हैं जिनमें Past Participle के साथ much के बदले very का प्रयोग होता है; जैसे—

very pleased, *very* tired, *very* dejected, *very* contented. ये प्रयोग की दृष्टि से शुद्ध हैं, पर इनके आधार पर नये phrases गढ़े नहीं जा सकते।

NOTE (b)—much/very much

Affirmative sentences में verb के साथ very much का प्रयोग होता है, पर Negative में केवल much आता है, very much नहीं; जैसे—

1. I like him very much.
2. I don't like him much.

Very much का प्रयोग इस प्रकार नहीं हो सकता—

I don't like him very much.

EXERCISE

Correct the following sentences.

(1) This question is much difficult but that is much easy. (2) You are much ugly but she is much lovely. (3) He is the much best boy of his class. (4) He was beaten much severely. (5) It is much amusing. (6) He was very ashamed of his conduct. (7) You are very the best boy. (8) I am very interested in your story.

Hints—(1) very difficult … very easy; (2) very ugly … very loverly; (3) the very best or much the best; (4) very; (5) very; (6) much; (7) the very best or much the best; (8) much interested

Rule V. Very much, Too much, Much too and Only too

Very much अर्थ होता है, 'पूर्ण रूप से' पर too much और much too से 'इतना अधिक जितना नहीं होना चाहिए, का बोध होता है। Only too से 'बहुत' (very) का बोध होता है, too (excess) का नहीं; जैसे—

1. I am *very much* obliged to my friend.
2. I am *very much* sorry for this boy.
3. It gives me *too much* pain.
4. It is *much too* painful.
5. I shall be *only too* glad to see you.

   = I shall be *very* glad to see you.

इस प्रकार आप देखते हैं कि only too का अर्थ too से भिन्न होता है। Too much के बाद noun आता है, पर much too के बाद adjective या participle.

इन वाक्यों को देखें—

1. He gave me *much too* pain.
2. It is *too* much painful.

यहाँ पहले वाक्य में too much का और दूसरे में much too का प्रयोग होना चाहिए।

Rule VI. Presently, Shortly and Directly

Presently के दो अर्थ होते हैं—1. शीघ्र (soon), 2. अभी (at present)। Shortly तथा directly का अर्थ होता है 'शीघ्र ही' (soon without delay)। याद रखें कि 'shortly' का अर्थ होता है 'शीघ्र ही' (soon without delay)। याद रखें कि shortly का अर्थ in short (संक्षेप में) और directly का अर्थ straight (सीधे, शीघ्र) नहीं होता।

सीधे (straight) के अर्थ में direct का प्रयोग होता है; जैसे—

1. He will go presently/shortly (शीघ्र).
2. He is presently a teacher (अभी).

Rule VII. Presently and Just now

शीघ्र (soon) के अर्थ में pesently का प्रयोग future action के लिए होता है, पर just now का past action के लिए; जैसे—

1. He *has come* just now. 2. I *shall go* presently.

इसलिए ये वाक्य अशुद्ध हैं—

1. I *shall go* just now. 2. He *has come* presently.

Rule VIII. Hard and Hardly

1. He works *hard.* 2. He *hardly* works.

पहले वाक्य का अर्थ है 'वह कड़ी मेहनत करता है' पर दूसरे का अर्थ है 'वह काम प्रायः नहीं करता'।

Hardly का अर्थ होता है scarcely. इसलिए hardly का प्रयोग इस प्रकार नहीं करें—

He always gets success since he hardly works.

Rule IX. Late and Lately/Recently

Late का अर्थ होता है 'देर से' और Lately/Recently का 'हाल ही में' जैसे—

1. He came *late.* 2. He has come *lately.*

पहले वाक्य का अर्थ है 'वह देर से आया' पर दूसरे का 'वह हाल ही में (recently) आया है'। याद रखें कि Lately के साथ सदा Present Perfect Tense का प्रयोग होता है, पर Recently के साथ Present Perfect या केवल Past Simple Tense का।

....

EXERCISE

Correct the following sentences.

(1) I give him much too freedom. (2) He is too much free. (3) What are you? Presently I am a student. (4) I shall go just now. (5) He has gone presently. (6) He wants to stand first in the University examination and so he works hardly. (7) As the boy came lately, he was fined.

Hints—(1) too much; (2) much too; (3) at present; (4) presently; (5) just now; (6) works hard; (7) came late

....

Rule X. Since/Ever since

जब Since के समय (time) का बोध होता है, तब इसका प्रयोग Preposition, Conjunction और Adverb तीनों ही प्रकार से होता है। इन तीनों प्रकार के प्रयोग में थोड़ा-थोड़ा अंतर है। यहाँ हम since के केवल adverbial प्रयोग पर विचार करें।

Adverb की भाँति प्रयुक्त होने पर since का अर्थ होता है 'तब से' (from then) और इसलिए इससे समय का बोध होता है। Since के प्रयोग के संबंध में इन नियमों का ध्यान रखें—

(i) Since के साथ Present Perfect Tense का प्रयोग होता है, पर Indirect Narration में Past Perfect का।

(ii) Since का स्थान वाक्य के अंत में रहता है। कभी-कभी इसके पहले ever/ever since का प्रयोग होता है; जैसे—

I first saw him five years ago and *have remembered him ever* since.

Rule XI. Else ... but

वाक्य में else के साथ *but* (else but) का प्रयोग होना चाहिए, *than* (else than) का नहीं; जैसे—

It is nothing *else but* pride.

यहाँ but के बदले than का प्रयोग अनुचित होता।

Rule XII. Seldom or never/Seldom if ever

वाक्य में seldom के बाद *or never* या *if ever* का प्रयोग होना चाहिए; जैसे—

1. He seldom *or never* tells lies.
2. He seldom *if ever* helps the poor.

ऐसे वाक्यों में seldom के बाद or ever का प्रयोग इस प्रकार नहीं होता—

He seldom or ever tells lies.

Rule XIII. Ago and That

यदि ago के बाद कोई clause आए तो उसे that से शुरू करना चाहिए, since से कभी नहीं (... ago + that + clause); जैसे—

It was twenty years *ago that* he died.

यहाँ that के बदले since का प्रयोग अशुद्ध होता। इसलिए यह वाक्य अशुद्ध है—

It was twenty years *ago since* he died.

इस नियम को न भूलें—

If **ago** *is used, and the event to be dated is given by a clause it must be one beginning with* **that,** *and not* **since.** —FOWLER

....

EXERCISE

Correct the following sentences.

(1) It was barely 50 years ago since it was introduced. (2) It was only twenty five years ago since he left this job.

Hints—Use 'ago that' in both the sentences.

....

Rule XIV. Before and Ago

इन दोनों का अर्थ 'पहले' होता है और इनसे समय (time) का बोध होता है।

Before के साथ Past Simple या Present Perfect Tense आता है, पर Ago के साथ सदा Past Simple Tense आता है, Present Perfect नहीं; जैसे—

1. I never before saw such a bad man. 2. I have seen this place before.
3. I came here an hour ago.
4. That happened ten years ago/long ago.

इसलिए ऐसे-ऐसे वाक्य न बनाएँ—

1. She has left a few minutes ago. 2. I have seen him a week ago.

NOTE—Ago and Back

इन दोनों से past time का बोध होता है; जैसे—

1. I saw him a week ago. 2. He saw me a few years back.

Rule XV. Present Perfect and Adverb

यदि वाक्य में Present Perfect Tense का प्रयोग हो, तो किसी ऐसे Adverb या Adverbial Phrase का प्रयोग नहीं होना चाहिए जिससे Past Tense का बोध हो; जैसे—

1. I *have* passed the examinaton *last year.*
2. He *has* died *yesterday.*
3. You *have* come back *last evening.*

Last year/yesterday/last evening से Past Tense का बोध होता है न! इसलिए यहाँ Present Perfect Tense के बदले Past Simple Tense का प्रयोग होना चाहिए। इससे यह स्पष्ट है कि यदि वाक्य में किसी ऐसे Adverb/Adverbial Phrase का प्रयोग किया जाए जिससे Past Tense का बोध हो, तो वाक्य में Past Simple Tense का प्रयोग करना चाहिए, Present Perfect का नहीं, जैसे—

I passed the examination last year.

....

EXERCISE

Correct the following sentences.

(1) He has come here the other day. (2) I have joined this college only last year. (3) You have said so last evening.

Hints—(1) He came …; (2) I joined …; (3) You said … .

....

Rule XVI. Yes/No/Not

Rule XVI (A). Affirmative sentence के साथ Yes का प्रयोग करें और Negative sentence के साथ No का; जैसे—

Are you well? 1. *Yes,* I *am.* 2. *No,* I *am not.*

आप इस प्रकार के उत्तर न दें—

1. Yes, I am not. 2. No, I am.

Yes/No के बाद केवल subject + auxiliary (सहायक क्रिया) का प्रयोग करें—

1. Does he know you? Yes he *does.* No, he *doesn't.*
2. Can you lift this box? Yes, I *can.* No, I *can't.*

Rule XVI (B). अपने कथन पर अधिक जोर डालने या विनम्रता प्रकट करने के लिए Yes/No के पहले Oh इस प्रकार आता है—

1. Could you give me some money? Oh, no, I can't.
2. Could you lend me your pen? Oh, yes, I can.

no + noun: auxiliary + not

Rule XVI (C). No का प्रयोग noun के पहले होता है और not का प्रयोग auxiliary के बाद; जैसे—

1. He has no money/car/house.
2. He has not (hasn't) got any money.
3. He does not (doesn't) have any money.
4. She cannot (can't) do this sum.

verb + not/so

Rule XVI (D). इन verbs के बाद not का प्रयोग noun clause के बदले में होता है—

hope, believe, think, expect, suppose, be afraid.

इन वाक्यों को लें—

1. Will he help you? I believe not.
   I believe not = I believe/that he will not help me.
2. Can you help me? I'am afraid not.
   I'm afraid not = I am afraid/that I can't help you.

इन verbs के बाद so का प्रयोग noun clause के बदले में होता है; जैसे—

1. Will he reach on time? Yes, I hope so.
   I hope so = I hope/that he will reach on time.
2. Is he right? Yes, I think so.
   I think so = I think/that he is right.

इस प्रकार, not और so की सहायता से वाक्य छोटे हो जाते हैं; क्योंकि इनका प्रयोग noun clause के बदले में होता है, अर्थात noun clause के छिप जाने पर होता है।

Rule XVI (E). not + infinitive/gerund

वाक्य में not आता है infinitive (to + verb) और gerund (verb + ing) के पहले; जैसे—

1. I asked him *not to sleep* in the class.
2. You are right in *not helping* him.

इसलिए इस प्रकार के वाक्य न बनाएँ—

1. I asked him *to not sleep* in the class.
2. You are right in ***helping not him*** or ***helping him not.***

Rule XVII. yet/still [अभी तक/अभी भी]

Yet का प्रयोग सामान्यतः वाक्य के अंत में होता है; जैसे—

1. He hasn't returned yet.
2. It is not 9 o'clock yet.

Still का प्रयोग auxiliary के बाद होता है, पर ordinary verb के पहले—

1. She is still in bed.
2. He still loves her.

Rule XVIII. yet/already

Affirmative sentences में already का प्रयोग होता है और इसका अर्थ होता है—**पहले ही**; जैसे—

1. I have done the work already.
2. It is 9 o'clock already.

Negative और Interrogative sentences में already के बदले yet आता है और ऐसे yet का अर्थ होता है—**अभी भी/अभी तक**; जैसे—

1. I haven't done the work yet. [not, already]
2. It is not 9 o'clock yet. [not, already]
3. She is not ready yet. [not, already]

Rule XIX. yet/already/so far/uptil now

इन adverbials के साथ सामान्यतः Present Perfect Tense आता है; जैसे—

1. He hasn't begun the work yet.
2. He has begun the work already.
3. He has not begun the work so far.
4. He has not begun the work uptil now.

Rule XX. just

Just के साथ सामान्यतः Present Perfect Tense आता है, पर American usage में just के साथ Past Simple का प्रयोग अधिक प्रचलित है; जैसे—

1. He has just begun the work. [British English]
2. He just began the work. [American English]

आप American English की नकल न करें, तो अच्छा हो।

Just के साथ past simple का भी प्रयोग होता है जब इसका अर्थ होता है only/barely; जैसे—

1. He just caught the bus.
2. She just managed to swim across.

Just का अर्थ at this very moment/exactly भी होता है; जैसे—

1. It is just 9 o'clock.
2. This is just what I want.
3. This is just the book I was looking for.
4. I am just going out.
5. The new edition of the book is just out.

Rule XXI. The Split Infinitive [to + adverb + verb]

किसी Adverb को to + verb [अर्थात infinitive] के बीच में रख देना गलत समझा जाता है; जैसे—

I request you to kindly grant me leave.

इस वाक्य में Infinitive 'to grant' को अलग कर दिया गया है और इन दोनों के बीच (to और grant के बीच) Adverb (kindly) को रख दिया गया है। व्याकरण में इसे Split Infinitive कहते हैं; क्योंकि Split का अर्थ होता है काटना। नियम यह है कि आप Adverb को Infinitive के पहले या बाद, अर्थ के अनुसार रखें, Infinitive को अलग कर उसके बीच में नहीं। इसलिए नियमानुसार यह वाक्य अशुद्ध है—

I advised him to carefully read.

यहाँ Infinitive 'to read' के बीच में Adverb (carefully) को रख दिया गया है। व्याकरण के नियमानुसार Adverb का स्थान यहाँ Verb (read) के बाद होना चाहिए—

I advised him *to read carefully.*

NOTE (a)—आजकल अच्छे-अच्छे लेखक भी Split Infinitive के दोष से बच नहीं पाते। इसलिए एक आचार्य ने कहा है—

The split infinitive is an ugly thing ... but it is one among several hundred ugly things ... Even that mysterious quality, 'distinction' of style, may in modest measure be attained by splitter of infinitives. —POWLER: *King's English*

And again,

We admit that separation of **to** *from its infinitive ... is not in itself desirable ... We will split infinitives sooner than be ambiguous or artificial; more than that, we will freely admit that sufficient recasting will get rid of any split infinitive.*

—FOLWER: *Modrn English Usage*

फाउलर साहब ने इस बात पर जोर दिया है कि जहाँ तक संभव हो, हम अपने वाक्य की बनावट इस प्रकार करें कि अर्थ भी स्पष्ट रहे और Split Infinitive का दोष भी न आए।

सिर्फ Split Infinitive के दोष से बचने के लिए वाक्य के अर्थ को नष्ट नहीं करें। कहने का तात्पर्य यह है कि फाउलर साहब की दृष्टि में यह कोई बहुत बड़ी गलती नहीं है। एक आचार्य ने तो स्पष्ट रूप से अपना मत इस प्रकार रखा है—

Split Infinitive with a single adverb may be allowed.

—G H VALLINS: *Better English*

इस संबंध में आप अमेरिका के एक प्रसिद्ध व्याकरणाचार्य का मत सुनें। उन्होंने यह वाक्य लिया है—

If you expect to eventually succeed, you must keep trying.

और इसपर अपना विचार इस प्रकार प्रकट किया है—

We have here an example of that notorious bugbear of academic grammar, 'the split infinitive' ... I am happy to be able to report to you that it is not only legal, it is also ethical, moral ... Benjamin Franklin, Washington Irving, Nathaniel Hawthorn, Theodore Roosevelt and Woodrow Wilson among many others, were unconscionable infinitive splitters. And modern writers are equally partial to the construction.

—NORMAN LEWIS: *Word Power*

वास्तव में, Split Infinitive का प्रचार और प्रयोग इतना अधिक हो गया है कि अब यह बड़ा दोष नहीं माना जाता। इसलिए, *infinitive* को *split* कर इसके बीच में एक-आध *Adverb* का प्रयोग धड़ल्ले से हो रहा है। हाँ, Infinitive को Split करके इसके बीच बहुत-से Adverbs की एक चेन बनाना आजकल भी दोष माना जाता है, क्योंकि इससे वाक्य भद्दा हो जाता है; जैसे—

I have asked him to *thoroughly, patiently* and *carefully* read his books.

यहाँ infinitive (to read) को split करके to और read के बीच तीन Adverbs का प्रयोग कर दिया गया है, जो काफी भद्दा लगता है। इससे अच्छा होता यदि इन तीनों Adverbs को books के बाद रखा जाता। अब इस वाक्य को देखें—

I request you *to kindly grant me* casual leave.

यहाँ Infinitive (*to grant*) को split करके to और grant के बीच एक Adverb (kindly) को रखा गया है। यह वाक्य भद्दा नहीं मालूम पड़ता। यों तो Nesfield तथा अन्य पुराने आचार्यों के मतानुसार यह वाक्य अशुद्ध समझा जाएगा, क्योंकि इसमें Split Infinitive का दोष आ गया है, पर Fowler, Vallins तथा Norman Lewis आदि आचार्यों के अनुसार यह कोई बहुत बड़ा दोष नहीं है।

इस संबंध में मेरा विचार है कि Infinitive को split करके to और verb के बीच में एक से अधिक Adverb का प्रयोग न करें, क्योंकि इससे वाक्य भद्दा हो जाता है। इसलिए किसी भी व्याकरणाचार्य ने, यहाँ तक कि Norman Lewis ने भी, ऐसे प्रयोग को अच्छा नहीं माना है। आप प्रयत्न तो यह करें कि to और verb के बीच में एक भी Adverb का प्रयोग न हो। यही सर्वोतम है, पर यदि आप एक Adverb का प्रयोग कर ही दें, तो लोगों को चाहिए कि आधुनिक प्रयोगानुसार, इस दोष को उदारतापूर्वक क्षमा कर दें और लेखक/परीक्षार्थी को इसके लिए दण्ड न दें।

NOTE (b)—not + to + verb : to + not + verb

Infinitive को काटकर to और verb के बीच में Adverb 'not' का प्रयोग भयंकर भूल है, क्योंकि not का स्थान सदा Infinitive के पहले रहता है। इन वाक्यों को लें—

1. He asked me *not to* go there.
2. He asked me *to not* go there.

यहाँ पहले वाक्य में 'not' का प्रयोग Infinitive (to go) के पहले है, जो शुद्ध है, पर दूसरे वाक्य में Infinitive (to go) को अलग कर दिया गया है और to तथा go के बीच में 'not' को रख दिया गया है। यह भी एक प्रकार का Split Infinitive ही है, क्योंकि 'not' भी Adverb है। ऐसा Split Infinitive प्रयोग में नहीं है। कोई भी लेखक या व्याकरणाचार्य इसे शुद्ध नहीं कह सकता और न कहता ही है।

EXERCISE

Correct the following sentences.

(1) He explained clearly the poem. (2) I do cheerfully my duties. (3) Describe briefly your classroom. (4) Express boldly your views. (5) He was enough pleased to help me. (6) I love my country enough dearly. (7) He looks never sad. (8) He comes late always. (9) He was told to not laugh. (10) I advised him to not make a noise.

Hints—(1) He clearly explained ...... poem or, he explained the poem clearly; (2) I cheerfully do my duties or, I do my duties cheerfully; (3) Briefly describe or, ... room briefly; (4) Boldly express or, ... views boldly; (5) pleased enough; (6) dearly enough; (7) never looks; (8) always comes; (9) not to laugh; (10) not to make ....

Rule XXII. Even, Only, Almost and At least

वाक्य में ऐसे Adverbs के स्थान का ध्यान रखना आवश्यक है। क्यों? इसलिए कि इनके स्थान (position) का बहुत ही गहरा प्रभाव वाक्य के अर्थ पर पड़ता है—

1. *Even ten per cent* of the students were not able to pass.
2. Ten per cent of the students were not able *even to pass.*

यहाँ पहले वाक्य में even का स्थान ten per cent के पहले है। इसलिए, इस वाक्य का अर्थ है—10 प्रतिशत भी लड़के पास नहीं कर सके। दूसरे वाक्य में even का स्थान pass के पहले है और इसलिए इस वाक्य का अर्थ है—10 प्रतिशत लड़के पास भी नहीं कर सके। तो इस प्रकार even के स्थान को बदल देने से इन वाक्यों के अर्थ में काफी अंतर पड़ गया है। इसलिए उचित अर्थ प्रकट करने के लिए इसे उचित स्थान पर रखें। एक-दो और उदाहरण लें—

1. *Only* Sheela sang.
2. Sheela *only* sang.

यहाँ पहले वाक्य का अर्थ है—सिर्फ शीला ने गाया, अर्थात और किसी ने नहीं गाया। दूसरे वाक्य का अर्थ है—शीला ने सिर्फ गाया, अर्थात उसने कोई और काम नहीं किया। तो यह स्पष्ट है कि इन वाक्यों के अर्थ में जो अंतर है वह only के स्थान पर निर्भर है। इसलिए वाक्य के अर्थ को स्पष्ट रूप से दूसरे लोगों तक पहुँचाने के लिए इन Adverbs को सावधानी से वाक्य में रखना चाहिए। यदि आप इन्हें यों ही कहीं भी रख देंगे, तो आपके कहने का अभिप्राय दूसरों को मालूम नहीं हो सकेगा। जब इनका प्रयोग वाक्य में हो तब आप उस वाक्य का अर्थ लगाएँ और अभिप्राय के अनुरूप इन Adverbs को उचित स्थान पर रखें; जैसे—

He *only died* yesterday.

इसका अर्थ है—"कल वह सिर्फ मर गया।" आप जानते हैं कि 'सिर्फ मरना' का कोई अर्थ ही नहीं हो सकता। वास्तव में, लिखने का अभिप्राय यह है कि "वह कल ही (सिर्फ कल) तो मरा।" इसलिए, यहाँ only का स्थान yesterday के पहले होना चाहिए—

He died *only* yesterday.

EXERCISE

Correct the following sentences.

(1) You can only pass when you work hard. (2) We can only come to a reasonable conclusion if we study the problem carefully. (3) One can almost get everything in the black market. (4) You at least should write to me twice a month. (5) He at least should have heard my prayer. (6) He only died last Monday. (7) These examinations can only be passed with great difficulty. (8) He only sent me five shillings.

Hints—(1) only when; (2) only if; (3) almost everything; (4) at least twice; (5) at least heard; (6) only last Monday; (7) only with great difficulty; (8) only five shillings or five shillings only

Rule XXIII. Position of Adverbs

Rule XXIII (A). Adjective/Adverb/Phrase/Clause and Adverb

Adverb का स्थान Adjective/Adverb/Phrase/Clause के ठीक पहले रहता है; जैसे—

1. I am *partly responsible* for this. [Adverb + Adjective]
2. He is working *very patiently.* [Adverb + Adverb]
3. He sat *just behind me.* [Adverb + Phrase]
4. I shall go *only when he comes.* [Adverb + Clause]

इसलिए ये वाक्य अशुद्ध हैं—

1. He sat behind me exactly. 2. I am responsible partly.

Rule XXIII (B). Auxiliary and Principal Verb and Adverb

Adverb का प्रयोग Auxiliary Verb (सहायक क्रिया) और Principal Verb (प्रधान क्रिया) के बीच में होता है; जैसे—

1. I have never seen it. 2. He is patiently doing it.

Caution—Not का प्रयोग Adjective और Infinitive के पहले होता है, पर Auxiliary तथा Principal Verb के बीच में; जैसे—

1. This is *not* bad. 2. He was asked *not* to smoke.

3. He has *not* seen me yet. 4. He will *not* come.

Interrogative sentences में not का प्रयोग Auxiliary Verb और Subject के बीच में होता है; जैसे—

1. Didn't he come? 2. Can't you help?

Rule XXIII (C). Adverbs of Time/Place/Manner

साधारणत: Adverbs of Time/Place/Manner (Quality) verb के बाद आते हैं, पर object रहने पर object के बाद; जैसे—

1. He came here. 2. I looked for him everywhere.

3. He is writing now. 4. He came here last year.

5. He walks quickly. 6. He speaks well.

7. He acted foolishly. 8. He did the act badly.

साधारणतः Adverb of Frequency का प्रयोग Auxiliary Verb के बाद होता है, पर अन्य verb के पहले; जैसे—

1. He is always late. 2. She is never late.

3. He can never do it. 4. They have hardly begun.

5. She always speaks the truth. 6. I seldom find time for this.

इसलिए ऐसे-ऐसे वाक्य न लिखें—

1. He smiles never. 2. He laughs always.

3. He tells always a lie. 4. She badly plays tennis.

Rule XXIII (D). Adverbs of Degree का प्रयोग Adjective/Adverb/Verb के पहले होता है। पर enough का प्रयोग सदा Adjective/Adverb के बाद होता है; जैसे—

1. He is very kind. 2. He was kind enough to help me.

3. It is too hot. 4. I am just going.

5. It is big enough. 6. He can't walk quickly enough.

Caution—Adverb का प्रयोग करते समय सावधानी से देखना चाहिए कि यह किस शब्द का गुण बतलाता है। अर्थ का ध्यान रखकर ही Adverb का प्रयोग करना चाहिए। इन वाक्यों को लें—

1. Tell me clearly what you saw.

2. Tell me what you saw clearly.

यहाँ पहले और दूसरे वाक्य के अर्थ में बहुत अंतर है। इस अंतर का कारण है clearly का स्थान। पहले वाक्य से 'साफ-साफ कहने' का बोध होता है, पर दूसरे से 'साफ-साफ देखने' का। तो, Adverb को वाक्य में यों ही रख देना कितना खतरनाक हो सकता है।

Caution—Adverb of Manner, Place and Time

कुछ वाक्यों में कई प्रकार के Adverbs का प्रयोग एक साथ ही हो सकता है। वैसे वाक्यों में पहले Adverb of Manner आता है, उसके बाद Adverb of Place और अंत में Adverb of Time, जैसाकि एक महान आचार्य का मंत है—

... the normal position of adverbs is at the end of a sentence in the order Manner, Place and Time. —W S ALLEN

इन वाक्यों को लें—

1. He will go to Mumbai today.

2. She will come here within a few hours.

इन्हें इस प्रकार न लिखें—

1. He will go today to Mumbai.

2. She will come within a few hours here.

इस संबंध में इस नियम का भी ध्यान रखना चाहिए—

The more particular expressions of time come before the more general.

—W S ALLEN

इस नियम के अनुसार वाक्य में पहले छोटे समय को सूचित करनेवाला adverb आना चाहिए और उसके बाद लंबे समय का बोध करानेवाला adverb; जैसे—

He was born at 7 o'clock in the morning on Monday in 1920.

Rule XXIV. Empty There

जब वाक्य का Subject अनिश्चित (vague) रहता है और स्थान (place) या समय (time) का बोध करानेवाले Adverb या Preposition का प्रयोग होता है, तब ऐसा वाक्य There से आरंभ होता है। There से जब किसी व्यक्ति या वस्तु के अस्तित्व (existence) का बोध हो, तब इसे Empty There कहा जाता है, क्योंकि इसका कोई अपना अर्थ नहीं होता। ऐसे वाक्यों में सामान्यतया verb 'be' का प्रयोग होता है; जैसे—

1. There is a book on the table.
2. There is a pen in his pocket.
3. There is a temple near this place.
4. There is a river by this town.
5. There is a party tonight/this night.
6. There is a meeting tomorrow.

ऐसे वाक्य There के बिना इस प्रकार लिखे नहीं जा सकते—

1. A book is on the table. 2. A meeting is tomorrow.

Rule XXV. All and Quite

Adverb की भाँति प्रयुक्त होने पर all और quite—इन दोनों का अर्थ completely या perfectly होता है। इसलिए adjective के पहले केवल all या quite का प्रयोग होना चाहिए, जैसे—

1. It is *quite right.* 2. It is *all right.*

To say anything is **quite right** *is quite right in grammar, but to say anything is* **quite all right** *is quite wrong in grammar ... the phrase* **quite right** *is as good as the phrase* **all right;** *they are interchangeable, but* **quite all right** *is an illiterate pleonasm.*

—WHITAKER-WILSON: *English Grammar*

अब इस वाक्य को लें—Oh, that's quite all right.

Quite all right का प्रयोग बोलचाल तक ही सीमित है।

NOTE—यहाँ यह बात ध्यान देने योग्य है कि quite का अर्थ बिलकुल/पूर्णतः (completely) तब होता है जब यह verb या degreeless/absolute adjective के पहले आता है; जैसे—

1. I quite agree with you. 2. I am quite alone.
3. His watch is quite right.

पर जब quite का प्रयोग ऐसे adjective के पहले होता है जिसकी degree होती है, तब इसका अर्थ होता है—fairly, not very, अर्थात यह बोध होता है कि adjective की मात्रा कुछ-कुछ तो है, पर **पूरी** या **बिलकुल** नहीं; जैसे—

He is quite a good poet/player.

यहाँ quite good का अर्थ है—कुछ-कुछ अच्छा; बहुत अच्छा नहीं। इस अर्थ का ध्यान रखकर ऐसे-ऐसे वाक्य न बनाएँ—

1. I like him because he is quite a good poet.
2. He got a gold medal because he is quite a good player.

Caution—All right के बदले Alright का प्रयोग न करें।

Rule XXVI. Preposition and Adverb

वाक्य में Adverb के पहले Preposition का प्रयोग करना भयंकर भूल है। इसलिए humbly, slowly, bravely आदि Adverbs के पहले with या किसी दूसरे Preposition का प्रयोग नहीं हो सकता। इन वाक्यों को लें—

1. *With* most *humbly* and *respectfully* I beg to state.
2. You write *with patiently* and *confidently*.

इन वाक्यों में with का प्रयोग सर्वथा अनुचित है। यदि आपको ऐसे वाक्यों में Preposition का प्रयोग करना ही हो, तो Adverbs को Nouns में इस प्रकार बदल दें—

You write with *patience* and *confidence*.

Caution—जब this/next/last/all के बाद समय-सूचक शब्द आते हैं (जैसे—morning, night, day, month, year, etc.) तब इनके साथ Preposition का प्रयोग नहीं होता, क्योंकि वैसी अवस्था में ये Adverb of Time का काम करते हैं। इन वाक्यों को लें—

1. He reached this morning.
2. He is reaching this evening.
3. I will start next morning.
4. He will come next Sunday.
5. He came here last month.
6. She was married last year.
7. We worked all day/night.
8. We worked all morning/evening.

पर जब समय-सूचक शब्द के पहले next/last आदि न आए, तब Preposition का प्रयोग अवश्य होता है; जैसे—

1. I will start in the morning.
2. He will come on Sunday.

NOTE—home as an adverb of place

Home एक noun है, पर जब इसके पहले कोई Adjective नहीं आता, तब इसका प्रयोग Adverb of Place की तरह होता है और इसलिए इसके पहले to नहीं आता। इससे यह भी स्पष्ट है कि Adverb की तरह प्रयुक्त होने पर home के पहले Adjective (my, his, etc.) नहीं आता; जैसे—

I go home every day. [not, to home]

....

EXERCISE

Correct the following sentences.

(1) One must work with honestly and sincerely. (2) I read this book with thoroughly. (3) He taught me with clearly.

....

Rule XXVII. Fairly and Rather

इन दोनों से Adjective/Adverb की मात्रा का बोध होता है, पर इनके प्रयोग में एक अंतर भी है। किसी Adjective/Adverb को पसंद करने पर उसके पहले fairly का प्रयोग होता है, पर उसे नापसंद करने पर rather का; जैसे—

1. Tea is fairly hot. 2. Tea is rather hot.

यहाँ fairly hot का अर्थ है—hot enough अर्थात पसंद आने योग्य गरम, पर rather hot का अर्थ है—too hot अर्थात पसंद न आने योग्य गरम।

इस नियम का ध्यान रखें और ऐसे वाक्य न लिखें—

1. I like her because she is rather tall.
2. I do not like her because she is fairly tall.

यहाँ पहले वाक्य में fairly का प्रयोग होना चाहिए और दूसरे में rather का। क्यों? इसलिए कि यहाँ एक ही वाक्य में दो विरोधी भावों (पसंद और नापसंद) को एक साथ मिला दिया गया है।

....

EXERCISE

Make five sentences like the following.

1. She is rather tall for her age.
2. She looks lovely because she is fairly tall.

....

Rule XXVIII. No/Not/None

Rule XXVIII (A). No का प्रयोग Noun, Adjective (Positive तथा Comparative Degree) और Adverb (Comparative Degree) के पहले होता है। इन वाक्यों को लें—

1. I have no *book.*
2. I have no *good* book.
3. I have no *better* book.
4. This car will carry you there no *sooner* than the train.

Rule XXVIII (B). जब Noun या Adjective के पहले a/an आता है, तब no के बदले not का प्रयोग इस प्रकार होता है—

1. Not *a drop* of water was available.
2. Not *a child* could be seen there.

3. There is not *a rich* boy in this class.

4. There was not *an intelligent* boy to answer this question.

NOTE—Verb के बाद not का प्रयोग इस प्रकार होता है—

1. He doesn't sing. 2. She didn't come.

जब वाक्य में Positive Degree का Adverb रहे या Adjective का Predicative use हो, तो उसके पहले not का प्रयोग होता है, no का नहीं; जैसे—

1. I am not *very* well today. 2. This answer is not *correct*.

Rule XXVIII (C). जब वाक्य में *too + adjective/adverb* या *the + Comparative adjective/adverb* आए, तब उसके पहले none का प्रयोग होता है—

1. Her health is none too good.

2. I am none the worse for this loss.

Rule XXVIII (D). *good* और *different* के पहले *no* का प्रयोग शुद्ध माना जाता है। क्यों? इसका आधार है भाषा-विज्ञान। ऐतिहासिक दृष्टि से, good एक Noun था जो बाद में Adjective बन गया। इसलिए आज भी उसका थोड़ा प्रभाव बना हुआ है और इस प्रकार के वाक्य शुद्ध माने जाते हैं—

1. It is no good repenting now.

2. This medicine is no good.

Rule XXVIII (E). वाक्य में different के पहले no का प्रयोग इसलिए होता है कि इस शब्द में तुलना (comparison) का भाव निहित है। इसलिए इस प्रकार का वाक्य शुद्ध माना जाता है—

This shirt is no different from that.

ऐसे वाक्यों में no के बदले not का प्रयोग अनुचित है।

Rule XXVIII (F). वाक्य में double negative का प्रयोग नहीं होना चाहिए—

1. I forbade him to smoke. [not, not to smoke]

2. He cannot stay any longer. [not, no longer]

3. She can't go any further. [not, no further]

....

EXERCISE

Make ten sentences like the following.

1. There is no easier method.
2. Not a person could tell the real story.
3. It is no good crying now.
4. There is not an idle boy in this class.

....

Rule XXIX. Sentence Adverbials/Sentence Connectors

कुछ Adverbs, Conjunctions और Phrases को Sentence Connectors या Sentence Adverbials कहा जाता है।

Sentence Connectors उन शब्दों को कहते हैं जो दो Sentences या Paragraphs के बीच संबंध (link) स्थापित करते हैं। ये किस प्रकार का संबंध स्थापित करते हैं? ये पहले sentence या paragraph के अर्थ (idea/meaning) को दूसरे sentence या paragraph में जारी रखते हैं, अर्थात पहले वाक्य में कही गई बात का संबंध दूसरे वाक्य से जोड़ते हैं। इसलिए ऐसे शब्दों को connectives या link words भी कहा जा सकता है।

इससे यह स्पष्ट है कि ऐसे दो वाक्यों के बीच संबंध अर्थ की दृष्टि से स्थापित होता है; वाक्य की बनावट (structure) की दृष्टि से नहीं।

बनावट की दृष्टि से, दोनों वाक्य स्वतंत्र रहते हैं, क्योंकि दूसरा वाक्य semicolon या full stop के बाद आता है। इसलिए दूसरा वाक्य पहले वाक्य का अभिन्न अंग नहीं होता।

यहाँ एक बात ध्यान देने योग्य है। Conjunctions के द्वारा बहुत-से clauses को जोड़ा जाता है और वे सभी clauses एक ही sentence के अभिन्न अंग होते हैं। पर sentence connectors दो sentence को जोड़ते हैं और इसलिए ये दोनों बनावट की दृष्टि से एक-दूसरे से स्वतंत्र रहते हैं।

इन वाक्यों को देखें—

1. *Mohan reads* **and** *Radha plays. [conjunction]*
   Mohan loves Radha **and** *Radha is not a good* **girl.** [*sentence connector*]
2. *He is not only a worker but a leader* **as well.**
   He has a big car. He has a new house **as well.** [*sentence connector*]

कुछ मुख्य sentence connectors ये हैं—

and, also, as well (भी), too (भी), at first, at last, any how, anyway, but, besides, even so, either (भी), however, moreover, likewise, otherwise, meanwhile, meantime, in the same way, in short, in other words, of course, on the other hand, on the contrary, to illustrate, to conclude, to cap, to be brief, for example, still (अभी भी), yet (अभी तक), so, therefore, then, thus, clearly, certainly, equally, frankly, possibly, fortunately, seriously, obviously, strictly speaking, to our regret/surprise

इन वाक्यों को देखें—

1. He didn't help me. On the contrary he harmed me.
2. Mohan is a farmer. His father is a farmer, too.
3. You neither read nor write. What do you do, then?
4. He can't dance. I can't dance either.
5. I don't like this car; besides (moreover) it is costly.
6. He is rather sickly; nevertheless he works hard.
7. He feels tired; he however goes on working.

REVISION TEST I

Correct the following sentences.

1. He had climbed to the top almost when a branch broke.

2. He only worked five sums.
3. I speak always the truth.
4. I enough well know about it.
5. He only succeeded in scoring two goals.
6. I only like her when she smiles.
7. I did not find him nowhere.
8. I want to at once go home.
9. He finished quicker than I expected.
10. Firstly, it is too weak.
11. Is it not much surprising?
12. It is nothing else than folly.
13. You seldom or ever come in time.
14. She can't hardly do so.
15. He will pay heavy for his folly.
16. Is it not wise to always avoid bad men?
17. He will pay dear for his misconduct.
18. He seldom or ever gets up early.
19. I never remember having seen you.
20. I like her too much.
21. Of course, he is a great man.
22. My son is too healthy.
23. I am quite sorry to receive this letter.
24. I hope to immediately see him.
25. Nothing happens by chance ever.

REVISION TEST II

Explain why the following sentences are correct or incorrect.

1. I have read very often this book.
2. He explained very clearly this rule.
3. I am enough pleased with you.
4. He only died a month ago.
5. It was very hotter yesterday than today.
6. I have received no letter, neither from father nor from mother.
7. I was too glad to hear this happy news.
8. I only eat when I feel hungry.
9. This man is much interesting.
10. Although he has plenty of money, but he is unhappy.
11. I wish to earnestly and emphatically advise you.

12. He only came a week ago.
13. She goes out seldom at night.
14. Are you tired? Yes, a few.
15. I have seen often this man.
16. He works very hardly so that he may pass.
17. She is enough kind to help me.
18. He began to suddenly beat her.
19. She soon will leave for Mumbai.
20. She does patiently her work.

REVISION TEST III

Match the words in A with the right words in B.

A	B
You are much	intelligent.
He is very	wiser.
Yes	I am not happy.
No	I am glad.
He came	next year.
She will come	last evening.

REVISION TEST IV

Choose right words.

1. She seldom $\frac{\text{or ever}}{\text{or never}}$ tells lies.
2. He was $\frac{\text{kind enough}}{\text{enough kind}}$ to help me.
3. He is $\frac{\text{too}}{\text{very}}$ small to touch the ceiling.
4. He is $\frac{\text{too}}{\text{very}}$ glad to see you.
5. That boy is $\frac{\text{much}}{\text{very}}$ intelligent.
6. She has come $\frac{\text{just now}}{\text{presently}}$.

7. I saw him a week $\frac{\text{ago}}{\text{before}}$.

8. She reached $\frac{\text{in this}}{\text{this}}$ morning.

9. It is $\frac{\text{no}}{\text{not}}$ good repenting now.

10. It is nothing else $\frac{\text{but}}{\text{than}}$ pride.

11. I forbade them $\frac{\text{to shout}}{\text{not to shout}}$.

12. I don't want $\frac{\text{anything}}{\text{nothing now}}$.

❒

A large number of the formal restrictions and ancient 'thou shalt nots' of academic grammar are now completely outmoded. —NORMAN LEWIS

Chapter V

TEST YOURSELF

I. *Correct or justify the following sentences.*

1. Both he as well as she is here.
2. Neither I can sit nor stand nor sleep.
3. He cannot read nor write anything.
4. I have no pen nor paper with me.
5. You will pass if you will work hard.
6. I will go home after the college will be closed.
7. This pen is not either cheap nor good.
8. The reason why he is poor is because he is idle.
9. I doubt that he will pass this time.
10. You should act fearlessly like I do.
11. I will not go out before I will finish the work.
12. Four years passed since I have come here.
13. It appears as if he is a bird.
14. Not only he gave me food but also money.
15. Take an umbrella in case it will rain.
16. I do not know that he is ill or not.
17. I will wait here until you will not come back.
18. I know that where he lives these days.
19. I can't say as to whether he is ill or not.
20. Unless you do not work hard, you can't pass.
21. He has no other aim but to earn money.

II. *Fill in the blanks with a word given in brackets.*

1. He cannot sit ...... sleep. [or, nor]
2. He has not seen me since I ...... here. [came, have come]
3. She work hard lest she ...... fail. [will, should]
4. He is no other ...... my brother. [but, than]
5. I will leave before he .... [will return, returns]
6. They made haste lest they ...... miss the train. [should, would, might]
7. Though she is poor ...... she is happy. [but, yet]
8. I don't know ...... he will come or not. [that, whether]

❐

CONJUNCTIONS

हिन्दी में Conjunctions को समुच्चयबोधक अव्यय कहा जाता है। अँगरेजी के conjunctions के प्रयोग हिन्दी की अपेक्षा कुछ अधिक जटिल हैं। इसलिए यहाँ ऐसे प्रयोगों पर विचार करें।

Rule I (A). The Correct Correlatives

Neither के बाद nor आता है, or नहीं और either के बाद or आता है nor नहीं। इसी प्रकार, both के बाद and आता है, as well as नहीं और though के बाद yet आता है, but नहीं। Hardly और Scarcely के बाद when या before आता है, than नहीं और no sooner के बाद than आता है, when नहीं—

neither … nor, either … or, both … and, hardly or scarcely … when/before, though … yet, no sooner … than; जैसे—

1. He is *neither* good *nor* bad.
2. It is *both* good *and* cheap.
3. *Hardly* had he left *when* his father came.
4. *No sooner* did the thief see the police *than* he ran away.

यहाँ neither के बाद nor आया है और both के बाद and; आप यह भी देखते हैं कि hardly के बाद when का प्रयोग हुआ है और no sooner के बाद than का। अतः, ये वाक्य शुद्ध हैं। यदि यहाँ neither के बाद or होता और both के बाद as well as, तो वाक्य अशुद्ध हो जाते। इसी प्रकार hardly के बाद than के आ जाने से और no sooner के बाद when के प्रयोग से वाक्य अशुद्ध हो जाते। इस छोटे-से नियम का ध्यान रखना कठिन नहीं, पर कुछ लोग ऐसा नहीं कर पाते। अब इन वाक्यों को देखें—

1. *Like the Persian noble of old I ask that I may* **neither** *command* **or** *obey.*

—EMERSON

2. *But I would suggest that the time has come when other methods should be evolved* **both** *for the benefit of labour* **as well as** *for the community at large.*

—JAWAHARLAL NEHRU: AIR AUG. 5, 1957

3. **Which** *differs from* **that** *and* **who** *in being used* **both** *as an adjective* **as well as** *a pronoun.* —H SWEET

यहाँ पहले वाक्य में or के बदले nor का और दूसरे तथा तीसरे वाक्यों में as well as के बदले and का प्रयोग होना चाहिए।

Rule I (B). *Not either* के बाद or आता है, nor नहीं—not either … or; जैसे—

That house is *not either* useful *or* beautiful.

Rule II. Position of Correlatives

कुछ ऐसे शब्द हैं जो बराबर एक साथ जोड़ा (pair) बनकर आते हैं और Conjunction का काम करते हैं। इन्हें ही Correlative कहा जाता है। ये हैं—

either … or, neither … nor, both … and,

not only … but also, as much … as

इनके प्रयोग के संबंध में इनके स्थान (position) का पूरा ध्यान रखना चाहिए, क्योंकि नियम यह है कि इनमें से एक भाग के साथ जिस Part of Speech का प्रयोग होता है वही दूसरे भाग के साथ भी प्रयुक्त होना चाहिए। यदि एक का स्थान Noun के पहले हो, तो दूसरे का भी Noun ही के पहले होना चाहिए, Verb/Adjective आदि के पहले नहीं। इसी प्रकार, यदि एक का स्थान Verb के पहले हो, तो दूसरे का भी Verb ही के पहले होना चाहिए, किसी दूसरे प्रकार के शब्द के पहले नहीं; जैसे—

1. I saw neither *Ram* nor *Mohan.*
2. I neither *saw* Ram nor *wrote* to him.

यहाँ पहले वाक्य में neither का स्थान Noun (Ram) के पहले है। इसलिए इसके जोड़े का स्थान (nor का) भी Noun (Mohan) के पहले है। दूसरे वाक्य में neither का स्थान Verb के पहले है और इसलिए nor का भी स्थान Verb ही के पहले है। यदि हम ऐसा लिखें—I neither saw Ram nor Mohan, तो यह अशुद्ध होगा, क्योंकि यहाँ 'neither' Verb के पहले है और 'nor' Noun के पहले।

अब इस वाक्य को लें—

He not only *gave* me a book but also *money.*

यहाँ not only के बाद verb आया है, पर but also के बाद noun (money). अतः यह वाक्य अशुद्ध है।

अब इस वाक्य को देखें—

He has read both in India and England.

यहाँ both के बाद preposition (in) आया है, पर and के बाद noun (England). इसका शुद्ध रूप होगा—

1. He has read both *in* India and *in* England.
2. He has read *in* both India and England.

अब इन वाक्यों को देखें—

1. **Both for** *good* **and evil** *almost everything that distinguishes our age from its predecessors is due to science.* —BERTRAND RUSSELL
2. *The poor* **both in** *town* **and country** *suffered terribly from the price of bread.* —G M TREVELYAN
3. *They have been used* **either to clear** *a very knotty problem in his mind* **or in** *that of its co-workers.* —*The Modern Review*: Feb. '57

यहाँ पहले दो वाक्यों में both के बाद Prepositions (for/in) आये हैं, पर and के बाद Nouns (evil/country), जो अशुद्ध है। यहाँ and के भी बाद (अर्थात evil/country के पहले) एक

Preposition का प्रयोग होना चाहिए। इसी प्रकार, तीसरे वाक्य में 'either' के बाद Infinitive (to clear) आया है, पर 'or' के बाद Preposition (in)। यदि either को problem के बाद रख दिया जाए तो either/or के दोनों ही भाग बराबर हो जाएँगे, क्योंकि इन दोनों ही के बाद Preposition का प्रयोग हो जाएगा और तब वाक्य शुद्ध हो जाएगा। देखिए, सावधानी से लिखनेवाले ऐसी गलती नहीं करते—

1. *The poet's command* **both of** *his experience* **and of** *his technique is perfect.*

   —F R LEAVIS

2. *The plays of Synge form rather a special case because they are based upon the idiom of a rural people whose speech is naturally poetic* **both in** *imagery* **and in** *rhythm.* —T S ELIOT

3. *Goodman is most successful with respect* **both to** *the control* **and to** *the development of his method.* —*The Kenyon Review*: Spring, 1955

4. *In this lecture I wish to consider* **both in** *history* **and in** *the present day the relation of the exceptional man to the community.* —BERTRAND RUSSELL

यहाँ इन वाक्यों में both ... and को काफी सावधानी से रखा गया है, क्योंकि both और and दोनों ही के बाद Preposition (of/in/to/in) का प्रयोग हुआ है। आप यह भी देखेंगे कि यहाँ Bertrand Russell ने सावधानी से काम लिया है, पर उनके प्रथम वाक्य में असावधानी के कारण अशुद्धि आ गयी है। तो, इससे यह स्पष्ट है कि Correlative की अशुद्धि बड़े-बड़े लोगों से भी कभी-कभी असावधानी के कारण हो जाती है। आप असावधानी के शिकार न हों।

....

EXERCISE

I. *Correct the following sentences.*

(1) I could neither help Ram nor Shyam. (2) He neither had gold nor silver. (3) She neither offended me nor my friend. (4) He both offended me and my friend. (5) He is as much noted for his bravery as for his charity. (6) He not only built a house but also a garage. (7) Latin is not only difficult to read but also to write. (8) I neither met Gopal nor his brother. (9) I have read both in England and America. (10) He has gone both to America and Russia. (11) Neither he comes nor writes. (12) I neither want to take nor give.

Hints—(1) help neither Ram ...; (2) had neither gold; (3) offened neither me ...; (4) offended both me ...; (5) He is noted as much for ... ; (6) He built not only ...; (7) difficult not only to read ...; (8) neither Gopal; (9) both in England and in America; (10) both to America and to Russia or ... gone to both America and Russia; (11) neither comes nor writes; (12) neither to take nor to give

II. *Correct the following sentences.*

(1) There was much agitation both in Dacca as well as in Karachi. (2) A thing cannot be both white as well as black at the same time. (3) No sooner had he reached the station when the train started. (4) Hardly had he left home than it began to rain. (5) He has

neither a pen or a pencil. (6) Though he is poor, but he is happy. (7) Your pen is not either good nor cheap.

Hints—(1) and in Karachi; (2) and black; (3) than the train …; (4) when it …; (5) nor a pencil; (6) yet; (7) or

. . . .

Rule III. Either and Either … or; Neither and Neither … nor

Rule III (A). Either और Neither का प्रयोग Adjective तथा Pronoun—दोनों ही प्रकार से होता है—

1. *Either* of the roads is long.
2. *Neither* of the roads is long.
3. *Either* road is long.
4. *Neither* road is long.

यहाँ पहले दो वाक्यों में either/neither का प्रयोग Pronoun की भाँति हुआ है और तीसरे तथा चौथे में Adjective की भाँति। आप जानते हैं कि जब इनका प्रयोग Pronoun/Adjective की भाँति होता है, तब ये केवल दो ही व्यक्तियों या वस्तुओं के साथ प्रयुक्त होते हैं, क्योंकि either का अर्थ होता है—*one of the two* और neither का—*not one or the other.*

Rule III (B). जब either के बाद or आ जाता है और neither के बाद nor, तब इन्हें Correlative भी कहा जाता है, क्योंकि इनके द्वारा एक ही श्रेणी के शब्दों को जोड़ा जाता है। ऐसी अवस्था में इनका प्रयोग दो से अधिक व्यक्तियों या वस्तुओं के साथ भी होता है, केवल दो ही के लिए नहीं, अर्थात वैसी अवस्था में either … or तथा neither … nor के द्वारा दो से अधिक Nouns/Pronouns/Verbs/Adjectives को जोड़ा जा सकता है—

Either *as a Conjunction, Adverb, or Correlative indicates that what immediately follows is the first of* **two or more** *alternatives—used before* **two** *or* **more** *coordinate words, phrases or clauses which are joined by* **or**. *—Webster's International Dictionary*

Neither *as a Conjunction or Adverb—Usually introducing the first of* **two or more** *coordinate words or clauses joined by* **nor**. *—Webster's International Dictionary*

Shorter Oxford Dictionary में भी either और neither के अर्थ क्रमशः ये भी दिए गए हैं—

1. Any one of more than two
2. None of more than two

इस प्रकार, यह स्पष्ट है कि Conjunction की भाँति प्रयुक्त होने पर either … or तथा neither … nor का प्रयोग दो से अधिक के साथ भी हो सकता है, और इसलिए either के बाद एक से अधिक or तथा neither के बाद एक से अधिक nor आ सकता है—

either … or … or … or; neither … nor … nor … nor

कुछ लोगों का मत है कि Conjunction की भाँति प्रयुक्त होने पर भी either/neither का प्रयोग केवल दो ही के लिए होना चाहिए, दो से अधिक के लिए कभी नहीं—

The correct correlatives are **either ... or** *and* **neither ... not.** *Strictly speaking, we should not add another* **or** *or* **nor,** *since* **either** *and* **neither** *imply* **two and two** *only.*

—G H VALLINS: *Better English*

मेरे विचार में Vallins साहब का यह मत मान्य नहीं, क्योंकि अँगरेजी की उच्च कोटि की Dictionary का भी मत उनसे नहीं मिलता। जहाँ तक आधुनिक प्रयोग का प्रश्न है, वह तो Vallins के मत को बिलकुल ही नहीं मानता। आप देखेंगे कि महान लेखकों ने either ... or तथा neither ... nor का प्रयोग दो से अधिक वस्तुओं के साथ किया है और इसलिए उनके वाक्यों में either के बाद एक से अधिक or और neither के बाद एक से अधिक nor रहते हैं—

1. *There was, that is to say, nothing to distract him from his interests or to corrupt these interests;* **neither** *the ambitions of parents or wife,* **nor** *the standards of society,* **nor** *the temptations of success.* —T S ELIOT
2. **Either** *from the moralist's point of view,* **or** *from the theologian's point of view,* **or** *from the psychologist's point of view,* **or** *from that of the political philosopher,* **or** *judging by the ordinary, standards of likeableness in human beings, Milton is unsatisfactory.* —T S ELIOT
3. *Which, as a matter of fact, are found* **neither** *in Shakespeare,* **nor** *in the Authorised Version of the Bible,* **nor** *in the poetical works of Milton, Pope, Cowper and Shelley.* —JESPERSON
4. **Neither** *the brilliancy of Hazlitt,* **nor** *the harmony of De Quincey,* **nor** *the vigour of Macaulay,* **nor** *the eloquence of Ruskin,* **nor** *the purity of Goldsmith could for a moment be thought capable of expressing the meaning of Lamb.*

—HUGH WALKER

इन वाक्यों में either ... or तथा neither ... nor का प्रयोग दो से अधिक व्यक्तियों या वस्तुओं के लिए हुआ है। Vallins साहब के मतानुसार ये सभी वाक्य अशुद्ध हैं। अपनी पुस्तक *Good English* में उन्होंने तीसरे वाक्य का खंडन भी किया है, जो उचित नहीं। व्याकरण के नियमानुसार भी ऐसे वाक्य शुद्ध होते हैं, क्योंकि अँगरेजी के सबसे महान व्याकरणाचार्य ने स्पष्ट कहा है—

This restriction to **two** *does not hold for the adverb* **(conjunction)—Neither** *fish* **nor** *flesh* **nor** *fowl.* —FOWLER: *Modern English Usage*

Fowler साहब के मतानुसार Neither fish nor flesh nor fowl शुद्ध है, क्योंकि यहाँ neither ... nor का प्रयोग Adverb (या Conjunction) की भाँति हुआ है। इसलिए, इस वाक्य के आधार पर Neither book, nor pen, nor paper आदि वाक्य शुद्ध हैं। यही प्रयोग में भी है। यदि Vallins साहब के मतानुसार इन्हें अशुद्ध माना जाए, तो लेखकों के लिए एक बड़ी जटिल समस्या उत्पन्न हो जाएगी और व्याकरण के छात्रों के लिए सिरदर्द।

Rule IV. No/Not/Never and Or

यदि वाक्य में no/not/never आए और उसके बाद पूरा clause रहे, तो no/not/never के बाद *or* का प्रयोग होता है, nor का नहीं; जैसे—

1. I have *no* pen *or* pencil.
2. I have *never* seen him *or* heard of him.
3. He can*not* laugh *or* weep.
4. I did *not* see her *or* write to her.

इन वाक्यों में nor का प्रयोग आधुनिक व्याकरण के नियमानुसार अशुद्ध होता, जैसा महान आचार्य ने कहा है—

I cannot read **nor** *write. I cannot read* **or** *write. The use of 'nor' in such sentences was formerly in fashion, and that of* **or** *is now in fashion.*

—FOWLER: *Modern English Usage*

वास्तव में no/not/never के बाद nor का प्रयोग Chaucer और Shakespeare के युग में होता था। आज का अच्छा लेखक ऐसी अवस्था में or का ही प्रयोग करता है—

Mr Whibley is **not** *a critic of men* **or** *of books.* —T S ELIOT

EXERCISE

Correct the following sentences.

(1) He cannot sit nor stand. (2) I do not sing nor dance. (3) He has not book nor paper. (4) He has no brother nor sister.

Hints—(1) or stand; (2) or dance; (3) or paper; (4) or sister

Rule V. The Uses of That

Rule V (A). That का प्रयोग सदा Indirect Narration में होता है, Direct में नहीं; जैसे—

He said that he would go home.

इसलिए यह वाक्य अशुद्ध है—

He said that, "I shall go home".

Rule V (B). That के बाद Imperative/Interrogative/Optative/Exclamatory sentences का प्रयोग भद्दी भूल है; जैसे—

1. He said *that* bring a glass of water.
2. I said *that* where does he live and how is he?
3. He said *that* how beautiful it was!
4. He said *that* may you live long!

ये सभी वाक्य अशुद्ध हैं। इनको शुद्ध करने के दो तरीके हैं। पहला तरीका तो यह है कि आप that को हटा दें और इन Clauses (that के बाद आनेवाले) को inverted commas के भीतर रख दें। दूसरा तरीका यह है कि आप प्रत्येक को Narration के नियम के अनुसार Indirect Narration में बदल दें, जिसकी चर्चा Narration के संबंध में विस्तारपूर्वक होगी।

Rule V (C). That का प्रयोग करने पर इसके बाद आनेवाले Verb के Tense का ध्यान रखना चाहिए, क्योंकि किसी वाक्य में that के पहले आनेवाले Clause में यदि Past Tense का प्रयोग हो, तो इसके बाद (That के बाद) आनेवाले Clause में भी Past Tense का प्रयोग करना पड़ता है; जैसे—

He said *that* he *would go* home.

यहाँ will का प्रयोग अशुद्ध होता। इस नियम पर Verb तथा Narration के संबंध में विस्तारपूर्वक विचार होगा।

Rule V (D). That से शुरू होनेवाले Clauses में Pronoun के प्रयोग में भी सावधानी की बड़ी आवश्यकता है, क्योंकि वैसी अवस्था में (परीक्षा भवन में) that के बाद आनेवाले 'I' से परीक्षार्थी (examinee) का बोध होता है और 'you' से परीक्षक (examiner) का।

इस वाक्य को लें—Sohrab tells Rustam that *you* are *my* father. इसका अर्थ है—"सोहराब रुस्तम से कहता है कि तुम (examiner) मेरे (examinee के) पिता हो।" यहाँ असावधानी के कारण वाक्य का अर्थ ही बदल गया है। इसका शुद्ध रूप यह होना चाहिए—

Sohrab tells Rustam that *he is his* (Sohrab's) father.

कुछ और वाक्य लें—

1. The spider tells the bee that *I* am rich but *you* are poor.
2. The old leaf tells the green leaf that *you* are foolish but *I* am wise.
3. The poet tells his beloved that *you* should not remember me after *my* death.
4. Anne says that *I* want to be the wife of a minister.

इन सभी वाक्यों में अर्थ का अनर्थ हो गया है। क्यों? इसलिए कि यहाँ I से परीक्षार्थी का बोध होता है, spider/old leaf/poet/Anne का नहीं। इसी प्रकार यहाँ you से परीक्षक का बोध होता है, bee/green leaf/beloved का नहीं। इस प्रकार, ऐसे वाक्य लिखकर परीक्षार्थी कभी तो अपने को गाली देते हैं और कभी परीक्षक को। इसलिए that के बाद (अर्थात Indirect Narration में) जब आप I और you का प्रयोग करें, तब सतर्कता से करें, नहीं तो आप भयंकर भूल के भागी बनेंगे।

NOTE—इस पक्ष पर Narration के अध्याय में विस्तारपूर्वक विचार किया जाएगा।

Rule V (E). यदि Interrogative Pronoun (who/which/what, etc.) या Interrogative Adverb (why/how/when/where/whether, etc.) से कोई Clause शुरू हो और उसके बाद कोई Principal Clause नहीं आए, तो Interrogative Pronoun/Interrogative Adverb के पहले that का प्रयोग नहीं होता; जैसे—

I do not know how he is.

यहाँ how से एक Clause (he is) शुरू होता है और इस Clause के बाद Principal Clause नहीं आया है। इसलिए how के पहले that का प्रयोग नहीं हुआ है। एक और वाक्य लें—

I do not know why he is absent.

इस वाक्य में why से एक Clause (he is absent) शुरू हुआ है, पर इसके बाद कोई Principal Clause नहीं आया है। इसलिए why के पहले that का प्रयोग नहीं हुआ है। अब इन वाक्यों को देखें—

1. I know *that when* he will come.

2. I cannot say *that where* he is these days.

3. You do not follow *that what* I say.

इन वाक्यों में when/where/what के पहले that का प्रयोग नहीं होना चाहिए, क्योंकि इन Clauses के बाद Principal Clause नहीं आया है।

NOTE—यदि Interrogative Pronoun/Interrogative Adverb से आरंभ होनेवाले Clauses के बाद Principal Clause आए, तो इनके पहले that का प्रयोग होना चाहिए; जैसे—

I know *that what* you say is right.

यहाँ what के बाद एक Clause (you say) आया है और इसके बाद एक Principal Clause (is right), इसलिए यहाँ what के पहले that का प्रयोग शुद्ध है। कुछ और वाक्य लें—

1. I know *that when* father will come, he will bring sweets for all his children.
2. I can say *that where* he lives is known to none.

इन वाक्यों में when/where के पहले that का प्रयोग शुद्ध है, क्योंकि इनके बाद Principal Clause आया है।

Rule V (F). याद रखें कि agree, assert, assume, aver, calculate, conceive, hold, learn, maintain, reckon, state, suggest और understand ऐसे Verbs हैं जिनके बाद that-Clause आने पर that को छिपा देना, आधुनिक प्रयोग के अनुसार, अच्छा नहीं समझा जाता; जैसे—

1. I understand he will come today.

2. I assert it is right.

3. I maintain it is all wrong.

यहाँ understand/assert/maintain के बाद that का प्रयोग अवश्य होना चाहिए।

NOTE—believe/presume/suppose/hope/think/be afraid के बाद, आधुनिक प्रयोगानुसार, that छिपा रहता है; जैसे—

1. I hope you are well.

2. I think you ar right.

....

EXERCISE

Correct the following sentences.

(1) I do not know that how and where he is. (2) I said to my servant that bring a chair and a glass of water. (3) In this poem the poet says that O, my beloved, you will remember me in your old age. (4) The withered leaf says to the green leaf that you are inexperienced but I am experienced. (5) Louisa says to her father that you have ruined my life. (6) Do not follow that what he says. (7) He said that he will not return within a week. (8) I know that when he will come here. (9) I cannot explain that why I like him so much. (10) I agree it is a nice proposal.

Hints—(1) know how; (2) I asked or ordered my servant to bring; (3) says "O … age" or says that she will remember him in her old age; (4) that she is … but he is; (5) that he has ruined her life or says to her father, "You … life." (6) follow what; (7) he would; (8) know when; (9) explain why; (10) agree that it is …

. . . .

Rule VI. Other/Rather and Than

Than का प्रयोग other, rather और comparative degree के adjective के भी साथ होता है। इन वाक्यों को देखें—

1. I would *rather* have a book *than* a pen.
2. He is no *other than* my father.
3. He has no *other* aim *than* to earn money.
4. He is much richer *than* she.

इन वाक्यों में to या but आदि का प्रयोग अशुद्ध होता।

. . . .

EXERCISE

Frame five sentences like the following.

1. I would rather have a cow than a horse.
2. She is no other than my sister.

. . . .

Rule VII. That and If/Whether

Rule VII (A). That का अर्थ होता है 'कि' पर If/Whether का कि नहीं/या नहीं। इसलिए whether के बाद or no या or not आता है, पर that के बाद वाक्य की बनावट इस प्रकार की नहीं हो सकती; जैसे—

I do not know *whether* he will come *or not.*

अब इस वाक्य को लें—

I do not know that he will come *or not.*

यहाँ that के बदले whether का प्रयोग होना चाहिए।

Rule VII (B). Affirmative sentence में doubt/doubtful के साथ whether का प्रयोग होता है, that का नहीं; जैसे—

1. I *doubt whether* he will come or not.
2. *Whether* he will come or not is *doubtful.*

NOTE (a)—यदि वाक्य Negative या Interrogative हो, तो doubt/doubtful के साथ that का प्रयोग शुद्ध माना जाता है; जैसे—

1. I do *not doubt that* he will come.

2. It is *not doubtful that* he will come.

3. *Is* there any *doubt that* he will come?

4. *Is* it *doubtful that* he will come?

NOTE (b)—वाक्य में whether के पहले as to का प्रयोग अनावश्यक है। इसलिए इस प्रकार न लिखें—

1. I doubt as to *whether* he will come or not.

2. I can't say as to *whether* he is ill or not.

. . . .

EXERCISE

Correct the following sentences.

(1) That he has been so misled is doubtful. (2) It was generally doubted that France would permit the use of her force. (3) It is extremely doubtful that he will succeed in this work.

Hints—(1) Whether he ……; (2) whether France; (3) whether he

. . . .

Rule VIII. Conjunctions of Comparison

कुछ ऐसे Conjunctions होते हैं जिनसे तुलना (comparison) का बोध होता है। ये हैं—

as … as, not so (as) … as, than

the + comparative degree … the + comparative degree

इन वाक्यों को देखें—

1. My shirt is as good as yours.

2. My pen is not as (so) good as yours.

3. My pen is better than yours.

4. The sooner you start, the better.

Rule IX. Conjunctions of Concession

कुछ Conjunctions ऐसे होते हैं जिनसे concession या supposition (यद्यपि … तथापि) का बोध होता है। ये हैं—

though, although, even if, however, whatever, no matter, for all, adjective/adverb + as

इन वाक्यों को लें—

1. Though he is black, he looks beautiful.

2. However hard he may work, he will fail.

3. Whatever may happen, I will help him.

4. No matter what he said, no one cared.

5. Black as he is, he looks beautiful.

6. For all you may say, he is not wise.

7. Even if he has abused me, I will not harm him.

कभी-कभी केवल may से भी 'यद्यपि ... तथापि' का बोध होता है—

He may be very poor, but he is happy.

ऐसे वाक्यों में may का अर्थ होता है though, पर याद रखें कि though के साथ yet का प्रयोग होता है। पर आजकल yet के बदले केवल comma से ही काम चल जाता है। हाँ, may के साथ but का प्रयोग अवश्य होता है; पर but का प्रयोग though के साथ नहीं होता। इसलिए but का प्रयोग इस प्रकार न करें—

Though he is poor, but he is happy.

....

EXERCISE

Complete the following sentences.

1. Though she is black ....
2. She may be black ....
3. Black as she is ....
4. However fast he may run ....
5. Whatever he might say ....

....

Rule X. As/Just as/Like

इनका अर्थ 'जैसे' या 'समान' होता है। पर, अंतर यह है कि 'as' Conjunction है, और 'like' एक Adjective, जो Preposition की तरह प्रयुक्त होता है। इसलिए like के बाद Objective Case का प्रयोग होता है और as के बाद Nominative का; जैसे—

1. I am like *him*. 2. I am as good as *he*.

आप ऐसे-ऐसे वाक्य नहीं लिख सकते—

1. I am like *he*. 2. He is as good as *me*.

आपको यह जानकर आश्चर्य होगा कि प्रसिद्ध वैज्ञानिक डारविन साहब ने यह वाक्य लिखा था—

Unfortunately, few have observed **like you have done.** —DARWIN

इस वाक्य में like के बाद you को Nominative Case में रख दिया गया है, जो फाउलर साहब के मतानुसार अनभिज्ञता का सूचक है। इस वाक्य में you के बाद पूर्णविराम होना चाहिए या like के बदले as का प्रयोग। अब इस वाक्य को देखें—

You should act like I do.

यहाँ like me या as I do होना चाहिए।

NOTE—As के बाद आनेवाला Noun/Pronoun सदा Objective Case में रहता है, यदि वह वाक्य में किसी Transitive Verb/Preposition का Object हो; जैसे—

You love her as much as *me*.

इससे यह स्पष्ट है कि यदि वाक्य में न Transitive Verb हो और न Preposition, तो as के बाद सदा Nominative Case का प्रयोग होना चाहिए।

....

EXERCISE

I. *Correct the following sentences.*

(1) Keep you body upright like I do. (2) Young Briam appeared for a few minutes in the part of Juliet just like boys did in Shakespeare's own time. (3) You are as dear to me as him.

Hints—(1) as I do; (2) as boys did; (3) as he.

II. *Fill in the blanks with as/just as/like.*

1. He talks ...... my master.
2. None has done ...... I have.
3. I will do ...... others.
4. She looks ...... a princess.

....

Rule XI. However and But

However के संबंध में यहाँ इतना ही कहना है कि इसके पहले but का प्रयोग (but however) नहीं होता। आप केवल but का प्रयोग करें या however का, पर दोनों को एक साथ मिलाकर नहीं। इसलिए ये वाक्य अशुद्ध हैं—

1. **But that, however,** is not hard.
2. **But one thing,** however, has not changed.

Rule XII. Conjunction of Condition

कुछ Conjunctions से कार्य होने की शर्त (condition) का बोध होता है। ये हैं—

if, unless, in case, provided, provided that, supposing that.

इन वाक्यों को लें—

1. **If you work hard, you will pass.**
2. **Unless you work hard, you won't pass.**
3. **You will pass provided you work hard.**
4. **Take an umbrella in case it rains.**

जब ऐसे वाक्यों के **Principal clause** में **Future Tense** आता है, तब शर्त बतानेवाले **clause** में **Present Simple Tense** आता है, **Future Tense** नहीं।

इसलिए ऐसे-ऐसे वाक्य न बनाएँ—

1. **You will pass if you will work hard.**
2. **Unless I will win a lottery, I won't buy a car.**
3. **Take an umbrella in case it will rain.**

Rule XII (A). Until and Unless

Until का अर्थ होता है 'जब तक नहीं' और इससे समय (time) का बोध होता है। Unless का अर्थ होता है 'अगर नहीं' और इससे केवल एक शर्त (condition) का बोध होता है। इसलिए condition के अर्थ में until का और time के अर्थ में unless का प्रयोग नहीं होना चाहिए। इन वाक्यों को देखिए—

1. I will wait here *unless* you come back.
2. You cannot succeed *until* you work hard.

यहाँ पहले वाक्य में unless के बदले until का प्रयोग होना चाहिए और दूसरे में until के बदले unless का। कुछ लोग unless के बदले कभी-कभी without/except का प्रयोग कर बैठते हैं, जो अशुद्ध है।

Until और unless Negative हैं। इसलिए Negative sense का बोध कराने के लिए इनके साथ not का प्रयोग इस प्रकार न करें—

1. *Unless* you *do not* labour hard, you cannot pass.
2. I will wait here *until* you *do not* come back.

इन वाक्यों में *do not* का प्रयोग अनुचित है। यदि आप negative (not) का प्रयोग करना ही चाहें, तो unless के बदले if का प्रयोग करें—

If you do not work hard, you cannot succeed.

Rule XII (B). Condition/Supposition

कुछ वाक्यों से condition/supposition (शर्त) का बोध होता है। ऐसे वाक्य निम्नांकित तीन प्रकार के होते हैं—

(i) वर्तमान या भविष्य में शर्त पूरी होने की अधिक संभावना

(ii) वर्तमान या भविष्य में शर्त पूरी होने की बहुत कम संभावना

(iii) जो भूतकाल में पूरी न हो सकी

ऐसे वाक्यों के दो भाग होते हैं और इनकी बनावट होती है—

If + Subordinate clause [condition] + Principal clause.

शर्त की दृष्टि से ऐसे वाक्य तीन प्रकार के होते हैं—

Structure I

If + SC [Present Simple] + PC [Future Simple]

इन वाक्यों को देखें—

1. If you work hard, you will pass.
2. If he starts early, he will catch the bus.
3. If she goes by air, she will reach soon.

ऐसे वाक्यों से यह बोध होता है कि वर्तमान/भविष्य में शर्त पूरी होने की आशा या संभावना बहुत अधिक है।

यह भी देखें कि ऐसे if + clause में Future Tense का प्रयोग इस प्रकार नहीं हो सकता—

1. If you will work hard, you will pass.
2. If he will start early, he will catch the bus.

Structure II

If + SC [Past Simple] + PC [Past Simple]

इन वाक्यों को लें—

1. If a tiger came here, all would run away.
2. If he won a lottery, he would buy a big car.
3. If I had wings, I would fly to you.

ऐसे वाक्यों से यह बोध होता है कि वर्तमान/भविष्य में शर्त पूरी होने की संभावना बहुत कम है या बिलकुल ही नहीं है।

इस प्रकार के वाक्यों के Past Tense से Present/Future Time का बोध होता है, Past Time का नहीं।

Structure III

If + SC [Past Perfect] + PC [Past Perfect]

इन वाक्यों को देखें—

1. If he had worked hard he would have passed.
2. If she had won a lottery she would have bought a car.
3. If I had been a Prime Minister I would have abolished examinations.

ऐसे वाक्यों से यह बोध होता है कि भूतकाल में शर्त पूरी न हो सकी और इसलिए कार्य न हो सका। इस प्रकार, भूतकालिक संभावना संभावना ही रह गई। यही कारण है कि हिन्दी में इसे हेतुहेतुमद्भूतकाल कहा जाता है।

जब इस प्रकार के वाक्यों में If का प्रयोग नहीं होता है, तब वाक्य Had से आरंभ होता है और वैसे Had का अर्थ होता है—यदि/अगर; जैसे—

If he had worked hard he would have passed.

= Had he worked hard he would have passed.

. . . .

EXERCISE

Correct the following sentences.

1. If you will play well you will win the match. 2. If he will wake up early he will catch the train. 3. If she will travel by bus she will reach later. 4. If a ghost will appear all would flee away. 5. If the police reached in time robbers have been caught. 6. Everything will be ruined if a world war broke out.

. . . .

Rule XIII. Conjunctions of Cause

कुछ Conjunctions ऐसे होते हैं जिनसे कारण (cause) का बोध होता है। ये हैं—as, because, since, that, considering that, seeing that, now that, in that, in as much as, noun + that, adjective + that.

इन वाक्यों को देखें—

1. As he started late, he missed the train.
2. He missed the train, because he started late.
3. Since he is poor, he can't buy a new dress.
4. Seeing that it is getting late, I had better start at once.
5. Now that the criminal has been caught, he should be punished.
6. I am not a fool that you expect me to believe you.
7. I am sorry that he has failed.
8. I am glad that he has come.

NOTE (a)—The reason is/The reason why

यदि वाक्य में the reason is या the reason why आए, तो इसके बाद आनेवाला Clause *that* से आरंभ होता है, because या due to से नहीं; जैसे—

1. The reason is *that* he is ill.
2. The reason why he is absent is *that* he is ill.

इन वाक्यों में that के बदले because/due to का प्रयोग अनुचित होता, क्योंकि नियम है—

After such openings as **The reason is, The reason why,** *the clause containing the reason must not begin with 'because' but with 'that'.*

—FOWLER: *Modern English Usage*

Grammar insists on 'that' following 'reason', never 'because'.

—C WHITAKER-WILSON

इस छोटे से नियम का उल्लंघन इस वाक्य में देखिए—

The reason why Denmark has been able to build up its trade and industries is **due to** *the advantages of transport ... .* —*The Eastern Economist*: Feb. 8, '57

यह वाक्य काफी भद्दा है। फिर भी, इसे इस प्रकार सुधारा जा सकता है—

The reason why ... is *that* it has the advantages of transport ... .

NOTE (b)—As-Clause and its Position

यदि वाक्य में कोई Clause 'as' से शुरू हो, जिसमें कोई कारण (cause) बताया जाए, तो वैसे as-Clause को वाक्य के आरंभ में रखना चाहिए, और उसके बाद Principal Clause को; जैसे—

As I am ill, I request you to grant me leave.

यहाँ as-clause कारण बताता है। इसलिए इसको वाक्य में पहले रखा गया है और इसके बाद Principal Clause (I request ... leave) को। यदि यहाँ Principal Clause को पहले रखा जाता

और उसके बाद as-clause को, तो शैली की दृष्टि से वह अच्छा नहीं समझा जाता। इस संबंध में कहा गया है—

To casual or explanatory **As-clauses** *if they are placed before the main sentence (As he only laughed at all my arguments, I gave it up) there is no objection. The reverse order (I gave it up, as he only laughed at all my arguments) is intolerable to anyone with a literary ear. All good writers instinctively avoid it, but being common in talk it is much used in print also by those who have not yet learnt that composition is an art and that sentences require arrangement.* —FOWLER: *Modern English Usage*

NOTE (c)—For एक Coordinating Conjunction है और इससे कारण (cause) का बोध होता है। पर उस cause के साथ-साथ inference (अनुमान) और explanation (कार्य की व्याख्या) का भी भाव व्यक्त होता है। इसलिए for का प्रयोग because के बदले नहीं होता—

1. He will fail, for all bad boys have to.
2. He fought well, for he was very brave.

EXERCISE

Complete the following sentences.

1. I am delighted that …… .
2. He can't buy an elephant …… .
3. As he reached late …… .
4. He will not succeed …… .
5. Now that …… .
6. Seeing that …… .

Rule XIV. Conjunctions of Time

कुछ ऐसे Conjunctions होते हैं जिनसे समय (time) का बोध होता है। ये हैं—

when, while, as, as soon as, before, after, till, until, since

इन वाक्यों को लें—

1. I will go when he comes back.
2. Make hay while the sun shines.
3. He will be remembered while the world lasts.
4. He reached as the clock struck one.
5. I will go before he comes back.
6. I will go after he comes back.
7. Five years have passed since he left this place.

NOTE (a)—Temporal Conjunctons and Tense

Principal Clause में Future Tense रहने पर भी while/when/till/until/as soon as/before/after आदि समयसूचक conjunctions से आरंभ होनेवाले clauses में Present Simple या Present Perfect Tense का प्रयोग होता है, Future Tense का नहीं। यह भी देखें कि after के बाद साधारणतः Present Perfect आता है, Present Simple नहीं; जैसे—

1. I will go out when the rain stops.
2. You should not get off the bus till it stops.
3. I will see you before I leave for home.
4. I will stay until you finish (have finished) writing.
5. I will return the book as soon as you need it.
6. I will buy a book after he has come back.

NOTE (b)—When and While

When का अर्थ होता है 'जब' और while का 'जब तक'। इसलिए when का प्रयोग तब होता है जब एक कार्य समाप्त होता है और दूसरा आरंभ होता है, पर जब दो कार्य एक साथ जारी रहते हैं, तो while का प्रयोग होता है; जैसे—

1. He saw a snake when he awoke.
2. While there is life there is hope.
3. While I write, he sits by me.

NOTE (c)—Since: cause

Since: cause

Conjunction की भाँति प्रयुक्त होने पर Since से कारण (cause) का बोध होता है और इसका प्रयोग 'क्योंकि' (because) के अर्थ में होता है; जैसे—

Since he is ill, he is absent.

Since: time

Since से समय (time) का भी बोध होता है और इसका अर्थ होता है 'जब से' (from the time when) या 'उस समय से'। ऐसे वाक्यों में since के प्रयोग से संबंधित इन नियमों का ध्यान रखें—

(i) Principal Clause में Present Perfect Tense का प्रयोग होता है।

(ii) Principal Clause में एक ऐसे समयसूचक शब्द का प्रयोग होता है जिससे Period of Time (कितने समय से) का बोध होता है।

(iii) Since + clause में Past Simple Tense का प्रयोग होता है; जैसे—

1. Seven years *have passed* since I *came here.*
2. Ten years *have passed* since *my father died.*

अब इन वाक्यों को देखें—

1. Seven years *passed* since I came here.
2. Ten years have passed since my mother *had died.*

यहाँ पहले वाक्य में Principal Clause में Period of Time का प्रयोग तो हुआ है, पर Present Perfect के बदले Past Simple का। अतः, यह अशुद्ध है। दूसरे वाक्य में Principal Clause में Period of Time क प्रयोग हुआ है और Present Perfect का भी, पर Since-Clause में Past Simple के बदले Past Perfect का, जो अशुद्ध है।

कुछ और वाक्य लें—

1. Twelve hours have passed since the patient *had fallen* asleep.

2. Either years have passed since I *had gone* there.

3. A year *passed* since his brother came.

यहाँ पहले दोनों वाक्यों में since के पहले Period of Time का प्रयोग हुआ है और Present Perfect का भी, पर since के बाद Past Simple के बदले Past Perfect का प्रयोग कर दिया गया है, जो गलत है। यहाँ had fallen के बदले fell और had gone के बदले went का प्रयोग होना चाहिए। तीसरे वाक्य में since के पहले Present Perfect के बदले Past Simple का प्रयोग कर दिया गया है। यहाँ Passed के बदले has passed होना चाहिए।

NOTE—ऐसे Principal Clauses में It is का भी प्रयोग होता है और वाक्य की बनावट होती है—

It is + period of time + since + clause [Past Simple]

1. It *is* a month since his father died. 2. It *is* a week since the holidays began.

3. It *is* ten years since she was married.

इन वाक्यों में is के बदले *was/has been* का प्रयोग अशुद्ध होता।

अब, इन वाक्यों को लें—

1. It is a year since I *have seen* him. 2. It is a week since he *has left* India.

इन वाक्यों में have seen के बदले saw और has left के बदले left का प्रयोग होना चाहिए।

EXERCISE

Fill in the blanks with a word given in brackets.

1. I will buy a new suit before I ...... for Chennai. [leave, will leave]
2. You will be surprised when you ...... the sight. [see, will see]
3. I will close the doors as soon as he ...... back. [will come, comes]
4. She will buy a house after her husband .... [has returned, will return]
5. Three years ...... since he joined this post. [passed, have passed]
6. It ...... a year since they were married. [is, was]

Rule XV. Or/Or else

कभी-कभी or का अर्थ होता है 'नहीं तो' (if not) और इसके द्वारा वाक्यों को जोड़ा जाता है। कुछ वाक्यों में or पर जोर देने के लिए or else का प्रयोग होता है, केवल else का नहीं; जैसे—

1. Come soon or you won't get any help.
2. Come soon, or else you won't get any help.
3. Put your coat on, or else you will catch cold.

ऐसे वाक्यों में केवल or या or else का प्रयोग हो सकता है, केवल else का नहीं। इसलिए केवल or का प्रयोग करें या or else का।

EXERCISE

Join the following sentences with 'or else'.

1. Hurry up. You will miss the train.
2. You must go home. If you don't, mother will get angry.

Rule XVI. As if/As though

इन दोनों का अर्थ होता है 'मानो' और इनसे शर्त या कल्पना का बोध होता है। इनके प्रयोग के संबंध में यह सदा याद रखें कि इनके बाद सदा Past Conditional Tense का प्रयोग होता है, Present या Future का नहीं—

> *These should invariably be followed by a past conditional, and not by a present form ('would', not 'will', 'could' not 'can', 'did' not 'does', 'was' or 'were' not 'is', 'had gone' not 'has', 'knew' not 'knows'.)* —FOWLER

इन वाक्यों को देखें—

1. He memorises *as if he were* a parrot.
2. It seems *as though he were* immortal.

इन वाक्यों में as if तथा as though का प्रयोग शुद्ध है।

कुछ और वाक्य लें—

3. *You have been promised a textbook, and I perhaps ramble on* **as if** *we* **had been** *taken outdoor to study botany.* —EZRA POUND
4. *Do you know I feel* **as though** *I* **were** *split in two?* —DOSTOEVSKY
5. *I do not want to give the impression that I regard his earlier and his later work almost* **as if** *they* **had been** *written by two different men.* —T S ELIOT
6. *Act* **as if** *you* **were** *already happy, and that will tend to make you happy.* —DALE CARNEGIE

इन सभी वाक्यों में as if और as though के बाद Past Conditional Tense का प्रयोग बड़ी ही सतर्कता से हुआ है। आप भी ऐसा ही करें।

NOTE—As if/As though के साथ Present या Future Tense का भी प्रयोग हो सकता है यदि कल्पना की मात्रा बहुत कम हो। पर, यदि कल्पना की मात्रा बहुत अधिक हो तो केवल Past Tense का प्रयोग होता है।

इस संबंध में इस मत पर विचार करें—

There is surely a distinction between '*He walks as if he were drunk*' (implying '*but he is not*') and '*He walks as if he is drunk*', meaning '*He is drunk*', judging from the way he walks. Similarly, we have '*It looks as if it is going to rain*' (= It is going to rain, by the look of it). *It looks as though we shall have to do the work ourselves. For these the indicative seems justifiable.* —F T WOOD

सामान्यतया as if/as though के साथ Past Tense का ही प्रयोग अधिक प्रचलित है।

EXERCISE

Correct or justify the following sentences.

(1) He behaves as if he is my master. (2) He pretends to read a book as if he does not know anything about the matter. (3) It appears as if a fresh calamity will come. (4) It appears as if he is a king. (5) He moves as if he is a snail.

REVISION TEST I

Correct the following sentences.

1. Several things have happened since I have joined this college.
2. He fled for life lest he might be arrested.
3. I shall not go except you permit me.
4. He boasts like his father does.
5. Directly the meeting commenced, a censure motion was moved.
6. Such dresses are seldom or ever used here.
7. He gave no more than he could help.
8. Scarcely had he slept than a thief broke into the house.
9. No sooner had he left but it started raining.
10. I do not know that how is he.
11. He is not only famous for his wealth but also for wisdom.
12. She sang when he played.
13. I am as rich or even richer than him.
14. Are you wiser than her?
15. He not only reads English but also science.
16. He is richer but not so popular.
17. It is very much like I expected.
18. I would neither help or harm.
19. I am not sure whether she likes me or no.
20. Do like he does.
21. No change took place since he has died.
22. Why do you not either read nor write?

23. Fools are both found in Asia and Europe.
24. Did he only die yesterday?
25. Does he not look as if he is a ghost?
26. I cannot read nor write.
27. I have received no help, neither from her nor from him.

Hints—1. I joined; 2. he should be; 3. unless you; 4. like his father or as his father does; 5. as soon as the meeting; 6. seldom or never; 7. than he could not help; 8. when a thief; 9. than it; 10. do not know he is (not, as to how); 11. famous not only for his wealth; 12. while he; 13. as rich as or even richer than he; 14. than she; 15. reads not only English; 16. richer than … as I; 17. as I expected; 18. not harm; 19. or not; 20. like him or as he does; 21. has taken place since he died; 22. or write; 23. are found in both Asia and Europe or are found both in Asia and in Europe; 24. only yesterday; 25. he were; 26. or write; 27. either from her or from him

REVISION TEST II

Explain why the following sentences are correct or incorrect.

1. Until you remain idle, you will not pass.
2. No sooner he had died, but his sons quarrelled.
3. It has been now a year since he had left.
4. The crops will die before the rains will fall.
5. Scarcely he had returned before his wife was taken ill.
6. Not only he was injured but ruined.
7. He rose early, lest he might not be late.
8. It was a week since the holidays had begun.
9. I am not a liar like you are.
10. Sports are not only good for the body but also for the mind.
11. He behaves as if he is a child.
12. Let me know that whether you will return or not.
13. Tell me that how much the book cost you.
14. Both the teacher as well as the student was there.
15. Unless you are not careful you will fall into trouble.
16. Seven years passed since I have come here.
17. She told me that I will help you.
18. I will keep quiet until I will know all the facts.

REVISION TEST III

Fill in the blanks with a conjunction from the box.

though	but	that	until	because	since
who	as soon as	whether	when	than	or unless

1. December is cold …… June is hot.
2. …… he is poor, he is honest.
3. I am glad …… he has passed.
4. I do not know the man …… is here.
5. I could not go to college …… it was raining.
6. No change has taken place …… I came over here.
7. I will wait here …… you come back.
8. Thieves fled for life …… the polic arrived.
9. I do not know …… he will come next week.
10. Hardly had he left …… his mother arrived.
11. No sooner did the thief see the police …… he fled away.
12. I have no pen …… pencil.
13. I doubt …… he will come.
14. I will not go …… he invites me.
15. I will tell you everything …… you will come back.

❐

Chapter VI

TEST YOURSELF

I. *Correct or justify the following sentences.*

1. He is a father of mine.
2. Our five-years plans are defective.
3. The gentries of the two have been invited.
4. She gave me a lot of informations.
5. New furnitures and machineries have been bought.
6. In his poetries Wordsworth has described lovely sceneries.
7. His mathematics are weak.
8. I am an examiner of the Patna and Bihar University.
9. The price of the book is three and a half rupees.
10. This book's rules are easy.
11. I have read Keats and Shelley's poems.
12. She is a fine sportswoman.
13. The news have spread quickly.
14. The clergies and the nobilities have no respect today.
15. She is my cousin sister.
16. We can't live without airs.
17. How many issues have you?
18. This table is made of woods.
19. He bought three pairs of shoes.
20. Most of the MA's are unemployed.
21. The poors and the sicks deserve help.
22. This is a five-rupees note.
23. The peasantry is still very poor.
24. This house is made of bricks.
25. She had her hairs cut.
26. The barber's is too full of customers today.
27. The datas are correct.
28. He is a man of words.

II. *Fill in the blanks with a noun/pronoun given in brackets.*

1. All the ...... have been checked. [data, datas]
2. What are the ......of selection? [criteria, criterions]

3. He has drawn up an …… for the meeting. [agendum, agenda]
4. I saw lovely …… in Kashmir. [scenes, sceneries]
5. He gave me several pieces of …… . [information, informatons]
6. He is my …… . [cousin, cousin brother]
7. Everyone should do …… duties. [her, his, their]
8. She is a …… . [statesman, stateswoman]
9. She is a …… doctor. [lady, woman]
10. She is a …… . [chairman, chairwoman]
11. Indians have black …… . [hair, hairs]

NOUNS

हिंदी-उर्दू में संज्ञा के प्रयोग, लिंग-विचार की दृष्टि से, अँगरेजी की अपेक्षा कुछ अधिक कठिन हैं, पर हिंदी-उर्दू में वचन के नियम अत्यंत ही सरल हैं। इसके विपरीत, अँगरेजी में **nouns** के प्रयोग, लिंग-विचार की दृष्टि से, अत्यंत सरल हैं, पर अँगरेजी में वचन के नियम कुछ टेढ़े-मेढ़े हैं। इन बातों का ध्यान रखकर हम यहाँ nouns के प्रयोग पर विचार करें।

Rule I. Numeral Adjective + Hyphen + noun

यदि Definite Numeral Adjective और Noun को Hyphen (-) से जोड़कर Compound Word बनाया जाए, तो वह Noun सदा singular रहता है; जैसे—

1. I have two *five-rupee* notes. 2. You have a *ten-rupee* note.

यहाँ पहले वाक्य में Definite Numeral Adjective और Noun ('five' तथा 'rupee') को hyphen से जोड़कर एक शब्द (five-rupee) बनाया गया है। इसलिए Plural Adjective (five) के रहने पर भी Singular Noun (rupee) का प्रयोग हुआ है, Plural (rupees) का नहीं। इसी प्रकार, दूसरे वाक्य में ten और rupee को मिलाकर एक शब्द बनाया गया है 'ten-rupee'। यहाँ ten-rupees का प्रयोग नहीं हो सकता। याद रखें कि ऐसे वाक्यों में hyphen के बाद आनेवाला Noun singular रहता है; जैसे—

1. You have twenty *rupees*. 2. I have two *ten-rupee* notes.
3. It is three *feet* in length. 4. It is a *three-foot* rule.
5. It is fifty *feet* in width. 6. It is a *fifty-foot* tape.
7. This is a *three-man* team. 8. This is a *five-year* plan.

अब इस वाक्य को देखें—

... and the only money I ever hoarded was money that I had no time to spend within the narrow compass of a **twenty – four hours** *day.* —ROBERT LYND

यहाँ hours के बदले hour का प्रयोग होना चाहिए। यह छपाई की भूल है या असावधानी? कारण जो भी हो, यहाँ hours के बदले hour का प्रयोग आवश्यक है।

. . . .

EXERCISE

Correct the following sentences.

(1) He is a fifty-years old man. (2) It is a five-pounds weight. (3) It is a seven-men committee. (4) There was a three-hours sitting. (5) The five-men subcommittee had a two hours conference this morning. (5) The Five-Years Plan is good. (6) India cannot accept the two-nations theory. (7) An all-parties conference was held to consider the food problem. (8) There is two-ways traffic here.

Hints—(1) fifty-year; (2) five-pound; (3) seven-man; (4) three hour; (5) five-man … two-hour …; (6) two-nation; (7) all party; (8) all-party; (9) two-way

. . . .

Rule II. Nouns Singular in form but Plural in use

कुछ Nouns ऐसे होते हैं जिनका प्रयोग plural के अर्थ में होता है, यद्यपि देखने में वे singular मालूम पड़ते हैं। इसलिए '*s*' या '*ies*' लगाकर उन्हें plural नहीं बनाया जा सकता। वे Nouns हैं—

admiralty, cavalry, clergy, cattle, gentry, infantry, nobility, poultry, peasantry, yeomanry, children; जैसे—

1. The *clergy have* always stood in the way of progress.
2. The *nobility have* oppressed the *peasantry* in several ways.

अब इन वाक्यों को देखें—

1. The gentries have come.
2. The infantries are ready.

यहाँ gentries के बदले gentry और infantries के बदले infantry का प्रयोग होना चाहिए।

NOTE (a)—Swine, vermin, mankind, police तथा public दोनों ही वचनों में प्रयुक्त होते हैं, यद्यपि इनका रूप दोनों ही वचनों में समान रहता है। इनमें 's' लगाकर इन्हें plural नहीं बनाया जाता। इसलिए plural अर्थ में भी police का polices और public का publics नहीं होता।

NOTE (b)—इनके प्रयोग के संबंध में कुछ लोगों के मन में एक भ्रम है कि ये सदा plural अर्थ में ही प्रयुक्त होते हैं, singular में नहीं; पर यह ठीक नहीं है। आप इन वाक्यों को देखें जिनके लेखक महान विद्वान हैं—

1. *These swine* **are** *a nuisance. He* **is** *a dirty swine.* —FOWLER
2. *The British public* **was** elated rather than dismayed. —H G WELLS
3. *Mankind* **is** *collectively engaged under the guidance of fools and with the ingenuity of slaves in exterminating itself.* —BERTRAND RUSSELL
4. … *at present mankind* **is** *demented.* —H G WELLS
5. *These vermin* **are** *an incessant torment. Such a vermin as you.* —FOWLER

इन उदाहरणों से यह स्पष्ट है कि इनका प्रयोग दोनों ही वचनों में होता है।

NOTE (c)—People का प्रयोग 'आदमी' के अर्थ में सदा plural number में होता है, पर 'राष्ट्र' के अर्थ में singular, क्योंकि ऐसी हालत में इसके पहले a का प्रयोग होता है; जैसे—a people. 'राष्ट्र' के अर्थ में people का plural हो जाता है peoples, पर 'आदमी' के अर्थ में people को peoples करना भूल है।

EXERCISE

Correct the following sentences.

(1) The peoples of India are marching ahead. (2) The people of Russia is hard-working. (3) The gentry of the town has assembled here. (4) Our peasantry is very poor. (5) These cattles are mine. (6) The infantries were ordered to march on. (7) Childrens are playing.

Hints—(1) people; (2) are; (3) have; (4) are; (5) cattle; (6) infantry; (7) children.

Rule III. Nouns Plural in form but Singular in use

कुछ Nouns ऐसे होते हैं जिनके अंत में 's' रहता है, और इसलिए ये plural मालूम पड़ते हैं, पर वास्तव में ये हैं singular; जैसे—news, gallows, summons.

1. This news *is* bad.
2. A summons *has* been issued.

अतः ये वाक्य अशुद्ध हैं—

1. The news *have* spread quickly.
2. Summons *have* not yet been served on him.

NOTE—कुछ लोग news का प्रयोग दोनों ही वचनों में कर बैठते हैं, जो आधुनिक प्रयोग के विपरीत है—

> *The number varied (The news is bad,* **are** *bad) for more than two centuries, but has now settled down permanently as singular.* —FOWLER

Rule IV. Nouns always Plural

कुछ Nouns के अंत में s आता है और ये सदा plural रहते हैं। ये हैं—

aborigins, alms, amends, annals, archives, ashes, arrears, athletics, auspices, bellows, belongings, breeches, bowels, braces, binoculars, billiards, brains, customs, curds, congratulations, cards, drawers, dregs, eaves, earnings, entrails, embers, fetters, fireworks, funds, glasses, guts, greens, knickers, lodgings, lees, mumps, measles, nuptials, odds, outskirts, pantaloons, pants, pioneers, particulars, proceeds, proceedings, regards, riches, remains, seals, savings, shambles, shears, scissors, spectacles, stairs, surroundings, tidings, troops, trousers, tongs, tactics, thanks, victuals, vegetables, valuables, wages, works (कृतियाँ)

इन वाक्यों को लें—

1. His earnings are small.
2. All his valuables were stolen away.

ध्यान दें—

(i) ऐसे Nouns के अंत में *s* अवश्य आता है। इसलिए *s* को हटाकर इन्हें singular नहीं बनाया जाता।

(ii) ऐसे Nouns को singular बनाकर इनके पहले a/an का प्रयोग नहीं किया जाता।

इसलिए ये वाक्य अशुद्ध हैं—

1. I gave him an alm. 2. He is a man of gut.

NOTE (a)—Innings का प्रयोग दोनों ही वचनों में होता है—

The plural 'Inningses' is colloquial only, 'innings' (originally plural) being used for either number—an innings, or several innings. —FOWLER

इसलिए नेसफिल्ड (Nesfield) साहब का यह कहना कि "*It is always used as a singular*" ठीक नहीं जँचता।

NOTE (b)—Means के वचन पर प्रकाश डालते हुए नेसफिल्ड (Nesfield) साहब ने कहा है—

This is now almost always used as singular.

पर एक दूसरे आचार्य का मत है—

In the sense 'income', etc., 'means' always takes a Plural Verb—'My means were (never 'was') much reduced.' In the sense 'way to an end', etc., **means** *takes a Singular Verb;* **means** *can be treated as either Singular Verb or Plural Verb—all means (Plural), every means (Singular)* —FOWLER

मेरा विचार है कि आप फाउलर साहब के मतानुसार चलें। यदि means का अर्थ 'आमदनी' हो, तो उसे plural में प्रयोग करें, पर यदि means के पहले *a* या *every* का प्रयोग हो (***a means, every means***) तो उसे शुद्ध singular मानें। यदि ***means*** के पहले a या every का प्रयोग नहीं हो, तो उसका प्रयोग 'तरीका' के अर्थ में आप singular या plural जिसमें चाहें, कर सकते हैं—

The means **do not** *or* **does not** *justify the end. The end is good but the means* **are,** *or* **is** *bad.* —FOWLER

. . . .

EXERCISE

Correct the following sentences.

(1) My means is small. (2) The house was reduced to an ashes. (3) Thanks is due to him. (4) Where is your spectacles? (5) His bowel is loose today. (6) Riches has wings. (7) I like vegetable. (8) The thief is in fetter. (9) Shear has been purchased for my garden. (10) He is suffering from measle.

Hints—(1) are; (2) to ashes; (3) are; (4) are; (5) bowels are; (6) have; (7) vegetables; (8) fetters; (9) Shears have been; (10) measles.

. . . .

Rule V. Nouns always Singular

कुछ Nouns सदा singular रहते हैं। ये हैं—

poetry, scenery, machinery, drapery, stationery, jewellery, sultery, crockery, luggage, baggage, knowledge, postage, breakage, haltage, wastage, percentage, foolish, polish, rubbish, dirt, dust, information, furniture, traffic, clothing, money, music, coffee

इन वाक्यों को देखें—

1. Tagore's poetry is immortal. 2. I saw lovely scenery in Nepal.
3. I am fond of music. 4. He bought new machinery.

ध्यान दें—

(i) ऐसे Nouns का plural नहीं होता।

(ii) ऐसे Nouns के पहले a/an का प्रयोग नहीं होता।

(iii) ऐसे निश्चित Nouns के पहले the का प्रयोग होता है। जब ये किसी Preposition/ Adjective clause के पहले आते हैं; जैसे—

1. The poetry of Tagore is immortal.

2. The poetry Tagore wrote is immortal.

इसलिए ये वाक्य अशुद्ध हैं—

1. Tagore's poetries are great.
2. I saw lovely sceneries in Nepal.
3. I am fond of a music.
4. He bought new machineries.
5. He gave me several informations.
6. These crokeries are costly.
7. He has several furnitures.
8. There were heavy traffics on the road.

ध्यान दें—

(i) Singular अर्थ में ऐसे Nouns/के पहले an item of/an article of/a piece of का प्रयोग होता है।

(ii) Plural अर्थ में ऐसे Nouns के पहले items of/articles of/kinds of/pieces of का प्रयोग होता है।

(iii) 'बहुत', अर्थात मात्रा के अर्थ में, ऐसे Nouns के पहले much/some/little/most/a lot of आदि Adjective of Quantity का प्रयोग होता है। ऐसे Nouns के साथ Adjective of Number (few, many/several) का प्रयोग उचित नहीं है।

इन वाक्यों को लें—

1. This is a piece of poetry. 2. He gave me a piece of information.
3. He has several articles of furniture. 4. He gave me a lot of information.

NOTE (a)—Number of *hair/work/word*

जब hair का प्रयोग सामान्य अर्थ में होता है, तब इसका plural नहीं होता। पर जब इसका प्रयोग, विशेष अर्थ में, Countable Noun की तरह होता है, तब इसका plural होता है—*hairs;* जैसे—

1. Her hair is dark.
2. I had my hair cut.
3. There are only two grey hairs on his head now.

जब work का सामान्य प्रयोग होता है और इसका अर्थ होता है काम/कार्य, तब इसका plural नहीं होता। पर जब work का अर्थ होता है **कृति** (मानसिक या काल्पनिक उपज) तब इसका plural होता है—*works*; जैसे—

1. He is without work.
2. He is fond of hard work.
3. The works of Tulsi Das are immortal.

जब word का अर्थ होता है **संदेश** या **पक्की बात** (प्रतिज्ञा) तब इसका plural नहीं होता। पर जब word का अर्थ होता है शब्द, तब इसका plural होता है—*words*; जैसे—

1. He sent me word.
2. He is a man of word.
3. Use these words in sentences.

NOTE (b)—Number of *brick/stone/wood/glass*

जब इनसे वस्तु/पदार्थ का बोध होता है, तब इनका plural नहीं होता; जैसे—

1. This house is made of brick/wood.
2. That house is made of stone/glass.

NOTE (c)—Number of the names of birds/animals

जब शिकार (hunting) के संबंध में किसी पशु-पक्षी का नाम आए, तो इसका प्रयोग सदा singular में होता है, पर इसके पहले a/an/the नहीं आता; जैसे—

1. I went to hunt elephant.
2. He wanted to shoot wild duck.

Rule VI. Nouns with one meaning in singular but another in plural

इन्हें देखें—

Singular	Plural
1. abuse [दुरुपयोग]	abuses [कुरीतियाँ]
2. advice [राय/परामर्श]	advices [सूचनाएँ]
3. air [हवा]	airs [दिखावटी आचरण]
4. alphabet [वर्णमाला]	alphabets [भाषाएँ]
5. compass [सीमा]	compasses [एक यंत्र]
6. good [लाभ]	goods [माल, सामान]
7. force [शक्ति]	forces [सेना]
8. iron [लोहा]	irons [कड़ी, जंजीर]
9. return [वापसी]	returns [हिसाब-किताब]
10. sand [बालू]	sands [रेगिस्तान]
11. water [पानी]	waters [समुद्र]
12. wood [लकड़ी]	woods [जंगल]

इसलिए अर्थ की दृष्टि से ये वाक्य अशुद्ध हैं—

1. We can't live without airs. 2. The table is made of woods.
3. This child is learning alphabets. 4. Man can't live without waters.

Rule VII. Nouns in the same form in both Numbers

कुछ Nouns का प्रयोग दोनों ही Numbers में होता है, पर इनका रूप (form) सदा एक-सा रहता है। ये हैं—

sheep, deer, swine, salmon, yoke, brace, gross, stone, hundredweight, police, public, means, innings, series, species, Japanese, Chinese, Burmese, Nepalese, etc.

इनमें 's' लगाकर इन्हें plural बनाने का प्रयत्न न करें। इन वाक्यों को देखें—

1. He has five *sheeps* and *seven deers.*
2. You have three *yokes* of oxen and four *braces* of bird.

इन वाक्यों में sheeps/deers/yokes/braces के बदले sheep/deer/yoke/brace का प्रयोग होना चाहिए।

NOTE—आजकल police का प्रयोग plural में ही अधिक प्रचलित है।

Rule VIII. Numeral Adjective and the Noun

कुछ Nouns ऐसे होते हैं जो Numeral Adjective (संख्यासूचक विशेषण) के बाद आने पर सदा singular रहते हैं, पर Indefinite Number (अनिश्चित संख्या) का बोध कराने पर plural भी बन सकते हैं; जैसे—

pair, dozen, stone, hundred, thousand, million, billion, score, gross

इन्हें देखें—

five dozen pens; six stone weight; three hundred rupees; four thousand rupees; two score; two pair of shoes

इन सभी Nouns के पहले Definite Numerals (निश्चित संख्यासूचक शब्द) आये हैं। इसलिए five dozens, six stones, three hundreds, four thousands इत्यादि तरह के प्रयोग अशुद्ध हैं। यदि इनसे अनिश्चित संख्या का बोध हो तो इनका plural अवश्य होता है; जैसे—

dozens of pens; hundreds of boys; in hundreds;
scores of men; thousands of books; in thousands;
several pairs of shoes; millions of men; in millions

. . . .

EXERCISE

Correct the following sentences.

(1) I have three dozens pins. (2) How many pair of shoes do you require? (3) There are two thousands boys in our college. (4) I have three hundreds books.

Hints—(1) dozen; (2) pairs; (3) two thousand; (4) three hundred.

. . . .

Rule IX. Nouns ending in 'ics'

कुछ Nouns ऐसे होते हैं जिनके अंत में 'ics' आता है; जैसे—

mathematics, politics, classics, economics, ethics

ऐसे शब्दों के Number के विषय में इस मत का ध्यान रखें—

This is not so simple a matter as it is sometimes thought … . The rules that seem to emerge are (i) Singular for the name of a science strictly so used; (ii) Plural for those names more loosely used, e.g., for a manifestation of qualitites, often recognizable by the presence of 'his', 'the', etc.—His matheatics **are** *weak. Such ethics* **are** *abominable. The Acoustics of the hall* **are** *faulty. (iii) The presence of a Singular noun complement often makes the verb singular—Mathematics, or even Athletics,* **is** *his strong point.* —FOWLER

फाउलर साहब का मत है कि इन शब्दों का (जिनके अंत में 'ics' रहता है) प्रयोग singular में होना चाहिए, यदि इनसे 'किसी विषय के नाम' का बोध होता हो; जैसे—

1. Physics *is* taught even in schools today.
2. Mathematics *requires* practice.

पर इनका प्रयोग plural में होना चाहिए, यदि इनसे 'गुणों' (quality or property) का बोध हो; जैसे—

1. His mathematics *are weak.*
2. Most men's politics *sit* much too loosely about them.

इन दोनों वाक्यों में mathematics/politics का प्रयोग plural में हुआ है, क्योंकि इनसे किसी विषय का बोध नहीं होता, बल्कि mathematical qualities/political qualities का बोध होता है। अब इन वाक्यों को देखें—

1. Mathematics *is* his favourite subject. 2. Politics *is* an interesting subject.

इन वाक्यों में mathematics और politics से किसी विषय का बोध होता है; इसलिए इनका प्रयोग singular में हुआ है। अब एक वाक्य देखें जिसमें politics का प्रयोग (political qualities के अर्थ में) plural में हुआ है, जो शुद्ध है—

Politics **are** the outcome rather than the cause of social change.

—G M TREVELYAN

Rule X. Plural of letters, figures and abbreviations

1. Nouns और Pronouns के अतिरिक्त अन्य शब्दों का plural साधारणतः नहीं होता। फिर भी, विशेष अर्थ में हम उनका plural 's लगाकर बना सकते हैं; जैसे—

if—if's; but—but's; shall—shall's; will—will's.

I do not like your if's and but's.

2. किसी Letter (अक्षर) का plural's लगाकर बनाया जाता है; जैसे—

p—p's; I—I's. This word is full of p's and I's.

3. संख्या का plural's लगाकर बनाया जाता है, यदि उसे अंक (figure) में लिखा जाए, शब्दों में नहीं; जैसे—

5—5's; 10—10's; 3—3's Your 5's are like 3's.

4. कुछ abbreviations (संक्षिप्त शब्द) का plural उनके पहले letter को दुहराने से बनता है; जैसे—

p—pp [pages]; l—ll (lines)

यहाँ p का अर्थ है page और pp का अर्थ है pages. इसी प्रकार, l से line का बोध होता है और ll से lines का।

5. कुछ abbreviations (संक्षिप्त शब्द) का plural *s* लगाने से बनता है, जब उनसे किसी व्यक्ति का बोध होता है; जैसे—

MP—MPs; MA—MAs; BA—BAs.

1. Most of our MPs are not honest.
2. Most of the BAs are unemployed.

यहाँ MP का अर्थ है Member of Parliament, और BA का Bachelor of Arts. इन शब्दों से किसी व्यक्ति का बोध होता है।

NOTE—यदि ऐसे शब्दों से degree (उपाधि) का बोध होता हो, तो उनका plural *'s* लगाकर बनाया जाता है; जैसे—

BA—BA's (degree); MA—MA's (degree).

6. Proper Nouns का plural तो साधारणतः नहीं होता पर विशेष अर्थ में यदि उनका plural बनाना हो तो *s* लगाकर plural बनाया जा सकता है; जैसे—

Mary—Marys (not *Maries*); Henry—Henrys (not *Henries*).

1. There are several Marys and Henrys in this town.
2. These Miltons and Shelleys write rubbish.

Rule XI. Latin Nouns ending in 'um'

Rule XI (A). *um = a.* Latin के कुछ एकवचन शब्द ऐसे होते हैं जिनके अंत में *um* आता है। उनका बहुवचन '*um*' के बदले 'a' का प्रयोग करके बनाया जाता है, उनमें 's' लगाकर नहीं; जैसे—

agendum—agenda; addendum—addenda; datum—data; dictum—dicta; ovum—ova; erratum—errata; memorandum—memoranda; medium—media; stratum—strata.

NOTE (a)—आधुनिक अँगरेजी में agenda और data का प्रयोग singular और plural दोनों ही में होता है। Agendum और datum का प्रयोग अब होता ही नहीं। अब इन वाक्यों को लें—

1. The *agenda has* been drawn up.
2. The *agenda* were drawn up.
3. The data *is* insufficient.
4. What are the data?

आजकल memorandum के दो बहुवचन रूप होते हैं—memoranda, memorandums.

आजकल लोग इस प्रकार नहीं लिखते—The agendum has been drawn up. कुछ लोग agendas और datas का भी प्रयोग कर बैठते हैं, जो भद्दी भूल है।

NOTE (b)—Medium का अर्थ जब means या agency होता है तब इसका plural 'media' होता है, पर आध्यात्मिक अर्थ (spiritualistic sense) में mediums होता है, media नहीं—

In the spiritualistic sense, the plural is always 'mediums'. —FOWLER

Rule XI (B). *um = um + s*—Latin के कुछ ऐसे शब्द हैं जिनके अंत में 'um' आता है। इनका बहुवचन 'um' में 's' लगाकर बनाया जाता है, 'um' के बदले 'a' का प्रयोग करके नहीं; जैसे—

asylum—asylums; decorum—decorums; forum—forums;

harmonium—harmoniums; museum—museums; nostrum—nostrums;

pendulum—pendulums; petroleum—petroleums; pomatum—pomatums;

premium—premiums; quorum—quorums.

NOTE—Premiums के बदले premia का प्रयोग उचित नहीं है। हाँ, formula के दो बहुवचन रूप होते हैं—formulas और formulae, पर साधारणतः formulas का प्रयोग होता है और विज्ञान के क्षेत्र में formulae का।

....

EXERCISE

Correct the following sentences.

(1) Collect all the datas carefully in support of your dictas. (2) Can you test these stratas of the earth? (3) The pendula of these clocks are not in order. (4) What datas have been prepared? (5) Do you know the agendums of the meeting?

Hints—(1) data ...... dicta; (2) strata; (3) pendulums; (4) data; (5) agenda

....

Rule XII. Latin Nouns ending in 'us'

कुछ ऐसे Latin शब्द हैं जिनके अंत में 'us' रहता है। इनका बहुवचन 'us' को 'i' में बदल देने से बनता है; जैसे—

alumnus—alumni; locus—loci; fungus—fungi; genius—genii

radius—radii; terminus—termini; syllabus—syllabi.

NOTE—Genius का बहुवचन 'प्रतिभाशाली व्यक्ति' के अर्थ में geniuses होता है, genii नहीं। Syllabus का बहुवचन Syllabuses भी होता है और वास्तव में यह syllabi की अपेक्षा अधिक लोकप्रिय है।

Rule XIII. Greek Nouns ending in 'is' or 'on'

Rule XIII (A). Greek के कुछ शब्द ऐसे हैं जिनके अंत में 'is' रहता है। इनका बहुवचन 'is' को 'es' में बदल देने से बनता है; जैसे—

analysis—analyses; basis—bases; crisis—crises;

hypothesis—hypotheses; oasis—oases; parenthesis—parentheses;

thesis—theses.

Rule XIII (B). कुछ ऐसे भी Greek शब्द हैं जिनके अंत में 'on' रहता है। इनका बहुवचन 'on' को 'a' में बदलने से बनता है; जैसे—

criterion—criteria; phenomenon—phenomena.

....

EXERCISE

Correct the following sentences

(1) Our country is proud of great genii like Gandhi and Nehru. (2) Our country is facing many crisises. (3) Most of the thesises are worthless. (4) It is a wonderful phenomena. (5) What are the criterions of selection? (6) There are not many oasises in a desert. (7) Wonderful phenomenons have suddenly appeared.

Hints—(1) geniuses; (2) crises; (3) theses; (4) phenomenon; (5) criteria; (6) oases; (7) phenomena

....

Rule XIV. Noun + preposition + noun (repeated)

यदि किसी Noun को Preposition के बाद दुहराया जाए तो वह Noun (जो Preposition के पहले और बाद में आता है) Singular Number में रहता है; जैसे—

Noun + Preposition + Noun (repeated)

1. City *after* city was destroyed.
2. Row *upon* row of delicate green is soothing to the eyes.
3. Ship *after* ship is sailing by.
4. One hour *after* another (hour) is passing away.
5. He begged from door *to* door.

इन वाक्यों में after/upon to के पहले तथा बाद आनेवाले Nouns को singular number में रखा गया है, जो शुद्ध है। इसलिए ऐसा न लिखें—

1. Cities after cities were destroyed.
2. Rows upon rows of delicate green are soothing to the eyes.
3. Ships after ships are sailing by.
4. Hours after hours are passing.

Rule XV. Article, Adjective and Noun

यदि and से संयुक्त सभी Adjectives के बाद एक ही Noun का प्रयोग हो और केवल एक ही Adjective के पहले Article आए, तो वह Noun plural number में रहता है। पर यदि प्रत्येक Adjective के पहले Article का प्रयोग हो, तो वह Noun singular number में रहता है; जैसे—

1. I am an examiner of *the* Patna and Bihar *Universities.*
2. I am an examiner of *the* Patna and *the* Bihar *University.*

यहाँ Patna/Bihar का प्रयोग Adjective की भाँति हुआ है जो and से संयुक्त हैं। पहले वाक्य में एक ही Adjective (Patna) के पहले Article आया है। इसलिए यहाँ Plural Noun

(Universitis) का प्रयोग हुआ है। पर दूसरे वाक्य में इन दोनों Adjectives (Patna और Bihar) के पहले Article आया है। इसलिए यहाँ Noun (University) singular है। यदि पहले वाक्य में Singular Noun का प्रयोग हुआ होता और दूसरे में Plural का, तो वह अशुद्ध हो जाता। इसकी चर्चा Numeral Adjective के Rule II के प्रसंग में भी हुई है।

....

EXERCISE

Correct the following sentences.

(1) The Chancellor of the Patna and Bihar University came to our college. (2) The Chancellor of the Patna and the Bihar Universities came to our college. (3) I very much like the literature of the 16th and the 17th centuries.

Hints—(1) universities; (2) university; (3) century

....

Rule XVI. Numeral Adjective + Fraction and the Noun

यदि Numeral Adjective के बाद 'a half' या 'a quarter' आए, तो Noun को (Numeral Adjective के Number को ध्यान में रखकर) Numeral Adjective के बाद में रखें और उस Noun के बाद 'a half' या 'a quarter' को; जैसे—

1. I have *one* rupee *and a half.*
2. You have *two* rupees *and a half.*

इन वाक्यों में Numeral Adjectives क्रमशः one और two का प्रयोग हुआ है, जिनमें 'one' singular है और 'two' plural. इसलिए पहले वाक्य में one के बाद rupee आया है, और rupee के बाद a half; दूसरे वाक्य में Plural Noun 'rupees' को Numeral Adjective के बाद रखा गया है और rupees के बाद a half को। अब इन वाक्यों को देखें—

1. I have one and a half rupees.
2. You have two and a half rupees.

ये अशुद्ध हैं, क्योंकि यहाँ Noun को Adjective के बाद रखने के बदले 'a half' के बाद रख दिया गया है। कुछ और उदाहरण लें—

1. I gave him three and a quarter mangoes.
2. The meeting was held for two and a half hours.

इन वाक्यों में भी Noun को क्रमशः 'a quarter' तथा 'a half' के बाद रखा गया है जो शुद्ध नहीं। इन्हें Adjective के बाद इस प्रकार रखना चाहिए—

1. I gave him *three* mangoes *and a quarter.*
2. The meeting was held for *two* hours *and a half.*

याद रखें कि ऐसे वाक्यों की बनावट इस प्रकार की होती है—

Numeral Adjective + Noun + Fraction.

इसलिए इस नियम के अनुसार यह वाक्य अशुद्ध है—

... between 1801 and 1831 the inhabitants of England, Wales and Scotland rose from eleven to sixteen and a **half millions.** —G M TREVELYAN

यहाँ sixteen and a half millions के बदले sixteen million and *a half* होना चाहिए।

NOTE—यदि Numeral Adjective तथा Fraction (a half या a quarter) को and से जोड़कर इसका प्रयोग गुण करने (multiply) के अर्थ में हो, तो वह Noun plural number में 'a half' या 'a quarter' के बाद आता है, Numeral Adjective के बाद नहीं; जैसे—

1. *One and a half* times.
2. *Two and a half* times.

हम इस प्रकार नहीं लिख सकते—

1. One time and a half.
2. Two times and a half.

EXERCISE

Correct the following sentences.

(1) The length of this table is one and half feet. (2) This pen has cost me seven and a quarter rupees. (3) The Britishers ruled India for two and a half centuries. (4) It is three times and a half as large as that.

Hints—(1) one foot and a half; (2) seven rupees and a quarter; (3) two centuries and a half; (4) three and a half times as large as that.

Rule XVII. Adjectives Used as Plural Nouns

Rule XVII (A). यदि Adjective का प्रयोग Plural Noun की भाँति हो, तो उसके पहले the आता है। इसलिए 's' या 'es' लगाकर उसे plural बनाना भद्दी भूल है। इन वाक्यों को लें—

1. The *poor* and the *sick* were helped.
2. The *poors* and the *sicks* were helped.

यहाँ पहला वाक्य शुद्ध है, पर दूसरा अशुद्ध। क्यों? इसलिए कि दूसरे वाक्य में poor और sick जो Adjectives हैं उनका plural 's' लगाकर बना दिया गया है।

Rule XVII (B). कुछ Adjectives ऐसे हैं जिनके बाद 'things' छिपा रहता है और इसलिए इनका प्रयोग एक plural noun की तरह होता है। ये हैं—

bitters, sweets, essentials, particulars, valuables, moveables, necessaries, breakables, disagreeables, explosives, goods, dues, odds, bygones

इन वाक्यों को देखें—

1. One has to taste the sweets and bitters of life.
2. All his valuables (moveables) were sold away.
3. The essentials (necessaries) of life must be available to all.
4. All the dues have been paid.

EXERCISE

Correct the following sentences.

(1) The lames and the blinds deserve our sympathy. (2) Neither the poors nor the riches can escape death. (3) The sicks are not properly looked after in hospitals. (4) The particular was supplied. (5) The odd was overcome.

Hints—(1) The lame and the blind; (2) the poor ... the rich; (3) The sick; (4) particulars were; (5) odds were

Rule XVIII. Nouns and their Gender

जिस Noun को एक बार Masculine/Feminine/Neuter माना जाए, उसका वही gender आरंभ से अंत तक रहना चाहिए। उसको एक बार Masculine Gender में और उसके बाद Feminine Gender में और फिर तुरंत ही Neuter Gender में प्रयोग करना भयंकर भूल है। यदि आप spider को Masculine Gender मानते हैं, तो इसके लिए he/his/him का प्रयोग होना चाहिए, it/she/its/her का नहीं। देखिए, इस वाक्य में लेखक ने Noun के Gender के साथ कैसा खिलवाड़ किया है—

> *It is not only in regard to India that Denmark has been able to increase its foreign trade; with western countries, too, she has increased her foreign trade considerably.*
>
> —*The Eastern Economist*: Feb. 8, 1957

यहाँ Denmark को एक बार neuter माना गया है, इसलिए its का प्रयोग हुआ है। पर तुरंत ही इसे feminine मानकर इसके लिए she/her का प्रयोग कर दिया गया है। ऐसा 'sex-change' कितनी भद्दी भूल है? आप इससे बचें और Noun/Pronoun के gender के बीच मेल (agreement) का संबंध इस प्रकार अवश्य स्थापित करें—

1. He is an actor. 2. She is an actress.

यहाँ पहले वाक्य में actress और दूसरे में actor का प्रयोग कितना हास्यास्पद होता।

EXERCISE

Match A with B, so as to make correct sentences.

A	B
She is a	hero
He is a	bride
She is my	nephew
He is your	niece
She is his	husband
He is her	wife

Rule XIX. Nouns/Pronouns of Common Gender [Dual Gender]

Rule XIX (A). कुछ Nouns ऐसे हैं जो Common Gender (उभयलिंग) में रहते हैं, अर्थात इनका प्रयोग male और female दोनों के लिए होता है। इसलिए इन्हें Dual Gender भी कहा जाता है—

artist, author, student, reader, baby, teacher, servant, engineer, lawyer, advocate, clerk, client, worker, conductor, poet, speaker, writer, typist, cyclist, lecturer, professor, musician, politician, minister, leader, dealer, secretary, enemy, parent, relation, cousin, child, friend, orphan, neighbour, pupil, person, president, monarch, statesman, publicman, chairman, sportsman, chair, person, spokesman, spokesperson

Distributive और Indefinite Pronouns भी common Gender में रहते हैं; जैसे—

each, either, neither, everyone, no one, nobody,

anybody, everybody, somebody.

Rule XIX (B). जब Common Gender (Dual Gender) के ऐसे Nouns/Pronouns का प्रयोग singular में होता है, तब इनके लिए Third Person Singular Pronoun और Masculine Gender (he/his/him) का प्रयोग होता है; जैसे—

1. Every teacher should do *his* duty.
2. Neither of them has done *his* duty.
3. Everyone should mind *his* own business.
4. No one should trouble *his* neighbour.

NOTE—ऐसे Nouns/Pronouns के साथ Gender के प्रयोग के संबंध में कुछ कठिनाई खड़ी हो जाती है, क्योंकि ये Common Gender (उभयलिंग) के हैं। इसलिए कुछ लोगों का कहना है कि ऐसी हालत में सिर्फ Masculine का प्रयोग उचित नहीं जँचता। वे चाहते हैं कि पुरुष और नारी को समान अधिकार मिले और इसलिए ऐसे Nouns/Pronouns के साथ वाक्य की बनावट इस प्रकार की हो—

1. Every student should do *his or her* duty.
2. Everyone should do *his or her* duty.
3. No one should neglect *his or her* duty.

इस संबंध में इतना ही कहा जा सकता है कि ऐसे वाक्य अशुद्ध तो नहीं हैं, पर अस्वाभाविक अवश्य हैं। ऐसी भाषा कचहरी में ही अच्छी लग सकती है। इसलिए जहाँ कानून आदि की बात हो, वहाँ आप Common Gender को *his or her* के द्वारा स्पष्ट कर दें, पर साधारणतः केवल *he/his/him* से काम लें।

कुछ लोगों ने *his or her* के बदले 'their' का प्रयोग किया है, क्योंकि ***plural*** बना देने से ***Common Gender*** की समस्या ही टल जाती है और *his or her* लिखने की आफत भी नहीं आती; जैसे—

1. *Everyone* should do *their* duty.
2. *No one* should trouble *their* neighbour.

ऐसा प्रयोग कुछ अच्छे लेखकों ने भी किया है—

1. **No one** *will ever gauge or measure English poetry until* **they** *know how much of it, how full a gamut of its qualities is already there on the pages of Chaucer.*

—EZRA POUND

2. *The first phase of* **anyone's** *writing always shows* **them** *doing something* **they** *have heard or read.*

—EZRA POUND

3. **Everybody** *was pleased to think how much* **they** *had always disliked Mr Darcey.*

—JANE AUSTEN

इन वाक्यों में no one/anyone/everybody के लिए Plural Pronoun का प्रयोग किया गया है। ऐसे प्रयोगों को Professor Bain ने अपनी पुस्तक *Higher English Grammar* में 'allowable' माना है जिसका अर्थ होता है कि ये प्रयोग अशुद्ध नहीं हैं। इस समस्या की चर्चा करते हुए कहा गया है—

There are three makeshifts—(a) Anybody can see for **himself or herself**. *(b) Anybody can see for* **themselves.** *(c) Anybody can see for* **himself**.

—FOWLER: *Modern English Usage*

Fowler साहब ने इस समस्या के तीन समाधान निकाले हैं—(i) Common Gender के लिए 'his or her' का प्रयोग करें या (ii) उसे plural बना दें या (iii) उसके लिए Third Person Singular Masculine Pronoun का प्रयोग करें। Ezra Pound तथा Jane Austen ने plural बनाकर समस्या का समाधान किया है और इसलिए Bain साहब ने ऐसे प्रयोग को अशुद्ध नहीं माना।

मेरे जानते ऐसी अवस्था में Plural Pronoun का प्रयोग अशुद्ध भले ही न हो, पर इससे कहीं अच्छा है Third Person Singular Masculine Pronoun (he/his/him) का प्रयोग। इसका कारण यह है कि एकवचन पुँल्लिंग से पुँल्लिंग और स्त्रीलिंग—दोनों का बोध होता है। यह एक सामान्य नियम है। Fowler साहब ने भी ऐसा ही मत प्रकट किया है—

'C' *is here recommended. It involves the convention that where the matter of sex is not conspicuous or important 'he' and 'his' shall be allowed to represent a person ....*

एक और आचार्य ने इस मत का समर्थन इस प्रकार किया है—

Use **his** *as common gender unless there is any real necessity to make the distinction—"Each member has paid his subscription"—not his or her.*

—F T WOOD

आधुनिक प्रयोग और साहित्य में भी ऐसी अवस्था में Singular Masculine Pronoun का ही प्रयोग अधिक प्रचलित है—

1. **Everyone,** *I believe, can remember some moment in life when* **he** *was completely carried away by the work of any poet. Very likely* **he** *was carried away by several poets ....*

—T S ELIOT

2. **Anyone** *who tries to write poetic drama even today should know that half of* **his** *energy must be exhausted in the effort to escape from ... the toils of Shakespeare.* —T S ELIOT

3. **Each** *must decide that question for* **himself.** —VIRGINIA WOOLF

4. *That question* **each** *of us can answer, perhaps, for* **himself.**

—FOWLER: *Modern English Usage*

इन लेखकों ने Common Gender के Singular Pronoun के लिए he/his/himself का प्रयोग किया है। मेरी राय है कि आप भी ऐसा ही करें और Pound तथा Austen की नकल कर Plural Pronoun का प्रयोग न करें।

Rule XIX (C). यदि Common Gender के Nouns के पहले girl/woman/lady/female का प्रयोग (girlfriend, girl-student, female-child, woman-student, woman-teacher, woman doctor, woman conductor आदि) हों, तो इनके लिए Feminine Gender के Pronoun (her) का प्रयोग होना चाहिए। इस वाक्यों को देखें—

A girl-student should not neglect *her* home.

Lady or woman?

Rule XIX (D). Common Gender के Nouns के पहले lady का प्रयोग हो या woman का? इस संबंध में इन मतों पर विचार करें—

I. *'Lady' prefixed to name indicating vocation as a mark of sex (lady doctor, author, clerk, etc.) is a cumbrous substitute for a feminine designation, which should be preferred when it exists or can be made; in default of that 'woman' or 'female' would be better than 'lady' not confusing the essential point with irrelevant suggestions of social position.* —FOWLER: *Modern English Usage*

II. For the mere indication of sex use *woman*:

woman teacher, woman doctor, women students, women writers

... *lady* is a courtsey term, and should be employed only (i) for direct address, and then only in the plural, as *Ladies and Gentlemen*, (ii) in the presence of the person concerned:

'Could you find this lady a seat, please?' 'If any lady owns this watch, will she please come forward and claim it?' —F T WOOD: *Current English Usage*

Wood साहब ने बहुत अच्छा समाधान निकाला है। इसलिए पेशे (profession) के अर्थ में woman doctor/teacher का प्रयोग होना चाहिए, पर शिष्टाचार की दृष्टि से उसे lady कहकर संबोधन (address) करना चाहिए। इसका अर्थ यह नहीं कि उसे lady doctor या lady teacher कहें। यहाँ एक बात ध्यान देने योग्य है। हिंदी में महिला शिक्षक/महिला डॉक्टर का ही प्रयोग होता है, औरत शिक्षक/डॉक्टर का नहीं। यही कारण है कि भारत में woman doctor/woman teacher जैसे शब्द शिष्टाचार की दृष्टि से लोकप्रिय नहीं हो पाए हैं, पर हमें यहाँ अँगरेजों का ही शिष्टाचार अपनाना है न!

इसलिए आप इस प्रकार लिखें—

1. A woman doctor has been sent for. [not, *lady doctor*]
2. A woman teacher teaches me English. [not, *lady teacher*]
3. It is a women students' common room. [not *lady students'*]
4. Is it a women's college? [not, *ladies' college*]

जब ऐसे nouns के लिए she का प्रयोग होता है तो woman की आवश्यकता ही नहीं पड़ती; जैसे—

1. She is a doctor. 2. She is a teacher.

ऐसे वाक्यों के she से ही sex का पता चल जाता है, तो woman की आवश्यकता ही क्या?

. . . .

EXERCISE

Correct the following sentences.

(1) India has rich mineral deposits and vast population and so it can be reasonably expected that she will be a great power in near future if all its resources are fully exploited for the implementation of her Second Five-Year Plan. (2) A reader should not blindly accept everything she finds in a book. (3) A husband must love her wife and a wife must love his husband. (4) He does not care for her daughter. (5) She is a lady doctor. (6) Lady writers have been invited.

Hints—(1) her resources, or it will be … its … its Second Fiver-Year Plan; (2) he finds; (3) his wife … her husband; (4) his daughter; (5) woman doctor; (6) Women writers.

. . . .

Rule XX. Nouns always in Feminine Gender

कुछ nouns ऐसे होते हैं जो सदा Feminine Gender में रहते हैं। ये है—

coquette, blonde, maid, midwife.

सामान्यत: bachelor का प्रयोग masculine gender में और virgin का feminine gender में होता है, पर आजकल bachelor/virgin का प्रयोग masculine और feminine—दोनों genders में हो रहा है—

1. He is a bachelor. 2. She is a bachelor girl.
3. He is a virgin. 4. She is a virgin.

Rule XXI. Nouns and the Nominative Case

यदि कोई Noun वाक्य का कर्ता हो, तो उसे Nominative Case (कर्ता कारक) में रहना चाहिए; जैसे—

1. Dickens is a Victorian novelist.
2. Keats is a Romantic poet.

यहाँ Dickens और Keats वाक्य के कर्ता हैं। इसलिए ये Nominative Case में हैं। अब इन वाक्यों को देखें—

1. Dickens's is well known for his humour.
2. Keats's was a great lover of nature.

इन वाक्यों में Dickens/Keats कर्ता हैं, पर इन्हें Possessive Case में रखा गया है, जो भयंकर भूल है। यहाँ Dickens's और Keats's के बदले Dickens/Keats होना चाहिए।

Rule XXII. Noun and the Possessive/Genitive Case

Rule XXII (A). यदि दो या दो से अधिक Nouns को and से जोड़ा जाए, तो इनके joint possession (सम्मिलित अधिकार) का बोध कराने के लिए केवल अंत में आनेवाले Noun में 's या (') लगाकर Possessive Case बनाया जाता है। पर यदि इनके separate possession (अलग-अलग अधिकार) का अर्थ प्रकट करना हो, तो इनमें से प्रत्येक Noun में (') या ('s) लगाकर इन्हें Possessive Case बनाया जाता है। इसे Group Genitive कहा जाता है—

1. J M Dent & Sons' shop
2. Keats's and Yeats's poems

यहाँ पहले उदाहरण में केवल अंत में आनेवाले Noun (Sons) में (') लगाकर इसे Possessive Case बनाया गया है, क्योंकि Dent & Sons' से joint possession का बोध होता है। दूसरे उदाहरण में Keats और Yeats दोनों ही में ('s) लगाकर इन्हें Possessive Case बनाया गया है, क्योंकि यहाँ separate possession का बोध होता है। इन्हें इस प्रकार लिखना उचित नहीं—

1. I have placed orders with J M Dent's & Sons'.
2. I have read Keats and Yeats's poems.

Rule XXII (B). यदि house/school/shop/church आदि nouns (जिनसे निश्चित स्थान/घर का बोध हो) का प्रयोग वाक्य में Object की भाँति हो और ये Possessive Case के Noun के बाद आएँ, तो ऐसे Nouns को छिपा दिया जा सकता है। इसे Local Genitive कहा जा सकता है। यदि ये Nouns वाक्य में Subject का काम करें, तो इन्हें छिपाया नहीं जा सकता; जैसे—

1. I went to *Blackwell's* (shop).
2. I went to the *barber's* (shop).
3. The *barber's* is full of customers.
4. *Blackwell's* is prompt in service.

यहाँ पहले दो वाक्यों में Blackwell's और barber's के बाद जो Noun (shop) आया है वह Objective Case में है। इसलिए इन वाक्यों में shop छिपा हुआ है, जो शुद्ध है। पर तीसरे और चौथे वाक्यों में barber's/Blackwell's के बाद Noun (shop) का प्रयोग अवश्य होना चाहिए। यहाँ इसको छिपा देना अनुचित है, क्योंकि यहाँ shop वाक्य का Subject है।

Rule XXII (C). प्राणिवाचक एकवचन संज्ञाओं में apostrophes ('s) जोड़कर Possessive Case बनाया जाता है। इसे S-genitive कहा जाता है—

1. Ram's house
2. Mohan's book
3. A dog's tail
4. A bird's eyes
5. James's coat
6. Keats's poems

इसके प्रयोग के संबंध में इस नियम का ध्यान रखें—

Generally speaking, the **S-genitive** *is favoured by the classes that are highest on the gender scale, that is, animate nouns, in particular persons and animals with personal gender characteristics.*

—RANDOLPH QUIRK and others: A *Grammar of Contemprary English*

Rule XXII (D). प्राणिवाचक बहुवचन संज्ञाओं में (जिनके अंत में s रहे) केवल apostrophe (') जोड़कर Possessive Case बनाया जाता है; जैसे—

1. Boys' school 2. Girls' hostel 3. Poor Boys' Fund

यदि प्राणिवाचक बहुवचन संज्ञाओं के अंत में s नहीं रहे, तो उनका Possessive Case 's जोड़कर बनाया जाता है; जैसे—

1. Children's toys 2. Men's dresses

Rule XXII (E). Compound nouns के अंत में 's इस प्रकार जोड़कर Possessive Case बनाया जाता है—

1. The government of Bihar's order 2. My son-in-law's house

Rule XXII (F). जिन संज्ञाओं से समय, स्थान, दूरी, वजन या मूल्य का बोध होता है उनमें 's जोड़कर Possessive Case बनाया जाता है; जैसे—

1. One day's leave 2. A week's holiday
3. A stone's throw 4. A razor's edge

Rule XXII (G). अप्राणिवाचक संज्ञाओं का Possessive Case बनाया जाता है of के द्वारा, 's के द्वारा नहीं। इसलिए इसे of-genitive कहा जाता है :

1. The doors of this house 2. The rules of this book
3. The water of this well 4. The leaves of this tree

इन्हें इस प्रकार लिखना अनुचित है—

1. This house's doors are weak. 2. This book's rules are easy.
3. This well's water is pure. 4. This tree's leaves are green.

Rule XXII (H). Pronouns and 's/of

प्राणिवाचक Indefinite Pronouns का Possessive Case बनाया जाता है 's जोड़कर, जैसे—

one's, nobody's, somebody's, anybody's, some one's, no one's,

nobody else's, somebody else's, some one else's

प्राणिवाचक Reciprocal Pronouns का Possessive Case बनाया जाता है 's जोड़कर; जैसे—

They are touching each other's/one another's fingers.

अप्राणिवाचक Indefinite Pronouns का Possessive Case बनाया जाता है of के द्वारा, जैसे—

1. The life of everything is short. [not, everything's life]
2. The colour of nothing is fast. [not, nothing's colour]

NOTE (a)—all, both, many, each, either, neither का Possessive Case बनाया जाता है of के द्वारा; जैसे—

1. The names of both are unknown. [not, both's names]
2. The price of each/either is high. [not, each's price]

NOTE (b)—कभी-कभी दो अप्राणिवाचक संज्ञाओं के बीच of नहीं आता है; जैसे—

street lamp, kitchen garden, gold ring, birthday party,

winter nights, ghost stories.

Double Genitive

Rule (I). कभी-कभी Double Genitive का भी प्रयोग होता है, अर्थात of के बाद आनेवाली संज्ञा में 's लगा रहता है या of के बाद कोई Possessive Pronoun (mine, ours, yours, theirs) आता है। संक्षेप में, इनकी बनावट इस प्रकार की होती है—

(i) singular noun + of + noun + 's

(ii) singular noun + of + possessive pronoun.

1. Mohan is a friend of Ram's.
2. He is a friend of mine.

ऐसे वाक्यों में of के पहले आनेवाली संज्ञा से one of the many (बहुतों में से एक) का बोध होता है, पर केवल 's + noun से एक निश्चित संज्ञा का भाव प्रकट होता है; जैसे—

1. Mohan is a friend of Ram's/mine. [बहुत मित्रों में से एक]
2. Mohan is Ram's friend. [एक निश्चत मित्र]

इस नियम को ध्यान रखकर इन वाक्यों पर विचार करें—

1. She is a wife of mine. 2. Is he a father of yours?

3. She is a mother of *Mohan*. 4. Is she a mother of hers?

ध्यान दें कि a wife of mine का अर्थ है—बहुतों मे से एक। इसी प्रकार, a father of yours/ a mother of Mohan's/a mother of hers का अर्थ है—बहुतों में से एक। लिखने/बोलने का अभिप्राय यह नहीं है न? इसलिए, इन्हें इस प्रकार लिखें—

1. She is my wife. 2. Is he your father?

3. She is Mohan's mother. 4. Is she her mother?

REVISION TEST I

Correct the following sentences.

1. There are not many gentries in this village.
2. What are the peoples of this place doing?
3. Whose poultries are these?
4. All the cattles have been sold away.
5. Why are there more os than es in this poem?
6. She is in her teen's.
7. Don't write 3s like 5s.

8. Is it a girl's school?
9. What is the this book's price?
10. He was paid two week's wages.
11. It is a nice poetry.
12. There are two females here.
13. He gave me five ten rupee's notes.
14. I gave him three and a half rupees.
15. How many MP's have come?
16. He is my cousin brother.
17. She is a stateswoman.

Hints—(1) gentry; (2) people; (3) poultry; (4) cattle; (5) o's than e's; (6) teens; (7) 3's like 5's; (8) girls'; (9) the price of this book; (10) weeks'; (11) is nice poetry or is a nice poem; (12) two women; (13) five ten-rupee notes; (14) three rupees and a half; (15) MPs; (16) He is my cousin; (17) statesman

Revision Test II

Explain why the following sentences are correct or incorrect.

1. He likes new poetries.
2. The sceneries of Ranchi are charming.
3. These news are very bad.
4. The Indians are brave peoples.
5. All the furnitures were burnt.
6. Help the deafs and blinds.
7. He gave me five and half rupees.
8. I gave him many good advices.
9. He is a student of three year's degree course.
10. This book has been recommended by the Bihar and the Bhagalpur Universities.
11. How many babys and ladys are there?
12. His teeths and feets were broken.
13. She is a good actor.
14. She is the hero of this movel.
15. What are the criterions of selection?
16. All your informations are wrong.
17. I bought two dozens of pens.
18. She is a lady student.
19. My means is much reduced.
20. The barber's is too full of customers.
21. The cattle is sold away.
22. He is a flirt.
23. I like Kabir and Mira's poetry.

❐

Chapter VII

TEST YOURSELF

I. *Correct or justify the following sentences.*

1. It is all India Radio.
2. Her either son passed the examination.
3. The two boys are beating one another.
4. This apple is sour. I want sweet one.
5. You, he and I tried my very best.
6. Neither of the three books is very useful.
7. Everyone of the two guests reached in time.
8. Neither of the two sisters had their own choice.
9. One must always do his duties sincerely.
10. Myself can do this work without your help.
11. Do you really know whom you are speaking?
12. The boy who is here he is my friend.
13. It is I who has broken this chair.
14. We enjoyed yesterday.
15. Received your letter and I thank you for the same.
16. It is me but this is him.
17. It is him who is really guilty.
18. She didn't avail of the offer.
19. This is the only book whom I like.
20. He is not such a man who can help me.
21. Each of the soldiers saluted their commander.
22. It is strictly between he and I.
23. She addressed to the chairperson.
24. It is no use to cry now.
25. I think wrong to travel without ticket.

II. *Fill in the blanks with a Pronoun given in brackets.*

1. …… of the two sisters is married. (None, Neither)
2. …… is she dancing with? (Who, Whom)
3. She does not love …… husband. (his, her)
4. He and I do …… duties well. (my, our)
5. …… of the two boys has come. (Each, Everyone)
6. Everyone of the ladies had a choice of …… own. (her, their)
7. None should harm …… neighbour. (her, his, their)

❒

PRONOUNS

अँगरेजी में Pronouns के प्रयोग के नियम कुछ जटिल हैं। Pronouns के Gender के नियम तो सरल हैं, पर इनके Number और Case से संबंधित नियम तथा प्रयोग कठिन हैं। विशेष कठिनाई इसलिए होती है कि व्याकरण के बहुत-से नियम अब पुराने पड़ गए हैं और उन्होंने आधुनिक प्रयोग के सामने घुटने टेक दिए हैं। यहाँ इन बातों पर हम विस्तारपूर्वक विचार करें।

Rule I. Each other and One another

पुराने आचार्यों ने इन दोनों के प्रयोग में यह अंतर माना है कि *each other* का प्रयोग दो व्यक्तियों या वस्तुओं के लिए होता है, जबकि *one another* का दो से अधिक के लिए—

'Each other' is used when two persons or things are concerned; 'one another' is used when more than two persons or things are concerned. —NESFIELD

आधुनिक आचार्यों ने इस अंतर को आवश्यक नहीं माना है। इस मत पर विचार करें—

The differentiation is neither of present utility nor based on historical usage.

—FOWLER

वास्तव में, दो व्यक्तियों या वस्तुओं के लिए भी one another का प्रयोग 18वीं सदी के गद्य में भी मिलता है—

They **both** *simpered and looked upon* **one another.** —RICHARDSON

आज के महान लेखक भी ऐसा प्रयोग निःसंकोच भाव से करते हैं—

1. *Whereas in Shakespeare the effect is due to the way in which the* **characters** *act upon* **one another** *in Jonson it is given by the way in which the* **characters** *fit in with* **each other.** —T S ELIOT
2. *The artistic result of Volpone is not due to any effect that Volpone, Mosca, Corvino, Corbaccio and Voltore have upon* **each other.** —T S ELIOT
3. *... neither the Chestnut nor the Oak spoke to* **one another.** —T F POWYS
4. *For you and I are foreigners to* **one another,** *foreigners in time.*

—ALDOUS HUXLEY

यहाँ पहले वाक्य में characters के लिए एक बार one another का प्रयोग हुआ है और दूसरी बार each other का। इससे यह स्पष्ट है कि लेखक each other और one another के बीच कोई भी अंतर नहीं मानता। दूसरे वाक्य में पाँच व्यक्तियों के लिए each other का प्रयोग हुआ है और तीसरे वाक्य में केवल दो (Chestnut and Oak) के लिए one another का, जो Nesfield साहब के नियमानुसार अशुद्ध है, पर Fowler साहब तथा आधुनिक प्रयोग के अनुसार शुद्ध। इसलिए, मेरा विचार है कि each other और one another के बीच कोई अंतर मानना आवश्यक नहीं। हाँ, यदि कोई ऐसा अंतर माने, तो उसे भी अशुद्ध नहीं कहा जा सकता। इसलिए, जब इस प्रकार के वाक्य शुद्ध करने को दिए जाते हैं—

1. The three sisters love *each other.*

2. The two sisters love *one another.*

तो ये प्रश्न ही गलत जान पड़ते हैं, क्योंकि ये वाक्य अशुद्ध हैं ही नहीं। यदि आप भी इस आधुनिक प्रयोग को मान लें, तो सुविधा होगी।

Rule II. Pronouns and their Position

यदि वाक्य में भिन्न-भिन्न Persons के Nouns/Pronouns आएँ, तो सबसे पहले Second Person आता है, उसके बाद Third Person और अंत में First Person, अर्थात ऐसे वाक्यों की बनावट इस प्रकार की होती है—2 + 3 + 1; जैसे—

You, he and *I are* going.

देखिए, इन वाक्यों में Pronouns को उचित स्थान नहीं मिला है—

1. *I, you* and *he went* there.

2. *I* and *you* are fast friends.

इनके शुब्द रूप ये होंगे—

1. *You, he* and *I went* there.

2. *You* and *I are* fast friends.

NOTE—हाँ, यदि वाक्य में किसी भूल या अपराध को स्वीकार किया जाए तो, सभ्य आचरण की दृष्टि से, आप सबसे पहले First Person को रख सकते हैं; जैसे—

I and *he* are guilty.

Rule III. Pronouns and their Number/Person

Rule III (A). यदि वाक्य में तीनों ही Persons के Nouns/Pronouns को जोड़ा जाए और उन सबके लिए एक ही (common) Pronoun का प्रयोग करना हो, तो वह Pronoun सदा First Person Plural (we) होना चाहिए—2 + 3 + 1 = 1 (we); जैसे—

1. *You, he* and *I are* doing *our* duties well.

2. *You, Ram* and *I* have tried *our* best.

इन दोनों वाक्यों में तीनों ही Persons के लिए एक ही Pronoun का प्रयोग हुआ है। इसलिए, First Person Plural 'we' का व्यवहार किया गया है। यहाँ my/their या किसी और Pronoun का प्रयोग करना अशुद्ध होता।

Rule III (B). यदि वाक्य में Second और Third Persons को जोड़ा जाए और उनके लिए एक ही Pronoun का प्रयोग करना हो, तो वहाँ Second Person Plural (you) का व्यवहार होना चाहिए—2 + 3 = 2 (you); जैसे—

You and he did not do *your* duties well.

इस वाक्य में Second और Third Persons को and से जोड़ा गया है। इसलिए, यहाँ your का प्रयोग हुआ है। यहाँ his/their का प्रयोग अशुद्ध होता।

Rule IV. Pronouns and their Case

Noun के समान, Pronoun भी किसी-न-किसी case में अवश्य रहता है—subject के समान प्रयुक्त होने पर Nominative Case (I/he) में, Object के समान प्रयुक्त होने पर Objective Case (me/him) में और possession/relation का बोध कराने के लिए Possessive Case (my/his) में।

इसलिए, जब Pronoun किसी Transitive Verb/Preposition के साथ आता है, तब इसे Objective Case में अवश्य रहना चाहिए। इस नियम का ज्ञान नहीं रहने पर लोग Objective के बदले Nominative का प्रयोग कर बैठते हैं। इन वाक्यों को लें, जिनमें इस नियम का पालन हुआ है—

1. It is between him and me.
2. Let him and me lead the procession.

आप जानते हैं कि 'between' एक Preposition है और 'let' है Transitive Verb. इसलिए, इन दोनों वाक्यों में Objective Case (him, me) का प्रयोग किया गया है। नियम भूलकर ऐसे-ऐसे वाक्य न लिखें—

1. It is between him and I. 2. Let him and I work together.

....

EXERCISE

Correct the following sentences.

(1) Let he and I work together. (2) There is friendship between you and I. (3) The book is liked by him and I. (4) Both he and me were asked to do it. (5) I and he are fast friends. (6) He and I have done my work together. (7) You and he did not do their duty well. (8) Let she and I do it. (9) Me and my husband have been invited.

Hints—(1) him and me; (2) you and me; (3) him and me; (4) he and I; (5) he and I; (6) our work; (7) your duty; (8) her and me; (9) my husband and I

....

Rule V. Either/Neither/Both

Pronoun की भाँति प्रयुक्त होने पर इनका प्रयोग केवल दो ही व्यक्तियों या वस्तुओं के लिए होता है, दो से अधिक के लिए कभी भी नहीं। दो से अधिक के लिए either के बदले *anyone*, neither के बदले *none* (no one) और both के बदले *all* का प्रयोग होता है; जैसे—

1. *Either* of the two *pens* will do.
2. *Neither* of the two pens will do.

इस प्रकार के वाक्य न लिखें—

1. *Either* of the three pens will do.
2. *Neither* of the three pens will do.
3. *Both* of the three pens will do.

इन्हें इस प्रकार लिखें—

1. *Anyone* of the three pens will do.

2. *None* (no one) of the three pens will do.

3. *All* the three pens will do.

NOTE—इन वाक्यों से यह स्पष्ट है कि *anyone, none* तथा *all* का प्रयोग सदा दो से अधिक व्यक्तियों या वस्तुओं के लिए होता है।

EXERCISE

Correct the following sentences.

(1) Gold, silver and copper—either will do. (2) None of the two guests turned up. (3) Answer anyone of the two questions. (4) Neither of the four books will do. (5) Either of the three careers will suit him. (6) None of my two pens writes well. (7) Anyone of the two men would be able to do this work.

Hints—(1) anyone will do; (2) Neither of the two; (3) either of the two; (4) None of the four books; (5) Anyone of the three careers; (6) Neither of my two pens writes well; (7) Either of the two men.

Rule VI. Each and Everyone

Each का प्रयोग दो या दो से अधिक वस्तुओं के लिए होता है, पर everyone का सदा दो से अधिक के लिए, दो के लिए कभी नहीं; जैसे—

1. *Each* of the two guests came.
2. *Each* of the ten guests came.
3. *Everyone* of the ten guests came.

ये वाक्य शुद्ध हैं, क्योंकि यहाँ दो या दो से अधिक के लिए पहले दो वाक्यों में each का प्रयोग हुआ है और दो से अधिक के लिए तीसरे वाक्य में everyone का। अब इन वाक्यों को लें—

Everyone of the two guests came.

यहाँ everyone के बदले each का प्रयोग होना चाहिए।

Rule VII. Distributive/Indefinite Pronouns and Gender

Rule VII (A). Distributive Pronouns (each, everyone, either and neither) तथा Singular Indefinite Pronouns (no one, nobody, anybody, anyone, someone and somebody) के लिए Third Person Singular Pronoun, Masculine Gender (he/his/him) का प्रयोग होता है; जैसे—

1. None should hate *his* neighbour.
2. Everyone should help *his* friend.

ऐसा ही प्रयोग अच्छे लेखक करते हैं—

It is almost impossible for **anyone** *to secure a correct impression of* **his** *own personal appearance or of the features of anyone in whom* **he** *is personally interested.* —I A RICHARDS

Rule VII (B). यदि Distributive Pronouns (each, everyone, either and neither) के बाद Feminine Gender के Noun का प्रयोग हो, तो Singular Feminine Gender के Pronoun (her) का प्रयोग अवश्य ही होना चाहिए, Masculine (he, his, him) का नहीं; जैसे—

1. *Neither* of the two sisters has paid *her* tuition fees.
2. *Neither* of the two women has a choice of *her* own.
3. *Either* of the two wives is dominated by her husband.
4. *Each* of the two girls has prepared a dress *for* herself.
5. *Everyone* of the women has a taste of *her* own.

यदि इन Feminine Nouns के बदले Plural Pronouns (us/you/them) या Masculine Gender के Nouns आते, तो यहाँ Singular Masculine Gender के Pronouns का प्रयोग होता; जैसे—

1. *Neither* of them has done *his* duty.
2. *Neither* of the boys has done *his* duty.

One/One's/Oneself

Rule VII (C). One एक ऐसा Singular Indefinite Pronoun है जिसके लिए सदा one/one's/oneself का प्रयोग होता है, he/his/him/himself का नहीं; जैसे—

1. *One* must do *one's* duty.
2. *One* must love *one's* country.

यहाँ one's के बदले his का प्रयोग अशुद्ध होता। इसलिए ये वाक्य अशुद्ध हैं—

1. One must take care of *his* health.
2. One should love not only *himself* but also others.

यहाँ one's/oneself का प्रयोग होना चाहिए। देखिए, इस नियम का कैसा उल्लंघन हुआ है इन वाक्यों में—

1. *One who jumps up and flourishes* **his** *toes three times before* **he** *comes to the ground, may have three hundred a year.* —OLIVER GOLDSMITH
2. *One should, therefore, be careful not to make* **himself** *obnoxious to others.*

—*The Searchlight*: March 12, 1957

इन वाक्यों में *one's/one/oneself* का प्रयोग होना चाहिए। देखिए, अच्छे लेखक इस नियम का पालन कितनी सावधानी से करते हैं—

But even when one is fully informed about Mr Pound's allusions, **one's** *recognition has no significant effect.* —F R LEAVIS

NOTE—one के लिए he/him/himself का प्रयोग American English में धड़ल्ले से होता है, पर British English के अनुसार यह प्रयोग अनुचित है। इसलिए, आप American English की नकल न करें।

Rule VII (D). adjective + one/ones

जब adjective के बाद singular noun को छिपा दिया जाता है, तब इसके बदले a + adjective + *one* आता है; जैसे—

This is a red car. I want a blue one. [a blue one = a blue car]

जब adjective के बाद plural noun को छिपा दिया जाता है, तब इसके बदले adjective + ones आता है; जैसे—

There are red cars. I want blue ones. [blue ones = blue cars]

ऐसे वाक्यों में adjective + *one* के पहले *a/an* आता है, पर adjective + *ones* के पहले *a/an* नहीं आता; जैसे—

a green one, an old one, green ones, red ones.

EXERCISE

Correct the following sentences.

(1) Everyone of the students have paid their tuition fees. (2) Everyone of the two alternatives is equally painful. (3) None should oppress their neighbours. (4) Neither of the two wives looks after his domestic affairs. (5) Each of the two sisters has a separate room of his own. (6) Neither of the two sons loves their father. (7) Either of the two daughters loves their mother. (8) One must not be blind to his own defects. (9) One can rise in life only when he puts forth his best not only for himself and his family but also for others. (10) Nobody should lose heart when they are in the teeth of difficulties. (11) Everybody should mind their own business. (11) It is an old car but I want new one.

Rule VIII. 'And' and the Number of Pronouns

Rule VIII (A) यदि and से जुड़े Singular Nouns से एक ही व्यक्ति या वस्तु का बोध हो, तो उनके लिए Singular Pronoun का प्रयोग होता है; जैसे—

1. The Principal and Secretary has tendered *his* resignation.
2. The Magistrate and Collector has prepared *his* statement.
3. The scientist and thinker has expressed *himself* against the use of atom bombs.

इन वाक्यों में the Principal and Secretary, the Magistrate and Collector तथा the scientist and thinker के लिए Singular Pronoun का प्रयोग हुआ है, जो शुद्ध है; क्योंकि इनसे एक ही व्यक्ति का बोध होता है। हाँ, his/himself के बदले their/themselves का प्रयोग अनुचित होता।

Rule VIII (B) यदि and से जुड़े Nouns के पहले each/every आए, तो उनके लिए Singular Pronoun का प्रयोग होना चाहिए; जैसे—

1. Every boy and girl did *his* or *her* best to win the match.
2. Each man and each woman should try to help *his* or *her* fellow beings.

इन वाक्यों में Singular Pronoun का प्रयोग शुद्ध है, क्योंकि and से जुड़े Nouns के पहले each/every का प्रयोग हुआ है। यहाँ their का प्रयोग अशुद्ध होता।

NOTE—इस संबंध में Rule III का ध्यान रखें।

....

EXERCISE

Correct the following sentences.

(1) Ram and Shyam are very irregular in his habits. (2) The poet and critic have a soft corner in their heart for Shakespeare. (3) The poet and the thinker has expressed his view clearly. (4) Every man and every woman have their own tastes. (5) Every scientist and thinker have a duty towards their society.

Hints—(1) their habits; (2) has ... his heart; (3) have expressed their ...; (4) has ... his or her; (5) has ... his society.

....

Rule IX (A). Reflexive and Emphasising Pronouns

कुछ Pronouns के अंत में self/selves इस प्रकार लग जाता है, जैसे—myself, ourselves. इन्हें Self-Pronoun कहा जा सकता है।

ऐसे Self-Pronoun का प्रयोग दो प्रकार से होता है—

1. Reflexive Pronoun. 2. Emphasising Pronoun

जब वाक्य के Verb का Object होता है Self-Pronoun तब वह Reflexive Pronoun कहा जाता है। ऐसे वाक्यों में वाक्य का Subject और Object—दोनों से एक ही व्यक्ति/वस्तु का बोध होता है; जैसे—

1. Ram loves himself. 2. I harmed myself.

यहाँ love के object (himself) और subject (Ram)—इन दोनों से राम का बोध होता है, किसी अन्य व्यक्ति का नहीं। इसी प्रकार, दूसरे वाक्य में फल भोगनेवाला myself है, जो I के लिए आया है। ऐसे object का अर्थ होता है—ownself. इसलिए Ram loves himself का अर्थ है—Ram loves his *ownself.* यही कारण है कि हिंदी-उर्दू में ऐसे Self-Pronoun का अर्थ होता है—खुद को, स्वयं अपने को।

Emphasising/Emphatic Pronoun

कभी-कभी वाक्य के subject या object को जोरदार बनाने के लिए pronoun + self/selves का प्रयोग होता है। इसलिए, इसे Emphasising या Emphatic Pronoun कहा जाता है।

ऐसे वाक्यों के subject को emphatic बनाने के लिए pronoun + self/selves का प्रयोग subject के बाद या object के बाद होता है; जैसे—

1. She cooks food *herself.* 2. She *herself* cooks food.

ऐसे वाक्यों के object को emphatic बनाने के लिए इसका प्रयोग सदा object के बाद होता है; जैसे—

1. I saw the chief minister himself.

2. I spoke to the princess herself.

NOTE (a)—Self-Pronoun का प्रयोग Subject की तरह नहीं करना चाहिए।

इन वाक्यों को लें—

1. Myself will go. 2. Himself will do it.

इन्हें इस प्रकार लिखें—

1. I myself will go. 2. He will do it himself.

NOTE (b)—Reflexive Pronouns ये हैं—

myself, ourselves, yourself, yourselves, himself, herself, itself, themselves

इसलिए, hisself/ourself/themself जैसे शब्द गढ़ने की कोशिश न करें।

Rule IX (B). Verbs and Reflexive Pronouns

कुछ Verbs ऐसे हैं जिनके बाद Reflexive Pronoun आता है। ये हैं—

absent, address, avail, pride, plume.

इन वाक्यों को देखें—

1. He *absents himself* from the college everyday.
2. I *availed myself* of casual leave.
3. He *prides himself* on his style.
4. He *addressed himself* to the chairperson.

यदि इन वाक्यों में Reflexive Pronouns का प्रयोग नहीं होता, तो ये अशुद्ध हो जाते। देखिए, इस वाक्य में नियम का पालन अत्यंत ही सावधानी से किया गया है—

I availed myself of it in Candida. —G B SHAW

NOTE (a)—Avail of का प्रयोग Passive Voice में नहीं होता। इसलिए I availed myself of an offer का Passive Voice—The offer was availed of—अशुद्ध है। इसकी चर्चा करते हुए कहा गया है—

We may notice here a curious blunder that is sometimes made with the reflexive verb **I avail myself of.** *The passive of this is never used, because there is no occasion for it ... .* —FOWLER: *King's English*

NOTE (b)—आजकल avail का प्रयोग American English में Reflexive Pronoun के बिना ही हो रहा है, पर इसे भारत तथा इंगलैंड में मान्यता नहीं मिली है। इसलिए आप इस American usage से बचें।

NOTE (c)—Enjoy के बाद object अवश्य आता है, जैसे—

We enjoyed the picnic last week.

पर जब enjoy के बाद कोई object नहीं आता है, तब इसके साथ Reflexive Pronoun एक object के रूप में अवश्य आता है, जैसे—

We enjoyed ourselves last week.

इसलिए, ऐसे-ऐसे वाक्य न बनाएँ—

1. I enjoyed yesterday. 2. He enjoyed last night.

Rule X (A). Such/as + noun + as

यदि वाक्य में किसी Noun के पहले such या as आए, तो उस noun के लिए as का प्रयोग होता है, who/which/that का नहीं; जैसे—

1. He is not *such* a good man *as* can help me.
2. *As* many questions *as* were set were answered.

यहाँ पहले वाक्य में man के पहले such आया है। इसलिए, इसके लिए (man के लिए) pronoun 'as' का प्रयोग हुआ है। दूसरे वाक्य में questions के पहले as आया है, इसलिए इसके बाद as का प्रयोग हुआ है। ऐसे वाक्य न लिखें—

1. He is not *such* a good man who/that can help me.
2. *As* many questions *which* were set were answered.

Rule X (B). The Same + noun + that/as

यदि वाक्य में noun के पहले the same का प्रयोग हो, तो वैसे noun के लिए as या that का प्रयोग इस नियम के अनुसार होता है— Verb के रहने पर the same के बाद that या as आता है, पर Verb के छिपे रहने पर as आता है; जैसे—

1. This is *the same* pen *that/as* I bought yesterday.
2. This is *the same* pen *as* yours (is).

पहले वाक्य में the same के बाद Verb (bought) आया है। इसलिए यहाँ the same के बाद that या as का प्रयोग हुआ है। दूसरे वाक्य में Verb (is) छिपा हुआ है। अतः, इस वाक्य में as का प्रयोग हुआ है, that का नहीं। यहाँ that का प्रयोग अशुद्ध होता। इस संबंध में आचार्यों के बीच थोड़ा मतभेद है। उनके मतों पर विचार करें—

The use of **that** *or* **as** *is guided by the following rules—(1) When a verb is expressed after it, we generally use* **that.** *(2) When the verb is understood we always use* **as.**

—J C NESFIELD

नेसफिल्ड साहब के अनुसार जब the same के बाद Verb आता है तब that का प्रयोग होता है, पर जब Verb छिपा रहता तब as का; जैसे—

1. This is *the same* man *that* came yesterday.
2. This is not *the same* book *as* mine (is).

अन्य आचार्यों के मतानुसार, दूसरे वाक्य में तो as ही का प्रयोग होना चाहिए, पर पहले वाक्य में that के बदले as का भी प्रयोग हो सकता है। उनका विचार है कि the same के बाद Verb के आने पर that और as में से किसी भी एक का प्रयोग होना चाहिए, केवल that ही का नहीं; जैसे—

1. *Is this* **the same** *as, or the same* **that,** *or the same, you showed me before?*

—*The Oxford Dictionary*

2. *This is* **the same** *timetable as you had last year. This is* **the same** *horse that won the race last year.*

—SOARES & MAZUMDAR

इन वाक्यों में the same के बाद Verb आने पर as या that का प्रयोग किया गया है, जो शुद्ध है। यह आवश्यक नहीं है कि the same के बाद Verb आने पर केवल that ही का प्रयोग हो। अतः, Nesfield साहब का मत आधुनिक प्रयोग के अनुरूप नहीं है।

NOTE—the same के बाद Verb आने पर as का प्रयोग होता है तब समानता (resemblance) का बोध होता है, पर पूर्ण एकत्व (identity) का बोध होने पर that का प्रयोग होता है; जैसे—

1. She has *the same* hair *as her* sister has. (resemblance)
2. She has *the same* coat *that her* sister has. (identity)

हाँ, यदि the same के बाद Verb नहीं आए, तो as का ही प्रयोग होना चाहिए, that का कभी नहीं; जैसे—

This is the same as yours.

Rule X (C). But = who not/which not

कभी-कभी but का प्रयोग एक Relative Pronoun की तरह होता है और इसका अर्थ होता है—who not/which not [जो ... नहीं]; जैसे—

1. There is no one *but* admires this book. [but admires = who doesn't admire]
2. There is no problem *but has* a solution. [but has = which doesn't have]

ऐसे *but-clause* सदा adjective clause होता है।

Rule XI. Relative Pronouns

Rule XI (A). Relative Pronouns (who/which/that/what/whose/whom) वाक्य में subject या object का कार्य करते हैं और clauses को एक साथ जोड़ते भी हैं। इस प्रकार Relative Pronoun noun का काम करता है और conjunction का भी; जैसे—

1. The book *that is* here is mine. (Subject)
2. The book *that I bought* is good. (Object)

Rule XI (B). Who तथा whom का प्रयोग प्राणिवाचक संज्ञा के लिए होता है और खासकर people तथा those के साथ; जैसे—

1. I know the *boy who* is here.
2. I know all *those who* are here.

Who तथा whom का प्रयोग निर्जीव संज्ञा के लिए नहीं होता; जैसे—

1. The *pen* who is here is mine.
2. The *pen whom* I bought is cheap.

यहाँ who/whom के बदले that/which का प्रयोग होना चाहिए।

Rule XI (C). Which का प्रयोग निर्जीव संज्ञा के लिए होता है और that का सजीव और निर्जीव दोनों प्रकार की संज्ञा के लिए; जैसे—

1. This is the *boy that* came here yesterday.
2. The *pen that* is here is good.

NOTE—That का प्रयोग खासकर इन शब्दों के बाद होता है—

all, much, little, anything, nothing, anybody, somebody, nobody, no one, none, superlative degree, the same + noun, the only + noun

इन वाक्यों को देखें—

1. He is the greatest man **that** ever lived. [not, who]
2. He is the only man **that** can do this work. [not, who]
3. He is the same man **that** saved her. [not, who]

Rule XI (D). whose/of which

Whose का प्रयोग संबंध बताने के लिए व्यक्ति और जानवर के लिए होता है और कभी-कभी अप्राणिवाचक संज्ञा के लिए भी; जैसे—

1. A girl whose hair is short looks like a boy.
2. A cow whose colour is black looks lovely.
3. The sun whose rays give us life is regarded as a god.

Of which का प्रयोग संबंध बताने के लिए निर्जीव वस्तु के लिए होता है; जैसे—

A house of which the door is weak is unsafe.

NOTE (a)—preposition + which = relative adverb

वाक्य को सरल और संक्षिप्त बनाने के लिए preposition + which को relative adverb में इस प्रकार बदल देना अच्छा माना जाता है—

in which/on which = when [time]

in which/at which = where [place]

for which = why [cause]

इन वाक्यों को लें—

1. I don't know the month *in which* he was born.
   = I don't know the month *when* he was born.
2. I haven't seen the house *in which* he was born.
   = I haven't seen the house *where* he was born.
3. I don't know the reason *for which* he came here.
   I don't know the reason *why* he came here.

NOTE (b)—of which + noun = with/without + noun

वाक्य को सरल और संक्षिप्त बनाने के लिए of which + noun को with + noun या without + noun में इस प्रकार बदल देना चाहिए—

1. A house *of which* the doors are weak is unsafe.
   = A house *with weak doors* is unsafe.
2. A tree of which leaves fall down looks ugly.
   = A tree *without leaves* looks ugly.

Rule XI (E). Restrictive sense/Continuative sense

जब Relative Pronoun का प्रयोग restrictive sense में होता है तब उसे defining clause कहा जाता है, अर्थात उसे adjective clause माना जाता है। ऐसे वाक्यों में noun और relative pronoun के बीच में comma नहीं आता है और इनकी बनावट होती है—

noun + no comma + relative pronoun + clause

इन वाक्यों को लें—

1. A man *who works hard* gets success.
2. My friend *who lives in London* has sent me a watch.

यहाँ noun (man/friend) और relative pronoun (who) के बीच में comma नहीं आया है। इसलिए ये adjective clause हैं।

जब Relative Pronoun का प्रयोग continuative sense में होता है तब उसे non-defining clause कहा जाता है, अर्थात उसे Principal clause माना जाता है। ऐसे वाक्यों में noun और relative pronoun के बीच में comma अवश्य आता है और इनकी बनावट होती है—

noun + comma + relative pronoun + clause

इन वाक्यों को देखें—

1. My mother, *who lives in London* has sent me a watch.
2. The pen, *which was broken yesterday* is now useless.

यहाँ noun (mother/pen) और Relative Pronoun (who/which) के बीच में comma आ गया है। इसलिए, ये Principal clause हैं, न कि Adjective clause.

इस प्रकार, comma की सहायता से restrictive sense (defining clause) और continuative sense (non-defining clause) को समझना बहुत ही आसान है।

Who + clause और which + clause का प्रयोग restrictive sense में तथा continuative sense में—दोनों प्रकार से हो सकता है। पर, that + clause का प्रयोग सदा restrictive sense में होता है, अर्थात that + clause हमेशा adjective clause होता है, Principal clause नहीं, क्योंकि noun और that के बीच में comma का प्रयोग होता ही नहीं; जैसे—

1. The book *that is lying here* is mine. [Adjective clause]
2. He is the only man *that can help me.* [Adjective clause]

NOTE—which = and this

कुछ वाक्यों में which पूरे clause के बदले प्रयुक्त होता है, केवल एक noun के बदले नहीं। याद रखें कि that का प्रयोग इस प्रकार नहीं होता, जैसे—

1. He killed all the soldiers, *which was a cruel act.* [Principal clause]
2. He says that he is poor, *which is not true.* [Principal clause]

ऐसे which का अर्थ होता है— 'and this'. ऐसा which clause सदा co-principal clause होता है, क्योंकि इससे सदा continuative sense का बोध होता है। ऐसे which के पहले comma अवश्य रहता है।

Analysis के संबंध में इन पक्षों पर विस्तारपूर्वक विचार किया जाएगा।

Zero Relative

Rule XI (F). कभी-कभी Relative Pronouns किसी Transitive Verb या Preposition के object के रूप में प्रयुक्त होते हैं। वैसे वाक्यों में Objective Case में Relative Pronouns (whom, which, that) का लोप हो जाता है। इसे zero relative कहा जाता है। इन वाक्यों को देखें—

1. This is the book *that* I bought yesterday.
   This is the book I bought yesterday.
2. The people *whom* I met yesterday are rich.
   The people I met yesterday are rich.
3. The doctor *whom* I consulted gave me some advice.
   The doctor I consulted gave me some advice.
4. This is the book *about which* I told you.
   This is the book I told you about.
5. The boy *at whom* you were looking is my brother.
   The boy you were looking at is my brother.
6. The book *which* I am reading is good.
   The book I am reading is good.

Caution—शुद्ध व्याकरण की दृष्टि से Objective Case में whom का प्रयोग होना चाहिए, क्योंकि Transitive verb और Preposition के साथ आनेवाला Noun/Pronoun सदा Objective case में रहता है। इसलिए, नियमानुसार Transitive verb + whom और Preposition + whom का प्रयोग आवश्यक है; जैसे—

1. The man *whom I invited* is my friend. [Transitive Verb + Object]
2. The man *whom I spoke to* is my friend. [Preposition + Object]

पर, आजकल whom का प्रयोग प्रायः होता ही नहीं। अब लोग व्याकरण के इस नियम की अवहेलना धड़ल्ले से कर रहे हैं, क्योंकि whom बहुत असुविधाजनक लगता है। इसलिए आजकल whom के बदले who/that का प्रयोग Nominative और Objective—दोनों ही case में हो रहा है; जैसे—

1. The man *who I invited* is my friend. [Transitive Verb + Object]
2. The man *who I spoke to* is my friend. [Preposition + Object]

ऐसे वाक्यों में who को Objective Case में रखना बहुत खटकता है। प्रयोग तो इसे उचित मानता है, पर व्याकरण इसे बिलकुल अनुचित समझता है। इसलिए प्रयोग तथा व्याकरण के बीच सामंजस्य स्थापित करने के लिए अब whom को बिलकुल छिपा दिया जाता है—

1. The man/I invited.
2. The man/I spoke to.

इस तरीके से प्रयोग की मान्यता और व्याकरण की प्रतिष्ठा—दोनों की रक्षा हो जाती है। आप भी इस तरीके से काम लें और whom को बिलकुल छोड़ दें।

NOTE—ध्यान दें कि whom/which के लोप होने पर preposition का स्थान बदल जाता है। उसका स्थान उस clause के अंत में इस प्रकार रहता है—

1. ... *about which* I told you = I told you *about.*
2. ... *at whom* you were looking = you were looking *at.*
3. ... *for what* you were trying = you were trying *for.*

Rule XI (G). कभी-कभी Relative Clause के बाद Verb 'to be' आता है और उसके बाद कोई Adjective. इस प्रकार के Clauses में Relative Pronoun और Verb 'to be'—इन दोनों ही का लोप हो जाता है। इन वाक्यों को लें—

1. The only man *who was present* there was the teacher.

   = The only man present there was the teacher.
2. This dog has been trained in the best way *that is possible.*

   = This dog has been trained in the best way possible.

Rule XI (H). Relative Pronoun के Antecedent को Possessive Case में नहीं रखना चाहिए। इन वाक्यों को देखें—

1. These are the *Principal's* orders *who must* be obeyed.
2. I went to Ram's house *who* is my friend.

पहले वाक्य में who का Antecedent *Principal's* है और दूसरे में *Ram's.* ये दोनों ही Possessive Case में हैं, जो अशुद्ध हैं। आप वाक्य की बनावट इस प्रकार करें—

1. These are the orders of the Principal *who* must be obeyed.
2. I went to the house of Ram who is my friend.

Rule XI (I). Relative Pronouns (who/which) के पहले and/but का प्रयोग (and who, but who, and which, but which) करके इन्हें Antecedent से अलग नहीं करें—

Do not separate the Relative Pronoun from its antecedent by 'and'.

—G H VALLINS

इस वाक्य को लें—

It is a good book, *and which* should be read by all.

यहाँ Relative Pronoun 'which' है और इसका Antecedent है book. इन दोनों (Relative Pronoun और Antecedent) को 'and' के द्वारा अलग कर दिया गया है। इसलिए यहाँ and का प्रयोग अशुद्ध है। एक और उदाहरण लें—

Ram is a good man *and who* is my friend.

यहाँ who के पहले and का प्रयोग करके Relative Pronoun 'who' और इसके Antecedent 'man' को अलग कर दिया गया है। इसलिए यहाँ and का प्रयोग अशुद्ध है। यदि वाक्य से and को हटा दें, यह शुद्ध हो जाएगा।

NOTE—Relative Pronoun के बाद and या but का प्रयोग तब होता है जब वाक्य में एक से अधिक Relative Pronouns जोड़े जाते हैं; जैसे—

It is a book *which* is useful *and which* everybody should read.

इस वाक्य में and which का प्रयोग शुद्ध है, क्यों? इसलिए कि यहाँ and के द्वारा दो Relative Pronouns (which और which) जोड़े गए हैं। यदि यहाँ एक ही which का प्रयोग होता, तो and का प्रयोग अशुद्ध होता।

....

EXERCISE

Correct the following sentences.

(1) I like Shaw's plays who was a good dramatist. (2) One likes to read Shakespeare's sonnets who was a great poet. (3) I have read your book and which is well-written. (4) He has bought a new house and which has cost him Rs 5000.

Hints—(1) the plays of Shaw; (2) the sonnets of Shakespeare; (4) book which; (5) house which

....

Rule XII. Interrogative Pronouns

Interrogative Pronouns (who, whom, whose, which, what) की सहायता से Interrogative Sentences बनाए जाते हैं। यहाँ इनके प्रयोग पर थोड़ा विचार करें—

Rule XII (A). What का प्रयोग निर्जीव संज्ञा (वस्तुओं या कार्यों) के लिए होता है—

1. What is there? 2. What has happened?

What का प्रयोग व्यक्ति के लिए भी होता है जब उसके पेशा या पद (profession or position) के संबंध में प्रश्न किया जाता है—

1. What is he? 2. What are you?

Rule XII (B). Which का प्रयोग चुनाव (selection) के अर्थ में व्यक्तियों और वस्तुओं—दोनों ही के लिए होता है—

1. Which is your pen? 2. Which book do you like best?

Rule XII (C). Who/Whose/Whom का प्रयोग व्यक्तियों के लिए होता है—Who का Nominative Case में; Whose का Possessive Case में और Whom का Objective Case में—

1. Who is he? 2. Who is there?
3. Whose house is that? 4. Whose pen is this?

Whom का प्रयोग Objective Case में होता है—*Transitive Verb* + *whom* या Preposition + whom; जैसे—

1. Whom have you *invited*? Transitive Verb + Object
2. Whom did you see yesterday?
3. Whom were you speaking *to*?
4. Whom is she dancing *with*? Preposition + Object.

व्याकरण की दृष्टि से ये वाक्य शुद्ध हैं, पर बहुत ही भद्दे और कठिन लगते हैं। इसलिए, आजकल Interrogative Sentences में whom का प्रयोग होता ही नहीं। सुविधा की दृष्टि से

आजकल whom के बदले who का ही प्रयोग होता है, जो व्याकरण की दृष्टि से भले ही अनुचित हो, पर प्रयोग की दृष्टि से उचित है। इसलिए आप Transitive verb + whom और Preposition + whom के बदले Transitive verb + *who* का प्रयोग इस प्रकार करें—

1. *Who* were you calling?
2. *Who* have you invited?
3. *Who* was he dancing *with*?
4. *Who* are you waiting *for*?

ध्यान दें—ऐसे वाक्यों में Preposition वाक्य के अंत में आता है।

Rule XII (D). कभी-कभी which तथा what के साथ preposition का प्रयोग होता है। वैसी अवस्था में preposition का स्थान वाक्य के अंत में रहता है (which/what ... + preposition). वाक्य के आरंभ में (Preposition + which/what) नहीं। इन वाक्यों को देखें—

1. What is this pen made *of*?
2. What is this *for*?
3. Which house do you live *in*?
4. Which place did he *go to*?
5. What train will you *go by*?
6. What year was he born *in*?
7. Which book are you looking *for*?
8. What is he laughing *at*?

इन वाक्यों में preposition का प्रयोग वाक्यों के अंत में हुआ है, जो उचित है। यहाँ which/what के पहले preposition का प्रयोग अनुचित होता।

Rule XIII. Possessive Adjective/Pronoun and Noun

Possessive Adjective (my, your, etc.) के बाद आनेवाले Noun को छिपाया नहीं जा सकता। इन वाक्यों को लें—

1. Your *letter* of the 10th ultimo is to hand.
2. I will go to your *house* next morning.

यहाँ 'your' Possessive Adjective है और इसलिए इसके बाद दोनों ही वाक्यों में Nouns (letter तथा house) का प्रयोग स्पष्ट रूप से किया गया है। यहाँ Possessive Adjective + Nouns को छिपाकर इनके बाद Possessive Pronoun का प्रयोग इस प्रकार नहीं किया जा सकता—

1. *Yours* of the 10th ultimo is to hand.
2. I will go to *yours* next morning.

NOTE—यदि वाक्य में एक बार Noun आ जाए, तो उसे छिपाकर उसके बदले Possessive Pronoun का प्रयोग करना उचित है—

If you come to my place, I will go to *yours.*

इस वाक्य में Noun 'place' का प्रयोग एक बार हो गया है। इसलिए, your place (Possessive Adjective + noun) के बदले yours का प्रयोग किया गया है।

EXERCISE

Correct the following sentences.

(1) I shall see you at yours this evening. (2) He came to mine this morning. (3) Yours of the 15th instant has been received. (4) I shall be at his by 2 p.m.

Hints—(1) at your house; (2) to my house; (3) your letter of; (4) at his house

Rule XIV. 'The same' as a Pronoun

The same का प्रयोग Pronoun की भाँति करना अच्छा नहीं समझा जाता, क्योंकि यह एक Adjective है, Pronoun नहीं। इन वाक्यों को देखें—

1. This is *the same* pen that I bought yesterday.
2. I gave him a pen and *the same* was returned to me.

यहाँ पहले वाक्य में the same का प्रयोग Adjective की भाँति हुआ है, क्योंकि यह pen का गुण बतलाता है। यह प्रयोग शुद्ध है। पर दूसरे वाक्य में the same का प्रयोग Pronoun की भाँति कर दिया गया है, क्योंकि यहाँ यह pen के बदले आया है। यह प्रयोग अनुचित है। एक और वाक्य लें—

Your letter of the 10th instant is to hand and I thank you for the *same.*

यहाँ भी the same का प्रयोग Pronoun की भाँति हुआ है क्योंकि यह letter के लिए आया है। आचार्यों का कहना है कि ऐसी अवस्था में the same के बदले साधारण Pronouns ('it', 'this', 'they') का ही प्रयोग होना चाहिए। आप इनके मत का ध्यान रखें—

It **(the same)** *has the peculiarity that it occurs chiefly in writing, not often in speech, and yet is avoided by all who have any skill in writing. As the working man puts on his Sunday clothes to be photographed, so the unliterary adorns himself with* **the same** *when he is to appear in print; each seems bent on giving the worst possible impression of himself.*

—FOWLER: *Modern English Usage*

The word **same** *must be regarded as an adjective—but never as a pronoun. This is thoroughly bad grammar: 'We thank you for your letter and in reply to the same ...' No, the writer is making 'same' to stand for 'letter' which it can never be. In reply to* **it** *is the answer because* **it** *is a pronoun and never anything else.*

—WHITAKER WILSON: *English Grammar*

इसलिए the same का प्रयोग जो Pronoun की भाँति हो चला है उसे कानून और व्यापार (law and business) के क्षेत्र तक ही सीमित रखा जाए, क्योंकि अन्य क्षेत्रों में ऐसा प्रयोग काफी भद्दा लगता है।

Rule XV. Double Nominatives/Redundant Pronouns

यदि वाक्य में किसी Finite Verb का Subject कोई Noun या Pronoun हो, तो उसी Verb के लिए एक और अतिरिक्त Pronoun का प्रयोग करना भयंकर भूल है; जैसे—

1. The *man* who is here *he is* my friend.

इस वाक्य में दो clauses हैं—(i) The man is my friend; (ii) who is here. पहले clause में is का Subject 'man' है और दूसरे का Subject 'who'. यहाँ he का प्रयोग अनावश्यक है।

याद रखें कि ऐसे ही Pronouns को Redundant Pronouns कहा जाता है। क्यों? इसलिए कि वाक्य में उनकी कोई आवश्यकता ही नहीं।

...

EXERCISE

Correct the following sentences.

(1) The cows that are grazing in the field they are mine. (2) He who works hard he is rewarded. (3) Those who kill time they are killed by time. (4) The boy who is here he is my brother. (5) The people of the world, when they heard of Gandhiji's death, they were rudely shocked. (6) A man when he becomes old, he behaves very much like a child.

Hints—(1) The cows that ...... field are mine; (2) He who ...... hard is rewarded; (3) Those who ...... time are killed by time; (4) The boy who ...... here is my brother. (5) The people ...... death were rudely shocked; (6) A man ...... old behaves ...... child.

...

Rule XVI. Verb 'To be' + Pronoun

व्याकरण के नियमानुसार Verb 'to be' के बाद आनेवाला Pronoun उसी Case में रहना चाहिए जिस Case में Verb 'to be' के पहले आनेवाला Noun/Pronoun रहता है; जैसे—

1. It is he. 2. It is I. 3. This is she.

यहाँ पहले वाक्य में Verb 'to be' (is) के पहले It आया है जो Nominative Case में है। इसलिए is के बाद आनेवाला Pronoun भी Nominative Case में (he) है। दूसरे तथा तीसरे वाक्यों में भी I और she को Nominative Case में रखा गया है, क्योंकि इनके पहले It/This Nominative Case में हैं।

अतः, व्याकरण की दृष्टि से ये वाक्य अशुद्ध हैं—

1. It is *him.* 2. It is *me.* 3. *This is her.*

NOTE (a)—आजकल इस नियम के विरुद्ध ऐसे वाक्य लिखें और बोले जाते हैं, जिन्हें प्रयोग (usage) की दृष्टि से, शुद्ध माना जाता है—

1. It is me. 2. This is her. 3. This is him.

ऐसे प्रयोग के संबंध में इन विचारों का ध्यान रखें—

> **Me** *is technically wrong in* **It wasn't me;** *the phrase being of its very nature coloquial, such a lapse is of no importance, and this is perhaps the only temptation to use* **me** *insted of* **I.** —FOWLER: *Modern English Usage*
>
> *It is reasonable to infer that subject and complement should both have the same, that is, the subject form. But the fact remains that few people would say or write* **It's**

I; This is he; That's she. *Usage, a little shamefacedly, admits the object form to such expressions*—**It's me; This is him; That's her.** —G H VALLINS: *Good English*

This violation of grammatical law has been completely sanctioned by current usage. —NORMAN LEWIS: *Word Power*

इस प्रकार, यह स्पष्ट है कि इन आचार्यों के मतानुसार It is *me*/This is *me*/This is *him*/That is *her* इत्यादि प्रयोग शुद्ध हैं, क्योंकि ये काफी प्रचलित हो गए हैं।

NOTE (b)—यहाँ एक बात याद रखने योग्य है। जब ऐसे वाक्यों में who/which that + clause आता है, तब Verb 'to be' के बाद सदा Nominative Case आता है, Objective नहीं। इन वाक्यों पर विचार करें—

1. It ws *he who* was really guilty.
2. It was *him who* was really guilty.

यहाँ पहले वाक्य में Verb 'to be' (was) के बाद he का प्रयोग हुआ है जो Nominative Case में है, क्योंकि इसके बाद who + clause आया है। यदि यहाँ who + clause नहीं आता (अर्थात केवल It was he रहता), तो he के बदले him का भी प्रयोग शुद्ध माना जाता; जैसे—

It was him.

पर who के आ जाने से यहाँ him का प्रयोग नहीं हो सकता, क्योंकि यह व्याकरण की दृष्टि से तो अशुद्ध है ही, प्रयोग के भी विपरीत है। अतः, दूसरा वाक्य अशुद्ध है। इसलिए जब आप देखें कि Verb 'To be' (is, was) के बाद एक Pronoun आता है और वाक्य उसके बाद समाप्त हो जाता है, तब यहाँ उस Pronoun को Nominative या Objective किसी भी Case में रख सकते हैं—

1. It is I. 2. It is me.

ये दोनों ही वाक्य शुद्ध माने जाएँगे, पर यदि Verb 'to be' के बाद आनेवाले Pronoun के बाद clause का प्रयोग हो, तो उस Pronoun को सदा Nominative Case में रखें; जैसे—

1. It is *he* who is to blame. 2. It is *she* who is guilty.

NOTE (c)—यदि *Verb* 'to be' के पहले आनेवाला Noun/Pronoun Objective Case में हो, तो इसके बाद आनेवाले Noun/Pronoun को भी Objective Case में ही रहना चाहिए, Nominative में नहीं; जैसे—

I know the man to be *him*.

यहाँ Verb 'to be' के पहले man आया है जो Transitive Verb (know) का Object है। इसलिए नियमानुसार और प्रयोगानुसार भी Verb 'to be' के बाद आनेवाले Pronoun (him) को Objective Case में रहना चाहिए। अतः, यह वाक्य शुद्ध है। यहाँ him के बदले he का प्रयोग किसी भी दृष्टि से—व्याकरण या प्रयोग की दृष्टि से—उचित नहीं होता।

EXERCISE

Correct the following sentences.

(1) It is me who is guilty. (2) It was them who were to blame. (3) I found it to be he. (4) I guessed the woman to be she. (5) We knew it to be she. (6) We thought the actress to be she.

Hints—(1) I who am; (2) they who; (3) him; (4) her; (5) her; (6) her

Rule XVII. It and This

Rule XVII (A). आप देखेंगे कि It कर्ता का काम करता है जब वाक्य से समय, दूरी, ऋतु/मौसम या अन्य प्राकृतिक घटना का बोध होता है। ऐसे It को Empty It कहा जाता है क्योंकि इसका कोई अर्थ नहीं होता है। जैसे—

1. It is morning. 2. It is 7 o'clock. 3. It is winter.
4. It is very cold. 5. It is raining. 6. It thunders.

Rule XVII (B). It का प्रयोग Infinitive, Gerund और Clause के बदले में भी होता है—

1. It is easy to say. 2. It is no use crying. 3. It is sad that he is ill.

Rule XVII (C). It का प्रयोग कथन पर जोर देने के लिए भी, वाक्य में कर्ता के समान होता है; जैसे—

1. It is I who called you. 2. It is he who said so.

Rule XVII (D). वाक्य में this कर्ता का काम करता है और इससे किसी व्यक्ति/वस्तु के नाम/पहचान/ परिचय (identity), समीपता आदि का बोध होता है; जैसे—

1. This is a pen. 2. This is a cow.
3. This is my brother. 4. This is 51181.
5. This is All India Radio. 6. This is Voice of America.

It और This के इन कार्यों से यह स्पष्ट हो जाता है कि नाम/परिचय का बोध कराने के लिए This का प्रयोग होना चाहिए, It का नहीं और समय/मौसम आदि अर्थों में It का प्रयोग होना चाहिए, This का नहीं। यही कारण है कि नाम/परिचय जानने के लिए प्रश्नवाचक वाक्यों में This आता है, It नहीं; जैसे—*What is this?*

Rule XVII (E). कुछ वाक्यों में Principal Clause के बाद *it + noun/adjective* का प्रयोग होता है, क्योंकि it के बाद is छिपा रहता है। ऐसे वाक्यों में it को *preparatory it* कहा जाता है। इस प्रकार के वाक्यों की बनावट होती है—

Principal Clause [subject + verb] + it + noun/adjective + infinitive/clause; जैसे—

1. I think that it is wrong to travel without ticket.
   = I think *it is wrong* to travel without ticket.
   = I think *it wrong* to travel without ticket.
2. I consider that it is a pity to waste time.
   = I consider *it is a pity* to waste time.
   = I consider *it a pity* to waste time.

ध्यान दें कि ऐसे वाक्य is के बिना तो लिखे जा सकते हैं, पर it के बिना नहीं। इसलिए इस प्रकार न लिखें—

1. I think wrong to travel without ticket.
2. I consider an honour to work here.

यहाँ think/consider के बाद it का प्रयोग आवश्यक है। इस प्रकार यह स्पष्ट है कि ऐसे वाक्यों में *that* और *is* दोनों का लोप हो जाता है—

1. I consider *that* it *is* my duty to help the poor.
   = I consider it is my duty to help the poor.
   = I consider it my duty to help the poor.

इसे इस प्रकार न लिखें—

I consider my duty to help the poor.

REVISION TEST I

Correct the following sentences.

1. He came with Mohan and myself.
2. Ram and myself will work together.
3. Myself found him stealing.
4. I am not one of those who believe everything I hear.
5. It is meant for you and myself.
6. I, you and he will go soon.
7. It's me who have helped you.
8. I am as good as him.
9. I answered more questions than him.
10. It is strictly between he and I.
11. I help everyone of my sons in their studies.
12. Is she taller than either of her three sisters?
13. The student who you praised so highly, has failed.
14. I do not know whom they are.
15. Everyone of them think that they are right.
16. One shouldn't be proud of his wealth.
17. Either of the five books will serve the purpose.
18. I am one of those who says what I feel.
19. None of the two books will do.
20. Whom do you think is the oldest of the two?
21. Someone gave me this letter but I don't remember whom.
22. It is him who I know full well.
23. The dog who is here it is mine.

24. She told you and I that herself will do the work.
25. He is a man whom I believe is honest.
26. I don't know who I should blame.
27. He is not such a man who can help me.
28. Neither of the eleven players turned up.
29. He who has come late, let him suffer.
30. Your watch is better than that of mine.

Hints—1. and I; 2. and I myself; 3. myself; 4. they hear; 5. and me; 6. You, he and 1; 7. it is I; 8. as he; 9. than he; 10. him and me; 11. his studies; 12. anyone of her three sisters; 13. whom you; 14. who they; 15. thinks that he is right; 16. one's wealth; 17. Anyone of; 18. who say what they; 19. Neither of; 20. who … the older; 21. remember who; 22. he whom; 23. which/that is here is mine; 24. you and me that she herself would; 25. the man who; 26. whom; 27. as can; 28. none of ; 29. He … late should suffer; 30. than mine

REVISION TEST II

Explain why the following sentences are correct or incorrect.

1. Each of us have our own problems.
2. One must take care of his health.
3. Let you and I do it together.
4. I am the person who have started this work.
5. He is one of the greatest poet who has ever lived.
6. None of the two brothers came.
7. It was me who caught the thief.
8. I am not one of they who criticise everything I come across.
9. I have read Plato's writings, who was a great philosopher.
10. I did not read either of the five books.
11. You are the man who wish to help all.
12. I have received a letter and replied to the same.
13. The magistrate and collector have tendered their resignation.
14. He and I are doing their duty well.
15. He, I and you will work together.
16. One who works hard he suceeds.
17. He does not love her wife.
18. Does she love his husband?
19. I consider an honour to serve here.

❐

Chapter VIII

TEST YOURSELF

I. *Correct or justify the following sentences.*

1. Your argument is besides the point.
2. He was prevented to speak.
3. It is strictly between you or I.
4. There is a treaty among the five great powers.
5. The whole property was divided between the three sons.
6. She has no taste in music.
7. It is raining since the last few days.
8. You must return before a week.
9. He insisted me to go there.
10. He is investigating into this case.
11. There is a treaty among these five nations.
12. We should prevent damage and theft of railway property.
13. He was afraid and alarmed at the sound.
14. None but he was called for interview.
15. It's 7 o'clock in my watch.
16. She covered her face by a piece of cloth.
17. She fell in a ditch.
18. He resigned from his post.
19. He resembles to his father.
20. He will come between 7 a.m. to 8 a.m.
21. He came and sat besides his wife.
22. The train is running in time.
23. They started in the morning of the 15th August.
24. He travelled in train but I by horseback.
25. That house was destroyed with fire.
26. All but him had fled away.

II. *Fill in the blanks with a suitable word given in brackets.*

1. The train is running ...... time. [to, in]
2. It ...... raining since Monday. [is, has been]
3. She has been ill ...... one month. [for, since]
4. You have to choose between death ...... disgrace. [or, and]

5. He is disqualified …… . [to compete, from competing]
6. We buy silk …… the metre. [by, with]
7. She will return …… a month. [by, within]
8. He is quick …… figures. [in, at]
9. She is good …… English. [in, at]
10. She died …… cholera. [of, from]
11. She is sitting …… an armchair. [in, on]

❐

PREPOSITIONS

जहाँ हिन्दी में कारक की केवल पाँच-सात विभक्तियों (को, से, में पर आदि) से काम चल जाता है, वहाँ अँगरेजी में दर्जनों Prepositions की सहायता लेनी पड़ती है। हिंदी के एक 'से' के लिए अँगरेजी में with, by, from, for, since आदि Prepositions हैं। कहीं 'से' का अनुवाद with होता है, तो कहीं by और यदि since या for का प्रयोग करना हो, तो एक अजीब आफत ही आ जाती है। यही कारण है कि Prepositions के प्रयोग में इतनी भूलें होती हैं। पर, याद रखें कि Prepositions का शुद्ध प्रयोग जाने बिना आप अँगरेजी भाषा का रसास्वादन कर ही नहीं सकते। इसलिए इनके प्रयोग पर विचार करें।

KINDS OF PREPOSITIONS

Prepositions की सहायता से भिन्न-भिन्न प्रकार के अर्थों का बोध होता है। इसमें प्रमुख ये हैं—

(i) Time [समय]—*at, by, between, before, after, during, in, on, to, from, for, since, throughout, till, until*

इन वाक्यों को देखें—

1. He came at 7 o'clock.
2. He came on Monday.
3. He will start after lunch.
4. She will return before dinner.
5. It has rained for a week.
6. It has been raining since Monday.
7. He will come by 7 o'clock.
8. He will come before 7 o'clock.
9. He will go out during Pujas.
10. He was here throughout summer.

(ii) Place/Position [स्थान/स्थिति]—*at, above, across, against, before, behind, in, on, over, under*

इन वाक्यों को देखें—

1. He is at home.
2. He is in his room.
3. He has no roof above his head.
4. There is an umbrella over his head.
5. There is a cap on his head.
6. Place a ladder against the wall.
7. The thief stood before the judge.
8. Place a ladder against the wall.
9. He is sitting under a tree.

(iii) Direction [दिशा]—*above, into, on, to, towards, up, down*

इन वाक्यों को देखें—

1. He is above me in rank.
2. He climbed up a tree.
3. He fell into a river.
4. He is going to school.
5. He is kind towards the poor.
6. He fired on the enemy.

(iv) Relative Position [संबंधसूचक स्थिति]—*between, among, amongst*

1. There is friendship between him and me.
2. There is unity among the boys.
3. There is a village among the hills.
4. There is no difference amongst us.

(v) Destination [गंतव्य स्थान]—*to, from*

1. He is going to market.
2. He is coming from school.

(vi) (a) State/Condition [दशा/अवस्था]—*at, in, on, under*

(b) Change of State [अवस्था में परिवर्तन]—*into, to*

1. Boys are at play.
2. He is at work.
3. That house is under repair.
4. The case is under consideration.
5. He is in good health.
6. He died in misery.
7. Translate into English.
8. Love turned into hatred.

(vii) Aim/Goal/Purpose/Target [लक्ष्य/उद्देश्य]—*for*

1. He bought a pen for Mohan.
2. I borrowed a book from the library.
3. He died for his society.
4. He lives for others.

(viii) Origin/Source [उत्पत्ति/उद्‌गम/स्रोत]—*from, of*

1. This road runs from Patna to Gaya.
2. I borrowed a book from the library
3. He comes of a rich family.
4. It is a poem of Dinkar.

(ix) Separation [अलग होना]—*from, of, off*

1. Leaves are falling from the tree.
2. He is off duty now.
3. He is away from home.
4. The dog jumped off the chair.
5. He was robbed of his money.

(x) Relation/Possession [संबंध/अधिकार]—*of*

1. This is the house of my friend.
2. He is a servant of my uncle.

(xi) Material/Ingredient [वस्तु/वस्तु का अंश]—*of, from*

1. This chair is made of wood.
2. We make butter from milk.

(xii) Part/Portion [भाग/अंश]—of

1. This is the window of this house.
2. This is the horn of my car.
3. Give me a piece of silk.

(xiii) Means/Instrument [साधन]—*by, in, with, without*

1. He came here by car.
2. This play was written by Mohan.
3. He was struck by lightning.
4. The house was destroyed by fire.
5. It is written in ink.
6. It is written in pencil.
7. He speaks in English.
8. She writes in Hindi.
9. We see with our eyes.
10. We can't see without eyes.

(xiv) Manner [ढंग/तरीका]—*like, with*

1. He is like his father.
2. I look upon this work with pride.
3. He treated me with kindness.
4. He heard me with sympathy.

(xv) Cause [कारण]—*from, of, for, with*

1. He died from loss of blood.
2. He died of cholera.
3. He will suffer for his bad habits.
4. He is sick with fever.
5. Her eyes are red with tears.

(xvi) Measurement/Standard [मानक/मापदंड]—*at, by, for, to*

1. Rice sells at Rs 4/- a kilogram.
2. Mangoes sell two to a rupee.
3. It is ten by my watch.
4. She is rather tall for her age.
5. He is good at painting.
6. She is bad at mathematics.
7. She is good at cooking.
8. He is clever at games.

(xvii) Accompaniment [साथ-साथ, एक साथ]—*with, without*

1. I played with them.
2. He came without his wife.

(xviii) Support/Opposition [पक्ष-विपक्ष]—*for, against*

1. I stand for my friend.
2. I am for the resolution.
3. He is against me.
4. He is against the motion.

(xix) Subject-matter [विषय-वस्तु]—*on, about*

1. I am reading a book on English grammar.
2. I told him about my school.

(xx) Exception [अपवाद]—*but, except*

1. None but I/me can do this work.
2. All except him have done well.

(xxi) Concession [यद्यपि/तथापि]—*in spite of*

1. In spite of poverty, he is happy.
2. In spite of difficulties, he rose high.

Prepositions: Meaning and correct usage

About

(i) के संबंध में—

1. He is careless about his duties.
2. What are you angry about?

(ii) स्थान का भाव—

1. She is walking about the town.
2. Books are lying about the room.

(iii) about + infinitive [कार्य तुरंत होने का भाव]

1. They are about to start.
2. She is about to die.

Above

(i) के ऊपर [स्थान का बोध]

1. The plane is flying above the clouds.
2. She has no roof above her head.

(ii) से परे/से ऊपर

1. She is above suspicion.
2. He married above his position.

Across

(i) के उस पार [स्थान का भाव]

He lives just across the road.

(ii) इस छोर से दूसरी छोर तक

There is a bridge across the river.

After

(i) के बाद [समय का बोध]

We went out after lunch/10 o'clock.

(ii) ठीक बाद में [समय का बोध]

She will go home the day after tomorow.

(iii) के अनुसार/की शैली में

This is a poem after Wordsworth.

(iv) दुहरावट के अर्थ में

We suffer day after day/week after week.

Among and Between

(a) Between के बाद जब दो Nouns या Pronouns आते हैं तब वे and द्वारा जुड़े रहते हैं, or या to के द्वारा नहीं; जैसे—

1. Please see me *between* 7 p.m. *and* 8 p.m.
2. You have to choose *between* death *and* disgrace.
3. One has to choose *between* this *and* that.

इन वाक्यों में and के बदले or या to का प्रयोग अशुद्ध होता। देखिए, इस वाक्य में लेखक ने ऐसी ही भूल की है—

The choice before the two countries lay **between** *a closer union negotiated on equal terms or the severance of the existing connection.* —G M TREVELYAN

यहाँ or के बदले and का प्रयोग होना चाहिए।

(b) Between के बाद कोई एक Plural Noun या Pronoun आता है या दो Nouns/ Pronouns जो and से जुड़े रहते हैं; पर इसके (between के) बाद Distributive 'each' या 'every' का प्रयोग नहीं हो सकता; जैसे—

1. He is between *two horns* of a dilemma.
2. It is between *us*.
3. I am between *two perils*.
4. It is between him *and* me.
5. He is between the devil *and* the deep sea.

अब इन वाक्यों को लें—

1. There is rivalry between *each* boy.
2. The batsman blew a whistle between *every* ball.

यहाँ पहले वाक्य में between के बाद each का और दूसरे में every का प्रयोग हुआ है। यह प्रयोग अशुद्ध है। यदि आप each/every को हटाकर इसके बाद आनेवाले Noun को Plural बना दें, तो वाक्य शुद्ध हो जाएँगे—between boys/balls.

(c) Between के बाद जो and द्वारा जुड़े हुए Nouns/Pronouns आते हैं वे सभी Objective Case में रहते हैं, Nominative में कभी भी नहीं; जैसे—

1. It is between *Ram* and *me*. 2. It is between *him* and *her*.

इन दोनों वाक्यों में and द्वारा जुड़े Nouns या Pronouns Objective Case में हैं, इसलिए ये वाक्य शुद्ध हैं। अब इन्हें देखें—

1. It is between *he* and *I*. 2. It is between *he* and *she*.

ये वाक्य अशुद्ध हैं, क्योंकि यहाँ and से जुड़े Pronouns को Nominative Case में रख दिया गया है। ऐसी भूलों से अवश्य बचें।

(i) इन दोनों ही का अर्थ होता है 'बीच में'; पर इनमें अंतर यह है कि between का अर्थ होता है केवल 'दो के बीच' और among का 'दो से अधिक के बीच'। इसलिए between का प्रयोग दो व्यक्तियों या वस्तुओं के साथ होता है, पर among का दो से अधिक के साथ; जैसे—

1. The money was divided *between* my *two* sons.

2. The money was divided *among* my *three sons.*

यदि यहाँ पहले वाक्य में among का प्रयोग होता और दूसरे में between का, तो भयंकर भूल हो जाती। इसलिए ये वाक्य अशुद्ध हैं—

1. The whole wealth was divided *between* the *five sons.*

2. The whole wealth was divided *among* his *two sons.*

(ii) Between का प्रयोग दो से अधिक के साथ भी होता है, जब उन सब वस्तुओं या व्यक्तियों के बीच परस्पर संबंध या सहयोग (reciprocal relation) का बोध होता है—

... between is always required when aggregation or co-operation is expressed: The **three** *children saved over* **a** *hundred pounds* **between** *them.*

—F T WOOD: *Current English Usage*

नेसफिल्ड साहब का भी ऐसा ही मत है—

But **between** *can be used for more than two things or persons to denote some* **reciprocal action** *or* **relation.** —NESFIELD: *Errors In English Composition*

इन वाक्यों को लें—

1. There is a treaty *between* the *five* great powers.

2. Our choice lies *between* these *four* candidates.

3. There is not much space *between* the *three* points.

इन वाक्यों में among का प्रयोग उचित नहीं होता, क्योंकि यहाँ परस्पर संबंध का भाव झलकता है।

Among and Amongst

इन दोनों के प्रयोग में बहुत अंतर नहीं, पर यह अवश्य कहा जा सकता है कि among का प्रयोग amongst से अधिक होता है। साधारण प्रयोग के लिए आप इस नियम को याद रखें—among या amongst के बाद यदि the आए, तो किसी भी एक का प्रयोग कर सकते हैं; पर यदि उसके बाद vowel आए, तो amongst का ही प्रयोग करना चाहिए—

amonst *the* men; among *the* men; amongst *us.*

इस संबंध में एक महान आचार्य ने अपना विचार इस प्रकार प्रकट किया है—

It may be said with some confidence that (i) **among** *is the normal word, (ii)* **amongst** *is more usual before vowels, but (iii) before* **the** *... the two forms are used quite indifferently.*

—FOWLER

Against

(i) के विरुद्ध/विपरीत

I am *against* this proposal.

(ii) से सटकर [स्थान का बोध]

Put a ladder *against* the tree.

(iii) की तुलना में

There were fifty murders this year *against* a hundred last year.

(iv) की तैयारी में

This is an injection *against* cholera.

At

(i) पर/में [समय का बोध]

1. She will reach *at* 10 o'clock.
2. They came *at* noon/night/midnight.

(ii) पर/में [छोटे स्थान का बोध]

1. She is *at* home.
2. He is *at* school.
3. He lives *at* Patna.

किसी देश के नाम के पहले in आता है, at नहीं, जैसे—

We live *in* India.

(iii) दिशा (direction) का बोध

1. She is looking *at* him.
2. He aimed his gun *at* the thief.

(iv) उम्र (age) का बोध

He left school *at* 10.

(v) अस्थायी रूप से कार्य में लगे रहने का बोध

1. They are *at* work = They are working now.
2. Boys are *at* play = Boys are playing now.

स्थायी कार्य/व्यवसाय के साथ in का प्रयोग होता है, जैसे—

1. He is *in* the army.
2. She is *in* politics.

(vi) कीमत/दर [price/rate]

1. Rice sells *at* Rs 5/- a kilogram.
2. I got this book *at* Rs 25.

(vii) गति (speed) की दर

The car is running *at* forty kilometres an hour.

(viii) के कारण [कारण का भाव]

We are delighted *at* your success.

On and At

समय का बोध कराने के लिए on का प्रयोग खास दिन (day) या तिथि (date) के पहले होता है, पर at का घण्टे (hour) के पहले; जैसे—

1. I will start *on* Monday.
2. I will start *on* the 2nd June.
3. I will start *at* 5 o'clock.

यहाँ पहले दो वाक्यों में at और तीसरे में on का प्रयोग अशुद्ध होता।

On और at से स्थान का भी बोध इस प्रकार होता है—

1. There is a book *on* the table.
2. There is no hair *on* his head.
3. My son is *at* school.
4. She is *at* home.

Beside and Besides

Beside का अर्थ होता है, 'बगल में', 'समीप' या 'बाहर' (by the side of या outside) और इससे स्थान का बोध होता है; पर besides का अर्थ होता है 'अतिरिक्त' (in addition to); जैसे—

1. There is a river *beside* my residence.
2. Your argument is *beside* the point.
3. *Besides* English, he knows many other languages.

अब इन वाक्यों को देखें—

1. He sat *besides* me.
2. Your answer is *besides* the point.
3. *Beside* a pen, he has a watch.

यहाँ पहले दो वाक्यों में *beside* का और तीसरे में *besides* का प्रयोग होना चाहिए।

Before

(i) से पहले [समय का बोध]

He will get back *before* 9 a.m./lunch.

(ii) से पहले [स्थान का बोध]

A comes *before* B.

(iii) के सामने [स्थान का बोध]

He stood *before* the judge.

Behind

(i) के पीछे [स्थान का बोध]

He is walking *behind* his mother.

(ii) के पीछे [तुलना का बोध]

He is *behind* others in his class.

By

(i) के समीप/के किनारे [से सटा हुआ]

1. He sat *by* me.
2. Here is a temple *by* this river.

(ii) तक [समय के पहले]

1. He will get back *by* 9 a.m.
2. He should be here *by* the evening.

(iii) यातायात का साधन [means of travel/transport]

1. We travel *by* car/bus/train/boat/ship/taxi/cycle.

2. We travel *by* land/sea/air.

3. We send something *by* post/hand.

NOTE—We travel *on* foot/*on* horseback.

By and In

जब car/taxi/bus के पहले a/an या a/an + adjective आता है तब उसे एक विशेष (special) प्रकार का यातायात का साधन माना जाता है और इसलिए उस साधन के पहले in आता है; by नहीं, जैसे—

1. He came *in* a new car. 2. She came *in* a yellow taxi.

By and On

इसी प्रकार, जब cycle के पहले a/an या a/an + adjective आता है, तब इसके पहले on का प्रयोग होता है; by का नहीं, जैसे—

1. He came *on* his own cycle/bike. 2. She came *on* a new cycle/bike.

(iv) By and With

सजीव साधन/कार्यकर्ता के साथ by आता है—

1. Hamlet was written *by* Shakespeare.
2. The Taj Mahal was built *by* Shahjehan.
3. He was beaten *by* his teacher.

पर निर्जीव साधन के साथ with का प्रयोग होता है—

1. He was beaten *with* a cane.
2. We see *with* our eyes.

NOTE—जब निर्जीव साधन सजीव कार्यकर्ता के समान कार्य करता है, तब इसके पहले by का प्रयोग होता है—

1. Roads are lighted *by* electricity.
2. That house was destroyed *by* fire.
3. He was killed *by* lightning.
4. We pay wages *by* cheque. [but in cash]

(v) माप/तौल/दर का बोध by के द्वारा इस प्रकार होता है—

1. We hire a taxi/scooter *by* the hour.
2. We pay wages *by* the day.
3. We buy eggs *by* the dozen.
4. We buy petrol *by* the litre.
5. This house is 20 ft. *by* 15 ft.

(vi) शरीर के किसी अंग को साधन की तरह प्रयोग करने पर उसके पहले by आता है—

1. I caught him *by* the neck.
2. I seized him *by* the hair.

(vii) के अनुसार का भाव

It is nine *by* my watch.

(viii) शपथ लेने का भाव

I swear *by* God.

(ix) तुलना का भाव

We won *by* three goals to one.

In and Into

In

(i) में [स्थान का बोध]

1. He lives *in* a village/*in* India.
2. He is sitting *in* an easy chair. [but, sitting *on* a chair without arms]
3. She is lying *in* bed. [but sitting *on* the bed]

(ii) में [समय का बोध]

He will come back *in* an hour/*in* a week.

He will come *in* the morning/evening.

(iii) में [पोशाक में]

He is *in* white/black.

(iv) में [अवस्था का बोध]

1. He is *in* good health.
2. He is *in* tears.

(v) में [साधन का बोध]

1. It is written *in* ink/pencil.
2. It is printed *in* two colours.

(vi) में [स्थायी कार्य/पेशा का बोध]

He is *in* the army/navy.

Into

(i) में [बाहर से भीतर की ओर गति]

1. He came *into* the house/garden.
2. She fell *into* a ditch.

(ii) में [दशा/अवस्था का परिवर्तन]

1. The *rain* has changed *into* snow.
2. Translate this passage *into* English.

In and At

Morning/evening/afternoon के पहले in आता है, पर night/midnight के पहले at का प्रयोग होता है। इन वाक्यों को देखें—

She will get back *in* the morning.

She will get back *at* night/midnight.

In and Within

जब वाक्य में Future Tense का प्रयोग होता है और period of time आता है तब in के **बाद** का बोध होता है और within से **पहले** का, जैसे—

He will come *in* a week. [एक सप्ताह के बाद]

He will come *within* a week. [एक सप्ताह के पहले]

इसलिए Future Tense में Period of Time के साथ after का प्रयोग इस प्रकार न करें—

He will come after a week.

In and After

Future Tense में Point of Time के साथ after का प्रयोग उचित है, जैसे—

He will come *after* 6 p.m./after sunset.

Past Tense में Period of Time के साथ in/after का प्रयोग इस प्रकार होता है—

He came *in* a week/*after* a week.

Past Tense में Point of Time के साथ after का प्रयोग इस प्रकार होता है—

He came *after* 9 a.m.

In and On

जब किसी वस्तु के area का बोध होता है, तब in आता है, पर जब इससे volume का भाव व्यक्त होता है, तब on आता है, जैसे—

area

in the world, *in* the town/village, *in* the park/field, *in* the room

volume

on the wall, *on* the roof/ceiling, *on* the farm, *on* the field

इन वाक्यों को देखें—

1. Horses are grazing *in* the field. [area]
2. Players are practising *on* the field. [volume/surface]

For

(i) के लिए [उद्देश्य का भाव]

I bought sweets *for* children/*for* them.

(ii) के लिए/की ओर

He set out *for* home.

(iii) के कारण

1. They danced *for* joy.
2. He got a prize *for* bravery.

(iv) राशि/संख्या का भाव

1. I paid Rs 10/- *for* this book.
2. The score is 250 runs *for* five wickets.

(v) पसंद का भाव

1. He has a liking *for* fish.
2. He has a taste *for* music.

(vi) समर्थन का भाव

I am *for* this proposal.

(vii) के रहते हुए भी [in spite of]

For all his wealth he is unhappy.

(viii) समय का बोध [period of time]

1. She has gone home *for* a week.
2. He stayed here *for* a few hours.

For and Since [से अब तक]

इन दोनों ही का अर्थ 'से' होता है। इनसे समय का बोध होता है, और यह भी बोध होता है कि जो काम भूतकाल में आरंभ हुआ था वह अभी भी जारी है। इनके प्रयोग के संबंध में इन नियमों का ध्यान रखें—

(i) For और Since के पहले Present Perfect/Past Perfect/Present Perfect Continuous Tense आता है।

(ii) For के साथ period of time (अवधि) का प्रयोग होता है और इससे यह बोध होता है कि कार्य कितने समय तक चला। For के साथ period of time बताने के लिए इनका प्रयोग होता है—

for + numeral adjective + hours/minutes/days

for + numeral adjective + week/month/year/a long time

(iii) Since के साथ point of time (निश्चित समय-सूचक शब्द) आता है और इससे यह बोध होता है कि कार्य कबसे आरंभ हुआ। Since के साथ point of time बताने के लिए इनका प्रयोग होता है—

Since + morning/evening/night/o'clock

Since + name of the day/month/year

Since + birth/death/marriage/arrival/departure

Since + name of an event/festival

इन वाक्यों को देखें—

1. It has been raining *since* 7 o'clock/morning.
2. It has been raining *for* five hours.
3. She has been working here *since* 1980.
4. She has been working here *for* five years.
5. I have'nt seen him *since* his birthday/marriage.

6. He has been ill *for* a week.

7. He has been ill *since* Monday.

8. I haven't written to him *since* May.

9. I haven't written to him *for* over a month.

अब इन वाक्यों को देखें—

1. He *is* here *since* Monday.

2. He has been ill *since* a week.

यहाँ पहले वाक्य में Monday से पता चलता है कि काम कब से शुरू हुआ, पर since के पहले Present Simple Tense का प्रयोग हुआ है, जो अशुद्ध है। यहाँ Present Perfect (has been) का प्रयोग होना चाहिए—

He has been here *since* Monday.

दूसरे वाक्य में since के पहले Present Perfect Tense का प्रयोग तो हुआ है पर इसके बाद a week का जिससे 'कितने समय' (Period of Time) का बोध होता है, 'कब से' (from when) का नहीं। इसलिए यहाँ since के बदले for का प्रयोग होना चाहिए—

He has been ill *for* a week.

अब इन वाक्यों को लें—

1. It is raining *since* last Thursday.

2. The school *was closed since* yesterday.

3. My father has been ill *since three* days.

4. The results have been known *since two* days.

यहाँ पहले वाक्य में is के बदले has been और दूसरे में was closed के बदले has been closed का प्रयोग होना चाहिए। तीसरे और चौथे में since के बदले for का प्रयोग होना चाहिए, क्योंकि three days/two days से Period of Time का बोध होता है, Point of Time का नहीं।

For and During

For और During—इन दोनों से Period of Time (अवधि) का बोध होता है, पर इनमें एक अंतर है। For के साथ Period of Time अनिश्चित होता है, पर During के साथ वह निश्चित (जाना हुआ) रहता है; जैसे—

1. *for* an hour, *for* a month, *for* ever, *for* a long time

2. *during* summer/winter/night,
during Puja holidays/Christmas,
during one's childhood, during 1942.

Since and From

इन दोनों ही का अर्थ 'से' होता है और इनका प्रयोग Point of Time के साथ होता है। इनमें अंतर यह है कि since का प्रयोग केवल Past Time बतलाने के लिए होता है, पर from का प्रयोग सभी

Tenses में होता है। इसलिए since का प्रयोग Future Tense का साथ करना अशुद्ध है। इन वाक्यों को लें—

1. He has been ill *since* Tuesday.
2. He will be absent *from* Tuesday.
3. He was absent *from* Tuesday to Thursday.

ये सभी वाक्य शुद्ध हैं, पर यह वाक्य अशुद्ध है—

He *will* be absent *since* Tuesday.

Last week/month/year के साथ since आता है, क्योंकि इससे Point of Time का बोध होता है, जैसे—

I have been ill since last week [not, **for**]

The last + week/month/year के साथ for का प्रयोग होता है, क्योंकि इससे Period of Time का बोध होता है, जैसे—

I have been ill for the last week. [not, **since**]

NOTE (a)—past simple + for

जब वाक्य में past simple के साथ for + period of time आता है तब इससे यह बोध होता है कि कार्य भूतकाल में समाप्त हो गया, जैसे—

1. I lived in Mumbai for five years.
   [पर अब मुंबई में नहीं रहता हूँ।]
2. I have lived in Mumbai for five years.
   [मुंबई में अभी भी रहता हूँ।]

NOTE (b)—present/future + for

जब for का अर्थ **के लिए** होता है तब वाक्य में present या future tense का प्रयोग इस प्रकार होता है—

1. She is going away for a week.
2. He will work for six hours a day.

NOTE (c)—distance/duration का भाव व्यक्त होने पर for का प्रायः लोप हो जाता है, जैसे—

1. We walked ten kilometres. [not, **for** ten kilometres]
2. The meeting lasted three hours [not, **for** three hours]
3. I stayed there one month. [not, **for** one month]

NOTE (d)—noun/verb + for noun + for/verb + for से इन अर्थों का बोध होता है—

in place of, in exchange for, on behalf of, in favour of, for the sake of, for the purpose of, in spite of, in the direction of

इन वाक्यों को लें—

1. I took him *for* a thief.
2. I bought a pen *for* Rs 5/-
3. Let us die *for* our country.
4. I bought a pen *for* Ram.
5. He left *for* Mumbai.
6. *For* all his wealth he is not happy.

Of/Off

Of

(i) स्रोत [origin/source]

He comes *of* a poor family.

(ii) कारण [cause]

1. He died *of* cholera. 2. She died *of* hunger.

(iii) किसी वस्तु का अंग

1. This is a nib *of* this pen. 2. These are the doors *of* this room.

(iv) माप-तौल

1. I want a piece *of* paper. 2. He bought a litre *of* petrol.

(v) बहुत में से एक

He is a friend *of* mine.

(vi) दूरी [distance]

The bus stop is *within* a kilometre *of* my house.

(vii) वस्तु [material]

1. This house is made *of* brick/stone/wood.
2. This cloth is made *of* cotton/silk.

Of and From

Of और from इन दोनों से material (वस्तु/सामान) का बोध होता है, पर इनमें एक अंतर है। इन वाक्यों को लें—

1. This house is *made of* brick. 2. Wine is *made from* grapes.

Make of से केवल यह बोध होता है वह वस्तु ज्यों-का-त्यों रह जाती है। पर *make from* से यह बोध होता है कि वह वस्तु दूसरी वस्तु में बदल जाती है। इन वाक्यों को भी देखें—

1. Butter is made from milk. 2. A bridge is made of steel.

Off

Off से अलग होने (separation) का भाव व्यक्त होता है—

1. He is *off* duty now. 2. The dog jumped *off* the chair.

On

(i) पर [स्थान का बोध]

1. He is sitting *on* a chair. 2. There is a ring *on* his finger.

(ii) को/पर [समय का बोध]

1. He will go home *on* Sunday. 2. The train arrived *on* time.
3. She reached *on* the morning of the Ist January.

NOTE (a)—In time का अर्थ होता है समय से कुछ पहले, पर on time का अर्थ होता है बिलकुल ठीक या निर्धारित समय पर।

NOTE (b)—Morning/evening/afternoon के पहले in आता है, पर जब इनके साथ of + date का प्रयोग होता है, तब इनके पहले on आता है, in नहीं, जैसे—

1. He came here *in* the morning.
2. He came here *on* the morning of the Ist January.

(iii) की ओर [दिशा का बोध]

1. He smiled *on* her.
2. She drew a dagger *on* him.

(iv) आधार या कारण का बोध

I acted *on* the lawyer's advice.

(v) कार्य/व्यवसाय का बोध

He is *on* tour/business.

(vi) के विषय/संबंध में

This is a book *on* grammar.

(vii) सदस्य या आधिकारिक रूप से रहने का भाव—

1. He is *on* the staff of the AIR.
2. I am *on* the finance committee.

To

(i) को [to + object]

1. He wrote *to* me.
2. She replied *to* my letter.
3. I spoke *to* him.
4. I gave a pen *to* each of them.

(ii) की ओर [दिशा का बोध]

He is going *to* college/market.

(iii) तक [स्थान का बोध]

He will go from Agra *to* Delhi.

(iv) तक [समय का बोध]

He works from 7 a.m. *to* 11 a.m.

(v) तुलना का बोध

1. This is superior/inferior *to* that.
2. We won by six goals *to* three.

(vi) के प्रति

It is our duty *to* our parents/teachers.

(vii) पहले [समय का बोध]

1. It is a quarter *to* nine.
2. It is ten *to* seven.

(viii) पर

He invited me *to* tea/lunch/dinner. [not, **at**]

With/Without

(i) से/के द्वारा [निर्जीव साधन का भाव]

1. He writes *with* a pen.
2. She is writing *with* a pencil.
3. We can't write *without* a pen.
4. We can't see *without* eyes.

NOTE—In and With

He is writing *with* a pencil.

He is writing *in* pencil.

जब pencil के पहले a आता है, तब इसके साथ with का प्रयोग होता है, पर जब pencil के पहले a नहीं आता, अर्थात जब इसे एक uncountable noun माना जाता है, तब इसके साथ in आता है।

(ii) के साथ/साथ-साथ का भाव

1. He is playing *with* a cat.
2. He came here *with* his wife.

(iii) से [कारण का भाव]

1. He is trembling *with* fear.
2. Her eyes are red *with* tears.

(iv) से [संबंध का भाव]

I have nothing to do *with* her.

(v) तरीका [manner] का भाव

1. He fought *with* courage.
2. He won the race *with* ease.

(vi) गुण/विशेषता का भाव

He is a boy *with* long hair.

She is a girl *with* big blue eyes.

(vii) जुदाई (separation) का भाव

I parted *with* him at the station.

(viii) सहमति/विरोध का भाव

1. I agree *with* him.
2. I will fight *with* the enemy.

(ix) के रहते हुए भी [in spite of]

With all his wealth he is unhappy.

(x) के साथ [समय का भाव]

It is good to rise *with* the sun.

Verb/Adjective + Preposition + Gerund

कुछ ऐसे Verbs और Adjectives होते हैं जिनके बाद Infinitive कभी भी नहीं आता। वैसी अवस्था में Infinitive के बदले Preposition आता है और Preposition के बाद सदा Gerund (verb + ing) आता है। इस प्रकार, वाक्य की बनावट होती है—preposition + verb + ing. ये हैं—

abstain from, aim at, assist in, bent on, confident of, debar from, desirous of, desist from, despair of, disqualified from, dissuade (one) from, excel in, excuse for, fortunate in, hinder (one) from, hopeful of, insist on, intend on, meditate on, negligent in, passion for, perceive in, persist in, prevent from, (to take) pride in, prohibit (one) from, proud of, refrain from, repent of, succeed in, successful in, think of

इस सूची की सहायता से याद रखें कि किस Verb/Adjective के बाद कौन उपयुक्त Preposition आता है और तब इन Prepositions के बाद Gerund का प्रयोग अवश्य करें। कुछ लोग ऐसे Verbs और Adjectives के बाद Preposition के बदले Infinitive का प्रयोग कर देते हैं, जो निस्सन्देह अशुद्ध है। इन वाक्यों को देखें—

1. He prevented me *to do* it.
2. He refrains *to do* it.
3. He is disqualified *to compete.*
4. I am desirous *to go.*
5. I am hopeful *to pass.*
6. He persists *to do so.*

इन वाक्यों में Infinitive का प्रयोग अशुद्ध है। उपयुक्त Preposition का प्रयोग इस प्रकार करें, उसके बाद Gerund का—*preposition + gerund,* जैसे—

1. He prevented me *from doing* it.
2. He refrains *from doing* it.
3. He is disqualified *from competing.*
4. I am desirous *of going.*
5. I am hopeful *of passing.*
6. He persists *in doing* so.

NOTE—Aim के बाद preposition + gerund (aim at returning) के बदले aim + infinitive का प्रयोग आजकल काफी तेजी से चल पड़ा है, जो एक अमेरिकी प्रयोग (American usage) है। शुद्ध अँगरेजी प्रयोग (British idiom) के अनुसार aim at + verb + ing होना चाहिए, aim to + verb नहीं, जैसाकि एक महान व्याकरणाचार्य का विचार है—

> *The Verb in the metaphorical sense of purpose or design or endeavour is idiomatically followed by* **at** *with the gerund and not by* **to** *with the infinitive ... . And the infinitive construction, though not good British, appears to be good American, since it is certainly a favourite with Emerson ... .*
>
> —FOWLER: *Modern English Usage*

मेरे जानते aim के बाद Infinitive का प्रयोग (aim to) अब केवल अमेरिका तक ही सीमित नहीं रह गया है। अँगरेजी के महान लेखकों ने भी इसको अपना लिया है। F R Leavis और T S Eliot साहब ने भी *aim to be/aim to return* का प्रयोग किया है—

> *Our second danger is to associate tradition with the immovable; to think of it as something hostile to all change; to* **aim to return** *to some previous condition which we imagine as having been capable of preservation in perpetuity, instead of* **aiming to stimulate** *the life which produced that condition in its time.* —T S ELIOT

Fowler साहब तथा अन्य आचार्यों के अनुसार यहाँ aim to return के बदले aim at returning और aiming to stimulate के बदले aiming at stimulating होना चाहिए। मेरी समझ में इस प्रयोग को अब Americanism कहकर टाल देना उचित नहीं। जब अँगरेजी के महान लेखकों ने इसे अपनाया है और साहित्य में इसे सम्मानपूर्वक स्थान दिया है, तो उचित यह है कि व्याकरण भी इसे ग्रहण कर ले, क्योंकि व्याकरण और प्रयोग के बीच जितना अंतर बढ़ता है वह उस भाषा के लिए उतना ही हानिकारक सिद्ध होता है। फिर भी, यह तो मानना ही पड़ेगा कि aim के बाद preposition + gerund का प्रयोग Infinitive से अधिक अच्छा है और प्रयोग में अधिकतर यही मिलता है।

EXERCISE

Correct the following sentences.

(1) Who can prevent me to go there? (2) Would yu assist me to do it? (3) He is bent to ruin himself. (4) Ram is confident to win. (5) I cannot hinder you to go there. (6) He is negligent to attend the class. (7) I am proud to have a friend like you. (8) He repented to do it. (9) He succeeded to do this work. (10) I have a passion to learn new things. (11) I prohibited him to do that work. (12) I insisted him to leave the place.

Hints—(1) from going; (2) in doing; (3) on ruining; (4) of winning; (5) from going; (6) in attending; (7) of having; (8) of doing; (9) in doing; (10) for learning; (11) from doing; (12) insisted on his leaving

Ellipsis in Preposition

Preposition के संबंध में आप एक और बात का ध्यान रखें। वाक्य में दो या दो से अधिक शब्दों को जोड़ने पर उनके लिए एक ही Preposition का प्रयोग होता है, यदि वह Preposition उनमें से प्रत्येक शब्द के लिए उपयुक्त (appropriate) हो। पर, यदि वे ऐसे शब्द हों जिनमें से प्रत्येक के लिए वह उपयुक्त नहीं हो (एक के लिए उपयुक्त और दूसरे के लिए नहीं), तो आप प्रत्येक शब्द के लिए उपयुक्त Preposition का अलग-अलग प्रयोग करें, उन सबके लिए एक ही (common) Preposition का नहीं, जैसे—

We should prevent *damage to* and *theft of* railway property.

यहाँ दो Nouns ('damage' और 'theft') को and से जोड़ा गया है। आप जानते हैं कि damage के बाद to आता है, पर theft के बाद of इन दोनों शब्दों के लिए अलग-अलग उपयुक्त Prepositions हैं। इसलिए इन दोनों ही Prepositions का प्रयोग किया गया है—damage to and theft of.

आप ऐसा नहीं लिख सकते—

We should prevent damage and theft *of* railway property.

यहाँ 'of' theft के लिए तो उपयुक्त है, पर damage के लिए नहीं। अब इस वाक्य को देखें—

He is not only hopeful but also confident *of* success.

यहाँ hopeful तथा confident दोनों ही के लिए एक Preposition 'of' का प्रयोग हुआ है, जो शुद्ध है, क्योंकि यह Preposition दोनों ही के लिए उपयुक्त है—of (hopeful + confident). एक-दो और उदाहरण लें—

1. He was neither ashamed nor sorry *for* his deeds.
2. He has interest and passion *for* sports.

ये दोनों वाक्य अशुद्ध हैं। पहले वाक्य में एक ही Preposition 'for' का प्रयोग किया गया है जो sorry के लिए तो उपयुक्त है, पर ashamed के लिए नहीं, क्योंकि ashamed के बाद of आता है। यहाँ 'for' common factor नहीं है। इसलिए इस वाक्य की बनावट इस प्रकार की होनी चाहिए—

He was neither *ashamed of* nor *sorry for* his deeds.

दूसरे वाक्य में भी 'for' common factor नहीं है, क्योंकि interest के बाद in आता है, for नहीं। अतः, इस वाक्य की बनावट इस प्रकार की होनी चाहिए—

He has *interest in* and *passion for* sports.

EXERCISE

Correct the following sentences.

(1) Please listen and reflect on this matter. (2) He was afraid and alarmed at the sound. (3) I neither object nor approve of it. (4) Let 4 be added or subtracted from 8. (5) It added rather than detracted from its beauty.

Hints—(1) listen to; (2) afraid of; (3) object to; (4) added to; (5) added to

Transitive Verb and Preposition

Transitive Verb के साथ Preposition का प्रयोग उचित नहीं; जैसे—

1. The poet describes *about* nature.
2. He discussed *on* this problem.

इन वाक्यों में 'describes' और 'discussed' Transitive Verbs हैं। इसलिए पहले वाक्य में about और दूसरे में on का प्रयोग अशुद्ध है। अब इन वाक्यों को देखें—

1. He investigated into the case.
2. He criticised upon my action.
3. He resembles to his mother.
4. I recommended for him.
5. I did not catch up his words.
6. He resigned from his post.

इन वाक्यों में into/upon/to/for/up/from का प्रयोग अनावश्यक है।

EXERCISE

Correct the following sentences.

(1) I asked from him a question. (2) A wife must love to her husband. (3) The conference discussed on the merits of the issue. (4) In these lines the poet has described about death. (5) I will investigate into the case. (6) He forgot about me. (7) He signed to the deed. (7) It does not answer to my purpose.

Hints—(1) asked him; (2) love her; (3) discussed the merits; (4) described death; (5) investigate the; (6) forgot me; (7) signed the deed; (8) answer my purpose

'But' and the Case

But का अर्थ जब *except* होता है, तब इसका प्रयोग Conjunction और Preposition दोनों ही प्रकार से होता है। इसलिए इसके बाद Nominative और Objective दोनों में किसी का भी प्रयोग शुद्ध है। हाँ, आधुनिक अँगरेजी में but के बाद आनेवाले Noun/Pronoun को Nominative Case में रखा जाता है, क्योंकि इसका प्रयोग Conjunction की भाँति हो रहा है। पर, इसका अर्थ यह नहीं कि but के बाद Noun/Pronoun को Objective Case में रखना अशुद्ध है। वास्तव में, बोलचाल की भाषा में, और खासकर American usage के अनुसार but के बाद अधिकतर Objective Case का ही प्रयोग होता है। इस संबंध में इन मतों पर विचार करें—

In colloquial use 'me', 'us', etc., are more common after 'but' than 'I', 'we', etc., and are equally correct. —*The Shorter Oxford Dictionary*

In Modern English the uses of 'but' followed by nouns and pronouns are regarded by most writers as conjunctive, although use as a preposition before pronouns is still prevalent in the spoken language, especially when the pronoun is in the final position. —*Webster's International Dictionary*

The answer is that **but** *was originally a preposition meaning outside; but is now usually made a conjunction, the Subjective Case being preferred after it when admissible ...* **all but he had fled** *exemplifies the normal modern, literary use,* **All but him** *is used by those who either do not know or do not care whether it is right or not, and accordingly it is* **still good colloquial** ... .—FOWLER: *Modern English Usage*

Custom has sanctioned the ungrammatical phrase **but he, but she, but they.** *But none need be afraid to say* **but him, but her, but them** *which would be far better grammar.* —NESFIELD: *Errors In English Composition*

इन सभी आचार्यों ने स्वीकार किया है कि but के बाद Nominative और Objective में से किसी एक का प्रयोग शुद्ध है—but him या but he. केवल इतना ही अंतर है कि but के बाद Nominative Case (but he) आधुनिक साहित्यिक प्रयोग (modern literary use) है, क्योंकि अब but को अधिकतर Conjunction ही समझा जाता है और but के बाद Objective Case (but him) बोलचाल का प्रयोग (colloquial) है, क्योंकि कुछ लोग अभी भी but को Preposition ही मानते हैं। ये दोनों ही प्रयोग शुद्ध हैं, पर यदि शुद्ध आधुनिक व्याकरण की दृष्टि से देखा जाए तो but के बाद Nominative Case का प्रयोग Objective Case से अधिक अच्छा है; जैसा कि Fowler

साहब ने भी बताया है। Nesfield साहब का विचार है कि but him/but her आदि but he/but she से अच्छा है, क्योंकि but she/but he आदि ungrammatical हैं। पर वास्तव में इनका यह विचार न तो युक्तिसंगत है और न आधुनिक ही, क्योंकि जैसा ऊपर कहा गया है, आजकल but का प्रयोग अधिकतर Conjunction की भाँति हो चला है। मेरा तो विचार है कि आप Fowler साहब के मतानुसार चलें और but him तथा but he दोनों ही को शुद्ध मान लें—पहले को प्रयोग की दृष्टि से और दूसरे को आधुनिक व्याकरण की दृष्टि से। इन दोनों में बेहतर कौन है—यह प्रश्न उठाना ठीक नहीं, क्योंकि यहाँ एक बहुत बड़ा प्रश्न उठ सकता है कि व्याकरण और प्रयोग में अधिक अच्छा या बड़ा कौन है। सबसे अच्छा विचार तो यह है कि व्याकरण और प्रयोग एक-दूसरे के पूरक हैं, शत्रु नहीं। इसी आधार पर इन दोनों वाक्यों को शुद्ध मानें—

1. All *but him* had fled away. 2. All *but he* had fled away.

Position of Preposition

Prepositons किसी Noun/Pronoun के पहले आते हैं और उनके बीच संबंध स्थापित करते हैं। पुरानी परिभाषा की दृष्टि से Preposition का स्थान Nouns/Pronouns के पहले रहता है। क्यों? इसलिए कि Pre का अर्थ होता है 'पहले' और position का अर्थ होता है 'स्थान', पर आधुनिक अँगरेजी में इन अवस्थाओं में Preposition का स्थान Nouns/Pronouns के बाद रहता है—

(i) Interrogative Pronouns के साथ; जैसे—

1. Who are you thinking *about*? 2. Who are you speaking *to*?
3. What are you looking *at*?

(ii) Relative Pronouns (object) के लोप होने पर; जैसे—

1. The boy you are looking *at* is my brother.
2. This is the book I told you *about*.

. . . .

EXERCISE

I. *Make five sentences like the following.*

1. Which train will you go by?
2. The man you were talking to is my brother.

EXERCISE WORKED OUT

[Exercise from Nesfield's Grammar]

(A)

1. I acquit you *of* all complicity in that crime; and hope you will be compensated *for* the annoyance entailed *upon* you *by* the groundless imputation.
2. I was horrified *at* the sight *of* so much distress.
3. He did not die *of* cholera but *from* the effects *of* overexposure *to* the sun *at* an unhealthy time *of* the year.

4. This shopkeeper deals *in* grain, but he did not deal honestly *by* me and I shall have no more dealings *with* him in future.
5. You will have to answer *to* me *for* your misconduct.
6. Forty students competed *with* one another *for* a single scholarship.
7. I must consult *with* you *on* that matter shortly.
8. Do not exult offensively *in* the victory you have won *over* your rival.
9. He is not possessed *of* much wisdom but possessed *with* a very high notion *of* his own importance.
10. Will you entrust me *with* that letter? No, I will entrust nothing *to* you.
11. Always be prepared *for* the worst.
12. That motive prevails *with* me.
13. I prevailed *on* him to make the attempt, but he could not prevail *over* his adversary.
14. I rejoiced not only *in* my own success, but also *at* yours.
15. We must provide *for* our children *against* the evil day.
16. Some men stick *to* their point.
17. Why do you stare me *in* the face? It is bad manners to stare *at* one in that manner.
18. The ship touched *at* Gibralter. He touched *upon* the subject of tides.
19. He supplied money *to* the men; and they supplied his horses *with* provender.
20. He could smile *at* their threats, for fortune continued to smile *on* him.
21. They proceeded *with* the business that they had commenced yesterday, before they proceeded *to* the consideration *of* any new questions.
22. Do not live *for* riches, but whatever you live *for*, live *by* honest labour; and if you have to live *on* a small income, live *within* your means.
23. He is labouring *under* a misapprehension, but he thinks he is labouring *on* a good cause and *for* the public welfare.
24. He once laid me *under* an obligation, and therefore, I am very unwilling to lay the blame *of* this affair *to* his charge.
25. He not only intruded *into* my house but *upon* my leisure, for I was engaged *at* that time *in* reading an interesting book.
26. The railways intersect *with* each other *at* this place.
27. Let me intercede *with* you *for* my friend.
28. I enquired *of* him *concerning* that matter.
29. He is impressed *with* that notion, and he desires to impress it *on* me.

(B)

1. The river *to* which I went *with* my brother abounds *in* fish; we took a boat and rowed *across* the stream *to* the opposite bank.
2. He promised to abide *by* the contract, and they relied *on* his honour *for* its fulfilment. But they were disappointed *of* their hopes, and found they could never trust their work *to* him again.

3. He lives *at* small cost, and he does so *by* abstaining *from* every kind of luxury and accustoming himself *to* humble fare such as is suitable *to* a person *of* small income.
4. The person who stood *before* the Judge yesterday was accused *of* throwing a stone *at* his neighbour's window, but nothing more came *of* the matter, and he was acquitted *of* the charge imputed *to* him.
5. A man *of* honour will adhere *to* his convictions, and act *from* a sense of duty, even if men rail *at* him and think him weak *of* understanding and wanting *in* common sense.
6. The intentions *of* that man admit *of* no doubt; we must agree *to* his terms, whether we approve *of* them or not, and there is no reason to be anxious *about* the result.
7. Aim *at* doing your duty *at* all risks, and do not be uneasy *in* mind *about* the consequences.
8. He was much alarmed *at* what he had just heard; and alluded *to* it as soon as he arrived *at* my house and alighted *from* his carriage.
9. The ship stopped a little way *off* the shore and an experienced man was at once appointed *to* the post *of* pilot *for* bringing her *into* port.
10. He had a great affection *for* his parents; but he had no taste *for* hard work and was not attentive *to* his studies.
11. One man complained *to* the Magistrate of A's dishonesty; another brought a complaint against A *about* some debt; in fact. A has made many enemies *for* himself.
12. When you attend school, attend *to* your studies. What has been the cause *of* your idleness, hitherto? Surely there was no just cause *for* such laziness.
13. He took advantage *of* my ignorance, but he gained no real advantage *over* me *in* the end.
14. I am vexed *with* him *for* what he has done.
15. A man is adapted *for* any occupation which is adapted *to* his capacities.
16. I am annoyed *with* him *for* saying that; and I am not easily annoyed *at* trifles.

(C)

1. Whatever you decide *on* stick *to* it and do your best *under* difficulties.
2. I understand *from* all I hear that, though he despairs *of* success, nothing will deter him *from* his purpose.
3. I differ *with* you *at* the exact point *in* which dogs differ *from* wolves *in* shape or kind. But there is no difference *of* opinion *as to* their comparative fierceness.
4. He is so weak that all food disagrees *with* him. Care must be taken that he does not die *from* weakness.
5. He was deprived *of* that very thing *in* which he delighted most.
6. I depended *on* his coming *at* four o'clock; but *notwithstanding* all the hopes I had formed he deviated *from* his purpose and did nothing to defend me *from* injustice.
7. I disapprove *of* your way *of* working, and must, therefore, dispense *with* your services.

8. A blind man cannot distinguish light *from* darkness. Death does not distinguish *between* the rich and the poor.
9. I can divide this apple *between* two persons, but it is too small to be divided *among* forty; for it cannot be divided *into* forty parts.
10. When they had disposed *of* all their wares, there was a dispute *about* the profits, each man differing *with* the other.
11. Dissuade him *from* this folly, if you can; but I fear he is weak *in* his head *from* constant overwork and anxiety.
12. I will have nothing to do *with* a man who tries to domineer *over* everyone and cavils *at* everything which does not coincide *with* his own opinion.
13. More things are wrought *by* prayer than this world dreams *of*.
14. He dwells *among* a simple-minded people, *at* the Kalpi village *in* the northern part *of* the district.
15. He dwelt *for* a long time *on* that subject but no one really knew what he was driving *at*.
16. The Magistrate's decision *on* that case was not *in* accordance with the evidence. We must appeal *to* a higher court, where perhaps this slur *on* our character will be removed.
17. He has an excellent appetite *for* his dinner; but no aspiration *for* anything higher.
18. The hill was veiled *in* a mist; and we were tired *of* waiting till the mist cleared *off*, besides being tired *with* our exertions.
19. I am reconciled *with* my opponent, but not *to* my loses.
20. He was disqualified *for* the post on account *of* age, but he was not disqualified *from* competing *for* a diploma.
21. It is better to be clothed *in* rags than to be clothed *with* shame.

(D)

1. He embarked *on* board the steamer, which was to take him *to* India, where we intended to embark *in* some kind of trade.
2. He was more popular than most men *with* the people *of* the country.
3. In some place the sea encroaches *on* the land, *in* others the land gains *on* the sea. This is so well-known that I need not expatiate *on* it any further.
4. As soon as he emerged *from* poverty, he entered *into* partnership *with* a man *of* wealth, and the two then entered *upon* a grand commercial career.
5. I will exchange this book *with* you *for* another, if you have a good one to offer me *in* exchange.
6. He rejoiced *in* his success, and exulted *over* his fallen rival. I am not familiar *with* that subject, so I cannot fall *in* with your views, *or* engage *in* this controversy any longer.

7. He fought *with* the robbers *for* his life. The Spaniards allied *with* the English fought *against* the French *in* what is called the Peninsular War.
8. While the cat was running *at* the mouse, the mouse ran *into* its hole and freed itself *from* danger.
9. Be so good as to furnish me *with* a copy of that letter. Furnish medicine *to* the sick.
10. A glance *at* this letter will convince you *of* its contents that he is grasping *at* your money. Everyone will grieve *for* your loss.
11. He increased *in* wisdom *with* the increase *of* age, and at last grew *out* of follies *of* his boyhood and youth. Thus *by* degrees he rose *to* eminence *in* his profession.
12. A young man should be *on* his guard *against* bad company, and beware *of* falling *into* their evil ways.
13. He loitered *about* this place *for* the greater part *of* the day, sometimes leaning *against* the wall, and sometimes strolling *to* the opposite side *of* the street.
14. Madagascar is an island *off* the east coast *of* Africa. The French could not prevail *upon* the inhabitants to surrender *without* an effort.
15. We must get rid *of* this difficult business at once. Let us enquire *about* the danger; and be ready *against* the evil day.
16. Your words are strange and quite *beyond* my comprehension. It is foolish to say what no one can understand and I thought you were *about* such folly.
17. This leaves no stain *on* his character, and no further prejudice *against* him should be entertained, as he has now cleared himself *of* all the faults imputed *to* him.
18. I have no liking *for* that man; in fact, I have taken a decided dislike *to* him. For all that, I wish to deal fairly *by* him.
19. My relations *with* him are now quite friendly and there is no ill feeling left *in* relation *to* that dispute.
20. Did you beg pardon *of* the teacher? No, I do not like to entreat anyone *for* mercy.
21. I cannot agree *with* you *in* this matter; and therefore I do not agree *to* your proposal.
22. I blush *at* my own fault more than I blush *for* your reputation.
23. Rhetoric might be compared *with* poetry.
24. I am in need *of* good advice, but there is no need *for* your reproaches.
25. There is no use *in* my purchasing that article, for I have no use *for* it.
26. I have failed *of* my purpose because I failed *in* my first attempt and was not allowed to make another.
27. He is invested *with* full authority *by* me to invest my money *in* that speculation.
28. He is profuse *in* his promises, but not at all profuse *of* his money.

(E)

1. You must apologise *to* him *for* what you have done, even though the act was not done *with* any bad intention.

2. You will have to answer *to* your master *for* that mistake and you may hope *for* pardon, if you ask *for* it *in* the proper way.
3. You can appeal *to* a higher court and apply *for* a fresh trial; but it will be wiser to appoint some man who is versed *in* such matters to act as arbitrator *between* you and the opposite party.
4. To continue arguing and disputing *with* a man, when you are certain that he will not assent *to* your own views is not wise *of* you; men will only blame you *for* wasting your time, and ascribe your conduct *to* obstinacy.
5. While he was battling *with* the sea, the wind rose and the waves beat *against* the shore; he begged *for* help *from* those persons who were *in* the boat, and they pulled him up *out of* the water.
6. I have bestowed great attention *on* that subject, and I bethought myself *of* one thing, namely that a bridge must be built at once *over* the river, and that this bridge should be *of* iron, not *of* wood or brick.
7. One man boasts *of* his wealth, another prides himself *on* his wisdom: we cannot help blushing *for* persons who are so wanting *in* modesty and who cannot blush *at* their own faults.
8. India borders *on* Burma, and is separated *from* it partly by the Bay of Bengal, which lies *between* them, and partly *by* a line *of* mountains situated *to* the north *of* the Bay.
9. A man should not brood *over* his troubles, however much he may be burdened *with* them.
10. She burst *into* tears, when she found that he did not care *for* her affection.
11. I am indifferent *to* heat and cold, because I have strong chest and there is no need *for* caution; I am sorry, however, that you have need *for* so such caution *with* every change *in* the weather.
12. He has a great capacity *for* mathematics and *in* respect of this subject his teacher has a great respect *of* his abilities.
13. In consideration *of* the fact that no one is perfect, you ought to show more consideration *for* other men's weaknesses, though there is no need to connive *at* their faults.

(F)

1. A drowning man will catch *at* a straw; and if he escapes, you need not caution him again *against* the danger *of* throwing himself *into* the water and bathing *out* of his depth.
2. Cease *from* speaking evil *of* others, and cling *to* charity. You will yourself be judged according *to* your judgment of others.

3. It is useless to clamour for what we cannot have. Do not complain *of* your lot. Be content *with* what you have already, and leave the future *to* Providence.
4. An eye *for* an eye, and a tooth *for* a tooth; this was the old law, but it has now been superseded *by* the duty *of* forgiveness.
5. They brought a complaint *before* the Magistrate against their neighbour who *without* asking their consent had dug a hole almost *under* the foundation *of* their house and thus rendered it unsafe *for* a dwelling place. The Magistrate complied *with* their request and issued a summons *against* him. He sentenced him *to* a fine for trespass.
6. A man who confides *in* a friend will not conceal anything *from* him, but will confer *with* him *on* all matters of real importance.
7. The wing *of* a bird corresponds *to* the arms of a man.
8. I had a long correspondence *with* him *on* the wisdom of conforming *to* custom, but he did not yield *to* my advice and remained unconvinced *of* his error. A man convinced *against* his will is *of* the same opinion still, as you know *from* the proverb. You cannot cure a man *of* his prejudices.
9. The culprit craved *for* pardon, and succeeded *in* getting it.
10. One cock crowed *over* the other *on account of* its victory, as one man boasts *of* having conquered another, and exults *over* his defeated rival.
11. You cannot compete *with* a man who is superior *to* yourself *in* resources. It is better to acquiesce *in* the fact that he has the advantage *over* you.
12. That trader there, who deals *in* cotton goods, has dealt hardly *by* his customers, and they must not concede *to* his demands *in* future.
13. The point you spoke *of* will be attended *to*. But if you ever touch *upon* it again, I hope you will speak *at* length *on* the wider question *on* which that point hinges.
14. This is an exception *to* the usual rule. I hope, therefore, you will make an exception *of* my son's case, and show some forbearance *for* his inexperience.
15. Live ameanably *to* reason, and independently *of* other men's help.
16. It is better even to be blind *of* one eye, than to be blind *to* one's own faults.
17. He is committed *to* a policy which he now dislikes and is not at all certain *of* its success.
18. He is blessed *in* his children, who have all turned out well, but he is not blessed *with* good health.
19. The ship is bound *for* India, and is bound by contract to arrive at Kolkata *by* the 18th of July.
20. He is accountable *to* his master *for* the money.
21. I do not concur *with* you *in* that opinion.

22. The decision *of* the dispute is left *to* me; but I have not yet given my decision *on* the matter.
23. I have had much experience *of* sicknesses, but none *in* curing them.
24. He guesses *at* his answer, for he has no genius *for* mathematics; in fact, he is not a genius *in* anything.
25. In old times an irruption was made *into* England *by* the Danes, who *at* first were more than a match *for* the Saxons.
26. I have no influence *over* that man and therefore, my advice has no influence *on* his actions.

REVISION TEST I

Correct the following sentences.

1. Everyone except she sang a song.
2. Nobody but me was able to answer the question.
3. Let it be divided between you and I.
4. Nothing can prevent me to do what I like.
5. Would he not accept of my invitation?
6. Why did you not reply my letter?
7. This problem has to be considered in every point of view.
8. How can I agree with your proposal?
9. Why should I differ from you?
10. Please write me at your earliest.
11. Can you connect the one to the other?
12. I will prefer death rather than dishonour.
13. Is she ill from fever?
14. This scheme is entirely different to what I planned.
15. Has he really profited from your loss?
16. He would prefer dying than begging.
17. She was presented with a nice gift.
18. I am not averse to play football.
19. Is he really addicted to gamble?
20. I am confident to secure victory.
21. He is expert to cook up stories.
22. I insisted to have my say in the matter.
23. He was justified to blame you.
24. Nothing can hinder me to go there.

25. He persisted to give me the same reply.
26. He thought to win over the enemies.
27. I decline saying anything at present.
28. I hope passing the examination.
29. She expects meeting her friends.
30. I am inclined holding this view.

Hints—1. except her; 2. but I; 3. you and me; 4. me from doing; 5. accept my invitation; 6. reply to; 7. from every; 8. agree to; 9. with you; 10. write to; 11. with the other; 12. death to dishonour; 13. ill of; 14. different from; 15. by your loss; 16. dying to; 17. presented a nice gift; 18. to playing; 19. to gambling; 20. confident of securing; 21. expert in cooking up; 22. insisted on having; 23. justified in blaming; 24. me from going; 25. persisted in giving; 26. thought of winning over; 27. decline to say; 28. hope to pass; 29. expects to meet; 30. inclined to hold

REVISION TEST II

Fill in the blanks with appropriate prepositions.

1. You are proficient ...... physics but deficient ...... chemistry.
2. One must conform ...... rules. One's actions must be ...... conformity ...... rules.
3. My views may be different ...... yours but you should not be indifferent ...... your interest.
4. He is endowed ...... divine gifts.
5. I differ ...... him but my pen does not differ ...... his. It does not differ ...... all respects.
6. I have now retired ...... service. I now wish to retire ...... a jungle.
7. While labouring ...... a noble cause, I had to labour ...... a lot of handicaps. I have laboured hard ...... my book.
8. He is not entitled ...... all the honours which have been showered ...... him.
9. Promotion acts as an incentive ...... hard work.
10. I have considerable influence ...... my students but I have no influence ...... any minister. Your suggestions had a remarkable influence ...... my career.
11. I am anxious ...... my son's result. I am anxious ...... avoid future litigation. I am anxious ...... my son's welfare.
12. He met me ...... my way home and I asked him to meet me ...... the office. My appeals ...... peace ...... the town met ...... a rather poor response.
13. He hindered me ...... leaving the meeting. Dowry system is a hindrance ...... suitable marriage.
14. What a contrast ...... his father! What a contrast ...... the two brothers!
15. He is greatly appreciated ...... his skill ...... acting.

16. India cannot yield ...... the ambition ...... the Chinese to take ...... force a portion ...... her northern borders.
17. A number ...... accidents are due ...... rash driving ...... the crowded roads ...... large cities.
18. The rules ...... grammar are essential parts ...... speech and usage peculiar ...... a language.
19. I am indebted ...... you ...... writing ...... me ...... time.
20. Most of the corruptions prevalent ...... our society are due ...... ambition ...... power. We should not be ambitious ...... fame ...... the cost ...... our society.
21. He is sitting ...... an examination.

Hints—1. in, in; 2. to, in, with; 3. from, to; 4. with; 5. with, from, in; 6. from, to; 7. for, under, at; 8. to, upon; 9. to; 10. over, with, on; 11. about, to, for; 12. on, in, for, of, with; 13. from, to; 14. to, between; 15. for, in; 16. to, of, by, of; 17. of, to, in, of; 18. of, of, to; 19. to, for, to, in; 20. in, to, for, of, at, of; 21. for

REVISION TEST III

Explain why the following sentences are correct or incorrect.

1. His father is ill since two months.
2. I sat under the feet of a great teacher.
3. Between you and I neither of us is to blame.
4. He is absent since two months.
5. Please excuse me being late by a few minutes.
6. I insisted my friend to call a doctor.
7. He is angry upon me.
8. He does not obey to my orders.
9. Who were you talking to?
10. I was prevented to go there.
11. I ordered for his dismissal.
12. All but him had fled away.
13. Here the poet describes about a lover.
14. He is justified to blame you.
15. I have great pleasure to introduce him to you.
16. When did he reach at the station?
17. He has not written me for a long time.
18. He asked from me a question.
19. He has been sitting at my application.

REVISION TEST IV

Match A with B, so as to make correct sentences.

A	B
He will come on	the morning.
He will go in	Tuesday.
He has been ill since	a week.
He has been absent for	Wednesday.
Mangoes were divided among	both the sons.
Sweets were distributed between	all the children.
She is reading	into her room.
A thief broke	in her room.
There is a cap	over his head.
Birds were flying	on his head.
He was killed in	a sword.
He was killed with	an accident.

REVISION TEST V

Fill in the blanks with an appropriate preposition.

1. She is …… home in mathematics.
2. He is quick …… figures.
3. They have no house to live …… .
4. Beware …… these mad dogs.
5. We are preparing …… examination.
6. She is blind …… one eye but he is blind …… his own faults.
7. He hanged himself …… a piece of cloth.
8. Please come and sit …… me.
9. He sells fish …… the kilogram.
10. They travelled …… horseback.
11. I will always stand …… you.
12. We buy eggs …… the dozen.
13. She is good …… translation.
14. What is he …… now?
15. He is guessing …… the meaning.

❒

Chapter IX

TEST YOURSELF

Correct or justify these sentences.

1. I should have liked to have seen the Taj Mahal.
2. You like fish, isn't it?
3. I have never known her to laugh.
4. He promised that he will help me.
5. He prevented me to go out.
6. No one has or can prove it.
7. I am seeing what you mean.
8. He reached the station after the train left.
9. She was happy because she could win a lottery.
10. As he is rich he needs not to work hard.
11. I teach grammar to her.
12. A triangle is having three sides.
13. If I win a lottery I am going to buy a car.
14. I request you to kindly help me.
15. Please excuse me coming later.
16. He had rather to die than to live.
17. He prefers to die than to live in misery.
18. Why do you avoid to see me?
19. He couldn't avail of that chance.
20. I would not do it if I was you.
21. He went to Rajgir for seeing old things.
22. Will I pass the examination this time?

❐

VERBS

1. Ordinary Verbs
2. Modal Verbs

Verb को दो भागों में बाँटा जा सकता है—

(i) Ordinary Verbs

to come, to go, to play, to write

(ii) Modal Verbs [Auxiliary Verbs]

be, do, have, dare, need, can, may, must, shall, will, ought, used

Ordinary Verbs

Ordinary verbs दो प्रकार के होते हैं—

1. Regular 2. Irregular

Regular Verb का वही Past Participle रूप होता है जो Past Simple का होता है, पर Irregular verb के Past Participle और Past Simple रूप में अंतर होता है, जैसे—

Regular Verbs	**Present**	**Past Simple**	**Past Participle**
	play	played	played
	live	lived	lived
	call	called	called
Irregular Verbs	go	went	gone
	eat	ate	eaten
	write	wrote	written

Modal Verbs [Auxiliary Verbs]

Auxiliary Verbs को Helping Verbs कहा जाता है। आधुनिक अँगरेजी में Auxiliary verbs को Anomalous Finites, Special Finites और Modal Verbs या Modals कहा जाता है। इन्हें '24 Friends of not' भी कहा जाता है। ऐसा क्यों? इसलिए कि इनके negative और interrogative रूप में do/does/did का प्रयोग नहीं होता और इनमें not (n't) सीधे आकर जुट जाता है।

Auxiliary Verbs को Modal Auxiliaries या Modals क्यों कहा जाता है? इसलिए कि इनसे verb के Mood (अवस्था/भाव) का बोध होता है और Mode है Mood का ही दूसरा नाम। इसी Mode या Mood को व्यक्त करते हैं ये Modal Auxiliaries या Modal Verbs.

इन Modal Verbs की संख्या 24 है—

am, is, are, was, were, have, has, had, do, does, did, shall, should, will, would, can, could, may, might, must, ought, need, dare, used

NOTE—Modal Verbs को छोड़कर अन्य सभी verbs को ordinary verbs कहा जाता है।

Functions of Modal Verbs

Rule I. Modal verbs की सहायता से Tense के भिन्न-भिन्न रूप बनाए जाते हैं; जैसे—

1. He is playing well. 2. He has played well.

Rule II. इनकी सहायता से Question-tags और short answers बनाए जाते हैं, जैसे—

1. He likes fish, doesn't he? 2. It is fine today, isn't it?

3. Do you like ice-cream? Yes, I do … No, I don't.

Rule III. इनका प्रयोग किसी कथन (statement) से सहमति (agreement) या असहमति (disagreement) प्रकट करने के लिए भी होता है, जैसे—

1. He is intelligent. Yes, he is.
No, he isn't.
2. It is too hot. So, it is.
3. He likes fish. Yes, he does.
No, he doesn't.
4. She doesn't have a car. But she has.

Rule IV. इनके प्रयोग से भिन्न-भिन्न प्रकार के भाव व्यक्त होते हैं, जैसे—

1. He can lift this box.—ability.
2. It may rain tonight.—possibility.
3. He has got to work hard.—obligation.
4. He has got a new car.—possession.

NOTE—Question-tag किस प्रकार बनाया जाता है इसपर इस अध्याय के अंत में Annexture A के अंतर्गत विचार किया जाएगा।

अब हम इनके प्रयोग पर विस्तारपूर्वक विचार करें।

To be: am/is/are/was/were

Rule I. Is and Am

ये दोनों ही singular हैं, पर इन दोनों में अंतर यह है कि 'is' Third Person Singular है, पर 'am' First Person Singular. इसलिए is का प्रयोग he/she/it के साथ होता है, पर am का I के साथ। ऐसा क्यों होता है? यह भाषाविज्ञान (philology) का विषय है जो यह बताता है कि am है 'eimi'/'asmi' आदि Verbs का ही एक परिवर्तित रूप—

Anglo-Saxon, ***Am, Eom*** *is akin to Gothik* **im,** *old Norse* **em,** *Lithuanian* **esmi,** *Latin* **sum,** *Greek* **eimi,** *Armenian* **em** *and Sanskrit* **esmi.**

—*Webster's New International Dictionary*

इसी प्रकार, is भी 'esti'/'asti' आदि का ही एक रूप है—

Is *is akin to Gothic* **ist**, *Lithuanian* **esti, est,** *Latin* **est,** *Greek* **esti,** *and Sanskrit* **asti.**

—*Webster's New International Dictionary*

आप जानते हैं कि 'eimi'/'asmi' आदि का प्रयोग First Person Singular Pronoun के साथ होता है और 'esti'/'asti' आदि का Third Person Singular Pronoun के साथ। इसलिए am का प्रयोग केवल First Person Singular Pronoun (I) के साथ होता है और is का Third Person Singular Pronoun (he/she/it) के साथ। यही इनके प्रयोग का ऐतिहासिक तथा वैज्ञानिक आधार है। इसलिए **I** के साथ is का प्रयोग और **he/she/it** के साथ am का प्रयोग हो ही नहीं सकता। हाँ, इंगलैंड के अल्पज्ञ ऐसा प्रयोग (I is) अवश्य कर बैठते हैं, पर हमें उनका अनुकरण नहीं करना चाहिए।

....

EXERCISE

Correct the following sentences.

(1) I is the Headmaster of this school. (2) I is he. (3) I is a teacher in an H E school. (4) Is I a thief? (5) Is I not innocent?

....

Rule II. Subject + Verb to be + Complement

बहुत-से वाक्यों में subject के साथ Verb *to be* (am/is/are/was/were) आता है और वह मुख्य क्रिया का काम करता है। ये Verbs सदा Intransitive रहते हैं और इसलिए वाक्य के अर्थ को पूरा या स्पष्ट करने के लिए इनके साथ एक noun/pronoun/adjective/adverb आता है, जो complement का काम करता है। ऐसे वाक्यों की बनावट इस प्रकार की होती है—

Subject + be (am/is/are/was/were) + complement (noun/pronoun/adjective/adverb)

ऐसे वाक्यों से किसी व्यक्ति/वस्तु के अस्तित्व (existence), स्थिति-स्थान (position), अवस्था (condition), नाम, उम्र, जाति-धर्म, स्वभाव, व्यवसाय (पेशा), रूप-रंग, आकार-प्रकार, गुण-दोष, समय-मौसम, भाव-मूल्य आदि अर्थों का बोध होता है; जैसे—

1. God is. 2. She is a nurse. 3. He is here.
4. It is spring. 5. It is 5 o'clock. 6. It is red.
7. This is a pen. 8. He is ten. 9. She is a Christian.

NOTE—Verb *to be* का एक रूप होता है *were* जो कभी-कभी वाक्य के आरंभ में आता है और इससे कोरी कल्पना या ऐसी इच्छा का बोध होता है जो पूरी न हो सके। ऐसे वाक्यों की बनावट इस प्रकार की होती है—

Were + subject + complement, [noun/adjective/adverb]; जैसे—

1. Were I a king! 2. Were I young! 3. Were he here!

Rule III. It + is + noun/adjective/infinitive

कुछ वाक्यों की बनावट इस प्रकार की होती है—

It + is + noun/adjective/infinitive/gerund/clause

ऐसे वाक्यों से किसी कार्य के सामान्य रूप से होने का बोध होता है। इन वाक्यों को देखें—

1. It is easy *to say so.* [infinitive]
2. It is foolish *behaving like this.* [gerund]
3. It is very sad *that he is ill.* [clause]

ऐसे वाक्यों की बनावट इस प्रकार की भी हो सकती है—

1. To say so is easy. 2. Behaving like this is foolish.

3. That he is ill is very sad.

ध्यान दें कि ऐसे वाक्यों में infinitive/Gerund/Clause वाक्य का subject हो जाता है और it का प्रयोग होता ही नहीं।

Rule IV. Static Verbs and Process (Inchoative) Verbs

Verb 'to be' (is/am/are/was आदि) से यह बोध होता है कि कोई वस्तु या व्यक्ति किसी एक अवस्था में स्थिर रूप से रहता है, क्योंकि verb 'to be' से एक स्थिर स्थिति या अस्तित्व का बोध होता है। इसलिए इन्हें static verb कहा जा सकता है।

कुछ Verbs ऐसे भी होते हैं जिनसे यह बोध होता है कि कोई वस्तु या व्यक्ति एक अवस्था से दूसरी अवस्था में बदल जाता है, अर्थात ऐसी क्रियाओं से किसी कार्य के आरंभ तथा विकास का बोध होता है। इसलिए इन्हें Process Verb या Inchoative Verb कहा जाता है। ये Verbs हैं—

come, go, get, fall, grow, begin, become, turn

इन वाक्यों को देखें—

1. Ram was a king. 2. Ram became a king.

पहले वाक्य से यह बोध होता है कि राम पहले से ही राजा था, पर दूसरे वाक्य से यह बोध होता है कि राम पहले राजा नहीं था; वह बाद में राजा बन गया। इसलिए was से यहाँ एक स्थिर अवस्था का बोध होता है, पर became से यह बोध होता है कि एक अवस्था दूसरी अवस्था में परिणत हो गई।

कुछ और वाक्य लें—

1. He was a king.	He became a king.
2. It is dark.	It is growing dark.
3. He is weak.	He is getting weak.
4. It is true	It will come true.
5. He was asleep.	He fell asleep.
6. He was mad.	He turned mad.

यहाँ is/was से एक स्थिर स्थिति का बोध होता है, पर grow/get/come आदि से एक अवस्था से दूसरी अवस्था में (विकास के फलस्वरूप) बदलने का अर्थ प्रकट होता है।

इसलिए Inchoative Verb का प्रयोग इस प्रकार नहीं किया जा सकता—

There became a meeting/quarrel/war.

Rule V. Subject + Verb 'to be' + Infinitive

कुछ वाक्यों की बनावट इस प्रकार की होती है—

Subject + am/is/are + Infinitive

1. I am to leave for Delhi next week.
2. He is to marry next year.

ऐसे वाक्यों से यह अर्थ प्रकट होता है कि कोई काम भविष्य में पूर्व-निर्धारित कार्यक्रम के अनुसार (आज्ञा या योजना के अनुसार) होगा।

Rule VI. ऐसे वाक्यों से आज्ञा/आदेश का भी बोध होता है, पर वह थोड़ा विनम्र (polite) और परोक्ष (indirect) ढंग का होता है; जैसे—

1. Candidates are to write their answers in their own words.
2. You are to arrange a party at once.

इन वाक्यों में 'are to write' के बदले 'must write' या 'have to write' और 'are to arrange' के बदले 'must arrange' या 'have to arrange' का भी प्रयोग हो सकता है, पर अर्थ में थोड़ा अंतर पड़ जाएगा। याद रखें कि 'must' से कड़े आदेश का बोध होता है और 'have to' से बाध्यता (लाचारी) का, जो फौजी दुनिया के लिए तो उचित हो सकता है, पर सभ्य समाज के लिए नहीं। शिक्षित समाज आज्ञा और आदेश को बुरा नहीं मानता, पर वह यह भी चाहता है कि उसे आदर मिले। आदर और आदेश—इन दोनों ही भावों का समन्वय *verb 'to be' + infinitive* या will + infinitive के द्वारा हो सकता है, must + infinitive या have + infinitive के द्वारा नहीं। इन्हें देखें—

1. You are to see me tomorrow.
2. You will see me tomorrow.
3. You must see me tomorrow.
4. You have to see me tomorrow.

तीसरे और चौथे वाक्य बहुत ही कड़ी चोट करते हैं न! इसलिए 'must' और 'have to' का प्रयोग जितना कम करें, इतना ही अच्छा। आप must या have to का प्रयोग केवल उन्हीं लोगों के लिए करें जो सभ्य भाषा समझ ही नहीं सकते।

Rule VII. Subject + was/were + Infinitive

कुछ वाक्यों की बनावट इस प्रकार की होती है—

Subject + was/were + Present Infinitive/Perfect Infinitive

1. My friend was to come.
2. They were to marry.
3. He was to have been married.

ऐसे वाक्यों से बोध होता है कि कोई काम जो किसी योजना के अनुसार भूतकाल में होनेवाला था, वह हो नहीं सका।

Rule VIII. Subject + Verb 'to be' + Present Participle (verb + ing)

बहुत-से वाक्यों में Verb 'to be' एक सहायक क्रिया (auxiliary verb) का काम करता है। इस रूप में वह अपने साथ आनेवाले Principal Verb में ing जोड़कर Imperfect Tenses (Present/Past/Future) बनाता है और समय का बोध कराता है। इनकी बनावट इस प्रकार होती है—

Subject + Verb 'to be' + verb + ing [Present Participle]

इस प्रकार के verbs से यह पता चलता है कि कोई काम अपूर्ण (imperfect) था या है या रहेगा। इन वाक्यों को देखें—

1. He is reading. 2. He was reading. 3. He will be reading.

ऐसे वाक्यों से यह बोध होता है कि कोई काम कुछ समय तक जारी है या था या रहेगा और वह कुछ समय के बाद समाप्त हो गया या हो जाएगा। इस प्रकार के वाक्यों से यह स्पष्ट आभास मिलता है कि कोई काम अनिश्चित समय तक जारी नहीं रहता, अर्थात उसका अंत निश्चित है।

NOTE (a)—Non-conclusive Verbs

अब इन क्रियाओं पर थोड़ा विचार करें—

think, feel, hope, love, desire, like, dislike, know, see (समझने के अर्थ में), *understand, want, wish*

इन क्रियाओं को non-conclusive verbs कहा जाता है। क्यों? इसलिए कि इनसे क्रिया की पूर्णता (स्थायित्व) का बोध होता है, थोड़े समय तक जारी रहकर समाप्त होने का नहीं। यही कारण है कि इन क्रियाओं का प्रयोग सामान्य अर्थ में Imperfect Tenses में नहीं होता। अब इन वक्यों को देखें—

1. I am writing English fairly well.
2. I am seeing what he means.

यहाँ Present Indefinite (simple) Tense का प्रयोग इस प्रकार करना चाहिए—

1. I know English fairly well.
2. I see what he means.

NOTE (b)—अब कुछ ऐसे verbs पर विचार करें जिनका संबंध शरीर के अंगों (कर्मेंद्रियों—senses) से रहता है। ये हैं—

see, hear, smell, taste, feel

ऐसे verbs के द्वारा किसी वस्तु का ज्ञान प्राप्त होता है और यह बोध होता है कि यह स्थायी काम है; कुछ समय तक जारी रहकर समाप्त होनेवाला नहीं। इस दृष्टि से (सामान्य अर्थ में) इनके लिए Imperfect Tenses का प्रयोग उचित नहीं। इन वाक्यों को लें—

1. We see with our eyes. 2. We hear with our ears.
3. The rose smells sweet. 4. This bed feels hard.

ऐसे verbs के साथ जब Imperfect (progressive) Tenses का प्रयोग होता है तब इनका अर्थ ही बदल जाता है, क्योंकि इनसे यह बोध होता है कि कोई काम बहुत थोड़े समय के लिए होता है—

1. He is smelling the fish to find whether it is fresh or rotten.
2. Who is hearing your case?
3. The doctor is feeling my pulse.

EXERCISE

Fill in the blanks with a verb in the Present Progressive Tense.

1. Cows …… in the field.
2. Boys …… kites.
3. He …… clothes.
4. She …… her pupils.

To have: have/has/had

Rule I. Subject + have + noun/have got + noun

कुछ वाक्यों में subject के बाद finite verb 'have' (has, have, had) आता है और उसके बाद कोई noun. ऐसे वाक्यों में have का प्रयोग Transitive verb की तरह होता है और इसके बाद आनेवाला noun उसका object होता है। ऐसे वाक्यों से भिन्न-भिन्न प्रकार के अर्थों का बोध होता है।

इन वाक्यों को देखें—

1. I have a horse. 2. She has got a book.
3. They have money. 4. I have got a servant.

ऐसे वाक्यों से ownership (स्वामित्व) का बोध होता है, अर्थात यह बोध होता है कि किसी व्यक्ति का किसी वस्तु/व्यक्ति के साथ मालिक और नौकर का संबंध है।

अब इन वाक्यों को लें—

1. I have two sons. 2. He has three daughters.
3. He has two wives. 4. I have two friends.

ऐसे वाक्यों से relationship (संबंध) का बोध होता है। यह संबंध पारिवारिक या सामाजिक आदि प्रकार का हो सकता है।

अब, इन वाक्यों पर विचार करें—

1. A man has two eyes. 2. A cow has two horns.
3. A horse has a tail. 4. A table has four legs.

ऐसे वाक्यों से आवश्यक गुण (inherent quality) का भाव व्यक्त होता है।

Rule II. Subject + have + noun

To 'have' से take/give/enjoy/experience आदि का भी बोध इस प्रकार होता है—

1. I have my breakfast at 7 a.m. [खाना]
2. I have my bath in the morning. [करना]
3. I had several letters from my son. [पाना]
4. I had no difficulty in finding his house. [अनुभव करना]

NOTE (a)—जब have से स्वामित्व/संबंध/आवश्यक गुण का बोध होता है, तब बोलचाल की भाषा (colloquial style) में have पर जोर देने के लिए have के साथ got (have + got) का प्रयोग होता है—

1. I have a house. I have got a house.
2. She has two sons. She has got two sons.

NOTE (b)—ऐसे वाक्यों का negative दो प्रकार से बनता है—

(i) Subject + have + no + noun या have + not any + noun.

1. I have no car. 2. I haven't any cars.

(ii) Subject + do + not + have + noun.

1. I don't have any cars.

NOTE (c)—ऐसे वाक्यों का Interrogative दो प्रकार से बनता है—

(i) Have + subject + other words?

Have you got a car?

(ii) Do + subject + have + other words?

Do you have a car?

NOTE (d)—जब have से स्वामित्व/संबंध/आवश्यक गुण का बोध होता है, तब have का having (अर्थात continuous tense) नहीं होता पर जब have से लेना, देना, करना (give/take आदि) का बोध होता है, तब have का having (अर्थात continuous tense) हो सकता है; जैसे—

1. A room has four walls. 2. They are having a birthday party.
3. I am having a nice time these days.

इसलिए इस प्रकार न लिखें—

1. He is having a small family. 2. I am having a servant.

EXERCISE

Make five sentences like the following.

1. Have you indigestion? 2. Do you have indigestion?
3. He has no cow. 4. He doesn't have a house.
5. I have my lunch at 1 p.m.

Rule III. Subject + have + Infinitive/have got + Infinitive

कुछ वाक्यों में subject + have + infinitive (to + verb) का प्रयोग होता है या subject + have got + infinitive का।

ऐसे वाक्यों में has/have/had एक Transitive verb का काम करता है और Infinitive उसका object होता है।

उस प्रकार के वाक्यों से आवश्यकता (necessity), अनिवार्यता (compulsion) या बाध्यता (obligation) का बोध होता है; जैसे—

1. He has to obey. He has got to obey. [बाध्यता]
2. He has to beg. He has got to beg. [आवश्यकता]

ऐसे अर्थ में must + infinitive का भी प्रयोग हो सकता है; जैसे—

1. He must obey.
2. He must beg.

NOTE—ऐसे वाक्यों का negative इस प्रकार बनता है—

(i) Subject + has/have/had + not + infinitive

(ii) Subject + do/does/did + no have + infinitive

(iii) Subject + need not + infinitive [without to]

इन वाक्यों को देखें—

1. He has to beg. (affirmative)
2. He has not to beg. (negative)
3. He does not have to beg. (negative)
4. He need not beg. (negative)

ध्यान दें कि ऐसे negative sentences से बाध्यता या आवश्यकता के अभाव का बोध होता है।

Rule IV. Subject + have + Object + Past Participle

कुछ वाक्यों में has/have/had के बाद noun/pronoun आता है और उसके बाद Past Participle (अर्थात Verb का तीसरा रूप)। ऐसे वाक्यों में have और past participle के बीच आनेवाला noun/pronoun एक object का काम करता है, क्योंकि वह Verb 'have' का object होता है।

इस प्रकार के वाक्यों से यह बोध होता है कि कोई काम किसी दूसरे के द्वारा (सहायता या प्रेरणा के द्वारा) होता है, स्वयं कर्ता के द्वारा नहीं। इसलिए ऐसी क्रिया को अँगरेजी में Causative Verb कहा जाता है और हिन्दी में प्रेरणार्थक क्रिया।

इन वाक्यों को लें—

1. Ram had a house built. 2. Shyam had a letter written.

इन वाक्यों का अर्थ यह है कि राम ने खुद घर नहीं बनाया और श्याम ने स्वयं पत्र नहीं लिखा। ऐसे वाक्यों में काम करनेवाला व्यक्ति कोई दूसरा ही होता है जो छिपा रहता है। ऐसे अदृश्य कर्ता का पता अनुमान से ही चल सकता है।

NOTE—इस प्रकार के वाक्यों में 'have' के बदले get का भी प्रयोग होता है, पर get की अपेक्षा have का प्रयोग अधिक अच्छा माना जाता है; जैसे—

1. I had my hair cut. 2. I got my hair cut.

EXERCISE

Make five sentences like the following.

1. I had a house built.
2. I got the road repaired.

Rule V. Subject + have + Object + Infinitive [without 'to']

कुछ वाक्यों में has/have/had के बाद कोई noun/pronoun आता है, जो एक object का काम करता है और उसके बाद एक Infinitive आता है, पर उसका to छिपा हुआ रहता है; जैसे—

1. I will *have him remember.* 2. I will *have you know this.*
3. Would you *have me believe this?*

ऐसे वाक्यों के have से इच्छा (wish) का बोध होता है। वाक्य की ऐसी बनावट और इसका अर्थ थोड़ा कठिन होता है। इसलिए यह लोकप्रिय नहीं है। यही कारण है कि ऐसे वाक्य इस प्रकार लिखे जाते हैं—

1. I wish him to remember. 2. I wish you to know this.

ध्यान दें कि इस प्रकार के वाक्यों में Infinitive का 'to' चिह्न छिपा हुआ नहीं रहता।

Rule VI. Subject + have + Object + Present Participle (verb + ing)

कुछ वाक्यों में have के बाद कोई noun/pronoun आता है, जो एक object का काम करता है और उसके बाद एक Present Participle (verb + ing) रहता है; जैसे—

1. I won't *have you behaving* like that.
2. I can't *have him wasting* his time.

ऐसे वाक्यों से अनुमति देने (allow) का बोध होता है। इसलिए ये वाक्य इस प्रकार भी लिखे जा सकते हैं—

1. I won't allow you to behave like that.
2. I can't allow him to waste his time.

NOTE—यहाँ यह ध्यान देने योग्य बात है कि allow के बाद कोई noun/pronoun (object) आता है और उसके बाद to + infinitive (to behave, to waste) आता है, present participle नहीं। इसलिए ऐसे वाक्यों की बनावट का सदा ध्यान रखें।

Rule VII (A). Subject + have + Past Participle

कुछ वाक्यों में has/have के बाद Past participle आता है, जिसे Present Perfect Tense कहा जाता है; जैसे—

1. He has come. 2. She has gone.

Present Perfect का प्रयोग तब होता है जब कोई काम वर्तमानकाल में तुरंत समाप्त हुआ हो। यही कारण है कि ऐसे अर्थ में has के बाद 'just' (अभी-अभी, तुरंत) का प्रयोग होता है; जैसे—

1. She has (just) gone out. 2. He has (just) left the place.

ऐसे वाक्यों से यह स्पष्ट है कि Present Perfect का संबंध वर्तमान काल से रहता है, भूतकाल (Past Tense) से नहीं। इसलिए Present Perfect के साथ किसी भी ऐसे शब्द या शब्द-समूह (phrase) का प्रयोग नहीं होता जो भूतकाल का सूचक हो। इन्हें देखें—

a moment ago, a few moments (minutes/days/weeks/months) ago, last night/ evening/week/year/winter/spring, the other day, yesterday

ये सब Adverbs of Time हैं और इनसे निश्चित रूप से Past Time का बोध होता है। इसलिए Present Perfect के साथ इनका प्रयोग हो ही नहीं सकता। आप Past और Present की खिचड़ी इस प्रकार न पकाएँ—

1. She has passed last year. 2. I have met him the other day.
3. I have seen him last evening. 4. He has come a week ago.

यदि आप ऐसे Adverbs को रखना ही चाहें, तो Present Perfect के बदले Past Simple (passed/met/saw/came) का प्रयोग करें।

Rule VII (B). Present Perfect and Adverb/Preposition

कभी-कभी कुछ Adverbs/Prepositions के प्रयोग से भूतकाल का संबंध वर्तमान काल (लिखने या बोलने के समय तक) से स्थापित किया जाता है, अर्थात इनसे यह बोध होता है कि जो काम भूतकाल में आरंभ हुआ था वह वर्तमानकाल तक जारी है। ऐसे वाक्यों में भी Present Perfect का प्रयोग होता है और उसके साथ कभी-कभी ये Adverbs/Prepositions आते हैं—

since, for, yet, just, already, ever, never, often, several times, today, this week/month, lately, recently, so far, uptil now, up to the present

इन वाक्यों को देखें—

1. She *has lived* in India *for* several years.
2. He *has not seen* me *since* 1970.
3. He *has not seen* me *for* several weeks.
4. He *has seen* me *already.*
5. He *has often seen* me here.
6. He *has seen* me *today* (*this week*).
7. He *has not seen* me *so far.*
8. I *have just finished* the work.

NOTE (a)—इन Adverbials of Time के साथ Past Simple Tense का प्रयोग नहीं होता है—

since, so far, uptil now, yet

इन वाक्यों को देखें—

1. He has already begun the work. [not, already *began* the work]
2. She has worked since 7 o'clock. [not, she *worked*]
3. He has not replied so far. [not, he *didn't reply*]

4. She has not reached uptil now. [not, he *didn't reach*]

5. He has not yet begun the work. [not, he *didn't* begin]

NOTE (b)—Just का प्रयोग Present Perfect के साथ होता है, जैसे—

I *have just begun* the work.

पर American English में just का प्रयोग Past Simple के साथ भी होता है, जैसे—

I just began the work.

Rule VIII. Subject + Verb (be) + Past participle [is gone/has gone]

कुछ वाक्यों में has/have + Past Participle के बदले is/are + Past Participle का प्रयोग Intransitive verb के साथ भी इस प्रकार होता है—

1. He is *gone* to London.
2. The snow *is melted.*

ऐसे वाक्यों से verb के परिणाम (result) या अवस्था (condition) का बोध होता है, अर्थात यह बोध होता है कि काम पूर्ण रूप से समाप्त हो जाने की अवस्था में है। यहाँ is gone का अर्थ है—जाने का काम बिलकुल पूरा हो चुका है और इसलिए वह लंदन पहुँच चुका है। इसी प्रकार, is melted का अर्थ है—पिघलने का काम बिलकुल पूरा हो चुका है और इसलिए अब कहीं भी बर्फ का पता नहीं।

अब इन वाक्यों को लें—

1. He has gone to London.
2. The snow has melted.

यहाँ पहले वाक्य से बोध होता है कि काम तुरंत समाप्त हुआ है, अर्थात वह लंदन के लिए तुरंत रवाना हुआ है, या लंदन तुरंत पहुँचा है। इसी प्रकार has melted से बोध होता है कि बर्फ तुरंत पिघली है, अर्थात पिघलने का काम अभी पूरा हो पाया है।

अब, इन वाक्यों को देखें—

1. The bell *is gone.* 2. The spring *is come.*

यहाँ is gone का अर्थ है—घंटी पूर्णरूप से समाप्त हो चुकी है (अभी तुरंत नहीं बजी है), अर्थात घंटी बजने के कारण (घंटी के अनुसार) सारे काम-काज आरंभ हो गये हैं। इसी प्रकार, is come का अर्थ है—आया हुआ है, अर्थात बसंत तुरंत नहीं आया है। वह पहले ही आ चुका है और इसलिए बसंतऋतु की शोभाएँ दिखाई पड़ रही हैं। देखिए, इस वाक्य में यह अर्थ कितनी सुंदरता से व्यक्त किया गया है—

Those days are gone. —Pandit Jawaharlal Nehru

NOTE (a)—is gone/is lost

इन वाक्यों को लें—

1. My bag *is gone.* 2. My bag *is lost.*

कभी-कभी 'go' का अर्थ होता है गुम हो जाना, खो जाना। ऐसे अर्थ में (go और lose के साथ) सदा is/was + Past Participle का प्रयोग होता है, has/have + Past Participle का नहीं।

इस संबंध में इस सिद्धांत का ध्यान रखें—

Before the past participle of certain intransitive verbs, like **go, come, arrive, fall, rise,** *expressive of* **motion or change of state or position,** *the auxiliary* **to be** *is permissible where we should normally expect* **have: e.g., He is gone to London. The Post is come. How are the mighty fallen! The sun is risen.** —F T WOOD: *Current English Usage*

NOTE (b)—gone to and **been to**

इन वाक्यों को लें—

1. Ram *has gone* to Mumbai.
2. Ram *has been* to Mumbai.

यहाँ पहले वाक्य का अर्थ है—राम मुंबई तुरंत गया है, अर्थात वह अभी यहाँ नहीं है। दूसरे वाक्य का अर्थ है—राम मुंबई में रह चुका है, अर्थात वह मुंबई जाकर वहाँ से वापस आ चुका है।

याद रखें—

gone to = left for a place

been to = gone to a place and come back

Rule IX. Subject + had + Past participle

कुछ वाक्यों में had के बाद Past Participle आता है जिसे Past Perfect Tense कहा जाता है। ऐसे वाक्यों के दो भाग होते हैं जो इन conjunctions के द्वारा जोड़े जाते हैं—*when, before, after.*

यदि Past Tense में दो काम समाप्त हो गए हों तो पहले समाप्त किए गए काम के लिए Past Perfect और बाद में समाप्त किये हुए काम के verb के लिए Past Simple का प्रयोग होता है; जैसे—

1. I had reached the station before the train came.
2. The train had arrived before I reached the station.

NOTE (a)—कभी-कभी ऐसे वाक्यों के दो भाग नहीं भी होते हैं और वाक्य में had + past participle का प्रयोग होता है। क्यों? इसलिए कि प्रसंग से ही स्पष्ट हो जाता है कि एक काम दूसरे काम के पहले समाप्त हो चुका था; जैसे—

1. I had already bought my ticket.
2. He had reached much earlier.

NOTE (b)—कुछ वाक्य ऐसे भी होते हैं जिनसे यह बोध होता है कि भूतकाल में एक काम दूसरे के तुरंत बाद हुआ या दोनों एक साथ (simultaneously) हुए। उनसे यह बोध नहीं होता कि एक काम के पूरे रूप से समाप्त होने पर दूसरा काम हुआ। इसलिए ऐसे वाक्यों के दोनों भागों में Past Simple का प्रयोग उचित है; जैसे—

1. She washed her face before she went to bed.
2. The train started before he reached the station.

इन वाक्यों से यह बोध होता है कि दो काम एक-दूसरे के तुरंत बाद हुए। ऐसा अर्थ व्यक्त होता है before से, after से नहीं। ध्यान दें कि after से यह बोध होता है कि एक काम पहले पूर्ण

रूप से समाप्त हो चुका था। इसलिए after वाले वाक्य में Past Perfect आता है, Past Indefinite नहीं; जैसे—

He reached the station after the train had already left.

NOTE (c)—Direct Narration के Past simple और Present Perfect के बदले Indirect Narration में Past Perfect का प्रयोग होता है, जब Reporting Verb Past Tense में रहता है; जैसे—

1. He said, "I saw a ghost."

   He said that he had seen a ghost.
2. He said, "I have seen a ghost."

   He said that he had seen a ghost.

NOTE (d)—कभी-कभी शर्त (condition), इच्छा या कल्पना (wish, supposition) के अर्थ में भी Past Perfect का प्रयोग इस प्रकार होता है—

1. Had I (if I had) been a king!
2. Had he (if he had) met me!
3. He behaved as if he had been my master.

Rule X. Subject + have had/had had/will have had + noun

कुछ वाक्यों में पहले have का प्रयोग Auxiliary Verb की तरह होता है और इसके बाद आनेवाले have का प्रयोग Principal Verb की तरह। ध्यान दें कि Principal Verb की तरह प्रयुक्त होने पर have का अर्थ होता है—

to take/get/enjoy/receive/experience

ऐसे अर्थ में Perfect tense बनाने पर have का रूप had हो जाता है। इसलिए ऐसे वाक्यों की बनावट इस प्रकार की हो जाती है—

1. I *have had* my breakfast in time. [have had = have taken. Present Perfect]
2. I *had had* my breakfast in time. [had had = had taken. Past Perfect]
3. I *shall have had* my breakfast in time.

   [shall have had = shall have taken. Future Perfect]

Rule XI. Subject + Past Perfect + Infinitive

Past Perfect से यह बोध होता है कि कोई काम भूतकाल में निश्चित रूप से पूरा हो गया। पर, कुछ ऐसे भी verbs होते हैं जिनके Past Perfect + Infinitive रूप से यह बोध होता है कि वे काम (आशा, इच्छा, कामना, कल्पना आदि) पूरे न हो सके। ये verbs हैं—

hope, expect, think, want, wish, intend (mean), suppose

इन वाक्यों पर विचार करें—

1. Ram had hoped (expected) to see me.
2. Ram had wished (wanted) to see me.
3. Ram had intended (thought) to see me.

इन वाक्यों से यह बोध होता है कि देखने का काम पूरा नहीं हो सका, अर्थात राम की आशा या इच्छा अधूरी ही रह गयी। इन वाक्यों से यह स्पष्ट है कि Past Perfect + Infinitive का प्रयोग सावधानी से करना चाहिए, क्योंकि यह अर्थ Past Perfect के सामान्य अर्थ के विपरीत है।

NOTE (a)—Past Simple + Perfect Infinitive

इन वाक्यों को लें—

1. Ram hoped to have seen me.
2. Ram intended to have seen me.

इन वाक्यों की बनावट इस प्रकार की है—

Past Simple + Perfect Infinitive [to have + past participle]

ऐसे वाक्यों से भी बोध होता है कि कोई काम (आशा, इच्छा आदि) भूतकाल में पूरा नहीं हो सका। इसलिए आप इन दोनों प्रकार के वाक्यों की बनावट का ध्यान रखें—

1. Past Perfect + Infinitive
2. Past Simple + Perfect Infinitive

इन दोनों की बनावट में अंतर है पर अर्थ में कोई अंतर नहीं। हाँ, पहली रीति दूसरी से कुछ अधिक अच्छी है और आसान भी।

NOTE (b)—Past Perfect + Perfect Infinitive

कुछ लोग वाक्य की बनावट इस प्रकार करते हैं—

Past Perfect + perfect infinitive [to have + past participle]

इन वाक्यों को देखें—

1. I had hoped to have seen him.
2. He had intended to have written to me.

ऐसे वाक्यों से भी यह बोध होता है कि कोई काम भूतकाल में पूरा न हो सका।

ऐसे वाक्य बहुत भद्दे समझे जाते हैं और इसलिए वाक्य के दोनों भागों में Perfect Tense का प्रयोग उचित नहीं माना जाता। इस संबंध में इन मतों पर विचार करें—

A Perfect Tense from, followed by a Perfect Infinitive, e.g., 'I should have liked to have stayed another week'. Only one of the verbs should be in the Perfect: either 'I should have liked to stay' or 'I should liked to have stayed' ... we must beware, however, of supposing that the use of the Perfect Infinitive after a Perfect Tense form is always wrong. Sometimes it is justifiable: e.g., 'I should have liked to have been able to comply with his request'. —F T WOOD

Wood साहब के मतानुसार Past Perfect Tense + Perfect Infinitive का प्रयोग कभी-कभी उचित हो सकता है, पर इतना तो अवश्य कहा जा सकता है कि ऐसा प्रयोग बहुत कम होता है। इसकी आवश्यकता भी नहीं है न! जब Past Simple + Perfect Infinitive और Past Perfect + Present Infinitive से यह बोध हो जाता है कि भूतकाल में कोई काम नहीं हुआ, तब Past Perfect + Perfect Infinitive से लाभ ही क्या?

शायद इसलिए Hornby साहब ने अपनी प्रसिद्ध पुस्तक *A Guide to Patterns and Usage in English* में वाक्य की ऐसी बनावट को स्थान ही नहीं दिया है। इसी प्रकार का मत फाउलर साहब का भी है—

After Past Tenses of **hope, fear, expect** *and the like, the* **perfect infinitive** *is used, incorrectly indeed and unnecessarily, but so often and with so useful an implication that* **it may well be counted idiomatic** *… . After past conditionally such as* **should have liked, would have been possible … the present infinitive is** *(almost invariably) the right form … .* —H W FOWLER

Only one of the verbs should be in the perfect. —F T WOOD

इसलिए आप Past Perfect + Perfect Infinitive का प्रयोग न करें तो अच्छा। इस नियम का ध्यान रखें।

May: may/might

Rule I. Subject + may + Infinitive [without 'to']

इस प्रकार के may से दो अर्थों का बोध होता है—

(a) अनुमति (permission)

(b) भविष्यत्कालिक संभावना + संदेह (possibility + doubt)

इन वाक्यों को लें—

1. May I go out, sir? [अनुमति माँगना]
2. You may play. [अनुमति देना]
3. May I use your pen? [अनुमति माँगना]
4. It may rain tonight. [संभावना + संदेह]

NOTE—आजकल अमेरिका में अनुमति (Permission) के अर्थ में भी may के बदले can का प्रयोग हो चला है। अमेरिका के एक आचार्य ने यह वाक्य लिखा है—

Mother, can I go out to play?

इसे शुद्ध बताते हुए अपना मत इस प्रकार प्रकट किया है—

'Mother' can I go out to play?'—Right. If you insist that your child should say **may** *and nothing but* **may,** *when asking for permission, modern parents may consider you old-fashioned and puristic.* **Can** *is not discourteous, incorrect, or vulgar—and the newest editions of the authoritative dictionaries fully sanction the use of* **can** *in requesting right, privileges or permission.* —NORMAN LEWIS: *Word Power*

Rule II. Subject + might + Infinitive [without 'to']

यदि काम होने की संभावना की मात्रा कम हो और संदेह या अनिश्चितता की मात्रा बहुत अधिक हो तो Might + Infinitive का प्रयोग इस प्रकार होता है—

1. It might rain tonight.
2. He might come today.

ऐसे वाक्यों में संभावना या संदेह की मात्रा निर्धारित करना लिखने या बोलनेवाले पर निर्भर रहता है—उसके ज्ञान और अनुभव पर।

Rule III. Subject + may + Perfect Infinitive [may have + past participle]

कुछ वाक्यों में May के बाद Perfect Infinitive आता है, पर Infinitive का 'to' छिपा रहता है। ऐसे वाक्यों की बनावट इस प्रकार की होती है—

May + Perfect Infinitive

इस प्रकार के may से भूतकालिक संभावना + संदेह (अनिश्चितता) का बोध होता है; जैसे—

1. You may have seen him.
2. He may have reached home.

ऐसे वाक्यों से यह बोध होता है कि भूतकाल में किए गए कार्य के होने की संभावना अधिक थी, पर यह पता नहीं कि कार्य पूरा हुआ या नहीं।

Rule IV. Subject + might + Perfect Infinitive [might have + past participle]

यदि ऐसे वाक्यों में Might + Perfect Infinitive का प्रयोग हो, तो यह बोध होता है कि भूतकाल में कार्य होने की संभावना थी, पर काम हुआ नहीं।

इन वाक्यों को लें—

1. He may have been killed. [मारे जाने की संभावना थी]
2. He might have been killed. [मारा नहीं गया]

Rule V. Subject + may + Infinitive [without 'to']

ऐसे वाक्यों से दो अर्थों का बोध होता है—

(a) उद्देश्य (purpose) और (b) इच्छा (wish)

इन वाक्यों को देखें—

1. He works hard that he may pass. [उद्देश्य]
2. May he live long! [इच्छा]

Rule VI. Might in Interrogative Sentences

अनुमति के अर्थ में may का प्रयोग होता है, पर अत्यंत नम्रतापूर्वक अनुमति का बोध कराने के लिए (Present Tense में) Interrogative Sentences में might का प्रयोग इस प्रकार होता है—

1. Might I use your knife?
2. Might I borrow your umbrella?

इस प्रकार के वाक्यों से संकोच, संदेह या द्विविधा का भाव झलकता है।

Rule VII. Might in Indirect Narration

Direct Narration के may के बदले Indirect Narration में might का प्रयोग होता है जब Reporting Verb Past Tense में रहता है; जैसे—

He told me, "I may help you."

He told me that he might help me.

EXERCISE

Make ten sentences like the following.

1. Could I use your pen?
2. Might I see you tomorrow?
3. May I go out?
4. He may have reached.

Can: can/could

Rule I. Subject + can/could + Infinitive

Rule I (A). Can + Infinitive [without 'to']

कुछ वाक्यों में Can के बाद Infinitive आता है, पर उसका 'to' चिह्न छिपा रहता है। ऐसे can से शक्ति/सामर्थ्य/क्षमता (power and ability) का बोध होता है, अर्थात यह बोध होता है कि किसी व्यक्ति या वस्तु को कोई काम करने की शक्ति/सामर्थ्य/क्षमता है। इसलिए जब can में not लग जाता है तब इससे यह बोध होता है कि काम करने की शक्ति और सामर्थ्य का अभाव (absence of power and ability) है; जैसे—

1. I can speak.
2. The dumb cannot speak.
3. I can see.
4. The blind cannot see.

ऐसे वाक्यों से काम करने की शक्ति या क्षमता का बोध होता है, पर यह बोध नहीं होता कि काम वास्तव में हुआ है। काम होने का भाव can के बदले Present Simple से इस प्रकार प्रकट होता है—

1. I speak.
2. I see.
3. I write.

Rule I (B). Subject + could + Infinitive/be able + Infinitive

Can + Infinitive से यह बोध होता है कि किसी व्यक्ति या वस्तु को शक्ति या सामर्थ्य है और could + Infinitive से यह बोध होता है कि उसे शक्ति/सामर्थ्य/क्षमता थी; जैसे—

1. He can walk fast.
2. He could walk fast.

ऐसे वाक्यों से यह बोध होता है कि काम करने की शक्ति/सामर्थ्य/क्षमता का अभाव नहीं था, पर यह बोध नहीं होता कि उस शक्ति और सामर्थ्य के कारण कोई कार्य पूरा हो सका या नहीं।

इसलिए भूतकाल में कार्य पूरा होने का बोध कराने के लिए Subject + was/were + able + infinitive या केवल Past Simple का प्रयोग होता है, could + infinitive का नहीं। इन वाक्यों को देखें—

1. He could pass the examination. — परीक्षा पास करने की शक्ति/क्षमता/सामर्थ्य थी, पर पास किया या नहीं यह मालूम नहीं।
2. He was able to pass the examination. — शक्ति और सामर्थ्य के कारण पास कर सका।

or

He passed the examination.

इस प्रकार, Subject + was/were + able + infinitive से कार्य करने की शक्ति/सामर्थ्य और कार्य की पूर्णता (ability + completion of action) का बोध होता है, पर could + infinitive से केवल शक्ति/सामर्थ्य (ability) का बोध होता है। यही कारण है कि कार्य की पूर्णता व्यक्त करने के लिए could + infinitive का प्रयोग नहीं हो सकता।

Rule I (C). Subject + shall/will be able + Infinitive

इसी प्रकार, भविष्य में कार्य करने की शक्ति और कार्य की पूर्णता का बोध कराने के लिए subject + shall/will be able + infinitive या केवल Future Simple का प्रयोग करना चाहिए, can का नहीं; जैसे—

1. I shall be able to help him.

   I shall help him.

2. He will be able to reach in time.

   He will reach in time.

NOTE—Negative वाक्य में was/were + not + able + infinitive के बदले could + not + infinitive का भी प्रयोग हो सकता है जैसे—

1. The luggage *was* so heavy that I *couldn't* carry it.
2. I *tried* to carry the box but *couldn't*.

ऐसे वाक्यों से यह बोध होता है कि कार्य भूतकाल में पूरा न हो सका।

Rule II. Can't से संभावना के अभाव का बोध होता है, अर्थात यह बोध होता है कि कार्य होने की संभावना (likelihood) नहीं है, जैसे—

1. The sky is bright and clear. It can't rain tonight.
2. He is a gentleman. He can't be a liar.

Rule III. Can't से अनुमति नहीं देने (refusal) का भाव इस प्रकार व्यक्त होता है—

Can I play here?

No, you can't.

Rule IV. Can have + past participle से भूतकाल में किए गए कार्य के संबंध में संभावना (posibility) और अनिश्चितता (uncertainty) का भाव व्यक्त होता है, जैसे—

He can have heard the news.

= It is probable but uncertain that he heard the news.

इस प्रकार, can have + past participle और may have + past participle—इन दोनों का एक ही अर्थ होता है, जैसे—

He can have caught the train.

= He may have caught the train.

ध्यान दें कि will have + past participle का भी यही अर्थ होता है, जैसे—

He may have caught the train.

= He will have caught the train.

Rule V. Subject + could + Perfect Infinitive

कुछ वाक्यों में Could + Perfect Infinitive का प्रयोग होता है। ऐसे वाक्यों से यह बोध होता है कि काम करने की शक्ति, क्षमता और सामर्थ्य होने पर भी भूतकाल में कोई कार्य पूरा न हो सका; जैसे—

1. He could have passed the examination. [पर पास न कर सका]
2. He could have caught the thief. [पर पकड़ न सका]

Rule VI. Could in Interrogatives: request

आजकल बोलचाल की भाषा में could का प्रयोग अत्यंत नम्र निवेदन (polite request) के अर्थ में होता है; जैसे—

1. Could I use your pen?
2. Could you lend me some money?
3. Could you give me 51181?

Rule VII. Can in Interrogatives: negative sense

कुछ Interrogative Sentences में can का प्रयोग होता है और उसका अर्थ *cannot* होता है। ऐसे can वाले वाक्य देखने में तो affirmative लगते हैं, पर अर्थ होता है negative. यह अर्थ निर्भर रहता है वाक्य के subject और verb के संबंध पर। आप देखेंगे कि ऐसे वाक्यों में verb जो कुछ बताता है वह subject के धर्म-स्वभाव (nature, quality) के विपरीत रहता है। यही कारण है कि can का अर्थ होता है cannot, जो can का बिलकुल विपरीत अर्थ प्रकट करता है।

इन वाक्यों को देखें—

1. Can the deaf hear?
2. Can human nature change?
3. Can God be unkind?
4. Can coal be white?

इन वाक्यों में can का अर्थ है—cannot.

Rule VIII. Can't = prohibition

कभी-कभी cannot से निषेध (prohibition) का बोध होता है, अर्थात यह बोध होता है कि काम करने पर रोक है। संक्षेप में, ऐसे वाक्यों के cannot का अर्थ लगभग वही होता है जो must not का होता है; जैसे—

1. You can't (cannot) shout like this.
2. You can't (cannot) smoke in the class.

याद रखें कि इस अर्थ में could not का प्रयोग हो ही नहीं सकता।

Rule IX. Can/Could in Indirect speech

Direct Narration के can का Indirect में could हो जाता है, जब Reporting Verb Past Tense में रहता है; जैसे—

He told me, "I can help you." He told me that he could help me.

ऐसे could का रूप तो Past Tense में रहता है, पर इससे बोध होता है Future Time का।

EXERCISE

Make ten sentences like the following.

1. Can the blind see?
2. He was not able to pass the examination.
3. She could have helped me.
4. You can't behave like this.

To do: do/does/did

Rule I. Ordinary verbs के negative तथा interrogative रूप में to do का प्रयोग इस प्रकार होता है, जैसे—

He knows Sanskrit.

1. He doesn't know Sanskrit.—Negative.
2. Does he know Sanskrit?—Interrogative.

Rule II. सकारात्मक कथन (positive statement) और आज्ञा-निवेदनसूचक वाक्य (imperatives) को जोरदार बनाने के लिए do का प्रयोग इस प्रकार होता है—

1. He likes this book. He does like this book.
2. She told me a lie. She did tell me a lie.
3. See me tomorrow. Do see me tomorrow.
4. Have a cup of coffee. Do have a cup of coffee.

EXERCISE

Make these sentences (a) negative, (b) interrogative and (c) emphatic.

1. He likes fish.
2. She stole my pen.
3. I bought some sugar.
4. He speaks the truth.

Shall: shall/should
Will: will/would
must/ought
shall/will and going to

Rule I. I/we + shall से यह बोध होता है कि कार्य सामान्य रूप से होगा, जैसे—

1. I shall be twenty next week.
2. Shall I get a medal this time?

Rule II. Second/third persons + will से यह बोध होता है कि कार्य सामान्य रूप से होगा, जैसे—

1. She will be twenty next week?
2. Will he get a prize this time?

NOTE (a)—Colourless Future/Coloured Future

Shall/will से सामान्य रूप से कार्य होने का भाव व्यक्त करने पर, अर्थात केवल future time का बोध कराने पर इसे Pure Future या Colourless Future कहा जाता है। पर जब shall/will से इच्छा/इरादा/संकल्प/प्रतिज्ञा/आदेश/निवेदन/चेतावनी (wish/will/intention/determination/promise/threat) आदि भावों का भी बोध होता है तब इसे Coloured Future कहा जाता है।

NOTE (b)—Would like or Should like?

First Person के साथ would like का प्रयोग होना चाहिए या should like का? व्याकरण के नियमानुसार like/prefer/care/be glad/be inclined रहने पर First person के साथ should का प्रयोग होना चाहिए, would का नहीं; जैसे—

1. I should like to suggest.
2. I should like to know.
3. I should be glad to see you.
4. I should be inclined to say so.

कुछ लोग ऐसे वाक्यों में should like के बदले would like का प्रयोग करते हैं। इस संबंध में आप इन आचार्यों के मत पर विचार करें—

In these **should**, *not* **would**, *is the right form.* —FOWLER

And again,

If the **shall** *and* **will** *idiom is worth preserving at all, I* **would like** *is wrong and I* **should like** *right.* —FOWLER

NOTE—इसके संबंध में इतना ही कहना है कि I would like का भी प्रयोग काफी हो रहा है, खासकर अमेरिका में। पर, यदि शुद्ध व्याकरण की दृष्टि से विचार किया जाए, तो I should like को शुद्ध मानना पड़ेगा और I would like को अशुद्ध, जैसाकि Fowler साहब का मत है। इसलिए अच्छे लेखक should like का ही प्रयोग करते हैं, would like का नहीं। इन वाक्यों को देखें—

1. *On the other hand, I* **should like** *to be clear that I am not defending a high-brow against a low-brow literature.* —T S ELIOT
2. *Might be continued—These are the words with which I* **should like** *to finish my coiners.* —ANDRE GIDE
3. *The phrases I* **should like** to underline in this statement are ... .

—*The Kenyon Review*: SPRING, 1955

फिर भी, प्रयोग को देखते हुए I would like को अशुद्ध मानना उचित नहीं जँचता। यही कारण है कि अमेरिका के एक व्याकरणाचार्य ने इस वाक्य को—I would like to ask you a question—शुद्ध बताते हुए कहा है—

In current American usage, **would** *may be used with* **I,** *though no die-hard purist will give a inch in this matter. Strict, old-fashioned rules demand* **I should** ... .

—NORMAN LEWIS: *Word Power*

अमेरिका ही में नहीं, इंगलैंड में भी I would like का प्रयोग काफी होता है। कुछ वर्ष पहले इंगलैंड की रानी (Her Majesty Elizabeth II) ने भी BBC से बोलते हुए I would like का प्रयोग किया था। इसलिए आप would like को अशुद्ध न समझें। हाँ, यह अवश्य कहा जा सकता

है कि I should like का प्रयोग I would like से अधिक अच्छा है, पर I would like अधिक लोकप्रिय है।

NOTE (c)—आजकल shall/will में प्रायः कोई अंतर नहीं माना जाता और इसलिए केवल future time व्यक्त करने के लिए भी I/we के साथ will का प्रयोग धड़ल्ले से होता है। हाँ, प्रश्नवाचक (questions) में I/we के साथ सदा shall का प्रयोग होता है, जैसे—

Shall I see you tomorrow? [not, will I?]

Rule III. I/we + will से कार्य करने के इरादे (intention) या संकल्प (determination) का बोध होता है, जैसे—

1. I will see her tomorrow.
2. We will play a match next week.

ऐसे वाक्यों में going to का प्रयोग अधिक अच्छा माना जाता है, जैसे—

1. I will see her tomorrow.
   = I am going to see her tomorrow.
2. I will buy a car next week.
   = I am going to buy a car next week.

Rule IV. Second/Third Persons + will से आदेश (command) का भी बोध होता है, जैसे—

1. You will wait here until I get back.
2. Boys will attend the function at 10 o'clock.

Rule V. Second/Third Persons + shall से आदेश/प्रतिज्ञा/चेतावनी (command/promise/threat) का भाव इस प्रकार व्यक्त होता है—

1. You/he/they shall pay a fine.
2. You shall get your money back.

Rule VI. Shall I? तथा Shall we? से किसी दूसरे व्यक्ति की इच्छा (wish) के संबंध में प्रश्न किया जाता है, जैसे—

1. Shall I wait here?
2. Shall we meet at the station?

Rule VI (A). Will you? Won't you? Would you? तथा Would you mind? से निवेदन/निमंत्रण (request/invitation) का भाव व्यक्त होता है, जैसे—

1. Will you/would you give me some money, please?
2. Won't you wait here, please?
3. Would you mind closing the gate?

Rule VII. Indirect Narration में shall/will बदल जाता है should/would में जब Reporting verb रहता है Past Tense में, जैसे—

1. He told me, "I *will* help you."
2. He told me that he *would* help me.

ऐसे should/would से *future time* का बोध होता है, past time का नहीं।

Rule VIII. Will से आदत (habit) या सामान्य सत्य (general truth) का भाव इस प्रकार व्यक्त होता है—

1. Boys will be boys everywhere.
2. The dog will sit by his master.

Rule IX. Would से यह भी बोध होता है कि कोई कार्य भूतकाल में कभी-कभी (occasionally) होता था—

1. We *would* often talk for hours.
2. He *would* often go for a ride.

Rule X. Would rather/would sooner से पसंद (preference) का बोध इस प्रकार होता है—

1. I would rather start now.
2. I would sooner resign my post.

Rule XI. Will have + past participle से भूतकाल के कार्य के संबंध में संभावना (likelihood) व्यक्त की जाती है—

1. He will have heard the news.
   = Probably he heard the news.

Rule XII. Would have + past participle से यह बोध होता है कि कार्य भूतकाल में नहीं हुआ, क्योंकि शर्त पूरी नहीं हुई, जैसे—

If he had gone to Delhi, he would have seen the Red Fort.

Rule XIII. जिस adverb clause से शर्त (condition) या समय (time) का बोध होता है उसमें will का प्रयोग नहीं होता, जैसे—

1. You will get wet if you go out in the rain. [not, **will go out**]
2. Wait here until I get back. [not, **will get back**]
3. The patient will die before a doctor arrives [not, **will arrive**]

NOTE—पर जब will से determination/insistence का भाव व्यक्त होता है तब if के साथ will का प्रयोग होता है, जैसे—

1. If you *will* keep your watch slow, you will be late for your office.
2. If you *will* eat so much of fat, you will get fat soon.

Rule XIV. If only तथा Wish के साथ would का प्रयोग होता है, will का नहीं; जैसे—

1. I wish you *would* join this club.
2. If only he *would* listen to reason.

Rule XV. Shall/will and Going to

Shall/will और Going to—इन तीनों से यह बोध होता है कि कार्य भविष्य में होगा।

I/We + shall और Second/Third Persons + will से यह बोध होता है कि कार्य भविष्य में सामान्य रूप से होगा। पर Going to से अन्य अर्थों का भी बोध होता है, जैसे—

1. I am going to buy a car.—intention
2. He is going to learn English.—intention

3. They are going to get married.—intention

4. It is going to rain tonight.—likelihood

5. The sun is going to come out.—likelihood

6. The patient is going to die.—likelihood

NOTE (a)—Going to का प्रयोग साधारणतया निकट भविष्य (immediate future) के लिए होता है, पर shall/will का प्रयोग immediate future तथा remote future दोनों के लिए होता है।

NOTE (b)—Going to का प्रयोग वैसे वाक्यों में प्रायः नहीं होता जिनमें time/condition/cause आदि सूचक clause का प्रयोग होता है। इसलिए वैसे वाक्यों में shall/will का ही प्रयोग होता है, जैसे—

1. If I have money, I will buy a cow. [now, **I am going to buy**]

2. I will wait here until you come back. [not, **I am going to wait here**]

3. I will see my friend when I get time. [not, **I am going to see**]

NOTE (c)—जब कोई कार्य सामान्य या स्वाभाविक रूप से होता है, तब shall/will का प्रयोग होता है, going to का नहीं, जैसे—

1. He *will be* forty next week. [not, **is going to be**]

2. It is Saturday today. Tomorrow *will be* Sunday. [not, **is going to be**]

Rule XVI. Will/Would/Should/Must/Ought से अनुमान (guess/assumption) का बोध इस प्रकार होता है—

1. What's her age? She would be twenty.

2. Who is at the door? That will be the postman.

3. Where is she? She will be at home by now.

4. He started early. He should/must reach here soon.

5. He started early. He ought to reach here soon.

Rule XVII. Should/Must/Ought से कर्तव्य (duty/obligation) का बोध होता है, जैसे—

1. We should/must love our country.

2. We ought to obey our teachers.

Rule XVIII. Should/Must/Ought से राय (advice) का भी भाव व्यक्त होता है, जैसे—

1. You should/must see a doctor. 2. He ought to eat simple food.

Rule XIX. Shouldn't/Mustn't/Oughtn't से भी कर्तव्य/राय का बोध होता है, जैसे—

1. You shouldn't/mustn't touch a live wire.

2. You oughtn't to play with fire.

3. We shouldn't/mustn't hate our neighbours.

Rule XX. Must से बाध्यता/अनिवार्यता (compulsion/necessity) का भाव व्यक्त होता है। ऐसे अर्थ में must के बदले have to या have got to का प्रयोग इस प्रकार होता है, जैसे—

You must obey your officer.

= You have to/have got to obey your officer.

NOTE (a)—ध्यान दें कि must का negative होता है needn't. याद रखें कि must का negative mustn't नहीं होता है, क्योंकि must और mustn't—दोनों से बाध्यता/अनिवार्यता का बोध होता है। पर needn't से बाध्यता/अनिवार्यता के अभाव (absence of obligation) का भाव व्यक्त होता है, जैसे—

1. You must go to school on time.
   —obligation/compulsion
2. You mustn't go to school late.
   —obligation/compulsion
3. You needn't go to school on Sundays.
   —absence of obligation/compulsion

NOTE (b)—ऐसे वाक्यों में needn't के बदले don't have to/haven't to/haven't got to का प्रयोग इस प्रकार हो सकता है—

I needn't go to school on Sundays.

I don't have to go to school on Sundays.

I haven't to/haven't got to go to school on Sundays.

Rule XXI. Should have और Ought to have से यह बोध होता है कि कोई कर्तव्य या उचित कार्य भूतकाल में पूरा नहीं हो सका; जैसे—

1. He should have taken the examination.
2. She ought to have obeyed her parents.

Rule XXII. Must have से यह बोध होता है कि कोई कार्य भूतकाल में अवश्य पूरा हुआ होगा। इसलिए must have से निश्चितता (certainty) का भाव व्यक्त होता है, जैसे—

He started early. He must have caught the train.

Rule XXIII. Must be/Must have been से भी निश्चितता (certainty) का भाव व्यक्त होता है, जैसे—

1. He always talks nonsense. He must be an idiot.
2. He looked ferocious. He must have been a robber.

Rule XXIV. Must का Past Tense और Future Tense नहीं होता। इसलिए भूतकाल की बाध्यता के लिए had और भविष्यत्काल की बाध्यता के लिए shall have to का प्रयोग इस प्रकार होता है—

1. He was very poor. He had to work hard.
2. He wants to win the race. He shall have to run fast.

Rule XXV. कभी-कभी Should का अर्थ होता है—if (अगर) और इसलिए इससे शर्त (condition) का भाव व्यक्त होता है, जैसे—

Should he see me I would certainly help him. [should = if]

Need: need/needn't

Rule I. जब need का अर्थ होता है **जरूरत होना**, तब इसका प्रयोग एक ordinary verb की तरह होता है, अर्थात need का प्रयोग subject के number/person के अनुसार होता है, जैसे—

1. I need a pen.
2. He needs a pen.
3. You need a pen.
4. She doesn't need a pen.

Rule II. जब need से बाध्यता का अभाव (absence of obligation) व्यक्त होता है तब singular और plural subjects—दोनों के साथ सदा needn't का प्रयोग होता है, जैसे—

1. I needn't work hard.
2. He needn't work hard.
3. You needn't see a doctor.
4. She needn't see a doctor.

Rule III. कुछ वाक्यों में needn't have + past participle का प्रयोग होता है और यह बोध होता है कि भूतकाल में जो कार्य हुआ वह अनावश्यक या अनुचित था, जैसे—

1. He needn't have gone to school on Sunday.
2. He has got a car. He needn't have travelled by bus.

Dare: dare/daren't

Rule I. जब dare का अर्थ होता है चुनौती देना (to challenge) तब इसका प्रयोग ordinary verb की तरह होता है। इसलिए subject के number/person के अनुसार dare/dares का प्रयोग होता है और negatives तथा interrogatives बनाने के लिए do का प्रयोग किया जाता है, जैसे—

1. They dare me to swim across this river.
2. He dares me to swim across this river.
3. They do not dare me to swim across this river.
4. He doesn't dare me to swim across this river.

Rule II. जब dare का अर्थ होता है हिम्मत होना (to have the courage), तब वाक्य की बनावट हो जाती है—

affirmative [dare]

1. I dare to challenge him.
2. He dares to slap her.

negative [daren't]

1. I daren't challenge him.
2. He daren't slap her.
3. She daren't go out.

ध्यान दें—

Rule II (A). जब ऐसे वाक्य negative बन जाते हैं, तब singular तथा plural subjects—दोनों के साथ सदा **daren't** का प्रयोग होता है। इसलिए **daresn't** का प्रयोग एक भयंकर भूल है।

Rule II (B). ऐसे affirmative वाक्यों में *infinitive with to* आता है, पर negative में *infinitive without to* का प्रयोग होता है, जैसे—

1. I dare *to challenge* him. 2. I daren't *challenge* him.

Rule III. कुछ वाक्यों में I dare say का प्रयोग होता है। ऐसे dare say का अर्थ होता है I suppose/It is likely, जैसे—

1. I dare say there will be taxis at the station.
2. I dare say he is right.

Used to

Rule I. Used to से यह बोध होता है कि कोई कार्य भूतकाल में लगातार होता था। इस प्रकार, इससे भूतकाल की आदत (habit) का बोध होता है, जैसे—

1. I used to play football at school.
2. He used to write to me every week.

जब वाक्य से यह बोध होता है कि कार्य भूतकाल में कभी-कभी होता था, तब would का प्रयोग होता है, use to का नहीं, जैसे—

1. He would often talk for hours.
2. She would often invite me to tea.

Rule II. Used का negative और interrogative इस प्रकार बनता है—

He used to live in London.

1. He *used not* (usedn't) *to* live in London.
2. *Used* he *to* live in London?

पर बातचीत में और विशेषकर question-tag में used का negative तथा interrogative बनाया जाता है do की सहायता से, जैसे—

He used to live in London.

1. He didn't use to live in London.
2. Did he use to live in London?
3. Didn't he used to live in London?
4. He used to live in London, didn't he?

Rule III. जब used to का अर्थ होता है आदी/अभ्यस्त (accustomed) होना, तब used to + noun/gerund का प्रयोग इस प्रकार होता है—

1. He is used to dust and smoke.
2. We are used to standing in queue.

Auxilliary Verb + Auxilliary Verb + Principal Verb

कुछ वाक्यों में दो या दो से अधिक Auxiliary Verbs के बाद एक ही Principal Verb का प्रयोग होता है, जब उन वाक्यों की बनावट इस प्रकार की होती है—

Auxiliary Verb + Auxiliary Verb + Principal Verb

1. He did not and will not *come*. 2. You can and should *do* it.

यहाँ पहले वाक्य में दो Auxiliary Verbs (did/will) के बाद एक ही Principal Verb (come) का प्रयोग हुआ है। दूसरे वाक्य में भी दो Auxiliary Verbs (can/should) के बाद एक ही Principal Verb (do) का व्यवहार किया गया है। ये दोनों ही वाक्य शुद्ध हैं, क्योंकि इन दोनों वाक्यों में Principal Verb का रूप अपने Auxiliary Verb का common factor है, अर्थात Principal Verb का रूप प्रत्येक Auxiliary Verb के लिए उपयुक्त है। आप जानते हैं कि come का प्रयोग did और will दोनों ही के बाद होता है। इसी प्रकार, do का प्रयोग can के साथ होता है और should के साथ भी। तो, इससे यह सिद्ध होता है कि यदि कई Auxiliary Verbs के लिए एक ही Principal Verb का प्रयोग हो, तो यह आवश्यक है कि उस Principal Verb का रूप उन Auxiliary Verbs के लिए common factor हो।

पर, यदि वह Principal Verb एक Auxiliary Verb के लिए उपयुक्त हो और दूसरे के लिए नहीं, अर्थात वह common factor नहीं हो, तो वैसे Principal Verb का प्रयोग प्रत्येक Auxiliary Verb के बाद अलग-अलग करना चाहिए; जैसे—

He has not *gone* and will not *go*.

यहाँ Principal Verb 'go' का प्रयोग दो Auxiliary Verbs के बाद अलग-अलग हुआ है—has के बाद gone का और will के बाद go का, क्योंकि यह Principal Verb दोनों Auxiliary Verbs का common factor नहीं है। आप जानते हैं कि has के बाद gone का प्रयोग होता है और will के बाद go का। इसलिए यदि हम यहाँ go और gone में से किसी एक ही का प्रयोग करें और दूसरे को छिपा दें, तो वह अशुद्ध होगा।

इन वाक्यों को देखें—

1. He has not and will not *go*. 2. You have and will *help* me.
3. He could not and has not *seen* me yet.

ध्यान दें कि इनमें Principal Verbs (go/helped/seen) अपने Auxiliary Verbs के लिए common factor नहीं हैं। यहाँ will के बाद go आया है जो will के लिए उपयुक्त है, पर has के लिए नहीं। इसी प्रकार help का प्रयोग will के साथ होता है पर have के साथ नहीं। फिर, तीसरे वाक्य में seen का प्रयोग has के साथ तो शुद्ध है पर could के साथ नहीं। इसलिए यहाँ Principal Verbs का प्रयोग इस प्रकार अलग-अलग होना चाहिए—

1. He has not *gone* and will not *go*.
2. You will *help* and have *helped* me.
3. He could not *see* and has not *seen* me yet.

....

EXERCISE

Correct the following sentences.

(1) No one has or can prove the existence of God. (2) He could and should have done the work. (3) No state has or can adopt such a measure. (4) You have and will help me in

future as well. (5) They did not and could not have known the truth. (6) I have never and shall never believe it. (7) I have never and shall never accuse a man.

Hints—(1) has proved or; (2) could do and; (3) has adopted or; (4) have helped and; (5) did not know, (6) have never believed and; (7) have never accused and

....

Position of Subject and Verb
[Inversion: verb + subject]

Rule I. Interrogative Sentences and Verb

Interrogative Sentence में Verb पहले आता है और उसके बाद Subject, जैसे—

1. *Are you* ill?
2. Where *is he* going?
3. What *do you* want?
4. Why *is he* angry?
5. Why *have you* beaten me?

इन सभी वाक्यों में Verbs (are/is/do) Subject के पहले आए हैं। अब इन्हें देखें—

1. You are ill?
2. Where he is going?
3. What you want?
4. Why he is angry?
5. Why you have beaten me?

ये सभी वाक्य अशुद्ध हैं।

इन वाक्यों से यह स्पष्ट हो जाता है कि Interrogative sentence की बनावट Verb और Subject के position (स्थान/क्रम) पर निर्भर करती है, केवल प्रश्नवाचक शब्द (why/where) पर नहीं।

....

EXERCISE

Correct the following sentences.

(1) Why the army insists so much on discipline? (2) What he is doing these days? (3) When you will see me? (4) Where you spent your last summer vacation? (5) Why I should help you? (6) How you came here from Patna? (7) Whom you are speaking of? (8) Why you did not reply to my letter? (9) When you will reply? (10) Where you are going? (11) What you did yesterday?

....

Rule II. Adverb/Conjunction/Verb [had/were]

यदि कोई वाक्य Negative Adverbs/Conjunctions से आरंभ हो, तो वाक्य में पहले Verb आता है और इसके Subject तथा अन्य शब्द।

Negative Adverbs/Conjunctions ये हैं—

seldom, hardly, scarcely, rarely, never, little, no sooner, in no other way, in no case, on no account, only by, only then, only when, only in this way, not only, nowhere, nor, neither, so

इन वाक्यों को देखें—

1. No sooner *had I* reached the station than the train started.
2. Hardly (Scarcely) *had he* started when his father came.
3. Never *did I* see such a scene before.
4. Rarely *is he* absent from duty.
5. Little *did I* know that he would betray me.
6. Nor *did he.* So *did he.* Neither *did he.*
7. So heavy *is the box* that I can't lift it.
8. *Were I* a bird I would fly to her.

इन सभी वाक्यों में Verb को Subject के पहले रखा गया है।

अब इन वाक्यों को देखें जिनकी बनावट नियम के विपरीत है—

1. Never I saw such a scene before.
2. Rarely he is absent.
3. Little I knew that.

NOTE (a)—यदि वाक्य इन Adverbs से शुरू नहीं हों, तो उनमें Subject पहले आता है और उसके बाद Verb, जैसे—

I had no sooner reached the station than the train started.

NOTE (b)—जो वाक्य इन Adverbs of Place से आरंभ होते हैं उनमें Verb पहले आता है और उसके बाद Subject—

in, up, out, down, over, back, round, forward

इन वाक्यों को लें—

1. *Down fell* a dozen mangoes.
2. *In came* the child crying.

पर यदि Subject कोई Pronoun हो, तो उसके पहले Verb का आना आवश्यक नहीं है; जैसे—

1. Down he fell.
2. In he came at once.

. . . .

EXERCISE

Correct the following sentences.

(1) No sooner I had reached home than it began to rain. (2) Hardly he had called me when I replied. (3) Scarcely he had heard the news, when he cried aloud. (4) No sooner he saw me than he ran away. (5) Never I will repeat this mistake. (6) In no other way he can be controlled.

. . . .

Position of Object and Complement

Rule I. Transitive Verb + Object

साधारणतः Object को Transitive Verb के बाद रखा जाता है; जैसे—

1. He *eats rice.*
2. He *bought* a *book.*

हाँ, यदि Object के पहले Adjective या Article का भी प्रयोग करना जरूरी हो, तो Verb के बाद सबसे पहले Article को रखना चाहिए, उसके बाद Adjective को और अंत में Object को। इसलिए ऐसे वाक्यों की बनावट इस प्रकार की हो जाती है—

Transitive Verb + Article + Adjective + Object; जैसे—

He *eats* a ripe *mango.*

इन अवस्थाओं में Object Verb के पहले आता है, बाद में नहीं—

(i) यदि Relative Pronoun Object का काम करे; जैसे—

1. This is the book *that he requires.*
2. This is *what I want.*

(ii) यदि Interrogative Pronoun Object के समान प्रयुक्त हो; जैसे—

1. *What* do you *want*?
2. *What* does she *like*?

NOTE—केवल एक object रहने पर Transitive verb को Mono Transitive कहा जाता है।

Rule II. Transitive Verb + object + object

कुछ Transitive Verbs के साथ दो-दो Objects आते हैं। उनमें से एक को Direct Object कहा जाता है और दूसरे को Indirect Object. जब Transitive Verb के साथ दो-दो objects आते हैं तब उसे Ditransitive कहा जाता है।

ऐसे वाक्यों की बनावट होती है—

(i) Subject + Verb + Indirect Object + Direct Object

1. He bought her a house.
2. He gave the place a new look.

(ii) Subject + Verb + Direct Object + to/for + Indirect Object

1. He bought a house for her.
2. He gave a new look to the place.

NOTE—यहाँ एक बात का ध्यान रखें। जब वाक्य में Direct Object पहले आता है तब दूसरे Object (Indirect Object) के पहले to या for का प्रयोग होता है। पर, जब Indirect Object पहले आता है, तो दूसरे Object (Direct Object) के पहले to या for नहीं आता। इससे एक बात स्पष्ट है कि जिस Object के पहले to या for का प्रयोग हो सकता है उसी को Indirect Object कहा जाता है और जिसके साथ to/for का प्रयोग नहीं हो सकता उसे Direct Object कहते हैं। यह आवश्यक नहीं है कि Direct Object सदा निर्जीव (lifeless object) हो और Indirect Object सदा सजीव (living) हो। इन वाक्यों को लें—

1. He gave the *country* a new *policy*.
2. He gave the *house* a new *look*.

इन वाक्यों में दोनों ही Objects निर्जीव हैं। यहाँ पहले वाक्य में Country और दूसरे में house हैं Indirect Objects. क्यों? इसलिए कि इनके पहले to का प्रयोग हो सकता है। इसी प्रकार, policy और house का प्रयोग Direct Object की तरह हुआ है, क्योंकि इनके साथ to/for का प्रयोग नहीं हो सकता। इसलिए याद रखें—

Object + to/for = Indirect Object

Object – to/for = Direct Object

वाक्य में पहले Direct Object को रखा जाए या Indirect Object को? इसके लिए इन दो नियमों की सहायता लें—

(i) जिस Object पर अधिक जोर देना हो, उसे पहले रखें; जैसे—

1. I gave *Ram* a book. [to Ram, not to anybody else]
2. I gave *a book* to Ram. [a book, not anything else]

(ii) जो Object छोटा हो (अर्थात जो कम शब्दों को मिलाकर बना हो) उसे पहले रखें, और जो Object बड़ा हो (अर्थात जो बहुत से शब्दों से बना हो) उसे बाद में रखें—

He gave a book to every student of my class.

यहाँ 'every student of my class' है Indirect Object और book है Direct Object. आप देखते हैं कि Indirect से छोटा है Direct Object. इसलिए वाक्य में Direct Object को पहले रखा गया है। इस वाक्य में book को अंत में रखना जरा भद्दा लगता है—

He gave every student of my class a book.

अब इस वाक्यों को लें—

He *gave me* books, pens, pencils and several other articles of daily use.

यहाँ me है Indirect Object और 'books ... use' है Direct Object. इस वाक्य में Indirect Object छोटा है। इसलिए इसे पहले रखा गया है। इसे इस प्रकार रखना अच्छा नहीं लगता—

He *gave* books, pens, pencils and several other articles of daily use *to me*.

इसलिए आप Direct तथा Indirect Object की लंबाई-चौड़ाई देखकर ही वाक्य में उन्हें उचित स्थान दें।

Rule III. Verb + preposition/adverb + noun

कुछ वाक्यों में Verb के साथ कोई Preposition/Adverb (on/off/up/down/in/out/away) आता है और Verb के बाद कोई noun/pronoun रहता है जो Object का काम करता है। ऐसे वाक्यों में जब Object (noun/pronoun) छोटा रहता है, तब Preposition का प्रयोग Object के बाद होता है। पर जब Object बड़ा रहता है, तो Preposition का प्रयोग Object के पहले होता है—

(i) Verb + Object + Preposition

(ii) Verb + Preposition + Object

इन वाक्यों को लें—

1. Put the hat *on.*
2. Take your shirt *off.*
3. Bring him *in.*
4. Look him *up.*
5. Take him *out.*
6. He knocked me *down.*

इन वाक्यों में Objects पहले आये हैं और उनके बाद Preposition. क्यों? इसलिए कि Objects छोटे-छोटे हैं।

अब इन वाक्यों को देखें—

1. Put *on* your new hat.
2. Take *off* your old shirt.
3. Bring *in* all the guests.
4. Lock *up* all the costly articles.
5. Take *out* all the cats and dogs.
6. He knocked *down* several children.

इन वाक्यों में Objects लंबे हैं। इसलिए Preposition का प्रयोग इनके पहले हुआ है।

NOTE—यही कारण है कि वाक्य में पहले Pronoun (Objective case में) आता है और उसके बाद noun या noun-equivalents (phrase/infinitive/clause) रखे जाते हैं; जैसे—

1. Cows give *us* milk.
2. I teach *her* English.
3. He showed *me* how to do it.
4. I advised *him* to buy a book.
5. I asked *her* where she lived.

इन वाक्यों में Pronouns पहले आये हैं और इनके बाद noun/phrase/infinitive/clause. क्यों? इसलिए कि ये Pronouns बहुत छोटे हैं। इन्हें इस प्रकार न लिखें—

1. Cows give milk *to us.*
2. I teach English *to her.*
3. I advised which book to buy *to him.*

ध्यान दें कि ऐसे वाक्यों की बनावट होती है—

Subject + Verb + Indirect Object + Direct Object (S + V + IO + DO)

इन्हें S + V + DO + IO कर देने से छोटा और सरल वाक्य भी बड़ा हो जाता है और भद्दा भी।

एक बात और। जब it/this वाक्य में Direct Object का कार्य करता है, तब Indirect Object के साथ to/for का प्रयोग अवश्य होता है और Indirect Object बाद में आता है (DO + to/for + IO); जैसे—

1. I bought *it* for him. 2. I gave *it* to her.

इन्हें इस प्रकार नहीं लिखा जा सकता, अर्थात इन्हें IO + DO में इस प्रकार बदला नहीं जा सकता।

1. I bought him it. 2. I gave him it.

Rule IV. Transitive Verb + object + complement

कुछ वाक्यों में object के बाद complement (पूरक) आता है, जैसे—

1. I made him captain. 2. We elected him president.

ऐसे Transitive verb को Complex Transitive कहा जाता है।

Rule V. Subject + make/get/have + object

ऐसे verb से subject को कार्य करने की प्रेरणा मिलती है; subject स्वयं कार्य नहीं करता। इसे हिन्दी में प्रेरणार्थक क्रिया और अँगरेजी में Causative Verb कहा जाता है, जैसे—

1. I made her sing. 2. I got a letter written.
3. I had him fined. 4. I got him to repair my watch.

Annexture A

Question-tags/tail questions

Question-tag को tail question भी कहा जाता है। इसकी बनावट होती है—

statement/command/request/proposal	*+ question-tag/tail question*
You like fish	don't you?
Make tea for me	will you?
Don't drive too fast	will you?
Let's start now	shall we?

ध्यान दें—

Rule I. Positive statement के साथ negative question-tag आता है और negative statement के साथ positive question-tag आता है—

1. It is fine today, isn't it? 2. She is not tall, is she?

NOTE—जब positive statement के साथ few, little, seldom, rarely, hardly, scarcely आदि negative अर्थ सूचित करनेवाले शब्द आते हैं, तब वह negative statement माना जाता है। इसलिए ऐसे negative statements के साथ positive question-tag आता है, जैसे—

1. Few people are happy, are they? 2. He is seldom late, is he?

Rule II. Question-tag का subject कोई pronoun होता है, noun नहीं, जैसे—

1. Radha is tall. Isn't she? 2. Mohan has a car, hasn't he?

NOTE (a)—जब statement का subject *no one/any one/someone/everyone/anybody/nobody/everybody* रहता है, तब question-tag में he या they का प्रयोग होता है। पर, they का प्रयोग अधिक प्रचलित तथा लोकप्रिय है, जैसे—

1. Anyone can do it, can't he/can't they?
2. No one can do it, can he/can they?

NOTE (b)—जब statement का subject *all of us/none of us/some of us/most of us/everyone of us* होता है, तब question-tag में we का प्रयोग होता है, जैसे—

All of us have seen the Red Fort, haven't we?

NOTE (c)—जब statement का subject *all of them/none of them/some of them/most of them/everyone of them* होता है तब question-tag में they आता है, जैसे—

All of them have seen the Taj Mahal, haven't they?

NOTE (d)—जब statement का subject *all of you/none of you/some of you/most of you/one of you* होता है, तब question-tag में you आता है, जैसे—

All of you know English, don't you?

NOTE (e)—जब statement में *There + auxilliary verb + subject* आता है, तब question-tag में केवल verb + there आता है; verb + pronoun नहीं, जैसे—

There is no hospital here, is there? [not, **is it there?**]

NOTE (f)—जब statement में *nothing/something/everything/anything* का प्रयोग subject की तरह होता है, तब question-tag में it आता है, जैसे—

Everything was stolen, wasn't it?

Nothing is lost, is it?

NOTE (g)—Statement के I am के लिए question-tag में aren't I आता है और used के लिए usedn't या didn't, जैसे—

1. I am still young, aren't I? [not, **am not I**]
2. I used to play football at school. [usedn't I/didn't I?]

ध्यान दें कि used के साथ didn't का प्रयोग अधिक प्रचलित है।

NOTE (h)—जब statement में *need/needs* आता है, तब question-tag में don't/doesn't आता है और needn't के लिए need का प्रयोग होता है, जैसे—

1. I need a bike, don't I?
2. She needs a car, doesn't she?
3. We needn't hurry, need we?
4. He needn't worry now, need he?

NOTE (i)—Positive request/command के साथ positive या negative question-tag (will you? या won't you?) आता है, पर negative request/command के साथ सदा positive question-tag (will you?) आता है, जैसे—

1. Close the gate, will you?
2. Close the gate, won't you?
3. Don't close the gate, will you?

NOTE (j)—जब Let से proposal (प्रस्ताव) या suggestion (सुझाव) का बोध होता है, तब question-tag में shall we? आता है, जैसे—

Let us play now, shall we?

पर जब Let (*Let him/her/them*) से अनुमति (permission) का भाव व्यक्त होता है, तब question-tag में will you? आता है, जैसे—

Let them play here, will you?

EXERCISE

Add question-tags.

1. We ought to help him.
2. He has finished the work.
3. Few people know him.
4. We laughed at the joker.
5. Don't pluck flowers.
6. Please give me some money.
7. He was late for lunch.
8. None of us can solve this problem.
9. Most of them are very poor.
10. Have a cup of coffee.

REVISION TEST I

I. *Match the sentences under A and B.*

A	B
The market was closed yesterday.	She must see a doctor.
He is neither in the office nor at home.	He can't lift this trunk.
She is very ill.	He may die soon.
He is vomiting blood.	He may have gone to Delhi.
He is just a baby.	She needn't have gone to market yesterday.
She is very poor.	She has got to work hard.
He has got a car.	He doesn't have to travel by bus.

II. *Correct these sentences.*

1. Why you are so sad?
2. Will I take the examination?

3. He doesn't like milk, nor I do.
4. Seldom he is late for dinner.
5. Sheep give wool to us.
6. Where he lives these days?
7. Take your old shirt off.
8. He dares not to refuse.
9. She needs not to worry.
10. I like music. So he does.

III. *Make these sentences (a) negative and (b) emphatic.*

1. He likes to read novels.
2. She bought a lot of fish.
3. She helps the poor.
4. I travelled by air.

REVISION TEST II

Transform these sentences as directed.

1. I must catch the first train [use *have got to*]
2. She doesn't have to borrow books. [use *needn't*]
3. He finished the work in time. [use *was able to*]
4. She has no books to read. [use *don't have*]
5. We shouldn't kill birds. [use *oughtn't*]
6. He had the capacity to help me but he didn't. [use *could have*]
7. There was a possibility of our winning the match but we didn't. [use *might have*]
8. It was not necessary for her to buy another car but she did. [use *needn't have*]
9. It is probable but not certain that you saw the Red Fort. [use *can have*]
10. It is probable but not certain that she has gone to Mumbai. [use *may have*]
11. It is certain that the news is not true. [use *can't*]
12. It is almost certain that he caught the train. [use *must have*]
13. Prices are likely to rise. [use *going to*]
14. She is likely to get back tonight. [use *may*]
15. It was not proper for you to cheat her. [use *shouldn't have*]

❐

Chapter X

TEST YOURSELF

I. *Correct these sentences.*

1. We go to college for getting knowledge.
2. She doesn't know to drive a car.
3. I will have you to behave well.
4. Newton saw an apple to fall.
5. I don't mind to wait for you.
6. I got him repair my watch.
7. She has an armchair to sit.
8. He did nothing but to play.
9. Reading in my room the clock struck twelve.
10. Standing on the roof a helicopter flew over me.
11. She had better to stay indoors.

II. *Complete these sentences with an infinitive/gerund.*

1. He was punished …… .
2. I don't mind …… .
3. We saw the plane …… .
4. She now avoids …… .
5. This is a pen for you …… .
6. I made her …… .
7. He prefers …… .

❐

NON-FINITE VERBS

1. Infinitive
2. Gerund
3. Participle

जब किसी verb का number/person वाक्य के subject के अनुसार होता है, तब उसे Finite verb (सीमित क्रिया) कहा जाता है, जैसे—

1. We know English.
2. He likes fish.

जब verb पर subject के number/person का प्रभाव नहीं पड़ता है, तब उसे Non-finite verb कहते हैं। Non-finite verbs तीन प्रकार के होते हैं—

(i) Infinitive (ii) Gerund (iii) Participle.

अब हम इनके प्रयोग पर विचार करें।

Rule I. Infinitive/Gerund का प्रयोग वाक्य में subject/object/complement की तरह इस प्रकार होता है—

1. To say so is easy.—subject
2. He likes to collect stamps.—object
3. I am to say that.—complement
4. Walking is good for health.—subject
5. He is found of catching fish.—object

NOTE (a)—जब Infinitive एक Subject का कार्य करता है, तब वाक्य की बनावट इस प्रकार की भी हो सकती है—

It is/was + Infinitive; जैसे—

1. To say so is easy. It is easy to say so.
2. To try was useless. It was useless to try.

NOTE (b)—जब Infinitive का प्रयोग इन Verbs के बाद Object की भाँति होता है, तब Infinitive के पहले how आता है—*how + infinitive.*

ये Verbs हैं—

decide, discover, observe, forget, see, learn, know, teach, wonder, show, ask/enquire, explain

इन वाक्यों को देखें—

1. Please show/teach me how to do it.
2. I don't know how to drive a car.
3. I explained how to answer questions.

ऐसे वाक्य how के बिना इस प्रकार लिखे नहीं जा सकते—

1. She doesn't know to cook fish.
2. Please teach me to speak well.

ऐसे वाक्यों में how का प्रयोग क्यों होता है? इसलिए कि इनसे कार्य करने की विधि/तरीका (method) का बोध होता है।

Rule II. Subject + Verb + Infinitive: purpose

कुछ वाक्यों में Infinitive का प्रयोग उद्देश्य (purpose) या परिणाम (result) का बोध कराने के लिए होता है, जिसे Infinitive of Purpose या Gerundial Infinitive कहा जाता है।

इन वाक्यों को देखें—

1. I want *to see* my friend. (उद्देश्य)
2. He went to market *to buy* a cow. (उद्देश्य)
3. She lived *to be* eighty. (परिणाम)
4. We came *to realise* our mistake. (परिणाम)

Caution—ऐसे अर्थों में Infinitive के बदले for + gerund (verb + ing) का प्रयोग इस प्रकार नहीं होता—

1. He went to market *for buying* books.
2. Pull chain *for stopping* the train.

इन वाक्यों में to buy/to stop का प्रयोग होना चाहिए।

Rule III. Subject + Verb + for + Gerund: cause

कारण (cause) का बोध कराने के लिए *for + gerund* का प्रयोग इस प्रकार होता है—

1. He was punished for committing theft.
2. I was rewarded for writing correctly.

Rule IV. Subject + happen, etc. + Infinitive

कुछ वाक्यों में happen/seem/appeal/chance के साथ Infinitive आता है और *Verb + Infinitive* एक साथ मिलकर काम होने का बोध कराते हैं; जैसे—

1. I happened to see him. 2. I seem to remember.
3. He appeared to forget me. 4. I chanced to meet him.

यहाँ happened + to see का अर्थ है *saw;* seem + to remember का अर्थ है *remember;* appeared + to forget का अर्थ है *forgot;* और chanced + to meet का *met.* ध्यान दें कि ऐसे वाक्यों के Verb में थोड़ी अनिश्चितता का भाव मिलाने के लिए ही happen/chance का प्रयोग किया जाता है।

Rule V. Subject + Verb + Noun/Adjective + Infinitive

कुछ वाक्यों में Noun/Adjective के बाद Infinitive आता है, जो उस Noun/Adjective का गुण बतलाता है; जैसे—

1. This is a house to let. 2. English is difficult to learn.

ऐसे वाक्यों में Infinitive Active Voice में रहता है। इसलिए यहाँ to let और to learn के Passive Voice (to be let/to be learnt) का प्रयोग अशुद्ध होता।

कुछ और वाक्य लें—

1. Radium is not easy to get.
2. I have nothing to show.
3. He has nothing to do.
4. She is difficult to please.
5. It is easy to promise.
6. Meat is hard to digest.
7. I have several books to sell.
8. Grapes are good to eat.

इन वाक्यों में Infinitive (to get/to show/to do/to please/to promise/to digest/to sell/to eat) को Passive Voice में रखना अशुद्ध होता। इसलिए ऐसे-ऐसे वाक्य न लिखें—

1. He has nothing to be done.
2. I have two mangoes to be eaten.
3. You are difficult to be pleased.
4. Gold is not easy to be found.

देखिए अच्छे लेखक ऐसे वाक्यों में Active Voice का ही प्रयोग करते हैं।

Put this way it is plainly not an easy question **to answer.** —I A RICHARDS

EXERCISE

Correct the following sentences.

(1) Mathematics is difficult to be learnt. (2) It is easy to be said but difficult to be done. (3) The work is easy to be performed. (4) Grain is hard to be digested. (5) She is difficult to be pleased.

Hints—(1) to learn; (2) to say … to do; (3) to perform; (4) to digest; (5) to please

---

Rule VI. Subject + Verb + Noun + Infinitive + Preposition

कुछ वाक्यों में Noun के बाद Infinitive आता है और उसके बाद एक उपयुक्त Preposition. ऐसे वाक्यों में Infinitive + Preposition का प्रयोग तब होता है, जब वह Noun किसी उद्देश्य के लिए एक साधन (means/instrument) का काम करता है; जैसे—

1. I have a house to live in.
2. She has a pen to write with.
3. I have a stick to beat with.
4. He has a chair to sit on.
5. She has an armchair to sit in.

ऐसे वाक्यों में उद्देश्य/साधन का बोध Preposition की सहायता से होता है। ये वाक्य मूल रूप में इस प्रकार के होते हैं—

1. I have a house *in which* I live.
2. She has a pen *with which* she writes.

जब clause को Infinitive में बदल दिया जाता है, तब Relative Pronoun (which) का लोप हो जाता है और Preposition वाक्य के अंत में चला जाता है। इसलिए ऐसे वाक्यों में Infinitive + Preposition का प्रयोग आवश्यक होता है। यही कारण है कि ऐसे वाक्य preposition के बिना इस प्रकार लिखे नहीं जा सकते—

1. He has a chair to sit.
2. I have a walking stick to walk.
3. I have a house to live.

Rule VII. Subject + Verb + Object + Infinitive

कुछ वाक्यों में Transitive Verb के बाद object आता है और object के बाद Infinitive. ऐसे Transitive Verbs ये हैं—

allow, advise, order, force, tell, permit, request, remind, invite, etc.

ऐसे वाक्यों की बनावट होती है—

Subject + Transitive Verb + Object + Infinitive; जैसे—

1. He ordered me to go out.
2. I forced him to open the gate.

ऐसे वाक्य object के बिना इस प्रकार लिखे नहीं जा सकते—

1. He ordered to go out.
2. I forced to open the gate.

Rule VIII. Subject + Verb/Adjective + Infinitive

कुछ Verbs/Adjectives ऐसे होते हैं जिनके साथ Infinitive का प्रयोग होता है, Gerund का नहीं। ये हैं—

agree, desire, dare, decide, hope, expect, want, wish, promise, refuse, eager, anxious, able, glad, happy, easy, hard, ready, fail, etc.

इन वाक्यों को लें—

1. I hope to see him.
2. I am ready to start.
3. They have decided to marry.
4. Why did he fail to come?

इसलिए ऐसे-ऐसे वाक्य न लिखें—

1. I wish helping him.
2. He is eager seeing me.

Rule IX. Subject + Verb + Infinitive/Gerund

कुछ Verbs ऐसे होते हैं जिनके साथ Infinitive का प्रयोग हो सकता है और Gerund का भी। पर ऐसे वाक्यों के अर्थ में अंतर पड़ जाता है। *Verb + gerund* (verb + ing) से यह बोध होता है कि कार्य सदा सामान्य रूप से होता है, पर *verb + infinitive* से यह बोध होता है कि कोई काम किसी विशेष अवसर पर या परिस्थिति में ही होता है; जैसे—

1. I like (dislike) singing.
2. I like to sing.
3. He stopped talking.
4. He stopped to talk.
5. He began talking.
6. He began to talk.

EXERCISE

Make ten sentences like the following.

1. It is easy to say.
2. I have decided to help him.
3. It is no use crying now.
4. He enjoys reading grammar.

Rule X. Gerund and Possessive Case

यदि वाक्य में Noun/Pronoun के बाद Gerund (verb + ing) का प्रयोग करना हो, तो उस Noun/Pronoun के Possessive Case का प्रयोग करना चाहिए और उसे Gerund के ठीक पहले रखना चाहिए [possessive case + gerund]; जैसे—

1. I ask the favour of *your granting* me leave.
2. Ram won by *Mohan's missing* a chance.
3. I prevented *his doing* this work.
4. Please don't mind *my coming* late.

ध्यान दें कि ऐसे वाक्यों में Objective Case का प्रयोग इस प्रकार नहीं होता—

I prevented him doing this work.

कुछ और वाक्य लें—

1. I object to *his being* promoted.
2. You may rely upon *my doing* all in my power.

यहाँ Pronouns (his/my) Possessive Case में हैं और इन्हें Gerund के पहले रखा गया है। इन वाक्यों में his/my के बदले him/me का प्रयोग अशुद्ध होता।

NOTE—यदि Gerund के पहले कोई निर्जीव संज्ञा (noun) आए, तो 's' जोड़कर उसे Possessive में रखने की कोशिश नहीं करनी चाहिए। इसी प्रकार, Demonstrative Pronouns (this/that/these/those) में *s* जोड़कर इन्हें Possessive Case में न बदलें।

इन वाक्यों को लें—

1. There is no chance of *that happening* again.
2. I look forward to *attention being* given.
3. I depend on the *wall being* built immediately.

यहाँ that के बदले **that's,** attention के बदले **attention's** और wall के बदले **wall's** का प्रयोग अनुचित होता। क्यों? इसलिए कि *'s* जोड़कर ऐसे nouns/pronouns का Possessive Case बनता ही नहीं।

Rule XI. Subject + Verb + Gerund

कुछ verbs ऐसे होते हैं जिनके साथ सदा Gerund (verb + ing) का प्रयोग होता है, Infinitive का नहीं। ये Verbs हैं—

avoid, consider, enjoy, excuse, feel, finish, mind, miss, can't help, go on, give up, it is no use/good, look forward to

इन वाक्यों को देखें—

1. It is no use/no good crying now.
2. Would you mind closing the gate?
3. He avoids doing his duties.
4. I can't help laughing.
5. I am looking forward to meeting you again.

इसलिए ऐसे-ऐसे वाक्य न लिखें—

1. He avoids to see me.
2. He gave up to drink.

Rule XII. Anaphoric 'to'

Infinitive (to + verb) की पुनरावृत्ति से बचने के लिए केवल to का प्रयोग होता है और to के साथ आनेवाले verb का लोप हो जाता है। इसे **Anaphoric to** कहा जाता है; जैसे—

1. Would you have a cup of tea? Yes, I should like *to.*
2. I wished him to help me but he didn't want *to.*

यहाँ पहले वाक्य में like to have के बदले केवल *like to* का प्रयोग हुआ और दूसरे वाक्य में want to help के बदले केवल want to का। यहाँ verb को छिपाकर पुनरावृत्ति के दोष से वाक्यों को बचाया गया है।

Rule XIII. Omission of Infinitive [infinitive without *to*]

Rule XIII (A). इन verbs के बाद Infinitive का to चिह्न छिपा रहता है—

hear, see, notice, observe, need not, dare not, feel, make, let, bid, behold, watch, shall, should, will, would, can, could, may, might, do, did, must; जैसे—

1. I saw an apple *fall.*
2. I heard him *cry.*
3. He need not *go.*
4. He dare not *do.*
5. I made him *laugh.*
6. Let him *read.*

इन वाक्यों में fall/cry/go/do/laugh/read के पहले to छिपा हुआ है, जो शुद्ध है। यहाँ to का प्रयोग अनुचित होता।

अब इन वाक्यों को देखें—

1. I bade him *to go.*
2. He made me *to laugh.*
3. I heard him *to whisper.*
4. I saw him *to take* my book.

इन वाक्यों में to का प्रयोग अशुद्ध है।

हाँ, जब ये Verbs Passive Voice में रहते हैं, तब to अवश्य आता है; जैसे—

1. He *was made to* sing.
2. He *was seen to take* my book.

यहाँ to को छिपाया नहीं जा सकता। हाँ, let के साथ ऐसा नहीं होता, क्योंकि Passive Voice में भी इसके बाद to नहीं आता; जैसे—

He was *let go.* [**not,** *to go*]

देखिए इस वाक्य को जिसमें make के बाद to का प्रयोग अशुद्ध है, क्योंकि 'make' Active Voice में है—

Let this public mercy to the Church of God make you to forget your private sorrow.

—OLIVER CROMWELL

Rule XIII (B). *better/had better/had rather/would rather/had sooner/had as soon as* के बाद to छिपा रहता है; जैसे—

1. Better *reign* in hell than *serve* in heaven.
2. I had rather *rest* than *work.*

यदि यहाँ reign/serve/go/rest/work के पहले to का प्रयोग कर दिया जाए, तो वह अशुद्ध होगा। अब इन वाक्यों को देखें—

1. I had better *to* sleep.
2. He had rather *to* die than *to* live.

यहाँ sleep/die/live के पहले to का प्रयोग अशुद्ध है।

Rule XIII (C). *but, except, than* तथा *as* के बाद to छिपा रहता है; जैसे—

He did nothing but *talk* and *laugh.*

यहाँ talk/laugh के पहले to का प्रयोग अशुद्ध होता।

Rule XIII (D). why/why not के बाद to छिपा रहता है; जब वाक्य में subject तथा verb का प्रयोग नहीं होता, जैसे—

1. Why not start today?
2. Why worry now?

यहाँ start/worry के पहले to का प्रयोग अनुचित होता।

Rule XIII (E). Subject + have + Object + Infinitive [without 'to']

कुछ वाक्यों में has/have/had के बाद कोई noun/pronoun आता है, जो एक object का काम करता है और उसके बाद एक Infinitive आता है, पर उसका to छिपा हुआ रहता है; जैसे—

1. I will *have him remember.*
2. I will *have you know this.*
3. Would you *have me believe this?*

ऐसे वाक्यों के have से इच्छा (wish) का बोध होता है। वाक्य की ऐसी बनावट और इसका अर्थ थोड़ा कठिन होता है। इसलिए यह लोकप्रिय नहीं है। यही कारण है कि ऐसे वाक्य इस प्रकार लिखे जाते हैं—

1. I wish him to remember.
2. I wish you to know this.

ध्यान दें कि इस प्रकार के वाक्यों में Infinitive का 'to' चिह्न छिपा हुआ नहीं रहता।

Rule XIII (F). जब वाक्य में make (causative verb) के बदले get का प्रयोग होता है, तब Infinitive का to चिह्न प्रकट हो जाता है, जैसे—

1. I made him *do* the work.
2. I got him *to do* the work.
3. I got a mechanic *to repair* my radio.

याद रखें—

1. Subject + make + object + infinitive [without to]
2. Subject + get + obect + infinitive [with to]

Rule XIII (G). जब know का अर्थ see या hear होता है और इसके साथ Past/Present Perfect Tense का प्रयोग होता है, तब object + infinitive without to आता है, जैसे—

1. I have never known her *get* angry.
2. I haven't ever known him *laugh* heartily.

यहाँ get/laugh के पहले to का प्रयोग अनुचित होता। हाँ, passive voice में to का प्रयोग इस प्रकार अवश्य होना चाहिए—

She has never been known *to get* angry.

Rule XIII (H). जब वाक्य में help का प्रयोग एक verb की तरह होता है, तब to छिप जाता है, जैसे—

1. I helped him *lift* the box. 2. I helped her *find* her purse.

यहाँ lift/find के पहले to छिपा हुआ है। यह एक अमरीकी प्रयोग (American usage) है, जो अब बहुत लोकप्रिय हो चुका है। हाँ, British usage के अनुसार ऐसे help के बाद to का प्रयोग शुद्ध माना जाता है, जैसे—

I helped her *to find* her purse.

Rule XIV. Prefer to/Rather than

Rule XIV (A). यदि prefer के बाद Noun/Pronoun/Gerund आए, तो to का प्रयोग करना चाहिए, than या rather than का नहीं; जैसे—

1. I prefer work *to* rest. 2. I prefer you *to* him.
3. I prefer walking *to* riding.

यहाँ पहले वाक्य में prefer के बाद दो Nouns 'work' और 'rest' आए हैं, दूसरे में दो Pronouns 'you' और 'him' और तीसरे में दो Gerunds walking और riding. इसलिए इन वाक्यों में to का प्रयोग किया गया है। इन वाक्यों में to के बदले than का प्रयोग अशुद्ध होता।

Rule XIV (B). यदि prefer के बाद Infinitive आए, तो to के बदले rather than का प्रयोग करना चाहिए, सिर्फ than का कभी भी नहीं; जैसे—

1. He prefers *to die rather than* pay.
2. He prefers *to live rather than* die.

इन दोनों वाक्यों में prefer के बाद to die/to live का प्रयोग हुआ है, जो Infinitive हैं। इसलिए Infinitive के बाद rather than का प्रयोग हुआ है। यहाँ rather than के बदले सिर्फ than या to का प्रयोग सर्वथा अनुचित होता। इस संबंध में आप इस नियम का ध्यान रखें—

> **Prefer** *has two constructions—'I prefer this (living) to that (dying)' and 'I prefer to do this rather than that'. The infinitive construction must not be used without* **rather.**
>
> —FOWLER: *Modern English Usage*

NOTE (a)—यदि Infinitive के बाद rather than का प्रयोग नहीं करना चाहें, तो Infinitive को Gerund में बदल दें और rather than के बदले to का प्रयोग करें; जैसे—

1. He prefers *to die rather than pay.*

2. He prefers *dying to paying.*

NOTE (b)—Prefer के साथ more/most का भी प्रयोग नहीं होता। इसलिए ऐसे-ऐसे वाक्य न लिखें—

1. Which do you prefer more? 2. Which do you prefer most?

इन्हें इस प्रकार लिखें—

Which do you prefer?

. . . .

EXERCISE

Correct the following sentences.

(1) He prefers to read than to write. (2) I prefer rice than bread. (3) You prefer walking than riding. (4) She prefers me than him. (5) I prefer to feed than to eat. (6) You prefer to sing than to talk. (7) Which do you prefer more—meat or fish?

Hints—(1) rather than write, or prefers reading to writing; (2) to; (3) to; (4) to; (5) rather than eat, or prefer feeding to eating; (6) rather than talk, or prefer singing to talking; (7) prefer—meat or fish?

. . . .

Participle

1. Present Participle [verb + ing]
2. Perfect Participle [having + past participle]
3. Past Participle [verb + ed/en]

Rule I. Present Participle तथा Past Participle का प्रयोग तब होता है जब वाक्य के सभी भागों का subject एक ही (common) रहता है और वाक्य में दो या दो से अधिक कार्य किये जाते हैं, अर्थात दो से अधिक verbs का प्रयोग होता है, जैसे—

1. Opening the drawer he took out his pistol.
2. Having worked hard he felt tired.

NOTE (a)—जब दो कार्य एक साथ (simultaneously) होते हैं या एक कार्य दूसरे कार्य के तुरंत (immediately) बाद होता है, तब Present Participle का प्रयोग होता है, जैसे—

1. Opening the drawer he took out his pistol.
2. Turning to the left you can see the temple.

जब एक कार्य पूर्ण रूप से पूरा (complete) हो जाता है और उसके बाद दूसरा कार्य आरंभ होता है तब Past Participle का प्रयोग होता है, जैसे—

1. Having worked hard he felt tired.
2. Having typed the letter he posted it.
3. Having killed the tiger he carried it home.

NOTE (b)—Present और Past Participle से कारण (cause) का भी बोध है, जैसे—

1. Knowing that he wouldn't get success, he gave up the attempt.
2. Fearing that it might rain he took an umbrella.
3. Having been injured he left the battlefield.
4. Being a student he doesn't meddle in politics.

Rule II. Unattached/Dangling Participle

जब Participle को उपयुक्त subject के साथ जोड़ा नहीं जाता, तब इस भूल को Unattached Participle कहा जाता है। इसे Wrongly Attached Participle/Misrelated Participle/Dangling Participle/Hanging Participle भी कहा जाता है। इसकी चर्चा करते हुए कहा गया है—

The Unattached or Wrongly Attached Participle is one of the blunders most common with illiterate or careless writers. —FOWLER: *King's English*

Participle का प्रयोग कहाँ करना चाहिए और कहाँ नहीं, इसके लिए इस वाक्य पर विचार करें—

Walking along the street, Ram gave me a pen.

उपर्युक्त वाक्य में दो भाग हैं—

1. Ram was walking along the street.
2. Ram gave me a pen.

आप जानते हैं कि Ram was walking along the street एक clause है और इसका संक्षिप्त रूप है—walking along the street. इस वाक्य से एक बात स्पष्ट है कि इसके दोनों ही भागों (clauses) का subject एक ही (same) है और वह है Ram. जब वाक्य के दोनों भागों का subject एक ही हो अर्थात वह दोनों के लिए common factor हो, तब पहले भाग (clause) के बदले Participle का प्रयोग होता है।

पर जब दोनों भागों के subjects भिन्न हों (अर्थात प्रत्येक भाग के लिए भिन्न-भिन्न subjects हों), तब Participle का प्रयोग नहीं होना चाहिए। वैसे वाक्यों में पूरे clause (while + subject + verb) का प्रयोग होना चाहिए। यदि वैसे वाक्यों में clause के बदले Participle का प्रयोग हो जाए, तो उसे ही Unattached Participle कहा जाता है। इस वाक्य को देखें—

While going to school, a dog jumped at Ram.

इन वाक्य में दो भाग हैं—

1. Ram was going to school.
2. A dog jumped at him (Ram).

यहाँ while going to school संक्षिप्त रूप है Ram was going to school का। आप ध्यान से देखें कि इन दोनों भागों के subjects भिन्न हैं, एक ही नहीं। पहले भाग का subject है Ram और दूसरे भाग का dog. इसलिए यहाँ Participle के प्रयोग से Unattached Participle का दोष आ गया है। इस दोष को दूर करने के लिए Participle के बदले पूरे clause का प्रयोग इस प्रकार करना चाहिए—

While Ram was going to school, a dog jumped at him.

अब, इन वाक्यों को लें—

1. Ploughing his field, Mohan got a hidden treasure.
2. Ploughing his field, a snake bit him.

पहले वाक्य के दोनों भागों का subject है Mohan; इसलिए इसमें Participle उपयुक्त subject से attached (जुड़ा हुआ) है, अर्थात यहाँ Participle का प्रयोग उचित है।

पर दूसरे वाक्य की बनावट भिन्न है। इसके पहले भाग का subject है he और दूसरे भाग का a snake. इस प्रकार, यहाँ Participle उपयुक्त subject से जुड़ा हुआ नहीं है, अर्थात यह Unattached Participle है। इसलिए इस वाक्य की बनावट इस प्रकार की होनी चाहिए—

While he was ploughing his field, a snake bit him.

कुछ और वाक्य लें—

1. Walking across the bridge, his walking stick broke.
2. Sleeping in my room, a thief suddenly appeared.

इन वाक्यों में भी Unattached Participle का दोष आ गया है। क्यों? इसलिए कि यहाँ प्रत्येक भाग के subjects भिन्न-भिन्न हैं। इसलिए इन्हें इस प्रकार लिखें—

1. While he was walking across the bridge, his walking stick broke.
2. While I was sleeping in my room, a thief suddenly appeared.

यदि यहाँ Participle का प्रयोग कर देंगे, तो वाक्य का अर्थ बदल जाएगा। तब पहले वाक्य का अर्थ होगा—'जब छड़ी टहल रही थी' और दूसरे का 'जब चोर सो रहा था'। इस प्रकार, Unattached Participle के कारण वाक्य का अर्थ ही बदल जाता है न! इसलिए इस दोष से बचने के लिए इस सरल सूत्र का ध्यान रखें—

Same subject in both parts = Participle + PC

Different subjects in both parts = Adverb Clause (while) + PC

NOTE—कभी-कभी तो Voice को ही बदल देने से Wrongly Attached Participle का दोष मिट जा सकता है; जैसे—

Standing upon this house, the whole village can be seen.

= Standing upon this house, one can see the whole village.

इस प्रकार, Unattached Participle के दोष से बचने के लिए आप Participle को clause में बदल दें या Active Voice को Passive Voice बना दें।

EXERCISE

Correct the following sentences.

(1) Sleeping in his room a thief entered and took away his books. (2) Reading in the room, my dog disturbed me. (3) Returning from the college, my hat blew off. (4) Ploughing his field a hidden treasure was discovered. (5) Walking in the field, a dead man was seen. (6) Sleeping in my room, a ghost haunted me.

Hints—(1) While he was sleeping in his room; (2) While I was reading in the room; (3) While I was returning from the college; (4) While a farmer was ploughing his field, he discovered a hidden treasure; (5) While I was working in the field, I saw a dead man; (6) While I was sleeping

Rule III. Participles used as Prepositions

कुछ Participles ऐसे होते हैं जो अब Preposition की भाँति प्रयुक्त होते हैं और इसलिए उनके प्रयोग में Unattached या Wrongly Attached Participle का दोष नहीं लगता। ये हैं—

considering, judging, concerning, regarding, referring, speaking, allowing और granting; जैसे—

1. Considering the circumstances, there is no better way.
2. Regarding my qualification, I beg to submit the following.
3. Allowing for exception, the rule may stand.
4. Referring to your letter, you do not state the fact clearly.

इन वाक्यों के subjects क्रमशः way, I, rule और your है, पर considering, regarding, allowing और referring का प्रयोग इन subjects के लिए नहीं हुआ है। इन Participles का संबंध वाक्य के Subject के साथ नहीं है, अर्थात ये Unattached हैं। फिर भी, इनका प्रयोग शुद्ध हैं, क्योंकि अब ये सिर्फ देखने ही में Participle मालूम पड़ते हैं, पर वास्तव में ये हैं Preposition.

Rule IV. Past Participles used as Adjectives

कुछ Participles ऐसे होते हैं जिनका प्रयोग केवल Adjective की भाँति होता है, अर्थात ये Noun को qualify करते हैं। ये हैं—

bounden, cloven, drunken, graven, molten, stricken, shrunken, shorn and sunken. bounden duty; cloven hoof; drunken barber; molten image; shrunken cloth; sunken ship; etc.

इन सभी उदाहरणों में Participles का प्रयोग Nouns के पहले हुआ है जिनका ये गुण बतलाते हैं। इसलिए ऐसे Participles का प्रयोग Verbs के साधारण Past Participles की भाँति करना उचित नहीं। इन वाक्यों को देखें—

1. He has *drunken* wine.
2. The ship has *sunken.*
3. The cloth has *shrunken.*

यहाँ drunken, sunken तथा shrunken के बदले क्रमशः drunk, sunk तथा shrunk का प्रयोग होना चाहिए, क्योंकि ये शुद्ध Past Participles हैं। इनका प्रयोग Adjectives की भाँति कभी भी नहीं होता।

कुछ Past Participles ऐसे होते हैं जिनका प्रयोग Adjective और Verb दोनों तरह से होता है। ये हैं—

born, broken, fallen, given, spoken, stolen, torn, written.

Adjective की भाँति प्रयुक्त होने पर ये Noun के पहले आते हैं; जैसे—

broken heart, written answer, spoken language, etc.

इस प्रकार, हम देखते हैं कि बहुत कम Past Participles का प्रयोग noun के पहले होता है। अधिकांश Past participles का प्रयोग noun के बाद (Passive Voice के रूप में) होता है; जैसे—

1. We should follow the *path shown by* Mahatma Gandhi.
2. It is a light *seen* already.

इसलिए shown path, seen light आदि का प्रयोग कभी न करें।

Rule V. Present Participle का भी प्रयोग Adjective की भाँति इस प्रकार होता है—

1. Don't get off a running bus.
2. There is not much drinking water here.
3. You can't kill a flying bird.
4. We must give good food to growing children.

❐

Chapter XI

TIME AND TENSE

क्रिया के रूप (form) को Tense कहा जाता है। रूप के अनुसार क्रिया के तीन भेद होते हैं—(i) Present, (ii) Past, और (iii) Future.

इनके चार-चार उपभेद होते हैं। इस प्रकार, रूप के अनुसार क्रिया के कुल बारह भेद माने जाते हैं। इसलिए Tense का संबंध क्रिया के रूप से रहता है।

Time का संबंध क्रिया के अर्थ (meaning) से रहता है। क्रिया के रूप से कार्य होने के Time का बोध नहीं होता।

इन वाक्यों को लें—

1. The sun rises in the East.
2. We see with our eyes.
3. The blind can't see anything.
4. Milk is white.

रूप के अनुसार ये क्रियाएँ हैं Present Tense में, पर अर्थ के अनुसार इनसे बोध होता है Present Time, Past Time और Future Time का।

अब इन वाक्यों को देखें—

1. He leaves for home tomorrow.
2. He is going to buy a car next week.

रूप के अनुसार ये क्रियाएँ हैं Present Tense में, पर अर्थ के अनुसार इनसे बोध होता है Future Time का।

अब इन वाक्यों पर विचार करें—

1. Now the Battle of Panipat begins.
2. Could I see you tomorrow?
3. It might rain tomorrow.
4. I wish I were a prince.
5. It is time we started.

यहाँ पहले वाक्य में Present Tense [begins] का प्रयोग हुआ है, पर इससे बोध होता है Past Time का। दूसरे तथा तीसरे वाक्यों में Past Tense [could/might] का प्रयोग हुआ है, पर इससे बोध होता है Future Time का। चौथे तथा पाँचवें वाक्यों की क्रियाएँ हैं Past Tense [were/started] के रूप में, पर इनसे Present Time का भाव व्यक्त होता है।

इस प्रकार, क्रिया के रूप से संबंधित Tense और इसके अर्थ से संबंधित Time में बहुत अंतर है।

इसलिए हम क्रिया के Tense और Time पर विस्तारपूर्वक विचार करें और देखें कि क्रिया के रूपों से किस प्रकार समय तथा अन्य प्रकार के भाव व्यक्त होते हैं।

FORMS OF VERBS: TENSES

Present Tense

Structure I. Present Simple

Subject + full verb

1. He plays. 2. She writes.

Structure II. Present Imperfect [Progressive]

Subject + am/is/are + verb + ing

1. He is playing. 2. She is writing.

Structure III. Present Perfect

Subject + has/have + Past Participle

1. He has played. 2. She has written.

Structure IV. Present Perfect Continuous

Subject + has been/have been/verb + ing

1. He has been playing. 2. She has been writing.

Past Tense

Structure V. Past Simple

Subject + full verb

1. He played. 2. She wrote.

Structure VI. Past Imperfect [Progressive]

Subject + was/were + verb + ing

1. He was playing. 2. She was writing.

Structure VII. Past Perfect

Subject + had + Past Participle

1. He had played. 2. She had written

Structure VIII. Past Perfect Continuous

Subject + had been + verb + ing

1. He had been playing.
2. She had been writing.

Future Tense

Structure IX. Future Simple

Subject + shall/will + Infinitive [without to]

1. He will play.
2. She will write.

Structure X. Future Imperfect [Progressive]

Subject + shall/will + be + verb + ing

1. He will be playing.
2. She will be writing.

Structure XI. Future Perfect

Subject + shall/will + have + Past Participle

1. He will have played.
2. She will have written.

Structure XII. Future Perfect Continuous

Subject + shall have been/will have been + verb + ing

1. He will have been playing.
2. She will have been writing.

MEANING OF VERBS: TIME

I. Present Simple/Indefinite

ऐसे वाक्यों की बनावट होती है—

Subject + full verb [Present Simple]

Rule I. ऐसे वाक्यों से चिरंतन सत्य (eternal truth) या सिद्धांत (principle) का बोध होता है और इसलिए इनसे Past, Present, Future तीनों प्रकार के Time का भाव व्यक्त होता है; जैसे—

1. The sun rises in the east.
2. The sun sets in the west.
3. Stars shine at night.
4. The earth moves round the sun.

5. A bad carpenter quarrels with his tools.

6. Water boils at 100°C.

Rule II. ऐसे वाक्यों से स्थायी कार्य (permanent activity) या स्वभाव (nature) का बोध होता है और इसलिए इनसे Past, Present, Future तीनों प्रकार के Time का भाव व्यक्त होता है; जैसे—

1. We hear with our ears. 2. We see with our eyes.

3. The rose smells sweet. 4. He lives in India.

Rule III. ऐसे वाक्यों से आदत (habit) या कार्य के बार-बार होने (repetition) का बोध होता है और इसलिए इनसे Past, Present, Future तीनों प्रकार का Time व्यक्त होता है; जैसे—

1. I like fish very much. 2. He knows English.

3. He always comes on time. 4. She never comes on time.

5. They often come late.

इस प्रकार के वाक्यों में इन Adverbs of Frequency का प्रयोग होता है—

always, often, sometimes, never, seldom, generally, regularly, usually, rarely, normally

Rule IV. ऐसे वाक्यों से भविष्य में होनेवाले कार्यक्रम/निर्णय (firm decision/plan/programme) का बोध होता है और इसलिए इनसे Future Time का भाव व्यक्त होता है; जैसे—

1. He leaves for home tomorrow. 2. The plane takes off at 9 a.m.

इस प्रकार के वाक्यों में Future Time बतानेवाले ऐसे Adverbs of Time का प्रयोग होता है—

tomorrow, next day, next week/month/year

Rule V. ऐसे वाक्यों में ऐतिहासिक वर्तमान (historical present) का बोध होता है और इसलिए इनसे Past Time का भाव व्यक्त होता है; जैसे—

1. Now the Battle of Panipat begins.

2. Now Sohrab rushes forward.

3. Now Akbar calls Birbal and asks.

Rule VI. ऐसे वाक्यों से समय (time) या शर्त (condition) का बोध होता है और Future Time का भाव व्यक्त होता है; जैसे—

1. You will pass if you work hard.

2. I will wait here until he comes back.

यहाँ if you work hard का अर्थ है—If you will work hard और Until he comes back का अर्थ है—Until he will come back.

II. Present Progressive/Imperfect

ऐसे वाक्यों की बनावट होती है—

Subject + am/is/are + verb + ing

Rule I. ऐसे वाक्यों से तात्कालिक वर्तमान (immediate present—Now) का बोध होता है; जैसे—

1. The sun is rising now. 2. They are catching fish now.

Rule II. ऐसे वाक्यों से भविष्य में होनेवाले कार्यक्रम/योजना (plan/programme) का भी बोध होता है और इसलिए इनसे Future Time व्यक्त होता है; जैसे—

1. He is leaving for home tomorrow.
2. She is taking her examination next week.

Rule III. ऐसे वाक्यों से कार्य करने के इरादे (intention) या संभावना (likelihood) का बोध होता है और इसलिए इनसे Future Time का भाव व्यक्त होता है; जैसे—

1. He is going to buy a car.—**intention**
2. The patient is going to die.—**likelihood**

Stative and Dynamic Verbs

Stative Verbs

NOTE—Stative Verbs का अर्थ होता है—fixed, अर्थात दृढ़, स्थिर, स्थायी; इसलिए ऐसे verbs से स्थायी कार्य (continued activity/permanent activity) का बोध होता है। यही कारण है कि इस प्रकार के verbs का, सामान्य अर्थ में, Progressive/Imperfect Tense नहीं होता। इसलिए इन्हें Non-progressive या Non-conclusive verbs भी कहा जाता है।

अर्थ की दृष्टि से Stative verbs का प्रयोग इन कार्यों के लिए होता है—

(a) Verbs of Perception/Cognition

हम अपने शरीर के अंगों या इन्द्रियों (जैसे—आँख, कान, नाक आदि) के द्वारा प्रत्यक्ष ज्ञान प्राप्त करते हैं। इसे perception या cognition कहा जाता है। ध्यान दें कि perception की सहायता से ज्ञान/अनुभव प्राप्त करने के लिए कोई प्रयास (efforts) या इच्छा नहीं की जाती। जब कोई वस्तु आँख के सामने आ जाती है, तब हम बिना प्रयास या इच्छा के भी उसे देख लेते हैं। जब कोई आवाज होती है, तब बिना प्रयास या इच्छा के भी उसे सुन लेते हैं। इस प्रकार, ज्ञान/अनुभव की प्राप्ति सहज, स्वाभाविक रूप में हो जाती है। तो, ऐसे कार्यों के लिए Stative verb का प्रयोग होता है और वह सदा Present Simple Tense में रहता है। ये verbs हैं—

see, hear, smell, taste

इन वाक्यों को देखें—

1. We hear with our ears. 2. We see with our eyes.
3. I feel that the bed is hard. 4. We smell with our nose.

जब ऐसे verbs (verbs of perception) का प्रयोग Progressive Tense में होता है, तब इनसे अस्थायी कार्य का बोध होता है, अर्थात यह बोध होता है कि कार्य अभी हो रहा है, पर वह सदा नहीं होता, जैसे—

1. He is smelling a rose. 2. The judge is hearing my case.

(b) Verbs of Permanent Mental States/Activities

Stative verbs का प्रयोग स्थायी, मानसिक अवस्था (permanent mental state) बताने के लिए भी होता है; जैसे—

agree, believe, consider, doubt, differ, know, forget, remember, recognise, think, understand

इन वाक्यों को लें—

1. I believe in God.
2. I think he is honest.
3. He knows English.
4. I understand grammar.

ये मानसिक अवस्थाएँ स्थायी हैं। इसलिए ऐसे verbs का प्रयोग Progressive Tense में नहीं हो सकता। आप इस प्रकार नहीं लिख सकते—

1. He is knowing English.
2. I am believing in God.

(c) Emotional States

Stative verbs का प्रयोग स्थायी भावना (emotion) व्यक्त करने के लिए भी होता है, क्योंकि भावनाएँ स्थायी होती हैं; जैसे—

like, love, hate, desire, dislike, hope, regard, want, wish

इन वाक्यों को लें—

1. I love her.
2. I hate him.

इन वाक्यों से स्थायी भावना का बोध होता है, क्योंकि प्रेम या घृणा करना आदि स्थायी भावनाएँ हैं। यदि ऐसे verbs का प्रयोग Progressive Tense में किया जाए, तो यह बोध होगा कि कार्य अभी हो रहा है, अर्थात कार्य स्थायी नहीं है।

इन वाक्यों को देखें—

1. I love her.—Permanent emotional activity
2. I am loving her.—Temporary emotional activity

(d) Static States

कुछ कार्य सदा स्थिर (static) या स्थायी रूप (अर्थात एक रूप) में पाए जाते हैं। ऐसे कार्यों के लिए भी Stative verbs का प्रयोग होता है; जैसे—

appear, belong to, consist of, contain, deserve, have, live, own, possess, remain, resemble, seem

इन वाक्यों को देखें—

1. This book belongs to me.
2. I own (possess) a house.
3. He resembles his father.
4. He deserves praise.

ऐसे verbs का प्रयोग Progressive Tense में नहीं हो सकता।

Dynamic Verbs

NOTE—Dynamic का अर्थ होता है—गतिशील, परिवर्तनात्मक। यह stative का उलटा है। इसलिए Dynamic verbs का प्रयोग वैसे कार्यों के लिए होता है जो अस्थायी (temporary) या क्षणिक (momentary) या परिवर्तनशील (transitional) होते हैं, अर्थात जो कार्य सदा नहीं होते। यही कारण है कि Dynamic verbs का प्रयोग Progressive Tense में भी होता है; जैसे—

1. He is running.
2. She is walking.

अर्थ की दृष्टि से Dynamic verbs का प्रयोग इन कार्यों के लिए होता है—

(a) Temporary Activity

अस्थायी कार्यों के लिए Dynamic verbs का प्रयोग Progressive Tense में इस प्रकार होता है—

1. She is cooking fish.
2. I am living in London.

(b) Bodily Sensation

शारीरिक उत्तेजना (sensation) व्यक्त करने के लिए Dynamic verbs का प्रयोग इस प्रकार हो सकता है—

1. He is feeling fine.
2. He is hurting me.
3. His teeth are aching.
4. My fingers are itching.

(c) Momentary Activity

क्षणिक कार्य व्यक्त करने के लिए भी Dynamic verbs का प्रयोग होता है; जैसे—

1. The sun is setting.
2. The plane is landing.
3. I am forgetting his name.
4. He is waiting outside.

(d) Deliberate Activity/Voluntary Activity

Dynamic verbs का प्रयोग वैसे कार्यों के लिए भी होता है जो सोच-समझकर या जान-बूझकर किए जाएँ, अर्थात जिनसे deliberate activity (सुनियोजित कार्य) या voluntary activity (इच्छापूर्वक कार्य) का बोध हो; जैसे—

1. The doctor is feeling her pulse.
2. He is smelling a rose.
3. I am seeing him tomorrow.
4. I am hearing him.

इन वाक्यों से यह बोध होता है कि शारीरिक अंगों या इन्द्रियों (bodily organs) के द्वारा जान-बूझकर कार्य किए गए हैं, अर्थात इनसे सुनियोजित कार्य (deliberate activity) या इच्छापूर्वक कार्य (voluntary activity) का भाव व्यक्त होता है।

ध्यान दें कि जब Stative verbs का प्रयोग Progressive Tense में होता है, तब वे Dynamic बन जाते हैं और उनसे अस्थायी कार्यों का बोध होता है; जैसे—

1. We *smell* with our nose. —Permanent [stative]
2. He *is smelling* a red rose. —Temporary [dynamic]
3. I *have* a nice house. —Permanent [stative]

4. I *am having* a nice time. —Temporary [dynamic]
5. This mango *tastes* sweet. —Permanent [stative]
6. He *is tasting* a mango. —Temporary [dynamic]
7. He *lives* in London. —Permanent [stative]
8. He *is living* in London. —Temporary [dynamic]
9. I *forget* what he said. —Permanent [stative]
10. I *am forgetting* his name. —Temporary [dynamic]

III. Present Perfect

Subject + has/have + past participle

Rule I. इससे यह बोध होता है कि कोई कार्य तुरंत समाप्त हुआ है और इसलिए इसका संबंध वर्तमान समय (Present Time) से नहीं रहता है; जैसे—

1. He has just gone out.
2. She has just left for home.
3. I have finished the work.
4. He has returned from Delhi.

Rule II. इससे यह भी बोध होता है कि कार्य का संबंध वर्तमान समय (present time) से जुड़ा हुआ है, क्योंकि इसका प्रभाव अभी भी जारी है; जैसे—

1. He has lived here since 1970.
2. I have known him for five years.
3. I have seen her several times.

IV. Present Perfect Continuous

Subject + has/have + been + verb + ing

इससे यह बोध होता है कि जो काम भूतकाल (past) में आरंभ हुआ था यह वर्तमान समय (present time) में जारी है; जैसे—

1. It has been raining since Monday.
2. He has been working here since January.
3. They have been playing all the time.
4. She has been working all day.

V. Past Simple

Subject + full verb [Past Simple]

Rule I. ऐसे वाक्यों से यह बोध होता है कि कोई कार्य भूतकाल में समाप्त हो गया और इसलिए इनसे Past Time व्यक्त होता है; जैसे—

1. He played well.
2. She wrote a novel last year.
3. Babar won the battle. [not, had or has won]
4. Columbus discovered America. [not, had or has discovered]

Rule II. ऐसे वाक्यों से भूतकाल में कार्य करने की आदत का भी बोध होता है, अर्थात यह बोध होता है कि कोई कार्य बराबर होता था; जैसे—

1. He always helped me.
2. He never touched wine.
3. He used to smoke.
4. She used to help me.
5. She is used to dust.
6. I am used to hard work.
7. He would often come late.
8. She would often help me.

इस प्रकार के वाक्यों में इन Adverbs of Frequency का प्रयोग होता है—

often, always, never, seldom, generally, usually

Rule III. Could, Might और Would हैं Past Tense में, पर इनसे Present Time का बोध होता है, जब इनसे निवेदन (request) का भाव व्यक्त होता है; जैसे—

1. Could I use your pen?
2. Could I see you tomorrow?
3. Might I use your pen?
4. Might I see you tomorrow?
5. Would you shut the door, please?
6. Would you see me tomorrow?
7. Would you mind shutting the door?

Rule IV. Had better/had rather/had sooner/would rather/would sooner हैं Past Tense में पर इनसे Present Time का बोध होता है, क्योंकि इनसे राय (advice/suggestion) का भाव व्यक्त होता है—

1. You had better go.
2. I would rather stay.
3. You had better go = It is better for you to do.

Rule V. Indirect Narration में would से Future Time का बोध होता है, यद्यपि यह है Past Tense में; जैसे—

He said, "I will go home."

He said that he would go home.

यहाँ would go का अर्थ है—will go.

Rule VI. शर्त व्यक्त करनेवाले वाक्यों में if-clause के Past Simple Tense से Present/Future Time का बोध होता है—

1. If he reached on time, he would get a prize.
2. If a ghost appeared here, all would flee away.

ऐसे वाक्यों से वर्तमान या भविष्य का बोध होता है और यह भी बोध होता है कि कार्य होने की संभावना बहुत कम है। इसलिए इस प्रकार का Past Simple Tense भूतकाल (past time) का बोध नहीं कराता, यद्यपि यह विशुद्ध Past Tense के रूप में रहता है।

Rule VII. इच्छा (wish) व्यक्त करनेवाले वाक्यों के Past Tense से Present/Future Time का बोध होता है और Past Perfect Tense से Past Time का; जैसे—

1. I wish I were a prince. [I wish to be a prince] —Present time
2. I wish I were rich. [I wish to be rich] —Present time
3. I wish I know him. [I don't know him] —Present time
4. I wish I had known him. [I didn't know him] —Past time
5. If only I knew him. [I don't know him] —Present time
6. If only I had known him. [I didn't know him] —Past time

Rule VIII. It is + time के बाद आनेवाले Past Tense से Present Time का भाव व्यक्त होता है; जैसे—

1. It is time we started. [It is time for us to start] —Present Time
2. It is time you finished. [It is time for you to finish] —Present Time

VI. Past Imperfect [Progressive]

Subject + was/were + verb + ing

Rule I. इससे यह बोध होता है कि कोई काम भूतकाल में हो रहा था—

1. She was writing. 2. He was playing.

Rule II. इससे यह भी बोध होता है कि भूतकाल में कार्य करने की आदत थी, अर्थात कार्य लगातार जारी था। ऐसे वाक्यों में always/often आदि Adverb of Frequency का प्रयोग होता है; जैसे—

1. She was always complaining. 2. He was always murmuring.

VII. Past Perfect

Subject + had + past participle

Rule I. जब भूतकाल में दो कार्य समाप्त हो गये हों, तो पहले समाप्त (complete) होनेवाले कार्य के साथ Past Perfect का प्रयोग होता है और बाद में समाप्त होनेवाले के साथ Past Simple/Indefinite का; जैसे—

1. When I had shut the door, I opened the safe.
2. After I had shut the door, I opened the safe.
3. Mohan had left before Sohan arrived.
4. Muni had finished before Manju began.

Rule II. पर जब ऐसे दो कार्य एक साथ (simultaneously) होने का बोध कराते हैं, या जब यह बोध होता है कि दूसरा कार्य पहले कार्य के तुरंत (immediately) बाद हुआ, तब दोनों ही कार्यों के लिए Past Simple/Indefinite का प्रयोग होता है; जैसे—

1. He washed his face before he went to bed.
2. The train started just before I reached the station.

ध्यान दें कि ऐसे वाक्यों से केवल इतना ही बोध होता है कि दो कार्य एक-दूसरे के तुरंत बाद हुए। इनसे यह बोध नहीं होता कि एक कार्य पूर्ण रूप से समाप्त (complete) हो गया था और तब दूसरा कार्य आरंभ हुआ। हाँ, *after* से यह बोध होता है कि काम समाप्त हो चुका था। इसलिए after वाले वाक्य में साधारणतः Past Perfect का प्रयोग होता है; जैसे—

I reached after the train had already left.

VIII. Past Perfect Continuous

Subject + had been + verb + ing

इससे यह बोध होता है कोई काम भूतकाल में बहुत समय तक जारी था—

1. He had been reading.
2. She had been writing.
3. They had been playing.
4. She had been working.

IX. Future Simple

(i) First Person + shall + Infinitive [without to]
(ii) Second/Third Person + will + Infinitive [without to]

Rule I. ऐसे वाक्यों से केवल Future time का बोध होता है, अर्थात यह बोध होता है कि कोई कार्य भविष्य में सामान्य रूप से होगा; जैसे—

1. I shall go to Mumbai tomorrow.
2. I shall be fifteen next year.
3. Tomorrow will be Monday.
4. My father will be forty next month.
5. He will start for Delhi tomorrow.

Rule II. कुछ वाक्यों की बनावट इस प्रकार की होती है—

(i) First Person + will + Infinitive [without to]
(ii) Second/Third Person + shall + Infinitive [without to]

ऐसे वाक्यों से भविष्यत्काल के अलावा इच्छा, संकल्प, चेतावनी (will/determination/intention/threat) आदि भावों का बोध होता है। इसलिए इसे coloured future कहा जाता है। इन वाक्यों को देखें—

1. I will take the examination next year. [intention/determination]

2. He shall pay the fine. [threat]
3. You shall not tell a lie. [moral duty]
4. They shall get sweets. [promise]
5. Members shall pay fees in time. [command]

Rule III. कुछ Interrogative Sentences इस प्रकार के होते हैं—

Shall + I + Infinitive [without to]

1. Shall I open the door? 2. Shall I make tea for you?

ऐसे वाक्यों से राय/परामर्श/निवेदन (advise/suggestion/request) का भाव प्रकट होता है और Present Time का बोध होता है।

Rule IV. कभी-कभी Future Simple से आदत या सत्य का भाव प्रकट होता है और इससे Past, Present, Future तीनों प्रकार के Time का बोध होता है—

1. Boys will be boys.
2. Accidents will happen.
3. A patient will complain of headache.

X. Future Imperfect [Progressive]

Subject + shall be/will be + verb + ing

Rule I. इससे यह बोध होता है कि कोई कार्य भविष्य में कुछ समय तक जारी रहेगा; जैसे—

1. I shall be reading a novel.
2. He will be staying here.

Rule II. ऐसे वाक्यों से भविष्य में होनेवाले कार्यक्रम/योजना का भी बोध होता है; जैसे—

I shall be seeing her tomorrow.

XI. Future Perfect

Subject + shall have/will have + past participle

Rule I. इससे यह बोध होता है कि कोई कार्य भविष्य में किसी निर्धारित समय तक समाप्त हो चुकेगा; जैसे—

1. He will have finished the work by next year.
2. She will have returned home by next month.

Rule II. Future Perfect से संभावना (likelihood) या अनुमान (inference) का भी बोध होता है। ऐसी संभावना या अनुमान का संबंध भूतकाल (Past) के कार्यों से रहता है, जैसे—

1. You will have heard this story. [शायद आपने सुना होगा]
2. You will have seen this man. [शायद आपने देखा होगा]

इस प्रकार, will have + past participle का वही अर्थ होता है जो may have + past participle और can have + past participle का होता है।

XII. Future Perfect Continuous

Subject + shall /will have been + verb + ing

इससे यह बोध होता है कि कार्य भविष्य में बहुत समय तक जारी रहेगा—

1. I shall have been writing a novel.
2. He will have been reading a novel.

....

EXERCISE 1

Give the missing forms of verbs in this table.

Present Simple	Past Simple	Past Participle
wear	—	—
—	—	sunken
—	won	—
—	swore	—
hear	—	—
drink	—	—
rise	—	—
—	—	sworn
—	—	woven
—	hanged	—
—	—	hung
choose	—	—
—	—	been
—	tore	—

EXERCISE 2

Supply correct forms of verbs given in brackets.

1. He (go) to school everyday.
2. She now (learn) English.
3. The sun now (set).

4. Columbus (discover) America.
5. He (buy) pen a week ago.
6. She (not see) me for a long time.
7. The sun (rise) in the east.
8. She (live) here since 1970.
9. He (know) me for five years.
10. She (wake up) at five everyday.
11. It (rain) during the rainy season.
12. It now (rain) cats and dogs.
13. The sun always (shine) in Egypt.
14. Bad boys never (work) hard.
15. The plane regularly (take off) at 9 a.m.
16. The train often (arrive) here late.
17. She (watch) the television now.
18. They (have) a swim now.
19. I (listen to) the radio now.
20. I (not hear) about her since 1980.
21. We (win) the match yesterday.
22. She often (come) late.
23. It (grow) dark now.
24. I asked her where she (live).
25. He promised that he (help) me.
26. I wish (I know) him.
27. I wish I (be) a prince.
28. It is time we (finish) the work.
29. If only I (know) her.
30. He already (finish) the work.
31. Would you mind (have) a cup of tea?

EXERCISE 3

*Match the words under **A** and **B** to make correct sentences.*

A	B
They are	since 9 o'clock.
He has been	reaches here tomorrow.
He takes his examination	I know him.
I have bought a car	last week.
She has been working	ill for a month.

The Prime Minister	next week.
I wish	selling fish.
She went to Mumbai	this year.

EXERCISE 4

Correct these sentences.

1. She was writing a letter now.
2. He leaves for Mumbai last week.
3. I have passed the examination last year.
4. He has come here the other day.
5. I am going to college daily at 10 a.m.
6. He lives in Mumbai now.
7. I will go out when she will return.
8. Don't get off a bus until it will stop.
9. You will catch the train if you will start early.
10. Take an umbrella in case it will rain.
11. He is have a rest now, because he felt tired.
12. What are you doing? I write a letter.
13. Bad students are never going to college in time.
14. He is regularly going to bed at 9 p.m.
15. I wish I was a princess.
16. It is time we will begin the work.
17. I have seen him a week ago.
18. The plane is normally landing at 10 a.m.

EXERCISE 5

Re-write these sentences as directed.

1. He will go home tomorrow. [use Present Simple]
2. She will buy a car next week. [use going to]
3. I will see him next month. [use Present Progressive]
4. We won the match. [use Present Perfect]
5. She is singing songs. [use Present Perf. Cont.]
6. The President reaches tomorrow. [use Future Simple]
7. The Prime Minister stays here. [use Present Progressive]
8. He will fly to London next month. [use Present Simple]

EXERCISE 6

Distinguish between these pairs of sentences.

1. (a) He lives in India.
   (b) He is living in India.
2. (a) He visits our school next week.
   (b) He is visiting our school next week.
3. (a) He will buy a cow next month.
   (b) He is going to buy a cow next month.
4. (a) I shall finish the work.
   (b) I will finish the work.
5. (a) He comes from Chennai.
   (b) He is coming from Chennai.
6. (a) The sun rises in the East.
   (b) The sun is rising in the East.
7. (a) He plays tennis.
   (b) He is playing tennis.

EXERCISE 7

Fill in the blanks with the correct form of verbs given in brackets.

1. He …… (work) here for five years.
2. She …… (live) here since 1975.
3. I …… (learn) English for three years.
4. He …… (teach) us since 1976.
5. Who …… (discover) the Law of gravitation?
6. I waited at the platform until the train …… (arrive).
7. You would succeed if you …… (try).
8. If I …… (be) you I wouldn't do it.
9. I …… (not see) him for the last three months.
10. I wish I …… (be) a bird.

EXERCISE 8

Use correct forms of verbs given in brackets.

1. A person who (catch) fish is called a fisherman.
2. He usually (have) breakfast at 8 a.m.
3. She (go) to the picture on Sundays.
4. He (leave) for London next week.
5. You won't pass unless you (work) hard.
6. Take an umbrella in case it (rain).
7. He can't catch the bus if he (not start) early.

8. I (know) him for the last five years.
9. She (cook) food since morning.
10. He (cry) because he is very hungry now.
11. What you (write) now? I (write) a story now.
12. When he (have) lunch? He (have) lunch at 1 p.m.
13. What is she doing? She (play) tennis.
14. I will go out as soon as he (come) back.
15. The train usually (arrive) at 4 p.m.
16. Would you mind (shut) the door?
17. It is time we (start) the work.
18. My father (be) sixty next year.
19. I wish I (know) him.
20. He reached the station after the train (leave).
21. If only I (know) him.
22. I (have) a nice time these days.

EXERCISE 9

Put a tick (✓) by the right words.

1. I reached the bus-stop after the bus $\frac{\text{left}}{\text{had left}}$.
2. He told me that he $\frac{\text{will}}{\text{would}}$ take the examination.
3. I wish I $\frac{\text{know}}{\text{knew}}$ her in time.
4. Would you mind $\frac{\text{wait}}{\text{waiting}}$ here a while?
5. Don't get off until the bus $\frac{\text{stops}}{\text{will stop}}$.
6. You will rise in life if you $\frac{\text{will work}}{\text{work}}$ hard.
7. It is time we $\frac{\text{leave}}{\text{left}}$ for home.
8. I will go out before she $\frac{\text{will come back}}{\text{comes back}}$.
9. She $\frac{\text{is working}}{\text{has been working}}$ here since 1984.
10. It $\frac{\text{has been raining}}{\text{is raining}}$ $\frac{\text{for}}{\text{since}}$ a week.

Chapter XII

VERBS: VOICE

Voice की दृष्टि से क्रियाएँ (verbs) दो प्रकार की होती हैं—

1. Active Voice 2. Passitve Voice

Active Voice को Passive में बदलने के लिए वाक्यों की बनावट तथा अर्थ का ध्यान रखें और इन नियमों पर विचार करें।

कुछ वाक्यों की बनावट इस प्रकार की होती है—

(A) Subject + transitive verb + object

इन्हें Passive Voice में बदलने के लिए इन नियमों का ध्यान रखें—

Rule I. Subject को Object बना दें और इसके पहले by का प्रयोग करें।

Rule II. Object को Subject बना दें।

Rule III. Verb के पहले एक verb 'to be' (am, is, are, was, were, be, been, being) का प्रयोग Subject के Number और Verb के Tense के अनुसार करें।

Rule IV. Verb को Past Participle (Verb के तीसरे) रूप में रखें।

इस प्रकार, वाक्य की बनावट इस तरह हो जाती है—

Subject + Verb 'to be' + Past Participle + by + Object

इन नियमों की मदद से voice को बहुत ही आसानी से बदल सकते हैं—

1. Mohan teaches Sohan. —*Active*

 Sohan is taught by Mohan. —*Passive*

2. We respect him. —*Active*

 He is respected. —*Passive*

NOTE (a)—कभी-कभी वाक्य का Subject अनिश्चित (vague) रहता है; जैसे—

1. People say. 2. They say. 3. Somebody (Someone) says.

ऐसे अनिश्चित Subjects को Passive Voice में इस प्रकार बदल दिया जाता है—

People say/They say/Everybody says. —*Active*

= It is said. —*Passive*

NOTE (b)—वाक्य का Subject अनिश्चित (vague) रहे, तो उसे Object बनाकर उसके पहले by का प्रयोग करना उचित नहीं, क्योंकि आधुनिक प्रयोग इसकी स्वीकृति नहीं देता; जैसे—

1. People (They) will help me. 2. Someone will help me. —*Active*

= I will be helped. [not, *them/someone*] —*Passive*

यहाँ by the people/by them लिखना आवश्यक नहीं। क्यों? इसलिए कि यहाँ 'by + agent' (noun/pronoun) अनिश्चित है और वह अत्यंत ही गौण है। याद रखें कि by + agent का प्रयोग तब होता है जब agent महत्त्वपूर्ण होता है और हमारा ध्यान उसकी ओर आकृष्ट कर यह बताया जाता है कि कार्य **किसके द्वारा** किया गया है।

(B) Subject + verb 'to be' + Infinitive

कुछ वाक्यों की बनावट Active Voice में इस तरह की रहती है—

Subject + am/is/are/was/were + infinitive (to + verb)

Rule I. ऐसे वाक्यों के Passive Voice में am/is/are/was/were के बाद to be आता है और to be के बाद Verb का Past Participle रूप; जैसे—

1. I am to help him. —*Active*

   He is to be helped (by me). —*Passive*

2. I was to help him. —*Active*

   He was to be helped (by me). —*Passive*

3. We are to help him. —*Active*

   He is to be helped (by us). —*Passive*

(C) Subject + verb 'to have' + Infinitive

कुछ वाक्यों की बनावट Active Voice में इस तरह की रहती है—

Subject + has/have/had + infinitive (to + verb)

Rule I. ऐसे वाक्यों के Passive Voice में has/have/had के बाद to be आता है और to be के बाद Verb का Past Participle रूप; जैसे—

1. I have to help him. —*Active*

   He has to be helped (by me). —*Passive*

2. We have to help him. —*Active*

   He was to be helped (by me). —*Passive*

3. You have to help us. —*Active*

   We have to be helped (by you). —*Passive*

(D) Subject + may/can/should/must/etc. + Infinitive

कुछ वाक्यों के Active Voice में can/could/may/might/should/must/would + infinitive verb रहता है। ऐसे वाक्यों के Passive Voice में can/could/may/might/should/would के बाद be आता है और be के बाद verb का Past participle रूप।

Rule I. जब ऐसे वाक्यों के Active Voice में have + past participle रहता है, तब Passive Voice में have been + past participle का प्रयोग होता है,

इन वाक्यों को देखें—

1. I can help him. —*Active*
   He can be helped (by me). —*Passive*
2. I must help him. —*Active*
   He must be helped (by me). —*Passive*
3. I should have helped him. —*Active*
   He should have been helped (by me). —*Passive*

(E) Subject + verb + preposition + object

कभी-कभी Verb के बाद कोई Preposition आता है और उसके बाद Object; जैसे—

I look *after* him.

यहाँ after एक preposition है और him एक object.

Active को Passive में बदलने पर ऐसे Preposition को ज्यों-का-त्यों रख दिया जाता है और Preposition के बाद by का प्रयोग इस प्रकार किया जाता है—

preposition + by + object

इन उदाहरणों को लें—

1. I look after him. —*Active*
   He is looked after (by me). —*Passive*
2. I am searching for him. —*Active*
   He is being searched for (by me). —*Passive*

NOTE—ऐसे वाक्यों में कभी-कभी Adverb of manner का भी प्रयोग इस प्रकार होता है—

I will look after you *well.*

इस प्रकार के Adverb का स्थान Passive Voice में उस verb के पहले रहना चाहिए जिसको वह modify करता हो; जैसे—

You will be well-looked after.

Caution—कुछ Verbs के बाद Passive Voice में by का प्रयोग नहीं होता; उनमें by के बदले किसी दूसरे उपयुक्त Preposition का प्रयोग होता है।

इन वाक्यों को देखें—

1. He satisfied everybody. —*Active*
   Everybody was satisfied *with* him. —*Passive*
2. He knows me. —*Active*
   I am known *to* him. —*Passive*
3. Her conduct shocked me. —*Active*
   I was shocked *at* her conduct. —*Passive*

4. His reply surprised me. —*Active*

   I was surprised *at* his reply. —*Passive*

5. This book has greatly interested me. —*Active*

   I have been greatly interested *in* this book. —*Passive*

(F) Subject + verb + object + complement

कुछ वाक्यों में Transitive verb के बाद Object आता है और उस Object के अर्थ को पूरा करने के लिए object के बाद एक Complement का प्रयोग होता है। वैसे Transitive verb को Factitive verb कहा जाता है और उसके साथ आनेवाले complement को Objective Complement कहते हैं; जैसे—

We elected him *chairman.*

यहाँ chairman है Objective Complement.

Rule I. ऐसे वाक्यों के Passive voice में Object को Subject बनाया जाता है।

Rule II. Objective Complement को verb के बाद रखा जाता है।

इन वाक्यों को देखें—

1. We elected him chairman. —*Active*

   He was elected chairman. —*Passive*

2. They made him king. —*Active*

   He was made king. —*Passive*

(G) Subject + verb + object + object

कुछ वाक्यों के Active Voice में verb के बाद दो-दो objects रहते हैं। उन objects में एक Direct होता है और दूसरा Indirect; जैसे—

He gave me a book.

यहाँ gave के बाद दो objects (me/book) आए हैं। इनमें me है Indirect object और book है Direct object.

याद रखें कि जिस object के पहले *to/for* का प्रयोग हो सकता है उसे Indirect object कहते हैं, पर जिसके पहले *to/for* का प्रयोग नहीं हो सकता उसे कहा जाता है Direct object. इस वाक्य में me के पहले to का प्रयोग हो सकता है, पर book के पहले नहीं; जैसे—

He gave a book to me.

इसलिए यहाँ book है Direct object और me है Indirect object.

ऐसे वाक्यों का Passive voice इस प्रकार बनाना चाहिए—

(i) Subject + verb be + past participle + object

(ii) Subject + verb be + past participle + to/for + object

इन वाक्यों को लें—

1. He gave me a book. —*Active*

   I was given a book. —*Passive*

   Or

   A book was given to me. —*Passive*

2. He bought me a ring. —*Active*

   A ring was bought for me. —*Passive*

(H) There + verb + noun (subject) + Infinitive

कुछ वाक्यों में noun (subject) के बाद infinitive (*to + transitive verb*) आता है। इनका Passive Voice इस प्रकार बनाया जा सकता है—

There + verb + noun (subject) to be + past participle

इन वाक्यों के परिवर्तन को देखें—

1. There is no time to lose.

   There is no time to be lost.

2. There is no money to waste.

   There is no money to be wasted.

ध्यान दें कि *to + infinitive* हो जाता है—*to be + past participle.*

(I) Subject + verb + object + Infinitive (without 'to')

कुछ वाक्यों में object के बाद infinitive (without 'to') आता है और पूरे वाक्य की बनावट इस प्रकार होती है—

Subject + verb + object + infinitive (without 'to')

इन्हें *Passive Voice* में इस प्रकार बदलें—

Rule I. Object को subject बना दें।

Rule II. Infinitive के to चिह्न का प्रयोग करें।

Rule III. Verb का रूप हो जाता है—verb 'be' + past participle.

इन वाक्यों को लें—

1. I saw her sing a song.

   She was seen to sing a song.

2. I found him cross the road.

   He was found to cross the road.

. . . .

EXERCISE

Change the voice of the following sentences.

(1) We saw a plane land. (2) I saw a boat sail. (3) There is no food to waste. (4) There aren't sweets to distribute. (5) I watched a plane take off. (6) I saw him run away.

. . . .

Interrogative Sentences

(A) Interrogative Sentences with Auxiliary

Interrogative Sentences के auxiliary verb/modal verb का परिवर्तन इस प्रकार करें—

(i) do/does/did = am/is/are/was/were + past participle

(ii) has/have/had = has been/have been/had been + past participle

(iii) other auxiliary verbs = auxiliary verb + be + past participle

इन वाक्यों को देखें—

1. Did he abuse you? —*Active*
   Were you abused by him? —*Passive*
2. Will he write a book? —*Active*
   Will a book be written by him? —*Passive*
3. Has he written a novel? —*Active*
   Has a novel been written by him? —*Passive*

(B) Interrogative Sentences with 'who'

कुछ Interrogative sentences में 'who' आता है। ऐसे वाक्य Passive Voice में इस प्रकार बदले जाते हैं—

(i) By whom + verb 'be' + subject + past participle

(ii) Who + verb 'be' + subject + past participle + by

इन वाक्यों के परिवर्तन को देखें—

1. Who gave you this book? —*Active*
   By whom was this book given to you? —*Passive*
   Who was this book given to you by? —*Passive*
2. Who can save our country? —*Active*
   By whom can our country be saved? —*Passive*
   Who can our country be saved by? —*Passive*

NOTE—आजकल *By whom* का प्रयोग प्रायः नहीं होता। इसलिए who ... by का ही प्रयोग करना चाहिए।

(C) Interrogatives: indirect question

कुछ Interrogative Sentences की बनावट Indirect Narration में इस प्रकार की होती है—

Subject + ask + object + if/whether + clause

Or

Subject + ask + object + question word + clause

इनका Passive Voice इस प्रकार बनता है—

Rule I. Reporting Verb (ask) के object को subject बना दें।

Rule II. Reporting Verb के पहले verb 'be' + past participle का प्रयोग करें।

इन वाक्यों को लें—

1. I asked Radha if she was will. —*Active*

   Radha was asked if she was ill. —*Passive*

2. He asked me when I would return. —*Active*

   I was asked when I would return. —*Passive*

Imperative Sentences

(A) Imperative Sentences: order/command

कुछ Imperative sentences से order या command (आज्ञा/आदेश) का बोध होता है। उन्हें Passive Voice में इस प्रकार बदलें—

Rule I. वाक्य में अपनी ओर से Let का प्रयोग करें और उसे वाक्य के आरंभ में रखें।

Rule II. वाक्य में *be + Past Participle* का प्रयोग करें, is/are आदि का नहीं।

इन वाक्यों को देखें—

1. Bring a glass of water. —*Active*

   Let a glass of water be brought. —*Passive*

2. Turn him out. —*Active*

   Let him be turned out. —*Passive*

NOTE—ऐसे वाक्यों में by you का प्रयोग नहीं करना चाहिए।

(B) Imperative Sentences: advice/request

कुछ Imperative sentences से परामर्श/प्रार्थना (advice/request) का भाव प्रकट होता है।

Rule I. ऐसे वाक्यों का परिवर्तन should be + Past Participle द्वारा करें; जैसे—

1. Love your country. —*Active*

   Your country should be loved. —*Passive*

2. Feed the poor. —*Active*

   The poor should be fed. —*Passive*

3. Help your friends. —*Active*

Your friends should be helped. —*Passive*

इनका परिवर्तन Let के द्वारा भी हो सकता है; जैसे—

Let the country be loved. —*Passive*

NOTE—यदि Imperative sentences में please/kindly आदि शब्द रहें तो उनका प्रयोग Passive Voice में न करें।

(C) Imperatives: indirect command/request

कुछ Imperative sentences की बनावट Indirect Narration में इस प्रकार की होती है—

Subject + ask/tell/request + object + infinitive

इनका Passive Voice इस प्रकार बनता है—

Rule I. Reporting Verb के object को subject बना दें।

Rule II. Infinitive तथा इससे जुड़े हुए शब्दों को ज्यों-का-त्यों रख दें।

Rule III. Reporting Verb के पहले verb 'be' + Past Participle का प्रयोग करें।

इन वाक्यों को देखें—

1. I asked/told Mohan to make tea.

Mohan was asked to make tea.

2. He requested her to lend him her book.

She was requested to lend him her book.

(D) Subject + causative verb + infinitive [without 'to']

कुछ वाक्यों में Subject के बाद causative verb आता है और उसके बाद infinitive [without 'to']; जैसे—

I made him laugh.

इनका Passive Voice इस प्रकार बनाया जाता है—

Rule I. ऐसे वाक्यों को Passive Voice में object को subject बनाया जाता है।

Rule II. Infinitive के पहले 'to' का प्रयोग किया जाता है, जो Active Voice में छिपा रहता है।

इन वाक्यों को देखें—

1. I made him *laugh*. —*Active*

He was made *to laugh*. —*Passive*

2. He made me *sing*. —*Active*

I was made *to sing*. —*Passive*

3. I saw him *go*. —*Active*

He was seen *to go*. —*Passive*

पर Let के साथ Passive में भी to का प्रयोग नहीं होता; जैसे—

I let him go. —*Active*

He was let go. —*Passive*

यहाँ let to go का प्रयोग अनुचित होता।

(E) Present Continuous + that + Noun clause [object]

कुछ वाक्यों में Present Continuous के transitive verb (believe/find/claim/consider/know/report/say/think) के बाद that आता है और इसके बाद एक Noun clause जो object का काम करता है; जैसे—

We know that some boys grow wise early.

ऐसे वाक्यों का रूप Passive Voice में हो जाता है—

(i) *Subject + verb 'be' + past participle + infinitive*

Or

Subject + verb 'be' + past participle + to be + noun/adjective

(ii) *It is + past participle + that + clause* [Noun clause]

इन वाक्यों के परिवर्तन देखें—

1. We know that some boys grow wise early. —*Active*

Some boys are known to grow wise early. —*Passive*

Or

It is known that some boys grow wise early. —*Passive*

2. People consider that he is wise. —*Active*

He is considered to be wise. —*Passive*

Or

It is considered that he is wise. —*Passive*

ऐसे वाक्यों का परिवर्तन इन नियमों के अनुसार होता है—

Rule I. Noun clause के subject को Passive में subject बना दें।

Rule II. Principal clause के subject का लोप कर दें।

Rule III. ऐसे वाक्यों में by + object का प्रयोग न करें।

(F) Present Continuous + that + Noun clause [in passive voice]

ऐसे वाक्यों में Noun clause का verb रहता है Passive Voice में; जैसे—

He wants that he *should be treated* as a minister.

इस प्रकार के वाक्यों का परिवर्तन होता है—

Present Continuous + to be + past participle

इन वाक्यों को देखें—

1. He wants that he should be treated as a minister. —*Active*

   He wants to be treated as a minister. —*Passive*

2. He likes that he should be rewarded. —*Active*

   He likes to be rewarded. —*Passive*

ध्यान दें कि ऐसे वाक्यों का परिवर्तन इन नियमों की सहायता से होता है—

Rule I. Noun clause [that + subject + verb] का लोप हो जाता है।

Rule II. Verb के बाद to be + past participle आता है।

....

EXERCISE

Change the voice of the following sentences.

1. We appointed him teacher.
2. I nominated him monitor.
3. I wrote him a letter.
4. Write a story.
5. Did he teach you?
6. Who taught him?
7. We believe that he is honest.
8. We find that novels are harmful.
9. They say that he is a thief.
10. He likes that he should be excused.
11. People believe that he is a thief.
12. Nobody has answered this question correctly.

EXERCISES WORKED OUT

1. The book *has* greatly *interested* me.

   I *have been* greatly *interested* in the book.

2. I found the boys laughing at me.

   I found myself *being laughed* at by the boys.

3. *Hew* down the bridge.

   Let the bridge *be hewn* down.

4. Tell him to leave the room at once.

   Let him *be told* to leave the room at once.

5. The house is rapidly *building.*

   The house *is being* built rapidly.

6. He *taught* her to read Hindi.

   She *was taught* to read Hindi by him.

7. The teacher *taught* me to speak English.

   I *was taught* to speak English by the teacher.

8. The students loudly *cheered* the Governor's speech.

   The Governor's speech *was* loudly *cheered* by the students.

9. Brutus *accused* Caesar of ambition.
   Caesar *was accused* of ambition by Brutus.
10. They *chose* him their leader.
   He *was chosen* their leader.

Quasi-Passive Verbs/Middle Voice

कुछ ऐसे Transitive Verbs होते हैं जो देखने में तो Active Voice के समान लगते हैं क्योंकि उनका रूप (form) Active Voice में रहता है, पर उनसे Passive Voice का अर्थ (sense) प्रकट होता है। ऐसे ही Verbs को Quasi-Passive या Middle Voice कहते हैं। ऐसे Verbs के बाद Adjective का प्रयोग होता है जब वह Adjective उस Verb के Subject का गुण बताता है, पर जब उस Verb ही का गुण बताया जाए, तब Verb के बाद Adverb आता है, Adjective नहीं; जैसे—

1. This fruit *tastes sour.*
2. The sofa *feels soft.*
3. That wooden chair *feels hard.*
4. The flower *smells sweet.*
5. His words *sound harsh.*
6. This silken shirt *feels soft.*
7. This house *looks nice.*
8. Fish *sells cheap.*

इन वाक्यों में Verbs के बाद Adjective का प्रयोग हुआ है, क्योंकि ये Adjectives वाक्य के Subject का गुण बतलाते हैं। यहाँ Adjectives के बदले Adverbs का प्रयोग उचित नहीं होता, क्योंकि Adverbs का प्रयोग करने पर वाक्य का कोई अर्थ नहीं लग सकता।

अब, इन वाक्यों को देखें—

1. The book *reads well.*
2. The book *sells well.*
3. The sentence *reads badly.*
4. The house *lets easily.*

इन वाक्यों में Verbs के बाद Adverbs का प्रयोग हुआ है, Adjectives का नहीं, क्योंकि यहाँ Verbs का गुण बतलाया गया है। इन वाक्यों में Adjectives का प्रयोग करने पर वाक्य का कोई अर्थ ही नहीं लग सकता। तो, इससे ये स्पष्ट है कि Quasi-Passive Verbs के बाद जो Adjective/Adverb आता है, वह वाक्य के अर्थ पर निर्भर रहता है।

EXERCISE

Correct the following sentences.

(1) This feather feels softly. (2) The tamarind tastes sourly. (3) This mango tastes nicely. (4) This flower smells sweetly. (5) My garden looks beautifully. (6) Your words sound harshly. (7) This fruit tastes bitterly.

Hints—(1) soft; (2) sour; (3) nice; (4) sweet; (5) beautiful; (6) harsh; (7) bitter

❒

Chapter XIII

COMMON ERRORS

इस अध्याय में हम ऐसी अशुद्धियों पर विचार करेंगे जो शब्द के अनुपयुक्त प्रयोग के कारण होती हैं। शब्दों के शुद्ध रूप और प्रयोग ब्रैकेट (brackets) के भीतर दिए गए हैं।

(A) One Word for Another

1. His *four fathers* were great men. (forefathers)
2. He is given free *boarding* and lodging. (board)
3. There is a *bevy* of boys. (bevy of girls)
4. This house is made of *bricks.* (brick)
5. There is a *crowd* of grapes. (bunch)
6. He has not paid the *fooding* charge. (food)
7. I enjoy *freeship.* (free-studentship)
8. He has applied for *lecturership.* (lectureship)
9. He doesn't like *teachery* as a profession. (teaching)
10. A *towny man* gets a lot of comforts. (A townsman)
11. The house is beyond *repairs.* (repair)
12. You are a man of *words.* (word)
13. He is true to his *words.* (word)
14. I did all my *works.* (work)
15. I have sent a *petition* for casual leave. (an application)
16. He is out of *door.* (doors)
17. I have placed *order* for a book. (orders)
18. He is out of *spirit.* (spirits)
19. I am out of *sort.* (sorts)
20. I am a man of *part.* (parts)
21. He applied himself to *study.* (*studies*)
22. I am resting in the *shadow* of a tree. (shade)
23. There is no *place* on this berth. (room)
24. I have no *rupees.* (money)
25. He *walked* on his cycle. (rode)
26. My salary is Rs 400/- *per month.* (per mensem or a month)

27. My salary is Rs 4800/- *per year.* (per annum or a year)
28. Please credit this amount to my *name.* (account)
29. *Good bye*, Ram, I am glad to see you. (Good evening)
30. *Good night,* sir, you are welcome. (Good evening)
31. The *weather* of this place suits me. (climate)
32. He is *devoted* to gambling (addicted)
33. You are *addicted* to literature. (devoted)
34. There is *lack of* poverty here. (absence of)
35. I gave him a cheque of Rs 500/-. (for)
36. This great poem is very *artful.* (artistic)
37. I like your *childish* nature. (childlike)
38. Shakespeare was an *imaginary* poet. (imaginative)
39. As he is *sick,* he is absent. (ill)
40. Please grant me *ill* leave. (sick leave)
41. What's the cause *for* delay? (of)
42. There is no cause *of* complain. (for)
43. She is *somewhat* tall for her age. (too, rather)
44. The great saint is *notorious* in the spiritual field. (famous)
45. You are a *luxuriant* man. (luxurious)
46. Please *shut* the tap. (turn off)
47. Bread is made *of* flour. (from)
48. He is very *coward.* (is a coward or is very cowardly)
49. He is our *mutual* friend. (common)
50. He rose by dint of *sheer* merit. (great)
51. They are fast *enemies.* (friends)
52. They are *sworn* enemies. (avowed)
53. I *richly* deserve this honour. (highly, greatly)
54. He *highly* deserves this punishment. (richly)
55. It is *utterly* right. (wholly, perfectly)
56. I have done *good* at the examination. (well)
57. The thief stood *in front of* the judge. (before)
58. It is 4.30 *in* my watch. (by)
59. It is *totally* good. (wholly)
60. It is *totally* clear to me. (perfectly, thoroughly)
61. It is *totally right.* (all right/perfectly right)
62. The pot is *vacant.* (empty)
63. I admire her *womanish* virtues. (womanly)
64. It is a historical event. (historic)

65. My tooth is paining. (aching)
66. I *took* my admission. (I was admitted or I got myself admitted)
67. I *took* my birth in 1920. (I was born)
68. He invited me but I *denied.* (declined)
69. He *denied* to help me. (refused)
70. She *gave* a speech. (made)
71. A lot of men *suspect* the existence of God. (doubt)
72. I don't like *that he should go out.* (I don't like him to go out)
73. The ship was *drowned* in the sea. (The ship sank)
74. Fish *float* in the river. (swim)
75. A piece of wood is *swimming.* (floating)
76. The picture was *hanged.* (hung)
77. I cannot *rise* it. (raise)
78. I will do it *some way* or another. (some way or other/one way or another)
79. Please *await* me here. (wait for)
80. He jumped *at* a conclusion. (to)
81. Neither of them saw *each other.* (saw the other)
82. The two cars followed *each other.* (One car followed the other)
83. My speech was *broadcasted.* (broadcast)
84. His words are as sweet as *sugar.* (honey)
85. I went there *especially* to see him. (specially)
86. I cannot stay here *any more.* (any longer)
87. He went with me *so far as* Mumbai. (as far as)
88. She refused to look at me, *much more* speak to me. (much less)
89. He was *hung* for murder. (hanged)
90. The smoke is *raising* from huts. (rising)
91. I *hope* that I shall fail. (I am afraid)
92. Columbus *invented* America. (discovered)
93. You *enjoy* bad health. (You have)
94. I didn't *approve* this marriage proposal. (approve of)
95. This scheme has been *approved of* by the VC. (approved by the VC)
96. I can't question his *bona fide.* (bona fides)
97. Please excuse *me* coming late. (my)
98. Will you *forego* your holiday? (forgo)
99. I *told* him good morning. (wished)
100. He *tells* me a fool. (calls)
101. He *stopped* at my house for a week. (stayed)
102. He *saw* my certificates. (looked into)

103. The doctor *saw* my pulse. (felt)
104. Have you *seen* all the examination papers? (examined)
105. *See* this word in the dictionary. (Look up)
106. The teacher *told* that the earth is round. (said)
107. *Whom* are you speaking to? (Who)
108. His *dear* half is ill. (better half/wife)
109. The matter *shook* in the balance. (trembled)
110. He is as gentle as a *cow.* (lamb, dove)
111. He is as greedy as a *cat.* (wolf)
112. He is as faithul as a *horse.* (dog)
113. He *turned every* stone. (He left no stone unturned)
114. My friend *tells* that the Five-Year Plan is good. (says, feels)
115. It is as white as *milk.* (snow)
116. I have *given* examination this year. (appeared at, taken)
117. He *broke the news* of my grand success. (communicated)
118. I could not help *to laugh.* (laughing)
119. My parrot *speaks.* (talks)
120. It is as heavy as *stone.* (lead)
121. He *talks* English well. (speaks)
122. He is as firm as a *hill.* (rock)
123. Do not *speak* a lie. (tell)
124. It is as soft as *velvet.* (butter)
125. It is a *forgone* conclusion. (foregone)
126. She is as busy as an *ant.* (as a bee)
127. *What to speak* of helping, he did not even see me. (Not to speak)
128. It is an apple of *contention.* (discord)
129. He *shook my hand.* (shook hands with me or shook me by the hand)
130. *Except for* your help I would have been ruined. (Without or But for)
131. His name is *full-known.* (well-known)
132. It is as clear as gold. (crystal, day)
133. He made a goal. (scored)

(B) Superfluous Words

1. She is a mother of mine. (She is my mother.)
2. He is my *own* father. (He is my father.)
3. The fact is *true.* (It is a fact.)
4. I am awaiting *for* your reply. (awaiting your reply)
5. He picked *up* a quarrel. (picked a quarrel)
6. He died at the age of seventy *years.* (seventy)

7. I met a *child of* five years *old.* (a five-year-old child)
8. The clock has struck *six hours.* (six)
9. It is *almost quite* right. (quite right or almost right)
10. He is a man of *good* position. (man of position)
11. It is *rather* unique. (It is unique)
12. I am a man of *good* principle. (man of principle)
13. I walked on *my feet.* (on foot)
14. I think *myself.* (I think)
15. I forbade him *not* to smoke. (him to smoke)
16. This is just the *right thing.* (just the thing)
17. He is my cousin *brother.* (cousin)
18. I ordered *for* his dismissal. (ordered his dismissal)
19. He was proved *to be* wrong. (proved wrong)
20. I consider it *as* a good thing. (consider it a good thing)
21. I think/consider him *to be* a good student. (him a good student)
22. The train is behind *due* time. (behind time)
23. You are my only *one* friend. (only friend)
24. There is no *other* alternative. (no alternative)
25. She made a *fine* figure. (made a figure)
26. The poet describes *about* nature. (describes nature)
27. I saw him *on* last week. (saw him last week)
28. I doubt as *to* whether he is honest. (doubt whether)
29. Let us discuss *about* the problem. (discuss the problem)
30. I am investigating *into* the case. (investigating the case)
31. I am contesting *for* a seat. (contesting a seat)
32. I recommended *for* him to the Principal. (recommended him)
33. Her face resembles *to* her mother. (resembles her mother's)
34. Wait here until I *do not* return. (until I return)
35. Unless you *do not* work hard, you will not pass. (Unless you work)
36. My watch is in *proper* order. (is in order)
37. She is in a *bad* temper. (in a temper)
38. He is out of *good* temper. (out of temper)
39. I am forty *years.* (I am forty or forty years old)
40. He will return *back* in a week. (return or come back)

(C) Words Omitted

1. This house is 200 years. (200 years old)
2. Please come to *mine.* (my house, place, residence)

3. *Yours* of the 10th instant is to hand. (Your letter of the 10th)
4. I *find hard* to do it. (find it hard)
5. *Suffice* to say. (Suffice it to say)
6. I *know him* a good man. (know him to be)
7. I consider wrong to use unfair means. (consider it wrong)
8. His services were *dispensed.* (dispensed with)
9. I have *disposed* the business. (disposed of)
10. She does not *listen* my advice. (listen to)
11. He does not *know* to read and write. (how to read and write)
12. It is *regarded* sacred. (regarded as)
13. I *took him* a thief. (for a thief)
14. I have a pen *to write.* (to write with)
15. You have a house to *live.* (to live in)
16. He resides in a *boarding.* (boarding house)
17. *Open* page 15. (Open at)
18. I *wrote him* to come. (wrote to him)
19. I *replied him.* (replied to him)
20. I *pray God.* (pray to God)
21. Go there and *enjoy.* (enjoy yourself)
22. He *met* an accident. (met with)
23. She is five feet. (five feet tall)
24. When he *grows* he will enter a college. (grows up)
25. She *avenged* on her enemy. (avenged herself)

(D) Words Wrongly Related

1. My *family members.* (Members of my family)
2. Many *worth seeing* places. (Many places worth seeing)
3. *All round* the year. (All the year round)
4. I saw a dead horse walking across the field.
   (Walking across the field I saw a dead horse.)
5. He shot himself dead after bidding his wife good-bye with a gun.
   (After bidding his wife good-bye, he shot himself dead with a gun.)
6. He was murdered, sleeping in cold blood.
   (He was murdered in cold blood while he was sleeping.)
7. A large number of seats have been occupied by scholars that have no backs.
   (A large number of seats that have no backs have been occupied by scholars.)
8. A motor car may be driven across the bridge which weighs less than two tons.
   (A motor car which weighs less than two tons may be driven across the bridge.)

9. The death occurred yesterday afternoon at his residence of Mr Brown.
   (The death of Mr Brown occurred … residence.)
10. He gave a stool to the servant that had four legs.
    (He gave the servant a stool that had four legs.)
11. Lost a cane by a gentleman with a carved head.
    (Lost by a gentleman a cane with a carved head.)
12. I told him that he would fail as plainly as possible.
    (I told him as plainly as possible that he would fail.)
13. The storm burst just when the king reached the shore with great violence.
    (The storm burst with great violence just when the king reached the shore.)
14. Wanted a piano by a gentleman with carved legs.
    (Wanted by a gentleman a piano with carved legs.)
15. Wanted a house by a government officer that has at least four bedrooms.
    (Wanted by a government officer a house that has at least four bedrooms.)
16. Waiting for a taxi a lizard fell on his head.
    (As he was waiting for a taxi … .)
17. While plucking flowers a wasp stung him. (While he was plucking … .)
18. Walking in the morning a snake bit him. (While he was walking … .)
19. Playing in the field a ghost was seen. (While we were playing … .)
20. Standing on the roof a helicopter flew over me. (While I was standing … .)

Chapter XIV

TEST YOURSELF

I. *Fill in the blanks with a suitable word given in brackets.*

1. I won but you …… . [fought, lost]
2. He will be rewarded but she …… . [punished, banished]
3. I will lend but he will …… . [borrow, sorrow]
4. He talks much but does …… . [nothing, little]
5. He was given a …… punishment. [corporal, corporeal]
6. This saint is very …… [beneficial, beneficent]
7. …… of everything is bad. [Access, Excess]
8. He is very …… of me. [zealous, jealous]
9. She gave me a piece of …… . [advice, advise]
10. He …… all the charges. [denied, refused]
11. Smoking is a …… [habit, custom]
12. I like his …… simplicity. [childish, childlike]
13. Barometer measures …… . [pressure, temperature]
14. Wood is hard but butter is …… . [soft, white]
15. He …… to help me. [refused, denied]

II. *Correct the following sentences.*

1. Coffee is a mild stimulus.
2. This door is meant for exodus.
3. Do you mind your date of birth?
4. He went to Mumbai via train.
5. Who is the tragical hero?
6. The President has given ascent to this Bill.
7. His behaviour is not descent.
8. He is not sensible to criticism.
9. He is an imminent poet.
10. He is stopping with his friend.

❐

WORD POWER

Vocabulary

शुद्ध-शुद्ध बोलने और लिखने के लिए सिर्फ व्याकरण के नियमों का ही ज्ञान पर्याप्त नहीं। इसके लिए शब्दों के अर्थ का ज्ञान अत्यावश्यक है। इसलिए इस अध्याय में Synonyms, Antonyms, Paronyms और Homonyms पर विचार करें और देखें कि शब्द किस प्रकार कितने तरह से प्रयुक्त होते हैं। इससे शब्दों की शक्ति समझने और उनका उचित प्रयोग करने में सहायता मिलेगी।

SYNONYMS

जिन शब्दों के अर्थ में कुछ समानता रहती है और साथ ही उनमें भिन्नता भी वर्तमान रहती है, वे Synonyms कहलाते हैं। एक-दो उदाहरण लें। Crime उस अपराध को कहते हैं जो राज्य के विरुद्ध किया जाए; vice वह अपराध है जो नैतिकता के विरुद्ध किया जाए; और sin वह अपराध है जो धर्म के विरुद्ध किया जाए। इसलिए crime, vice और sin को हम synonyms कह सकते हैं। यहाँ हम कुछ Synonyms पर विचार करें—

1. **Assent** का अर्थ है agreement (स्वीकृति), किंतु यह फैसले के विषय से संबंधित रहता है; जैसे—

   The Chancellor has given his *assent* to this proposal.

   Consent का भी अर्थ है agreement (स्वीकृति), किंतु यह प्रबंध की बातों से संबंधित है; जैसे—

   The Chancellor has given his *consent* to preside over the function.

2. **Addicted** (बुरे गुणों के अर्थ में) — He is *addicted* to drinking.

   Devoted (अच्छे गुणों के अर्थ में) — I am *devoted* to my duties.

3. **Avenge** (to punish evil doers on behalf of one who is weak or oppressed)—He will *avenge* the murder of his bosom friend.

   Revenge (is a Noun and a Verb—to punish person for wrongs done to oneself or someone else)—The robber took *revenge* on the officer who had arrested him.

4. **Battle** (between large organised armies)—Three important *battles* were fought at Panipat.

   Fight (between persons or parties but without the aid of army)—The Hindus and the Muslims often *fight* for nothing.

   War (between nations with the aid of large armies—is the biggest type of armed conflict between nations)—A third world *war* will destory everything.

5. **Begin** (is used in a non-official sense)—I will *begin* the work soon.

   Commence (is used in an official sense)—The Principal has notified that the examination shall *commence* on the 15th of May, 1962.

6. **Confer** (to give—as an act of authority)—The President of India *confers* titles on great men.

   Bestow (to give—as an act of charity)—Many presents were *bestowed* on the flood-victims.

7. **Confess** (to accept responsibility or guilt)—The thief *confessed* his guilt at last.

   Admit (to accept as true)—My previous decision, I *admit,* was not helpful.

8. **Crime** (offence against law or state)—Theft is a *crime.*

   Vice (offence against moral law)—Drinking is a *vice.*

   Sin (offence against religion)—Telling lies is a *sin.*

9. **Custom** (general practice in a society, an established code of action)—Old *customs* are not always bad.

   Habit (a particular tendency in an individual)—*Habit* is the second nature of man.

10. **Deficient** (lacking in)—He is *deficient* in manners.

    Defective (having faults)—His language is very *defective.*

11. **Deny** (to declare something as false or untrue)—The thief *denied* all the charges against him.

    Refuse (not to accept)—He *refused* to help me.

    We cannot say, "He *denied* to help me."

12. **Discover** (to find something that existed before—to bring to light something that lay hidden for others)—A new planet has been *discovered.*

    Invent (to produce something new—to create what did not exist before)—Many deadly weapons have been *invented* these days.

13. **Drown** (is used for living objects only)—The body was *drowned* in the river.

    Sink (is used for both living and lifeless objects)—The ship *sank* into the ocean.

14. **Famous** (having importance in a good sense)—India is *famous* for her fine silk.

    Notorious (having importance in a bad sense)—He is a *notorious* criminal.

    Notable (is used in a good sense—Having a rare quality)—Mr Nehru was a *notable* citizen.

15. **Liberty** (absence of any check or restraint)—You are at *liberty* to do anything you like.

    Freedom (absence of dependence)—India has now achieved political *freedom.*

16. **Peaceable** (attracted towards peace, as opposed to war)—The world today requires men of *peaceable* nature.

    Peaceful (a state of peace)—Everybody by nature likes a *peaceful* life.

17. **Practice** (Noun—a habit—repetition of an action)—Mathematics requires *practice.*

    Practise (Verb—to do repeatedly)—A false preacher only preaches, he does not *practise.*

18. **Shade** (a place sheltered from the sun)—Cows are resting in the *shade* of this tree.
Shadow (a dark figure projected by a body)—This *shadow* dance was very nice.
19. **Stimulant** (that which produces artificial energy for some time)—Tea is a mild *stimulant*.
Stimulus (that which rouses to activity)—Promotion is a *stimulus* to efficiency.
20. **Vacant** (not filled or occupied)—The house is *vacant.*
Empty (not containing anything)—The pitcher is *empty.*

ANTONYMS

किसी शब्द का अर्थ यदि दूसरे शब्द के विपरीत हो तो वह उस शब्द का Antonym कहलाता है। अँगरेजी में Antonyms तीन प्रकार से बनाए जाते हैं—

(i) कुछ शब्दों के पहले dis, il, im, in, ir, un prefixes (उपसर्ग) जोड़कर; जैसे—

pleasant—unpleasant	courtsey—discourtesy
possible—impossible	pleased—displeased
important—unimportant	known—unknown
decent—indecent	convenience—inconvenience

(ii) कुछ शब्दों के अंत में आनेवाले suffix (प्रत्यय) full/less को बदलकर; जैसे—

hopeful—hopeless	careless—careful

(iii) अनियमित रूप से, अर्थात नए शब्द की रचना के द्वारा; जैसे—

good—bad	ugly—beautiful

यहाँ इन Antonyms को सावधानी से देखें—

Ability (योग्यता)	Incompetence (अयोग्यता)
Above (ऊपर)	Below (नीचे)
Accept (स्वीकार करना)	Reject (अस्वीकार करना)
Acknowledge (पहुँच स्वीकार करना)	Deny (नहीं मानना)
Acquit (मुक्त करना)	Convict (सजा देना)
Advance (आगे बढ़ना)	Retreat (पीछे हटना)
Advantage (लाभ, सुविधा)	Disadvantage (हानि, असुविधा)
Adversity (विपत्ति)	Prosperity (उन्नति)
Affirm (स्वीकार करना)	Deny (इनकार करना)
Agree (सहमत होना)	Differ (असहमत होना)
Agreeable (सहमत होना)	Disagreeable (अमान्य)
Allow (अनुमति देना)	Disallow (अनुमति न देना)

Always (सर्वदा)	Never (कभी नहीं)
All (सब)	None (कोई नहीं)
Angel (देवदूत)	Devil (दुष्ट)
Ancient (प्राचीन)	Modern (आधुनिक)
Appear (प्रकट होना)	Disappear (लुप्त हो जाना)
Arrival (आगमन)	Departure (प्रस्थान)
Ascend (ऊपर उठना)	Descend (नीचे गिरना)
Attach (जोड़ना)	Detach (अलग करना)
Attract (आकर्षित करना)	Repel (दूर हटाना)
Attack (आक्रमण करना)	Defend (रक्षा करना)
Armament (शस्त्रीकरण)	Disarmament (नि:शस्त्रीकरण)
Ample (पर्याप्त)	Meagre (अपर्याप्त)
Activity (क्रियाशीलता)	Passivity (निष्क्रियता)
Ayes (हाँ)	Noes (ना)
Bad (खराब)	Good (अच्छा)
Barbarous (असभ्य)	Civilized (सभ्य)
Barren (बंजर)	Fertile (उर्वर)
Beautiful (सुंदर)	Ugly (कुरूप)
Beginning (प्रारंभ)	End (अंत)
Belief (विश्वास)	Disbelief (अविश्वास)
Benevolence (उपकार)	Malevolence (अपकार)
Bitter (तीता)	Sweet (मीठा)
Blessing (वरदान)	Curse (अभिशाप)
Blunt (भोथा)	Sharp (पैना)
Bold (साहसी)	Timid (कायर)
Bottom (पेंदा)	Top (शीर्ष)
Bravery (वीरता)	Cowardice (कायरता)
Bright (चमकीला, चुस्त)	Dull (फीका, सुस्त)
Broad (चौड़ा)	Narrow (सँकरा)
Buy (खरीदना)	Sell (बेचना)
Care (परवाह करना)	Neglect (उपेक्षा करना)

Cause (कारण)	Effect (परिणाम)
Cheap (सस्ता)	Dear (महँगा)
Cheerful (प्रसन्न)	Cheerless (उदास)
Civil (विनम्र)	Uncivil (उद्दण्ड)
Classicism (पौराणिकता)	Romanticism (आधुनिकता)
Clean (साफ)	Dirty (गंदा)
Clever (चालाक)	Stupid (मूर्ख)
Cold (ठण्ढा)	Hot (गर्म)
Come (आना)	Go (जाना)
Comedy (सुखांत नाटक)	Tragedy (दुखांत नाटक)
Common (साधारण)	Rare (असाधारण)
Condemn (तिरस्कार करना)	Approve (प्रशंसा करना)
Confess (स्वीकार करना)	Deny (अस्वीकार करना)
Confidence (विश्वास)	Diffidence (अविश्वास)
Consent (सहमति)	Dissent (असहमति)
Considerable (बहुत)	Inconsiderable (अल्प)
Create (बनाना)	Destroy (नष्ट करना)
Credit (उधार)	Cash (नकद)
Crude (अपरिष्कृत, भोंढ़ा)	Refined (परिष्कृत)
Cruel (क्रूर)	Kind (दयालु)
Death (मृत्यु)	Life (जीवन)
Debtor (ऋणी, खददुक)	Creditor (ऋणदाता, महाजन)
Decent (भद्र)	Indecent (अभद्र)
Decision (निश्चय)	Indecision (अनिश्चय)
Decided (निश्चित, तय)	Undecided (अनिश्चित)
Deep (गहरा)	Shallow (छिछला)
Defendant (प्रतिवादी, मुद्दालह)	Plaintiff (वादी, मुद्दई)
Defensive (रक्षात्मक)	Offensive (आक्रमणात्मक)
Dependent (परतंत्र)	Independent (स्वतंत्र)
Deposit (जमा करना)	Withdraw (निकालना)
Destructive (ध्वंसात्मक)	Constructive (रचनात्मक)

Difficult (कठिन)	Easy (सरल)
Diligent (उद्यमी, मेहनती)	Idle (अनुद्यमी, काहिल)
Diminish (घटना)	Increase (बढ़ना)
Disease (रोग)	Health (स्वास्थ्य, आरोग्य)
Domestic (पालतू)	Wild (जंगली)
Dry (शुष्क)	Wet (आर्द्र)
Do (करना, बनाना)	Undo (बिगाड़ना)
Ebb (भाटा)	Flow (प्रवाह)
Early (पहले, शीघ्र)	Late (बाद, देर से)
Empty (खाली)	Full (भरा हुआ)
Employment (रोजगार, नौकरी)	Unemployment (बेकारी)
Encourage (उत्साहित करना)	Discourage (हतोत्साहित करना)
Entrance (प्रवेश)	Exit (निकास)
Evil (बुरा)	Good (भला)
Exclude (छोड़ना)	Include (शामिल करना)
Exterior (बाहरी)	Interior (भीतरी)
Extraordinary (असाधारण)	Ordinary (साधारण)
Experienced (अनुभवी)	Inexperienced (अनुभवहीन)
Extravagant (अपव्ययी)	Frugal, Thrifty, Economical (मितव्ययी)
Exhaustible (समाप्त होनेवाला)	Inexhaustible (असीम)
Examiner (परीक्षक)	Examine (परीक्षार्थी)
Failure (असफलता)	Success (सफलता)
Fair (अच्छा)	Foul, Unfair (बुरा)
Faithful (विश्वासी)	Faithless (अविश्वासी)
Fall (पतन)	Rise (उत्थान)
Falsehood (असत्यता)	Truth (सत्यता)
Familiar (परिचित)	Strange (अपरिचित)
Far (दूर)	Near (निकट)
Fast (तेज)	Slow (सुस्त)
Fat (मोटा)	Thin (पतला)
Foolish (मूर्ख)	Wise (बुद्धिमान)

Fortunate (भाग्यवान)	Unfortunate (भाग्यहीन)
Fortune (सौभाग्य)	Misfortune (दुर्भाग्य)
Freedom (स्वतंत्रता)	Slavery (दासता)
Fresh (ताजा)	Stale (बासी)
Friend (मित्र)	Foe, Enemy (शत्रु)
Friendliness (मैत्रीपूर्ण, अनुकूल)	Unfriendliness (रूखापन, प्रतिकूल)
Friendship (मित्रता)	Enmity (शत्रुता)
Gain (लाभ)	Loss (हानि)
Giant (भीमकाय, विशाल)	Dwarf (लघुकाय, बौना)
General (साधारण)	Particular (विशेष)
Great (बड़ा)	Small (छोटा)
Guest (अतिथि)	Host (आतिथेय)
Happiness (सुख)	Misery (दुःख)
Hard (कठोर)	Soft (कोमल)
Haste (शीघ्रता)	Delay (विलम्ब)
Heavy (भारी)	Light (हलका)
Heaven (स्वर्ग)	Hell (नरक)
High (ऊँचा)	Low (नीचा)
Honest (सच्चा, ईमानदार)	Dishonest (झूठा, बेईमान)
Honour (आदर, सम्मान)	Dishonour, Shame (निरादर, अपमान)
Hope (आशा)	Despair (निराशा)
Humble (विनम्र)	Proud (घमंडी)
Important (महत्त्वपूर्ण)	Unimportant, Trivial (साधारण)
Increase (वृद्धि)	Decrease (कमी)
Inferior (घटिया)	Superior (श्रेष्ठ)
Inhale (साँस लेना)	Exhale (साँस छोड़ना)
Initial (प्रारंभिक)	Final (अंतिम)
Interested (इच्छुक)	Uninterested (अनिच्छुक)
Interesting (रोचक)	Uninteresting (अरोचक)
Innocent (निर्दोष)	Guilty (दोषी)
Joy (हर्ष)	Sorrow (विषाद)

Junior (छोटा, निम्न)	Senior (बड़ा, उच्च)
Justice (न्याय)	Injustice (अन्याय)
Known (ज्ञात)	Unknown (अज्ञात)
Kind (दयालु)	Unkind (निष्ठुर)
Knowledge (ज्ञान)	Ignorance (अज्ञान)
Lad (लड़का)	Lass (लड़की)
Legal (कानूनी)	Illegal (गैर-कानूनी)
Lend (कर्ज़ देना)	Borrow (कर्ज लेना)
Like (समान)	Unlike (असमान)
Like (पसंद करना)	Dislike (नापसंद करना)
Literate (साक्षर)	Illeterate (निरक्षर)
Living (जीवित)	Dead (मृत)
Logical (तर्कपूर्ण)	Illogical (तर्कशून्य)
Legitimate (जायज)	Illegitimate (नाजायज)
Long (लंबा)	Short (नाटा)
Loyal (आज्ञाकारी, विश्वासी)	Disloyal (अवज्ञाकारी, विश्वासघाती)
Make (बनाना)	Mar (नष्ट करना)
Many (बहुत)	Few (कुछ)
Material (भौतिक, पार्थिव)	Spiritual (अभौतिक, अपार्थिव)
Masculine (पुंल्लिंग)	Feminine (स्त्रीलिंग)
Maximum (अधिकतम)	Minimum (न्यूनतम)
Merit (गुण)	Demerit (दोष)
Modest (विनम्र)	Immodest (उदंड)
Mortal (नाशवान)	Immortal (अमर)
Movable (चल)	Immovable (अचल)
Much (बहुत)	Little (थोड़ा)
Natural (अकृत्रिम, स्वाभाविक)	Artificial, Unnatural (कृत्रिम)
Negative (नकारात्मक)	Positive, Affirmative (स्वीकारात्मक)
Noble (उदार)	Ignoble (नीच, अधम)
Neither (कोई नहीं)	Either (कोई)
Obey (आज्ञापालन करना)	Disobey (आज्ञोल्लंघन करना)

Old (वृद्ध)	Young (युवा)
Optimist (आशावादी)	Pessimist (निराशावादी)
Oral (मौखिक)	Written (लिखित)
Partial (पक्षपाती)	Impartial (निष्पक्ष)
Peace (शांति)	War (युद्ध)
Permanent (स्थायी)	Temporary (अस्थायी)
Permisson (अनुमति)	Prohibition (रोक, निषेध)
Persuade (राजी करना)	Dissuade (रोकना, मना करना)
Please (प्रसन्न करना)	Displease (अप्रसन्न करना)
Pleasant (रुचिकर)	Unpleasant (अरुचिकर)
Pleasure (आनंद)	Pain (कष्ट), Displeasure (अप्रसन्नता)
Plenty (प्रचुरता)	Scarcity (अभाव)
Polite (नम्र)	Impolite (अनम्र, कटु)
Praise (प्रशंसा करना)	Blame (दोष देना)
Presence (उपस्थिति)	Absence (अनुपस्थिति)
Profit (लाभ)	Loss (हानि)
Proper (उचित)	Improper (अनुचित)
Private (निजी)	Public (सार्वजनिक)
Punctual (समयनिष्ठ)	Unpunctual, Late (देरी से आनेवाला)
Punish (दंड देना)	Reward (पुरस्कृत करना)
Pure (शुद्ध)	Impure, Adulterated (अशुद्ध)
Rational (विवेकपूर्ण)	Irrational (विवेकशून्य)
Religious (धार्मिक)	Secular (धर्म-निरपेक्ष)
Recover (प्राप्त करना)	Lose (खोना)
Regular (नियमित)	Irregular (अनियमित)
Reject (अस्वीकृत करना)	Accept (स्वीकृत करना)
Remember (याद रखना)	Forget (भूल जाना)
Reasonable (उपयुक्त, उचित)	Unreasonable (अनुपयुक्त, अनुचित)
Rich (धनवान)	Poor (निर्धन)
Rough (रुखड़ा)	Smooth (चिकना)

Raw (कच्चा)	Ripe (पका हुआ)
Social (सामाजिक)	Unsocial (असामाजिक)
Satisfied (संतुष्ट)	Dissatisfied (असंतुष्ट)
Satisfactory (संतोषजनक)	Unsatisfactory (असंतोषजनक)
Thick (मोटा)	Thin (पतला)
Transparent (स्पष्ट, पारदर्शी)	Opaque (अपारदर्शी)
Unite (मिलाना)	Disunite (अलग करना)
Uniform (एक रूप का)	Varied (भिन्न-भिन्न रूप का)
Vague (अनिश्चित)	Definite (निश्चित)
Victory (विजय)	Defeat (पराजय)
Visible (दृश्यवान)	Invisible (अदृश्य)
Violence (हिंसा)	Non-violence (अहिंसा)
Virtue (गुण, पुण्य)	Vice (अवगुण, पाप)
Voluntary (ऐच्छिक)	Compulsory (अनिवार्य)
Warm (उष्ण)	Cool (शीतल)
Wicked (पापी)	Virtuous (पुण्यात्मा)
Wild (जंगली)	Domestic (पालतू)
Win (जीतना)	Lose (हारना)
Wisdom (विवेक)	Folly (मूर्खता)
Yes (हाँ)	No (नहीं)

EXERCISE

Add the right prefix to each of these words to make a word opposite in meaning.

regular, friendly, pleasure, known, religious, natural, exhaustible, please, kind, noble, movable, satisfied, satisfactory, visible, rational.

PARONYMS

जिन शब्दों के रूप मिलते-जुलते हों या जिनकी उत्पत्ति एक ही शब्द से हुई हो, पर अर्थ में भिन्नता हो वे Paronyms कहलाते हैं; जैसे—artful, artistic और artificial; इन तीनों शब्दों की उत्पत्ति art से हुई है, किंतु तीनों के अर्थ में अंतर है। जो लोग शुद्ध ढंग से अँगरेजी लिखना या बोलना चाहते हैं उन्हें इस सूची से बहुत सहायता मिलेगी—

1. **Artist** (one skilled in fine arts, viz., painting, music, poetry, etc.)—A poet is an *artist.*

   Artisan (one who practises some handicraft)—A potter is an *artisan.*

   Artiste (a performer in singing or dancing)—The opera company had quite a large number of *artistes.*

2. **Artistic** (beautiful)—This poem is *artistic.*

   Artful (clever)—He succeeded by *artful* means.

   Artificial (not natural)—Modern life is getting *artificial.*

3. **Barbarism** (uncivilized condition)—*Barbarism* still prevails in some parts of the world.

   Barbarity (cruelty)—Great conquerors have committed seveal acts of *barbarity.*

4. **Beneficial** (useful—it is applied to things)—The University Act is very *beneficial.*

   Beneficent (kind—it is applied to persons)—My college is run by the *beneficent* person of the place.

5. **Ceremonious** (an excess of formality)—A friend's manners should not be *ceremonious.*

   Ceremonial (relating to rites or ceremonies)—His *ceremonial* dress is very costly.

6. **Comprehensive** (extensive, that which includes a good deal)—'The Discovery of India' gives us a *comprehensive* survey of the glories of ancient India.

   Comprehensible (that which can be understood)—Your ideas are not very clear and *comprehensible.*

7. **Confident** (quite sure)—A good student is *confident* of success.

   Confidant (one who is entrusted with a secret)—It is not safe to make everybody your *confidant.*

8. **Contemptible** (mean, नीच)—Iago's conduct was highly *contemptible.*

   Contemptuous (hateful, घृणित)—He dismissed the servant with a *contemptuous* look.

9. **Continuous** (without gap or break)—Rainfall has been *continuous* at Patna today.

   Continual (with occasional breaks)—My dog keeps up a *continual* barking at night.

10. **Continuance** (duration, time of remaining)—He will get all the privileges during his *continuance* in the service.

    Continuation (completion or resumption of something left 'incomplete')—The *continuation* of the work is delayed.

11. **Corporal** (relating to the body)—*Corporal* punishment at school was allowed till recently.

    Corporeal (material)—Saints avoid *corporeal* pleasures.

12. **Childish** (is used in a bad sense and means 'silly')—You are now fairly grown-up but your habits are *childish.*

Childlike (is used in a good sense and means 'simple' and 'innocent')—Aurobindo's *childlike* simplicity pleased everyone.

13. **Dependent** (is an adjective, meaning depending on)—My career is *dependent* upon this plan.

    Dependant (is a noun, meaning one depending on others)—The *dependants* of the college employees are granted full free-studentship.

14. **Disinterested** (unselfish, free from prejudice)—A great leader renders *disinterested* service to his society.

    Uninterested (indifferent, lacking in interest in a thing)—I am *uninterested* in local politics.

15. **Diverse** (different, not alike)—Our opinions on this point are as *diverse* as sky and earth.

    Divers (several)—*Divers* men have tried to bring about social reforms.

16. **Effective** (having a powerful effect)—Antony's funeral speech on the death of Caesar was *effective.*

    Efficient (competent, योग्य)—*Efficient* officers do not practise red-tapism.

    Efficacious (sure to produce the desired effect)—'Anacin' proves *efficacious* in all types of pain.

17. **Enviable** (producing or causing envy)—The performance of my college team was *enviable.*

    Envious (the feeling of envy, डाह)—A good man is not *envious* of the prosperity of his neighbours.

18. **Elemental** (relating to the elements, such as air, fire, etc.). The ship reached the shore in spite of *elemental* difficulties.

    Elementary (primary, introductory)—*Elementary* education is now free in India.

19. **Formalism** (observance of external forms)—We should give up the *formalism* of religions.

    Formality (formal or ceremonial act)—A thanksgiving ceremony is often a mere *formality.*

20. **Ghastly** (fearful)—I trembled at the *ghastly* sight.

    Ghostly (relating to ghost—भूत-प्रेत-जैसा)—The *ghostly* figure in the dark was a creation of my own brain.

21. **God-like** (above ordinary mortals)—An act of charity is *god-like.*

    Godly (religious, virtuous)—Vinoba Bhave leads a *godly* life.

22. **Graceful** (handsome)—Cleopatra had a *graceful* appearance.

    Gracious (merciful)—God save our *gracious* President!

23. **Honorary** (holding office without pay, conferred as an honour)—He got an *honorary* degree. The post of the Secretary is *honorary.*

    Honourable (worthy of honour)—Pandit Nehru was an *honourable* man.

24. **Human** (belonging to mankind)—Struggle for existence is deeply-rooted in *human* nature.

Humane (kind)—We must adopt a *humane* attitude towards animals.

25. **Humiliation** (loss of prestige, dishonour, अपमान)—He suffered great *humiliation* as a result of his failure.

Humility (politeness, नम्रता)—Right type of education produces *humility* in students.

26. **Imaginary** (unreal, fanciful)—The equator is an *imaginary* line.

Imaginative (having creative imagination)—No poet can be great without *imaginative* power.

27. **Industrious** (laborious, active)—There is nothing impossible for an *industrious* man.

Industrial (relating to commerce and industry)—Mumbai is an *industrial* town.

28. **Judicial** (impartial, pertaining to a judge or court of law)—A *judicial* enquiry has been recommended.

Judicious (wise, sensible)—A *judicious* selection of books is essential to success.

29. **Lovable** (worthy of love, that which should be loved)—He has many *lovable* qualities.

Lovely (nice, beautiful)—Rose is a *lovely* flower.

30. **Luxuriant** (having rich growth)—Castor oil helps *luxuriant* growth of hair.

Luxurious (having much of comfort and luxury)—The Zamindars led a *luxurious* life before Zamindari abolition.

31. **Memorable** (worth remembering)—The 26th of January is a *memorable* day in India.

Memorial (a statue, etc., which helps us remember something or somebody)—The Taj Mahal is a *memorial.*

32. **Momentous** (very important)—The first battle of Panipat was a *momentous* event in the history of India.

Momentary (short-lived)—Physical comforts give only *momentary* pleasure.

33. **Negligent** (careless)—A great man is *negligent* about his dress.

Negligible (extremely unimportant or small)—The difference between the head examiner and the co-examiner in marking is *negligible.*

34. **Observation** (the act of watching closely, making a remark)—*Observation* in an important source of knowledge. He made a significant *observation* in his speech.

Observance (keeping rules and rites strictly)—A superintendent of examination must be strict in the *observance* of all the rules of examinations.

35. **Official** (as a noun means an 'officer', and as an adjective means 'connected with an office')—All the *officials* have some *official* secrecy.

Officious (interfering, too ready to offer help that is not wanted)—His *officious* manner is simply disgusting.

36. **Pitiable** (creating or arousing pity)—The victims of the flood are in a *pitiable* condition.

    Pitiful (feeling pity)—God cannot be *pitiful* if you are not merciful to your neighbours.

    Piteous (miserable)—Her *piteous* cry attracted a big crowd.

37. **Practical** (opposed to what is merely theoretical)—*Practical* classes will be started soon.

    Practicable (possible, that which can be performed)—The scheme of Three-year Degree Course is not *practicable.*

38. **Popular** (having the quality to please)—Browning was a great poet but not a *popular* poet.

    Populous (thickly populated)—China is a *populous* country.

39. **Refuge** (shelter)—Refugees have found no *refuge* as yet.

    Refuse (i) as a Verb means 'not to accept' and (ii) as a Noun means 'worthless materials, rubbish', etc.—He *refused* to lend me a book. The vast heaps of *refuse* could not be cleared in a day.

40. **Sensible** (having sense and reason)—Every *sensible* man can follow such a *sensible* suggestion as yours.

    Sensitive (touchy, easily affected)—A *sensitive* person is pleased or displeased too quickly.

41. **Sensuous** (capable of affecting the senses)—The poetry of Keats is *sensuous.*

    Sensual (is used in a bad sense and means 'indulging in bodily pleasures')—*Sensual* men lose both health and wealth.

42. **Social** (relating to society or small group)—A lot of *social* reforms are necessary.

    Sociable (fond of society or company)—Government servants should now be *sociable.*

43. **Spirituous** (pertaining to alcohol)—The Government is now discouraging *spiritous* drinks.

    Spiritual (opposed to material; pertaining to soul or spirit)—Material progress at the cost of *spiritual* progress is harmful.

44. **Temporal** (opposed to eternal and spiritual)—The lust for *temporal* power is at the root of all conflicts.

    Temporary (short-lived)—I cannot accept a *temporary* job.

45. **Union** (act of uniting)—A workers *union* has been formed.

    Unity (oneness)—Hindu-Muslim *unity* is essential.

46. **Willing** (ready without hesitation)—I am *willing* to help you.

    Wilful (deliberate, conscious)—Acts of *wilful* negligence will ruin your career.

47. **Womanly** (is used in a good sense and means 'tender', 'affectionate', 'that which is worthy of a woman')—The *womanly* qualities of Lady Macbeth could not remain suppressed.

    Womanish (is used in a bad sense and means 'weak and cowardly')—It is *womanish* on a soldier's part to leave the battlefield.

48. **Verbal** (relating to words, oral)—*Verbal* orders for firing were given.

    Verbose (having too many words, having more words than necessary)—His early style is *verbose.*

HOMONYMS

Such words as have the same form but different meanings are called Homonyms. Homonyms, strictly speaking, are separate words that are identical in form but different in meaning. For example, *pole* which means a 'stake' or 'shaft' is an English word and *pole* which means 'the terminal point of axis' is of Greek origin. But, broadly and loosely speaking, Homonyms are all those words that have the same form but different meanings. The following list is only a small part of hundreds of Homonyms—

1. **Arms**—His *arms* (बाँह) are broken. India is receiving *arms* (अस्त्र-शस्त्र) from America.
2. **Bat**—A *bat* (चमगादड़) becomes blind during day. I hit the ball with my *bat* (बल्ला).
3. **Band**—This is a nice *band* (दल) of musicians. The military *band* (बाजा) is playing national anthem.
4. **Bar**—He drinks every evening at the local *bar* (शराबखाना). The *Bar* (वकील, बैरिस्टर) and the Bench are not on good terms. I have crossed the *bar* (बाधा, रुकावट). The window *bars* (छड़) were broken. The criminals were put behind the *bars* (कैदियों के खड़े होने का स्थान, जेल). Have you ever tasted the *bar* (एक प्रकार की समुद्री मछली)?
5. **Base**—He is very mean and *base* (नीच). The *base* (नींव) is too weak.
6. **Become**—He *becomes* angry. It does not *become* (शोभा देना) you.
7. **Bridge**—Do you play *bridge* (एक प्रकार क ताश का खेल)? There is a *bridge* (पुल) across the river.
8. **Bear**—It is a Russian *bear* (भालू). I cannot *bear* (सहना) this loss. The tree *bears* (पैदा करना) sweet fruit.
9. **Bore**—He *bore* (सहा) his losses calmly. He *bores* (छेद करना) a hole in the wall. You are a *bore* (बकवास से जी उबा देनेवाला) in our company.
10. **Board**—He gets free *board* (भोजन) and lodging in the college hostel. This factory is managed by a *board* (मंडल, काउन्सिल) of directors. When do you *board* (चढ़ना) the train today? The black-*board* (श्यामपट्ट) is now almost white. This card-*board* (कूट, गत्ता) is quite thick.
11. **Can**—*Can* you do it? It is a milk *can* (बरतन).

12. **Cat**—I love my *cat.* They were whipped with a *cat* (कोड़ा या चाबुक) for criminal offences.
13. **Capital**—Patna is the *capital* (राजधानी) of Bihar. I lost not only the interest but also the *capital* (मूलधन). He was awarded *capital* punishment (मृत्युदण्ड).
14. **Certain**—It is not *certain* (निश्चित) whether he will come. There lived a hermit in a *certain* (किसी, अनिश्चित) village.
15. **Charge**—How much do you pay as food *charge* (मूल्य)? There is a serious *charge* (दोषारोपण) against him.
16. **Close**—Please *close* (बंद करना) the door. He is my *close* (नजदीकी, निकट का) relation.
17. **Composed**—He remained calm and *composed* (अविचलित) even in the teeth of difficulties. Keats has *composed* (रचा) this poem.
18. **Correspond**—This *corresponds* (मिलता-जुलता है) to that. I do not *correspond* (पत्र-व्यवहार करना) with him these days.
19. **Contract**—The *contract* (करार, ठीका) is now broken. Almost every thing *contracts* (सिकुड़ना) in winter.
20. **Country**—Our *country* (देश) is passing through a crisis. He is a *country* (देहाती) doctor. Do you like *country* (देशी) wine?
21. **Credit**—The goods were supplied on *credit* (उधार). It is to his *credit* (गुण). Please *credit* (जमा करना) this amount to my account.
22. **Cricket**—Do you play *cricket* (एक प्रकार का खेल)? Keats found beauty even in a *cricket's* (झींगुर, एक प्रकार का कीड़ा) music.
23. **Custom**—All old *customs* (प्रथा) are not bad. The officer failed to collect all the *customs* (कर, टैक्स).
24. **Date**—What is your *date* (तारीख) of birth? Do you like the taste of *date* (खजूर)?
25. **Dear**—Foodstuff is rather *dear* (महँगा) these days. He is very *dear* (प्यारा) to me.
26. **Down**—The signal is *down* (नीचे). It is as light as *down* (कोमल रोआँ). Even these lonely *downs* (खुला तथा ऊँचा धरातल; पठार) look lovely today.
27. **Exact**—Give me the *exact* (ठीक-ठीक) time of your arrival. Officers *exact* (बलपूर्वक वसूल करना) payment of loans from poor farmers.
28. **Fast**—It is a *fast* (पक्का) colour. I observe *fast* (उपवास) today. Your watch is too *fast* (तेज).
29. **Fair**—Have you ever been to the Sonepur *fair* (मेला)? He writes a *fair* (साफ) hand. His complexion is *fair* (गोरा). It is not a *fair* (अच्छा) business.
30. **Fit**—He is not *fit* (योग्य) for this post. She fell into a *fit* (मूर्च्छा).
31. **Fix**—I am in a *fix* (उधेड़-बुन). Please *fix* (मजबूत करना, स्थिर या निश्चित करना) your attention upon this object.
32. **Fine**—It is a *fine* (सुंदर, अच्छा) poem. He had to pay a *fine* (जुर्माना) of Rs 5.
33. **Firm**—I am *firm* (दृढ़, स्थिर) in my view. This *firm* (दूकान, कंपनी) is making a rapid progress.

34. **Fly**—Birds *fly*, but man cannot. Don't kill this poor *fly* (मक्खी).
35. **Ground**—The *ground* (जमीन) is slippery. He was granted help on the *ground* (कारण, आधार) of poverty.
36. **Hang**—He *hangs* criminals (फाँसी पर लटकाना). She *hangs* pictures (दीवाल पर लटकाना).
37. **Hand**—A man has two *hands* (हाथ). How many *hands* (नौकर, कर्मचारी) are required in your department? Neither *hand* (सूई) of my wristwatch moves.
38. **Hide**—Why do you *hide* (छिपाना) yourself? This *hide* (चमड़ा) is too coarse.
39. **Hood**—The *hood* (गाड़ी का छत) of my jeep is new. He is still in boy*hood* (बालपन). The *hood* (साँप का फण) of this cobra is terrible. A graduate wears *hood* (एक प्रकार का वस्त्र या टोपी जो उपाधिग्रहण के अवसर पर पहनी जाती है) and gown on the occasion of university convocation.
40. **Import**—The *import* (आयात) of food from America costs us much. The *import* (अभिप्राय, अर्थ) of his speech is not very clear.
41. **Interest**—What is the rate of *interest* (सूद)? I do not take *interest* (रुचि) in games.
42. **Industry**—*Industry* (परिश्रम) and intelligence must go hand in hand. It is an iron and steel *industry* (उद्योग).
43. **Issue**—She is my first *issue* (संतान). It is an important *issue* (समस्या, घटना). Who will *issue* (निकालना) this notice?
44. **Just**—He is perfectly *just* (ईमानदार). He has reached here *just* (ठीक) now.
45. **Kite**—Boys are flying *kites* (पतंग, गुड्डी). *Kites* (चील) are devouring the dead body.
46. **Lie**—He *lies* (लेटना) quietly in his bed. Do not tell a *lie* (झूठ).
47. **Like**—I do not *like* (पसंद करना) this picture. Ram is *like* (समान) Shyam.
48. **Light**—The *light* (रोशनी) is dim. The load is rather *light* (हलका).
49. **Lead**—Who will *lead* (नेतृत्व करना) the procession? *Lead* (राँगा, सीसा) is very heavy.
50. **Long**—It is very *long* (लंबा). I *long* (इच्छा करना) to see him.
51. **Low**—The roof is too *low* (नीचा). Cows *low* (बोलना, डकरना).
52. **Matter**—What is the *matter* (बात, विषय)? *Matter* (पदार्थ) is perishable.
53. **Mean**—What does it *mean* (अर्थ होना)? He is very *mean* (नीच). It is a golden *mean* (मध्यवर्ती, औसत).
54. **Minute**—Wait a *minute* (मिनट). He gave *minute* (बारीक) details of the incident.
55. **Mole**—A *mole* (छछूँदर) gives out foul smell. There is a *mole* (तिल, काला मस्सा) on her check.
56. **Move**—Please *move* (हिलाना) it. Who will *move* (पेश करना) this resolution? Her tears *moved* (द्रवित करना) me at once. Asia is on the *move* (प्रगति, क्रांति, परिवर्तन).
57. **Object**—A transitive verb has an *object* (कर्म). It is an *object* (विषय, कारण) of envy. He clearly explained his aims and *objects* (उद्देश्य). I do not *object* (विरोध करना) to your plan.

58. **Present**—He is *present* (हाजिर) here. I gave him several *presents* (उपहार).
59. **Patient**—He is a TB *patient* (रोगी). Be *patient* (शांत, स्थिर, धैर्यपूर्ण) for some time more.
60. **Pole**—The North *Pole* (ध्रुव) is too cold. It is a bamboo *pole* (खंभा). He is a *Pole* (पोलैंड का निवासी).
61. **Right**—You are *right* (ठीक). It is my *right* (दाहिना) hand. A citizen has several *rights* (अधिकार).
62. **Rest**—I must take *rest* (आराम) now. *Rest* (बाकी) is OK. A house *rests* (टिकना, स्थिर रहना) on poles and pillars.
63. **Reel**—Please wind this thread on a *reel* (धागा या तार लपेटने की रोल). His head *reels* (चक्कर खाना).
64. **Save**—Please *save* (रक्षा करना) me. All have left *save* (अलावा) and except Ram.
65. **Set**—I gave him a *set* (समुदाय, संग्रह) of books. The sun *sets* (डूबना) in the west. All the questions have been *set* (चुनना). A costly stone has been *set* (जड़ना) on my ring.
66. **Second**—I will not wait even for a *second* (सेकण्ड). Is she your *second* (दूसरी) wife? I *second* (समर्थन करना) this proposal.
67. **Sentence**—It is a negative sentence (वाक्य). He is *sentenced* (दंडित होना) to death.
68. **Sole**—A thorn pierced into my *sole* (तलवा). The *sole* (जूते का तल्ला) of my shoe has rubbed out. Man is the *sole* (एकमात्र, अकेला) judge of truth.
69. **Sort**—What *sort* (तरह) of man is he? The postman *sorts* (अलग-अलग करना, छाँटना) out letters.
70. **Subject**—A finite verb agrees with its *subject* (कर्ता). The king did not care for his *subject* (प्रजा). What is the *subject* (विषय) of your speech? The price of the book is *subject* (आश्रित, निर्भर) to changes from time to time.
71. **Suit**—I have a woollen *suit* (सूट). This does not *suit* (शोभा देना, अच्छा लगना) you. This programme does not *suit* (अनुरूप होना) me. It is a civil *suit* (मुकदमा).
72. **Top**—Boys like to spin a *top* (लट्टू). He is standing at the *top* (चोटी) of a hill. You will *top* (सबसे आगे बढ़ जाना) the list of successful candidates.
73. **Too**—It is *too* (उचित से अधिक) hot. He, *too* (भी), will join us.
74. **Trumpet**—The *trumpet* (तुरही, एक प्रकार का बाजा) has inspired our soldiers. Elephants *trumpet* (चिग्घाड़ना).
75. **Void**—Dr Rajendra Prasad's death has created a *void* (शून्य स्थल) in our public life. The law is now null and *void* (बेकार).
76. **Well**—It is a deep *well* (कुआँ). I am all *well* (स्वस्थ). I have done *well* (अच्छा, सफलतापूर्वक). Water is *welling* up (निकलना). *Well* (अच्छा), I will see to it.
77. **Will**—Who *will* go? God *willed* (इच्छा करना) that man should die. He left a *will* (वसीयतनामा) after his death.
78. **Wind**—The *wind* (हवा) is blowing hard. Please *wind* (चाभी देना) the watch. Let us now *wind* up (समेटना, बंद करना) the discussion.

79. **Word**—Proper use of *word* (शब्द) is essential for good style. He sent me *word* (संदेश) that he would come. He gave me *word* (जबान, वादा) that he would help me. He does not obey my *word* (कहना).

HOMOPHONES

Such words as are similar in look or sound but different in meaning are called Homophones; for example, Birth and Berth. Beach and Beech. The following list of Homophones deserves special attention—

1. **Access** (reach)—Students should have *access* to their teachers.

   Excess (too much)—*Excess* of everything is bad.

2. **Accept** (take)—He *accepted* with thanks some humble presents from me.

   Except (excluding)—None could compete *except* him.

3. **Accident** (a mishap, दुर्घटना)—Road *accidents* are common today.

   Incident (an event, घटना)—A great man's life is full of important *incidents.*

4. **Adapt** (adjust, suit)—Education helps us *adapt* ourselves to even unfavourable circumstances.

   Adept (expert, skilful)—Hitler was an *adept* in the art of public speaking.

   Adopt (choose)—One must always *adopt* right means.

5. **Advice** (a piece of opinion—Noun)—I gave him a piece of *advice.*

   Advise (to give opinion—Verb)—I *advised* him to read this book.

6. **Affect** (pretend, influence)—The criminal *affected* (pretended) madness. This simple failure should not *affect* (influence) your career.

   Effect ('result' if used as a Noun and 'to bring about' if used as a verb)—Every *effect* must have its cause. Mahatma Gandhi *effected* great political and social reforms.

7. **Altar** (a place for offering in a temple or church, बलिवेदी)—Several goats were sacrificed at the *altar.*

   Alter (change)—Nothing can *alter* my opinion now.

8. **Allusion** (indirect reference)—In this poem there is an *allusion* to Gandhiji's death.

   Illusion (deceptive appearance, भ्रम, माया)—Some philosophers regard the world as an *illusion.*

9. **Apposite** (suitable, proper)—The remarks of the Prime Minister on the defects of the present system of education were *apposite.*

   Opposite (contrary, quite different)—Your opinions are *opposite* to mine.

10. **Avocation** (secondary occupation, गौण पेशा)—My *avocation* is painting.

    Vocation (regular profession, पेशा)—Your *vocation* is teaching.

11. **Bare** (uncovered, खाली)—It is not safe to walk *barefoot.*

    Bear (tolerate)—I cannot *bear* such insults.

12. **Birth** (coming into life)—What is your date of *birth*?

    Berth (a seat in a cabin or carriage)—I have reserved a *berth* in a first class compartment.

13. **Bridal** (relating to marriage)—A *bridal* ceremony should be simple.

    Bridle (rein, etc., लगाम आदि)—The new *bridle* has been put on the horse.

14. **Board** (a piece of wood, etc.)—This is a card *board.*

    Bored (felt tired and dull)—His talks *bored* me.

15. **Border** (edge)—The *border* of the *sari* is fine.

    Boarder (one who lives with somebody)—He is a *boarder* of his hostel.

16. **Cannvas** (rough cloth of hemp or flax)—My shoe is made of *canvas.*

    Canvass (solicit votes or some favour)—A candidate for the Assembly has to *canvass* for votes from door to door.

17. **Casual** (accidental, occasional, आकस्मिक)—*Casual* leave to teachers is granted by the Principal.

    Causal (having the relation between cause and effect)—There is no *causal* reaction between wealth and happiness.

18. **Check** [(i) restrain or prevent, (ii) test]—I cannot *check* him from smoking. I have *checked* (tested or examined) all accounts.

    Cheque (a written order to bank for money)—He was paid by *cheque*.

19. **Cession** (surrender of something or transfer of a territory)—The *cession* of a part of West Bengal has been demanded by Pakistan.

    Session (a term or period)—The college *session* has started.

    Cessation (stopping)—The UNO is trying hard for the *cessation* of armed conflict in the Congo.

20. **Coarse** (rough)—I cannot wear coarse cloth.

    Course (line of action)—I do not know which *course* to adopt.

21. **Cease** (to stop)—Rain has *ceased.*

    Seize (to take possession)—Stolen articles were *seized.*

22. **Corpse** (dead body)—The *corpse* was covered with flowers.

    Corps (a body of troops)—The national Cadet *Corps* is doing much service.

23. **Complement** (that which completes)—Milk is a good *complement* of our diet.

    Compliment (regards, courtesy)—Pay my best *compliments* to mother.

24. **Conscious** (aware)—I am *conscious* of my duties.

    Conscientious (honest, obedient to one's conscience)—It is only a *conscientious* worker who always does his duties.

25. **Credible** (believable)—The news is too good to be *credible.*

    Creditable (worthy of praise and honour)—Your performance at the examination is really very *creditable.*

    Credulous (ready to believe easily)—*Credulous* persons fall victims to cheats.

26. **Council** (a group of men to give advice)—The council of ministers has taken this decision.

    Counsel (advice)—He was given a *counsel* to keep off bad days.

27. **Defy** (challenge)—He dare not *defy* my orders.

    Deify (to worship as a god)—Mahatma Gandhi is now *deified* by the Indians.

28. **Descent** (downward slope)—This hill has a sharp *descent.*

    Dissent (differ)—I *dissent* from you on several points.

    Decent (proper)—A student's manner must always be *decent.*

29. **Diseased** (suffering from a disease)—The milk of a *diseased* cow is harmful.

    Deceased (dead)—The *deceased* has left his will.

30. **Draught** (the quantity of liquid drunk at a time, current of air)—The thirsty beggar is crying for a *draught* of water. If you sit in *draught,* you will fall ill.

    Drought (want of rain)—Bihar is very often visited by serious *droughts.*

    Draft (to draw up a rough sketch, प्रारूप)—I have to *draft* all the letters. The *draft* of the letter has been approved.

31. **Dual** (divided into two)—There is *dual* control over this house.

    Duel (fight between two)—A *duel* between Ram and Shyam took place last month.

32. **Eminent** (prominent, famous)—Newton was an *eminent* scientist.

    Imminent (impending, about to happen)—Mr Shastri is sure that war is not *imminent.*

33. **Emigrant** (a man who leaves his country and settles in another)—He is an *emigrant* from Pakistan.

    Immigrant (a man who comes to live in a foreign country)—In India all the *immigrants* enjoy the rights of a citizen.

34. **Eligible** (fit to be chosen)—Persons holding at least a second class Master's Degree are *eligible* for lectureship.

    Illegible (that which cannot be read)—*Illegible* handwriting is a very great defect for a writer.

35. **Elicit** (to draw out by question and answer)—The police succeeded in *eliciting* some necessary information.

    Illicit (unlawful)—He was charged with *illicit* sale of opium.

36. **Eruption** (bursting up)—Volcanic *eruptions* in Japan are common.

    Irruption (sudden invasion)—The *irruption* of the Chinese into Indian borders was condemned by almost all the nations of the world.

37. **Fair** [(i) just, (ii) a show]—All's *fair* in love and war. The Sonepur *fair* is very famous.

    Fare (passage money)—What is the train *fare* from Gopalganj to Patna?

38. **Gate** (door)—The *gate* is closed.

    Gait (manner of walking, चाल)—She has a charming *gait.*

39. **Gamble** (play for stakes, money)—*Gambling* has ruined many rich men.

Gambol (to play or dance about, फुदकना)—Young lambs are *gamboling* on the green.

40. **Hoard** (to store)—A miser does nothing but *hoards* money.

Horde (a gang)—A *horde* of tribesmen have attacked the Indian borders.

41. **Ingenious** (clever, skilful)—Robinson Crusoe was an *ingenious* person.

Ingenuous (frank and simple)—An *ingenuous* person is liked everywhere.

42. **Jealous** (envious)—A *jealous* person has no peace of mind.

Zealous (full of enthusiasm, जोश और उमंग से भरा हुआ)—Mr Nehru was a *zealous* reformer.

43. **Knows** (to know)—He *knows* me.

Nose (an organ of smell)—His *nose* is red.

44. **Later** (more late in time)—He came *later* than I.

Latter (opposed to former)—Keats and Shelley are great poets but the former is greater than the *latter*.

45. **Loose** (as an Adjective 'not tight', as a Verb 'to release')—Your coat is *loose*. It is not safe to let *loose* this wild dog.

Lose (suffer loss)—A liar has to *lose* much.

46. **Lessen** (to make less)—His importance has been *lessened*.

Lesson (something to be learnt)—I taught him a *lesson*.

47. **Monetary** (relating to money)—Do not be guided by *monetary* motives.

Monitory (giving warning or advice)—We should respect the *monitory* counsel of our trusted friends.

48. **Mist** (water vapour in the air)—The hills were hidden in the *mist*.

Missed (failed to hit or catch)—I *missed* the bus.

49. **Persecute** (oppress, अन्यायपूर्ण ढंग से तंग करना)—Money-lenders still *persecute* simple villagers.

Prosecute [(i) to bring before a court, (ii) to pursue]—He was *prosecuted* on a charge of cheating. This boy is unable to *prosecute* his studies further.

50. **Place** (space)—He has an important *place* in the society.

Plaice (a flat fish)—I don't like the taste of *plaice*.

51. **Pray** (make devout request)—I *pray* to God every day.

Prey (victim)—Bihar has fallen a *prey* to flood and disease.

52. **Prescribe** (to give directions for the use of)—The doctor has *prescribed* very costly medicines. This book is *prescribed* for Intermediate and Degree Examinations.

Proscribe (to prohibit)—Indecent films should be *proscribed* by the Government.

53. **Precede** (to go before)—A storm is *preceded* by a peculiar lull.
Proceed (to go ahead, आगे बढ़ना)—He *proceeded* with a great work in spite of difficulties.

54. **President** (one who presides over a meeting)—The *President* spoke very well.
Precedent (that which goes before, a previous example for illustration)—The lawyer quoted several *precedents* on this point.

55. **Plane** [(i) level, (ii) a tool]—You must have a high *plane* of thinking. A carpenter smoothes wood with his *plane.*
Plain (simple, easy)—*Plain* living without high thinking is not a very helpful principle.

56. **Principal** (chief, head of a college, capital)—The *principal* streets were nicely decorated. The *principal* has granted me full free-studentship. The interest on the *principal* is low.
Principle (fundamental law or truth, सिद्धांत)—Nobody today believes in the *principle* of 'might is right'. A man of *principle* often suffers but he does not give up his *principles.*

57. **Quite** (altogether)—It is *quite* impossible.
Quiet (silent)—The place is calm and *quiet.*

58. **Root** (part of plant in the soil)—The plant has taken *root.*
Rout (a way taken or planned)—I found a new *route* to the forest.

59. **Stationary** (Adjective—fixed) The earth is not *stationary.*
Stationery (Noun—writing materials—paper, envelopes, etc.)—Much *stationery* is wasted in offices these days.

60. **Stare** (to look fixedly)—He is *staring* at me.
Stair (fixed steps)—These *stairs* are slippery.

61. **Story** (an account of events)—He told me a *story.*
Storey (floor in a building)—It is a house of two *storeys.*

62. **Symbol** (mark)—Whiteness is a *symbol* of purity.
Cymbol (a musical instrument)—The orchestra has a *cymbol.*

63. **Soldier** (member of an army)—One *soldier* was injured.
Shoulder (part of the body)—There is pain in his *shoulders.*

64. **Umpire** (a referee in a game of cricket)—No player can disobey the *umpire.*
Empire (dominion)—The British *Empire* has now become much smaller.

65. **Waive** (to forgo, छोड़ देना)—My claims were *waived.*
Wave—*Waves* are rising in the sea.

66. **Wait** (stay where one is)—Please *wait* here.
Weight (measurement by scale-balance)—My *weight* is sixty kilograms

EXERCISE

Make sentences with the following pairs of words.

cease—seize	stair—stare
root—route	board—bored
wait—weight	advice—advise

List of Single-word Substitution

(A) *Single word for a group of words*

1. agenda—Items of business to be considered at a meeting.
2. aggressor—One who attacks first.
3. alien—One who lives in a country without citizenship.
4. anarchist—One who plans to destroy all governments.
5. arbitrator—One appointed by parties to settle disputes.
6. amateur—One who does something for pleasure.
7. autocracy—Government by one.
8. atheist—One who does not believe in the existence of God.
9. antidote—A medicine to nullify (counteract) the effect of poison.
10. autobiography—The life-history of a man written by himself.
11. bankrupt (insolvent)—Unable to pay one's debts.
12. bigot—One with narrow religious views.
13. bigamy—The state of having two wives or husbands at a time.
14. biography—The life-history of a person written by another.
15. bilingual—One who speaks two languages.
16. brittle—That which can be easily broken.
17. bureaucracy—Government by officials.
18. cannibal—One who eats human flesh.
19. credulous—One who easily believes.
20. colleagues—Those who work in the same department or office.
21. catalogue—List of books or other articles.
22. carnivorous—Eater of flesh.
23. celibacy—The state of being without wife.
24. circumlocution—A round-about way of writing or speaking.
25. cemetery—A place of burial.
26. contemporary—Living in the same age (one who lives at the same time as another).

27. cosmopolitan—Of or different parts of the world.
28. democracy—Government by the representatives of the people.
29. diplomacy—The art practised by statesmen.
30. drought—Want of rain.
31. emigrant—One who leaves one's country to settle elsewhere.
32. epidemic—A disease that spreads over a large area.
33. egoist—A man who thinks only of himself.
34. edible—That which is fit to be eaten.
35. extempore—Speech without any preparation.
36. exchange—Giving and receiving.
37. efficacious—That which produces the desired effect.
38. fastidious—Hard to satisfy one's taste.
39. fatalist—One who believes in fate.
40. fratricide—Killing of one's brother.
41. foreigner—A man residing in a country of which he is not a citizen.
42. honorary—An office without pay.
43. homicide—killing of a man.
44. herbivorous—Animals living on herbs.
45. invisible—That which can't be seen.
46. inaudible—That which can't be heard.
47. illegible—That which can't be read.
48. ineligible—Not qualified to be elected or selected under rules.
49. invincible—That which can't be conquered.
50. inaccessible—That which can't be approached.
51. inexplicable—That which can't be explained.
52. incorrigible—That which can't be corrected.
53. inimitable—That which can't be imitated.
54. indispensable—That without which one can't do.
55. indelible—That which can't be blotted.
56. inevitable—That which can't be avoided.
57. incurable—That which can't be cured.
58. incomparable—That which can't be compared.
59. inexhaustive—That which can't be exhausted.
60. inscrutable—That which can't be scrutinised.
61. indisputable—That which can't be disputed.
62. irrevocable—That which can't be changed.
63. irritable—Easily excited to anger.
64. irrelevant—That which is not to the point.

65. incredible—That which can't be believed.
66. infallible—That which never fails.
67. inflammable—Liable to catch fire easily.
68. insecticide—A medicine that kills insects.
69. invulnerable—That which can't be hurt.
70. inimitable—That which can't be imitated.
71. irrepressible—That which can't be checked.
72. insolvent—One who can't pay debts.
73. illegal—Against law.
74. illicit—A trade prohibited by law.
75. linguist—One who knows several languages.
76. matricide—Killing of one's mother.
77. martyr—One who dies for a noble cause.
78. migratory—A bird that comes and goes with seasons.
79. maiden speech—The first public speech.
80. monogamy—The practice of having one wife.
81. misanthrope—A hater of mankind.
82. materialistic—An attitude that measures everything in terms of matter.
83. matinee—A film show in the afternoon.
84. mercenary—The motive to earn money.
85. neurotic—One suffering from nervous disorder.
86. narcotic—A medicine that induces sleep.
87. notorious—Having a bad reputation.
88. obsolete—No longer in use.
89. optimist—One who looks at the bright side of life.
90. orator—One who makes an eloquent speech.
91. orphan—A child whose parents are dead.
92. omnipotent—One who is all-powerful.
93. omnipresent—One who is present everywhere.
94. omniscient—One who knows everything.
95. patricide—Killing of one's father.
96. patriot—One who has great love for one's country.
97. posthumous—Born after the father's death or published after the author's death.
98. patrimony—Property inherited from father and ancestor.
99. philanthropist—One who does good to mankind.
100. pessimist—One who looks at the dark side of life.
101. parasite—That which exists by living upon others.
102. post-mortem—Medical examination of dead body.
103. polygamy—Practice of marrying more than one wife at a time.

104. panacea—Remedy for all diseases.
105. prodigal—One who wastes money.
106. popular—To be liked by everybody.
107. recluse—One who lives by alone and avoids people.
108. reticent—Reserved in speech.
109. regicide—Murder of a king.
110. somnambulist—One who walks in sleep.
111. somniloquist—One who talks in sleep.
112. sinecure—An office with no work but high pay.
113. soliloquy—The act of speaking aloud one's thought when alone.
114. unanimous—All of the same opinion.
115. unambiguous—Which is not vague.
116. unavoidable—Which can't be avoided.
117. unimaginable—Which can't be imagined.
118. unknowable—Which can't be known.
119. unthinkable—Which can't be thought of.
120. unreliable—Which can't be relied upon.
121. unbelievable—Which can't be believed.
122. unparalleled—Which has no parallel/match.
123. unusual—Which is not common.
124. unforeseen—Which is not seen before.
125. verbose—Which is full of words.
126. vegetarian—One who lives on vegetables.
127. veteran—One with long experience.
128. wardrobe—Place where clothes are kept.
129. waterproof—That which can keep water out.
130. widow—A woman whose husband is dead.
131. widower—A man whose wife is dead.

EXERCISE

Give single words which mean the following.

1. That which can't be heard.
2. That which can't be believed.
3. That which can't be imitated.
4. That which can't be imagined.
5. That which can't be avoided.
6. That which can't be known.
7. That which can't be thought of.
8. That which is not vague.
9. One who lives on vegetables.
10. One who attacks first.

FORMATION OF WORDS

अँगरेजी में शब्द-निर्माण (word formation) prefix (उपसर्ग) और suffix (प्रत्यय) की सहायता से होता है। इन्हें देखें—

Prefix + Words

1. *im*—im + possible = impossible, im + proper = improper, impure, impolite, improbable, imperfect.
2. *in*—in + discipline = indiscipline, in + action = inaction, incomplete, inefficient, inability, indecent, invisible, ineffective, incapable.
3. *ir*—ir + religious = irreligious, ir + responsible = irresponsible, irrelevant, irregular, irreparable.
4. *il*—il + legal = illegal, il + literate = illiterate, illogical, illegitimate, illegible, illiberal.
5. *em*—em + power = empower, em + body = embody, embalm, embitter.
6. *en*—en + able = enable, en + danger = endanger, enrich, enlarge.
7. *re*—re + write = rewrite, re + build = rebuild, recall, reopen, remind, recur.
8. *un*—un + kind = unkind, un + happy = unhappy, un + necessary = unnecessary, un + load = unload, un + ripe = unripe, un + wanted = unwanted, un + wise = unwise, un + lock = unlock.
9. *de*—de + value = devalue, de + train = detrain, de + throne = dethrone, de + compose = decompose, de + control = decontrol.
10. *dis*—dis + agree = disagree, dis + like = dislike, dis + honest = dishonest, dis + obedient = disobedient, dis + please = displease, dis + honour = dishonour.
11. *mis*—mis + take = mistake, mis + understand = misunderstand.
12. *pre*—pre + fix = prefix, pre + paid = prepaid, pre + war = prewar, pre + mature = premature, pre + historic = prehistoric, pre + judge = prejudge.
13. *non*—non + violence = nonviolence, non + sense = nonsense, non + vegetarian = nonvegetarian.

Words + Suffix

1. *ar/er/or*—beg + ar = beggar, teach + er = teacher, drive + er = driver, sail + or = sailor.
2. *age*—marry + age = marriage, postage, breakage.
3. *er*—small + er = smaller, cheap + er = cheaper.
4. *es*—box + es = boxes, bench + es = benches, go + es = goes.
5. *ed*—look + ed = looked, laugh + ed = laughed.
6. *est*—small + est = smallest, cheap + est = cheapest.
7. *ing*—go + ing = going, drink + ing = drinking.

8. *ism*—Hindu + ism = Hinduism, social + ism = socialism.
9. *ic*—hero + ic = heroic, emphatic, specific, economic, artistic, tragic, comic.
10. *an/en*—India + an = Indian, Russian, American, European, republican, golden, silken.
11. *al*—arrive + al = arrival, culture + al = cultural, natural, denial, trial.
12. *sl's*—boy + s = boys, boy + 's = boy's, write + s = writes, sing + s = sings.
13. *cal*—history + cal = historical, social, political.
14. *ish*—boy + ish = boyish, self + ish = selfish, green + ish = greenish, fool + ish = foolish, child + ish = childish, girl + ish = girlish.
15. *ful*—care + ful = careful, beauty + ful = beautiful, mouth + ful = mouthful, hand + ful = handful, use + ful = useful, hopeful, sinful, fearful.
16. *less*—sense + less = senseless, care + less = careless, harm + less = harmless, tact + less = tactless.
17. *ness*—happy + ness = happiness, bold + ness = boldness, kind + ness = kindness, firm + ness = firmness.
18. *logy*—sociology, psychology, biology, radiology, pathology.
19. *sion/ion/tion*—decision, suspicion, action, relation.
20. *dom*—wisdom, freedom, kingdom.
21. *hood*—boyhood, childhood, girlhood.
22. *ship*—friendship, free-studentship, membership.
23. *ment*—movement, payment, judgement.
24. *ous*—fame + ous = famous, virtuous, ambitious, courageous.
25. *ly*—brother + ly = brotherly, friendly, manly, kindly, cowardly, lovely, faithfully, sincerely, bravely, slowly, quickly.
26. *y*—water + y = watery, misty, sandy, creamy, windy, rainy, stormy, dirty, noisy, rosy.

अब देखें कि इनकी सहायता से एक प्रकार के शब्द दूसरे प्रकार में किस प्रकार बदल जाते हैं—

1. Noun + al/en/y/ly = adjective

nature + al = natural, personal, social, national, elemental.

gold + en = golden, silken, woollen, wooden.

rose + y = rosy, dirty, snowy.

brother + ly = brotherly, friendly, lovely.

2. Noun + ic/ish/ous/ful/less/like = adjective

artist + ic = artistic, scientific, dramatic, tragic.

girl + ish = girlish, childish, tigerish, foolish.

fame + ous = famous, virtuous, ambitious.

care + ful = careful, fearful, hopeful, beautiful.

care + less = careless, charmless, harmless, fearless.

war + like = warlike, businesslike, childlike.

3. Verb + al/er/or/age/ment = noun

arrive + al = arrival, trial, denial, refusal.

teach + er = teacher, preacher, driver, leader.

conduct + or = conductor, inspector, instructor.

marry + age = marriage, carriage, breakage.

move + ment = movement, agreement, payment.

4. Verb + ce/ture/tion/sion/ion = noun

defend + ce = defence, offence, insistence, reliance.

depart + ture = departure, mixture, fixture.

select + tion = selection, starvation, competition, reduction.

decide + ion = decision, suspicion.

admit + sion = admission.

5. Adjective + ty/ness/dom = noun

safe + ty = safety, purity, reality.

happy + ness = happiness, boldness, kindness.

free + dom = freedom, wisdom, officialdom.

6. Noun + ise/ify = verb

memory + ise = memorise, criticise, sympathise.

beauty + ify = beautify, certify, classify.

7. Adjective + ify/en = verb

simplify, purify, justify.

blacken, widen, quicken, lengthen.

8. Em/en + noun/adjective = verb

empower, emitter, enrich, enlist, enable.

9. Adjective + ly = adverb

slowly, quickly, quietly, attentively, patiently.

❐

Chapter XV

FIGURES OF SPEECH

1. Simile—Comparison between two dissimilar (different) things or persons on certain points is called *simile*. From this it follows that likeness between two different things is shown on a few points only. The words commonly used to introduce a *simile* are:

like, as, just … in the same way, even at … so, as … so.

Examples

(a) Thy soul was *like* a star … .

(b) Her eye *as* stars of twilight fair,
Like twilight's too, her dusky hair.

(c) My heart is *like* a singing bird.

(d) *Like* to the summer's rain,
Or as the pearls of morning dew;
Ne'er to be found again.

In all the examples, two dissimilar things have been compared and some points of similarity have been discovered between them. It should, however, be noted that in ultimate analysis the two dissimilar objects remain dissimilar. The presence of *as* or *like* shows that the things compared are only similar, not identical. In case of metaphors, the things compared are treated as one and the same.

2. Metaphor—Comparison between two dissimilar things or persons on all points (or in all respects) is called *metaphor.* The qualities of one object are thus completely transferred to another and there is cent per cent correspondence between the two objects compared. It is an essential function of a metaphor, for metaphor means 'transferring'. From this it is clear that the two things cease to be different, and become one. It is possible only when complete identity between two things is discovered in a fit of imagination. Naturally, *like, as*, etc., which show similarity on a few points only are not used to introduce a metaphor.

Examples

(a) He is the *star* of the family.

(b) Was your hope *drunk*
Wherein you *dressed* yourself?

(c) The camel is the *ship* of the desert.

(d) This news is a *dagger* to my tender heart.

In all these examples, two different objects have been compared. The comparison is so complete that the two objects become one and the same. A simile creates the impression that the objects compared are no doubt similar but they are still different from each other.

3. Allegory, Parable, Fable—*Allegory, parable and fable are fictitious* stories that teach some moral. At times, it is difficult to distinguish between a parable and an allegory, for, as Mr Fowler puts it, 'Every parable is an allegory and every allegory a parable.' There are, however, certain points of difference between them. A parable is a story that aims at answering a single question or suggesting a single principle and offering a definite moral. But an allegory is a story of greater length and the aim is not so clearly didactic. Allegory has been defined in the Oxford English Dictionary as 'an extended continued metaphor'. Mr Fowler rightly comments that the definition would have been better suited to *parable* than to *allegory.* Since an allegory is of greater length, worked out in greater details, we should accept the definition gien by Mr Fowler—'It may fairly be said that parable is an extended metaphor and allegory an extended simile.' Spenser's *Faerie Queene* and Bunyan's *Pilgrim's Progress* are allegories. *The Bible* (New Testament) has several parables meant to teach some moral lesson.

A fable, too, is a type of story that teaches a moral. In most of the fables birds and beasts and even insects are treated like human beings and so they are made to think, feel, speak and act like men and women. Swift's *The Spider and the Bee* and *Aesop's Fables* are nice specimens of a fable.

4. Personification—Sometimes lifeless things are treated as if they were human beings. This is called *personification.*

Examples

(a) Nature might stand up
And say to all the world
This was a man.

(b) Death lays his icy hand on kings.

In the above examples, *Nature* and *Death* which are lifeless objects have been treated as persons, i.e., living beings.

5. Apostrophe—Sometimes lifeless things are addressed as human beings. This is called *apostrophe.* Apostrophe, too, is a sort of personification, but in personification things are not addressed.

Examples

(a) O Death! come soon.

(b) O Liberty! Why are you so dear?

(c) Come, Peace of mind … .

In these examples, *Death, Liberty* and *Peace of mind* have been addressed by name, as living beings are addressed as Ram or Shyam.

6. Pathetic Fallacy—Sometimes nature is regarded as taking active interest in human affairs. *Pathetic fallacy,* too, therefore is a kind of personification; but the difference between them is that the element of nature's interest in man's destiny is not present in personification. In pathetic fallacy, nature is happy or sorry at the vise or fall of man.

Examples

Earth felt the wound, and nature from her seat sighing through all her works, gave signs of awe that all was lost.

In the above lines, earth and nature have been shown to be in sorrow at the loss in man's life. They are actively interested in human affairs.

7. Climax—This is a Greek word meaning a ladder. As in a ladder so in *climax*, the sense rises step by step to what is more and more important. The different ideas are arranged in ascending order of importance. The least important idea is placed first and the most important last.

Examples

(a) He was abused, beaten and killed.

(b) She sobs, groans and cries.

(c) I came, I saw, I conquered.

8. Anticlimax or Bathos—It is a sudden descent (fall) from something grand and great to something extremely small. In this way, something serious and important is mixed up with what is extremely light and unimportant. The total effect of this arrangement is one of humour and ridicule.

Examples

(a) No louder shrieks by dames to heaven are cast.

When *husbands* die or *lap-dogs* breathe their last.

Here husbands and lap-dogs have been placed side by side to make the whole thing ridiculous.

(b) Who in course of one revolving moon was *lawyer, statesman, fiddler* and *buffoon.*

Here, too, something great (lawyer and statesman) has been mixed up with what is trivial (fiddler and buffoon).

9. Zeugma—It literally means 'yoke'. By *zeugma,* two nouns are joined (yoked) to only one verb and this verb suits only one of the nouns joined. Naturally, such a verb gives two entirely different meanings and produces humour. Zeugma is, therefore, very much like bathos.

Examples

(a) He took his *hat* and his *leave.*

(b) The *moment* and the *vessel* passed.

10. Antithesis—In this figure of speech, one set of words or phrases in the first part of a sentence is set against another in the second part. There is some sort of contrast between the two sets of words or phrases and they are balanced against each other.

Examples

(a) *United* we *stand, divided* we *fall.*

(b) *Man proposes, God disposes.*

In the first example, one set (united we stand) is set against another (divided we fall). These two sets of ideas are contrasted and balanced. In the second sentence, 'proposes' is set against 'disposes' and 'man' against 'God'.

(c) *To err is human, to forgive divine.*

11. Epigram—Maximum of sense in the minimum of space is *epigram.* That is to say, a statement is called epigram if it is extremely concise. Only a few words convey a lot of sense and the statement is witty.

Examples

(a) Crying is the refuge of plain women, but the ruin of pretty ones.

(b) Studies serve for delight, for ornament and ability.

12. Oxymoron—In this figure of speech, two terms which are opposite is meaning are placed side by side and they form one lovely phrase.

Examples

(a) A *noiseless noise* among the leaves.

(b) And all its *aching joys* are no more.

13. Paradox—There are statements that appear at first to be meaningless and even absurd but on second thought, they are found to be quite significant. A *paradox,* too, like epigram, is a precise statement having a lot of sense at bottom but almost no sense on the surface.

Examples

(a) There is none so *poor* as a *wealthy miser.*

(b) He who *goes against the fashion* is himself its *slave.*

14. Metonymy—It means 'name-change'. *Metonymy* is the use of an attribute (quality) for the things. This attribute suggests the thing associated with it.

Examples

Crown for *king, pen* for *writer* and *purse* for *money.*

The *pen* is mightier than the *sword.*

Here 'pen' is used for 'writer' and 'sword' for 'soldier'.

15. Synecdoche—The mention of a part of a thing for the whole or *vice versa* (i.e., whole for the part) is called *synecdoche.*

Examples

(a) He can no longer earn his *bread.* (necessaries)

(b) Five more *hands* are needed. (men)

'Bread' is only a part of the necessaries of life and, 'hand' is only a part of man. But here the part of a thing suggests or stands for the whole of it—'bread' for all the necessaries of life and 'hands' for men.

16. Irony—*Irony* is a type of statement which has double meaning—*surface meaning* and *inner meaning.* The inner meaning is opposite to the surface meaning and the intention of the speaker is to convey this inner meaning. It is only the careless or ignorant audience that can accept the surface meaning. In Shakespeare's *Julius Caesar,* Antony again and again describes Brutus and his friends as 'honourable men' but what he really wishes to suggest is that they are not honourable at all. Here 'honourable' means 'dishonourable'. In this way, irony is a sort of veiled (hidden) attack.

17. Sarcasm—*Sarcasm* is a direct attack, and aims at censure, ridicule or contempt. The essence of sarcasm is giving pain by the use of bitter words. Irony, too, cuts quite deep, but sarcasm cuts with an iron dagger. It does not cut as cleverly as irony. Swift describes mankind as 'the most pernicious race of little odious vermin'. It is a bitter and direct statement.

18. Innuendo—*Innuendo,* too, is a sort of censure or ridicule but it is never direct. It is only hinted at cleverly as in irony, but it lacks the double meaning of irony. It is, therefore, different from both irony and sarcasm, for sarcasm is a direct censure whereas innuendo is an indirect one.

Examples

He was born of rich *but* honest parents.

Here the use of 'but' indirectly suggests (hints) that the rich are not honest. It is bitter censure but is not stated in plain words.

19. Hypallage or Transferred Epithet—Sometimes an *Epithet* (adjective) is transferred or attached to a word with which it is associated instead of to a word to which it really belongs. In other words, the position of an adjective is transferred and so it qualifies not the right noun but some other noun placed near it.

Examples

(a) He lay sobbing on his *sleepless* pillow.

(b) He passed a *restless* night.

In these examples, the adjectives (sleepless and restless) have been transferred from 'he' to some other noun (pillow and night). These adjectives really belong to 'he' and not to 'pillow' or 'night'. Hence these two adjectives (epithets) are here *transferred epithets.*

20. Litotes—It is a figure of speech in which a negative (no, not) is used with some other word to express a strong affirmative. *Litotes* is a type of understatement (meiosis) that aims at enhancing the impression. A clearly positive statement is often not as effective as an understatement.

Examples

He is *no mean* scholar.

Here 'no mean' means 'very great' and it is a more effective and impressive statement than 'very great'. In the same way, 'not a few' means 'a large number', and 'not bad' means 'excellent'.

21. Hyperbole or Exaggeration—It is an overstatement as opposed to understatement (litotes) and statement of facts. Litotes and *hyperbole* do not make a statement of facts as they are. Litotes understates whereas hyperbole overstates them. Both of them, however, aim at the same thing—to create a powerful effect. In hyperbole, things are represented as much greater or smaller than they actually are.

Examples

Ten thousand saw I at a glance.

Forty thousand brothers could not … make up the sum.

Here the number (ten thousand, forty thousand) is not a literal statement of facts. It is a definite exaggeration (overstatement) to create a strong impression.

22. Euphemism—The use of a good, agreeable or auspicious word instead of an evil, disagreeable or inauspicious word is called *euphemism.* It aims at avoiding blunt or bitter truth and hence it avoids such words as are not polite or pleasing. For instance, 'to breathe one's last' is used for 'death' and 'a light fingered person' for 'thief'. 'Death' and 'thief' and such other words are rather blunt or plain descriptions and so they are avoided in a decent society.

23. Periphrasis or Circumlocution—It means a piece of writing that is neither plain nor precise. On the contrary, even a plain and simple thing is expressed in a roundabout way. The result is that one has to use much more words than are necessary. In euphemism, too, there is a roundabout way of putting things and hence several unnecessary words are used for a single word. But there is a difference between euphemism and periphrasis. The former adopts a roundabout method because it wishes to avoid words that are disagreeable, but the latter has no such intention. Euphemism aims at decency but *periphrasis* aims just at verbal beauty. It is, therefore, very often difficult to make any head or tail of it and one has the feeling of reading nothing but a group of lovely words. It is, therefore, considered to be a faulty style.

Examples

(a) The flaming orb of the day = the sun

(b) One's prominent feature = one's nose

(c) The shining leather = boots

24. Tautology or Pleonasm—Repetition of the same idea in different words is called *tautology.* Tautology, too, like periphrasis is a faulty style because one has to use a lot of such words as can easily be avoided. It is in a sense the opposite of precis and, to say the least, is a careless piece of writing.

Examples

(a) He is *an extremely old* man of hundred years.

(b) He rejoiced at the *happy* sight.

In the first sentence, the use of 'extremely old' is unnecessary for it merely repeats the idea in 'man of hundred years'. Can a man of hundred years be ever young? In the second example, the word 'rejoice' presupposes that the sight must have been happy, for one cannot possibly rejoice at an unhappy sight. Then why use 'happy' at all? It is thus clear that tautology serves no useful purpose. It can, however, be justified when it lays emphasis.

25. Repetition—Sometimes the key word (important word) in a sentence is repeated. *Repetition* in itself is a fault, as in tautology, but it is fully justifiable if it aims at giving expression to some deep emotion. In that case, it tries to create a powerful effect, as in the following lines:

(a) O *dark, dark, dark* amid the blaze of moon.

(b) *Alone, alone,* all, all *alone.*
Alone on a *wide, wide* sea.

In the first line, 'dark' is repeated thrice to suggest a sense of utter darkeness. The impression cannot be created without repetition. In the second example, the poet tries to describe the feeling of terrible loneliness and hence repetition here is welcome and even essential.

26. Interrogation—It is a kind of question to which there is only one answer—either a strong affirmative or a strong negative. The very nature of the question determines the answer. The reason is that it contains some truth or fact which has to be either affirmed or denied.

Examples

(a) *Is there anybody here* who does not love his mother and his motherland?

(b) If you succeed, do *you not rejoice?*

The answer to the first question is a strong negative 'No' and the answer to the second one is a strong affirmative 'Yes'. The questions are such that no other answer is possible. So, the answer to an *interrogation* is inevitable and it is the same answer as the writer expects the reader to give.

27. Exclamation—It is a strong expression of some powerful feeling. Naturally, the rules of grammar very often fail to control the writer. The effect, however, is very strong. In fact, it is stronger than a full grammatical sentence can ever create.

Examples

(a) A horse! a horse! a kingdom for a horse!

(b) … and oh!

The difference to me!

The rush of intense emotion sweeps the poets away. They cannot but write broken sentences like these. But mark their effect. Well, it is tremendous.

28. Pun—*Pun* is a play on words. Lots of words we know have more than one meaning. Pun is a play on the different meanings of a word. It is rather a light work and so it may be said that the pun is a playing upon words. In fact, it is generally for some fun that pun is used.

Examples

(a) If a woman loses her husband, she pines for a *second.* (sixtieth part of a minute; another)

(b) An ambassador *lies* abroad for the good of his country. (lives; tells lies)

In the above examples, 'second' and 'lies' each has two meanings, and pun lies in using the words in different senses.

29. Alliteration—The use of words beginning with or containing the same letter or sound is called *alliteration.* Generally, it aims more at beauty than at utility and hence it is not a serious work of art.

Examples

(a) After life's fitful fever he sleeps well.

(b) In a summer season when soft was the sun.

In the first sentence, 'f' is repeated and in the second 's'. So, there is a lot of 'f' sound in the first sentence and 's' sound in the second. Alliteration, therefore, aims at producing a particular type of sound. If this sound suggests proper sense, it does serve some useful purpose.

30. Onomatopoeia—It means 'name-making' and is based upon the principle of imitation. *Onomatopoeia*, therefore, is the formation of a name (or word) by imitating the natural sound that is associated with the object. An onomatopoeic word is suggestive of the sound or the quality of the object. 'Babble', 'croak' and 'puff-puff' are some of the instances on the point. These words have been formed by imitating the natural sounds or qualities of the objects associated with them. Such words aim at suggesting or echoing the sense and are, therefore, highly effective.

EXERCISE

Point out the Figures of Speech in the following and give your comments.

1. Her hair is as black as night and as soft as velvet. The enemy came down like a wolf. Money is like manure, not good unless it is spread. It is as swift as an arrow. He is as thin as a stick. Time, like an over-rolling stream, bears all its sons away.

Hints—There are similes—are apt (appropriate) but hackneyed—not fresh—so they fail to add force to a description.

2. The camel is the *ship* of the desert. Hope is the *anchor* of the soul. She has *stony* heart. The leader put *all his cards* on the table. I have *caught* cold. Don't *shut your eyes* to your faults. The ambassador was *bombarded* with questions. He is the *salt* of the earth.

Hints—These are metaphors—are so old that they have almost ceased to be metaphors and have become a part of common speech.

3. (a) It is no use beating about the bush. You had better hit the nail on the head before it is too late.
   (b) The soldier put his foot in it right up to the hilt.
   (c) Life is an illusion. It is a shadow that bursts in on time and leaves mere ashes behind.

Hints—(a) Mixed metaphor—hunting and hammering mixed up—is rather far-fetched and confused. (b) Mixed Metaphor—foot and sword mixed up—strained and confused—lacks force and fails to add clearness to the description. (c) Mixed Metaphor—Life has been compared to a number of things one after another—illusion, shadow, bubble (*bursts* suggests that life is a bubble) and fire (life burnt to ashes by fire)—the mind at work seems to be confused.

4. "How far that little candle throws its beams!
   So shines a good deed in a naughty world."

Hints—It is a simile, although *as* or *like* has not been used. A simile may be expressed by placing two objects side by side. This arrangement suggests certain points of similarity between them. This device has been employed in the above two lines. A good deed in a wicked world is like a candle in darkness.

5. (a) "Here, thou great Anna! whom three realms obey.
   Dost sometimes counsel take—and sometimes tea."
   (b) She has lost her health, her wealth, her reputation and her handkerchief all at once.
   (c) "Miss Bolo went home in a flood of tears and a sedan chair."

Hints—Bathos or Anticlimax. In all the examples something great has been mixed up with something hopelessly trivial. This produces humour and ridicule.

6. (a) O death, where is thy sting?

   (b) O Solitude where are the charms,

   That sages have seen in thy face?

Hints—Apostrophe.

7. (a) "The moon doth with delight.

   Look round her when the heavens are bare."

   (b) "the grey-eyed morn smiles on the frowning night."

   (c) "Knowledge is proud that he has learnt so much,

   Wisdom is humble that he knows no more."

Hints—Personification. In (a) there are two figures—personification in "The moon … her" and periphrasis in "when the heavens are bare" for *the sky is clear.*

8. (a) "So frowned the mighty combatants, that hell Grew darker at their frown."

   (b) "Here's the smell of blood still: all the perfumes of Arabia will not sweeten this little hand."

   (c) She grew so weak that you could knock her down with a feather.

Hints—Hyperbole.

9. (a) "Men must work and women must weep."

   (b) "Men have many faults; women only two."

Hints—Antithesis.

10. (a) He had no little difficulty.

    (b) There are no fools here: they have all become leaders.

    (c) You must have "a heart to resolve, a need to continue, and a hand to execute."

    (d) He took his hat and his leave.

    (e) "What a piece of work is man!"

    (f) "He who can, does, he who cannot, teaches."

    (g) "Life is bitter sweet!"

Hints—(a) Litotes; (b) Innuendo; (c) Climax; (d) Bathos (or better call it Zeugma); (e) Exclamation; (f) Epigram; (g) Oxymoron.

....

Chapter XVI

SIMILAR EXPRESSIONS DISTINGUISHED

1. (a) The dinner is *already* on the table.

   (The dinner is placed from before.)

   (b) The dinner is *all ready* on the table.

   (The dinner is fully prepared.)

3. (a) It cost me *almost* thirty pounds.

   (*Almost* means *'about'* and is a mere statement of price, i.e., about thirty pounds.)

   (b) It cost me *nearly* thirty pounds.

   [Here *'nearly'* suggests that the price (about thirty pounds) was more than I wished to pay.]

3. (a) I have *always* tried. (at all times)

   (b) I have tried *all ways.* (every possible way)

4. (a) *Anyone* will do. (one of the persons)

   (b) *Any one* will do. (one of the things)

5. (a) She dislikes you as much as *I.*

   (She dislikes you as much as I dislike you.)

   (b) She dislikes you as much as *me.*

   (She dislikes both you and me in equal degree.)

6. (a) He walks *as if he were* drunk.

   (The sentence suggests that *he is not drunk.*)

   (b) He walks *as if he is* drunk.

   (The sentence suggests that *he is drunk.*)

7. (a) She helped him, *as well as I.* (She and I both helped him.)

   (b) She helped him *as well as me.*

   (She helped both him and me.)

8. (a) There are, *too,* many people who accept bribe.

   (Here *too* is separated from *many* and means *also.*)

(b) There are *too many* people who accept bribe.

(Here *too* is attached to 'many'. Thus *too many* means 'more than the proper number'.)

9. (a) He was *familiar to* me.

(*Familiar to* means 'known to'. The sentence therefore, means—I recognised him without any difficulty, because he was known to me already).

(b) He was *familiar with* me.

(*Familiar with* means 'having a fairly good knowledge of', 'to know intimately'. The sentence, therefore, means—He treated me in a friendly manner as though he knew me intimately.)

10. (a) *My friend* is ill.

(*My friend* suggests a definite person whose identity is well known.)

(b) *A friend of mine* is ill.

(It suggests 'someone with whom I am friendly'. It is not definite and specific.)

11. (a) It is a *gold* ring. (It is a ring made of gold.)

(b) It is a *golden* ring. (The ring has the colour of gold.)

12. (a) *Have* you constipation?

(Do you suffer from constipation at this moment?)

(b) *Do* you *have* constipation?

(Do you generally or habitually suffer from constipation?)

13. (a) Will you see *if* Ram has arrived yet?

(*If* is used when the speaker wishes or hopes for a positive answer.)

(b) Will you see *whether* Ram has arrived yet?

(*Whether* suggests a mere enquiry and the speaker is prepared for a positive or negative answer.)

14. (a) I feel *ill.*

(I am unwell.)

(b) I feel *sick.*

(*I feel nausea or vomiting tendency.*)

15. (a) *Only* he read a book.

(Nobody else read.)

(b) He *only* read a book.

(He read but he didn't understand it.)

(c) He read *only* a book.

(He read a book but he didn't read anything else.)

16. (a) She *often* thinks of marrying.

    (She now thinks of getting married.)

    (b) She thinks of marrying *often.*

    (She thinks of getting married several times.)

17. (a) Ram will have *written* a letter.

    (That is, the letter will be written by Ram.)

    (b) Ram will have a letter *written.*

    (That is, the letter will not be written by Ram.)

18. (a) He is *a* greater *soldier* than *statesman.*

    (He is both a soldier and statesman but he is greater as a soldier.)

    (b) He is *a* greater *soldier* than a statesman.

    (He is a greater soldier than a statesman is. That is, he is a soldier but not a statesman.)

19. (a) My dog is better than *Mohan's.*

    (My dog is better than *Mohan's* dog.)

    (b) My dog is better than *Mohan.*

    (My dog is better than Mohan himself.)

20. (a) *Who* is he?

    (What is his name or parentage?)

    (b) *What* is he?

    (What is his profession or social status?

    (c) *Which* is he?

    (The question inquires about a particular person out of a group of persons.)

21. (a) I *must do* this work.

    (It indicates some internal compulsion.)

    (b) I *have to do* this work.

    (It indicates some external compulsion.)

    (c) I *should do* this work.

    (It indicates a sense of duty.)

22. (a) *Happily,* his father did not die.

    [His father did not die and it was a happy (fortunate) thing.]

    (b) His father did not die *happily.*

    (His father died and his death was not a happy one.)

23. (a) *The poet and philosopher* has said so.

    (The same person is both poet and philosopher and he has said so.)

(b) *The poet and the philosopher* have said so.

(There are two persons. One is a poet and the other a philosopher and both have said so.)

24. (a) He *has black and white* cat.

(He has two cats. One is black and the other is white.)

(b) He *has a black and white* cat.

(He has only one cat. It is partly black and partly white.)

25. (a) He loves Sheela more than *I.*

(He and I love Sheela but he loves her more than I do.)

(b) He loves Sheela more than *me.*

(He loves Sheela and me but he loves her more than he loves me.)

26. (a) He is not *at home.*

(He is not in the house.)

(b) He is not *yet home.*

(He has not yet returned home from outside.)

27. (a) She is a *woman.*

(*Woman* denotes sex.)

(b) She is a *lady.*

(*Lady* denotes social rank. The sentence, therefore, suggests that she is not an ordinary woman.)

28. (a) Do you like *this kind of wine?*

(Wine of this brand or make)

(b) Do you like *wine of this* kind?

(Wine of this quality)

29. (a) You will not find that book *so easy.*

(That book is rather difficult.)

(b) You will not find that book *so easily.*

(It would be difficult for you to get that book.)

30. (a) It is not *worth saving.*

[It (something) is so small or insignificant that it does not deserve to be saved.]

(b) It is not *worthwhile* saving.

(Saving is rather useless. It is no use saving money.)

31. (a) I shouldn't do that if I were you.

(I should refrain from doing that if ...)

(b) I wouldn't do that if I were you.

(I should refuse to do that if ...)

32. (a) I went *to college.*

(I went there to learn or teach.)

(b) I went *to the college.*

(I went just to see or visit the place.)

33. (a) He was *surprised by* the police.

[He was taken by surprise (caught unawares.)]

(b) He was *surprised at* the police.

(He was filled with surprise at the sight of the police.)

34. (a) The police *searched* the thief.

(The thief was caught and the police were searching his pockets, etc.)

(b) The police *searched for* the thief.

(The thief was absconding. The police were trying to trace him out.)

35. (a) What *sort of* musician is he?

(It inquires about his classification whether he is in a band or an orchestra.)

(b) What *sort of* a musician is he?

(It inquires about his capabilities whether he is great or average or bad.)

36. (a) These books have been bought for *Leela* and *Sheela's* sake.

(Here the two persons are thought of together.)

(b) These books have been bought for *Leela's* and *Sheela's* sake.

(Here the two persons are thought of separately.)

37. (a) The tea is *fairly* hot.

(It is as hot as it should be.)

(b) The tea is *rather* hot.

(It is too hot. It is more hot that it should be.)

38. (a) Did she do it *then*?

(Here 'then' is a part of the sentence meaning 'at that time'.)

(b) Did she do it, *then*?

(Here 'then' stands apart from the sentence. It is an introductory adverb, and not an adverb of time.)

39. (a) He *lives* in India.

(He lives in India permanently.)

(b) He *is living* in India.

(He is in India at present but does not live here permanently.)

40. (a) I *dare to* say.

(I have the courage to say. I am bold enough to say.)

(b) I *dare* say.

(I believe or think likely.)

41. (a) He is *dying.* (expiring, on the point of death)

(b) He is *dyeing.* (colouring a piece of cloth)

42. (a) It is *lawful.* (not against law)

(b) It is *legal.* (sanctioned and recognised by law)

43. (a) Which do you like *best*?

(*The sentence indicates that one's liking is dependent upon a comparison between the qualities of the things amongst which one has to choose.*)

(b) *Which do you like most*? (The sentence indicates that one's liking is a mere personal preference without any comparison.)

In other words, the sentence means—'What is your choice?' without giving reasons for it.)

44. (a) I should have liked *to go.*

(The sentence expresses a desire that is a past one.)

(b) I should like *to have gone.* (The sentence expresses a desire that is a present one.)

45. (a) He *may* have been injured. (There was a possibility of his being injured.)

(b) He *might* have been injured. (He was not injured.)

46. (a) I am *at fault.* (I am puzzled.)

(b) I am *in fault.* (I am to blame.)

47. (a) I am *tired of* writing. (I am exhausted.)

(b) I am *tired with* writing. (I am disgusted.)

48. (a) She is the *best poetess.* (best of all the female poets)

(b) She is the *best poet.* (best of all the poets, male and female taken together)

49. (a) Speak *or* die. (You shall die if you do not speak.)

(b) Speak *and die.* (You shall die if you speak.)

50. (a) He appears *to be ill.* (He seems to be ill at present.)

(b) He appears *to have been ill.* (He was ill but is not so now.)

51. (a) He *may have gone.* (I am not sure if he has gone.)

(b) He *might have gone.* (He did not go although he could.)

52. (a) Poor *as* he is. (although he is poor)

(b) *As* he is poor. (because he is poor)

53. (a) He reached *safe.* (He was safe and sound when he reached.)

(b) He reached *safely.* (He reached without any trouble on his way.)

54. (a) He works *hard.* (He labours hard.)

(b) He *hardly* works. (He does not labour.)

55. (a) He went *to market.* (to buy something)

    (b) He went *to the market.* (for some other purpose, not to buy anything)

56. (a) He *thinks little* of me. (He has a poor opinion about me.)

    (b) He *little thinks* of me. (He does not remember me.)

57. (a) Go to college *direct.* (Go without stopping anywhere on the way.)

    (b) Go to college *directly.* (Go without stopping anywhere on the way.)

58. (a) Ram *alone did it.* (Nobody except Ram did it.)

    (b) Ram *did it alone.* (Ram did it without anybody's help.)

59. (a) She is *still* standing. (continues to stand)

    (b) She is standing *still.* (standing motionless)

60. (a) Tell me clearly what you saw. (telling clearly)

    (b) Tell me what you saw clearly. (seeing clearly)

❐

Chapter XVII

REWRITING IN SIMPLE ENGLISH

1. Slang
2. Colloquialism
3. Circumlocution
4. Euphemism
5. Glamorous words

इनके प्रयोग और अर्थ पर विचार करें।

Euphemism/circumlocution

कभी-कभी कुछ कथन बहुत ही कटु और अरुचिकर होते हैं। ऐसी अप्रिय अभिव्यक्ति (unpleasant expression) को कम अप्रिय बनाने के लिए साधारण बात भी घुमा-फिराकर कही जाती है। इसे प्रियोक्ति (euphemism = यूफिमिज्म) कहा जाता है। जैसे—

1. He gave up the ghost = He died.
2. This is a public toilet = This is a public lavatory.

कभी-कभी छोटी या साधारण बात भी घुमा-फिराकर (roundabout way से) कही जाती है और इसलिए बहुत-से अनावश्यक शब्दों का प्रयोग किया जाता है। इसे व्यास शैली या वाग्जाल (circumlocution/periphrasis—सर्कमलॅक्यूशॅन/पॅरिफ्रसिस) कहा जाता है, जैसे—

He is a light-fingered person. = He is a pick-pocket.

यहाँ देखें कि euphemism/circumlocution को Simple English में कैसे व्यक्त किया जा सकता है।

Euphemism/circumlocution	Simple English
He breathed his last.	
He has passed away.	
It is all over with him.	He is dead.
He gave up the ghost.	
He went the way of all flesh.	

Euphemism/circumlocution	Simple English
He paid the debt to Nature.	
He closed his busy life.	
He has departed from the world.	
He has gone to the next world.	
Death laid his icy hand on him.	He is dead.
He has joined the great majority.	
He was gathered to his forefathers.	
He sleeps the sleep that knows no breaking.	
His soul has left for its heavenly abode.	
He is gone to kingdom come.	
He is not quite exact in his statement.	He is telling a lie.
His statement suffers from terminological inexacitude.	
The hand that rocked the cradle has kicked the bucket.	Mother is dead.
The heavens are bare.	The sky is clear.
Night's candles are burn-out.	It is morning now.
He is his Majesty's guest.	He is in prison.
He is fond of the fragrant weed.	He is fond of tobacco.
He is a meat purveyor.	He is a butcher.
He is an operative.	He is a workman.
He is no mean thinker.	He is a great thinker.
This is a canine specimen.	This is a dog.
He partook of his meal.	He ate his meal.
I feel an aching void.	I feel hungry.
The inner man must be satisfied.	The stomach must be satisfied.
He has reached the evening of his life.	He has grown old.
Silver and gold have I none.	I have no money.
He fables not.	He speaks the truth.
He is a professor of the tonsorial art.	He is a barber.
We partook of a cup that cheers but not inebriates.	We had tea/coffee.
Finny denizens of the deep	Fish
Lord of creation	Man
Weaker vessel	Woman

Euphemism/circumlocution	Simple English
Adverse climatic conditions	Bad weather
A gentleman's gentleman	An attendant
One's prominent feature	One's nose
A succulent bivalve	An oyster
The sacred page	The Bible
A call-girl	A prostitute hired by telephone.
Culinary department	Kitchen
Culinary knowledge	The art of cooking
Tonsorial art	The art of hair-cutting
Lady-dog	Bitch
The nuptial tie	Marriage
A medical attendant	A doctor
One's snowy locks	One's grey hair
The animal that brouses on thistle	An ass
The viewless couriers of air	The winds
A lot of transformation of capital	A lot of expenditure
A minatory expression	A threat
A hair-dresser	A barber
To trip the light fantastic toe	To dance
Watcher of the skies	An astronomer
The shining leather that covers our limbs	Our skin
Nocturnal watch.	Night watch
Natal day	Birthday
The festive board	The dinner-table
On one's sleepless pillow	Without sleep
Mortal remains	Dead body
One's mistress	One's concubine
A light-fingered person	A pick-pocket
To be in the family way	To be pregnant
To get the green light	To get permission to go ahead

Colloquialism

अँगरेजी में कुछ शब्दों का प्रयोग बोलचाल में होता है जिसे बोलचाल की शैली या चलती भाषा (colloquialism, कॅलोक्विलिज्म) कहा जाता है, जैसे—

1. I bought a lot of eats = I bought a lot of food.
2. This is an A[1] (A one) party = This is an excellent party.
3. He is a big gun = He is an important person.

यहाँ colloquialism के कुछ और नमूने देखें—

Colloquialism	**Simple English**
An ace player/driver	An expert/first rate player/driver
Ad lib	Without restraint
Ad-man	A composer of advertisements
All-time high/low	Highest/lowest level
An ape	A clumsy person
Apple sauce	Nonsense/flattery
Ask for trouble	Invite trouble
Auto	Automobile
To get the axe	Be dismissed from a job
To baby (verb)	To treat like a baby
To be in bad with	To be in disfavour
Not bad/not so bad	Quite good
To feel bad	To feel sorry
To be in the soup	
To be in hot water	To be in trouble
A Ladies	A public toilet for woman
Full of go/Have plenty of go	Full of energy
To be on the go	Very busy
To have a go at something	To make an attempt
A piece of goods	A young girl
Plenty of guts	To have courage
The gutter press	Newspapers giving prominence to scandals/ scoops
A hair-do	Dressing of a woman's hair
Better half	Wife
Not care a hang	Not care at all
Hanky	Handkerchief
Hanky-panky	Trickery
Hash	Hashish

Colloquialism	**Simple English**
A hawk	One who favours the use of military force
To have something on	To have an engagement
To have nothing on	To have no engagement
Neither here nor there	Not to the point
That's him/her	That's he/she
It's me/us	It's I/we
Honey	Sweatheart
Honeys	Little children
Hubby	Husband
A hush affair	A secret affair
Jack	Man
Jolly	Very
I bet	I am certain
He is a clever old bird	He is a clever old man
A cat-nap/A cat-sleep	A short sleep in a chair
A bitch	A spiteful girl/woman
A big gun	A powerful person
Bum	Buttocks
Best of the bunch	Best of the lot
A capital speech/idea	An excellent speech/idea
To carry on with somebody	To have a love-affair with somebody
Champ	Champion
Chum	A close friend
Chummy	Very friendly
To chuck away	To throw away
A decent dinner	A good dinner
To a degree	To the highest degree
To doctor a cold/child	To give medical treatment
Dad/Daddy	Father
Doggy/Doggie	A dog
Dolly	A doll
A fan	Supporter of something/somebody

Colloquialism	Simple English
Fan mail	Letters from fans
Fellow	Man/Boy
A fib	A lie
A fibbler	A liar
Fishy	Suspicious
A Gents	A public toilet for men
To give the sack	To dismiss
To get the sack	To be dismissed
See you [soon]	Goodbye [while parting]
All the best	With warmest wishes [while parting]
Rattish	Irritable
A smash hit	Very successful
A raw deal	A harsh treatment
Ta	Thank you
Ta-ta	Goodbye
Talkies	Cinema films
That	So
[She isn't that tall]	[She isn't so tall]
A tidy sum	A large sum of money
To get tight	To have too much of drinks
Tonsorial art	Hair-cutting
To have a sweet tooth	To be fond of sweets
To give some teeth	To make something effective
Tough luck	Bad luck
Tremendous	Big/great
[He is a tremendous eater.]	[He is a big eater]
Tummy	Belly
An ugly customer	A person difficult to deal with
Up [verb]	To happen
[What is up?]	[What is happening?]
Vac	Vacation
Vet	A veterinary surgeon

Colloquialism	**Simple English**
Vim	Energy
A vulture	A greedy person
A whacking lie	A big lie
A white lie	A harmless type of lie
A walkie-talkie	A portable radio set
Wooly/woolies	Woollen garments, specially a sweater
To spin a yarn [She spins a long yarn about her adventures.]	To make up a story
To be saucy [She is a saucy young girl.]	To be smart
To sauce [verb] [How dare you sauce your teachers?]	To be rude
To have the cheek [How have you the cheek to talk like this?]	To be rude/to have the courage
To be cheeky [She is very cheeky in her talk.]	To be rude

Slang

अँगरेजी में कुछ शब्दों का प्रयोग गँवारू बोली में होता है जिसे अपभाषा (slang, स्लैंग) कहा जाता है, जैसे—

1. She is in the family way.	She is pregnant.
2. He is a big bug. He is a big noise.	He is a powerful person.
3. She is a chicken.	She is a young girl.
4. She is a bird.	She is a girl companion.
5. He always cares for number one.	He always cares for himself.
6. We had plenty of eats.	We had plenty of food.

यहाँ slang के कुछ और नमूने देखें—

Slang	**Simple English**
On appro	On approval
A babe	A young girl
A baby	A sweetheart
Bags of money	A lot of money
Baloney	Nonsense

Slang	Simple English
To be with at a bean	To be without money
Had best	Had better
[You had best stay here.]	[You had better stay here.]
A bird	A girl companion
Blind drunk	Highly drunk
Bobby/Cop	Policeman
To go like a bomb	Be efficient
To bug [verb]	To cause annoyance
[He always bugs me.]	[He always annoys me.]
A bum	A begger/loafer
A piece of cake	Something very easy
To carry the can	To take the blame
To chew the rag	To discuss old grievances
A chicken	A young girl
A chick	A girl
To chuck	To throw
To clip somebody's ear	To hit or punch sharply
Cooky/cookie	Biscuit
A doll	A pretty but brainless girl
[She is just a doll.]	
Dolly	An attractive girl who is gorgeously dressed
Eats [plural noun]	Food/eatables
In the family way	Be pregnant
Floozy/Floozie	A prostitute/A careless woman
Footer	Football
Small fry	An insignificant person
To be in a funk	To be in fear
Gone	Lost/dead
[The purse is gone.]	
Guy	A person
[He is an old guy.]	[He is an old man.]
A bad hat	A bad person
A hoodlum	A dangerous criminal

Slang	Simple English
Hood	Hoodlum
To get into a jam	To be in a difficult situation
Jolly	Very
Just	Absolutely
Killer	Murderer
Lib [women's lib]	Liberation
The likes of [The likes of Gandhi are rare]	Similar persons/things
A good-looker	A good-looking person
A love/flame [An old love/flame of mine]	A sweetheart
Ma'dm	Madam
Man [They are man and wife]	Husband
Mummy	Mother
Maxi	Woman's ankle-length shirt
Mini [This is a mini bus/shirt.]	Of small size or length
To earn a mint of money	To earn a large amount
Met office	Metereological office
Mortal [I am an ordinary mortal.]	Man
It's no-go [noun]	It can't be done
Noes [noun]	Those saying no
Pa/Papa	Father
Pop music/star	Popular music/star
Posh hotel	First-rate
Posh friends	Smart
Puppy-love	First love-affair
A puppy	A conceited young man
A kid	A young person
A kiddy	A child
To kip	To go to bed

Slang	Simple English
A know-all	One who claims to know everything
To monkey about with [Don't monkey about with a blade.]	To play mischievously
Nix	Nothing
A big noise	An important person
A nosy/nosey Parker	An inquisitive person
An old sweat	A person with a long experience of his job
Odd	A person who is aloof from society
Number one	Oneself/self-interest
A packet [This car has cost me a packet.]	A considerable amount
To rag [Don't rag these girls)	To tease/to play jokes
Rag trade	Business of making/selling
A big shot [He can help us. He is a big shot.]	An important or powerful person
A shrimp [He can't help us. He is just a shrimp.]	A very small person
To throw a party	To give a party
To give somebody the glad eye	To give an amorous look [प्यार भरी नजर]
To give somebody the glad hand	To offer the hand of welcome

Glamorous words

कभी-कभी छोटे और सरल शब्दों (plain words) के बदले कठिन या मोहक शब्दों (glamorous words) का प्रयोग कर दिया जाता है। कुछ लोग अपनी अभिव्यक्ति (expression) को आकर्षक और मोहक बनाने के लिए glamorous words का प्रयोग इस प्रकार करते हैं—

1. We extinguished the conflagration. We put out the fire.
2. He died in indigent circumstances. He died in poverty.

Glamorous words के इन नमूनों को भी देखें—

Glamorous words	Simple English
She sustained injuries.	She was injured.
The train is running with great velocity.	The train is running fast.
The generality of leaders is dishonest.	Most of the leaders are dishonest.

Glamorous words	Simple English
I don't find myself in entire agreement with you.	I don't fully agree with you.
He reached at the psychological moment.	He reached at the right moment.
She was conveyed to the place of her residence.	She was carried home.
He is labouring under the delusion of a serious nature.	He is committing a mistake.
Your case is of a hopeful nature.	Your case is hopeful.
A vastly huge concourse of populace gathered.	A huge crowd gathered.
It is an investigation of an impartial character.	It is an impartial investigation.
He made a speech of an offensive character.	He made an offensive speech.
Your remark produces awfully painful sensations.	Your remark hurts.
You will get assisatance from me in the eventuality of this being the case.	If this is so, I will help you.
What is the ordinary beverage of the urban population?	What is the usual drink of townsman?
The situation with regard to export of sugar has shown a slight improvement.	Sugar export has improved a little.
Owing to repeated deviations from the recognised principles of honesty he received orders for dismissal.	He was dismissed for dishonesty.

❒

Pompous words	Simple English
I don't find myself in entire agreement with you.	I don't fully agree with you.
He reached at the psychological moment.	He reached at the right moment.
She was conveyed to the place of her residence.	She was carried home.
He is labouring under the delusion of a serious nature.	He is committing a mistake.
Your case is of a hopeful nature.	Your case is hopeful.
A vastly huge concourse of populace gathered.	A large crowd gathered.
It is an investigation of an important character.	It is an important investigation.
He made a speech of an offensive character.	He made an offensive speech.
Your remark produces awfully painful sensations.	Your remark hurts.
You will possess assistance from me in the eventuality of this being the case.	If this is so, I will help you.
What is the ordinary beverage of the urban population?	What is the usual drink of town people?
The situation with regard to export of sugar has shown a slight improvement.	Sugar export has improved a little.
Owing to repeated deviations from the recognized principles of honesty, he received orders for dismissal.	He was dismissed for dishonesty.

Chapter XVIII

ANALYSIS

Analysis का अर्थ होता है वाक्य के अंगों या अंशों को अलग-अलग कर उनकी जाँच करना। सुविधा की दृष्टि से इस कार्य को हम तीन भागों में बाँट सकते हैं—

(A) *First stage:* वाक्य के Clauses को अलग-अलग करना

(B) *Second stage:* उन Clauses का नामकरण करना

(C) *Third stage:* वाक्य का नामकरण करना

(A) FIRST STAGE

How to Find Out Clauses

सबसे पहले हमें यह देखना है कि clause किसे कहते हैं, क्योंकि इसके बिना clauses को अलग-अलग किया ही नहीं जा सकता। कुछ लोग दिये हुए वाक्य को अंदाज से कई टुकड़ों में बाँट देते हैं। यह तरीका ठीक नहीं। यह तो सच है कि clause किसी sentence का एक भाग होता है; पर sentence का हर भाग clause नहीं भी हो सकता है।

Sentence के उस भाग (part) को clause कहते हैं जिसमें Subject और Finite Verb हों। यदि Subject और उसके Finite Verb का पता लग जाए, तो clauses आप-से-आप अलग हो जाएँगे, पर कुछ लोगों को इनका (Subject और Verb का) पता ही नहीं चलता। इसलिए यहाँ इन दोनों पर विस्तारपूर्वक विचार करना आवश्यक है।

How to Find Out the Subject

आप जानते हैं कि केवल Noun या उसके equivalents (जो शब्द Noun का काम करें) ही Subject हो सकते हैं; जैसे—

1. NOUN—This *book is* good.
2. PRONOUN—*He* is a good man.
3. INFINITIVE—*To walk* is healthy.
4. GERUND—*Walking* is good.
5. PHRASE—*What to do* is difficult to decide.
6. CLAUSE—*What he says* is quite right.

How to Find Out the Finite Verb

Finite Verb उस Verb को कहते हैं जिसका Number और Person Subject के अनुसार होता है; जैसे—

1. We go home. 2. He goes home.

पहले वाक्य का Subject (We) Plural है। इसलिए यहाँ Verb (go) plural है। अतः, *go* Finite Verb है। इसी प्रकार, दूसरे वाक्य में Verb (goes) singular है, क्योंकि subject (He) singular है। इसलिए goes भी Finite Verb है।

NOTE (a)—जिस Verb का Number और Person Subject के अनुसार नहीं होता, अर्थात जो Subject की परवाह नहीं करके सदा स्वतंत्र रूप में रहता है, उसे Absolute Verb कहते हैं। ये Absolute Verbs तीन प्रकार के होते हैं—

1. Infinitive—I like *to walk.*
2. Gerund—I am fond of *walking.*
3. Participle—
   (i) Present Participle—*Going* there he saw a tiger.
   (ii) Past Participle—*Having gone* there he saw a tiger.

तो, इस प्रकार Finite Verb और Absolute Verb में बहुत अंतर है। Finite Verb सदा Subject के अनुसार होता है, पर Absolute Verb कभी भी Subject के अनुसार नहीं होता; जैसे—

1. *Having gone* there *he* saw a tiger.
2. *Having gone* there *they* saw a tiger.

पहले वाक्य में Subject (he) Singular है और दूसरे में (they) Plural; पर Verb का रूप एक ही है। यही लक्षण Infinitive और Gerund का भी है।

इसलिए Absolute Verb को कभी भी Finite Verb नहीं समझना चाहिए, नहीं तो clauses ठीक-ठीक अलग हो ही नहीं सकते।

NOTE (b)—कभी-कभी Infinitive (to + verb) का *to* चिह्न छिपा रहता है और केवल verb का प्रयोग होता है। इन वाक्यों को लें—

1. He can *speak.* 2. He should *speak.*
3. He must *speak.* 4. He had better *speak.*
5. I made him *speak.* 6. He did nothing but *speak.*

यहाँ speak है Infinitive, Finite Verb नहीं। इसे Infinitive without *to* कहा जा सकता है। इसलिए ऐसे Infinitive को Finite Verb का एक भाग मान लेना चाहिए; इसे Finite Verb नहीं समझना चाहिए। इस सभी वाक्यों में केवल एक-एक Finite Verb है—can speak, should speak, must speak, had better speak.

Elliptical (Contracted) Sentences

Rule I. आपको कुछ ऐसे वाक्य मिलेंगे जिनमें दो-दो Subjects रहते हैं, पर उनके लिए एक ही Verb का प्रयोग होता है। ऐसा होता है उन वाक्यों में जिनमें *or, nor, as well as, and not, but,* *not only ..., but also* या *and therefore* का प्रयोग होता है। ऐसे वाक्यों को अलग-अलग clause का रूप देना चाहिए और यह तभी हो सकता है जब आप दोनों Subjects के लिए अलग-अलग Verb का प्रयोग करेंगे। इन वाक्यों पर ध्यान दें—

1. Neither *this man came* nor *that.*
   (a) Neither this man came.
   (b) Nor that (man) came.
2. *He* as well as *I is* to blame.
   (a) He is to blame.
   (b) I am to blame.
3. *He is* poor *but* meritorious.
   (a) He is poor.
   (b) But (he) is meritorious.
4. He, *and not* I, is guilty.
   (a) He is guilty.
   (b) I am not guilty.
5. *Not only* he *but also* his friends were arrested.
   (a) He was arrested.
   (b) His friends were arrested.
6. He is rich, *and therefore* happy.
   (a) He is rich.
   (b) He is happy.

NOTE—जब एक से अधिक Subjects को and के द्वारा जोड़ा जाता है, तब उन सभी Subjects को एक ही माना जाता है और इसलिए उन्हें अलग-अलग clauses में बाँटना नहीं चाहिए; जैसे—

Ram, Mohan and Sohan are friends.

इस वाक्य में एक ही clause है, तीन नहीं। यदि इसका Analysis इस प्रकार कर दिया जाए—(a) Ram is a friend. (b) Mohan is a friend. (c) Sohan is a friend.—तो यह अनुचित होगा।

Rule II. अब आप ऐसे वाक्यों को देखें जिनमें एक ही Subject रहता है, पर एक से अधिक Verb—

He *came* and *gave* me a letter.

ऐसे वाक्यों में जितने Finite Verbs रहते हैं उतने ही clauses होते हैं। इसलिए उन सभी छिपे हुए Subjects को प्रकट कर देना चाहिए और तब clauses का अलग-अलग रूप देना चाहिए; जैसे—

1. He came and gave me a letter.
   (a) He came.
   (b) He gave me a letter.

एक और उदाहरण लें—

2. He lifted a gun, took aim and fired.

(a) He lifted a gun.

(b) He took aim.

(c) He fired.

Rule III. As और Than के बाद कभी-कभी Subject तथा Verb दोनों ही छिपे हुए रहते हैं। ऐसे clauses को अलग करते समय उन्हें प्रकट कर देना चाहिए और उन्हें अलग-अलग clauses का रूप देना चाहिए; जैसे—

1. Come as soon as you can.

(a) come.

(b) As soon as you can (come).

2. He writes as fast as possible.

(a) He writes.

(b) As fast as (it is) possible.

3. This is the same pen as mine.

(a) This is the same pen.

(b) As mine (my pen) is.

4. He is better than I.

(a) He is better.

(b) Than I (am).

Rule IV. इस संबंध में यह भी जान लेना अच्छा होगा कि कभी-कभी if, though, when, unless, till, while और whether ... or के बाद *Subject* और *Verb (to be)* छिपे रहते हैं। इसलिए clauses को अलग करते समय छिपे हुए Subject और Verb को प्रकट कर देना चाहिए और तब उन्हें clause का रूप देना चाहिए; जैसे—

1. Though badly defeated, he did not leave the field.

(a) Though (he was) badly defeated.

(b) He did not leave the field

2. He lost his way while walking at night.

(a) He lost his way.

(b) While (he was) walking at night.

3. I will send papers if (when) called for.

(a) I will send papers.

(b) If (they are) called for.

4. His argument, whether right or wrong, goes on endlessly.

(a) His argument goes on endlessly.

(b) Whether (it is) right or wrong.

5. It should be preserved till required/necessary.

(a) It should be preserved.

(b) Till (it is) required.

Rule V. As if या As though से शुरू होनेवाले clause को एक ही Subordinate Clause मानना चाहिए; जैसे—

He memorised his lesson as if he were a parrot.

(a) He memorised his lesson.

(b) As if he were a parrot.

कुछ लोग as if को दो clauses मानते हैं, क्योंकि वे समझते हैं कि as if = as + if.

इस दृष्टि से ऊपर दिए गए वाक्य के तीन clauses इस प्रकार हो जाएँगे—

(a) He memorised his lesson.

(b) As he would have memorised.

(c) If he were a parrot.

पर आप as if या as though को एक ही conjunction मानें, तो अच्छा हो।

ऊपर दिए गए इन नियमों की सहायता से आप आसानी से clauses को चुन लेंगे और आपको यह भी पता चल जाएगा कि ये clauses Principal हैं या Suboridanate. इस प्रकार आप Analysis के First Stage को आसानी से पार कर लेंगे।

(B) SECOND STAGE
How to Name Clauses

अब हम Analysis की दूसरी और सबसे बड़ी मंजिल में प्रवेश करते हैं। यहाँ यह विचार करना होता है कि अमुक clauses किस प्रकार के हैं। तो प्रश्न उठता है कि clauses कितने प्रकार के होते हैं। हम सभी clauses को पहले दो भागों में बाँट दे सकते हैं—

1. Principal or Main or Independent. 2. Subordinate or Dependent.

Subordinate Clauses तीन प्रकार के होते हैं—

1. Adverb Clause 2. Adjective Clause 3. Noun Clause

How to Find Out Principal and Subordinate Clauses

Rule I. जो clauses इन Subordinating conjunctions से आरंभ होते हैं वे Subordinate Clauses होते हैं और जो clauses इन subordinating conjunctions से आरंभ नहीं होते वे Principal Clauses होते हैं। Subordinating conjunctons ये हैं—

as, as if, as though, as much as, as far as, according as, after, as soon as, so long as, before, because, since, that, so that, provided, provided that, notwithstanding that, in that, than, now that, though, in order that, so much so that, although, who, which, what, how, if, whether, until, unless, when and where

इन वाक्यों को लें—

1. *As* he is ill, he is absent.
2. He behaves *as if* he were a king.
3. I will help you *as far as* I can.
4. I do not know *when* he will come.
5. I know *where* he lives.

इन वाक्यों में as, as if, as far as, when और where से आरंभ होनेवाले clauses Subordinate हैं और बाकी Principal.

NOTE (a)—*Who/Which/When/Where* से आरंभ होनेवाले clauses Principal भी हो सकते हैं जब इनका प्रयोग continuative sense में होता है, restrictive sense में नहीं। यह समस्या वहाँ उठती है जहाँ इनके पहले Noun और Comma दोनों ही रहते हैं, जिसकी चर्चा More Hints On Principal Clause and Subordinate Clause के प्रसंग में विस्तारपूर्वक की जाएगी।

NOTE (b)—कभी-कभी *But* का प्रयोग Relative Pronoun की तरह होता है और उसका (but का) अर्थ होता है *Who not/that not* (जो नहीं)। ऐसे but-clauses सदा Subordinate Clauses होते हैं; जैसे—

There is no teacher/but loves good students.

Rule II. कभी-कभी *Should, Were* और *Had* का अर्थ 'अगर' (if) होता है; जैसे—

1. *Should* you appoint him, he would be obliged.
2. *Were* he here, he would help me.
3. *Had* there been rain, there would have been good crops.

ऐसी अवस्था में Should/Were/Had + clause सदा Subordinate Clause होता है। आप आगे देखेंगे कि ऐसे clauses सदा Adverb Clauses होते हैं।

Rule III. जब *Once* का अर्थ 'अगर एक बार' ('एक बार' नहीं) हो तो, वह clause Subordinate होता है और सदा Adverb Clause होता है; जैसे—

Once you move ahead, you cannot go back.

यहाँ once का अर्थ 'अगर एक बार (if once)' है। इसलिए यहाँ once + clause Subordinate है।

Rule IV. कुछ ऐसे भी वाक्य होते हैं, जिनका पहला clause Imperative sentence होता है और दूसरा Assertive (Imperative + and + Assertive); जैसे—

Give me blood, and I will give you freedom.

ऐसे वाक्यों के पहले clause से (अर्थात Imperative sentence से) एक condition (शर्त) का बोध होता है। यहाँ Give me blood का अर्थ है—If you give me blood. इसलिए ऐसे Imperative sentences को Subordinate Clause मानना चाहिए। आप आगे देखेंगे कि ये सदा Adverb Clause होते हैं। यहाँ आप इतना ही देखें कि ऐसे वाक्यों में Imperative sentence और Assertive sentence के बीच and आता है और and के पहले Comma रहता है।

Rule V. कुछ वाक्यों की बनावट इस प्रकार की होती है—

The + Comparative Degree, *the* + Comparative Degree; जैसे—

The more you have, *the more* you want.

ऐसे The ...... The-clauses से Degree का बोध होता है। इसलिए ऐसे वाक्यों का पहला The-clause Subordinate (Adverb) होता है और दूसरा Principal.

Rule VI. For से शुरू होनेवाला clause coordinate to Principal होता है। कुछ लोग ऐसे clause को subordinate मानते हैं, जो उचित नहीं। इसका कारण यह है कि *for-clause* से सूचना/व्याख्या (information/explanation) का बोध होता है, कारण (cause) का नहीं।

Rule VII. However से शुरू होनेवाला clause Principal होता है और Subordinate भी। जब however के पहले और बाद भी comma रहता है तब वह Principal Clause होता है, पर जब सिर्फ इसके पहले comma रहता है (पर बाद में नहीं) तब वह Subordinate Clause होता है; जैसे—

1. You have committed a grave offence, *however,* I excuse you this time.
2. You will fail, *however* hard you may try.

यहाँ पहले वाक्य में however से शुरू होनेवाला clause Principal Clause है, पर दूसरे में Subordinate.

Rule VIII. जब दो clauses के बीच न comma रहे और न Conjunction, तो पहला clause Principal होता है और दूसरा Subordinate. याद रखें कि ऐसे वाक्यों में that, which, whom, when आदि Relative Pronouns/Relative Adverbs छिपे रहते हैं। इन वाक्यों को देखें—

1. I hope you are well = I hope that you are well.
2. The food you eat is pure = The food that (which) you eat is pure.

इसलिए यहाँ you are well तथा you eat हैं Subordinate Clauses और I hope तथा The food is pure हैं Principal Clauses.

कुछ और वाक्य लें।

1. The book/I bought yesterday/is mine.
2. The boy/you are looking at/is my brother.
3. The man/you are speaking to/is my uncle.
4. The time/he came/was good.

यहाँ I bought yesterday, you are looking at, you are speaking to तथा he came हैं Subordinate Clauses और बाकी हैं Principal Clauses.

NOTE (a)—Coordinate Clauses

Coordinate clause का अर्थ होता है—of equal rank, अर्थात बराबर श्रेणी का। यही कारण है कि Principal clause का भी coordinate होता है और Subordinate clause का भी।

दो या दो से अधिक Principal clauses तब coordinate होते हैं जब वे Coordinating conjunctions से जोड़े जाते हैं। इन वाक्यों को देखें—

1. He took aim/*and*/fired.
2. He went home/*and*/saw his mother.
3. He is poor/*but*/very intelligent.
4. He/*as well as*/she is very intelligent.

इन वाक्यों के दोनों ही भाग (clauses) Principal Clause हैं। इसलिए पहले भाग को PC कहा जाता है और दूसरे को Coordinate to PC; जैसे—

1. He took aim and fired.
   (a) He took aim, ... PC.
   (b) He fired .... Coordinate to PC.

जब एक ही प्रकार के दो या दो से अधिक Subordinate clauses किसी Coordinating conjunctons से जोड़े जाते हैं, तब वे Coordinate clauses होते हैं; जैसे—

1. Tell me/where she lives/*and*/when she will return.
2. I don't know/when he will take his examination/*or*/whether he will take his examination at all.

यहाँ दो-दो Noun clauses (NC) जोड़े गए हैं Coordinating conjunction (and/or) के द्वारा। इसलिए ये Coordinate Noun clause हैं—

(a) Tell me .... PC.
(b) Where she lives .... NC.
(c) When she will return .... Coordinate to NC (b).

Coordinate conjunctons ये हैं—

and, both ... and, as well as, but,
not only ... but also, or, either ... or,
neither ... nor, for

NOTE (b)—Interrogative Clauses

Principal और Subordinate Clauses पर विचार करते समय हम जरा एक विशेष प्रकार के Interrogative sentences को भी देखें—

1. The weather is very fine today, isn't it?
2. These things will not be needed any more, will they?

यहाँ पहले वाक्य में दो clauses हैं—(a) The weather is very fine today और isn't it? इसी प्रकार, दूसरे वाक्य में भी दो clauses हैं—(a) These things will not be needed any more, (b) will they?

कुछ लोगों का मत है कि ऐसे Interrogatie sentences के दोनों ही clauses को Principal Clauses माना जाए। आप भी ऐसा कर सकते हैं। पर मेरा विचार है कि ऐसी अवस्था में आप इन दोनों ही clauses को केवल एक Principal Clause मानें, क्योंकि ऐसे दो clauses एक ही वाक्य के अभिन्न अंग होते हैं। इस दृष्टि से ऊपर दिए गए दोनों ही Interrogative sentences का analysis इस प्रकार होगा—

1. The weather is very fine today, isn't it?—Principal Clause
2. These things will not be needed any more, will they?—Principal Clause

कुछ लोग ऐसे clauses को Interrogative Clauses के नाम से पुकारते हैं, पर यदि आप इन्हें Principal Clauses मानें, तो अच्छा हो।

NOTE (c)—Parenthetical Clauses

इन वाक्यों की बनावट पर ध्यान दें—

1. Experience, they say, is the best teacher.
2. You are all well, I hope.
3. You see, we lost our way in the forest.

यहाँ पहला वाक्य है—Experience is the best teacher और इसके साथ they say को लगा द्रिया गया है। वास्तव में, they say का वाक्य से कोई भी संबंध नहीं है और इसलिए comma के द्वारा इसे वाक्य से अलग कर दिया गया है। दूसरे वाक्य में भी I hope का वाक्य से कोई संबंध नहीं और इसलिए इसे भी comma के द्वारा वाक्य से अलग कर दिया गया है। तीसरे वाक्य में भी you see को comma के द्वारा वाक्य से अलग रखा गया है, क्योंकि वाक्य से इसका कोई भी संबंध नहीं है। आप देखेंगे कि बहुत-से वाक्यों में I hope, I expect, I believe, I suppose, they say, you see इत्यादि प्रकार के clauses लगे रहते हैं, पर वास्तव में, वाक्य से इनका कोई भी संबंध नहीं रहता। इसलिए ये comma या dash के द्वारा वाक्य से अलग रखे जाते हैं। ऐसे clauses को Parenthetical Clauses कहा जाता है। इसका अर्थ यह है कि ये न तो Principal Clauses होते हैं और न ही Subordinate Clauses।

आप देखेंगे कि ऐसे clauses कभी तो वाक्य के आरंभ में रहते हैं, कभी बीच में और कभी अंत में, पर ये comma या dash के द्वारा वाक्य से अलग रखे जाते हैं। आप इन्हें Principal Clause मत समझ लें। याद रखें कि जब I hope, I believe, they say इत्यादि clauses Principal Clauses होते हैं, तब इनके बाद comma या dash का प्रयोग कभी भी नहीं हो सकता। इन वाक्यों को देखें—

1. You are well, I hope.
2. I hope you are well.

यहाँ पहले वाक्य में I hope एक Parenthetical Clause है, क्योंकि इसके पहले comma आ गया है, पर दूसरे वाक्य में I hope के बाद Comma नहीं आया है और न आना ही चाहिए, क्योंकि यहाँ यह एक Principal Clause है। इस नियम का ध्यान रखकर इसका analysis इस प्रकार करें—

1. You are well, I hope.
   (a) You are well—Principal Clause
   (b) I hope—Parenthetical Clause
2. I hope you are well.
   (a) I hope—Principal Clause
   (b) You are well—Subordinate Clause (SC)

कुछ और उदाहरण लें—

1. Experience, they say, is the best teacher.
   (a) Experience is the best teacher.—Principal Clause (PC)
   (b) They say—Parenthetical Clause

2. They say experience is the best teacher.

(a) They say—PC

(b) Experience … teacher—SC

इस प्रकार Principal और Subordinate Clauses को चुन लेने के बाद हमें यह देखना चाहिए कि Subordinate Clauses किस प्रकार के हैं। इसलिए अब तीनों प्रकार के Subordinate Clauses को लें और उन्हें पहचानने का प्रयत्न करें।

How to Find Out Adverb Clauses

Rule I. जो clauses इन Subordinating conjunctions से आरंभ होते हैं वे Adverb Clause होते हैं—

as, as if, as though, as soon as, as long as, as far as, as much as, after, before, because, considering that, if, in order that, in case, in that, in as much as, lest, not withstanding that, provided, provided that, since, so far as, so that, now that, that, than, though, until, unless, where, wherever, when, whenever, while, whether … or not, however + adjective/adverb

इन वाक्यों को देखें—

1. As he is ill, he is absent.
2. Play while you play.
3. He went home after he had finished his work.
4. Don't get down until the train stops.
5. You won't pass unless you work very hard.
6. He won't pass however hard he may work.
7. He works hard that (so that) he may pass.
8. He was late since it was raining.
9. Two hours have passed since he fell asleep.
10. Though (although) he is poor, he is very happy.
11. Take an umbrella in case it rains.
12. Now that he has surrendered, he sould be pardoned.

वाक्य में Adverb clauses भिन्न-भिन्न प्रकार के भाव व्यक्त करते हैं। इस पर विस्तारपूर्वक विचार करें।

(I) Principal Clause + Adverb Clause of Time

कुछ Adverb clauses से समय (time) का भाव व्यक्त होता है और इनकी बनावट इस प्रकार होती है—

I

PC	+Adverb Clause (Showing Time)
I saw her	as (while) she was getting off the bus.
Please wait here	until I come back.
No sooner had I started	than it began to rain.
I will go out	after she comes back.
Hardly/Scarcely had I started	when it began to rain.

II

Adverb Clause (Showing Time)	+PC
When he returned home	he found the gate closed.
Whenever he comes here	he brings sweets.
While there is life	there is hope.

इन वाक्यों को भी देखें—

1. He finished the work before he went to bed.
2. We thought only of our past glories when we were slaves.
3. She cooked fish, while I listened to the radio.
4. As soon as he fell asleep, he had a dream.
5. No sooner did he go to bed than he fell asleep.
6. Hardly (scarcely) had he started when it began to rain.
7. The patient died the moment the doctor arrived.
8. As long as I live, I shall remain grateful to him.
9. I will finish the work, as quickly as I can.
10. I haven't seen him since he left this place.

Adverb Clause of Time इन Subordinating conjunctions से आरंभ होते हैं—

as, after, as soon as, as long as, as quickly as, before, when, whenever, while, since, till, than, until, the moment/the minute

NOTE (a)—No sooner से आरंभ होनेवाला clause होता है Principal और than से आरंभ होनेवाला होता है Adverb Clause; जैसे—

No sooner had the thief entered than I woke up.

(a) No sooner had the thief entered—Principal Clause

(b) Than I woke up—Adverb Clause

NOTE (b)—As soon as से आरंभ होनेवाला clause होता है Adverb और दूसरा होता है Principal; जैसे—

As soon as he started, it began to rain.

(a) As soon as he started—Adverb Clause

(b) It began to rain—Principal Clause

NOTE (c)—Hardly/Scarcely से आरंभ होनेवाला clause होता है Principal Clause और when से आरंभ होनेवाला होता है Adverb Clause; जैसे—

Hardly/Scarcely had I started when it began to rain.

(a) Hardly (Scarcely) had I started—Principal Clause

(b) When it began to rain—Adverb Clause

NOTE (d)—The moment/the minute से आरंभ होनेवाला clause होता है Adverb Clause, क्योंकि इसका अर्थ होता है—**ज्योंही/जिस समय।**

Exercise 1. *Make meaningful sentences from this table.*

1	2	3	4	5
No sooner	did	the teacher leave the class	when	I climbed a tree.
Scarcely	had	he gone to bed	than	he got a shock.
No sooner	did	a tiger appear	when	pupils began to quarrel.
Hardly	had	he touched the wire	than	he fell asleep.

Exercise 2. *Complete these sentences.*

1	2	3	4	5
Hardly	had	I reached the bus stop	when	....
No sooner	did	the police arrive	than	....
No sooner	did	the sun set	than	....
No sooner	did	we start the play	than	....
Scarcely	had	the train stopped	when	....
Hardly	had	the bus arrived	when	....
No sooner	did	I start writting	than	....

(II) PC + Adverb Clause of Place

कुछ Adverb Clauses से स्थान (place) का बोध होता है और इनकी बनावट इस प्रकार होती है—

PC	+ Adverb Clause (Showing Place)
I play	where they play.
He helps everybody	wherever he goes.

कुछ और वाक्य लें—

1. I live where he lives.
2. He feels happy wherever he lives.
3. Where there is a will there is a way.

ध्यान दें कि Adverb Clause of Place निम्नांकित Subordinating conjunctions से आरंभ होते हैं—

where, wherever

Exercise 3. *Match the sentences under A and B.*

A	B
The air is hot	where there is a sea.
The place is noisy	where there are honest men.
The air is cool	where there is a desert.
The place is good	where there is a bus-stop.

(III) PC + Adverb Clause of Condition

कुछ Adverb Clauses से शर्त (condition) का बोध होता है और इनकी बनावट इस प्रकार होती है—

PC + Adverb Clause [Showing Condition]
Or
Adverb Clause [Showing Condition] + PC

1. If you work hard, you will get success.
2. Unless you work hard, you can't get success.
3. Write to me in case you need money.
4. He has to do the work, whether he likes it or not.
5. Had he gone to Delhi, he would have seen the Red Fort.
6. Were I the Chief Minister, I would abolish examinations.
7. You may stay here so long as you behave well.
8. Whether I get bouquets or brickbats, I will do my duties well.
9. Supposing it rains, what will you do?
10. You may take this book provided you return it to me in a week.

ध्यान दें कि ऐसे Adverb Clauses इन Subordinating conjunctions से आरंभ होते हैं—

if, unless, in case, supposing, provided, provided that, on condition that, so long as, whether … or, whether … or not.

NOTE (a)—Should/Were/Had = If [अगर]

कभी-कभी वाक्य में if का प्रयोग नहीं होता और if (अगर) का अर्थ प्रकट करने के लिए वाक्य के आरंभ में should/were/had का प्रयोग होता है। इसलिए इनसे आरंभ होनेवाले clauses भी Adverb Clauses of Condition होते हैं—

1. Should you like this book, please write to me.

2. Were I a bird, I would fly to her.

3. Had I visited Delhi, I would have seen the Red Fort.

NOTE (b)—कुछ लोग *in case + clause* को Adverb Clause of Purpose मानते हैं।

NOTE (c)—Once = if once [अगर एक बार]

कभी-कभी once का अर्थ होता है—**अगर**। इसलिए ऐसे once से आरंभ होनेवाला clause होता है Adverb Clause of Condition.

1. Once you decide, you should stick to your decision.
2. Once you make a promise, you must keep it.

NOTE (d)—Imperative + and + Imperative/Assertive [अगर]

कुछ वाक्य ऐसे होते हैं जिनका पहला clause होता है Imperative sentence और दूसरा Assertive या Imperative. ऐसे दोनों clauses जोड़े जाते हैं and के द्वारा। इस प्रकार पहले clause (imperative sentence) से शर्त (condition) का भाव व्यक्त होता है, क्योंकि इसका अर्थ होता है—**अगर।** इसलिए ऐसा clause होता है Adverb Clause of Condition और दूसरा clause होता है Principal; जैसे—

1. Give me bullets, and I will drive away the enemy.
2. Spare the rod, and spoil the child.
3. Give me blood, and I will give you freedom.

NOTE (e)—So long as + clause होता है Adverb Clause of Condition, क्योंकि इससे शर्त (condition) का बोध होता है, पर **as long as + clause** होता है Adverb Clause of Time, क्योंकि इससे समय (time) का बोध होता है, जैसे—

1. You may play in the park so long as you don't pluck flowers.
2. You may play in the park as long as you like.

So long as ...... flowers.—Adverb Clause of Condition

As long as ...... like.—Adverb Clause of Time

ध्यान दें कि इन दोनों का अर्थ होता है **जब तक,** पर इनके अर्थ में अंतर है।

Exercise 4. *Complete these sentences.*

1	2	3
If/Unless	I were a king	....
	he had reached on time	....
	I were a bird	....
	I had known him well	....
	I were a minister	....
	he works hard	....
	he were a monkey	....

If/Unless	he had received the telegram	....
	he were a donkey	....
	she were a fairy	....
	man were a god	....
	I were a examiner	....
	he goes to Delhi	....
	she goes to Agra	....

Exercise 5. *Match the clauses under A and B to make meaningful sentences.*

A	B
If you work hard	you can't get a prize.
If you are honest	you can't rise high.
Unless a doctor is sent for	the patient can be saved.
Unless you work hard	you will get success.
If you start early	you can't catch the bus.
Unless you are honest	you will get respect.
If you give this medicine	he can't be cured.
Unless you start at once	you will catch the train.

Exercise 6. *Complete these sentences.*

1. If I had known her in time ....
2. If he had not warned me ....
3. If she had visited Agra ....
4. If I were an examiner ....
5. If I were the President of India ....
6. If she were a fairy ....
7. All the fields would have been swept away ....
8. He would have seen the Red Fort ....
9. She would have died of starvation ....
10. I would have eaten up all the mice ....

Exercise 7. *Complete these sentences.*

1. Unless he gets some help ....
2. Unless his condition improves ....
3. Unless she studies hard ....

4. Unless there is timely rain ....
5. Unless we get good books ....
6. Unless you go to Agra ....
7. Unless you know your culture ....
8. You can't be cured ....
9. You can't rise high ....
10. We can't win the race ....

Exercise 8. *Match the clauses under A and B to make meaningful sentences.*

A	B
Take this medicine	in case electricity fails.
Take this blanket	in case you need money.
Don't eat sweets	in case it is too hot.
Light this lamp	in case you fall ill.
Send me a telegram	in case you feel cold.
Don't go out	in case you suffer from diabetes.

(IV) PC + Adverb Clause of Comparison

कुछ Adverb Clauses से तुलना (comparison) का बोध होता है और इनकी बनावट इस प्रकार की होती है—

(i) PC [with as + adjective/adverb] + Adverb Clause [with as]
(ii) PC [with not + adjective/adverb] + Adverb Clause [with as]
(iii) PC [with comparative adjective/adverb] + Adverb Clause [with than]
(iv) Adverb Clause [with the + comparative] + PC [the + comparative]

1. Mohan is as rich as Sohan.
2. Mohan is not as wise as Sohan.
3. Radha is richer than Mohan.
4. Radha runs faster than Mohan.
5. The more you have, the more you want.
6. The older we grow, the wiser we become.

ध्यान दें कि ऐसे Adverb Clauses इन शब्दों से आरंभ होते हैं—

as, than, the + comparative degree

NOTE—ध्यान दें कि पहला the + comparative clause होता है Adverb Clause और दूसरा होता है Principal Clause.

Exercise 9. *Match the clauses under A and B to make meaningful sentences.*

A	B
This boy is as old	as his father.
The more you love	the more confused they grow.
The nearer an object is	the smaller it looks.
He is as clever	as his friend.
The more she has	the sooner I reach home.
The farther the plane is	the larger it gets.
The faster the train is	the more she wants to have.
The more they thought	the better it is for you.
The longer you work	the thicker it grows.
The longer you boil milk	the worse you feel.

(V) PC + Adverb Clause of Concession

कुछ Adverb Clauses से **यद्यपि-तथापि** (concession) का बोध होता है। इसलिए Adverb Clause में जो कुछ कहा जाता है उसके विपरीत (contrast) Principal Clause में कहा जाता है। ऐसे वाक्यों की बनावट इस प्रकार की होती है—

PC + Adverb Clause [Showing Concession] **Or** **Adverb Clause [Showing Concession] + PC**

1. Though he is poor, he is happy.
2. Although he started late, he caught the bus.
3. Even if/though she deceives me, I won't harm her.
4. Whatever happens, I won't tell lies.
5. Come what may, I must help him.
6. Say what you will, he is honest.
7. For all you say, he is sincere.
8. No matter what I said, nobody cared for me.
9. Fast as he ran, he couldn't win the race.
10. Rich as he is, he is unhappy.
11. However rich he may be, he is not happy.
12. However hard he may work, he can't get success.
13. Wherever he may go, he can't be happy.

14. Much as I like to help you, I am helpless.
15. Considering/admitting that he is very old, he is in good health.
16. He is in good health notwithstanding that he is eighty years of age.
17. It doesn't matter how wise you are, you can't solve this problem.

Adverbs of Concession निम्नांकित शब्दों से आरंभ होते हैं, क्योंकि इनका अर्थ होता है—**यद्यपि**

though, although, even if, even though, for all, no matter, it doesn't matter, come what may, say what you will, however + adjective/adverb, adjective/adverb + as, much + as, whatever (चाहे कुछ भी), wherever (चाहे कहीं भी), considering that, admitting that, notwithstanding that.

Exercise 10. *Match the clauses under A and B to make meaningful sentences.*

A	B
Even if I suffer	he is a miser.
Even if he hates me	she looks beautiful.
However hard he may try	he won't be fined.
Though he is rich	I can't be dishonest.
Black as she is	I will still help him.
Even if he comes late	he won't get success.
Even if he is tired	she won't beg.
Although he is a child	I will go out.
Even if she is poor	he will continue to work.
Even if it is too hot	he is very wise.

(VI) PC + Adverb Clause of Cause

कुछ Adverb Clauses से कारण (cause) का बोध होता है और इनकी बनावट इस प्रकार होती है—

PC + Adverb Clause [Showing Cause]
Or
Adverb Clause [Showing Cause] + PC

1. He missed the train because he started late.
2. As he was ill, he was absent yesterday.
3. Since he is poor, he should he helped.
4. Now that he is dead, we shouldn't criticise him.
5. I am glad that he has passed.
6. I am sorry that she has failed.

7. I am glad in that you agree with me now.

8. He needn't be punished in as much as he offers an apology.

ध्यान दें कि ऐसे Adverb Clause of Causes इन शब्दों से आरंभ होते हैं—

as, because, since, now that, considering that, in that, in as much as, seeing that, noun + that, adjective + that

NOTE—ऐसा adjective + that + clause तब Adverb Clause होता है जब adjective से मनोभाव (emotion) का बोध होता है—

I am glad/that he passed.

याद रखें—

adjective [expressing emotion] + that + clause = Adverb Clause of Cause.

NOTE—जब **Interrogative sentence** या **Negative Exclamatory sentence** में *noun + that + clause* आता है, तब वह (that + clause) Adverb Clause होता है। क्यों? इसलिए कि इससे कारण (cause) का भाव व्यक्त होता है, जैसे—

1. Am I a *child that* you give me poppins?
2. I am not a *child that* you give me poppins.
3. Am I a *fool that* you expect me to believe you?
4. I am not a *fool that* you expect me to believe you.

Exercise 11. *Match the clauses under A and B to make meaningful sentences.*

A	B
As it was raining	I gave him some food.
Now that he offers an apology	he must be punished.
I am glad	that she is very ill.
Since he was hungry	he reached late.
As he committed a serious mistake	he should be excused.
I am sorry	that you have won a prize.

(VII) PC + Adverb Clause of Purpose

कुछ Adverb Clauses से उद्देश्य (purpose) का बोध होता है और इनकी बनावट इस प्रकार होती है—

PC	+ Adverb Clause [Expressing Purpose]
He works hard	that he may pass.
She runs fast	so that she may win the race.
Keep a diary	so that you may not forget even trifles.
Start early	lest you should miss the bus.

1. We work that/so that/in order that we may be happy.
2. He died that/so that/in order that man might learn a lesson.
3. Note down the point, lest you should forget it.

ध्यान दें कि ऐसे Adverb Clauses इन शब्दों से आरंभ होते हैं—

that, so that, in order that, lest

Exercise 12. *Match the clauses under A and B to make meaningful sentences.*

A	B
They fought hard	so that you may not forget it.
Send for a doctor	so that he may remember your case.
I started early	so that I may learn English.
Send him a letter	so that the patient may be saved.
Note it down	so that they might win.
I read this book	so that I might catch the bus.

(VIII) PC + Adverb Clause of Result/Consequence

कुछ Adverb Clauses से कार्य होने के परिणाम/फल (result/consequence) का बोध होता है और Principal Clauses से कारण (cause) का भाव व्यक्त होता है। ऐसे वाक्यों की बनावट इस प्रकार होती है—

(i) PC [with so + adjective/adverb] **(ii) PC [with such + noun]**	**+ Adverb Clause [with that]** **+ Adverb Clause [with that]**
So heavy is the box	that I can't lift it.
The box is so heavy	that I can't lift it.
He is so intelligent	that he solves problems quickly.
I worked so hard	that I felt tired.
He gave such a talk	that none liked it.

कुछ और वाक्य लें—

1. She is so beautiful that she attracts everybody.
2. He is so great that he forgives even his enemies.
3. The door is so high that the baby can't reach it.
4. She ran so fast that she won the race.

5. It rained so heavily that houses were swept away.

6. He is not such a man that he will tell lies.

ध्यान दें कि ऐसे Adverb Clauses आरंभ होते हैं that से और Principal Clause में so या such आता है। इस प्रकार, वाक्य में so ... that/such ... that का प्रयोग होता है।

Exercise 13. *Complete these sentences by stating result, as in the example.*

(A) The sun is very bright. (B) We can't look at it.

(A) The sum is very difficult. (B) ....

(A) The ceiling is very high. (B) ....

(A) This place is very dirty. (B) ....

(A) He spoke very clearly. (B) ....

(A) The rope is very strong. (B) ....

(A) She is very poor. (B) ....

(A) The car stopped very suddenly. (B) ....

(A) The thief came very quickly. (B) ....

Exercise 14. *Join these sentences by using a clause of result as in the example.*

She sings very sweetly. Everybody likes her songs.

= She sings so sweetly that everybody likes her songs.

1. She played very well. She won the match.
2. He is very rich. He can buy a car.
3. She is very weak. She can't run fast.
4. He is very wise. He can solve this problem.
5. The hall is very big. It can accommodate hundreds of people.
6. Her condition is extremely pitiable. You can hardly imagine it.
7. North Pole is unbearably cold. Water is frozen there.
8. The earthquake was very severe. Houses were reduced to dust.
9. He is a fool. He can't understand me.
10. He is a big man. He can help us all.

NOTE—ध्यान दें कि इन्हें जोड़ने पर—

(i) **adverb + adverb** के बदले **so + adverb** होता है; जैसे—

very sweetly = so sweetly

(ii) **adverb + adjective** के बदले **so + adjective** आता है; जैसे—

very poor = so poor

(iii) **noun or adjective + noun** के बदले **such + noun or such + adjective + noun** का प्रयोग होता है; जैसे—

man = such a man. a big man = such a big man.

(iv) पूरे वाक्य की बनावट इस प्रकार हो जाती है—

PC [subject + verb + so + adjective/adverb] Or PC [subject + verb + such + noun]	+ that + clause + that + clause
He ran so fast	that I couldn't catch him.
She is so poor	that she can't buy a pen.
He is such a rich man	that he can buy a car.

Exercise 15. *State the result in B for the cause in A.*

A. This bag is very small. B. ....
A. This rod is very strong. B. ....
A. This flower is very beautiful. B. ....
A. He is speaking very loudly. B. ....
A. She is running very fast. B. ....
A. The palm-tree is very tall. B. ....
A. This book is very easy. B. ....

Exercise 16. *Match the clauses under A and B to make meaningful sentences.*

A	B
This dress is so costly	that he can't tell lies.
This house is so small	that she fell ill.
He is so gentle	that everybody likes it.
He is so honest	that a poor person can't buy it.
She worked so hard	that he can't harm anybody.
This book is so good	that a big family can't live in it.

(IX) PC + Adverb Clause of Manner

कुछ Adverb Clauses से कार्य करने की रीति/ढंग (manner) का बोध होता है। ऐसे वाक्यों की बनावट इस प्रकार होती है—

PC	+ Adverb Clause [Expressing Supposition]
He talked	as if he were mad.
He walks	as though he were drunk.
It appeared	as if the night wouldn't end.
Do the experiment	as I have explained.

ध्यान दें कि ऐसे Adverb clauses आरंभ होते हैं *as, as if/as though* से।

Exercise 17. *Rewrite these sentences as in the example.*

He talked as if he were mad.

He appeared to be mad but he wasn't so.

1. It appeared as if the forest would never end.
2. He talked as though he were a parrot.
3. The house looked as if it were haunted.
4. The platform looked as though it were a fish market.
5. She cried as if she were in great trouble.

Exercise 18. *Match the clauses under A and B to make meaningful sentences.*

A	B
She looks	as if it would rain.
She sings	as if he had seen a ghost.
The rope looked	as if he were mad.
He memorises	as if it were fish.
It looks	as though she were a nightingale.
He behaved	as if it were a snake.
He laughed	as if she were a fairy.
It tastes	as if he were a parrot.

Exercise 19. *Make sentences of these patterns.*

1. PC + Adverb Clause [result]
2. PC + Adverb Clause [cause]
3. PC + Adverb Clause [condition]
4. PC + Adverb Clause [supposition]
5. PC + Adverb Clause [time]
6. PC + Adverb Clause [concession]
7. PC + Adverb Clause [unless + clause]
8. PC + Adverb Clause [since + clause]
9. PC + Adverb Clause [however + clause]
10. PC + Adverb Clause [in case + clause]

Exercise 20. *Pick out Adverb Clauses.*

1. I play where he plays.
2. If you think I am telling lies you are mistaken.
3. He died because the doctor didn't reach in time.

4. Ten years have passed since he came over here.
5. Hardly had I started when it began to rain.
6. Black as she is she is beautiful.
7. It apeared as if the forest would never end.
8. Had he run fast he would have won a prize.

How to Find Out Noun Clauses

Noun Clauses निम्नांकित शब्दों से आरंभ होते हैं—

who, which, what, when, where, whether, why, if, how, that

(I) PC + Noun Clause [As Object]

Noun Clause, एक Noun के समान, Transitive Verb या Preposition के Object (कर्म) के रूप में आता है। ऐसे वाक्यों की बनावट होती है—

(i) PC [with Transitive Verb] **(ii) PC [with Preposition]**	**+ Noun Clause [As Object]** **+ Noun Clause [As Object]**
I think	that he is poor.
I know	that she is rich.
It depends on	what your plan is.

ध्यान दें कि—

Rule I. Who/Which आदि से आरंभ होनेवाला clause NC तब होता है जब यह PC में आए हुए Transitive Verb या Preposition का Object होता है।

Rule II. Who/Which/That आदि का अर्थ हिन्दी में ऐसा शब्द होता है, जो **क** से आरंभ होता है; जैसे—

कि, कौन, क्या, कब, कहाँ

इन वाक्यों को देखें—

1. I don't know/who has stolen my pen. **who = कौन**
2. I don't know/which book he wants. **which = कौन**
3. I don't follow/what you say. **what = क्या**
4. Tell me/where he lives. **where = कहाँ**
5. Inform me/when he will come. **when = कब**
6. I don't know/if he is ill. **if = कि**
7. I don't know/whether she is poor. **whether = कि**
8. Tell me/how you have come. **how = कैसे**

9. I find/that he is not honest. **that = कि**

10. I will judge you by/what you do. **what = क्या**

11. I now feel/that it is wrong. **that = कि**

12. I still remember/that he helped me. **that = कि**

इन वाक्यों में NC एक Object का काम करता है। किसका Object? PC में आए हुए Transitive Verb या Preposition का।

NOTE—कभी-कभी Transitive Verb के बाद that छिपा रहता है। फिर भी, ऐसे Verb के बाद आनेवाला clause होता है NC, क्योंकि यह Object का काम करता है। ध्यान दें कि अनुवाद करने पर छिपे हुए that के लिए भी **कि** का प्रयोग होता है; जैसे—

1. I think/he is honest. [मैं समझता हूँ **कि** वह ईमानदार है।]
2. I hope/you are well. [मैं आशा करता हूँ **कि** आप स्वस्थ हैं।]

यहाँ he is honest और you are well हैं Noun Clauses. ऐसे clauses को PC न समझ बैठें।

Exercise 21. *Match the words to make meaningful sentences.*

1	2	3
I know	whether	my father is honest.
Tell me	when	the hospital is.
I hope	that	I will fail.
I asked him	that	he was ill.
Inform me	where	you will come.
I think	that	I will pass.
I can't rely on	how	he says.
She asked him	who	he had laughed.
I don't know	what	he escaped.
I don't know	why	stole my pen.

(II) Noun Clause [Subject] + PC

Noun Clause, एक Noun के समान, Subject का कार्य करता है। ऐसे वाक्यों की बनावट इस प्रकार की होती है—

Noun Clause	+ PC [Verb + Other Words]
What he says	is right.
That he is honest	is known to all.
Why he killed her	is a mystery.

ध्यान दें—

Rule I. Who/Which/That आदि से आरंभ होनेवाला clause NC तब होता है जब यह PC में आए हुए verb का subject होता है।

Rule II. Who/Which आदि का अर्थ हिंदी में ऐसा शब्द होता है जो **क** से आरंभ होता है।

Rule III. NC के बाद PC का Verb आता है और Verb से संबंधित अन्य शब्द। इस प्रकार, ये सभी शब्द (Verb तथा अन्य शब्द) मिलकर PC की रचना करते हैं।

इन वाक्यों को देखें—

1. What he spoke/was not heard. **what = क्या**
2. That the earth is round/is known to all. **that = कि**
3. When he will come/is uncertain. **that = कब**
4. How he came here/is a mystery. **how = कैसे**
5. Where she lives/is not known. **where = कहाँ**

ध्यान दें कि ऐसे वाक्यों में NC एक Subject का काम करता है। किसका Subject? PC में आए हुए Verb का।

यह भी ध्यान दें कि PC का अपना अलग Subject नहीं होता। इसका Subject होता है NC. इसलिए ऐसे-ऐसे वाक्य न गढ़ें—

1. That the earth is round it is known to all.
2. What he spoke it was not heard.

Exercise 22. *Complete these sentences.*

Noun Clause	**+ Principal Clause**
That the earth is flat	....
What I should do	....
Where he is hiding	....
Why she is angry	....
How he entered the house	....
What he has written	....

(III) PC + Noun Clause [as Component]

Noun Clause, एक Noun के समान, पूरक (complement) का कार्य करता है। ऐसे वाक्यों की बनावट इस प्रकार होती है—

Principal Clause	**+ Noun Clause [Component]**
My opinion is	that he is clever.
I am sure	that she is mad.
This is	how he became poor.
This is	what we like.
The problem is	how it should be done.

ध्यान दें—

Rule I. Who/Which/That आदि से आरंभ होनेवाला clause NC तब होता है जब यह PC में आए हुए Intransitive Verb का पूरक (complement) होता है।

Rule II. Who/Which आदि का अर्थ हिंदी में ऐसा शब्द होता है जो **क** से आरंभ होता है।

इन वाक्यों को लें—

1. My opinion is/that he is poor. **that = कि**
2. The mystery is/how he came here. **how = कैसे**
3. The mystery is/who killed her. **who = कौन**
4. The question is/whether he will return. **whether = कि**
5. The problem is/what should be done. **what = क्या**
6. I am sure/he will pass. **that = कि**
7. I am afraid/she will fall ill. **that = कि**

ध्यान दें कि ऐसे वाक्यों में NC एक पूरक (complement) का कार्य करता है। किसका complement? PC में आये हुए Intransitive Verb का। ऐसा complement क्यों आता है? उत्तर है—Intransitive Verb के अर्थ को पूरा (complete) करने के लिए।

NOTE—कभी-कभी Intransitive Verb के बाद that का प्रयोग नहीं होता। फिर भी, ऐसे verb के बाद आनेवाला clause होता है NC. ध्यान दें कि that के लुप्त रहने पर भी अनुवाद में **कि** का प्रयोग अवश्य होता है; जैसे—

1. It seems/he is poor. [लगता है **कि** वह गरीब है।]
2. I am afraid/she will fail. [मुझे आशंका है **कि** वह फेल करेगी।]
3. I am sure/he will pass. [मुझे विश्वास है **कि** वह पास करेगा।]

यहाँ he is poor, she will fail और he will pass—तीनों ही Noun Clauses हैं।

Exercise 23. *Complete these sentences.*

Principal Clause	**+ Noun Clause [Complement]**
This is	....
The question is	....
The problem is	....
The fact is	....
The pity is	....
The mystery is	....
I am afraid	....
I am doubtful	....

(IV) PC + Noun Clause [In Apposition]

Noun Clause, एक Noun के समान, apposition का कार्य करता है, अर्थात Noun की व्याख्या करके उसे स्पष्ट करता है। ऐसे वाक्यों की बनावट इस प्रकार होती है—

PC [With A Noun]	+ NC [In Apposition]
I haven't heard the news	that he has resigned.
I don't believe in the principle	that might is right.
I hold the view	that she is guilty.
I haven't heard the rumour	that he has been arrested.

ध्यान दें—

Rule I. ऐसा NC आरंभ होता है That से

Rule II. ऐसा NC आता है PC में आए हुए Noun के बाद और यह उस noun की व्याख्या करके उसे स्पष्ट करता है।

Rule III. ऐसे That का अर्थ होता है **कि**

NOTE—ऐसा NC सटा रहता है Noun से जैसे—

the **news that ...**, the **principle that ...**

(V) Noun + NC [in apposition] + PC

ऐसे वाक्यों की बनावट इस प्रकार की होती है—

Noun	+ NC [In Apposition]	+ PC
The fact	that wine is harmful	is known to all.
The news	that he has resigned	is correct.
The principle	that might is right	is old.
The view	that she is guilty	is wrong.
The rumour	that he has been arrested	is baseless.

ध्यान दें—

Rule I. ऐसा NC [in apposition] आरंभ होता है that से

Rule II. ऐसा NC आता है एक Noun के बाद और यह उस Noun की व्याख्या करता है; जैसे—

The **news that** ... resigned.

Rule III. ऐसे that का अर्थ होता है **कि**

Rule IV. ऐसे वाक्यों में NC के पहले आनेवाला noun PC का subject होता है और NC के बाद आनेवाला verb होता है PC का verb. इस प्रकार, noun और verb आदि शब्द मिलकर PC की रचना करते हैं; जैसे—

The news/that he has resigned/is correct.

(a) The news is correct—PC

(b) That he has resigned—NC [in apposition to **news**].

NOTE—ऐसे वाक्यों की रचना करते समय NC को उपयुक्त noun के साथ जोड़ना चाहिए; जैसे—

1. The **rumour that** he has been arrested is baseless.
2. The **belief that** God is merciful is known to all.

ऐसे NC को अनुपयुक्त noun के साथ जोड़ने पर वाक्य अर्थहीन हो जाता है, इसलिए इस प्रकार के वाक्य न लिखें—

1. The **news that** God is merciful is known to all.
2. The **rumour that** might is right is old.

(VI) PC + NC [In Apposition to It]

ऐसे वाक्यों की बनावट इस प्रकार की होती है—

PC [It + is + noun/adjective]	**+ NC [In Apposition to it]**
It is sure	that he will pass.
It is evident	that he is a criminal.
It is a pity	that she is not tall.
It is a mystery	how he came here.
It is a mystery	where she is living.
It so happened	that the steam got stuck.

ध्यान दें—

Rule I. ऐसा NC आरंभ होता है that, how, where आदि से

Rule II. ऐसे that/how आदि का अर्थ हिंदी में ऐसा शब्द होता है जो **क** से आरंभ होता है।

Rule III. ऐसा NC व्याख्या करता है PC में आए हुए It की, अर्थात PC के subject की और इस प्रश्न का उत्तर देता है—What?

इन वाक्यों को लें—

1. It is sure. What is sure? He will pass.
2. It is evident. What is evident? He is a criminal.

कुछ और वाक्य लें—

1. It is certain that he will win a prize.
2. It is strange that she is so unkind.
3. It is sad that she is very ill.
4. It is a tragedy that he is very poor.

5. It is a mystery what he always does.
6. It is a mystery how the thief escaped.

NOTE—ऐसे Noun Clause (In apposition) को Noun Clause (as subject) में आसानी से बदला जा सकता है—

1. It is certain/that he will win a prize.
   = That he will win a prize/is certain.
2. It is strange/that she is so unkind.
   = That she is so unkind/is strange.

ऐसे वाक्यों की बनावट हो जाती है—

NC (As Subject)	+ PC (Verb + Other Words)
That he will win a prize	is certain.
That she is so unkind	is strange.

ध्यान दें—

Rule I. PC के It (subject) का लोप हो जाता है।

Rule II. PC का स्थान NC के बाद रहता है।

NOTE—ऐसे वाक्यों के साथ उपयुक्त कथन (statement) का प्रयोग करना चाहिए जिससे कार्य होने के कारण (cause) का बोध हो। उपयुक्त कथन का पता why के द्वारा प्रश्न करने पर आसानी से चल जाता है। इन वाक्यों को देखें—

1. (a) It is certain that he will win a prize. **Why?**
   (b) He is working very hard.
2. (a) It is likely that it will rain today. **Why?**
   (b) The clouds look very black.
3. (a) It is possible that she will return tomorrow. **Why?**
   (b) A letter from her has just been received.

Exercise 24. *Change these Noun Clauses in apposition into Noun Clauses as subject. One example is done for you.*

It is evident that he is guilty.

= That he is guilty is evident.

1. It is known to all that she is gentle.
2. It is a pity that he is too tall.
3. It is unfortunate that he betrayed me.
4. It is likely that he will return tomorrow.
5. It is doubtful that she will pass this time.

Exercise 25. *Make meaningful sentences from this table.*

Noun	NC (In Apposition)	+ PC
The news	that God is merciful	is false.
The rumour	that vitamins are essential for health	is baseless.
The argument	that the earth is flat	is strong.
The principle	that milk is the best food	is known to everybody.
The view	that he is dead	is true.
The fact	that he has been arrested	is known to all.
The remark	that bad men prosper	is harmful.
The fact	that all men are equal	is a noble one.
The theory	that he is innocent	is wrong.
The belief	that all men are dishonest	is hasty.

Exercise 26. *Pick out Noun Clauses.*

1. It is a pity that he has failed.
2. I am not sure if he is ill.
3. I do not know whether he is alive.
4. It is true that he is very poor.
5. I do not know where he lives.
6. What he says is not correct.
7. I think he will come soon.
8. I do not know who is lying here.
9. Do you know why he is absent today?
10. It is a fact that he is poor.

Exercise 27. *Match the words from this table to make meaningful sentences.*

1	2	3
This is	that	he became rich.
Tell me	when	the bus-stop is.
I don't know	why	you will reach here.
Write to me	where	he was absent.
I think	how	she is honest.

Exercise 28. *Complete these sentences with Noun Clauses.*

1. I can't say where …… .

2. It is true that ....
3. I don't know which ....
4. I am not sure that ....
5. The difficulty is that ....
6. My argument is that ....
7. It is necessary that ....
8. I don't know when ....

Exercise 29. *Make sentences of these patterns.*

(i) Principal clause + NC [as object to a Verb].
(ii) Noun clause [as subject] + Principal Clause.
(iii) Principal clause + NC [as complement to a Verb].
(iv) Principal clause + NC [as apposition to a Noun].
(v) Principal clause + NC [as object to a Preposition].
(vi) Principal clause + NC [that + clause].
(vii) Principal clause + NC [what + clause].
(viii) Principal clause + NC [as apposition to a Noun].

Exercise 30. *Match the clauses under A and B to make meaningful sentences.*

A	B
What he did	he will fail.
I am sure	is known to all.
It so happened	that he will win the race.
Where he lives	who will bell the cat.
I am afraid	was not proper.
That she is honest	she will return today.
It is certain	that he fell into a well.
The question is	a mystery.

How to Find Out Adjective Clauses

Adjective Clauses इन शब्दों से आरंभ होते हैं—

that, who, which, why, when, where, how

(I) PC [With Noun] + Adjective Clause

Adjective Clause, एक Adjective के समान, किसी noun की विशेषता बताता है। ऐसे वाक्यों की बनावट इस प्रकार की होती है—

PC [With Noun]	+ Adjective Clause
I know the girl	who is dancing.
I have read the book	that is lying here.
I don't know the place	where he lives.
I don't know the time	when she will return.

ध्यान दें—

Rule I. Who/Which/That आदि से आरंभ होनेवाला clause Adjective Clause तब होता है जब यह PC में आये हुए Noun की विशेषता बताता है।

Rule II. ऐसे Noun और Adjective Clause के बीच कॉमा नहीं रहता।

Rule III. Who/Which/That आदि का अर्थ हिंदी में ऐसा शब्द होता है जो **ज** से आरंभ होता है; जैसे—

जो, जैसा, जब, जहाँ

इन वाक्यों को लें—

1. I don't know the man/**who** is standing thee. **who = जो**
2. I like the food/**that** is simple. **that = जो**
3. I know the method/**how** I should do it. **how = जैसे**
4. I don't know the reason/**why** he is absent. **why = जो**
5. He doesn't know the place/**where** he was born. **where = जहाँ**
6. He doesn't know the time/**when** he will reach. **when = जब**

Exercise 31. *Match the clauses under A and B to make meaningful sentences.*

A	B
I don't know the date	who has long hair.
I haven't read the book	where he is staying.
I don't know the reason	when she will be married.
I don't know the boy	how a language is taught.
I don't know the hotel	that is in your hand.
He doesn't know the method	why she was absent.

(II) Noun + Adjective Clause + PC

कुछ वाक्यों की बनावट ऐसी होती है—

Noun	+ Adjective Clause	+ PC [Verb + Other Words]
The boy	who is here	is intelligent.
The book	that is here	is useful.

The place	where he was born	is known to all.
The time	when he will come	is uncertain.
The reason	why she was absent	is not known.

ध्यान दें—

Rule I. Who/Which/That आदि से आरंभ होनेवाला clause Adjective Clause तब होता है जब यह Noun के बाद आता है और उस Noun की विशेषता बताता है।

Rule II. Who/Which आदि का अर्थ हिंदी में ऐसा शब्द होता है जो **ज** से आरंभ होता है।

Rule III. Adjective Clause के पहले आनेवाला Noun/Pronoun होता है PC का Subject और Adjective Clause के बाद आनेवाला Verb होता है PC का Verb. इस प्रकार, Subject और Verb तथा अन्य शब्द मिलकर PC की रचना करते हैं; जैसे—

The boy/who is here/is intelligent.

(a) The boy is intelligent—Principal Clause

(b) Who is here—Adjective Clause

(III) Noun + Comma + Who/Which + Clause

यदि Noun के बाद comma रहे और इसके बाद who/which आए, तो वह (who/which + clause) होता है Principal Clause, Adjective Clause नहीं। क्यों? इसलिए कि ऐसा who/which उस Noun को qualify या define नहीं करता। यही कारण है कि ऐसे who/which + clause को Non-defining Clause या Nonrestrictive Clause कहा जाता है।

ऐसे वाक्यों की बनावट इस प्रकार होती है—

Noun	**+ Comma**	**+ Who/Which + Clause**	**+ PC [Verb + Other Words]**
My father	,	who lives in London	is returning today.
Pt Nehru	,	who was born in a rich family	suffered a lot for the country.
Dr Rajendra Prasad	,	who was the President of India	was a very simple man.
My watch	,	which was damaged	is now useless.

इस प्रकार के वाक्यों में comma के बाद आनेवाला *who/which + clause* होता है Principal Clause [अर्थात Coordinate to PC], Adjective Clause नहीं।

NOTE—Adjective Clauses की रचना इस प्रकार होती है—

1. **Present Participle + noun** [verb + ing + noun]

   a running train = a train which is running

   a flying bird = a bird which is flying

   a dazzling light = a light that is dazzling

2. **Past Participle + noun** [verb + ed/en + noun]

   a faded flower = a flower which has faded

   a broken chair = a chair that is broken

3. **Noun + preposition + noun**

   a boy with long hair = a boy who has long hair

   a chair in the corner = a chair that is in the corner

(IV) Noun + Adjective Clause [Without Conjunction] + PC

कुछ वाक्यों की बनावट इस प्रकार की होती है—

Noun	**+ Adjective Clause [Without Conjunction]**	**+ Principal Clause [Verb + Other + Words]**
The food	you eat	is not pure.
The book	I bought	is very useful.
The day	he was married	was a holiday.
The boy	you help	is my brother.

ध्यान दें—

Rule I. ऐसा Adjective Clause किसी Noun के बाद आता है और उसकी विशेषता बताता है।

Rule II. ऐसा Adjective Clause किसी Conjunction से आरंभ नहीं होता, क्योंकि वह छिपा रहता है। वह क्यों छिपा रहता है? इसलिए कि ऐसा Conjunction आता है Object के रूप में। किसका Object? उत्तर है Adjective Clause में आए हुए Transitive Verb का; जैसे—

1. The food/you eat/is not pure.
2. The boy/you help/is my brother.

यहाँ पहले वाक्य में that/which छिपा हुआ है। क्यों? इसलिए कि यह eat का object है। इसी प्रकार दूसरे वाक्य में who/whom छिपा हुआ है, क्योंकि यह help का object है।

Rule III. Which/Who/Whom/That आदि के छिपे रहने पर भी अनुवाद करने पर इसका अर्थ हिन्दी में ऐसा शब्द होता है जो **ज** से आरंभ होता है; जैसे—

1. The food/you eat/is not pure. [वह भोजन **जो** आप खाते हैं, शुद्ध नहीं है।]
2. The boy/you help/is my brother. [वह लड़का **जिसकी** आप मदद करते हैं, मेरा भाई है।]

Rule IV. Adjective Clause के पहले आनेवाला Noun होता है PC का Subject और Adjective Clause के बाद आनेवाला Verb होता है PC का Verb. इस प्रकार, Subject तथा Verb और अन्य संबंधित शब्द मिलकर PC की रचना करते हैं—

The food/you eat/is not pure.

(a) The food is not pure—PC

(b) You eat—Adjective Clause

(V) Noun + Adjective Clause [Without Conjunction] + Preposition + PC

कुछ वाक्यों की बनावट ऐसी होती है—

Noun	+ Adjective Clause [Without Conjunction] + Preposition	+ PC
The room	he lives in	is small.
The pen	I write with	is red.
The air	you breathe in	is not pure.
The chair	he sits on	is weak.
The man	you are speaking to	is my friend.
The star	you are looking at	is very bright.
The train	you are travelling by	is very fast.

ध्यान दें—

Rule I. ऐसा Adjective Clause किसी Noun के बाद आता है और उसकी विशेषता बताता है।

Rule II. ऐसा Adjective Clause किसी Conjunction से आरंभ नहीं होता, क्योंकि वह छिपा रहता है। वह क्यों छिपा रहता है? इसलिए कि ऐसा Conjunction आता है एक Object के रूप में। किसका Object? उत्तर है—Adjective Clause में आए हुए Preposition का; जैसे—

The room he lives in is small.

यहाँ which छिपा हुआ है, क्योंकि यह Preposition (in) का Object है। यह वाक्य वास्तव में ऐसा है—

The room **in which** he lives is small.

यहाँ which छिप गया है और Preposition चला गया है Adjective Clause के अंत में। जब Preposition + Conjunction आता है तब—

(a) Conjunction का लोप हो जाता है।

(b) Preposition का स्थान बदल जाता है और वह Adjective Clause के अंत में चला जाता है।

इन वाक्यों को लें—

1. The chair **on which** he sits is weak.

   = The chair he sits **on** is weak.

2. The man **to whom** you are speaking is my friend.

   = The man you are speaking **to** is my friend.

3. The star **at which** you are looking is very bright.

   = The star you are looking **at** is very bright.

Rule III. Which/Whom आदि के छिपे रहने पर भी अनुवाद करने पर इसका अर्थ हिंदी में ऐसा शब्द होता है जो **ज** से आरंभ होता है; जैसे—

1. The room he lives in is small.

   [वह कोठरी **जिसमें** वह रहता है, छोटी है।]

2. The star you are looking at is bright.

   [वह तारा **जिसको** आप देख रहे हैं, चमकीला है।]

Rule IV. Adjective Clause के पहले आनेवाला Noun होता है PC का Subject और Adjective Clause के बाद आनेवाला Verb होता है PC का Verb. इस प्रकार, Subject और Verb मिलकर PC की रचना करते हैं।

(VI) PC [With Noun] + Adjective Clause [Without Conjunction]

कुछ वाक्यों की बनावट इस प्रकार की होती है—

PC [With Noun]	+ Adjective Clause [Without Conjunction]
I don't like the food	she prepares.
I like the coffee	you make.
I like the book	he has written.
I don't know the time	she will reach.

ध्यान दें—

Rule I. ऐसा Adjective आता है एक Noun के बाद जो PC में प्रयुक्त होता है और उस Noun की विशेषता बताता है।

Rule II. ऐसा Adjective Clause किसी Conjunction से आरंभ नहीं होता। क्यों? इसलिए कि यह Object के रूप में आता है। किसका Object? उत्तर है—Adjective Clause के Transitive Verb का; जैसे—

I don't like the food/she prepares.

यहाँ which she prepares के बदले she prepares का प्रयोग हुआ है। यहाँ which क्यों छिप गया है? इसका कारण यह है कि which है Transitive Verb (prepares) का Object. ध्यान दें कि जब who/which, whom/that + transitive verb आता है, तब who/which आदि का लोप हो जाता है।

Rule III. Who/Whom/Which आदि के छिपे रहने पर भी अनुवाद करने पर इसका अर्थ हिन्दी में ऐसा शब्द होता है जो **ज** से आरंभ होता है; जैसे—

1. I like the coffee you make.

   [मैं वह कॉफी पसंद करता हूँ **जो** तुम बनाते हो।]

2. I don't like the food she prepares.

   [मैं वह भोजन पसंद नहीं करता **जो** वह तैयार करती है।]

(VII) PC [With Noun] + Adjective Clause [Without Conjunction] + Preposition

कुछ वाक्यों की बनावट ऐसी होती है—

PC [With Noun]	+ Adjective Clause [Without Conjunction] + Proposition
I haven't seen the house	she lives in.
I have seen the well	he fell into.
This is the pen	I write with.

This is the chair	he sits on.
That is the bus	he will go by.
This is the book	I talked about.

ध्यान दें—

Rule I. ऐसा Adjective Clause आता है PC में प्रयुक्त Noun के बाद और यह उस Noun की विशेषता बताता है।

Rule II. ऐसा Adjective Clause किसी Conjunction से आरंभ नहीं होता। क्यों? इसलिए कि यह Object होता है Adjective Clause में प्रयुक्त Preposition का; जैसे—

I haven't seen the house/she lives in.

यहाँ which छिप गया है, क्योंकि यह Preposition (in) का Object है। यह वाक्य वास्तव में इस प्रकार का है—

I haven't seen the house **in which** she lives.

यहाँ which का लोप हो गया है और Preposition चला गया है Adjective Clause के अंत में। ऐसे वाक्यों में—

(a) Conjunction छिप जाता है।

(b) Preposition आता है Adjective Clause के अंत में।

Rule III. Which, Whom आदि के छिप जाने पर भी अनुवाद करने पर इसका अर्थ हिंदी में ऐसा शब्द होता है जो **ज** से आरंभ होता है; जैसे—

1. I haven't seen the house/she lives in.
   [मैंने वह घर नहीं देखा **जिसमें** वह रहती है।]
2. This is the pen/I write with.
   [यह वही कलम है **जिससे** मैं लिखता हूँ।]

(VIII) PC + Adjective Clause [With As/But]

कुछ वाक्यों की बनावट इस प्रकार की होती है—

PC	+ Adjective Clause [With As/But]
That is not such a pen	as I should buy.
He is not such a man	as I should help.
This is the same pen	as I have got.
There is no teacher	but loves good students.
There is no one	but likes this book.

ध्यान दें—

Rule I. As/But से आरंभ होनेवाला clause Adjective Clause तब होता है जब यह PC में प्रयुक्त Noun के बाद आता है और उस Noun की विशेषता बताता है।

Rule II. As का प्रयोग such या the same के बाद होता है—

Such/the same + noun + adjective clause

Rule III. As का अर्थ **जो** होता है, जैसाकि **who/that/which** का होता है।

Rule IV. But का अर्थ होता है—**who not** [जो नहीं]।

इन वाक्यों को देखें—

1. This is not such a pen/as I should buy. [यह ऐसी कलम नहीं है **जो** मुझे खरीदनी चाहिए।]
2. There is no one/**but** likes this book. [ऐसा कोई नहीं है **जो** इस किताब को पसंद नहीं करे।]

Exercise 32. *Make meaningful sentences from this table.*

PC	+ Adjective Clause + Preposition
This is the river.	he belongs to
This is the school	she lives in
This is the dagger	he fell into
This is the family	he was drowned in
This is the plane	we all read at
That is the house	he was killed with
This is the man	I get water from
That is the person	I stand for
That is the ditch	he will travel by
This is the tape	I want to speak to
This is the well	he was hanged by
This is the principle	I always believe in
This is the lady	I measure with
This is the paper	I told you about
This is the book	I write on

Exercise 33. *Pick out Adjective Clauses.*

1. There is no teacher but loves good students.
2. The man who wrote this letter is coming today.
3. The book I bought yesterday is a novel.
4. The man I met on the road is honest.
5. The eggs I bought yesterday are not good.
6. There is a shop here that sells pictures.

7. This is the place where he died.
8. The lady who is here is my aunt.
9. The bed I sleep on is hard.
10. The man she married is old.

Exercise 34. *Complete the following sentences.*

1. The people ...... live in glass-houses shouldn't throw stones.
2. What's the name of the man ...... son has run away?
3. Where is the man ...... buys and sells cars?
4. This is the book ...... I bought last month.
5. The pen ...... is lying on the table is not mine.

Exercise 35. *Make sentence of these patterns.*

(i) Principal clause + Adjective clause [who + clause].
(ii) Principal clause + Adjective clause [that + clause].
(iii) Principal clause + Adjective clause [whom + clause].
(iv) Principal clause + Adjective clause [where + clause].
(v) Noun + who + verb + verb + other words.
(vi) Noun + that + verb + verb + other words.
(vii) Noun + where + Subject + verb + verb + other words.
(viii) Noun + whom + Subject + verb + verb + other words.
(ix) Principal clause + Adjective clause [with **but**].
(x) Principal clause + Adjective clause [**that/which** understood].
(xi) Principal clause + Adjective clause + Preposition.

More Hints on Principal and Subordinate Clauses

इन नियमों की मदद से आप Principal और Subordinate Clauses को पहचान लेंगे और उनका नामकरण भी कर लेंगे, लेकिन Analysis पर विजय प्राप्त करने के लिए इतना ही काफी नहीं। इसके लिए Relative Adverbs (when and where) और Relative Pronouns (who and which) पर अधिकार प्राप्त करना होगा, क्योंकि इनसे शुरू होनेवाले clauses Principal, Adverbial, Adjective और Noun—चारों ही हो सकते हैं। इनकी चर्चा इस पुस्तक में जहाँ-तहाँ हुई है, पर विस्तारपूर्वक नहीं। इसलिए हम यहाँ इन्हें एक-एक कर लें और विचार करें।

Rule I. समयसूचक Noun + Comma + When

यदि समयसूचक Noun के बाद Comma रहे और उसके बाद When का प्रयोग हो, तो वह (when-clause) Principal Clause (Principal Clause का Coordinate) होता है, Adjective या Adverb Clause नहीं; जैसे—

I stayed there for a *week, when I received a letter.* [Coordinate to PC]

ऐसे वाक्यों में when का अर्थ होता है—'*and then*'.

NOTE—यदि ऐसे वाक्यों में Comma + When के पहले समयसूचक Noun न रहे (अर्थात कोई ऐसा Noun रहे जिससे समय का बोध न हो) तो when-clause एक Adverb Clause होता है; जैसे—

He sold the *book, when it was the best he had.* [Adverb Clause]

Rule II. स्थानसूचक Noun + Comma + Where

यदि स्थानसूचक Noun के बाद Comma रहे और उसके बाद Where का प्रयोग हो, तो (where-clause) Principal Clause (Principal Clause का Coordinate) होता है, Adjective या Adverb Clause नहीं; जैसे—

I went to *Mumbai, where I received a letter.* [Coordinate to PC]

ऐसे वाक्यों में where का अर्थ होता है—'*and there*'.

NOTE—यदि ऐसे वाक्यों में Comma + Where के पहले स्थानसूचक Noun न रहे, अर्थात कोई ऐसा Noun रहे जिससे स्थान का बोध न हो तो where-clause एक Adverb Clause होता है; जैसे—

We find *grass, where we expected flowers.* [Adverb Clause]

Rule III (A). Noun + Comma + Who/Whose/Whom/Which/As + Clause

यदि Noun के बाद Comma रहे और उसके बाद Who/Whose/Whom/Which आए तो वह Principal Clause (Coordinate to PC) होता है; Adjective Clause नहीं; जैसे—

1. The watch, *which was damaged,* is now useless. [Coordinate to PC]
2. The boy, *who is here,* is very intelligent. [Coordinate to PC]
3. The Taj Mahal, *as we all know,* is one of the wonders of the world. [Coordinate to PC]

Rule III (B). Principal Clause + Comma + Which

यदि Principal Clause के बाद Comma रहे और उसके बाद Which, तो वह (which-clause) Principal Clause (Coordinate to PC) होता है; जैसे—

He killed all the prisoners, *which was a cruel act.* [Coordinate to PC]

ध्यान दें कि ऐसे वाक्यों में which पूरे Principal Clause के बदले में प्रयुक्त होता है, केवल एक noun के बदले नहीं। इसलिए ऐसे which का अर्थ होता है—'*and this*'.

Rule III (C). Noun + Comma + Who

यदि Noun के बाद Comma रहे और उसके बाद Who, तो वह (who-clause) Adverb Clause या Principal Clause (Coordinate to PC) होता है। जब ऐसे वाक्यों के who-clause से कारण (cause) का बोध होता है, तब वह Adverb Clause होता है। पर जब उससे (who से) कारण का बोध नहीं होता, तब वह Principal Clause (Coordinate to PC) होता है। संक्षेप में, इन नियमों का ध्यान रखें—

Noun + Comma + who = because [Adverb Clause]

Noun + Comma + who = and he/she [Principal Clause]

इस वाक्य पर विचार करें—

Ravan, *who was found guilty,* was killed.

यहाँ PC में Why लगाकर यह प्रश्न करें—Why was Ravan killed?

उत्तर मिलता है—He (who) was found guilty.

यह उत्तर संतोषजनक है। क्यों? इसलिए कि Principal Clause में कार्य किया गया है उसका कारण (cause) यहाँ बताया गया है। इसलिए यह who-clause Adverbial है।

एक दूसरा वाक्य लें—

I saw my father, *who gave me a book.*

PC में *why* लगाकर यह प्रश्न करें—Why did I see my father?

उत्तर मिलता है—He (who) gave me a book.

यह उत्तर संतोषजनक नहीं क्योंकि Principal Clause में जो कार्य किया गया है उसका cause यहाँ नहीं बताया गया है। वास्तव में, किताब का पाना तो पिता के मिलने के बाद हुआ न! तो यह कारण हो कैसे सकता है? इसलिए यह who-clause Principal Clause है।

Caution—Noun + Who/Which/Where/Whom का अर्थ होता है—बहुत में से एक (one of the many). ऐसा क्यों? इसलिए कि ऐसा clause सदा Adjective Clause होता है, और Adjective Clause किसी Noun की संख्या को limit/restrict (कम या सीमित) करता है जो एक Adjective का काम (function) है। प्रत्येक Adjective किसी Noun का गुण बताकर उसकी संख्या को कम करता है। इसलिए horses से सभी horses का बोध होता है, पर white horses से कम horses का। यही काम Adjective Clause भी करता है। इस सिद्धांत का ध्यान रखकर इन वाक्यों पर विचार करें—

1. My mother who lives in Mumbai is returning today.
2. My father who returned today gave me sweets.

यहाँ mother who का अर्थ है—one of the mothers और father who का अर्थ है—one of the fathers. यहाँ अर्थ का अनर्थ हो गया है न! लिखने/बोलने का अभिप्राय दूसरा था। इसलिए जब who/which के पहले आनेवाले noun/pronoun की संख्या को restrict नहीं करना हो (अर्थात one of the many का अर्थ न हो) तो Who/Which के पहले Comma का प्रयोग अवश्य होना चाहिए। याद रखें कि Comma + Who/Which का अर्थ होता है—and he/she/it. इसलिए Definite Singular Noun (जो सदा singular रहता है; जैसे—father, mother, God, India, Russia, Ram, Mohan आदि) और Who/Which के बीच Comma का प्रयोग continuative (non-defining) sense में ही करना उचित है।

इन वाक्यों को देखें—

1. Her husband who is ill is going to London next week.
2. Her husband, who is ill is going to London next week.

husband who = *one of the husbands.*

husband + comma + who = *and he.*

यदि किसी को एक से अधिक husband हो (one of the many) तो पहला वाक्य शुद्ध और अर्थपूर्ण माना जा सकता है, पर यदि उसे एक ही husband हो, तो उसे दूसरे वाक्य का प्रयोग करना चाहिए। इस विश्लेषण से यह स्पष्ट हो जाता है कि Definite Singular Noun के साथ *who* या *comma + who* का प्रयोग बहुत ही सतर्कता से करना आवश्यक है।

(C) THIRD STAGE

How to Name a Sentence

इस प्रकार, clause को पहचान लेने के बाद, अंत में हमें यह देखना चाहिए कि अमुक वाक्य किस तरह का है। कुछ लोग वाक्य को पहले ही पहचानकर clauses को अलग करते हैं और तब नामकरण करते हैं। मेरी समझ में यह तरीका तो घोड़े के आगे गाड़ी रखने के समान है। हम वाक्य का नामकरण कर ही कैसे सकते हैं, जब तक यह पता ही न चले कि अमुक वाक्य में कितने clauses हैं और वे किस प्रकार के हैं? इसलिए sentence का नामकरण अंत में होना चाहिए। पर, यह किया कैसे जाए? इसके लिए यह जानना आवश्यक है कि वाक्य कितने प्रकार के होते हैं।

बनावट की दृष्टि से Sentence चार प्रकार का होता है—

(i) Simple, (ii) Compound, (iii) Complex, (iv) Mixed

(i) Simple Sentence = 1 Principal Clause

(ii) Compound Sentence = at least 2 Principal Clauses

(iii) Complex Sentence = Simple Sentence + Subordinate Clause

(iv) Mixed Sentence = Compound Sentence + Subordinate Clause

इस प्रकार हम देखते हैं कि Simple और Compound Sentences में Subordinate Clause नहीं रहता, पर इन दोनों में अंतर यह है कि Simple में एक ही Principal Clause रहता है और Compound में एक से अधिक (अर्थात कम-से-कम दो) Principal Clauses.

Complex Sentence में सिर्फ एक ही Principal Clause रहता है जैसे कि Simple में, पर Complex में कम-से-कम एक Subordinate Clause का रहना आवश्यक है।

Mixed Sentence में कम-से-कम दो Principal Clauses और कम-से-कम एक Subordinate Clause का रहना आवश्यक है।

EXERCISES WORKED OUT

1. If man had a skin thickly covered with hair or wool, as an ape or sheep has, he could not have moved from one climate to another with comfort, and so he is made naked, but not without the power of improving his condition, wherever he may be.

(a) If man …… wool—Adverb Clause

(b) As an ape has—Adverb Clause

(c) Or as a sheep has—Adverb Clause

(d) He could not …… comfort—Principal Clause

(e) And so …… naked—Coordinate to (d).

(f) But not without …… condition—Coordinate to (e).

(g) Wherever he may be—Adverb Clause

It is a mixed sentence.

2. Sir Issac Newton, after deep meditation, discovered that there was a law in nature called attraction, by virtue of which every particle of matter that the world is composed

of draws towards itself every other particle of matter with a force which is proportionate to its mass and distance.

(a) Sir Issac Newton …… discovered—Principal Clause

(b) That there was …… attraction—Noun Clause

(c) By virtue of which …… force—Adjective Clause

(d) The …… of—Adjective Clause

(e) Which is …… distance—Adjective Clause

It is a complex sentence.

3. A blind man, carrying a lantern is his hand and a pitcher on his shoulder, was walking alone one night, when he was met by a thoughtless young fellow who laughed at him and said, "O fool! day and night must be alike to you; of what use can this lamp be to you?"

(a) A blind man …… one night—Principal Clause

(b) When he was …… fellow—Coordinate to PC (a)—'when'—is used here in continuative sense.

(c) Who laughed at him—Adjective Clause

(d) And (who) said—Adjective Clause

(e) O fool! …… you—Noun Clause

(f) Of what use …… you?—Noun Clause

It is a mixed sentence.

4. They expected that the king would either treat the matter as a pleasant jest or threaten the insolent darwesh with punishment; but to their surprise, he was neither amused nor angry but seriously attentive to the words of the darwesh.

(a) They expected—PC

(b) That the king …… matter—Noun Clause

(c) As (he would treat) …… jest—Adverb Clause

(d) Or …… punishment—Noun Clause

(e) But to their surprise …… angry—Coordinate to PC (a)

(f) But …… darwesh—Coordinate to (e).

It is a mixed sentence.

5. After his schooling was finished, his father, desiring him to be a merchant like himself, gave him a ship freighted with various sorts of merchandise, so that he might go and trade about the world and grow rich, and become a help to his parents, who were now advanced in age.

(a) After his schooling was finished—Adverb Clause

(b) His father …… merchandise—Principal Clause

(c) So that he might go—Adverb Clause

(d) And trade …… world—Adverb Clause

(e) And grow rich—Adverb Clause

(f) And become …… age—Adverb Clause (showing *Cause*).

(g) Who were …… age—Adverb Clause (*showing Cause*).

It is a complex sentence.

NOTE—Clause No. (g) may be regarded also as an Adjective Clause qualifying 'parents' in (f).

6. Sometimes you may trace a river to a definite spring, but you very soon assure yourself that such springs are fed by rain which has percolated through the rocks or soil, and which, through some orifice that it has found or formed, comes to the light of day.

(a) Sometimes you …… spring—Principal Clause

(b) But you …… yourself—Coordinate to Principal Clause (a)

(c) That …… rain—Noun Clause

(d) Which has …… soil—Adjective Clause

(e) And which …… day—Adjective Clause

(f) That it has found—Adjective Clause

(g) Or formed—Adjective Clause

It is a mixed sentence.

7. The rootlets at the ends of these fibres strike into the ground, and when they have become well-fixed in the earth, the sap which previously was flowing downward changes its direction and flows upward.

(a) The rootlets …… ground—Principal Clause

(b) And when …… earth—Adverb Clause

(c) The sap changes its direction—Coordinate to Principal Clause (a)

(d) And flows upward—Coordinate to (a)

(e) Which …… downward—Adjective Clause

It is a mixed sentence.

8. With some men at that time of life so great a hurt would have been difficult to cure or might even have occasioned death; but with Carnaro, whose body was in the soundest condition, it was cured in a very short time.

(a) With some men …… cure—Principal Clause

(b) Or might …… death—Coordinate to (a)

(c) But with …… time—Coordinate to (a)

(d) Whose body …… condition—Adverb Clause (showing *cause*.)

NOTE—Clause No. (d) may be treated as an Adjective Clause as well.

It is a mixed sentence.

9. When the Piper claimed his pay, the Mayor declared that the promise which he had made before the town was cleared of rats, was only a joke, as the piper very well knew.

(a) The Mayor declared—Principal Clause

(b) When the Piper claimed his pay—Adverb Clause

(c) That the promise was only a joke—Noun Clause

(d) Which he had made—Adjective Clause

(e) Before the town ...... rats—Adverb Clause

(f) As the Piper well ...... knew—Adverb Clause

It is a complex sentence.

10. However, upon my way, I met a poor woman all in tears, who told me that her husband had been arrested for a debt he was not able to pay, and that his eight children must now starve, bereaved as they were of his industry.

(a) I met ...... tears—Principal Clause

(b) Who told me—Coordinate to Principal Clause

(c) That her husband ...... debt—Noun Clause

(d) (Which) he ...... pay—Adjective Clause

(e) That his ...... starve—Noun Clause

(f) Bereaved ...... industry—Adverb Clause

It is a mixed sentence.

11. I do not know what others may think of what I have done, but to myself I appear like a child who is picking up pebbles on the shore whilst the great ocean of truth lies unexplored before me.

(a) I do not know—Principal Clause

(b) What others may think of—Noun Clause

(c) What I have done—Noun Clause

(d) I appear ...... child—Principal Clause Coordinate to (a)

(e) Who is ...... shore—Adjective Clause

(f) Whilst ...... me—Adverb Clause

It is a mixed sentence.

12. The fox, who had been very much alarmed, now judged that there was no reason for fear, and demanded of the ass how he had dared to put on a skin which but a little while ago had belonged to an animal so noble that he was regarded as the King of the Forest.

(a) The fox now judged—Principal Clause

(b) Who had been ...... alarmed—Adverb Clause (showing *cause*).

(c) That there was ...... fear—Noun Clause

(d) (The fox) demanded of the ass—Coordinate to Principal Clause

(e) How he had …… skin—Noun Clause

(f) Which …… noble—Adjective Clause

(g) That he was regarded—Adverb Clause

(h) As the King of the Forest (was regarded)—Adverb Clause

It is a mixed sentence.

EXERCISE 1

Analyse the following sentences.

1. When I was a child, I spoke as a child, I understood as a child, I thought as a child, but when I became a man, I put away childish things.
2. I once put a wasp into the nest, but when the spider came out in order to seize it as usual, upon perceiving what kind of enemy it had to deal with, it instantly broke all the bonds that held it fast, and contributed all that lay in its power to disengage so formidable an antagonist.
3. The charts of the world which have been draw up by modern science have thrown into a narrow space the expression of a vast amount of knowledge, but I have never yet seen any one pictorial enough to enable the spectator to imagine the kind of contrast in physical character which exists between northern and southern countries.
4. When such a man perceives that if he fails, everyone will be able to understand the risk that has been incurred, but that if he succeeds no one will estimate the danger that has been silently overcome, he bows nevertheless to the supreme dictates of his judgement.
5. The lowest mechanic, however, looks upon it as his duty to be a watchful guardian of his country's freedom and often uses a language that might seem haughty even in the mouth of the great emperor who traces his ancestry to the moon.
6. The brute look and drank and evidently enjoyed the wine which was new to him and swilled again at the flagon and entreated for more and prayed to Ulysses to tell him his name that he might bestow a gift upon the man who had given him such brave liquor.
7. My friend's talk made so odd an impression upon my mind, that soon after I was abed, I fell insensibly into a most unaccountable reverie that had neither moral not design in it and cannot be so properly called a dream as a delirium.
8. When contrary to the wicked hopes he had formed, his brother proved victorious, his envy knew no bounds, and he swore he would burn the chamber where Orlando slept.

9. When the ship fell over and the mast became horizontal, he crawled out to the mizzentop and sat there till the spar gave away and plunged him into the waves whence he was dragged into one of the boats.
10. If you put the end of an iron rod in the fire and hold it there, you do something more than heat that end, for you heat the whole of it up to the end that you hold in your hand.
11. The governor of the town, who was present, cried out with a loud voice and ordered Androcles to explain how a savage beast could have so forgotten its innate disposition all of a sudden, that it became converted into a harmless animal which preferred rather to spare its victim than to devour him.
12. History says that Socrates, when he was given the cup of hemlock, continued to talk to the friends who were standing around him as he drank it.
13. There is nothing that shocks me so much as that which I hear very often that a man does not know how he can make his life happy.
14. I have noticed it often among my own people that the strong skilful men are often the gentlest to women and children, and it is pretty to see them carrying the little babies as if they were no heavier than little birds.
15. This put Viola in mind of her own sorrow and she longed to serve the lady, but the captain said that was impossible for she would admit none.
16. When we reached the gate, I told him I could go no further as I was expecting visitors and must return to receive them.
17. Everyone who knows you acknowledges, when he considers the case calmly that you have been wronged.
18. When the father came home, he found that, although he had been away for a long time, the children who had been left alone, had behaved quite well.
19. The governor who was himself young sympathised with the youngman but reminded him that it was the duty of an officer to fight when his country was at war with another.
20. The people of one country thought that they were better than others who lived in other countries and they fought with those others.
21. He had it proclaimed throughout his kingdom that he would give a great reward to anyone who would teach him what was the right time for every action.
22. I find it difficult to persuade my juniors that I was once as young as they are, and yet it is a fact that I was appointed editor at the age of twenty-three.
23. I do not know what others think of what I have done, but to myself I appear like a child who is picking up pebbles on the shore whilst the great ocean of truth lies unexplored before me.

24. As soon as a student receives his paper he should read carefully the instructions at the top and then glance at all the questions although this may take more time than he thinks he can afford.
25. The streets will be swept, thieves and other enemies driven out, and in the hive will be heard the soft sound of the strange hymns of rejoicing, which would seem to be the chant that denotes the presence of the queen.
26. After a flower has died, the cotton boll becomes larger and grows so fat that it bursts out of the leaves, and the feathery cotton boll can be seen.
27. While I was doing this, I found the tide began to flow, though very calm, and I had the mortification to see my coat, shirt and waistcoat, which I had left on the shore upon the sand, swim away.
28. Dr Rejendra Prasad, who was very fond of learning, said that students should cultivate the habit of reading books which are the treasure of knowledge.
29. Pandit Nehru said that India which is following the policy of neutrality, will never join any group, as it is not proper for the country.
30. The old beggar, who cried as if his heart would break, told me that he had no food to eat for three days.
31. I felt secure when I got home to my little tent and lay with all my wealth about me, but it blew very hard all that night, and in the morning, when I looked out, no more ship was to be seen.
32. Nothing can describe the confusion of thought which I felt when I sank into the water.

EXERCISE 2

I. *Complete the following sentences.*

1. If I were a monkey …… .
2. If she were a queen …… .
3. No sooner did I go to …… .
4. Everyone knows …… .
5. I believe …… .
6. The boy who has long hair …… .
7. Seven years have passed …… .
8. I missed the bus …… .
9. …… he is happy …… .
10. …… you can't rise high …… .
11. …… is not true …… .
12. …… is uncertain …… .

II. *Match the clauses under A and B to make meaningful sentences.*

A	B
She worked so hard	who wrote this novel.
However fast you may run	as if he were a parrot.
Were I a bird	is known to all.
I don't know	in case it rains.
What he spoke	that he is not honest.
Take an umbrella	I would fly to you.
That honesty is the best policy	you can't win the race.
My objection is	if he is ill.
I don't know the man	that she fell ill.
He memorises	was not heard clearly.

Chapter XIX

SYNTHESIS

Synthesis एक ऐसी विधि है जिसके द्वारा बहुत-से वाक्यों को जोड़कर एक वाक्य बनाया जाता है, जो Simple, Compound, Complex या Mixed हो सकता है। यहाँ हमें देखना है कि किन-किन विधियों (methods) के द्वारा वाक्यों को जोड़कर उन्हें Simple, Compound, Complex या Mixed Sentence का रूप दिया जाता है।

SIMPLE SENTENCES INTO A SINGLE SIMPLE SENTENCE

आप जानते हैं कि Simple Sentence में एक ही clause रहता है जो Principal Clause होता है; उसमें एक भी Subordinate Clause नहीं रहता। इसका अर्थ यह है कि Simple Sentence में केवल एक ही Finite Verb रहता है। इसलिए जब बहुत-से Simple Sentences को जोड़कर उन्हें एक Simple Sentence बनाना पड़ता है, तब यह कोशिश की जाती है कि एक ही Finite Verb का प्रयोग हो। इस लक्ष्य की पूर्ति के लिए बहुत-सी विधियाँ हैं जिनमें ये मुख्य हैं—

(A) *Use of Participle*

(B) *Use of Nominative Absolute*

(C) *Use of Noun or Phrase in Apposition*

(D) *Use of Infinitive*

(E) *Use of Preposition*

(F) *Use of Object + Infinitive*

(G) *Use of Too*

(H) *Use of Enough*

अब हम इन विधियों को एक-एक कर लें और देखें कि इनके द्वारा किस प्रकार बहुत-से Simple Sentences को जोड़कर एक Simple Sentence बनाया जाता है। हमें यह भी विचार करना होगा कि किस अवस्था में किस विधि का प्रयोग कब करना चाहिए। आज तक ऐसा कोई नियम नहीं बन पाया है कि किस विधि का प्रयोग कब होता है। लोग सुविधानुसार ही इनका प्रयोग करते हैं; पर मेरे जानते यदि वाक्यों के अर्थ को ठीक से समझा जाए तो उन विधियों के प्रयोग करने के नियम कुछ मोटे तौर पर निकल सकते हैं।

(A) USE OF PARTICIPLE

Participle के द्वारा Simple Sentences को तब जोड़ा जाता है, जब

Rule I. सभी Simple Sentences के Verbs का कर्ता Common (सामान्य कारक या common factor) हो, अर्थात एक ही व्यक्ति या वस्तु उन सभी Simple Sentences में कर्ता का काम करता हो; और

Rule II. जिन Simple Sentences के Verbs को देखने पर ऐसा लगे कि एक काम दूसरे के बाद हुआ है और इसलिए वे एक-दूसरे से बँधे हुए हैं; जैसे—

He raised his gun. *He* took aim. *He* shot the tiger.

इन तीनों वाक्यों का कर्ता *He* है, अर्थात *He* तीनों Verbs का Common Subject है—He (raised + took + shot).

Caution—इसके अतिरिक्त एक और बात पर ध्यान दें। इन तीनों Verbs से यह पता चलता है कि तीन कार्य किए गए हैं; पहले बन्दूक उठाने का, उसके बाद निशाना साधने का और अंत में बन्दूक चलाने का। इस तरह एक के बाद दूसरा काम किया गया है। इसलिए इन तीनों Simple Sentences को Participle के द्वारा जोड़ना चाहिए।

How to Use Participle

Participle के द्वारा वाक्यों को जोड़ने का नियम यह है—

Rule I. जो कार्य (Verbs) पहले हुआ हो, उसे Participle में बदल दें और जो कार्य या क्रिया अंत में हो, उसे Finite रहने दें; जैसे—

He *raised* the gun. He *took* aim. He *shot* the tiger.

इन तीनों वाक्यों में सबसे पहले कार्य की चर्चा पहले वाक्य में हुई है, उसके बाद दूसरे में और अंत में तीसरे वाक्य में। अतः, इन्हें इस प्रकार जोड़ दें—

Having raised the gun and *taken* aim, he *shot* the tiger.

कुछ और उदाहरण लें—

1. He *drew* his sword. He *rushed* at the man.
   = *Having drawn* his sword, he *rushed* at the man.
2. *Turn* to the left. You *will then see* the post office.
   = *Turning* to the left, you *will see* the post office.
3. They were *too late* for the train. They *tried* to hire a taxi. They *hoped* to see the princess.
   = *Being too late* for the train, they *tried* to hire a taxi, *hoping* to see the princess.
4. He *worked* hard. He *felt* tired.
   = *Having worked* hard, he *felt* tired.
5. I *spoke* to the teacher. I *sat* at the table. I *held* the book in my hand.
   = *Seated* at the table and *holding* the book in my hand, I *spoke* to the teacher.

(B) USE OF NOMINATIVE ABSOLUTE

Nominative Absolute का प्रयोग होता है, जब

Rule I. वाक्यों के कर्ता भिन्न-भिन्न व्यक्ति या वस्तु होते हैं, एक ही वस्तु या व्यक्ति नहीं।
Rule II. उन वाक्यों के Verbs से ऐसा मालूम पड़ता है कि जो कार्य एक-दूसरे के बाद होते हैं, उनके बीच एक प्रकार का causal relation (कारण और उसके परिणाम का संबंध) है; जैसे—

The *sun* rose. The *fog* disappeared.

यहाँ पहले वाक्य का कर्ता sun है और दूसरे का fog. हम यह भी देखते हैं कि यहाँ दो Verbs (rose and disappeared) आए हैं, जिनमें एक प्रकार का causal relation मालूम पड़ता है, क्योंकि यह स्वाभाविक है कि सूर्य के उगने से कुहासा विलीन हो जाता है। इसलिए इन वाक्यों को इस प्रकार जोड़ना चाहिए—

The sun having risen, the fog disappeared.

इन वाक्यों को भी देखें—

The *agreement* was signed. *All* were satisfied.

= *The agreement being signed,* all were satisfied.

इन वाक्यों को Nominative Absolute के द्वारा जोड़ा गया है, क्योंकि इनके कर्ता अलग-अलग हैं और जिन कार्यों की चर्चा हुई है उनके बीच कारण-फल का संबंध है—समझौते पर दस्तखत कारण है और लोगों का संतोष उसका फल।

How to Use Nominative Absolute

Nominative Absolute उस कर्ता (nominative) को कहते हैं, जो वाक्य में स्वतंत्र (absolute) रहता है, क्योंकि वैसे कर्ता का कोई भी असर वाक्य के Verb पर नहीं पड़ता। ऊपर के वाक्यों में *sun* और *agreement* Nominative Absolute हैं। इन वाक्यों के nominative क्रमशः fog और all हैं।

Nominative Absolute के प्रयोग की विधि यह है—

Rule I. जो कार्य पहले हो (जो कारण का काम करे) उसके कर्ता को Participle के पहले रख दें और जो कार्य पीछे हो (जो कारण का फल हो) उसके कर्ता को Nominative मान लें। ऊपर दिए गए वाक्यों में ऐसा ही किया गया है। पहले सूर्य का उगना हुआ और उसके बाद कुहासा का विलीन होना। इसलिए पहले वाक्य के कर्ता (sun) को Participle (having risen) के पहले रखा गया, अर्थात sun को Nominative Absolute बना दिया गया और दूसरे वाक्य के कर्ता (fog) को Nominative माना गया। इन उदाहरणों को भी देखें—

1. The leader was slain. The rioters were seized with panic.

   = The leader *having been slain* (*or being slain*), the rioters were seized with panic.

2. The steamer was delayed by a storm. We left by train.

   = The steamer *having been* (*or being*) *delayed* by a storm, we left by train.

3. Your son has been ill during the greater part of this term. His studies have fallen into arrears. I am unable to give him promotion. = Your son *having been ill* … term, and his studies *having fallen* into arrears, I am unable to give him promotion.
4. The town was well-stocked with provisions. The guns were well-stocked with ammunitions. The enemies were forced to raise the siege.

   = The town *being well-stocked* with provisions and the guns with ammunitions, the enemies were … siege.
5. The siege was over. The enemy withdrew. The city opened its gates.

   By this, it means its trade and prosperity rapidly revived.

   = The siege *being over*, the enemy *having withdrawn* and the city *having opened its gates,* trade and prosperity rapidly revived.
6. The business will now prosper. He and I have come to terms.

   = He and I *having come* to terms, the business will now prosper.
7. The fog was dense. No one could see his way through the streets.

   = The fog *being dense,* no one could … streets.

(C) USE OF NOUN OR PHRASE IN APPOSITION

Rule I. Appositon का प्रयोग तब होता है जब एक वाक्य में कही गई बातों (कार्यों या गुणों, अर्थात Verbs or Adjectives) की विस्तारपूर्वक व्याख्या अन्य वाक्यों में की जाती है; जैसे—

Byron had some of the great qualifications of a **great poet.** He possessed great *command of language.* He was a *keen observer of nature.* He had an *accurate knowledge of men and nature.*

यहाँ पहले वाक्य में Byron की योग्यताओं (गुणों) की चर्चा की गई है और अन्य तीन वाक्यों में उन गुणों की एक प्रकार से व्याख्या की गई है, अर्थात यह बताया गया है कि वे गुण क्या-क्या थे—भाषा पर अधिकार, प्रकृति-निरीक्षण की शक्ति और मानव का ज्ञान।

इसलिए इन वाक्यों को Apposition की विधि से जोड़ना चाहिए; जैसे—

Byron had some of the great qualifications of **a great poet,** *a great command of language, a keen observation of nature and an accurate knowledge of men and nature.*

इन वाक्यों को भी देखें—

Siraj-ud-daulah perpetrated **many atrocities.** He *oppressed the British merchants. He oppressed his own people no less.* He was defeated at the battle of Plassey.

ऊपर पहले वाक्य में सिराजुद्दौला के कठोर कार्यों (गुणों) की चर्चा हुई और अन्य वाक्यों में उन्हीं कार्यों पर विशेष प्रकाश डाला गया है, क्योंकि उनकी चर्चा विस्तारपूर्वक की गई है।

अतः, इन्हें इस प्रकार जोड़ा गया है—

Siraj-ud-daulah, **the perpetrator of many atrocities,** *oppressor of the British merchants and of his own people,* was defeated at the battle of Plassey.

How to Use Noun or Phrase in Apposition

Rule I. Apposition का अर्थ होता है 'side by side' और इसलिए किसी noun या phrase को उस noun के बगल में रखा जाता है जिसकी व्याख्या की जाती है। जो noun या phrase Apposition में रहता है, उसे दो कौमा (Commas) के बीच रखा जाता है। पहले दिए गए उदाहरणों के वाक्यों में comma का प्रयोग करके noun को Apposition में रखा गया है। कुछ और उदाहरण लें—

1. John Bunyan wrote "The Pilgrim's Progress". He had once been a thoughtless youngman. Later he became a religious penitent.

   = John Buńyan, *the author of "The Pilgrim's Progress", once a thoughtless youngman,* later became a religious penitent.

2. Mahatma Gandhi was a lover of peace. He had once been a *lawyer.* He preached *non-violence.*

   = Mahatma Gandhi, *a lover of peace, once a lawyer,* preached non-violence.

(D) USE OF INFINITIVE

Rule I. Infinitive के प्रयोग द्वारा वाक्यों को तब जोड़ा जाता है, जब सभी वाक्यों से मालूम पड़ता है कि उनमें अन्योन्याश्रय (*interdependence*) का संबंध है। वह संबंध कभी-कभी कारण और परिणाम (cause and effect) का रहता है, पर यह आवश्यक नहीं है। हाँ, इतना तो अवश्य है कि उनमें गहरा संबंध रहता ही है। ऐसे वाक्यों को Nominative Absolute के द्वारा जोड़ा नहीं जा सकता, क्योंकि Nominative Absolute उन वाक्यों को जोड़ता है (जैसाकि पहले कहा जा चुका है) जिनके कर्ता भिन्न-भिन्न होते हैं और इसलिए उन कार्यों में भिन्न-भिन्न बातें कही जाती हैं। इसके अतिरिक्त, उन वाक्यों से बोध होता है कि एक कार्य के समाप्त होने पर दूसरा कार्य तथा दूसरे के बाद तीसरा कार्य होता है और उनमें कारण-परिणाम का संबंध है। पर Infinitive उन वाक्यों को जोड़ता है, जिनसे यह मालूम पड़ता है कि कार्यों के बीच तो कारण-परिणाम का या अन्योन्याश्रय संबंध है, लेकिन एक कार्य दूसरे के बाद नहीं होता, बल्कि वे कार्य एक ही साथ होते हैं, मानों वे एक कड़ी से जुड़े हुए हों; जैसे—

His house and goods were sold. His debts had to be paid.

= His house and goods were sold *to pay* his debts.

यहाँ दूसरे वाक्य में कारण बतलाया गया है और पहले में उसका परिणाम। इन वाक्यों को Infinitive के द्वारा जोड़ा गया है, Nominative Absolute के द्वारा नहीं, क्योंकि इन वाक्यों से ऐसा पता नहीं चलता कि एक कार्य के समाप्त होने पर दूसरा कार्य उसके परिणामस्वरूप हुआ। एक और उदाहरण लें—

He could not prepare well for the examination. He had not sufficient time.

= He had not sufficient time *to prepare well* for the examination.

यहाँ भी दूसरे वाक्य में कारण बतलाया गया है और पहले में इसका परिणाम। इन वाक्यों में भी दो कार्यों की चर्चा हुई है, पर एक कार्य दूसरे के बाद नहीं हुआ, बल्कि वे दो कार्य एक ही साथ हुए, जिस प्रकार कारण और परिणाम एक ही साथ रहते हैं, अलग-अलग नहीं। इन वाक्यों को भी देखें—

1. He had a large family. He must provide for them.

   = He has a large family *to provide* for.

2. He stayed up at nights working out problems in mathematics. It was a pleasure to him.

   = It was a pleasure to him *to stay up* ... mathematics.

3. He must confess his fault. He will be fined otherwise.

   = He must confess his fault *to escape* fine.

4. The child grew worse every day. The parents were therefore grieved.

   = The parents were grieved *to see* the child grow worse every day.

5. The General has just come. The inspection of the volunteers is his object.

   = The General has just come *to inspect* the volunteers.

6. That man cheated all his creditors. He must have been mad.

   = That man was mad enough *to cheat* his creditors.

7. The head guides the rest of the body. It was made for this purpose.

   = The head was made *to guide* the rest of the body.

8. My father was very much delighted. He had heard of my brother's success.

   = My father was very much delighted *to hear* of my brother's success.

9. He wants to pass his examination. He works hard for that.

   = He works hard *to pass* his examination.

10. I received his letter. I was glad.

    = I was glad *to receive* his letter.

11. I will go to market. I want to buy books.

    = I will go to market *to buy* books.

(E) USE OF PREPOSITION

1. He was punished. He had stolen my book.

   = He was punished **for** stealing my book.

2. She sings songs. She earns money.

   = She earns money **by** singing songs.

3. The train went by. It did not stop.

   = The train went by **without** stopping.

4. I thanked him. He had helped me.

   = I thanked him **for** helping me.

ऐसे वाक्यों में Preposition का प्रयोग तब होता है जब इनसे कारण (cause) या साधन (means) आदि भावों का बोध होता है।

(F) USE OF OBJECT + INFINITIVE/OBJECT + PRESENT PARTICIPLE (Verb + ing)

1. I watched the children. They were playing.
   = I watched the children playing.
2. I heard the girls. They were singing.
   = I heard the girls singing.
3. He sang. I heard him.
   = I heard him sing.
4. The mango fell. I saw.
   = I saw the mango fall.

ऐसे वाक्यों के **Verb + Object + Infinitive** या **Verb + Object + Present Participle** से कार्य होने की अवस्था (State of action) का बोध होता है।

. . . .

EXERCISE

Change these into Simple Sentences as directed.

1. She teaches children. She earns money. [use **By**]
2. He ran away. He didn't look behind. [use **Without**]
3. He was fined. He came late. [use **For**]
4. She reached home. She saw her mother. [use **Participle**]
5. I met my friend. I was very glad. [use **Infinitive**]
6. He went to fair. He wanted to sell his cow. [use **Infinitive**]
7. The sun rose. Darkness disappeared. [use **Noun Absolute**]
8. The window closed. I heard. [use **Verb + Object + Infinitive** without **to**]
9. The aeroplane landed. I saw it. [use **Verb + Object + Infinitive** without **to**]
10. We saw the soldiers. They were marching.
    [use **Verb + Object + Present Participle**]
11. I saw her. She was climbing a tree. [use **Verb + Object + Present Participle**]
12. They watched the boat. It was crossing a river.
    [use **Verb + Object + Present Participle**]

. . . .

(G) USE OF TOO + ADJECTIVE/ADVERB

जब एक Simple Sentence से कार्य नहीं होने का कारण (cause) बताया जाता है और दूसरे Simple Sentence में इसका फल (result), तब इन्हें **too + adjective/adverb** की सहायता से जोड़ा जाता है। जैसे—

1. She is poor. She can't buy a new dress.

 = She is too poor to buy a new dress.

2. He is weak in English. He can't pass.

 = He is too weak in English to pass.

ध्यान दें कि इन्हें जोड़ने पर

(i) कारण बतलानेवाला वाक्य पहले आता है।

(ii) फल बतलानेवाले वाक्य के subject तथा verb का लोप हो जाता है और इसका verb बदल जाता है Infinitive (to + verb) में, जैसे—

buy = to buy

pass = to pass

(H) USE OF ADJECTIVE/ADVERB + ENOUGH

जब एक Simple Sentence से कार्य होने का कारण (cause) बताया जाता है और दूसरे से फल (result) का बोध होता है, तब इन्हें **adjective/adverb + enough** से जोड़ा जाता है; जैसे—

1. She is rich. She can buy a new car.

 = She is rich enough to buy a new car.

2. He is strong. He can lift this box.

 = He is strong enough to lift this box.

ध्यान दें कि इन्हें जोड़ने पर

(i) कारण बतलानेवाला वाक्य पहले आता है।

(ii) फल बतलानेवाले वाक्य के subject और verb का लोप हो जाता है और इसका verb बदल जाता है Infinitive में; जैसे—

buy = to buy

lift = to lift

EXERCISE

I. *Join these sentences using* **too + adjective + infinitive.**

1. This doll is very big. It can't go into the bag.
2. The ceiling is very high. She can't touch it.
3. The shirt is very small. I can't wear it.
4. These shoes are very big. He can't use them.
5. The sum is difficult. We can't do it.
6. It is very hot. We can't go out.
7. The wall is very strong. It can't collapse.
8. She is very tired. She can't work.

9. He is very young. He can't go alone.
10. You are very late. You can't catch the bus.

II. *Join these sentences using* **adjective + enough + infinitive**.

1. He was kind.	He helped me.
2. She is intelligent.	She can solve the problem.
3. He is tall.	He can reach the ceiling.
4. He is strong.	He can break this rope.
5. He works hard.	He can get grand success.
6. He is stupid.	He throws stones on others.
7. She is lucky.	She can win a lottery.

SIMPLE SENTENCES INTO A COMPOUND SENTENCE

Compound Sentence में कम-से-कम दो Principal Clauses रहते हैं और उसमें Subordinate Clause नहीं रहता। इसे ध्यान में रखकर ही Simple Sentences को एक Compound Sentence का रूप दिया जा सकता है। कहने का अभिप्राय यह है कि उन्हें Compound Sentence बनाते समय कम-से-कम दो Principal Clauses का प्रयोग अवश्य करें और Subordinate Clause का प्रयोग कभी भी नहीं करें। इससे यह स्पष्ट है कि यह कार्य Coordinating Conjunctions की सहायता से ही हो सकता है और Subordinating Conjunctions की जरूरत नहीं पड़ सकती। आप जानते हैं कि वे Coordinating Conjunctions हैं—

and, both ... and, also, too, as well as, not only ... but also, either ... or, neither ... nor, otherwise, or, but, yet, however, so, therefore, for. इन conjunctions के द्वारा वाक्यों को जोड़ते समय वाक्यों के अर्थ पर अवश्य ध्यान देना चाहिए। यदि वाक्यों को पढ़ने से ऐसा मालूम हो कि facts या statements के बीच विरोध (contrast) का भाव है, तो but, yet आदि का प्रयोग करना चाहिए; जैसे—

He is poor. He is happy.

आप जानते हैं कि poverty और happiness दो विरोधी भाव व्यक्त करते हैं। अतः, इन्हें but या yet के द्वारा जोड़कर compound sentence बनाया जाना चाहिए—

1. He is poor *but* happy. 2. He is poor, *yet* he is happy.

इस प्रकार, यदि ऐसे वाक्य मिलें जिनमें एक के आधार पर दूसरे वाक्य में अनुमान (inference) निकाला जाए या एक वाक्य में कारण (cause) बतलाया जाए और दूसरे में उसका परिणाम (consequence), तो उन्हें so या therefore के द्वारा जोड़ें; जैसे—

He took bribe. He was dismissed.

= He took bribe, *therefore* he was dismissed.

यदि ऐसे वाक्य मिलें जिनमें बहुत-सी चीजों के बीच एक को पसंद या सबको नापसंद करने की बात कही जाए, तो either ... or या neither ... nor का प्रयोग करना चाहिए; जैसे—

1. Do not do this. Do not do that.

   = *Neither* do this *nor* (do) that.

2. Take all. Take nothing.

   = *Either* take all *or* take nothing.

यदि ऐसे वाक्य रहें जिन्हें पढ़ने से मालूम हो कि प्रत्येक वाक्य में statement (कथन) है, तो उन्हें and, as well as, both ... and या not only ... but also के द्वारा जोड़ें; जैसे—

He cried. He wept.

= He cried *and* wept.

या He *not only* cried *but also* wept.

या He *both* cried *and* wept.

या He cried *as well as* wept.

EXERCISES WORKED OUT

Combine the following sentences into a Compound Sentence.

1. Two cats had stolen some cheese. They could not decide how to divide it equally between them. They decided on asking a monkey to settle the dispute for them. They went to the monkey at once for that purpose.

   = Two cats, having stolen some cheese, and not being able to decide how to divide it equally between them, decided on asking a monkey to settle the dispute for them, and went to the monkey at once for that purpose.

2. The monkey agreed to hear and decide the case. He called the two cats before him. He held out a pair of scales. He put one piece of cheese in one scale and one in another.

   = The monkey agreed to hear and decide the case, and having called the two cats before him, he held out a pair of scales, one piece of cheese being put in one scale, and the other in the other.

3. In all labour there is profit. Mere talking tends only to failure.

   = In all labour there is profit; but mere talking tends only to failure.

4. A certain rumour was current. He was said to have been taken seriously ill. He was quite well. He wrote to me that very day. He informed me by letter of his intention to extend his business.

   = According to a current rumour, he was taken seriously ill; but in point of fact he was quite well, and by a letter written that very day he informed me of his intention to extend his business.

5. In private life he was amiable. In private life he was even fond of amusement. In public life he was severe. In public life he was a rigorous dispenser of justice.

= In private life he was amiable and even found of amusement; but in public life he was severe, and a rigorous dispenser of justice.

6. It was now six o'clock in the evening. It was too late to start on our journey. We postponed starting till the following morning.

   = At six o'clock in the evening it was too late to start on our journey; so we postponed starting till the following morning.

7. The people of this place are thrifty. They are industrious. I noticed the fertility of their fields. Their cottage were neat. Their persons were clean.

   = The people of this place are thrifty and industrious; and I noticed the fertility of their fields, the neatness of their cottages, and the cleanliness of their persons.

8. I have no knowledge of the person referred to. I am unable to say any good of him. I am unable to say any evil of him.

   = I have no knowledge of the person referred to, and am, therefore, unable to say anything about him, good or evil.

SIMPLE SENTENCES INTO A COMPLEX SENTENCE

आप जानते हैं कि Complex Sentence में केवल एक ही Principal Clause होता है और उसमें कम-से-कम एक Subordinate Clause भी रहता है। इसलिए Simple Sentences को जोड़कर उन्हें एक Complex Sentence बनाते समय उसमें एक ही Principal Clause रखें और अन्य वाक्यों को Subordinate Clause का रूप दे दें।

Subordinate Clauses तीन प्रकार के होते हैं—(1) Noun Clause, (2) Adjective Clause और (3) Adverb Clause. ये तीनों प्रकार के Subordinate Clauses *Relative Pronouns/Relative Adverbs/Subordinating Conjunctions* से आरंभ होते हैं जिनमें निम्नांकित मुख्य हैं—

that, who, which, what, because, since, so that, in order that, as, as if, as soon as, though, before, after, if, when, where, till, until.

किस Subordinating Conjunction का प्रयोग कहाँ और कब होता है या (दूसरे शब्दों में) कब और कहाँ Noun Clause या Adjective Clause या Adverb Clause का प्रयोग करके वाक्यों को Complex Sentence बनाया जाता है, यह वाक्यों के अर्थ पर ही निर्भर करता है। यह काम नीचे दिए गए नियमों की सहायता से आसानी से कर लें सकते हैं।

How to Use Adverb Clause

Rule I. यदि वाक्यों से मालूम हो कि उनके बीच cause (कारण), condition (शर्त), contrast (विरोध), comparison (तुलना), time (समय) या place (स्थान) का संबंध है, तो Adverb Clause के द्वारा वाक्यों को जोड़ना चाहिए। इन्हें देखें—

1. He succeeded. He laboured hard.

   = He succeeded *because* he laboured hard.

2. He has been very unfortunate. He is always cheerful.

= *Though* he has been very unfortunate, he is always cheerful.

3. He is a clever boy. No other boy in the class is more clever.

= No other boy in the class is cleverer *than* he is.

4. You must sign your name. He will then agree to your terms.

= He will agree to your terms, *if* you sign your name.

5. Men may sow much or little. They will reap accordingly.

= Men will reap *according as* they sow much or little.

6. You have treated me in a certain way. I will treat you in the same way.

= I will treat you *as* you have treated me.

इन वाक्यों को Adverb Clauses के द्वारा जोड़कर Complex Sentence बनाए गए हैं। पहले दो वाक्यों में cause का संबंध है। इसलिए इन्हें because के द्वारा जोड़ा गया है। दूसरे दो वाक्यों के बीच contrast का संबंध है और तीसरे दो वाक्यों के बीच comparison का। अतः, दूसरे दो वाक्यों को though के द्वारा और तीसरे दो वाक्यों को than के द्वारा जोड़ा गया है। चौथे दो वाक्यों से condition का बोध होता है। इसलिए, इन्हें according as तथा as के द्वारा जोड़ा गया है।

Rule II. समय (time) का बोध करानेवाले वाक्यों को इनकी सहायता से जोड़ा जाता है—

after, before, until

इन वाक्यों को लें—

1. He finished the work. Then he went out.

He went out *after* he had finished the work.

He had finished the work *before* he went out.

2. I wrote a letter. Then I read the newspaper.

I read the newspaper *after* I had written a letter.

I had written a letter *before* I read the newspaper.

3. I finished the book. Then I went to bed.

I went to bed *after* I had finished the book.

I had finished the book *before* I went to bed.

4. The bus stopped. Then I got off.

I did not get off the bus *until* it stopped.

5. She finished the work. Then she went out.

She did not go out *until* she finished the work.

इन नियमों का ध्यान रखें—

(i) पहले समाप्त होनेवाले कार्य के साथ *before* का प्रयोग होता है, पर बाद में समाप्त होनेवाले कार्य के साथ *after* आता है।

(ii) Until से आरंभ होनेवाले clause में *not* नहीं आता, पर Principal Clause में not का प्रयोग होता है।

How to Use Adjective Clause

(I) Adjective Clause के द्वारा भी Simple Sentences को जोड़कर एक Complex Sentence बनाया जाता है। यदि वाक्य में किसी व्यक्ति या वस्तु की चर्चा हो और अन्य वाक्यों में उसी के गुणों पर प्रकाश डाला जाए, तो Adjective Clauses बनाने के लिए who, which, that, when या where का प्रयोग होता है; जैसे—

I suffered *anxiety.* The *anxiety* was extreme.

= The anxiety *that* I suffered was extreme.

यहाँ पहले वाक्य में anxiety के विषय में बताया गया है और दूसरे में उसी शब्द पर और प्रकाश डाला गया है। इसलिए इन्हें Adjective Clause के द्वारा जोड़ा गया है। एक और उदाहरण लें—

A small *house* stood at the foot of the hill. We stayed *there* for the night.

= We stayed for the night at a small house *which* stood at the foot of the hill.

यहाँ पहले वाक्य में house की चर्चा हुई है और दूसरे में उसी शब्द पर प्रकाश डाला गया है। (We stayed *there* for the night.)। इसलिए इन्हें भी Adjective Clause के द्वारा जोड़ा गया है।

इन वाक्यों को भी देखें—

1. He had received a good *education. This* raised him above many men.

   = The good education *that* he had received raised him above many men.

2. That is the *house.* He was born *there.*

   = That is the house *where* he was born.

3. This is the *book.* I wanted to buy *it.*

   = This is the book *that* I wanted to buy.

4. Daniel came alive out of the *den.* In that den lions were kept.

   = Daniel came alive out of the den in *which* lions were kept.

5. I went down a *footpath.* At the end of the *footpath* there was a chasm. The depth of the *chasm* was about twenty feet. The *dead body* of a man was lying there. A faithful dog was still seated by *its side.*

   = I went down a footpath, at the end of *which* there was a chasm about twenty feet deep, with the dead body of a man lying there, and a faithful dog still seated by its side.

NOTE—Who/Which/That के द्वारा जब Adjective Clause बनाया जाता है, तब इनका अर्थ हिन्दी में कोई भी ऐसा शब्द होता है जो 'ज' से आरंभ होता है; जैसे—**जो, जिस** आदि। विशेष जानकारी के लिए Analysis के अध्याय को देखें।

How to Use Noun Clause

Rule I. जब एक Simple Sentence के कथन (fact, opinion, belief, hope आदि) को दूसरे में स्वीकार (affirm) या अस्वीकार (deny) किया जाता है, तब ये *that* के द्वारा जोड़ जाते हैं। ऐसा that + clause होता है Noun Clause और वह वाक्य हो जाता है Complex; जैसे—

1. Better luck may be in store for us. We hope so.
   = We hope that better luck may be in store for us.
2. He is honest. I know this.
   = I know that he is honest.

इन वाक्यों को देखें—

1. He is honest. I do not doubt it.
   = I do not doubt *that* he is honest.
2. He will come today. I am sure of it.
   = I am sure *that* he will come today.
3. You have acted wrongly. I believe so.
   = I believe *that* you have acted wrongly.
4. A lazy man injures no one but himself. This is not true.
   = It is not true *that* a lazy man injures no one but himself.
5. Someone has been making a great noise. I should like to know the person.
   = I should like to know *who* has been making a great noise.
6. The messengers told us something about that matter. I heard it.
   = I heard *what* the messengers told us about that matter.
7. Your hopes about your son's future may or may not be fulfilled. Time alone will show.
   = Time alone will show *whether* your hopes about your son's future will be fulfilled or not.

NOTE—ऐसे वाक्यों को जोड़ने पर it/this/that/so का लोप हो जाता है।

Rule II. Simple Sentences को इन शब्दों की सहायता से जोड़ा जाता है—

who, which, whom, whose, what, when,
where, why, how, if, whether

इन्हें जोड़ने पर who + clause/which + clause आदि Noun Clauses होते हैं और पूरा वाक्य complex बन जाता है; जैसे—

Assertive + Interrogative = Assertive + Assertive; जैसे—

1. I don't know. Who is she?
   = I don't know who she is.
2. I can't say. Is he ill?
   = I can't say if/whether he is ill.

Imperative + Interrogative = Imperative + Assertive; जैसे—

1. Tell me. Where is he?
   = Tell me where he is.
2. Inform me. When will he come?
   = Inform me when he will come.

Interrogative + Interrogative = Interrogative + Assertive; जैसे—

1. Do you know? Why is she sad?
   = Do you know why she is sad?
2. Can you tell me? How have you come?
   = Can you tell me how you have come?

Assertive + Exclamatory = Assertive + Assertive; जैसे—

1. How well he plays! Nobody can believe.
   = Nobody can believe how well he plays.
2. No one can imagine. What a great man he is!
   = No one can imagine what a great man he is.

Assertive + Assertive = Assertive + Assertive; जैसे—

1. Somebody called me. I don't know who.
   = I don't know who called me.
2. He will come. I can't say when.
   = I can't say when he will come.

Rule III. जब एक Simple Sentence से प्रबल इच्छा का बोध होता है और दूसरे से इच्छापूर्ति का अभाव व्यक्त किया जाता है, तब इन्हें इस प्रकार जोड़ा जाता है—

Simple Sentence + ['that' understood] + Subject + Were + Other Words

Simple Sentence + ['that' understood] + Subject + Verb (Past Tense) + Other Words

इन वाक्यों को देखें—

1. I wish to be a king. I am not a king.
   = I wish I were a king.
2. I wish to know him. I don't know him.
   = I wish I knew him.
3. I wished to know him. I didn't know him.
   = I wished I had known him.

EXERCISE

Join these into Complex Sentences.

1. I can't swim. I wish to swim.
2. I am not a Prime Minister. I wish to be a Prime Minister.
3. I am not a bird. I wish to be a bird.
4. She is black. She is beautiful.
5. There is a cow in the field. It is mine.
6. He was late. He missed the bus.
7. She will pass. I hope so.

8. I used a candle. Electricity failed at that time.
9. The train arrived. I have reached the station before.
10. I started for Mumbai. I received a telegram at that moment.
11. A doctor arrived. She died before his arrival.
12. An eruption begins. Clouds of steam and ashes burst out.
13. Mother is making tea. Father is watching TV.
14. It may rain. I will take an umbrella in that case.
15. He worked very hard. He felt tired.
16. He is honest. He is honest in spite of poverty.
17. The police arrived. Thieves fled away.

....

SIMPLE SENTENCES INTO A MIXED SENTENCE

Mixed Sentence में कम-से-कम दो Principal Clauses रहते हैं और कम-से-कम एक Subordinate Clause. इन नियमों का सदा ध्यान रखें—

(i) *Simple Sentence—One Principal Clause.*

(ii) *Compound Sentence—At least two Principal Clauses.*

(iii) *Complex Sentence—Simple + Subordinate Clause.*

(iv) *Mixed Sentence—Compound + Subordinate Clause.*

तो, इससे यह स्पष्ट है कि Simple Sentence को एक Mixed Sentence बनाने के लिए आपको उन्हीं नियमों की सहायता लेनी पड़ेगी जो Compound और Complex Sentence के संबंध में बताए गए हैं। आप Coordinating और Subordinating Conjunctions के द्वारा यह काम आसानी से कर सकते हैं, जिसकी चर्चा पहले ही हो चुकी है।

EXERCISES WORKED OUT

Combine the following Simple Sentences into a Complex or Mixed Sentence.

1. The murder was proved. The judge then ordered the man to be executed. The man had been four days under trial.

   = The murder having been proved, the judge ordered the man, who had been four days under trial, to be executed.

2. The supply of pasture often runs short. The nomads of Tartary then shift their abode. They search for new pasture elsewhere.

   = When the supply of pasture runs short, the nomads of Tartary shift their abode in search of new pasture elsewhere.

3. We heard the sad news. We immediately started for the afflicted house. There we found the mourners.

= On hearing the sad news, we immediately started for the afflicted house, where we found the mourners.

4. They spoke in defence of their absent friend. They could not have spoken better.

   = They could not have spoken better than they did in defence of their absent friend.

5. He behaved prudently under the circumstances. Few men would have acted so prudently.

   = Few persons would have acted so prudently as he did under the circumstances.

6. Siraj-ud-daulah was defeated. He fled from the field of battle. His horse could not carry him more than a few miles. His horse was of the purest Arab blood.

   = When Siraj-ud-daulah was defeated he fled from the field of battle on his horse, which though it was of the purest Arab blood, could not carry him more than a few miles.

7. His difficulties become greater and greater. He shows more and more energy.

   = The greater his difficulties, the more energy he shows.

8. I will visit your house in June next. You have frequently asked me to do so. I will not disappoint you any longer.

   = I will visit your house in June next, as you have frequently asked me to do; and I will not disappoint you any longer.

9. Richard I, King of England, was seized with remorse. He had rebelled against his father. The father at that time was an old man. He was much attached to all his sons.

   = Richard I, King of England, was seized with remorse for having rebelled against his father, who was at that time an old man and much attached to all his sons.

10. I am very sorry. He has lost all hope. He has given up work. He worked hard last year. He has excellent abilities.

    = I am very sorry that he has lost all hope and given up work; for he worked hard last year, and has excellent abilities.

11. I left him to his fate. He persisted in refusing help. I offered him help on all occasions. On such occasions he needed it.

    = I left him to his fate, as he persisted in refusing the help which I offered him whenever he needed it.

Chapter XX

NARRATION

अँगरेजी में बोलने और लिखने के दो तरीके हैं—

(क) किसी के कथन को ठीक-ठीक उसी के शब्दों में रख देना, जिसे Direct Narration कहा जाता है।

(ख) किसी के कथन का सारांश लेकर उसे अपने शब्दों में व्यक्त करना, जिसे Indirect Narration कहा जाता है।

Direct Narration का प्रयोग करने पर हम किसी के कथन को Inverted Commas "......" के भीतर रखते हैं, पर Indirect Narration में Inverted Commas का प्रयोग नहीं होता; जैसे—

1. Ram said to Mohan, "I shall help you."—*Direct Narration*
2. Ram told Mohan that he would help him.—*Indirect Narration*

इस प्रकार हम देखते हैं कि Indirect Narration का प्रयोग होने पर कथन की भाषा में परिवर्तन हो जाता है। यह परिवर्तन कैसे होता है, इसके कुछ नियम हैं, जिन्हें हम General Rules और Special Rules कह सकते हैं। पर इन नियमों को समझने के पहले हमें Narration से संबद्ध कुछ पारिभाषिक शब्दों पर विचार करना चाहिए।

(A) Reporting Verb/Introductory Verb/Verb of the Reported Speech—आप देखेंगे कि Direct Narration में Inverted Commas के बाहर कम-से-कम एक वाक्य रहता है। उसी वाक्य के Verb को Reporting Verb या Introductory Verb कहते हैं।

जो वाक्य Inverted Commas के भीतर रहता है, उसे Reported Speech कहा जाता है और उस वाक्य के Verb को ही Verb of the Reported Speech कहते हैं।

(B) Kinds of Sentences—Narration में हमें वाक्य के अर्थ से प्रयोजन रहता है, उसकी बनावट से नहीं। बनावट की दृष्टि से वाक्य simple, compound, complex या mixed होते हैं, जो Analysis का विषय है। अर्थ के विचार से वाक्य के पाँच भेद होते हैं—

1. Assertive
2. Imperative
3. Interrogative
4. Optative
5. Exclamatory

Narration में हमें इन्हीं भेदों का ध्यान रखना है, क्योंकि Direct को Indirect में बदलने का, संक्षेप में, अर्थ होता है Inverted Commas के भीतर जितने प्रकार के वाक्य रहते हैं, उन्हें बदलना। यदि हम उन वाक्यों को पहचान नहीं सकें, तो फिर उन्हें नियमानुसार बदल ही कैसे सकेंगे? इन वाक्यों की चर्चा हम विस्तारपूर्वक आगे करेंगे जब Special Rules पर विचार होगा। अभी यहाँ हम पहले General Rules पर विचार करें।

GENERAL RULES

General Rules उन नियमों को कहते हैं, जो प्रत्येक प्रकार के वाक्य के साथ लागू होते हैं। Inverted Commas के भीतर किसी भी प्रकार का वाक्य क्यों न हो, इन नियमों की सहायता लेनी पड़ती है। इन नियमों को हम तीन भागों में बाँट सकते हैं—

(i) Change of Person

(ii) Change of Tense

(iii) Change of other Parts of Speech

I. CHANGE OF PERSON

Direct Narration को Indirect में बदलने पर Inverted Commas के भीतर जितने Person (first, second और third) रहते हैं, वें इस नियम के अनुसार बदल जाते हैं—

SON, जिसे आप **SON-Formula** भी कहते हैं।

यहाँ **S** का अर्थ है Subject, **O** का Object और **N** का None या No change. इसके अनुसार Inverted Commas के भीतर जो First Person (I, my, we, our, me, us) रहता है, वह Reporting Verb के Subject के अनुसार बदल जाता है; जैसे—

Ram told me, "*I* shall do *my* work."

Ram told me that *he* would do *his* work.

यहाँ Reporting Verb 'told' का Subject है Ram जो Third Person में है। इसलिए Inverted Commas के भीतर जो First Person (I और my) है, वह Third Person में बदल गया है। इसी प्रकार, यदि Inverted Commas के भीतर Second Person (you, your आदि) रहे तो वह Reporting Verb के Object के अनुसार बदल जाता है; जैसे—

Ram told *me*, "*You* should do *your* work."

Ram told *me* that *I* should do *my* work.

यहाँ Reporting Verb 'told' का object है me जो First Person में है। इसलिए Inverted Commas के भीतर जो Second Person (you और your) है, वह First Person में बदल गया है। यदि Inverted Commas के भीतर Third Person (he, she आदि) रहे, तो वह ज्यों-का-त्यों रहता है, अर्थात उसमें कोई परिवर्तन नहीं होता; जैसे—

Ram told *me*, "*He* will do *his* work."

Ram told me that *he* would do *his* work.

यहाँ Inverted Commas के भीतर Third Person है। इसलिए इसमें कोई परिवर्तन नहीं हुआ। तो संक्षेप में, आप इन नियमों को इस प्रकार याद रखें—

1. *First Person is changed into the person of the* **Subject.**
2. *Second Person is changed into the person of the* **Object.**
3. *Third Person requires* **No change.**

NOTE—Person के बदलने पर उसका Number और Case वही रहता है, जो Inverted Commas के भीतर रहता है; जैसे—

He told me, "I shall try *my* best to help you."

He told me that *he* would try *his* best to help me.

Caution—Reporting Verb without Object

कभी-कभी Reporting Verb के बाद object [say + to + me/him/her] नहीं आता है, जैसे—

1. He said, "You are an idiot, Suresh."
2. He said, "You are telling a lie, Leela."
3. He said, "Where are you going, mother?"
4. He said, "Don't make a noise here."
5. He said, "Bring a chair at once."

ऐसी अवस्था में दो समस्याएँ खड़ी होती हैं—

(i) Second Person के Pronoun का परिवर्तन कैसे करें?

(ii) Say के बदले ask/tell/order/request/wish के बाद किस Pronoun का प्रयोग करें?

इन समस्याओं का समाधान इस प्रकार करना चाहिए—

(a) वाक्य में प्रयुक्त संबोधन कारक (Vocative Case) के noun के अनुसार Second Person का परिवर्तन

(b) यदि वाक्य में संबोधन कारक का प्रयोग नहीं हुआ हो और प्रसंग (Context) से भी कुछ पता न चले, तो Second Person का First Person या Third Person में परिवर्तन

इन वाक्यों को लें—

1. He said, "You are an idiot, Suresh."
   = He said to Suresh, "You are an idiot."
   = He told Suresh that he (Suresh) was an idiot.
2. He said, "You are telling a lie, Leela."
   = He said to Leela, "You are telling a lie."
   = He told Leela that she (Leela) was telling a lie.
3. He said, "Where are you going, mother?"
   = He said to mother, "Where are you going?"
   = He asked mother where she was going.
4. He said, "Don't make a noise."
   = He said to me/him/her, "Don't make a noise."
   = He asked me/him/her not to make a noise.
5. He said, "Bring a chair."
   He said to me/him/her, "Bring a chair."
   He ordered me/him/her to bring a chair.
6. He said, "How are you?"
   He said to me/him/her, "How are you?"
   He asked me/him/her how I/he/she was.

7. He said, "Open the gate."

He said to me/him/her/us/them, "Open the gate."

He told me/him/her/us/them to open the gate.

यहाँ एक बात ध्यान देने योग्य है। जब Exclamatory Sentence अधूरा रहता है, तब उसमें Subject और Verb नहीं रहते हैं।

वैसे Exclamations में कुछ टूटे-फूटे शब्द रहते हैं जिन्हें fragments कहा जा सकता है। तब किस Person का प्रयोग किया जाए? मेरी राय में ऐसे Exclamations को परिवर्तित करते समय First Person (I/me) का प्रयोग करना अधिक अच्छा है और उचित भी, जैसे—

1. He said, "Congratulations!"

He congratulated **me.**

2. She said, "liar!"

She called **me** a liar.

कुछ लोगों की राय है कि जब Reporting Verb के बाद Object नहीं आता है, तब सदा Third Person (he/him/his/she/her/them) का प्रयोग होना चाहिए, पर मेरी राय में ऐसा मत उचित नहीं जँचता। इसलिए ऐसे वाक्यों में आप First Person या Third Person किसी का भी प्रयोग करें। हाँ, Exclamations में First Person का ही प्रयोग करें, तो अच्छा।

अपने मत के समर्थन में कुछ महान आचार्यों के उदाहरणों को देखें। अपनी प्रसिद्ध पुस्तक *Living English Structure* में W S Allen ने इन वाक्यों का परिवर्तन इस प्रकार किया है—

1. He said, "Bring me a book."

He asked her (him/us, etc.) to bring him a book. (Page 258)

2. He said, "Don't do it."

He asked me (her/us, etc.) not to do it. (Page 259)

3. He said, "Hello! Where are you going?"

He greeted me and asked (me) where I was going. (Page 276)

इसी प्रकार, A J Thompson ने अपनी लोकप्रिय पुस्तक *A Practical English Grammar* में इन वाक्यों का परिवर्तन इस प्रकार किया है—

1. He said, "What have you got in your bag?"

He asked me what I had got in my bag. (Page 182)

2. He said, "Why didn't you put on the brake?"

He asked her why she hadn't put on the brake. (Page 182)

3. He said, "What do you want?"

He asked them what they wanted. (Page 182)

4. He said, "Would you like a drink?"

He asked me if I would like a drink. (Page 183)

5. "Shut the door, will you?" he shouted.

He told us to shut the door. (Page 185)

6. "Will you stop talking?" he said.

He told them to stop talking. (Page 185)

7. He said, "When you go out lock both doors."

He told me to lock both doors when I went out. (Page 185)

8. He said, "Thank you."

He thanked me. (Page 188)

9. He said, "Good morning!"

He wished me a good morning. (Page 188)

10. He said, "Happy Christmas!"

He wished me a happy Christmas. (Page 188)

11. He said, "Congratulations!"

He congratulated me. (Page 188)

12. He said, "Liar!"

He called me a liar. (Page 188)

संक्षेप में, याद रखें कि जब Reporting Verb के साथ Object नहीं रहता है, तब

(i) Second Person = First or Third Person

पर जब Reporting Verb के साथ Object रहता है तब

(ii) Second Person = Object

यह भी याद रखें कि जब Reporting Verb का Subject होता है First Person और Object नहीं रहता है तब

(iii) Second Person = Third Person [not, First Person]

इन वाक्यों को देखें—

1. I said, "You are a liar."

I told him/her/that he/she was a liar. [not, I/me]

2. I said, "Congratulations!"

I congratulated him/her/them. [not me]

3. I said, "Fool!"

I called him/her a fool [not me]

II. CHANGE OF TENSE

Rule I. यदि Reporting Verb Present या Future Tense में रहे, तो Reported Speech के Verb का Tense ज्यों-का-त्यों रहता है; जैसे—

1. Ram says, "I *shall go*/I *went*."

Ram says that he *will go*/he *went*.

2. Ram will say, "I *go/shall go.*"

Ram will say that he *goes/will go.*

यहाँ पहले वाक्य में Reporting Verb 'says' Present Tense में है। इसलिए Reported Speech का Future Tense (shall go) और Past Tense (went) Indirect Narration में नहीं बदला है। इसी प्रकार, दूसरे वाक्य में Reporting Verb Future Tense में है और इसीलिए Reported Speech के Present Tense (go) और Future Tense (shall go) को ज्यों-का-त्यों रख दिया गया है।

Rule II. यदि Reporting Verb Past Tense में हो और Reported Speech का Verb Present या Future Tense में, तो वह Present या Future Tense corresponding Past Tense में बदल दिया जाता है; जैसे—

1. He said, "I *will go.*"

   He said that he *would go.*

2. He said, "I *am going.*"

   He said that he *was going.*

3. He said, "I *have gone.*"

   He said that he *had gone.*

4. He said, "I *have been going.*"

   He said that he *had been going.*

इन सभी वाक्यों में Reporting Verb (said) Past Tense में है। इसीलिए Inverted Commas के भीतर जितनी भी Future और Present Tense की क्रियाएँ हैं, वे corresponding Past Tense में बदल गई हैं—

1. Present Indefinite = Past Indefinite
2. Present Imperfect = Past Imperfect
3. Present Perfect = Past perfect
4. Present Perfect Continuous = Past Perfect Continuous

Rule III. यदि Reporting Verb Past Tense में हो और Reported Speech का भी verb Past Tense में हो, तो

(a) Reported Speech का Past Indefinite बदल जाता है Past Perfect में—

Ram said, "The train *reached* late."

Ram said that the train *had reached* late.

(b) Reported Speech का Past Imperfect बदल जाता है Past Perfect Continuous में—

Ram said, "The boy *was reading.*"

Ram said that the boy *had been reading.*

(c) Reported Speech का Past Perfect का Past Perfect Continuous ज्यों-का-त्यों रह जाता है।

Exception: Universal Truth

अभी हमने देखा है कि यदि Reporting Verb Past Tense में हो, तो Reported Speech का Verb Past Tense में बदल जाता है; पर इस नियम का एक अपवाद भी है, जो बहुत महत्त्वपूर्ण है। यदि Inverted Commas के भीतर कोई ऐसा कथन हो जिससे आदत या चिरंतन सत्य या सिद्धांत (habitual या universal truth या principle) का बोध हो, तो Reporting Verb के Past में रहने पर भी Reported Speech के Verb का Tense नहीं बदलता; जैसे—

1. The teacher *said*, "The earth *is* round."
   The teacher said that the earth *is* round.
2. He *said*, "Honesty *is* the best policy."
   He said that honesty *is* the best policy.
3. The preacher *said*, "Man *proposes* and God *disposes*."
   The preacher said that man *proposes* and God *disposes*.

इस संबंध में याद रखें कि Inverted Commas के भीतर जो Proverbs (मुहावरे) रहते हैं, उनसे भी universal truth का बोध होता है और इसलिए वैसे वाक्यों के Verbs के भी Tense नहीं बदलते; जैसे—

1. He *remarked*, "A bad carpenter *quarrels* with his tools."
   He remarked that a bad carpenter *quarrels* with his tools.
2. I *said*, "Birds of a feather *flock* together."
   I said that birds of a feather *flock* together.

Caution—कभी-कभी Reported Speech में must का प्रयोग होता है। ऐसे must को साधारणतः has/have to + verb में बदल देना चाहिए; जैसे—

He said, "I must go."

He said that he *had to go*.

इस संबंध में एक बात का ध्यान रखें। यदि must से किसी नियम या सिद्धांत (rule or principle) का बोध हो, तो must ज्यों-का-त्यों रह जाता है; जैसे—

He said, "Students must respect their teachers"

He said that students *must* respect their teachers.

III. CHANGE OF OTHER PARTS OF SPEECH

जब Reporting Verb Past Tense में रहता है, तब Reported Speech के केवल Verb का Tense ही नहीं बदलता वरन Reported Speech में (Inverted Commas के भीतर) जितने भी निकटता-सूचक (expressing nearness) Adjectives, Adverbs और Verbs रहते हैं, वे सब-के-सब दूरी-सूचक (expressing distance) शब्दों में बदल जाते हैं; जैसे—

This	*into*	That	Tomorrow	*into*	Next day
These	"	Those	Yesterday	"	The previous day

Here	into	There	Last Night	into	The previous night
Now	”	Then	Next week/year	”	The following week/year
Thus	”	So	Hence	”	Thence
Come	”	Go	Today	”	That day
A year, etc., ago	”	A year before			

Caution—इस संबंध में यह बात ध्यान देने योग्य है कि यदि Reported Speech में प्रयोग किए गए Adjective या Adverb से ऐसा मालूम पड़े कि वे चीजें वक्ता के साथ या सामने हैं, तो उस हालत में निकटता-सूचक शब्दों को दूरी-सूचक शब्दों में नहीं बदला जाता है; जैसे—

Ram said, "*This* is my pen."

Ram said that *this* was his pen.

यहाँ this को ज्यों-का-त्यों रख दिया गया है; इसे that में बदला नहीं गया, क्योंकि यहाँ जिस pen की चर्चा हुई है, वह वक्ता (राम) के साथ है या उसके सामने मौजूद है।

अब, इन वाक्यों को लें—

This morning he said, "I will go out *today*."

This morning he said that he would go out *today*.

यहाँ today के बदले that day का प्रयोग उचित नहीं। क्यों? इसलिए कि कार्य उसी दिन से संबंध रखता है जिस दिन की चर्चा Direct Speech में है।

SPECIAL RULES

अब हमें Special Rules पर विचार करना है, जो भिन्न-भिन्न प्रकार के वाक्यों के लिए भिन्न-भिन्न हैं। यदि Inverted Commas के भीतर Assertive sentence रहे, तो एक प्रकार के नियमों की आवश्यकता होती है और यदि Imperative रहे, तो दूसरे प्रकार के नियमों की। अगर Inverted Commas के अंदर Interrogative sentence हो, तो एक तीसरे प्रकार के नियम लगाए जाते हैं और Exclamatory के लिए चौथे प्रकार के। तो, इससे यह स्पष्ट है कि Special Rules लगाकर Direct को Indirect में बदलने के पहले हम यह अवश्य समझ लें कि Inverted Commas के अंदर किस प्रकार का वाक्य है। इसको पहचानने में कोई खास कठिनाई नहीं होती, क्योंकि वाक्य के अर्थ को समझकर और फिर विराम-चिह्न (punctuation marks) को देखकर हम आसानी से कह सकते हैं कि अमुक वाक्य किस प्रकार का है।

Interrogative sentence से प्रश्न का बोध होता है और वाक्य के अंत में प्रश्नवाचक चिह्न [Note of Interrogation (?)] आता है; जैसे—

1. Are you ill? 2. What is he doing?

इसी प्रकार, Imperative sentence में आज्ञा, प्रार्थना या परामर्श (order, request, advice या proposal) का बोध होता है; जैसे—

1. Go there. 2. Please help me. 3. Let us go.

Assertive sentence को पहचानने में कोई कठिनाई नहीं होती, क्योंकि वैसे वाक्यों से यह साफ झलकता है कि कोई बात सीधे रूप से हाँ या न (affirmative या negative) में कही गई है; जैसे—

1. You are a good man. 2. You are not a good man.

ऐसे वाक्यों से न तो प्रश्न का भाव झलकता है और न आज्ञा या प्रार्थना का ही।

Optative और Exclamatory sentences को भी पहचानना कठिन नहीं, क्योंकि Optative से option (इच्छा) का बोध होता है। यदि वाक्य से अभिशाप (curse) या आशीर्वाद (blessing) आदि प्रकार की अच्छी या बुरी इच्छाओं का बोध हो, तो उसे Optative समझना चाहिए; जैसे—

1. May you live long! 2. May he die!
3. A plague split you! 4. Long live the king!

यदि वाक्यों से हर्ष-उल्लास, शोक-संताप या आश्चर्य-घृणा आदि प्रकार की आंतरिक प्रबल भावनाओं का बोध हो, तो उन्हें Exclamatory sentence कहा जाता है; जैसे—

1. Alas! he is dead. 2. Hurrah! we are victorious.

इस प्रकार Inverted Commas के भीतर जितने वाक्य हों, उन्हें ठीक से पहचान कर आप Special Rules का प्रयोग करें।

I. SPECIAL RULES: ASSERTIVE SENTENCES/STATEMENTS

Rule I. Inverted Commas को that में बदल दें।

Rule II. Reporting Verb 'say' को **tell + object** में बदल दें यदि say + to + object का प्रयोग हो। पर यदि to + object न रहे, तो say को ज्यों-का-त्यों रहने दें।

इस प्रकार, Indirect में वाक्य की बनावट हो जाती है—

subject + say + that + clause

Or

subject + tell + object + that + clause

इन वाक्यों को देखें—

1. He said, "The earth is round."

   He said that/the earth is round.

2. He said to his friends, "I will return on Monday."

   He told/his friends/that he would return on Monday.

NOTE (a)—यदि Inverted Commas के भीतर Terms of Address (संबोधन के शब्द) आएँ, तो उन्हें object में बदल दें या उन्हें address ... as के बाद रखें।

इन वाक्यों को लें—

1. The teacher said, "Ram, I am pleased with you."

   The teacher *told Ram* that he was pleased with him.

2. The leader said, "Ladies and gentlemen, I should thank you all."

   The leader *addressed* the public *as* ladies and gentlemen and said that he should thank them all.

ऐसे वाक्यों का परिवर्तन इस प्रकार न करें—

The teacher said, "Ram, I am pleased with you."

The teacher said *that, Ram,* he was pleased with him.

NOTE (b)—यदि Inverted commas के अंदर O, well, You, See आदि प्रकार के शब्द संबोधन के लिए प्रयोग किए जाएँ, तो सबसे आसान तरीका यह है कि आप उन्हें उड़ा दें, अर्थात उनको बिलकुल ही छोड़ दें; जैसे—

The teacher said, "Well, Mohan, I shall punish you."

The teacher said to Mohan that he would punish him.

यहाँ well का बिलकुल लोप हो गया, पर इससे वाक्य के अर्थ पर कुछ भी आघात नहीं पहुँचता। वास्तव में, ऐसे शब्द निरर्थक होते हैं, क्योंकि बोलने के सिलसिले में ये यों ही प्रयुक्त हो जाते हैं। इसलिए ऐसे शब्दों को हटा देने से कोई हर्ज नहीं।

NOTE (c)—यदि Inverted Commas के अंदर स्वागत या बिदाई, 'welcome or farewell' (जैसे good morning, good night) आदि प्रकार के शब्द आएँ, तो Idiom के अनुसार इनके पहले bid या wish जोड़कर इन्हें Reporting Verb के पहले रख देना चाहिए, that के बाद नहीं; जैसे—

My friend said to me, "*Good morning*. I am happy to see you."

My friend wished me *good morning* and said that he was happy to see me.

NOTE (d)—यदि Inverted Commas के बीच एक से अधिक Assertive Sentence रहें तो उन्हें and से जोड़ देना चाहिए या further added आदि का प्रयोग कर सभी वाक्यों को मिला देना चाहिए, क्योंकि बार-बार say या tell का प्रयोग करने पर वाक्य भद्दा हो जाता है; जैसे—

The king said, "It is enough. My mother is yet alive. I will go and see her before I die."

The king said that it was enough; that his mother was yet alive; *and that* he would go and see her before he died.

यहाँ Inverted Commas के अंदर तीन वाक्य हैं, जो Assertive हैं और इसलिए Indirect Narration में तीनों ही को एक वाक्य बना दिया गया है। यही कारण है कि यहाँ and का प्रयोग हुआ है। यहाँ इसका Indirect form इस प्रकार भी हो सकता है—

The king said that it was enough and that his mother was yet alive. He *further added* that he would go and see her before he died.

NOTE (e)—कुछ ऐसे भी Assertive sentences होते हैं जो अधूरे रहते हैं, खासकर किसी प्रश्न के उत्तर में जो Elliptical (अधूरे) वाक्य कहे जाते हैं; जैसे—yes, no, very well, not at all इत्यादि। वैसी अवस्था में प्रश्न के उत्तर का अर्थ समझकर आप वैसे वाक्यों को पूरा कर दें या उन्हें इस प्रकार बदल दें—replied in the affirmative या replied in the negative आदि; जैसे—

I asked him, "Are you ill?" He said, "Yes, I am."

पहले वाक्य पर हमलोग Interrogative sentence के संबंध में विचार करेंगे, पर दूसरे वाक्य को दो प्रकार से बदला जा सकता है—

1. He said (replied) that he was ill.

2. He replied *in the affirmative.*

यहाँ Yes, I am का पूरा अर्थ है—I am ill. इसलिए ऐसे अधूरे वाक्यों को जरा सावधानी से Indirect में बदलना चाहिए। इन वाक्यों का परिवर्तन देखें—

1. He asked, "Do you feel hungry?" I said, "Yes, I do."

   = I replied that I felt hungry.

   Yes, I do = I feel hungry.

2. He asked, "Would you like to buy a new book?" I said, "I would like to."

   = I replied that I would like to buy.

   I would like to = I would like to buy.

II. SPECIAL RULES: INTERROGATIVE SENTENCES

Interrogatives: Questions

Rule I. Reporting Verb को ask में बदल दें।

Rule II. यदि Interrogative sentence का उत्तर सिर्फ Yes या No में दिया जा सके तो inverted Commas को If या Whether में बदल दें। पर यदि ऐसा संभव न हो, अर्थात Interrogative sentence का उत्तर Yes या No न होकर कोई वाक्य हो, तो सिर्फ Inverted Commas का लोप कर दें और if/whether का प्रयोग न करें।

Rule III. Interrogative sentence को Assertive में बदल दें।

NOTE—कभी-कभी इसमें कुछ कठिनाई होती है। इसलिए यहाँ एक-दो बातों पर विचार कर लेना अच्छा होगा। जितने Interrogative sentences होते हैं, वे दो भागों में बाँटे जा सकते हैं—(1) जिनमें Auxiliary Verb 'do' का प्रयोग होता है, और (2) जिनमें Auxiliary Verb 'do' का प्रयोग नहीं होता। जिन Interrogative sentences में Verb 'do' का प्रयोग होता है वे दो प्रकार के होते हैं—(a) जिनमें not लगा रहता है, जैसे—do not, did not, does not और (b) जिनमें not नहीं लगा रहता है।

यदि Interrogative sentences में do के साथ not लगा रहे, तो वैसे वाक्यों को इस प्रकार Assertive बनाएँ—

Subject के बाद Verb को रख दें; जैसे—

1. Did he not go? He did not go.

2. Does he not read? He does not read.

3. Do you not laugh? You do not laugh.

यदि Interrogative में do के साथ not नहीं आए, तो वैसे वाक्यों को इस प्रकार Assertive में बदलें—

Auxiliary Verb 'do' को बिलकुल हटा दें; जैसे—

1. Do you go? You go.

2. Did he go? He went.
3. Does he go? He goes.
4. What do you want? What you want.

यदि Interrogative sentence में Verb 'do' के बदले अन्य Verbs (is/have/will) का प्रयोग हो, तो उन्हें इस प्रकार Assertive बनाएँ—

Subject के बाद Verb को रख दें; जैसे—

1. Are you ill? You are ill.
2. Where is he? Where he is.
3. How will you go? How you will go.
4. Can you do it? You can do it.

इस प्रकार, Indirect में ऐसे वाक्यों की बनावट होती है—

subject + ask + object + if/whether + clause [assertive]
Or
subject + ask + object + question-word + clause [assertive]

इन वाक्यों को देखें—

1. Ram told Shyam, "Will you help me?"
   Ram asked Shyam if/whether he would help him.
2. Mohan told Sohan, "What do you want?"
   Mohan asked Sohan/what he wanted.
3. I told my friend, "Why are you sad?"
   I asked my friend/why he was sad.
4. Sita told Radha, "Are you ill?"
   Sita asked Radha if/whether she was ill.

Interrogatives: Question-tags

कभी-कभी Inverted Commas के भीतर Question-tags का प्रयोग होता है। ऐसे Interrogatives को Indirect में इन नियमों के अनुसार बदलें—

Rule I. Assertive sentence (Statement) को बिलकुल छोड़ दें।

Rule II. Question-tags को सामान्य नियमों के अनुसार बदलें, पर Question-tags को पूरे वाक्य का रूप अवश्य दें, जैसे—

1. He told me, "You are rich, aren't you?"
   = He told me, "Aren't you rich?"
2. She told me, "You like fish, don't you?"
   = She told me, "Don't you like fish?"

इन वाक्यों के परिवर्तन को देखें—

1. Ram told me, "*You are rich,* aren't you?"
   Ram asked me if I was rich.
2. Mohan told me, "*You like fish,* don't you?"
   Mohan asked me if I liked fish.

ध्यान दें कि यहाँ Assertive sentence को छोड़ दिया गया है और केवल Question-tags को Indirect में बदला गया है।

यह भी देखें कि Question-tags को पूरे वाक्य का रूप देकर इन्हें Indirect में बदला गया है।

Interrogatives: Shall I?

कुछ Interrogative sentences में Shall I? का प्रयोग होता है। इसके दो अर्थ होते हैं—

(i) Future Tense का बोध, (ii) Request का बोध

जब Shall I? का अर्थ होता है Future Tense, तब Indirect में Shall I? हो जाता है—*he/she would.* पर जब Shall I? से Request का भाव व्यक्त होता है, तब Shall I? हो जाता है—*he/she should;* जैसे—

1. He told me, "Shall I pass?"

   He asked me if he *would* pass—Future
2. She told me, "Shall I go to the picture?"

   She asked if she *should* go to the picture.—Request
3. He told me, "Shall I open the door?"

   He asked me if he should open the door.—Request

NOTE (a)—Interrogative sentence को Indirect में बदलने पर that का प्रयोग भूलकर भी मत करें। ऐसा तो Assertive sentence में होता है न!

NOTE (b)—Inverted Commas के अंदर बहुत-से Interrogative sentences रहने पर उन्हें and से जोड़ें या further asked आदि उपयुक्त शब्दों का प्रयोग करें।

NOTE (c)—Assertive sentence के संबंध में जो कुछ Note (a) से (d) तक कहा गया है, उसका ध्यान आप Interrogative sentences को Indirect Narration में बदलते समय भी रखें। उन्हीं नियमों से काम चल जाएगा। हाँ, say या tell के बदले यहाँ ask या enquire का प्रयोग होना चाहिए।

Caution—कुछ लोग who, which, what, when, why, where, whether आदि के पहले *as to* का प्रयोग इस प्रकार कर देते हैं—

1. He said to me, "Are you ill?"
   He asked me *as to* whether I was ill.
2. He said to me, "Why are you sad?"
   He asked me *as to* why I was sad.

इन वाक्यों में as to का प्रयोग अशुद्ध है; कम-से-कम अनावश्यक तो है ही। आप ऐसे वाक्यों में as to का प्रयोग न करें।

III. SPECIAL RULES: IMPERATIVE SENTENCES

Imperative: Order/Advise/Request

Rule I. Reporting Verb को, अर्थ के अनुसार, order/request/pray/suggest/ask/advise में बदल दें।

Rule II. Inverted Commas को to में बदल दें। Indirect में वाक्य की इस प्रकार बनावट हो जाती है—

subject + ask/request + object + infinitive

इन वाक्यों को देखें—

1. Ram said to me, "Go there."

   Ram *ordered/asked* me *to go* there.

2. The doctor told me, "Take medicine in time."

   The doctor *advised* me *to take* medicine in time.

3. I said to my father, "Please give me more money."

   I *requested* my father *to give* me more money.

NOTE (a)—Inverted Commas के अंदर Please, Kindly आदि प्रकार के शब्द Indirect में हटा दिए जाते हैं, क्योंकि उनका अर्थ तो Reporting Verb से ही स्पष्ट हो जाता है।

NOTE (b)—Assertive sentence के सिलसिले में जो कुछ Note (a) से (c) तक कहा गया है, उसका यहाँ भी ध्यान रखें और उन नियमों के अनुसार जितने भी संबोधन के शब्द Inverted Commas के भीतर मिलें, उन्हें Indirect में Reporting Verb के पहले रख दें। हाँ, केवल say या tell के बदले अर्थानुसार order/ask या request आदि का प्रयोग होना चाहिए।

Negative Imperative: Prohibition

NOTE (c)—यदि Inverted Commas के भीतर *do not + infinitive* आए तो उसे Indirect में इस प्रकार बदलें—

Rule I. Reporting Verb को forbid में बदल दें।

Rule II. Inverted Commas को to में बदल दें।

Rule III. Not को to के पहले रखें। इस प्रकार, वाक्य होगा—

not + infinitive

इन वाक्यों में परिवर्तन को देखें—

1. The teacher told us, "Don't write on tables."

   The teacher *forbade* us *to write* on tables.

2. He told me, "Don't shout in the class."

   He *forbade* me *to shout* in the class.

   Or

   He asked me *not to shout* in the class.

इस प्रकार, Negative Imperative की बनावट हो जाती है—

subject + forbid + object + infinitive [to + verb]

Or

subject + ask + object + not + infinitive [to + verb]

NOTE (d)—यदि Inverted Commas के भीतर Imperative में केवल Do रहे, तो साधारण नियम के अनुसार Reporting Verb को ask/request/order में बदल दें और Inverted Commas को to में; जैसे—

I said to him, "*Do* that at once."

I ordered *him to do* that at once.

Emphatic Imperatives

कुछ Imperative sentences के पहले do का प्रयोग वाक्य को जोरदार (emphatic) बनाने के लिए किया जाता है; जैसे—

1. Do have a cup of tea.
2. Do come tomorrow.

ऐसे Emphatic Imperative को Indirect में बदलते समय—

Rule I. Do का लोप कर दें।

Rule II. Do के बाद आनेवाले verb के पहले to का प्रयोग करें—

to + verb; इस प्रकार यह infinitive में बदल जाएगा।

इन वाक्यों के परिवर्तन को देखें—

1. I told Ram, "Do have a cup of tea."
   I requested Ram *to have* a cup of tea.
2. I told her, "Do come tomorrow."
   I requested/asked her *to come* next day.

More Hints On Imperative Sentences

आप देखेंगे कि कुछ Imperative sentences 'let' से शुरू होते हैं। इनको Indirect में बदलने के लिए इन नियमों की मदद लें—

(A) Let: Order

कुछ वाक्य Let से आरंभ होते हैं और उनसे परोक्ष आज्ञा (indirect command) का बोध होता है। इनका परिवर्तन इस प्रकार होता है—

(i) subject + say + that + subject + be + infinitive [with 'to']

(ii) subject + order/command + that + subject + should + infinitive [without 'to']

इन वाक्यों का परिवर्तन देखें—

The Principal said, "Let no one come late."

= The Principal said that no one *was to come* late.

The Principal ordered that no one should come late.

ध्यान दें कि Indirect Speech में let का प्रयोग नहीं होता और Inverted Commas के बदले that का प्रयोग होता है।

(B) Let + Us: Proposal

यदि Let वाले वाक्य से किसी प्रस्ताव (Proposal) का बोध हो, तो

Rule I. Reporting Verb को propose/suggest में बदल दें।

Rule II. Inverted Commas को that में बदल दें।

Rule III. Let को should में बदल दें।

Rule IV. Objective case (us) को Nominative (we) में बदल दें।

Rule V. Auxiliary Verb 'should' को Subject (we) के बाद रखकर अन्य शब्दों को रखें।

इस वाक्य को लें—

Ram said to me, "*Let* us sing together."

Ram *proposed* that *we should* sing together.

NOTE—ध्यान रहे कि साधारणतया वैसे let वाले वाक्यों से proposal का बोध होता है, जिनमें let के बाद 'us ...' आता है। अतः, ऐसे वाक्यों में ऊपर बताये गये नियमों (1 से 5 तक) का प्रयोग होना चाहिए।

(C) Let: Wish/Desire

कुछ वैसे भी Let वाले वाक्य होते हैं जिनसे proposal का बोध नहीं होता। उन वाक्यों में let के बाद me, him, her, them या there be का प्रयोग होता है। वैसे वाक्यों से वक्ता की इच्छा (wish) का बोध होता है; जैसे—

1. The boy said, "Let me go out, sir."
2. The lover said, "Let her rest in peace."
3. God said, "Let there be light", and there was light.
4. I said, "Let him do what he likes."
5. He said, "Let me help you."

ऐसे वाक्यों को Indirect में बदलने के लिए इन नियमों की सहायता लें—

Rule I. Reporting Verb को wish में बदल दें, क्योंकि ऐसा करने से वक्ता की इच्छा या अनुमति माँगने या देने का भाव स्पष्ट हो जाता है।

Rule II. Inverted Commas को that में बदल दें।

Rule III. Let को should में बदल दें और Objective Case (me, him, her इत्यादि) को Nominative (I, he, she इत्यादि) में बदलकर उसे should के पहले (I should, he should आदि) रख दें।

इन नियमों के अनुसार ऊपर दिए गए पाँच वाक्यों के indirect रूप क्रमशः इस प्रकार होंगे—

1. The boy *wished* that he should go out.
2. The lover *wished* that she should rest in peace.

3. God *wished* that there should be light and there was light.

4. I *wished* that he should do what he liked.

5. He *wished* that he should help me.

(D) Let: Supposition

कभी-कभी Let there be या Let it be से शुरू होने पर वाक्य से कल्पना (supposition) का भाव झलकता है; जैसे—

The teacher said, "Let it be a triangle."

ऐसे वाक्य को Indirect में बदलने के लिए—

(i) Reporting Verb को suppose में बदल देना चाहिए।

(ii) Let को गायब कर देना चाहिए; जैसे—

The teacher *supposed* that to be a triangle.

(E) Let it: Wish

कुछ वाक्यों के *Let it* से इच्छा (wish) का बोध होता है; जैसे—

1. Let it be so. 2. Let is rain.

वाक्यों से भिन्न-भिन्न प्रकार की इच्छा के भाव झलकते हैं। इसका भाव किसी प्रसंग में ही प्रकट हो सकता है। मान लें कि कोई दुखी है और वह घर छोड़कर बाहर चला जाना चाहता है। उसी समय वर्षा आरंभ होती है। यदि वैसी अवस्था में वह कहता है—"Let it rain. I must go."—तो वहाँ let it rain का वास्तव में अर्थ यह है कि "मुझे वर्षा की परवाह नहीं।" अतः, वहाँ इस वाक्य का Indirect रूप होगा—

He said that he did not care for rain.

अब मान लें कि सारे प्राणी गर्मी से व्याकुल हैं। उस समय वर्षा होती है और कोई कह उठता है—"Let it rain." वहाँ इस वाक्य से खुशी का बोध होगा, क्योंकि वह चाहता है कि वर्षा हो और उसके लिए उसे खुशी है। वैसे प्रसंग में उसका Indirect रूप होगा—

He wished that it should rain.

कहने का तात्पर्य यह है कि let के बाद it का प्रयोग होने पर उस वाक्य से हर्ष (joy), शोक (sorrow), अनुमति (approval) या उदासीनता (indifference) का भाव प्रकट हो सकता है। ऐसे वाक्यों का परिवर्तन अर्थानुसार होना चाहिए।

(F) Let: Even if [Concession]

Let के संबंध में एक और बात का ध्यान रखें। आप देखेंगे कि कुछ let वाले वाक्यों से even if (concession—यद्यपि) का बोध होता है—

1. Let it be ever so difficult. I must do it.

2. Let it rain ever so hard, I will go today.

ऐसे वाक्यों में Let it के बाद ever so अवश्य आता है—

Let it ... ever so. ऐसे वाक्यों को indirect में बदलने के लिए आप इन नियमों की सहायता ले सकते हैं—

Rule I. Reporting Verb को ज्यों-का-त्यों रहने दें।

Rule II. Inverted Commas को that में बदल दें।

Rule III. Let को even if में बदल दें।

Rule IV. Even so का लोप कर दें।

इस वाक्य को देखें—

Ram said, "Let it rain *ever so* hard, I will go today."

Ram said that *even if* it rained hard he would go that day.

(G) Imperative + Question-tag

कुछ Imperative sentences के बाद Question-tag आता है। ऐसे वाक्यों को Indirect में इस प्रकार बदलें—

(i) Question-tag को छोड़ दें।

(ii) Reporting Verb को *tell/ask/request* में बदल दें और इनके बाद to + verb (infinitive) का प्रयोग करें।

इन वाक्यों को देखें—

1. He told me, "Shut the door, will you?"

   He asked/requested me *to shut* the door.

2. She told me, "Give me some money, will you?"

   She requested me *to give* her some money.

ध्यान दें कि यहाँ question-tag को बिलकुल छोड़ दिया गया है।

(H) Interrogative: Order/Request

कुछ वाक्य देखने में तो Interrogative लगते हैं, पर वास्तव में वे एक विशेष प्रकार के Imperative sentence होते हैं, क्योंकि उनसे आज्ञा (permission/order), प्रार्थना (request), निमंत्रण (invitation) इत्यादि का बोध होता है। ऐसे वाक्यों को Indirect में बदलते समय Reporting Verb को उपयुक्त verb में (वाक्य के अर्थानुसार) बदल देना चाहिए। इन वाक्यों का परिवर्तन देखें—

1. He said, "Will you shut the door?"—polite order

   = He asked (requested) me to shut the door.

2. He said, "Will you lend me a book please?"—request

   He requested (asked) me to lend him a book.

3. He said, "Will you have tea with me tomorrow?"
He said, "Could you come to lunch tomorrow?" } —invitation
= He invited (asked) me to tea/lunch next day.
4. He said, "Could (May) I use your pen?"—permission
He asked if he could use my pen.

(I) Interrogative: Shall I? [request]

कभी-कभी Shall I? से प्रार्थना (request) का बोध होता है, केवल future time का नहीं। ऐसे वाक्यों के shall का should हो जाता है; जैसे—

1. He said, "Shall I open the door?"
He asked if he *should* open the door.
2. She said, "Shall I thread the needle?"
She asked if she *should* thread the needle.

IV. SPECIAL RULES: OPTATIVE SENTENCES

Rule I. Reporting Verb को curse, bless, pray, या wish में, वाक्य के अर्थानुसार बदल दें, क्योंकि ऐसे वाक्यों से अभिशाप, आशीर्वाद, प्रार्थना या इच्छा का बोध होता है।

Rule II. Inverted Commas को Assertive में बदल दें।

Rule III. Optative sentence को Assertive में बदल दें और वह इस प्रकार—

(a) वाक्यों में Subject को पहले रखें और उसके बाद Verb को।

(b) Note of Exclamation (!) को Full stop (.) में बदल दें; जैसे—

May God pardon you!—*Optative*

God *may* pardon you.—*Assertive*

इन वाक्यों के परिवर्तन को देखें—

1. Father said to me, "May you live long!"
Father *blessed* me that I might live long.
2. The preacher said to me, "May God help you!"
The preacher *prayed* that God might help me.
3. He said to me, "May you die!"
He *cursed* that I might die.

NOTE—यदि Optative sentence में may का प्रयोग नहीं हो, तो उसे (may को) वाक्य के आरंभ में जोड़ देना चाहिए; जैसे—

1. God save the king = *May* God save the king!
2. A plague split you = *May* a plague split you!

इस प्रकार, may जोड़कर वाक्य को पूरा कर देना चाहिए।

इस प्रकार, Indirect में ऐसे वाक्यों की बनावट हो जाती है—

subject + verb [bless/pray] + that + clause

V. SPECIAL RULES : EXCLAMATORY SENTENCES

Rule I. Reporting Verb को exclaim with joy/sorrow/surprise/anger/contempt/applause आदि प्रकार के शब्दों में, Reported Speech के अर्थानुसार बदल दें।

Rule II. Inverted Commas को that में बदल दें।

Rule III. Interjections (विस्मयादिबोधक शब्द) का लोप कर दें क्योंकि इनके भाव तो Reporting Verb से स्पष्ट हो ही जाते हैं।

Rule IV. Note of Exclamation (!) के बदले Full Stop (.) का प्रयोग करें।

Rule V. Exclamatory sentences को Assertive में बदल दें।

यदि Exclamatory sentences में how/what आए, तो इन्हें हटा दें और वाक्य को इस प्रकार बदल दें—

(i) What + noun = adjective + noun

1. What a place! = A lovely/strange place.
2. What a fool! = A big/great fool.

(ii) What + adjective + noun = adjective + noun

1. What a fine place! = A fine place.
2. What a good film! = A good film.

(iii) How + adjective/adverb = very + adjective/adverb

1. How well she sings! = She sings very well.
2. How handsome he is! = He is very handsome.

इस प्रकार, Indirect में इनकी बनावट हो जाती है—

subject + verb [exclaim] + that + clause

इन वाक्यों के परिवर्तन को देखें—

1. He said, "Alas! I am ruined."
   He *exclaimed* with sorrow that he was ruined.
2. She said, "Ah! he is dead."
   She *exclaimed* with sorrow that he was dead.
3. We said, "What a place it is!"
   We *exclaimed* with joy/surprise that it was a very fine place.
4. He said, "How sweetly she sings."
   He *exclaimed* with joy that she sang very sweetly.

NOTE (a)—यदि Exclamatory sentences अधूरे हों, तो Verb तथा अन्य शब्द जोड़कर उन्हें पूरा कर दें और तब उन्हें Indirect में बदलें; जैसे—

1. He said, "What a fall!"
   = He said, "What a fall it is/was!"
   = He exclaimed with sorrow that it was a big fall.
2. I said, "Oh, enough."
   = I said, "Oh, it is enough."
   = I exclaimed with disgust that it was enough.
3. She said, "Nonsense!"
   = She said, "It is nonsense."
   = She exclaimed that it was nonsense.

NOTE (b)—कुछ ऐसे अधूरे वाक्यों का परिवर्तन इस प्रकार करना चाहिए—

Rule I. Reporting Verb को एक उपयुक्त Transitive Verb में बदल दें।

Rule II. Reported Speech के शब्दों को Object का रूप दे दें।

इन वाक्यों के परिवर्तन को देखें—

1. He told me, "Fool! Liar!"
   He *called* me a fool and liar.
2. He said to me, "Thank you."
   He *thanked* me.
3. He told me, "Good morning!"
   He *wished* me good morning.
4. He said to me, "Happy Diwali!"
   He *wished* me a happy Diwali.
5. He told me, "Congratulations!"
   He *congratulated* me.

NOTE (c)—Inverted Commas के भीतर आनेवाले संबोधन के शब्दों को that के पहले रखें, जैसाकि Assertive sentences के संबंध में बताया गया है। ध्यान दें कि संबोधन या विस्मयादिबोधक शब्द that के बाद कभी भी नहीं आ सकते। वे या तो उड़ा दिये जाते हैं या उनके अर्थानुसार that के पहले वैसे शब्दों का प्रयोग होता है, जिनसे उन शब्दों का अर्थ स्पष्ट हो जाए।

MORE HINTS ON NARRATION

I

अभी तक भिन्न-भिन्न प्रकार के वाक्यों को Indirect में बदलने के संबंध में जिन General और Special Rules पर विचार किया गया है, उनकी सहायता से आप आसानी से उन्हें Indirect Narration में बदल सकते हैं। फिर भी, परीक्षा की दृष्टि से एक-दो बातों पर विचार करना आवश्यक है। आप देखेंगे कि Inverted Commas के अंदर कभी-कभी दो-तीन प्रकार के वाक्यों को रख कर उन्हें Indirect में बदलने को कहा जाता है; जैसे—

Ram told Shyam, "Please take your seat. I am very glad to see you.

Where had you been so long?"

यहाँ Inverted Commas के भीतर तीन वाक्य हैं, जिनमें पहला Imperative है, दूसरा Assertive और तीसरा Interrogative. इसलिए इन तीनों वाक्यों को भिन्न-भिन्न प्रकार के Special Rules की मदद से Indirect में बदलना चाहिए; जैसे—

Ram requested Shyam to take his seat. He told him that he (Ram) was glad to see him and asked him where he had been so long.

यहाँ पहले वाक्य को Imperative sentence के Special Rules की मदद से, दूसरे को Assertive sentence के Special Rules और तीसरे को Interrogative sentence के Special Rules की सहायता से indirect में बदला गया है और General Rules भी प्रत्येक के साथ लगाए गए हैं। तो, जब Inverted Commas के भीतर अलग-अलग तरह के वाक्यों को Indirect में बदलना होता है, तब Inverted Commas के बाहर जितने शब्द रहते हैं उन्हें उन सभी वाक्यों का common factor मान लिया जाता है और इसलिए भिन्न-भिन्न प्रकार के Special Rules के अनुसार उन्हें बार-बार बदलना पड़ता है; जैसे—

I told my friend, "Please help me. I am out of pocket. Can you help me? I hope you will."

I told my friend, "Please help me."

I told my friend, "I am out of pocket."

I told my friend, "Can you help me?"

I told my friend, "I hope you will."

यहाँ आप देखते हैं कि Inverted Commas के भीतर चार वाक्य हैं—पहला Imperative, दूसरा Assertive, तीसरा Interrogative और चौथा फिर Assertive. यहाँ "I told my friend" Inverted Commas के बाहर है और इसलिए इसको common factor मानकर इन चारों वाक्यों को अलग-अलग कर दिया गया है। अब इन्हें भिन्न-भिन्न Special Rules की मदद से Indirect में बदलना आसान है। यदि आप इन सभी वाक्यों को केवल Imperative या केवल Interrogative sentence के Special Rules की मदद से बदल देंगे, तो वह अशुद्ध होगा। सबको एक ही लाठी से हाँकने की कोशिश उचित नहीं है न!

II

हिंदी-उर्दू (तथा अन्य भारतीय भाषाओं) के छात्र that के बाद न तो Pronoun का ध्यान रखते हैं, न Tense का और न वाक्य के Structure (गठन) का ही। इसका कारण यह है कि भारतीय भाषाओं में Narration के नियम अत्यंत सरल हैं। इन भाषाओं में Inverted Commas से Direct Narration का बोध होता है और 'कि' से (Inverted Commas के हट जाने पर) Indirect Narration का। 'कि' के बाद वे वाक्य ज्यों-के-त्यों रख दिए जाते हैं; उनमें न तो Pronoun बदलता है, न Tense और न ही वाक्य का Structure; जैसे—

1. राम ने कहा, "मैं कल घर जाऊँगा।"
   राम ने कहा कि मैं कल घर जाऊँगा।

2. राम ने मुझसे पूछा, "आप कहाँ जा रहे हैं?"
   राम ने मुझसे पूछा कि आप कहाँ जा रहे हैं।

हिंदी-उर्दू के छात्र 'कि' के बाद आनेवाले वाक्यों का अँगरेजी अनुवाद ज्यों-का-त्यों कर देते हैं। वे भूल जाते हैं कि अँगरेजी में Narration के नियम बिलकुल भिन्न हैं और इसलिए वे भयंकर भूल कर बैठते हैं। आप ऐसी भूलों से अवश्य बचें।

EXERCISES WORKED OUT

1. The violent man said, "What violence have I done? What anger have I been guilty of?" Then the others laughed and said to him. "Why should we speak? You have given us ocular proof of your violent temper."

   Indirect—The violent man *asked what* violence *he had done,* and what anger he *had been* guilty of. Then the others laughed and *asked why they* should speak. They *further said that he had given them* ocular proof of *his* violent temper.

   Or, Then the others laughed and said that there was no need for them to speak, because he had given them ocular proof of his violent temper.

2. "What do you mean?" asked the man. "How can a rope be used for binding flour?" "A rope may be used for anything," replied the man, "when I do not wish to lend it."

   Indirect—The man *asked what he meant, and* how a rope *could* be used for binding flour. The man replied *that* a rope *might* be used for anything, when *he did* not wish to lend it.

3. The robber said to Alexander, "I am thy captive. I must hear what thou art pleased to say, and endure what thou art pleased to inflict. But my soul is unconquered and if I reply at all to thy reproaches, I will reply to thee like a free man."

   Indirect—The robber said to Alexander *that he was his* captive, and (he) must hear what *he* (Alexander) *was,* pleased to say and endure what *he was* pleased to inflict. He *further told him that his* soul *was* unconquered, and *if he replied* at all to *his* reproaches, *he would* reply to him like a free man.

4. Joseph said to James, "I can tell you what strikes me as the most useful machine in the world." James replied, "Can you Joseph? I should like to hear of it. What is it used for?"

   Indirect—Joseph said to James that he *could* tell *him* what *struck him* as the most useful machine in the world. James *asked Joseph if he could, and said that he would* like to hear of that. He *further inquired of* him (Joseph) *what* it *was* used for.

5. And Judah said unto his brethren, "What profit is it, if we slay our brother and conceal his blood? Come, let us sell him to the Ishmaelites, and let not our hand be upon him, for he is our brother and our flesh."

   Indirect—And Judah *asked* his brethren *what* profit it was if *they slew their* brother and *concealed* his blood. He *advised* them to sell ***(proposed to them that they should sell)*** him to the Ishmaelites and *wished that they should* not lay *their hand* upon him, for he was *their* brother and *their* flesh.

6. "What is this strange outcry?" said Socrates. "I sent the women away mainly in order that they might not offend in this way; for I have heard that a man should die in peace. Be quiet and have patience."

Indirect—Socrates *asked* them *what that* strange outcry *was.* He *said that he had sent* the women away mainly in order that *they might* not offend in that way; for *he had heard* that a man should die in peace. He (Socrates) *advised them to be quiet* and have patience.

7. The teacher became angry with the student and said, "Why have you disturbed the class in this way? I have told you before that when I am speaking, you should be silent. Leave the room, and do not return again today."

   Indirect—The teacher became angry with the student and *asked him why he had disturbed* the class in *that* way. He *said* to the student *that he had told him* before that when he *was* speaking, *he* (student) should be silent. The teacher *ordered* him *to* leave the room and *not to* return *(forbade him to return)* again that day.

EXERCISE

I. *Change the following from Direct to Indirect.*

1. "Gentlemen," I said, "there are more things in heaven and on earth than are dreamt of in your philosophy. Do not be astonished at my statement. Is it fair to judge me by appearance only?"
2. "Let me hire you as a nurse for my poor children," said a Butterfly to a quiet Caterpillar. "See these little eggs. I don't know how long it will be before they come to life, and I feel very sick and poorly and if I should die, who will take care of my baby butterflies when I am gone? Will you kind, mild, green Caterpillar?"
3. "Well", cried I, "my good boys, how do you like your bed? I hope you are not afraid to sleep in this room." "No papa", said Dick, "I am not afraid to be anywhere where you are."
4. "Cast thy eyes eastward", said the genius to Mirza, "and tell me what thou seest." "I see", said Mirza, "a huge valley and a prodigious file of water flowing through it." "The valley that thou seest", said the genius, "is the vale of misery, and the tide of water than thou seest is part of the great tide of eternity." "What is the reason", said Mirza, "that the tide rises out of a thick mist at one end, and loses itself in a thick mist at the other?"
5. I said, 'Do not brood over the past. Is there not something in every life which it is happiness to forget? I have so much to remember here,.so much to learn, and so much to repay."
6. They said, "Brothers and Sisters, hear what I tell you. The enemy approaches and you ought to know what will happen when they come here. Do not expect peace; for there will be none. They will rule over you and make you slaves."
7. An old lion said to a fox, "Please come near me in my cave. Come, let us talk of your health." The fox said, "Quite so, sir, but I am afraid the talk will not be beneficial for my health."

8. "You are old", said the youth. "One would hardly suppose that your eye was as steady as ever. What made you so awfully clever?" "I have answered three questions, and that is enough. Don't give yourself airs. Be off or I will kick you downstairs", said his father.
9. The ant said to the cricket, "What were you doing all the summer? Why do you beg from others instead of earning your own food? If you can while away the summer in singing and dancing, then you can pass the autumn in the same way."
10. The farthing said, "I thus rambled from pocket to pocket. It would be tedious to relate all my adventures. Soon I grew old and was disfigured by constant use. Then came the fatal end of my life. Along with many other coins I was thrown into a furnace. but strangely enough I did not die. I only rose out of the furnace with greater beauty and brightness than I ever had before."
11. *Teacher*—That is true, it is very cold indeed. But climbers wear very warm clothes. It is not often the cold that stops them.

    The child—How do they spend the nights there and where do they get their food?

    Teacher—Good. You have thought of other great difficulties which climbers must overcome. Remember, however, they take many strong coolies with them and these men carry their food and tents in which they sleep at night. But there are other and greater difficulties than these.
12. *Teacher*—Who knows which is the highest mountain in the world?

    First child—I do, Sir. It is Kanchanjunga in Sikkim.

    Teacher—No, wrong. Who knows? That is a very high mountain but not the highest of all.

    Second child—Is it, Mount Everest, Sir?

    Teacher—Yes, that's right. And it is over twenty-nine thousand feet high, you know. It is covered with snow all the year round, even in summer.
13. The youngest Princess took her father's hand in hers and said, "Father dear, I love you better than salt." The king looked at her in amazement and cried. "Do you measure your love for me by common salt? Your sisters have spoken of gold and gems. Have you nothing better to say?" The princess shook her head and again replied, "I love you, father, more than salt." At this the king was enraged and said to the Princess, "I bid you not to come near me or speak to me in future."
14. The Duke said to Shylock, "How can you hope for the mercy of God if you show mercy to none?" Shylock replied, "What judgement of God shall I fear, having done no wrong? You have your slaves. Shall I say to you, 'Let them be free'. You will answer, 'The slaves are ours'. So do I answer you: The pound of flesh is mine and I will have it."
15. (a) He said, "Mohan and I helped each other when we were at school."

    (b) The teacher told me, "You had better (had rather) wait for sometime."

    (c) She said, "I bought the car a year ago."

(d) I said, "I have not seen the Taj."

(e) He said, "I visited Delhi last year."

(f) I told him, "Did you reply to my letter?"

(g) I said, "How sweetly she sings!"

II. *Put a tick (✓) by the suitable word(s).*

1. He told me that [he / I] [will buy / would buy] a car in a week.
2. He asked [to me / me] [to not / not to] sleep in the class.
3. She told me that she [has / had] been working since morning.
4. He asked her [that why / why] [you are / she was] crying.
5. I asked her [that / whether] she [we / would] help me.
6. He requested me [to have / that have] a cup of tea.
7. He exclaimed with joy [that she sang sweetly / that how sweetly she sang]
8. The teacher [told / said] that the earth [moves / moved] round the sun.
9. She asked [me / from me] [if / that] [I will / I would] go to the picture.
10. I asked him [where / that where] [he was / I was] living.

❒

Chapter XXI

TRANSFORMATION

Transformation का अर्थ होता है—*to change the form,* इससे यह स्पष्ट है कि हम किसी sentence के अर्थ को नहीं बदल सकते; हमें केवल उसके form (रूप या बनावट) को बदलना चाहिए। इसका अर्थ यह नहीं कि हमें sentence के अर्थ से कोई मतलब ही नहीं। इसके विपरीत, दिए हुए sentence के अर्थ को ध्यानपूर्वक समझना चाहिए; क्योंकि अर्थ समझे बिना sentence के form को बदलना संभव हो ही नहीं सकता। इसलिए हम भिन्न-भिन्न प्रकार के वाक्यों को लें और देखें कि उन्हें किस प्रकार transform किया जा सकता है।

Sentences Expressing Excess

कुछ वाक्यों में *too* का प्रयोग होता है और इनसे किसी गुण की अतिशयता (excess) का भाव व्यक्त होता है और इसलिए उस गुण के बदले दोष का बोध होता है। ऐसे वाक्यों की बनावट इस प्रकार होती है—

Subject + verb + too + adjective/adverb

इन वाक्यों को लें—

1. She is too weak.
2. He is too angry.
2. It is too hot.
4. He runs too fast.

ऐसे वाक्यों को transform करने के लिए इन नियमों की सहायता लें—

Rule I. Too को हटा दें।

Rule II. Too के बाद आनेवाले Adjective/Adverb को Comparative Degree में रखें।

Rule III. Than के बाद अर्थानुसार should + infinitive/should be + adjective या it is/proper का प्रयोग करें।

इन वाक्यों को लें—

1. The weather is *too hot.* = The weather is hotter *than it is proper* या *than it should be.*
2. He is too weak. = He is weaker *than it is proper* या *than* he *should be.*
3. He runs too slowly. = He runs *more* slowly *than it is proper* या *than* he *should.*
4. He is too negligent. = He is *more* negligent *than it is proper* या *than he should be.*
5. The news is too shocking. = The news is *more* shocking *than it is proper* या *than it should be.*

इस प्रकर, Subject + verb + too + adjective/adverb हो जाता है—

Subject + verb + comparative adjective/adverb + than + clause

Sentences Expressing Cause

कुछ वाक्यों में *too + adjective/adverb + infinitive* का प्रयोग होता है। ऐसे वाक्यों के *too + adjective/adverb* से कारण (cause) का बोध होता है और *infinitive* से परिणाम (result) का। ऐसे वाक्यों की बनावट इस प्रकार होती है—

Subject + verb + too + adjective/adverb + infinitive

इन वाक्यों को देखें—

1. He is too weak to run.
2. She is too slow to win the race.

ऐसे वाक्यों को transform करने के लिए इन नियमों का ध्यान रखें—

Rule I. Too को हटा दें और इसके बदले *so* का प्रयोग करें।

Rule II. So के बाद adjective/adverb को रखें।

Rule III. इसके बाद that + clause (adverb clause) का प्रयोग करें।

इन वाक्यों के परिवर्तन को देखें—

1. He is too weak to run.
   He is *so weak/that he cannot run.*
2. She is too slow to win the race.
   She is *so slow/that she cannot win the race.*
3. He is too selfish to be a friend.
   He is *so selfish/that he cannot be a friend.*
4. He is too old to learn new tricks.
   He is *so old/that he cannot learn new tricks.*

इस प्रकार, Subject + verb + too + adjective/adverb + infinitive हो जाता है—

Subject + verb + so + adjective/adverb + that + clause

NOTE—कुछ वाक्यों में too + adjective + for + noun/pronoun आता है। ऐसे वाक्यों के too + adjective से कारण (cause) का बोध होता है और *for + noun/pronoun* से परिणाम (result) का। ऐसे वाक्यों की बनावट होती है—

Subject + verb + too + adjective + for + noun/pronoun

इन वाक्यों पर विचार करें—

1. She is too slow for a runner.
2. He is too dull for a sportsman.
3. His sorrow is too deep for tears.
4. It is too much for us.

ऐसे वाक्यों को transform करने के लिए निम्नांकित नियमों की सहायता लें—

Rule I. Too को हटा दें और इसके बदले so का प्रयोग करें।

Rule II. इसके बाद that + clause (adverb clause) का प्रयोग करें और इस clause में verb का प्रयोग सावधानी से करें, क्योंकि वाक्य में for + noun/pronoun के बाद कोई verb नहीं आता है।

Rule III. यदि too के बाद much (too much) आए, तो so bad/so shocking आदि का प्रयोग करें।

इन वाक्यों के परिवर्तन को देखें—

1. He is too dull for a sportsman.

   He is so dull that he cannot be a sportsman.

2. It is too much for us.

   It is so bad/shocking that we can't bear it.

इस प्रकार, Subject + verb + too + adjective/too much + for + noun/pronoun हो जाता है—

Subject + verb + so + that + clause

EXERCISES WORKED OUT

1. The news is too good to be true.

   = The news is *so* good *that* it *cannot* be true.

2. He arrived at the station too late to catch the train.

   = He arrived at the station *so* late *that* he *could not* catch the train.

3. He was too deeply affected to speak.

   = He was *so* deeply affected *that* he *was not* able to speak.

4. The sun is too hot for us to go out at present.

   = The sun is *so* hot *that* we *cannot* go out at present.

5. He is too proud to learn.

   = He is *so* proud *that* he *cannot* learn.

6. Her sorrow is too deep for tears.

   Her sorrow is *so* deep *that* she *can't* express it in tears.

. . . .

EXERCISE

Transform the following sentences.

(1) You are too lazy. (2) You are too dull to succeed. (3) It is too late to mend yourself. (4) You were too late. (5) It is too late for you. (6) She is too poor. (7) She is too poor to buy this dress. (8) Her son's death is too much for her. (9) I am too old to learn new ways. (10) You are too young to do this work. (11) She is too young for the old man.

. . . .

Sentences Expressing Condition

कुछ वाक्य ऐसे होते हैं जिनमें दो भाग होते हैं—एक भाग में कोई condition (शर्त) रहता है और दूसरे भाग में उसके consequence (परिणाम) की चर्चा होती है; जैसे—

If you work hard, you will succeed.

ऐसे वाक्यों की बनावट होती है—

Principal clause + Adverb clause [condition].

वाक्य में जो condition रखा जाता है, उसे इन शब्दों के द्वारा व्यक्त किया जाता है—

If, When, Unless, Supposing, Provided, Provided that, Were, Should, Had, But for, In case, One more, Once, Imperative sentence + and + Clause, Interrogative sentence + Imperative sentence beginning with 'then'

इन वाक्यों को देखें—

1. If you read this book, you will learn English.
2. Unless you read this book, you can't learn English.
3. Should you work hard, you would pass.
4. Take an umbrella in case it rains.
5. Work hard, and you will pass.
6. Do you want to pass? Then read this book.

ऐसे वाक्यों को transform करने के लिए इन्हें एक-दूसरे के रूप में बदल दें; जैसे—

1. If you read this book, you will learn English.

   = Unless you read this book, you can't learn English.

   Or

   Should you read this book, you would learn English.

   Or

   Do you want to learn English? Then read this book.

   Or

   Read this book, and you will learn English.

   Or

   Read this book in case you want to learn English.

2. *In case* you allow me, I will do the work at once.

   = *If* you allow me, I will do the work at once.

3. *Provided* you promise support, I will help you.

   = *If* you promise support, I will help you.

4. *Supposing* you fall ill, there is medical aid here.

   = *If* you fall ill, there is medical aid here.

5. *One more* effort, *and* you will pass.

= *If* you make one more effort, you will pass.

6. *But for* his help, I would not have succeeded.

= *If it had not been for* his help, I would not have succeeded.

7. If he *were* to meet me, I would recognise him at once.

= *Should* he meet me, I would recognise him at once.

ऐसे वाक्यों का transformation आसानी से किया जा सकता है, पर कभी-कभी किसी खास तरीके से transform करने को कहा जाता है। वैसी अवस्था में उन्हीं तरीकों को निर्देश के अनुसार अपनाना चाहिए। कुछ उदाहरण लें—

Transform by Using If

1. I get wet, *when* I go out in the rain.

= I get wet, *if* I go out in the rain.

2. *Had* you not taught me so well, I would not have passed.

= *If* you had not taught me so well, I would not have passed.

3. *Should* you be tired of working all day, go out for a walk.

= *If* you be tired of working all day, go out for a walk.

Transform by Using Conjunctional Phrase

1. You will be punished for talking in the class.

= You will be punished *in case* you talk in the class.

2. *Should* he awake, send for the doctor.

= *In case* he awakes, send for the doctor.

3. *Supposing* the house catches fire, we shall ring up the fire brigade at once.

= *In case* the house catches fire, we shall ring up the fire brigade at once.

Transform by Using Participle

1. *If* the rain does not fall soon, the crops will be spoilt.

= *Supposing* the rain does not fall soon, the crops will be spoilt.

2. *Had* you taken greater care, this could not have happened.

= *Supposing* you had taken greater care, this could not have happened.

3. *In case* Hari does not turn up, Jadu will play.

= *Supposing* Hari does not turn up, Jadu will play.

EXERCISES WORKED OUT

1. *One more* word, *and* I will send you out of the room.

= *If* you say another word, I will send you out of the room.

2. *Supposing* the house catches fire, we shall extinguish it with the water of this tank here.

   = *If* (*In case*) the house catches fire, we shall ....

3. *Had* you been more careful, such a calamity would not have befallen us.

   = *If* you had been more careful ....

4. *But for* your interference, everything would have gone smoothly.

   = *Had it not been for your* interference ...... of *If you had not interfered,* everything would ....

5. Persevere, *and* you will succeed in the end.

   = *If* you persevere, you will succeed in the end.

6. *Provided* we are all agreed, the resolution can at once be passed.

   = *If* we are all agreed, the resolution ....

Sentences Expressing Concession

कुछ ऐसे वाक्य होते हैं जिनमें दो भाग होते हैं। एक भाग में कुछ कहा जाता है और दूसरे भाग में उसके विपरीत कहा जाता है; जैसे—

Though he is poor, he is honest.

ऐसे वाक्यों की बनावट होती है—

Principal Clause + Adverb Clause [Concession]

वाक्य में Contrast/Concession (विपरीत का भाव) प्रकट करने के लिए इन शब्दों का प्रयोग होता है—

Though, Although, Despite, In spite of, Even if, No matter, Whatever, For all, Admitting that, Granting that, Supposing that, May + Infinitive, May be + Noun/Adjective, However + Adjective/Adverb, Adjective + As, Indeed ... but, All the same, Nevertheless

इन वाक्यों को देखें—

1. Though (although) he is poor, he is honest.
2. Poor as he is, he is honest.
3. He is poor indeed, but he is honest.
4. Despite (In spite of) his poverty, he is honest.
5. However poor he may be, he is honest.

ऐसे वाक्यों को transform करने के लिए इन्हें एक-दूसरे के रूप में बदल दें; जैसे—

1. Though she is black, she is beautiful.

   = Black as she is, she is beautiful.

   Or

   Despite (In spite of) her blackness, she is beautiful.

Or

However black she may be, she is beautiful.

Or

Granting that she is black, she is beautiful.

Or

Even if she is black, she is beautiful.

Or

For all her blackness, she is beautiful.

2. Poor *as* he is, he is honest.

= Though he *is* poor, he is honest.

3. *However* poor he may be, he is honest.

= Though he is poor, he is honest.

4. He is poor *indeed, but* he is honest.

= Though he is poor, he is honest.

5. He is poor, he is honest *all the same.*

= He is poor; *at the same time* he is honest.

= Though he is poor, he is honest.

6. He is poor, *nevertheless* he is honest.

= Though he is poor, he is honest.

7. Though he is poor, he is honest.

= He is indeed *poor, but* he is honest.

= Poor *as* he is, he is honest.

NOTE—जब *adjective + as* का प्रयोग contrast को व्यक्त करता है, तब *as* का प्रयोग Adjective के बाद होता है (*Poor as* he is, *Rich as* he is), clause के आरंभ में नहीं। जब as का प्रयोग किसी clause के आरंभ में होता है, तब इसका अर्थ हो जाता है— 'चूँकि' (because); जैसे—

As he is ill, he is absent.

EXERCISES WORKED OUT

1. He was poor *indeed, but* he was always happy.

= *Though* he was poor, he was always happy.

2. It is true that we have failed, *but* it is not through our own fault.

= We have failed *indeed,* but it is … fault.

3. The weather, *though* hot, is not unbearable.

= Hot *as* the weather is, it is not unbearable.

4. *Supposing* that he was rich, that was no reason for his bad behaviour.

= I *grant indeed* that he was rich, *but* that was … .

5. *Though* he succeeded in everything, he was never vain.

   = He succeeded in everything, *at the same time* he was never vain.
6. His mother still trusted him, *though* he had deceived her so often.

   = He had deceived his mother so often, she trusted him *all the same.*
7. He finished first, *though* he began late.

   = He began late *indeed, but* he finished first.
8. This man is never satisfied, *no matter* what we do for him.

   = This man is never satisfied, *whatever* we do for him. या This man is never satisfied *although* we may do everything for him.
9. *Admitting* that he has no means, yet he dresses pretty well.

   = *Though* he has no means, he dresses pretty well.
10. Poor *as* he is, he will never do a dishonest act.

    = He is poor *indeed, but* he will never do a dishonest act.

Sentences Expressing Comparison

वाक्य में जितने Adjectives के प्रयोग होते हैं, वे किसी-न-किसी Degree में अवश्य ही रहते हैं—Positive, Comparative या Superlative में। एक प्रकार की Degree को दूसरे में बदल सकते हैं और उनके अर्थ में भी कोई अंतर नहीं आता। ऐसा परिवर्तन किस प्रकार होता है, इनपर विचार करें।

(A) Interchange of Positive and Comparative Degree

बहुत-से Positive Degree के Adjectives दो as (as ... as) के बीच रखा जाता है; जैसे—

as dull *as, as* good *as.*

ऐसे वाक्यों को transform करने के लिए इन नियमों की सहायता लें—

Rule I. दोनों as (as ... as) को हटा दें।

Rule II. Adjective को (जो दो as के बीच में रहता है) Comparative Degree का रूप दे दें।

Rule III. यदि वाक्य Affirmative हो, तो उसे Negative बना दें और यदि Negative हो तो उसे Affirmative बना दें।

Rule IV. वाक्य के दूसरे भाग को नये वाक्य में पहले लिखें और पहले भाग को अंत में; जैसे—

1. Ram is *as* dull *as* Shyam. = Shyam is *not duller* than Ram.
2. You are *as* good *as* I = I am *not better* than you.
3. Ram is *not as* dull *as* Shyam. = Shyam is *duller* than Ram.
4. You are *not as* good *as* I = I am *better* than you.

इसी प्रकार, Comparative Degree को Positive Degree में बदलने के लिए निम्नांकित नियमों की सहायता लें।

Rule I. Comparative Degree के Adjective को Positive में बदल दें।

Rule II. Adjective को दो as (as … as) के बीच में रख दें।

Rule III. यदि वाक्य Affirmative हो, तो उसे Negative बना दें और यदि Negative हो, तो Affirmative.

Rule IV. वाक्य के दूसरे भाग को नये वाक्य में पहले रखें और पहले को अंत में; जैसे—

1. He is *better* than you. = You are *not as* good *as* he.
2. He *is not better* than you. = You are *as* good *as* he.

(B) Interchange of Comparative and Superlative Degree

यदि Comparative Degree में *all other* या *any other* का प्रयोग हो, तो उसे निम्नलिखित प्रकार से Superlative Degree में बदला जाता है—

Rule I. All other या any other को हटा दें।

Rule II. Comparative Degree के Adjective को Superlative में बदल दें—

1. He *is better* than *any other* boy in the class.—Comparative
   He is the *best* boy in the class.—Superlative
2. This book is *more* useful *than any other* in the market.—Comparative
   This is the *most* useful book in the market.—Superlative

NOTE—इसी प्रकार, Superlative Degree को भी Comparative में बदल देना चाहिए।

यदि Comparative Degree के साथ *most other* लगा रहे, तो इसकी Superlative Degree इस प्रकार बनाएँ—

Rule I. Most other के बदले one of the का प्रयोग करें।

Rule II. Comparative Degree के Adjective को Superlative में बदल दें—

1. He is more wicked than *most other* boys.—Comparative
   He is *one of the most wicked* boys.—Superlative
2. Iron is *more* useful than *most other* metals.—Comparative
   Iron is *one of the most* useful metals.—Superlative

NOTE—इसी प्रकार Superlative Degree को भी Comparative में बदल सकते हैं।

(C) Interchange of Positive and Superlative Degree

जब वाक्य में Positive Degree को दो as (as … as) के बीच में रखा जाता है और उसके पहले *no other* का प्रयोग होता है, तब उसकी Superlative Degree इस प्रकार बनाई जाती है—

Rule I. No other तथा as … as को हटा दें।

Rule II. Adjective को Superlative Degree का रूप दे दें; जैसे—

1. *No other* boy is *as* poor *as* Ram.—Positive
   Ram is the *poorest* boy.—Superlative
2. *No other* bookshop is *as* good *as* Pustak Mahal.—Positive
   Pustak Mahal is *the best* bookshop.—Superlative

यदि वाक्य में Positive Degree को दो as (as ... as) के बीच रखा जाए और Very few का प्रयोग हो, तो Positive Degree को Superlative में इस प्रकार बदलना चाहिए—

Rule I. as ... as तथा very few के बदले one of the का प्रयोग करें।

Rule II. Adjective को Superlative का रूप दे दें; जैसे—

1. *Very few* men were *as* great *as* Mahatma Gandhi.—Positive
   Mahatma Gandhi was *one of the greatest* men.—Superlative
2. *Very few* flowers are *as sweet as* rose.—Positive
   Rose is *one of the sweetest* flowers.—Superlative

EXERCISES WORKED OUT

1. The younger brother is *cleverer* than the elder.—Comparative
   The elder brother is not *so clever as* the younger.—Positive
2. Gold is *one of the heaviest* metals.—Superlative
   Gold is *heavier* than *most other* metals.—Comparative
   Very few metals are *as heavy as* gold.—Positive
3. This man has *more debts* than cash.—Comparative
   This man has not *as much cash as* he has debts.—Positive
4. That man has *more money than* brain.—Comparative
   That man has not *as much brain as* he has money.—Positive
5. He treats the poor with the *same respect as* he does the rich.—Positive
   He treats the poor with *no less respect* than the rich.—Comparative
6. You know his ways quite *as well as* I do.—Positive
   I do *not* know his ways *any better* than you do.—Comparative
7. I would *as soon die as* tell a lie.—Positive
   I would *rather die than* tell a lie.—Comparative
   I would *sooner die than* tell a lie.—Comparative
8. A live ass is *stronger* than a dead lion.—Comparative
   A dead lion is *not so strong as* a live ass.—Positive
9. *Very few* countries are *as hot as* India.—Positive
   India is *hotter* than *most other* countries.—Comparative
   India is *one of the hottest* countries.—Superlative
10. Platinum is *as heavy as* gold.—Positive
    Gold is *not heavier than* platinum—Comparative
11. *No other* singer in the school is *so good as* Hari.—Positive
    Hari is the *best singer* in the school.—Superlative
    Hari is *better* than *any other* singer in the school.—Comparative

12. He was *one of the greatest* of Indian rulers.—Superlative

He was *greater* than *most other* Indian rulers.—Comparative

Very few Indian rulers were *so great as* he.—Positive

Sentences Expressing Time

(A) Sentences with Point of Time

कुछ वाक्यों में Verb के साथ Point of Time (at/in + time) आता है। इन्हें transform करने के लिए इन नियमों का ध्यान रखें—

Rule I. वाक्य को Negative बना दें और Perfect Tense का प्रयोग करें।

Rule II. Point of Time के पहले since का प्रयोग करें। इन वाक्यों के परिवर्तन को देखें—

1. I met him at 9 o'clock.

   I haven't met him since 9 o'clock.

2. I saw her in 1982.

   I haven't seen her since 1982.

3. He gave me presents on my birthday.

   He hasn't given me presents since my birthday.

(B) Sentences with Last … When

कुछ वाक्यों में *last … when* आता है।

इन वाक्यों को देखें—

1. I last saw him when I visited Delhi.

   I have not seen him since I visited Delhi.

2. He last met me when he came here.

   He has not met me since he came here.

3. I last travelled by air when I went to England.

   I have not travelled by air since I went to England.

इन नियमों का ध्यान रखें—

Rule I. Since के बाद आनेवाले clause में Past Simple Tense का प्रयोग करें।

Rule II. Since के पहले आनेवाले clause (अर्थात PC) में Perfect Tense का प्रयोग करें और इसे Negative बना दें।

(C) Sentences with Ago

कुछ वाक्यों में Ago का प्रयोग होता है और इनसे समय का बोध होता है। इन्हें इस प्रकार transform किया जा सकता है—

Rule I. Ago के बदले for का प्रयोग करें।

Rule II. वाक्य को Negative बना दें और इसमें Perfect Tense का प्रयोग करें।

इन वाक्यों के परिवर्तन को देखें—

1. He helped me a month ago.
   He hasn't helped me for a month.
2. She wrote to me a week ago.
   She hasn't written to me for a week.

. . . .

EXERCISE

Transform these sentences.

1. She ate at 9 o'clock.
2. I went to the picture a week ago.
3. It rained a month ago.
4. I saw him in 1980.
5. She came here in 1981.
6. A storm caused damage in 1982.
7. I received a letter from him in 1983.

. . . .

Interchange of Interrogative and Assertive Sentences

कुछ ऐसे sentences होते हैं जो रूप के अनुसार Interrogative, पर अर्थ के अनुसार Assertive होते हैं। इसलिए ऐसे Interrogative sentences को Assertive में इस प्रकार बदलें—

Rule I. वाक्य में पहले Subject को रखें और उसके बाद Verb को।

Rule II. प्रश्नवाचक चिह्न (Note of Interrogation) के बदले Full Stop का प्रयोग करें।

Rule III. यदि Interrogative sentence में not नहीं रहे, तो Assertive में not का प्रयोग करें; पर यदि Interrogative sentence में not रहे, तो Assertive में not का प्रयोग नहीं करें; जैसे—

1. Who *would not* run from a lion? —Interrogative
   Everyone *would* run from a lion. —Assertive
2. *Can* the deaf hear? —Interrogative
   The deaf *cannot* hear. —Assertive
3. *Can* human nature change? —Interrogative
   Human nature *cannot* change. —Assertive
4. *Doesn't* God *help* helpless men? —Interrogative
   God *helps* helpless men. —Assertive

5. *Shouldn't* you love your mother? —Interrogative
You *should* love your mother. —Assertive

EXERCISES WORKED OUT

1. If you prick us, *don't we bleed*? —Interrogative
If you prick us, *we bleed.* —Assertive
2. If you poison us, *don't we die?* —Interrogative
If you poison us, *we die.* —Assertive
3. *Weren't* you *sent* to school to study? —Interrogative
You *were sent* to school to study. —Assertive
4. *Who is* here so rude as not to love his country? —Interrogative
There is *none* here so rude as not to love his country. —Assertive
5. *Haven't* I *warned* you of this danger over and over? —Interrogative
I *have warned* you of this danger over and over. —Assertive
6. This *is not* the kind of dress to wear in school. —Assertive
Is this the kind of dress to wear in school? —Interrogative
7. There *is nothing* better than hard work to cure nerves. —Assertive
Is there *anything* better than hard work to cure nerves? —Interrogative
8. No *one* can put up with such conduct. —Assertive
Can *anyone* put up with such conduct? —Interrogative
9. The beauty of nature *is* beyond description. —Assertive
Isn't the beauty of nature beyond description? —Interrogative
10. We could not have succeeded without your help. —Assertive
Could we have succeeded without your help? —Interrogative

Change of Assertive and Interrogative Sentences

Assertive sentences को Interrogative में इस प्रकार बदलें—

Rule I. यदि वाक्य में am/is/are/may/can/have/shall/will/should/ought आदि प्रकार की सहायक क्रिया आए, तो ऐसी क्रिया को वाक्य के आरंभ में रखें और इसके बाद कर्ता को।

Rule II. पूर्ण विराम (Full Stop) के बदलें Note of Interrogation का प्रयोग करें।

Rule III. यदि वाक्य में पूरी क्रिया (Full Verb, जैसे—come/go/read/write आदि) आए, तो वाक्य के आरंभ में so/does/did का प्रयोग करें और इसके बाद कर्ता को रखें।

इन वाक्यों को देखें—

1. This is a car.
Is this a car?

2. They are farmers.
Are they farmers?

3. He has a car.
Has he a car?

4. They have got a house.
Have they got a house?

5. I may go home.
May I go home?

6. He can help me.
Can he help me?

7. He will come soon.
Will he come soon?

8. He should work hard.
Should he work hard?

9. He plays tennis.
Does he play tennis?

10. They know English.
Do they know English?

11. He won a lottery.
Did he win a lottery?

12. She sells fish.
Does she sell fish?

13. You help her.
Do you help her?

14. He went home.
Did he go home?

यदि वाक्य में कोई प्रश्नवाचक शब्द (question words—what/how/where/when/why) आए, तो क्रिया को पहले रखें और इसके बाद subject को; जैसे—

1. What your name is.
What is your name?

2. Where you live.
Where do you live?

3. When he will come.
When will he come?

4. Why you are sad.
Why are you sad?

5. How he is now.
How is he now?

6. What he said.
What did he say?

7. What you want.
What do you want?

8. What he is doing.
What is he doing?

EXERCISE

Change these into Interrogative sentences.

1. Mohan has got a car.
2. He must wait here.
2. She will buy a car.
4. He can lift this box.
5. Where she lives these days.
6. When he will finish the work.
7. Why you reached late.
8. How you have come here.
9. She went to market.
10. He helps his neighbour.

Interchange of Affirmative and Negative Sentences

Rule I. Negative sentences को Affirmative में बदलने के लिए Negative Verbs, Adverbs, Adjectives और Pronouns को Positive में बदलना पड़ता है; जैसे—

none but the brave = the brave alone; none but a coward = the coward alone or only a coward; not always = sometimes; not gone far = gone a little way; no one nation = more than one nation; cannot but = bound to; no one = everyone; never again = for the last time; no sooner … than = as soon as

इन वाक्यों को देखें—

1. *None but* a coward would flee from his duty. —Negative
   Only a coward would flee from his duty. —Affirmative
2. Learned men are *not always* judicious —Negative
   Learned men are *sometimes* wanting in judgement. —Affirmative
3. *No sooner* had they heard the bell *than* they ran outside. —Negative
   As soon as they heard the bell, they ran outside. —Affirmative
4. He *cannot but* give me thanks. —Negative
   He is *bound to* give me thanks. —Affirmative
5. *No one* will *deny* that your son has done his best. —Negative
   Everyone will *admit* … best. —Affirmative
6. He left *no plan untried.* —Negative
   He *tried every plan.* —Affirmative
7. His temper *did not improve* with age —Negative
   His temper became *worse* with age. —Affirmative

इस प्रकार, यदि Affirmative sentence को Negative में बदलना हो, तो Positive Verbs/Adverbs/Adjectives/Pronouns को Negative में बदल दें, जैसे—

doubtful = not sure; always = never; as soon as = no sooner … than; all = none; quick understanding = slow understanding

इन वाक्यों के परिवर्तन को देखें—

1. It *always* pours when it rains. —Affirmative
   It *never* rains but it pours. —Negative
2. *As soon as* the master entered the room, everyone was silent. —Affirmative
   No sooner did the master enter the room *than* everyone was silent. —Negative
3. *Only* a little child would talk like this. —Affirmative
   None but a little child would talk like this. —Negative
4. Where there is *smoke,* there is fire. —Affirmative
   There is *no smoke* without fire. —Negative
5. *You alone* were to blame for this. —Affirmative
   None but you were to blame for this. —Negative
6. *As soon as* he saw her, he ran away. —Affirmative
   No sooner did he see her *than* he ran away. —Negative

Rule II. कुछ ऐसे भी Affirmative और Negative sentences होते हैं, जिनके Adjectives की Degree बदलकर वाक्य को transform किया जाता है; जैसे—

1. You are *not taller than* he is. —Negative
   He is *as tall as* you are. —Affirmative
2. I am *not so clever as* you. —Negative
   You are *cleverer than* I. —Affirmative
3. You are *not better* than your sister. —Negative
   Your sister is *as good as* you. —Affirmative

ऐसे वाक्यों को Affirmative से Negative और Negative से Affirmative बनाते समय Adjective की Degree बदल देनी चाहिए; जैसे—

(i) Comparative को Positive में और Positive को Comparative में।

(ii) Negative को Positive में बदलना चाहिए (not को हटाकर) तथा Positive को Negative में (not जोड़कर)।

(iii) वाक्य की बनावट बदल देनी चाहिए (वाक्य के दूसरे भाग को पहले लिखकर तथा पहले भाग को अंत में रखकर)।

Interchange of Assertive and Exclamatory Sentences

(A) What + Noun/How + Adjective/Adverb

यदि Exclamatory sentence में How/What आए तो उसे Assertive में परिवर्तित करने के लिए इन नियमों की सहायता लें—

Rule I. How/What को हटा दें।

Rule II. How + Adjective/Adverb को Very + Adjective/Adverb में बदल दें; जैसे—

1. How well he plays!
   = He plays very well.
2. How fast he runs!
   = He runs very fast.
3. How sweetly she sings!
   = She sings very sweetly.

Rule III. What + Noun को Adjective + Noun में बदल दें; जैसे—

1. What a sight it is!
   = It is a lovely sight.
2. What a boy he is!
   = He is a peculiar boy.

Rule IV. What + Adjective/Noun को Adjective + Noun में बदल दें; जैसे—

1. What a fine time it is!
   = It is a fine time.
2. What a good place it is!
   = It is a good place.

कुछ और वाक्यों का परिवर्तन देखें—

1. What a *problem* it is! —Exclamatory

   It is a *great* problem. —Assertive

2. What a *lame* excuse! —Exclamatory

   That was a *very* lame excuse. —Assertive

3. What a *piece* of work is man! —Exclamatory

   Man is a *wonderful (great)* piece of work. —Assertive

4. O what a *foolish* question to ask! —Exclamatory

   It is a *very* foolish question to ask. —Assertive

5. What *sweet* delight a quiet life brings! —Exclamatory

   A quiet life brings *very* sweet delight. —Assertive

6. How *sad* was the sight of the deserted city! —Exclamatory

   The deserted city presented a *very* sad sight. —Assertive

NOTE (a)—यदि Exclamatory sentences में Subject और Verb छिपे हुए हों, तो Assertive में बदलते समय उन्हें स्पष्ट रूप से (अर्थानुसार) प्रकट कर देना चाहिए; जैसे—

How foolish!

= How foolish it is!

अब इस Exclamatory sentence को Assertive में आसानी से बदल जा सकता है—

It is very foolish.

इसी प्रकार, इस वाक्य को देखें—

What a lame excuse!

= What a lame excuse it is or was!

अब इसे Assertive में बदलें—

It is (was) a very lame excuse.

(B) O that/Oh that, etc. + That

कुछ Exclamatory sentences की बनावट होती है—

O that/Oh that + clause
Would that + clause
Alas/Alas that + clause
O to be/Oh to be + phrase

इन्हें Assertive बनाने के लिए इनकी बनावट इस प्रकार करें—

Subject + Verb (wish) + Clause
It is sad + that + clause

इन वाक्यों को लें—

1. Would that I had not wasted my time! —Exclamatory
   I wish I had not wasted my time. —Assertive
2. O that the desert were my dwelling place! —Exclamatory
   I wish the desert were my dwelling place. —Assertive
3. O that he had a son! —Exclamatory
   I wish he had a son. —Assertive
4. O to be at home! —Exclamatory
   I wish I were at home. —Assertive
5. Alas that he should die so young! —Exclamatory
   It is sad that he should die so young. —Assertive
6. Alas! He is dead. —Exclamatory
   It is sad that he is dead. —Assertive

(C) If only + Clause

कुछ Exclamatory sentences आरंभ होते हैं *If only* से। इन्हें Assertive में इस प्रकार बदलें—

(i) *Subject + Verb (wish) + Infinitive*

(ii) *Subject + Verb (wish) + Clause*

इस वाक्यों के परिवर्तन को देखें—

1. If only I could see him once! —Exclamatory
   I wish to see him once. —Assertive
2. If only I could get one more chance! —Exclamatory
   I wish to get one more chance. —Assertive
   I wish I could get one more chance. —Assertive

(D) Infinitive + Other Words

कुछ Exclamatory sentences आरंभ होते हैं *Infinitive (to + verb)* से। इन्हें Assertive में इस प्रकार बदलें—

It is + Adjective (strange) + That + Clause.

इन वाक्यों के परिवर्तन को देखें—

1. To think of his coming so late! —Exclamatory
   It is strange that he should come so late. —Assertive
2. To imagine my seeing a snake! —Exclamatory
   It is strange that I should see a snake. —Assertive

(E) How + Adjective + Of + Other Words

कुछ Exclamatory sentences में *How + adjective + of* आता है। इन्हें इस प्रकार बदलें—

(i) *Subject + Verb + Adjective + Enough + Infinitive*

(ii) *It is/was + Adjective + Of + Object + Infinitive*

इन वाक्यों के परिवर्तन को देखें—

1. How kind of him to lend me money! —Exclamatory

   He was kind enough to lend me money. —Assertive

   It was kind of him to lend me money. —Assertive

2. How foolish of them to throw stones! —Exclamatory

   They were foolish enough to throw stones. —Assertive

   It was foolish of them to throw stones. —Assertive

(F) Word + And + Word

कुछ Exclamatory sentences में *word + and + word* आता है। इनका परिवर्तन इस प्रकार होता है—

It is + Adjective [strange/shocking/mean] + That + Clause.

इन वाक्यों का परिवर्तन देखें—

1. A fireman and afraid of sparks! —Exclamatory

   It is strange that a fireman should be afraid of sparks. —Assertive

2. A soldier and such a coward! —Exclamatory

   It is shocking that a soldier should be such a coward. —Assertive

(G) Bravo/Hurrah/Fie + Sentence

कुछ वाक्यों में Bravo का प्रयोग होता है और इससे प्रशंसा (praise) का भाव व्यक्त होता है। कुछ वाक्यों में Hurrah का प्रयोग होता है और इससे खुशी (joy) का भाव प्रकट होता है। कुछ वाक्यों में Fie, Fie आता है और इनसे घृणा (contempt) का बोध होता है। ऐसे Exclamatory sentences को Assertive में इस प्रकार बदलना चाहिए—

(i) *Bravo + sentence = It is a matter of praise + that + sentence.*

(ii) *Hurrah + sentence = It is a matter of joy + that + sentence.*

(iii) *Fie, Fie + sentence = It is a matter of contempt + that + sentence.*

इन वाक्यों को लें—

1. Bravo! He stood first.

   It is a matter of praise that he stood first.

2. Hurrah! We have won the race.

   It is a matter of joy that we have won the race.

3. Fie! Fie! You are a coward.

It is a matter of contempt that you are a coward.

EXERCISES WORKED OUT

1. *If* only I could see him reproach him for his ingratitude! —Exclamatory
   I wish I could see ... ingratitude. —Assertive
2. *O* for the might that laid the traitor down! —Exclamatory
   I wish I had (possessed) the might that ... down. —Assertive
3. O my son! *would that* I were dead and you alive! —Exclamatory
   I *wish* that I were dead and my son alive. —Assertive
4. *What* a piece of work is man! —Exclamatory
   Man is a *wonderful* piece of work. —Assertive
5. *O that* I were young again! —Exclamatory
   I *wish* that I were young again. —Assertive
6. *O* that she were living to this day! —Exclamatory
   I *wish* that she were living to this day. —Assertive
7. *O if* I could only raise the cover and look inside! —Exclamatory
   I wish to raise the cover and look inside. —Assertive
8. *A horse! a horse!* my kingdom for a horse! —Exclamatory
   A horse I must have, even at the price of my kingdom. —Assertive
9. *Too late! too late!* you cannot come in now! —Exclamatory
   It is now *too late* for you to come in. —Assertive
10. *If* I could only gain the first prize! —Exclamatory
    I *wish* to gain the first prize. —Assertive
11. Well done! —Exclamatory
    That was well done. }
    You have done well. } —Assertive
12. A fireman, and afraid of sparks! —Exclamatory
    It is strange that a fireman should be afraid of sparks. —Assertive
13. *I wish* I had known that long ago. —Assertive
    Would that I had known that long ago! —Exclamatory
14. *I wish* I had never left my home. —Assertive
    Would that I had never left my home! —Exclamatory
15. We had a *very merry* time of it last night. —Assertive
    What a merry time we had of it last night! —Exclamatory
16. A little knowledge is a *dangerous* thing. —Assertive
    How dangerous a thing is a little knowledge! —Exclamatory

17. I should like to see my native land again. —Assertive
If only I could see my native land again! —Exclamatory

18. To think of our meeting in this lonely place! —Exclamatory
It is strange that we should meet in this lonely place. —Assertive

19. He was the *tallest* man in the town. —Positive
There was *no man* in the town *who was taller than* he was. —Negative

20. *All must admit* that he was a great writer. —Positive
No one can deny that he was a great writer. —Negative

21. He *did not take long* to read this book. —Negative
He read the book *very quickly*. —Positive

22. Should not everybody be taught his native language? —Interrogative
Everybody should be taught his native language. —Assertive

23. This story is *very* beautifully told. —Assertive
How beautifully this story is told! —Exclamatory

24. Read this book to write English correctly. —Simple
Read this book *and* you will write English correctly. —Compound
If you read this book you will write English correctly. —Complex

....

EXERCISE

I. *Transform the following sentences as directed.*

1. I wish I had never left the place. (Turn into exclamatory)
2. As soon as he saw a tiger, he fled. (Turn into negative)
3. America is one of the richest countries. (Turn into positive)
4. He was too sad to speak a word. (Remove 'too')
5. How low has he fallen! (Turn into assertive)
6. The police is searching for the thief. (Turn into passive)
7. This fact is too evident to require proof. (Remove 'too')
8. He leads a miserable life. (Turn into exclamatory)
9. Can I ever forget him? (Turn into passive)
10. Who would not love his country? (Turn into assertive)
11. No one saw a brighter day than this. (Turn into interrogative)
12. This is the most beautiful pearl I have ever seen. (Turn into positive)
13. We shall be blamed by our countrymen. (Turn into active voice)
14. I found him laughing at me. (Turn into passive voice)
15. I made him sing a song. (Turn into passive voice)
16. I wrote him a letter. (Turn into passive voice)

17. I wish I had never left my home. (Turn into exclamatory)
18. You are not taller than he is. (Rewrite without a negative)
19. He was too deeply affected to speak a word. (Remove 'too')
20. As soon as he saw the tiger, he fled. (Turn into negative)
21. America is one of the richest countries. (Change from superlative to positive)
22. The news is too good to be true. (Remove 'too')
23. Whom do you search for? (Turn into passive)
24. How low has he fallen! (Turn into assertive)
25. India is the poorest country. (Change superlative into positive)
26. But for your help, I would have been ruined. (Turn into a complex sentence)
27. This fact is too evident to require proof. (Remove 'too')
28. There is no smoke without fire. (Turn into affirmative)
29. The beauties of Nature are beyond description. (Turn into interrogative)
30. He leads a miserable life. (Turn into exclamatory)
31. Mumbai is the best seaport in India. (Change from superlative to positive)
32. As soon as the master entered the room, everyone was silent. (Turn into negative)
33. Shall I ever forget those happy days? (Turn into passive)
34. Only the evening star has yet appeared? (Replace 'only' by 'none')
35. O that I were safe at home! (Turn into assertive)
36. A live ass is stronger than a dead lion. (Change from comparative to positive)
37. The sun is too hot for us to go out. (Remove 'too')
38. Platinum is as heavy as gold. (Change to comparative degree)
39. It is said that the money has been stolen by Rama. (turn into active voice)
40. Who would not love his country? (Turn into assertive)
41. No sooner did the thief see the police than he took to his heels. (Turn into affirmative)
42. As soon as he came here they left. (Turn into negative)
43. No one saw a brighter day than this. (Turn into interrogative)
44. It was an evil day when I first met that man. (Turn into exclamatory)
45. We shall be blamed by our countrymen. (Turn into active voice)
46. This is the most beautiful pearl I have ever seen. (Change from superlative to positive)
47. Very few countries are as hot as India. (Change into superlative)
48. Grapes cannot be gathered from thistles. (Change into active voice)
49. It was an evil day when I first met that man. (Change into interrogative)
50. None could do better under the circumstances. (Change into interrogative)
51. As soon as the master entered the room everybody was silent. (Change into negative)
52. Tell him to leave the room at once. (Change into passive voice)
53. How sad was the sight of the deserted city! (Change into assertive)
54. No sooner did he enter the compartment than the train started. (Turn into affirmative)

55. Everybody believed in his honesty. (Change into negative)
56. Very few Indian rulers were as great as Ashoka. (Turn into comparative degree)
57. Only a little child could talk like this. (Change into negative)
58. Who is here so rude as not to love his country? (Turn into assertive)
59. That was a very happy ending. (Change into exclamatory)
60. Pandora was scolded by Epi for breaking promise. (Turn into active voice)
61. No city in India is as big as Kolkata. (Change into superlative degree)
62. Can a man live for ever? (Change into negative)
63. He made the pupils do the work. (Turn into passive voice)
64. None but the brave deserves the fair. (Turn into assertive)
65. Gold is the heaviest metal. (Change into positive)
66. The sun is too hot for us to go out. (Remove 'too')
67. Bad health is a more terrible enemy than poverty. (Turn into positive degree)
68. He showed me the greatest respect. (Turn into passive voice)
69. Shall I ever forget those happy days? (Change into assertive)
70. London is the richest city in the world. (Change into negative)
71. Iron is the most useful of all metals. (Turn into positive degree)
72. He ordered the police to pursue the thief. (Change into passive voice)
73. Is this the kind of dress to wear in school? (Turn into negative)
74. What a fall was there, my countrymen! (Turn into assertive)
75. No sooner did he see the tiger than he fled. (Turn into affirmative)
76. If I could only gain the first prize! (Turn into assertive)
77. The beauties of Nature are beyond description. (Turn into interrogative)
78. Pass that bill today. (Change into passive voice)
79. Akbar was one of the greatest of kings. (Change into positive degree)
80. As soon as he saw the tiger, he fled. (Change into negative)
81. This church is the biggest in London. (Change into positive degree)
82. Who taught you grammar? (Change into passive voice)
83. Oh that I were safe at home! (Turn into assertive)
84. It is never too late to mend. (Remove 'too')
85. The news is shocking. (Change into exclamatory)
86. Actions speak louder than words. (Change into positive degree)
87. The criminal must be jailed. (Use 'has to')
88. This pencil is too small to write with. (Remove 'too')
89. Man cannot go against destiny. (Turn into interrogative)

II. *Change the following statements into (a) negatives and (b) questions.*

1. She can read English.
2. He sells books.

3. He swims well.
4. She loves her husband.
5. He must read now.
6. The police caught that thief.

III. *Change the structures (forms) under A into the structure under B, as in the example.*

A	B
I had a happy time.	What a happy time I had!
The Raj Bhawan looks lovely.	
He is an intelligent boy.	
This novel is very interesting.	
It is a pity.	
She plays very well.	

IV. *Change the structures under A into the structure under B, as in the example.*

A	B
She is so poor that she can't buy books.	She is too poor to buy books.
He is so weak that he can't run.	
She is so tired that she can't work.	
The rope is so strong that I can't break it.	

V. *Change the structures under A into the structure under B, as in the example.*

A	B
He sells fish.	Does he sell fish?
She returned yesterday.	
She plays tennis well.	
He will reach tomorrow.	
He has caught cold.	
She gave me a pen.	
He likes fish.	

....

❐

Chapter XXII

PUNCTUATION

व्याकरण में Punctuation (विराम चिह्न) का महत्त्वपूर्ण स्थान होता है। इन चिह्नों की सहायता से वाक्यों को पढ़ने, बोलने और उनके अर्थ समझने में बड़ी सुविधा होती है। इसलिए Punctuation के इन चिह्नों को हम एक-एक कर लें और इनके प्रयोग पर विचार करें।

The Comma

Comma का प्रयोग वहाँ होता है जहाँ कम ठहरने की जरूरत पड़ती है। इन नियमों को देखें—

Rule I. एक ही Parts of Speech के बहुत-से शब्द (पर कम-से-कम तीन शब्द) जब and से जोड़े जाते हैं, तब उनके पहले Comma आता है। इन वाक्यों को देखें—

1. Anil, Sudhir and Bashir are good boys.
2. He is tall, fair and strong.
3. She works slowly, carefully and patiently.
4. He reads Hindi, English, Physics and Chemistry.

NOTE—And के बाद Comma का प्रयोग कभी भी नहीं होता, पर and के पहले Comma का प्रयोग हो भी सकता है और नहीं भी।

Rule II. Yes और No के बाद Comma का प्रयोग अवश्य होता है, जब इनके बाद कोई वाक्य आता है; जैसे—

1. Yes, I like this book.
2. No, I don't like that book.
3. Yes, I will go at once.
4. No, I will not go there.

Rule III. वाक्य के Apposition पद के पहले और बाद में Comma का प्रयोग होता है, अर्थात Apposition पद को Commas के बीच में रखा जाता है; जैसे—

I, Mohan, am a student.

इस वाक्य में Mohan एक Apposition पद है, जो I के अर्थ को स्पष्ट करने के लिए आया है। इसलिए इसे Commas के बीच में रखा गया है। एक-दो और वाक्य लें—

1. Ram, the son of Dashrath, killed Ravan.
2. He, the son of a rich man, is very happy.

Rule IV. जो Noun या Pronoun संबोधन कारक (Vocative Case) में रहता है, उसके बाद Comma आता है; जैसे—

1. Gentlemen, I appeal to you for help.

2. Sir, may I go out for a minute?

3. You, come here at once.

NOTE— जब ऐसे Nouns या Pronouns वाक्य के अंत में आते हैं तब Comma का स्थान उनके पहले रहता है, बाद में नहीं; जैसे—

1. Get out, Shyam.

2. May I go out, Sir?

3. Is that you, Mohan?

एक और बात का ध्यान रखें। Nouns या Pronouns कभी-कभी वाक्य के बीच में रहते हैं। वैसी अवस्था में इनके पहले और बाद में भी Comma आता है, अर्थात इन्हें Commas के बीच में रखा जाता है; जैसे—

1. I ask you, Mohan, to go at once.

2. Now, gentlemen, I come to the main point.

Rule V. वाक्य में Parenthesis के पहले और बाद में Comma अवश्य आता है, अर्थात Parenthesis को Commas के बीच में रखा जाता है; जैसे—

1. He is, to speak the truth, a bad boy.

2. You will, I hope, agree with me.

Rule VI. कभी-कभी वाक्य के भीतर कोई Phrase या Conjunction घुसा हुआ रहता है। वैसी अवस्था में इनको Commas के बीच में रखा जाता है; जैसे—

1. She did not, however, like the idea.

2. My father, therefore, decided not to help me.

Rule VII. वाक्य में Direct Narration रहने पर Comma का प्रयोग होता है; जैसे—

1. He said, "I will help you."

2. She told me, "I don't like you."

3. "Man", he said, "is a political animal."

Rule VIII. कुछ वाक्यों में verb का लोप हो जाता है। वैसी अवस्था में Subject के बाद एक Comma आता है; जैसे—

He is going today; she, tomorrow.

Rule IX. वाक्य में Adverbial phrase, Participle phrase या Absolute phrase के बाद Comma का प्रयोग होता है; जैसे—

1. At present, I am helpless.

2. At last, he decided to help me.

3. The sun having set, all went home.

4. Walking along the road, I saw a snake.

Rule X. वाक्य में Principle clause और Adverb clause के बीच Comma का प्रयोग होता है; जैसे—

1. He was absent, because he was ill.

2. I will help you, when you come next time.

3. I will go, if he comes back in time.

NOTE (a)—जब वाक्य में than या as well as के द्वारा तुलना की जाती है, तब Comma का प्रयोग नहीं होता; जैसे—

1. He did as well as she did. 2. He likes him better than me.

NOTE (b)—जब before या after से कोई clause आरंभ होता है, तब Comma का प्रयोग नहीं होता; जैसे—

I will go before (after) she returns.

Rule XI. वाक्य में who, which, when या where का प्रयोग जब Continuative या Non-defining अर्थ में (Coordinate clause की तरह) होता है, तब इनके पहले Comma अवश्य आता है, पर जब इनका प्रयोग Restrictive या Defining अर्थ में (अर्थात Adjective clause की तरह) होता है, तब Comma का प्रयोग नहीं होता। इन वाक्यों को देखें—

1. My father, who came here, gave me a book.
2. He went to Patna, where he stayed for a week.
3. The time, when he will come, is not yet known.

Some Don'ts

(i) Noun clause के पहले Comma का प्रयोग न करें। इन वाक्यों को देखें—

1. I told him that I would help him.
2. I do not know what he wants.
3. I do not know where he lives.

(ii) वाक्य में कभी-कभी verb के बाद that छिपा हुआ रहता है और उस verb के बाद Noun clause या Adjective clause आता है। वैसे वाक्यों में verb के बाद Comma का प्रयोग नहीं होता; जैसे—

1. I think he is right. 2. I hope you are well.
3. The food you eat is not pure.

(iii) आवेदन-पत्र (Application) में To के बाद Comma का प्रयोग नहीं होता, पर Sir और Yours faithfully के बाद Comma अवश्य आता है; जैसे—

To

The Headmaster,

………

Sir,

………

………

Yours faithfully,
Shailendra

Semicolon

Comma से कुछ अधिक ठहराव के लिए Semicolon का प्रयोग किया जाता है। इस संबंध में एक बात का ध्यान रखें। वाक्य में बहुत-से भाग रहते हैं; पर व्याकरण की दृष्टि से उनमें कोई संबंध नहीं रहता। वे एक-दूसरे पर निर्भर नहीं रहते। उनके बीच केवल विचार (notion) का संबंध रहता है, वाक्य की बनावट का नहीं।

Rule I. इसलिए व्याकरण की दृष्टि से ऐसे भाग अलग-अलग स्वतंत्र वाक्य भी हो सकते हैं। वाक्य के ऐसे ही भागों के बाद Semicolon का प्रयोग होता है—

1. He is an honest person; even his enemies say so.
2. One can't expect it to be good; it is so cheap.

Rule II. Semicolon का प्रयोग Coordinate clauses के बीच में होता है जब वे किसी Conjunction के द्वारा जुटे नहीं रहते और उन clauses के Subjects अलग-अलग होते हैं—

People could be counted by thousands; the playground was full of women and children; there were vendors and hawkers, too.

Rule III. Semicolon का प्रयोग Coordinate clauses के बीच होता है जब वे किसी Conjunction के द्वारा जुटे रहते हैं और उन clauses के भिन्न-भिन्न भाग Comma के द्वारा अलग किये हुए रहते हैं—

The place, where the meeting was held, was full of men and women, all in their gala dresses; and every corner was occupied by hawkers who, in order to attract people, were crying up their goods.

NOTE—याद रखें कि एक ही Subject के लिए यदि वाक्य में बहुत-से verbs आयें, तो verbs के बीच में Comma का प्रयोग होता है, Semicolon का नहीं; जैसे—

He called, cried, shouted and wept but nobody came to his help.

The Colon

Rule I. Colon का प्रयोग किसी quotation के आरंभ में होता है; जैसे—

He said: 'God is our father.'

NOTE—ऐसे वाक्यों में Colon के बदले अधिकतर Comma का ही प्रयोग किया जाता है।

Rule II. किसी सूची (list) या उदाहरण (example) को आरंभ करने के लिए Colon का प्रयोग होता है; जैसे—

The following words are used both as nouns and as verbs: love, look and labour.

NOTE—ऐसे वाक्यों में Colon के बाद dash का भी प्रयोग किया जाता है।

The Full Stop

Rule I. Full Stop का प्रयोग वाक्य के अंत में होता है; पर याद रहे कि Optative, Exclamatory और Interrogative sentences के अंत में Full Stop का प्रयोग नहीं होता।

इन वाक्यों को देखें—

1. He is my friend.
2. Is he my friend?
3. What a good man he is!
4. He is a good man.

NOTE—याद रखें कि Imperative sentences के अंत में Full Stop आता है, Note of Interrogation नहीं। आप ऐसे वाक्य मत लिखें—

Describe a railway journey? Bring a book?

इन वाक्यों के अंत में Full Stop का प्रयोग होना चाहिए।

Rule II. संक्षिप्त शब्दों (Abbreviation) के बाद प्रायः Full Stop का प्रयोग नहीं होता है; जैसे—

BA, MA, SDO, DM, PhD, BC, AD, DC

NOTE (a)—आजकल केवल कुछ ही शब्दों में Full stop का प्रयोग होता है; जैसे—

e.g., i.e., ect,, a.c., d.c., a.m., p.m., a.c., d.c., co.

NOTE (b)—आप यह भी याद रखें कि Ist, 2nd, 3rd, 4th आदि के बाद Full Stop का प्रयोग नहीं होता।

The Note of Exclamation

Rule I. Note of Exclamation का प्रयोग Optative तथा Exclamatory sentences के बाद होता है; जैसे—

1. Alas! Hurrah! Nonsense!
2. What a fool he is!
3. May you live long!

NOTE—Note of Exclamation का प्रयोग Salutation (अभिवादन) के लिए नहीं होता। वैसी हालत में Comma का प्रयोग होता है; जैसे—

Dear friend, Sir, Dear Sir

इसलिए आप इस प्रकार मत लिखें—Dear friend! Dear Sir!

The Note of Interrogation

Rule I. Note of Interrogation का प्रयोग Interrogative sentences के बाद होता है; जैसे—

1. Where is he?
2. What is he?
3. Who is he?

NOTE (a)—Indirect question के बाद Full Stop का प्रयोग होता है, Note of Interrogation का नहीं; जैसे—

He asked me when I would return. I asked him how he was.

NOTE (b)—कुछ वाक्यों में who, how, when, where, what आदि के बाद Subject आता है और उसके बाद Verb. वैसे वाक्यों के अंत में Full Stop का प्रयोग होना चाहिए, Note of Interrogation का नहीं; जैसे—

1. Who he is.
2. Where he is.
3. How he is.

ऐसे वाक्यों में जब Subject के पहले verb आता है, तब अंत में Note of Interrogation का प्रयोग होता है; जैसे—

1. Who is he? 2. Where is he? 3. How is he?

Inverted Commas

Rule I. किसी quotation के आरंभ और अंत में Inverted Commas का प्रयोग होता है; जैसे—

He said, "The earth is round."

इससे यह स्पष्ट है कि Inverted Commas का प्रयोग Direct Narration में होता है, Indirect में नहीं। इसलिए आप ऐसे वाक्य मत लिखें—

He said, that, "he would help me."

Double and Single Inverted Commas

Rule I. Double Inverted Commas ("......") का प्रयोग Direct Narration में होता है; पर Single Inverted Commas ('......') का प्रयोग किसी वाक्य के एक अंश या शब्द के लिए होता है; जैसे—

1. He said, "Man is mortal."
2. I do not know what is meant by 'democracy'.

Rule II. कभी-कभी वाक्य में quotation के भीतर quotation रहता है। वैसी अवस्था में प्रधान quotation के लिए Double Inverted Commas का प्रयोग होता है और भीतरी quotation के लिए Single Inverted Commas का; जैसे—

He said, "Do you know the origin of the word 'boycott'?"

....

EXERCISE

Use the correct punctuation marks in these given paragraphs to make meaningful sentences.

1. I know they are talking nonsense Alice thought to herself and it is foolish to cry about it so she brushed away her tears and went on as cheerfully as she could at any rate i'd better be getting out of the wood for really it is coming on very dark do you think it is going to rain.
2. At length casting his eyes upon the bee and gathering causes from the events the spider said a plague split you is it you with a vengeance that have made this litter could not you look before you do not think I have nothing else to do but no mend and repair after you.
3. What do you think sir of that head in the corner done in the manner of jicone there's the true keeping in it is my own face and though there happens to be no likeness a countess offered me one hundred for its fellow I refuse her for hang it that would be mechanical you know.

4. Step forward cried he since I have broken your pine-tree we'll try which is the better man at a wrestling match aha then I will soon satisfy you shouted the giant for if there was one thing on which he prided himself more than another it was his skill in wrestling villain i'll fling you where you can never pick yourself up again.
5. In every way they tried to trap jeanne d' are but she was unafraid if you kill me she cried I will say no other thing and if I were in the fire I would say no more and till death I will hold that what I have said is truth.
6. You will think as some others did rahul that bapu and ba must have been quite comfortable as they were kept in a palace but this palace was only a palace in name it was a huge ugly building its rooms were dark and even when it was day you had to light a lamp to see there was a big garden around it but with no lovely flowers only dried up bushes it was full of mosquitoes too so it is no wonder poor ba felt as though she were being suffocated all the time.
7. All through the night my mind was full of the strange idea of my friend soon after I fell asleep I had a dream it seemed to me that the shilling that lay upon the table raised itself upon its edge it turned its face towards me.

❐

Chapter XXIII

TEST YOURSELF

I. *Match A with B, so as to make meaningful sentences.*

A	B
He was beaten	in black and white
She protested	black and blue
He passed because he worked	by fits and starts
He failed because he worked	heart and soul
It was raining	tooth and nail
They were fighting	cats and dogs
He got over	the examination
She got through	his difficulty
My attention	was called in
A doctor	was called off

II. *Fill in the blanks with suitable words.*

1. She was shedding …… tears.
2. He had to face the …… for negligence of duties.
3. Life is not a bed of …… .
4. Her son is the …… of her eye.
5. He is a …… gun.
6. It is a nine days' …… .
7. He proved to be a …… in the grass.
8. Even big leaders accept …… money today.
9. A fifth …… betrays his country.
10. He was paid back in the same …… .
11. Some newspapers indulge in yellow …… .
12. She is a woman of …… virtue.
13. He lives under …… government.
14. The Prime Minister of Russia was given a red …… .
15. The Parliament was adjourned sine …… .

IDIOMS AND PHRASES

I. COMMON MISCELLANEOUS PHRASES

(A)

I do not know even the *ABC* (साधारण ज्ञान) of science.

Old men cannot enjoy *animal spirits* (स्वस्थ युवावस्था की प्रफुल्लता)।

Kashmir is an *apple of discord* (कलह की वस्तु) between India and Pakistan.

Everything in this office is in *apple-pie* order (बिलकुल ठीक हालत में)।

My son is the *apple of my eye* (प्यारा, दुलारा)।

The Argus-eyed (ईर्ष्यापूर्ण, पैनी दृष्टिवाला) lover watched his rival.

Many politicians have always their own *axe to grind* (स्वार्थ सिद्ध करना)।

(B)

My father's death was a *boat from the blue* (आकस्मिक विपत्ति) for me.

He won through *back-stairs influence* (अनुचित रूप से)।

There is *bad blood* (शत्रुता) between Russia and America.

Our reading-room is often turned into a *bear garden* (हल्ला और झगड़े का स्थान)।

Life is not a *bed of roses* (आनंदप्रद वस्तु)।

Pt Nehru was a *big gun* (महत्त्वपूर्ण व्यक्ति) in world politics.

I took a *bird's-eye view* (सरसरी नजर) of the whole place.

Birds of a feather (एक तरह के लोग) flock together.

There is *black sheep* (नीच व्यक्ति) in every society.

The Nobel Prize is *a blue ribbon* (सर्वोच्च सम्मान) for a scholar.

Don't be proud of *blue blood* (उच्च कुल)।

This piece of land is a *bone of contention* (द्वेष एवं झगड़े की वस्तु) between the two families.

Jagdish is my *bosom friend* (सच्चा एवं विश्वासी मित्र)।

My *brown study* (अर्द्धजाग्रत अवस्था का स्वप्न) was rudely shaken.

All the measures to remove corruption have ended in a *blind alley* (जहाँ से निकलने की गुंजाइश न हो)।

(C)

Capital punishment (मृत्यु-दण्ड) is rare now.

Patel was a man of *cast iron will* (दृढ़—जो मुड़ न सके)।

The issue was decided by *a casting vote* (निर्णायक मत)।

Do not always build *castles in the air* (हवाई किला, ख्याली पुलाव)।

A soldier must not be *chicken-hearted* (कायर)।

A *close-fisted* (कृपण) man is not happy.

There was a *close vote* (पक्ष और विपक्ष में लगभग बराबर वोट) in my constituency.

There was a *cold blooded* (अकारण एवं निर्दयतापूर्ण) *murder* of the child.

There is a *cold war* (अमैत्रीपूर्ण संबंध) between Russia and America.

That Shri Subhas Chandra Bose is yet alive is a *cock-and-bull story* (मूर्खतापूर्ण, अविश्वसनीय बात)।

She shed *crocodile tears* (दिखावटी आँसू) over the death of her step-son.

His case could not stand *cross-examination* (जिरह) in the court.

All protests against price rise are *a cry in the wilderness* (अरण्यरोदन, व्यर्थ वस्तु)।

He had a *close shave* (बाल-बाल बचना) in the accident.

(D & E)

I am tired of my neighbour's *dog-in the-manger policy* (जिस सिद्धांत से न अपना लाभ हो और न दूसरे का)।

A graduate is a *drag in the market* (जिस वस्तु की माँग न हो) in our country.

Wine gives you *Dutch courage* (नशे का जोश) which goes down soon.

She is a woman of *easy virtue* (नैतिकताहीन)।

(F)

A candidate gets credit for a *fair hand* (साफ लिखावट)।

He is in *fine (high) feather* on his birthday (प्रसन्न, प्रफुल्लित मुद्रा)।

The *fair sex* (नारी) is tender by nature.

A *fair-weather friend* (सुख का साथी) leaves us in trouble.

One has to pay a *fancy price* (मनमाना दाम) in the black market.

My woollen suit has *fast colour* (पक्का रंग)।

No religion encourages *fast living/fast life* (भोग-विलास का जीवन)

In the company of old men I feel like a *fish out of water* (कष्टप्रद या प्रतिकूल अवस्था में होना)।

The liberation of Bangladesh is a feather in India's cap (गौरवपूर्ण काम)।

Flesh and blood (मानव-स्वभाव, मनुष्य-जाति) can bear it no longer.

If you hope to pass, you are in a *fool's paradise* (झूठी आशा में)।

One likes to enjoy *forty winks* (दिन में थोड़ी नींद) in summer.

The coughing of this old man at the music conference was a *fly in the ointment* (दूध में मक्खी जो मजा किरकिरा कर दे)।

A *fifth-columnist* (ऐसा व्यक्ति जो गुप्त रूप से अपने देश के विरुद्ध काम करे) betrays his country in the hours of crisis.

He is a *freelance* (स्वतंत्र) politician.

The student was fined for taking *French leave* (बिना आज्ञा या सूचना की अनुपस्थिति)।

At the time of my brother's appointment I found in Ram a *friend at court* (समय पर सहायता करनेवाला)।

(G)

Holi is a *gala day* (आनंद-उत्सव का दिन) for the Hindus.

Mere *gift of the gab* (चतुराईपूर्वक धारा-प्रवाह बोलने की शक्ति) is not enough.

This boy does nothing. He is just a *gentleman at large* (जिसे ऐश-आराम के लिए काफी धन और समय हो)।

You can be happy only when you follow the *golden mean* (मध्यम मार्ग)।

Both hard labour and capital are needed to keep it a *going concern* (चालू कारबार)।

He proved a *good Samaritan* (दयालु व्यक्ति) to me in my time of need.

All the actors dressed themselves in the *green room* (जिस कमरे में नाटक के पात्र तैयारी करते हैं)।

(H)

In the accident he had a *hair-breadth escape* (बाल-बाल बचना)।

A *hen-pecked husband* (पत्नी की झिड़की सुनने और सहनेवाला) cannot help his brother.

Even big leaders of our country accept *hush money* (घूस) today.

(I)

The riot was suppressed with an *iron hand* (कड़ाई से)।

Hitler was a man of *iron will* (दृढ़ निश्चय)।

(J)

If you are a *jack of all trades* (जो आदमी किसी भी काम में निपुण न हो, पर सभी में हाथ डाले) you are master of none.

You should not employ a *jail bird* (नामी अपराधी जो बराबर जेल ही में रहे) to guard your house.

Don't look at this problem with a *jaundiced eye* (द्वेष के साथ, पक्षपात की दृष्टि से)।

(L)

The commander's *laconic speech* (अलंकार-रहित छोटा भाषण) was effective.

His foolish argument made him the *laughing stock* (मजाक की चीज) of all.

To call Mahatma Gandhi the greatest leader of the Hindus is to pay him a *left-handed compliment* (प्रशंसा के रूप में शिकायत)।

Every teacher must have a bit of *learned leisure* (विद्योपार्जन का अवकाश)।

Even today capital gets *lion's share* (अनुचित रूप से बहुत बड़ा हिस्सा) in production.

That woman *in labour* (प्रसव-पीड़ा में) was carried to a nursing home.

Labour pain = प्रसव-पीड़ा

The police couldn't detect the *light-fingered person* (छोटी-छोटी चोरी में चुस्त-चालाक आदमी) who took away my pen.

A student must be a *light sleeper* (श्वान-निद्रावाला)।

The *long and short* (सारांश) of what I mean to say is that you must be honest.

Do not make *lame excuses* (फालतू बहाना) for coming late to school.

(M)

Mrs Smith's *maiden name* (विवाह के पहले का नाम) was Miss Jones.

The MP's *maiden speech* (जीवन में प्रथम सार्वजनिक भाषण) was not impressive.

Dr Jha was a *man of letters* (विद्वान, साहित्यिक)।

Pandit Nehru was a *man of parts* (असाधारण गुणवाला मनुष्य)।

One must be a *man of spirit* (साहसी मनुष्य)।

What help can you expect from a *man of straw* (अविश्वसनीय, तुच्छ) ?

Modern English poetry is not meant for the *man in the street* (साधारण आदमी)।

His discovery of a gold mountain proved to be a *mare's nest* (झूठा आविष्कार)।

This bill is still a *moot point* (बहस की बात, बिना निर्णय किया हुआ विषय)।

Birbal is well known for his *mother wit* (स्वाभाविक चतुराई)।

(N)

He reached in the *nick of time* (ऐन मौके पर) and saved the boy.

Hitler's conquest was a *nine days' wonder* (जो कुछ समय तक हलचल पैदा कर समाप्त हो जाए)।

I am not close to the CM, I have just a *nodding acquaintance* (बहुत कम जान-पहचान) with him.

(O)

An *oily tongue* (मीठी, खुशामदी जबान) is a master-key to wordly success.

A reader must have an *open mind* (खुला मस्तिष्क) about a poem before he has read it.

Zamindari abolition is no longer *an open question* (अनिश्चित, बिना फैसला किया हुआ विषय)।

It is an *open secret* (जो गुप्त बात सबको मालूम हो) that corruption in the country is rampant.

The situation is *out of hand* (वश के बाहर)।

(P)

Shakespeare wrote his plays during the *palmy days* (सुख-समृद्धि क समय) of Elizabeth's reign.

Several inventions have proved to be a *Pandora's box* (वरदान के रूप में अभिशाप) for mankind.

This work seems to be a *Penelope's web* (जिस काम का अंत न हो)।

Do not *play the fool* (बेवकूफ की तरह व्यवहार करना) in the classroom.

Every nurse gets *pin money* (वस्त्रादि के लिए भत्ता)।

The refugees did not find it all *plain sailing* (आसानी से बढ़ना) when they settled down in new places.

He refused *point blank* (स्पष्ट रूप से) to help me.

You should take up the issue only after you have weighed the *pros and cons* (पक्ष और विपक्ष में तर्क) connected with it.

(Q)

He is a *queer fish* (झक्की आदमी, सनकी) and so cannot pull on with anybody.

Our mud-built Assembly Hall was surely a *quixotic project* (मूर्खतापूर्ण, हास्यास्पद योजना)।

(R)

The Prime Minister of Russia was given a *red carpet welcome* (शाही, शानदार, स्वागत)।

One must lay by something against the *rainy day* (दुर्दिन)।

Raw spirits (नशीली शराब) made him almost mad.

There is no *ready money* (नकद रुपया) with me now.

The 15th of August is a *red-letter day* (सौभाग्यपूर्ण, महत्त्वपूर्ण दिवस) in India.

Grammar to some people is like a *red rag to a bull* (डराने/भड़कानेवाली वस्तु)।

Inefficient officers practise *red-tapism* (दफ्तर का तौर-तरीका)।

Most of our films are meant for the *riff-raff* (छोटे लोग), not for the people of taste.

During the last world war Russia and England were tied together with a *rope of sand* (आसानी से टूटनेवाला बंधन)।

Every work can't be done by the *rule of thumb* (विवेकहीन व्यावहारिक अनुभव)।

I cannot depend on him, because he is a *broken reed* (अविश्वसनीय आदमी)।

All the schools and colleges should be taken over by the government for the welfare of *the rank and file* (साधारण जनता)।

(S)

The black-marketeer got off *scot free* (बिना सजा/जुर्माना के मुक्त)।

Men like Mahatma Gandhi are the *salt of the earth* (उत्तम कोटि के लोग)।

When one has to choose between friend and country, one is between *Scylla and Charybdis* (उभय संकट)।

There is a *screw loose* (मानसिक दोष) in him.

Religion is the *sheet-anchor* (प्रधान सहारा) of life.

There is no *short cut* (सीधा और छोटा रास्ता) to real progress.

That college was closed *sine die* (अनिश्चित काल तक) on account of disturbances.

When the ship sank people escaped with the *skin of their teeth* (प्राण बचाकर, पर सब कुछ गँवाकर)।

The business is going down because of my *sleeping partner* (निष्क्रिय साझेदार)।

This work cannot be done quickly by a *slow coach* (सुस्त और बेवकूफ आदमी) like my servant.

Even a *small fry* (साधारण लोग) like me can do some service to the country.

When he failed to get wealth and fame he now calls them *sour grapes* (खट्टे अंगूर कौन खाये)।

A *snake in the grass* (छिपा हुआ शत्रु) is more dangerous than an open enemy.

You must use *soft sawder* (खुशामद) to win his favours.

Power and prestige are *sour grapes* (खट्टे अंगूर) to disappointed leaders.

Mango is a *stone fruit* (कड़ा बीजवाला)।

My friend's house is not more than a *stone's throw* (समीप) from mine.

Let us help these *street Arabs* (अनाथ बच्चे)।

The 'Death Of The Month' is the *swan song* (मृत्यु के ठीक पहले की रचना या कथन) of Virginia Wolf.

The threat of famine on the eve of Holi hangs like the *sword of Damocles* over our heads (खुशी के बीच खतरा)।

(T)

One must work, for mere *tall talk* (घमण्डभरी लंबी-चौड़ी बात) won't do.

Most of the villagers do not know even the *three R's* (पढ़ना-लिखना)।

(U)

Most of the candidates were quite *up to the mark* (उचित योग्यता के अनुरूप)।

There is no room for the *upper ten* (उच्च वर्ग के रईस) in a socialistic pattern of society.

The *ups and downs* (सुख-दुख, परिवर्तन) of life make you wiser.

The idea of world brotherhood is a *utopian scheme* (काल्पनिक आदर्शवादी योजना जो पूरी न हो सके)।

(W)

Most of his arguments were *wide of the mark* (निशाने/बिंदु से दूर)।

When the ship sank, several men met a *watery grave* (जलसमाधि, डूबने से मृत्यु होना)।

The old man's presence threw a *wet blanket* (जोश एवं खुशी को कम करनेवाला आदमी या वस्तु) on his children's mirth.

A motor car is a *white elephant* (जिस सम्पत्ति से लाभ के बदले हानि हो) for a teacher.

India needs field-workers, and not only *white-collar people* (ऑफिस में बैठकर काम करनेवाला)।

The unscientific Gogra Project is a *wild goose chase* (मूर्खतापूर्ण साहसिक कार्य)।

Wool gathering = अन्यमनस्कता (absent mindedness)

Witch hunt = विरोधियों की खोजकर उन्हें सताना

(Y)

Yellow journalism = something cheap and sensational in newspapers to attract readers.

Yeoman's service = help in times of need.

II. IDIOMS WITH VERBS

[A] IDIOMS WITH VERBS **To Be**

He has *been after* (खोज में रहना) an employment but in vain.

I should *be up to* (समान होना) the tricks of my enemy.

A farmer must *be up and doing* (क्रियाशील होना) in the rainy season.

Indian farmers *are* not *well off* (धनी, खुशहाल)।

Nehru *was born with a silver spoon in his mouth* (धनी परिवार में जन्म लेना या होना)।

If you *are born under a lucky star* (शुभ नक्षत्र में जन्म लेना) you rise by leaps and bounds.

I *am sick of* (तंग आ जाना) his misconduct.

To a hungry beggar every slice of bread *is worth its weight in gold* (बहुत कीमती होना)।

All his hard labour *was of no avail* (बेकार होना)।

I *am ill at ease* (परेशानी में होना) with drunkards.

The thief *was caught red-handed* (रँगे हाथ पकड़ा जाना)।

I *was all ears to* (ध्यान से सुनना) his speech.

She *is a capital hand* (निपुण होना) at cooking.

Stalin *was a host in himself* (महान शक्तिशाली होना)।

His wild talks show that he *is off his head* (मानसिक संतुलन नष्ट होना)।

I have a servant *at my beck and call* (इशारे पर नाचना)।

Communists and capitalists *are at daggers-drawn* (गहरी शत्रुता होना)।

Ramanujan was quite *at home in* (निपुण होना) mathematics.

Thieves *are at large* (निरंकुश, स्वतंत्र होना) at night.

I *am at a loss* (घबड़ा जाना) to decide what to do.

I am not at one (एक राय का होना) with you.

The boy *is* quite *at sea* (संभ्रांत होना) in general knowledge.

Books are lying *at sixes and sevens* (तितर-बितर होना)।

When he failed, he *was at his wit's end* (किंकर्तव्यविमूढ़ होना)।

Who *is in the chair* (सभापति होना) at this meeting?

When monsoon fails, farmers look as though they *were in the doldrums* (उदासीन एवं उत्साहहीन होना)।

The boy *was in a fix* (संकट और घबड़ाहट में पड़ जाना) when his pen broke in the examination hall.

His action *is in keeping with* (समान होना) his speech.

A good boy *is in the good books* (कृपाभाजन होना) of his teacher.

If you *are in your teens* (तेरह से उन्नीस वर्ष के बीच की अवस्था का होना), you can't get a responsible job.

Vinobaji *is in the van* (आगे रहना) of thinkers.

In the event of a world war America will find that she *is in the wrong box* (प्रतिकूल या बुरी दिशा में पड़ना)।

The Indian army *is on the alert* (सजग होना)।

Capitalism *is on the wane* (धीरे-धीरे घटना) now.

He *is out of temper* (क्रुद्ध होना) even at trifles.

Colonialism *is on its last legs* (अंतिम घड़ी में होना)।

He was absent, because he *was out of sorts* (थोड़ा अस्वस्थ होना) today.

To fight in a church *is out of place* (असंगत होना)।

She has been *out of her mind* (पागल होना) since her husband died.

I do not care if you go against me, because your opposition *is neither here nor there* (महत्त्वहीन होना)।

An upstart is *full of himself* (घमण्डी होना)।

[B] IDIOMS WITH OTHER VERBS

(A)

My lawyer *acts for* (बदले में काम करना) me.

I *act from* (भाव-प्रेरित होकर) a sense of duty.

Heat *acts on* (असर डालना) metals.

You should *act up to* (अनुसार काम करना) my advice.

You must *attend to* (ध्यान देना, सेवा करना) your work.

(B)

He helped me in the beginning but *backed out* (खिसक जाना, पीछे हट जाना) later.

You must *back up* (मदद करना) your friend.

My evidence will *bear out* (समर्थन करना) the charge.

Come to the point instead of *beating about the bush* (इधर-उधर की बातें करना)।

Our enemy had to *bite the dust* (अत्यधिक अपमानित होना) in the last war.

Blow out (फूँककर बुझाना) the candle.

He always *blows his own trumpet* (अपना राग अलापना) and never cares for others.

The farmer *is breaking ground* (योजना, काम शुरू करना)।

When all were silent, I *broke the ice* (मौन भंग करना)।

I *broke the news* (दुःखद समाचार कहना) to him about his father's death.

I saw the thief but he *broke away* (भाग जाना)।

Sending armed forces to control these children is like *breaking a fly on the wheel* (छोटे काम के लिए बड़ी शक्ति का प्रयोग)।

He *breaks in* (ट्रेनिंग देना) his horse every morning.

A thief *broke into* (अचानक बलपूर्वक घुसना) my house.

The lover's engagement is *broken off* (खत्म होना)।

Pox has *broken out* (अचानक फैलना) in the town.

The college *broke up* (समाप्त या बंद होना) for holidays.

Gandhiji *brought about* (किसी चीज के होने का कारण बनना) a great change in our country.

High prices have been *brought down* (नीचे ले आना या नीचा दिखाना)।

Trees *bring forth* (जन्म देना) new leaves in spring.

The thief was *brought to book* (सजा देना)।

This inquiry *brought out* (प्रकाश में लाना) hidden things.

I ws *brought up* (लालन-पालन होना या किया जाना) by my mother.

Don't *brood over* (चिंतामग्न होना) the past.

India and Pakistan are now trying to *bury the hatchet* (पुरानी दुश्मनी को समाप्त करना)।

(C)

My friend *called at* (किसी के घर पर भेंट करना) my house.

Call in (बुला भेजना) a doctor at once.

He was bold enough to *call a spade a spade* (साफ-साफ कहना, खरी-खोटी सुनाना)।

The cry *called off* (ध्यान खींचना) my attention.

I *called on* (भेंट करना) my friend this morning.

A drowning man *calls out* (चिल्लाना) for help.

I cannot *call up* (याद करना) that old incident.

The teacher *called over* (नाम पुकारना) the roll numbers.

It is useless to *carry on* (आगे बढ़ाना) this business.

He *carried out* (आदेशानुसार काम करना) my wishes.

I *carried my point* (बहस में हराना) in the debate.

Our college team *carried the day* (जीतना) in the match.

The SP *carries matters with a high hand* (कठोरता से पेश आना)।

My book *cast* all the others *into the shade* (फीका कर देना)।

Don't *cast a slur upon* (कलंक लगाना) your great family.

When I *caught his eye* (ध्यान खींचना), I called him.

A drowning man will *catch at a straw* (संकट में तिनके का सहारा लेना)।

America has *caught a Tartar* (बड़े शत्रु से पाला पड़ना) in Russia.

He faced the disaster that *came upon* (एकाएक आना) him.

The secret has now *come to light* (मालूम होना)।

How did the accident *come to pass* (होना)।

His result *came (fell) short of* (आशा से कम होना) my expectation.

At the MA Examination my brother *came off with flying colours* (सफलता पाना)।

I *count upon* (विश्वासपूर्वक निर्भर होना) my friend's vote.

A merchant *cries up* (बड़ाई करना) his own goods but *cries down* (छोटा समझना) those of others.

She *cut a sorry figure* (बुरा हाल होना, अच्छा न करना) on the stage.

Cut short (संक्षिप्त करना) your speech.

His misbehaviour *cut me to the quick* (मार्मिक चोट पहुँचाना)।

India alone can *cut the Gordian knot of* (पेंचीली समस्या को असाधारण रूप से सुलझाना) world peace.

His speech *cut no ice* (प्रभाव पैदा न कर सकना)।

(D)

This merchant *deals in* (व्यापार करना) rice.

You should *deal well by* (बरताव करना) your servant.

Please *deal out* (बाँटना) the cards.

I have *nothing to do* (कोई नाता नहीं रखना) with politics.

Do the story *into* verse (अनुवाद करके रूप बदलना)।

I am *done up* (थकना) under the pressure of work.

What does your argument *drive at* (लक्ष्य करना) ?

The enemy was *driven out* (भगा दिया जाना, निकाल दिया जाना)।

The speaker *dwelt on* (विस्तारपूर्वक बोलना या सोचना) the subject well.

He *dwells in* (रहना—to reside) a dirty house.

(E)

Lady Macbeth *egged* Macbeth *on* (उकसाना) to murder.

(F)

That officer had to *face the music* (डाँट सुनना) for his negligence.

Why do you *fight shy* (नजर बचाना) of your teacher?

Is it proper to *fall foul of* (विरोध होना) one's master?

Boys were asked to *fall in* (एक कतार में खड़ा होना)।

Sometimes even fast friends *fall out* (झगड़ा करना)।

Old laws are *falling into abeyance* (व्यवहार में न रहना)।

He *fell a prey* (शिकार होना—victim) to cholera.

My resolution *fell to the ground* (व्यर्थ होना) for want of support.

You must have something to *fall back upon* (सहारा लेना) in old age.

All my appeals *fell flat* (असर न होना) on the mob.

His performance *fell short of* my expectation (कम होना)।

I had to *foot the bill* (खर्च का भार ढोना) of the party.

Smugglers tried to *fish in troubled waters* (संकटकालीन स्थिति से लाभ उठाना) during the war.

(G)

I *got ahead* (आगे बढ़ जाना) of others in the race.

It is through inquiry that we *get at* (पहुँचना) the truth.

I have *got back* (वापस पाना) the book from him.

While passengers were *getting down* (उतरना) and *getting in* (चढ़ना) the train, I lost my bag.

I *got over* (विजय पाना) the difficulty at last.

The boy was asked to *get out* (बाहर निकलना)।

My son *got through* the examination (सफल होना, पूरा करना)।

Don't *get drunk* (शराब पीकर बेहोश हो जाना) on duty.

One must *get rid of* (बुरी चीज से छुटकारा पाना) bad habits.

He *got into hot water* (संकट में पड़ना) for committing a theft.

If you quarrel with your boss, you will *get into a scrape* (बुरी स्थिति में पड़ना) and then it is not easy to *get out of the scrape* (बुरी स्थिति से निकलना)।

We *got wind of* (अफवाह सुनना) the proposed taxation beforehand.

Sita was *given away* (पूर्ण रूप से दे दिया जाना) to Ram in marriage.

In the end the enemy *gave in* (झुकना)।

A flower *gives out* (बाहर निकालना) its perfume.

He *gave over* (सुपुर्द करना) charge to the new officer.

One must *give up* (पूर्ण रूप से छोड़ना) bad habits.

A student should *give himself to* (अपने को लगाना) studies.

When the boy came late again, I *gave him a bit of my mind* (डाँटना)।

Don't *give the cold shoulder* (उदासीन भाव से बरताव करना) to your friend.

The house *gave way* (गिर जाना) during rains.

We should *give a wide berth to* (दूर रहना) bad company.

Please *give ear* (ध्यान देना) to my prayer.

Don't *give currency* (ज्ञात करना) to baseless rumours.

A poet *gives vent to* (व्यक्त करना) his own feelings.

My dog *went after* (पीछा करना) the thief.

I have *given the go-by* (छोड़ना) to silly customs.

If I *go on* (जारी रखना) with my work, I will do it.

America and Russia cannot *go hand in hand* (मेल से एक साथ रहना)।

Russia's recent attitude will *go a long way* (बहुत हद तक जाना) in easing the world situation.

Let us *go to law* (कानून की मदद लेना) to decide the case.

Law can't *go out of the way* (नियमित मार्ग से हटना) to help us.

We cannot say that those who try to reach the moon *go on a fool's errand* (मूर्खतापूर्ण काम में लगना)।

I am prepared to *go through fire and water* (सभी संकटों एवं बाधाओं का सामना करना) to help my friend.

(H)

He always *hankers after* (for) (तीव्र इच्छा/आकांक्षा होना) money.

I can't take up your work, because I *have my hands full* (बहुत कामों में लगा रहना)।

If a businessman *has clean hands* (ईमानदार रहना), he will prosper.

I *have a hand (voice) in* (काम में हाथ होना) the construction of the college building.

I have English Grammar *at my finger's ends* (पूर्ण रूप से वश में रखना)।

This rule *holds good* (जारी रहना) even today.

One *has a short memory* (स्मरणशक्ति दुर्बल होना) in old age.

The boy *had not the face (cheek)* (दुस्साहस होना) to argue with the principal.

Some of the printing presses *have too many irons in the fire* (इतने अधिक काम में लग जाना कि कुछ काम खराब या अधूरा रह जाय)।

The talkative boy was asked to *hold his tongue* (चुप रहना)।

A great man is humble; he does not *hold his head high* (घमंड से सिर ऊँचा करना)।

I *hold it true* (सत्य मानना) that duty is rewarded.

Hold true = to continue to be true.

The advancing army was *held back* (पीछे हटा दिया जाना)।

The spirited horse was *held in* (रोककर रखा जाना)।

The judgement in this case is *held over* (स्थगित रखा जाना)।

(K)

He went to the picture just to *kill time* (समय काटना/बरबाद करना)।

Keep in with (मेल में रहना) your neighbour.

There is a danger here. *Keep out* (दूर रहना)।

Keep off (अलग रहना) singing.

Military plans are *kept dark* (छिपाकर रखा जाना)।

Flatteres should be *kept at arm's length* (दूर रखा जाना)।

You must live economically to *keep your head above water* (कर्ज या कष्ट से अलग रहना)।

If you *keep good hours* (सबेरे घर लौटना या सोना) it will keep you fit, but if you *keep bad hours* or *late hours* (देर से घर लौटना या सोना) you will fall ill.

Many labourers do not get as much as would *keep their body and soul together* (जिन्दा रहना)।

Our farmers work hard to *keep the wolf from the door* (गरीबी या भुखमरी से बचना)।

(L)

Our simple villagers are easily *led by the nose* (नाक पकड़कर घुमाना) by clever leaders.

He *looked blank* (चकित होना, घबड़ाना) when he was informed of his failure.

I *laughed in my sleeve* (मन-ही-मन हँसना) at his funny dress.

Even lovely places are *laid waste* (बरबाद होना या किया जाना) in war.

I have to *labour under handicaps* (प्रतिकूल परिस्थिति में काम करना)।

The dog was *let loose* (खुला छोड़ देना)।

The enemy's plan was *laid bare* (भेद खोल दिया जाना)।

A tiger *lies in wait* (छिपकर रहना) for its prey.

A hunter *lays* (sets) *a trap* (जाल बिछाना) for wild beasts.

One must *lay up for the rainy day* (संकट के लिए प्रबंध करना)।

The drunken husband returned late and said, *"Let me in."* (भीतर आने देना)।

The thief was caught but *let off* (छोड़ दिया जाना)।

The son *lived up to the expectation* (आशानुसार) of his father.

Animals *live on* (खाकर जीना) grass.

He is *looking into* (जाँच करना) the case.

A mother *looks after* (देखभाल करना) her children.

One should not *look down* upon (घृणा से देखना) the poor.

You must *look sharp* (जल्दी करना) about it.

(M, N)

I fail to *make out* (समझना) what you say.

The enemy was asked to *make up* (पूरा करना) the loss.

You should *make up* your mind (तय करना) soon.

The rival parties *made peace* (समझौता करना) at last.

Please *make room* (जगह देना) for me in the bus.

I excused the student when he *made a clean breast of* (साफ-साफ कहना) the whole matter.

A teacher works hard to *make both ends meet* (जीवन की आवश्यकताओं को पूरा करना)।

Though young, Netaji *made his mark* (बड़ा काम या नाम करना) in politics.

Modern essayists *make a mountain out of a molehill* (तुच्छ वस्तु को महत्त्व देना, तिल का ताड़ बनाना)।

(*"To make much ado about nothing"* also has a similar meaning.)

He writes in such a confused way that I can *make neither head nor tail* (कुछ भी समझ में न आना) of it.

Don't *make little (light) of* (तुच्छ समझना) others.

Don't *make much of* (बड़ा समझना) yourself.

You caused me a heavy loss, and you should, therefore, *make* it *good* (क्षति पूरी करना)।

Let us *make the best (most) of* (अधिक-से-अधिक उपयोग करना) what we have.

Life is very sad but one must *make the best of a bad bargain* (बुरी चीज से भी लाभ उठाना)।

The time for work has come and so we should *make hay while the sun shines* (अवसर से लाभ उठाना)।

When my friend called at my house, I requested him to *make himself at home* (घर में होने की तरह रहना, आराम से रहना)।

He *met with* (भिड़न्त होना, अचानक मिलना) an accident.

The ringleader was caught and so the plot was *nipped in the bud* (आरंभ में ही नष्ट कर दिया जाना)।

(P)

I *pin* my *faith/hope* (दृढ़ आशा) on my trusted friend.

He abused me and I *paid him back in the same (his own) coin* (जैसे को तैसा मिलना, ठीक वैसा ही व्यवहार करना जैसा पाना)।

There are men who instead of doing useful work *pick holes in others (other's coat)* (दोष देखना)।

When there was an exchange of hot words and blows, my advice *poured oil on the troubled waters* (क्रोध और अशांति को शांत करना)।

Even college students very often *play truant* (काम पर या क्लास में जाने के बदले इधर-उधर भटकना)।

Congressmen *played second fiddle* (अधीन रहकर काम में गौण या अप्रधान भाग लेना) to Pt Nehru.

One should just *play the game* (नियम का पालन करना) and not care for success.

A real friend never *plays one false* (धोखा देना)।

The Britishers *played a double game* (दोहरी चाल चलना, धोखा देना) in our country and created a rift between the Hindus and the Muslims.

On account of her obstinate nature she has now to *plough a lonely furrow* (अकेले रहना या काम करना)।

Don't *put off* (स्थगित करना) till tomorrow what you can do today.

You should *put off* (छोड़ देना) these tattered clothes.

The meeting was *put off* (स्थगित करना)।

We *put on* (धारणा करना) woollen clothes in winter.

Put *out* (शरीर के अंगों या अन्य साधनों की मदद से बुझाना) the fire/light. [यंत्र आदि साधन (mechanical aid) की मदद से बुझाने के लिए switch off का प्रयोग होता है।]

Most of us *put up* (रहना) in bad houses and have to *put up with* (सहन करना) the worst nuisance.

The enemy was *put to the sword* (कत्ल कर दिया जाना)।

Your friend is *put to (on) trial* (परीक्षित होना) in your need.

I should not *put in my ear* (दखल देना) in your affairs.

He must *put the screw on* (रोकना) his extravagant son.

It is *putting the cart before the horse* (उलटा काम करना) if you qualify yourself after appointment.

Let India *put her shoulder to the wheel* (दूसरे से नहीं माँगकर स्वयं परिश्रम करना) to implement her plans.

Please *put down* (लिखना) what you have to say.

He has *put a spoke in my wheel* (बाधा डालना)।

At the very start of his career he *put his foot in it* (भारी गलती करना)।

(R)

Do not *run after* (पीछा करना, खोज में रहना) money.

The deer was *run down.* My health has *run down* (थककर गिरना)।

If you don't spend well, you may *run into debt* (कर्ज या खतरे में पड़ना)।

My money has *run short* (खत्म हो जाना)।

That elephant *ran amuck* (पागल, उन्मत्त हो जाना) and killed two persons.

(S)

I will *see to* (ध्यान देना) it.

I very well *see through* (चाल समझना) his motive.

All the prisoners were *set free* (मुक्त करना, छोड़ देना)।

Set about (शुरू करना) your work without delay.

My objections were *set aside* (ठुकराया जाना)।

Rainy season has *set in* (शुरू होना)।

I want to *set off* (प्रस्थान करना) for home today.

The one was *set on* (उकसाया जाना) the other to fight.

I can work hard but lack the capacity to *set the Thames on fire* (असाधारण कार्य करना)।

You should *set your face against* (दृढ़ता से रोकना) temptations.

Let us try to *set our own house in order* (घर सँभालना)।

There was a rift when leaders *set people by the ears* (घृणा का भाव पैदा करना, उकसाकर झगड़ा करना)।

That soldier was punished for *showing the white feathers* (कायरता दिखाना)।

Some critics *split hairs* (बाल की खाल खींचना)।

This house *stands in need of* (जरूरत होना) repair.

During the last flood my boat *stood me in good stead* (संकट में या समय पर काम आना)।

The German soldiers could not *stand their ground* (अपने स्थान पर दृढ़ रहना) against the Russians.

If bad times come, you should *stand to your guns* (डटे रहना) and not shed idle tears.

The new teacher often *stops short* (बीच में रुक जाना) in the middle of his lecture.

You must *steer clear* (अलग रहना) of bad men.

That charming girl *steals everybody's heart* (दिल जीतना) away.

He *stole a march* (कार्य पहले करके लाभ पाना) on his opponent.

(T–W)

I was *taken in* (धोखा खाना) by that clever man.

Children *take after* (सदृश होना) their parents.

I *took him for* (एक चीज को दूसरी चीज समझना) a thief.

Before deciding, I shall *take your views into account* (विचार करना)।

I was *taken aback* (चकित होना) at the sight of a lion.

When the dog barked, the thieves *took to their heels* (भाग जाना)।

You, boy, *take off* (हटाना) your clothes.

You should *take up* (आरंभ करना) the work now.

You should act and not merely *talk big* (डींग हाँकना) about yourself.

A dwarf should not *take a leaf out of* (अनुकरण करना) a giant's book.

If you face a strong opposition, *you should take the bull by the horns* (साहसपूर्वक सामना करना)।

I *took a leap in the dark* (बिना सोचे खतरनाक काम करना) in buying a new company's shares.

By procuring his dismissal for your own appointment you have *taken the bread out of his mouth* (जीवन-निर्वाह का साधन छीनना)।

Don't *throw cold water upon* (उत्साह भंग करना) my plan.

By his flattery he tried to *throw dust in my eyes* (आँख में धूल झोंकना, धोखा देना)।

The whole village *turned out* (जमा होना) to welcome her.

Please *turn out* (बंद करना) the tap.

He was *turned out* (निकाल दिया जाना) of the examination hall.

Please *turn yur chair round* (घुमाना) to the fire.

Politicians very often *turn their coat* (एक पार्टी/सिद्धांत को छोड़कर दूसरी पार्टी में मिलना) for selfish ends.

Sometimes even sinners *turn over a new leaf* (बुरे आचरण को अच्छी दिशा में बदलना, नया जीवन आरंभ करना) and become saints.

In the man-to-man fight between the Russians and the Germans, the latter *turned tail* (पीठ दिखाना, कायरतापूर्वक भाग जाना) at last.

A servant always *waits* (सेवा करना, हाजिर रहना) on him.

III. IDIOMS WITH PAIR OF WORDS

[A] NOUNS THAT GO IN PAIRS

The English left India *bag and baggage* (सब सामान के साथ)।

Hitler carried *fire and sword* (विनाश) wherever he went.

If you work by *fits and starts* (अनियमित रूप से), you cannot succeed.

Do not try to earn money *by hook or by crook* (किसी भी तरह से)।

Let us work *heart and soul* (मन से) [Not *with heart and soul*].

Do not adopt a *hole and corner* (गुप्त और बुरी) policy to serve your interest.

I know his *ins and outs* (पूर्णविवरण)।

His secretary is, *to all intents and purposes,* (सभी अर्थों में, वास्तव में), his master.

I love my *kith and kin* (सगे-संबंधी)।

India is progressing *by leaps and bounds* (तीव्र गति से)।

A worker should not be eager for the *loaves and fishes* (आर्थिक लाभ) of office.

This bag is meant for *odds and ends.* In newspapers there is a column for *odds and ends* (इधर-उधर की बची हुई चीज, फुटकर पदार्थ)।

Kashmir is a *part and parcel* (अभिन्न अंग) of India.

A dishonest man goes to *rack and ruin* (नाश)।

A leader should respect the opinion of the *rank and file* (सर्वसाधारण)।

He was dismissed without *rhyme or reason* (कारण)।

Social inequality should be destroyed *root and branch* (जड़ से, पूर्ण रूप से)।

His speech was mere *stuff and nonsense* (बेकार)।

Time and tide (समय, अवसर) cannot wait for anyone.

Let us oppose capitalism *tooth and nail* (पूरी चेष्टा से)।

Ways and means (साधन, आय) to run the college sould be found out.

A mill-owner provides for the *wear and tear* (क्षय) of machinery.

[B] ADJECTIVES THAT GO IN PAIRS

He is *all in all* (सर्वेसर्वा) in his family.

The patient is getting from *bad to worse* (बदतर)।

India voiced her protest in *black and white* (लिखित)।

The thief was beaten *black and blue* (बुरी तरह पीटा जाना)।

If you are *fair and square* (न्यायी, निष्पक्ष) you will be respected.

One can't be *free and easy* (स्वाभाविक रूप से स्वच्छंद) with strangers.

The *hard and fast* (कड़ा, बँधा हुआ) rules of grammar must be observed.

The Act was declared *null and void* (निकम्मा, बेकार)।

Slow and steady (मंद, नियमित गति) wins the race.

IV. ADVERBIAL PHRASES

You should love your friends and relations, but *above all* (सबसे बढ़कर) your country.

Gandhiji's plan was always *above board* (साफ, स्पष्ट)।

Man, *after all* (आखिर), is man and not a beast.

If you try *again and again* (बार-बार) you will succeed.

NOTE—'*Over and over again*' and '*Time and again*' have a similar meaning.

A library is *as it were* (मानो) a faithful friend.

He talks *as if* (मानो) he were my master.

He does not read *at all* (एकदम)।

I do not know where or how he is or whether he is alive *at all* (भी)।

The train was late today, *as usual* (पहले जैसा)।

Go *at once* (तुरंत)।

He is a poet and thinker *at once* (साथ-साथ)।

It is bad; *at any rate* (किसी भी हालत में), not good.

At first—पहले। *At last*—अंत में। *At least*—कम-से-कम।

I can give you *at most* (अधिक-से-अधिक) ten rupees.

Don't kick the ball *at random* (यों ही, बिना लक्ष्य के)।

At times (कभी-कभी) even a sinner feels ashamed of himself.

By and by (थोड़े समय के बाद) my family joined me.

I have spoken enough and will speak to you more in future, but *by the by* (प्रधान विषय को छोड़कर, बीच में) let me know whether you follow me.

My book is *far and away* (निश्चय ही) the best of all.

This news has spread *far and near/far and wide* (सर्वत्र)।

Happy days are *few and far between* (बहुत कम)।

Our *first and foremost* (सर्वप्रथम) duty is to know ourselves.

A good man is remembered *for long* (बहुत दिनों तक)।

This book is meant for students *in general* (साधारण रूप से) and for college students *in particular* (खासकर)।

In a nutshell or *In short*—संक्षेप में

Do every work *in time* (ठीक समय पर)

Honesty is rewarded *in time* (समय आने पर, कभी-न-कभी, अंत में)।

Truth wins *in the long run* (कभी-न-कभी)

A great man does not care for criticism *in the least* (जरा भी)

A doctor was called in but *in vain* (व्यर्थ सिद्ध होना)।

Though in London, he remembers me *now and then* (अकसर)।

He passed and, *of course* (फलतः), he was happy.

If you work *off and on* (अनियमित रूप से) you can't succeed.

If you work *on and on* (नियमित रूप से), you will succeed.

One should always be *on the alert* (सावधान)।

He did not help me; *on the contrary* (बल्कि, इसके विपरीत), he harmed me.

He has nothing to say *to the contrary* (विपरीत, विरोध में)।

Once again, once more and *over again* (एक बार और)

Can you do it *once again* (*once more, over again*)?

Read this lesson *once and again* (बार-बार, कई बार)।

I go to the pictures *now and again* (कभी-कभी)।

He is ruined *once for all* (सदा के लिए)।

He was beaten, and abused *over and above* (भी अलावा)।

I got wet *through and through* (पूर्ण रूप से)।

I walked *to and fro* (आगे-पीछे) in a confused state of mind.

Man thinks, feels, wills and *what not* (और क्या नहीं)।

V. PREPOSITIONAL PHRASES

As to (संबंध में) my qualification, I beg to submit that I am an MA.

NOTE—*As regards, with regard to, with respect to,* and *in connection with* have a similar meaning. The phrases *at home in, at the top of, at enmity with,* and *at variance with* have been explained under 'Idioms With Verb To Be'.

Because of, on account of और *owing to*—कारण से

He is absent *because of* (*on account of, owing to*) illness.

Caution—Due to का भी अर्थ, इन तीनों के समान, 'कारण से' होता है, पर इसका प्रयोग सामान्यतः verb **be** के बाद होता है; जैसे—

The *accident* was *due to* carelessness. *This is due* to that.

He rose high in life *by dint of* labour [*By dint of* और *By force of* = शक्ति (power) द्वारा]।

Some men get honour *by means of* (वस्तु द्वारा) money.

He *is* a member *by virtue of* (निहित गुण द्वारा) his office.

I told you this *by way of* (रूप में) advice.

The thieves fled away *for fear of* (डर से) dogs.

One must work *for the sake of* (लिए, वास्ते) the country.

He died *for want of* (अभाव में) medicine.

I went *in accordance with* (अनुसार) his wishes.

I acted *on behalf of* my father.

On behalf of; instead of और *In lieu of* = बदले में।

NOTE—On behalf of के बदले In behalf of का प्रयोग गलत है।

I gave him a pen *instead* (in lieu) *of* a pencil.

अर्थ एक रहने पर भी इनमें अंतर यह है कि instead of तथा in lieu of का प्रयोग निर्जीव पदार्थ के लिए होता है, पर on behalf of का सजीव प्राणी तथा संख्या के लिए।

He will drop his studies *in case of* (परिस्थिति में, in the event of) failure.

You are guilty *in common with* (साथ-साथ) others.

In consequence of (फलस्वरूप) famine many men died.

In consideration of (दृष्टिकोण से, In view of) his poverty he should be helped.

In course of (सिलसिले में) talk he told me this news.

A mother pleads *in defence of* (रक्षा में) her son.

He murdered a child *in defiance of* (खिलाफ) law.

I retired *in favour of* (पक्ष में) my friend.

There is a park *in front of* (आगे, सामने) our college.

Nehru gave a dinner *in honour of* (सम्मान में) Russian leaders.

Your action should be *in keeping with* your speech. [*In keeping with, in accord with, in harmony with, in agreement with* और *in unison with* = मेल में]।

He is junior to me *in point of* (दृष्टि से, in respect of) service.

In prospect of और *In hope of* = आशा से

Men work *in prospect of* reward.

In quest of और *In search of* = खोज में

I am *in quest of* knowledge.

In spite of (रहते हुए भी) poverty he did well in life.

One should not bend even *in the teeth of (in the face of)* (विरोध तथा बाधा आदि के बीच) dangers.

He labours hard *in order to* (उद्देश्य-प्राप्ति के लिए) pass.

He is not paid *in proportion to* (अनुपात में) his labour.

The world is *on the brink of* (निकट, सीमा पर) ruin.

We had a dinner, *on the eve of* (कुछ पहले) the Pujas.

On the ground of और *on the score of* = आधार पर।

You are excused *on the score of* ignorance.

Wars are fought *on the pretence of* (बहाने) religion.

I saw him *with a view to* (उद्देश्य से) seeking help.

Let us work *with an eye to* (ध्यान में रखकर) future.

EXERCISE

I. *Fill in the blanks with a suitable word from the box.*

sword	tongue	hand	for	by
bud	ear	heart	on	off

1. Please hold your …… .
2. He was put to the …… .
3. He gave …… to my prayer.
4. That plan was nipped in the …… .
5. The situation is out of …… .
6. He is working …… and soul.
7. I took him …… a thief.
8. Cows live …… grass and hay.
9. He is working …… and on.
10. He is rising …… leaps and bounds.

II. *Match **A** with **B**, so as to make meaningful sentences from this table.*

A	B
Thieves were	at sixes and sevens.
I am at a loss	with you.
Hidden things were	brought up by me.
Books are lying	at large.
I am at one	to decide.
She was	brought out by him.
The speaker	ran short.
My money	stopped short.

Chapter XXIV

TEST YOURSELF

I. *Fill in the blanks with a suitable word from the box.*

omnipotent	pessimist	honorary
omniscient	optimist	wardrobe
catalogue	colleague	autocracy

1. We keep our clothes in a ....
2. He holds an ...... post.
3. One who is all-powerful is called ....
4. One who looks at the bright side of life is called ....
5. One who knows everything is called ....
6. One who looks at the dark side of life is called ....
7. Please prepare a ...... of books.
8. He is not on good terms with his ....
9. ...... is a government by one.

II. *Match A with B, so as to make meaningful sentences.*

A	B
A style that is too full of words is called	migratory
That which can't be read is called	ineligible
One who walks in sleep is called	a somniloquist
One who is not qualified to apply is called	illegible
A bird of passage is called	verbose
One who talks in sleep is called	a somnambulist

❐

PRECIS-WRITING

Precis फ्रांसीसी भाषा का एक शब्द है। इसका अर्थ होता है 'संक्षिप्त और ठीक-ठीक वर्णन'। Precis के अभ्यास से हम गद्यांश या पद्यांश को समझने और उसे संक्षेप में लिखने की कला सीखते हैं। इसकी आवश्यकता आधुनिक युग में बहुत ही बढ़ गई है, क्योंकि आज आदमी को बहुत अधिक पढ़ने का समय नहीं मिलता। इसके अतिरिक्त, precis-writing के द्वारा विचारों को आसानी से शीघ्र ही समझने और स्पष्ट रूप से सोचने का अभ्यास होता है, जिससे जीवन के प्रत्येक क्षेत्र में लाभ होता है।

Precis-writing के लिए हमें तीन बातों का ध्यान रखना चाहिए—

I. Meaning II. Language III. Length

I. MEANING

1. दिए हुए पद्यांश या गद्यांश का अर्थ (meaning या idea) समझना आवश्यक है। इसके लिए आप उसे सावधानी से पढ़ें। प्रत्येक शब्द का अर्थ जानना जरूरी नहीं। पूरी गद्यांश या पद्यांश को दो-तीन बार पढ़ जाएँ। अर्थ समझ में आ जाएगा।
2. इसके बाद उसका उपयुक्त शीर्षक (title) चुनें। यह काम कठिन नहीं है, क्योंकि प्रत्येक गद्यांश या पद्यांश में कोई-न-कोई प्रधान विचार अवश्य रहता है। वह विचार किसी समस्या के विषय में हो सकता है या किसी देश या व्यक्ति के विषय में। उसमें किसी दृश्य का वर्णन हो सकता है या किसी वस्तु का। आप ध्यान से देखें कि उसका विषय (matter) क्या है।
3. इसके बाद आप प्रधान विचारों को चुन लें और अप्रधान को छोड़ दें। यदि title का ध्यान रखकर विचारों को चुनेंगे, तो काम बहुत ही आसान हो जाएगा, क्योंकि उस title से संबंधित विचार ही प्रधान होंगे और जो उससे संबंधित नहीं होंगे, वे अप्रधान समझे जाएँगे।
4. इस प्रकार, प्रधान विचार को चुनकर आप उन्हें क्रम (order) में रखें, अर्थात उन्हें इस प्रकार रखें कि एक विचार दूसरे से संबंधित हो। इसी को natural order या logical sequence कहते हैं। ऐसा करना इसलिए जरूरी है कि बात तुरंत ही समझ में आ जाए। कुछ लोग दिए हुए गद्यांश या पद्यांश के विचारों की एक सूचीमात्र बना लेते हैं, पर यह ध्यान नहीं देते कि पहले किसको रखें और उसके बाद किसको। यह आवश्यक नहीं है कि आप भी उसी क्रम को मानें जैसा गद्यांश या पद्यांश में रहता है। इसके विपरीत, यदि आप अपनी सुविधा के अनुसार और अर्थ को स्पष्ट रूप से प्रकट करने की दृष्टि से, विचारों के क्रम को बदल दें, तो इसके लिए आपको विशेष श्रेय प्राप्त होगा।
5. कुछ लोग कुछ वाक्यों को छोड़ देते हैं और कुछ को चुनकर उन्हें यों ही रख देते हैं। वह तो precis नहीं, वह तो reproduction है न! आप ऐसा न करें।

II. LANGUAGE

दिए हुए पद्यांश या गद्यांश का अर्थ समझकर उसे अपनी भाषा में लिखें।

1. ध्यान रखें कि भाषा व्याकरण के नियमानुसार हो, टेलिग्राम (telegram) वाली नहीं। आप इस प्रकार लिखें जिससे मालूम हो कि विचार दूसरे का है, पर भाषा आपकी अपनी। यदि भाषा

आपकी नहीं है, तो इसका अर्थ यह होगा कि आपने दिए हुए गद्यांश को समझा नहीं और इसलिए उसी के कुछ वाक्यों को जोड़-तोड़कर यों ही रख दिया है। हाँ, जो छोटे-मोटे साधारण प्रयोग के शब्द हों, उनका प्रयोग आप कर सकते हैं, पर उन्हें भी अपना बनाकर, अर्थात अपने वाक्यों में रखकर प्रयोग करें।

2. Precis-writing में सदा Third Person Pronoun (he, she, it, they) का प्रयोग करें, First Person (I) का नहीं। इसका कारण यह है कि 'I' के प्रयोग से मालूम होगा कि विचार आपके हैं, पर आपके विचार तो ये हैं ही नहीं! ये विचार तो किसी अन्य व्यक्ति के हैं। इसलिए Third Person का प्रयोग उचित है।
3. Tense के संबंध में कुछ लोगों के मन में काफी भ्रम है। कुछ लोगों का मत है कि precis में सदा Past Tense का प्रयोग होना चाहिए। यह विचार ठीक नहीं। मेरे जानते precis-writing में उसी Tense का प्रयोग होना चाहिए जो दिए हुए गद्यांश में रहता है। मान लीजिए कि किसी गद्यांश में लेखक आधुनिक समस्या का वर्णन करता है। तो, उसे Past Tense में कैसे लिखा जा सकता है? इसी प्रकार, कोई लेखक या कवि भविष्य की कल्पना करता है। उसे Future Tense में ही लिखना चाहिए, Past Tense में नहीं। यही तर्कसंगत जँचता है।
4. Precis सदा Indirect Narration में लिखा जाता है। इसलिए जो वाक्य inverted commas ("............") के अंदर रहें उन्हें आप Indirect Narration में लिखें। यदि dialogue या conversation (वार्तालाप) का precis करना हो, तो उसे Indirect में रखें। पूरी dialogue का सारांश समझकर उसे Indirect Narration में लिखना चाहिए।

III. LENGTH

दिए हुए गद्यांश का precis कितना बड़ा या छोटा हो, इस संबंध में लोगों के बीच थोड़ा मतभेद है। Sri R P Ghosh ने *Good English* में लिखा है कि precis दिए हुए गद्यांश का 1/4 या 1/5 होना चाहिए, पर करीब-करीब सभी अच्छे लेखकों ने माना है कि यह 1/3 होना चाहिए। विश्वविद्यालयों में भी यही परिपाटी मान्य है। इसलिए आप भी precis लगभग 1/3 अंश में लिखें। यह काम बहुत कठिन नहीं। दिए हुए गद्यांश के सभी शब्दों को गिन लें और उसे तीन से भाग दें। इस प्रकार 1/3 अंश में लिखें। इसका यह अर्थ नहीं कि आप कुछ कम या कुछ अधिक शब्दों का प्रयोग कर ही नहीं सकते। हाँ, 1/3 से बहुत कम या बहुत अधिक न हो। कुछ लोग दिए हुए गद्यांश के 1/3 वाक्यों को चुनकर उन्हें यों ही रख देते हैं, पर आप यह न भूलें कि वह precis नहीं। वह तो कुछ और ही चीज है। दिए हुए अंश को 1/3 करने के लिए आप इन तरीकों की मदद लें।

1. Omission of Figures of Speech

Omission का अर्थ है 'छोड़ना'। इसके अनुसार दिए हुए अंश में जितने भी अलंकार (figures of speech) और उद्धरण (quotation) रहें, उन्हें छोड़ दें और उनका अर्थ सरल भाषा में लिखें। इससे दो लाभ होंगे—शब्दों की संख्या कम हो जाएगी और ऐसा मालूम पड़ेगा कि भाषा भी आपकी अपनी है।

एक उदाहरण लें—

He is as brave *as a lion.*

यहाँ as a lion एक अलंकार है जिसे simile कहते हैं। precis बनाने के लिए आप ऐसे अंश को छोड़ दें और इस प्रकार लिखें—He is brave.

Precis में आलंकारिक भाषा नहीं होनी चाहिए।

2. Method of Substitution

'Substitution' का अर्थ होता है 'बदलना'। इसके अनुसार दिए हुए अंश में जो phrases, group of words या clauses रहें, उन्हें single word (एक शब्द) में बदल दें; जैसे—

1. Books are lying *at sixes and sevens.*
2. I beat him *black and blue.*

आप जानते हैं कि *at sixes and sevens* और *black and blue* phrases हैं। इसलिए इनके लिए एक शब्द (single word) का प्रयोग वाक्यों में इस प्रकार हो सकता है—

1. Books are *scattered.* 2. I beat him *severely.*

इसी प्रकार group of words (शब्द-समुदाय) को भी single word में बदला जा सकता है; जैसे—

1. *To love one's own country* is not enough. = *Patriotism* is not enough.
2. He will be remembered *for all times to come*. = He will be remembered *for ever*. = He will *always* be remembered.

आप clause के बदले भी single word का प्रयोग इस प्रकार कर सकते हैं—

1. *Whether he will be successful or not* is doubtful. = *His success is* doubtful.
2. *That you are honest* is well-known. = *Your honesty* is well-known.

NOTE—Method of Substitution को समझने के लिए "Single word for a group of words" की सूची Word Power के अंतर्गत दी गई है। उसे दो-चार बार अवश्य देखें।

3. Avoidance of Repetition

Repetition का अर्थ होता है 'दुहरावट' या 'पुनरावृत्ति'। Repetition किसी idea (विचार) का हो या word (शब्द) का, आप उसे अवश्य छोड़ें, क्योंकि दुहराने से शब्दों की संख्या बढ़ेगी, घटेगी नहीं। आप देखेंगे कि लेखक अपने विचार को समझाने के लिए एक ही बात कई तरह से रखता है। वह कभी-कभी उसकी व्याख्या (explanation) भी करता है। आप ऐसा न करें, क्योंकि Precis में explanation नहीं चाहिए। एक बात और। साधारण लेखक छोटी बातों को भी बहुत-से शब्दों की सहायता से व्यक्त करता है। अतः, स्वभावतः कुछ शब्दों का repetition (पुनरावृत्ति) हो जाता है; जैसे—

He is a *very very old* man of *100 years.*

यहाँ very very old की आवश्यकता नहीं, क्योंकि जिसकी अवस्था 100 वर्ष की है वह तो बहुत बूढ़ा है ही, फिर very very old लिखने की आवश्यकता ही क्या? कुछ और उदाहरण लें—

1. The resolution was *unanimously* supported *by all.*
2. We reached the *final conclusion.*

ऊपर के पहले वाक्य में unanimously (सर्वसम्मति से) और by all का प्रयोग हुआ है, पर दोनों का अर्थ एक ही है। अतः, इस वाक्य में by all की कोई आवश्यकता नहीं है। इसी प्रकार, दूसरे वाक्य में final की कोई जरूरत नहीं, क्योंकि conclusion तो सदा final होता ही है। Conclusion में final का अर्थ निहित है। इसलिए आप ऐसे शब्दों को बिलकुल ही छोड़ दें। आप देखेंगे कि वाक्य में बहुत-से Adjectives और Adverbs का कोई प्रयोजन नहीं रहता। वैसी अवस्था में आप उनका प्रयोग न करें, तो अच्छा।

4. Use of Voice

Precis में Passive Voice का प्रयोग जहाँ तक हो, कम करें और बिलकुल ही न करें, तो और भी अच्छा। क्योंकि Passive Voice के प्रयोग से शब्दों की संख्या बढ़ती है और Active Voice से संख्या घटती है; जैसे—

1. Ravan *was* killed *by* Ram. —*Passive*
2. Ram killed Ravan. —*Active*
3. Good boys *are* loved *by* teachers. —*Passive*
4. Teachers love good boys. —*Active*

आप जानते हैं कि Passive Voice में Verb 'To be' और by का प्रयोग हो जाता है जिसकी जरूरत Active Voice में नहीं पड़ती। इसलिए Active Voice का ही प्रयोग अच्छा है।

5. Use of Article

आप जानते हैं कि जब Common Noun Singular Number में रहता है, तब उसके पहले a या an का प्रयोग करना पड़ता है और उससे शब्दों की संख्या बढ़ जाती है। यदि बिना अर्थ बदले ही plural कर दिया जाए तो a या an की आवश्यकता ही नहीं पड़ेगी; जैसे—

(i) A good boy is loved by teachers.

(ii) Good boys are loved by teachers.

दूसरे वाक्य में a की जरूरत नहीं पड़ी; क्योंकि boy को boys कर दिया गया और इससे एक शब्द (a) कम हो गया। इस प्रकार थोड़ी भी सावधानी से काफी लाभ होता है।

6. Use of Conjunction

Conjunction के प्रयोग से भी शब्दों की संख्या बढ़ या घट सकती है। आप जानते हैं कि as well as और and के अर्थ में कोई अंतर नहीं, पर as well as में तीन शब्द हैं और and में केवल एक। तो, यह स्पष्ट है कि Precis में as well as के बदले and का ही प्रयोग अच्छा है; जैसे—

He *as well as* I is guilty. = He *and* I are guilty.

इसी प्रकार, both ... and के बदले केवल and से ही काम चल सकता है—

Both Ram *and* Shyam are guilty. = Ram and Shyam are guilty.

अब आप no sooner ... than और as soon as लें। No sooner ... than के प्रयोग से वाक्य में एक शब्द बढ़ जाता है, पर as soon as के साथ ऐसा नहीं होता—

No sooner *did* he start than it began to rain.

= As soon as he started it began to rain.
इसलिए as soon as का ही प्रयोग करना अच्छा होता है।

7. Avoid Author's Name

Precis लिखने में लेखक का नाम और उसका परिचय नहीं दिया जाता। मालूम रहने पर भी आप उसका नाम-पता नहीं लिखें। नाम के बदले the writer, the author या the poet लिखना ही काफी है।

NOTE—Precis के शीर्षक (title) में जिन शब्दों का प्रयोग किया जाता है उन्हें छोड़ कर 1/3 अंश में Precis होना चाहिए। उन शब्दों की गिनती नहीं होती। Precis तैयार कर लेने के बाद शब्दों की संख्या (जितने शब्दों में Precis बनाया गया हो) अंत में लिख देनी चाहिए।

EXERCISES WORKED OUT

I

Now Jumman had an old relation, a maternal aunt, who had some property. This she transferred to him by a deed on the understanding that she would be well-looked after. So long as the deed remained unregistered, none was so obliging to the old lady as her nephew, none so considerate to her. Her every wish was anticipated and cheerfully carried out. But everything changed the moment the deed was registered. Jumman who used to wait dotingly on his old aunt now became supremely indifferent. His wife, Kariman, went even further. She grudged even the little food that the old lady ate. No meal was now served to her without Kariman letting loose a barb or two dipped in gall or poison. The very bread that the aunt ate seemed to be seasoned with the meal of abuse. And this went on mounting. Kariman would say, "How long is the old hag going to live? By giving us a few acres of waste land, she thinks she has bought us. She is a great lady who can't swallow a morsel without her *dal* being seasoned with ghee! We could have purchased a whole village with the money spent on her feeding." (202 words)

Precis

Title—INGRATITUDE

Jumman had an old aunt. She had some property. She gave it to Jumman on assurance that he would maintain her. Before the registration of deed he was hospitable to her but after registration he neglected her. His wife's treatment was worse. She abused her while giving even the little food she (aunt) ate and wished her early death. The aunt's troubles increased every day. (66 words)

II

Marlow: What a tedious uncomfortable day have we had of it! We were told it was but forty miles across the country and we have come above three score.

Hastings: And all, Marlow, from that unaccountable shyness of yours that would not let us inquire more frequently on the way.

Marlow: I own, Hastings, I am unwilling to lay myself under an obligation to everyone I meet and often stand the chance of an unmannerly answer.

Hastings: At present, however, we are not likely to receive any answer.

Tony: No offence, gentleman. But I'am told you have been inquiring for one Mr Hardcastle in these parts. Do you know what part of the country you are in?

Hastings: Not in the least, Sir, but I should thank you for information.

Tony: Nor the way you came?

Hastings: No, Sir, but if you can inform us.

Tony: Why gentleman, if you know neither the road you are going, nor where you are, nor the road you came, the first thing I have to inform you is that you have lost your way.

(171 words)

Precis

Title—THE TWO TRAVELLERS

Marlow complained of their too long and tedious journey for which Hastings blamed his (Marlow's) shyness. Marlow replied that he did not like to receive discourteous replies by asking his way frequently. Meanwhile, Tony interrupted and remarked that as they did not know which way they came or where they were, they were lost. (53 words)

III

The very abundance of books, an increasing and confusing abundance in our days, makes it important to know how to choose promptly and judiciously among them if one is not to spend as much time in the mere choice as in the perusal of the books that are selected. On this subject the first advice I venture to submit is to secure and to read only the best books. There are plenty of them, far more than you will ever find time to read. And when a wide range of excellent works is so readily obtainable, it is surely unfortunate to waste valuable minutes on any others. You may ask what I mean by best books. Passing by for the moment those publications which in each of the great languages of the world we call classics, I mean by the best books those from which you receive most, and can carry away most in the form of either knowledge or stimulation. When you want to learn something about a subject in which you are interested, do not turn to the first volume which you have heard or which professes by its title to deal exhaustively with the subject. Consult your teacher or any well-read friend, or the librarian of the nearest public library. (213 words)

Precis

Title—CHOICE OF BOOKS

Innumberable books are published nowadays. Naturally, there is no time to read even the best ones which are available in large numbers. One should, therefore, read only the best books. Besides classics, best books are those that give maximum of wisdom and inspiration. For quick and correct choice, the advice of teachers, well-read friends or public librarians, and not advertisements, is really helpful. (66 words)

IV

Kiran was a universal favourite with her family and neighbours, so that when she fell seriously ill they were all anxious. The village wiseacres thought it shameless for the husband to make so much fuss about a mere wife and even to suggest a change of air and asked if Sharat supposed that no woman had ever been ill before or whether he had found out that the folk of the place to which he meant to take her were immortal. Did he imagine that the writ of fate did not run there? But Sharat and his mother turned a deaf ear to them thinking that the life of their darling was of greater importance than the united wisdom of a village. So, Sharat went to Chandar Nagar, and Kiran recovered though she was still very weak. There was a pinched look on her face which filled the beholders with pity, and made their heart tremble, as they thought how narrowly she had escaped death. (180 words)

Precis

Title—KIRAN'S ILLNESS

Popular Kiran's serious illness grieved her relations and neighbours. Her husband, Sharat, desired her climatic change but the so-called wise villagers opposed the idea as foolish and shameless, but to her husband and mother-in-law, her life was dearer than village opinion. Therefore, they took her to Chandar Nagar where she recovered, although still too weak. She had a narrow escape from death. (60 words)

....

EXERCISES

I

Hetty was quite used to the thought that people liked to look at her, and she knew that Adam Bede—tall, clever, brave Adam Bede, of whom the people round about thought so well, who was often rather severe to others, and who was not often seen talking to girls—could be made to turn pale or red any day by a look or a word from her. Hetty did not know many men, but she couldn't help seeing that Adam was a greater man than most of the men she knew, and she was certain that her uncle Poyser wanted her to marry Adam, who had always been given welcome at Hall Farm.

But Hetty had other ideas about her marriage. She liked to be admired by a wise strong man, liked to know that he would always be there if she had need of him, but she had not thought of marrying Adam. She thought of him as a poor workman. When she had a husband, he must be a rich man who could give her all the things she dreamed about: a big house, servants, fine clothes and a life of ease. If Adam could have given her these things, she liked him well enough to marry him.

Aids

Used to—habituated (आदत पड़ना)। *People round about*—neighbours (पड़ोसी)। *Severe*—strict, serious, grave (कड़ा, गंभीर)। *Turn pale*—fade (मुरझा जाना, फीका पड़ना)। *Couldn't help seeing*—had to see (देखना या समझना पड़ता था)। *Ease*—comfort (आराम)।

II

It was a long journey to Windsor. There were no trains in those days, and Hetty had not enough money to travel by coach all the way; so sometimes she rode, sometimes walked, buying as little food as possible, and staying the nights at some inn or cottage. At noon on the seventh day she reached Windsor, with only a shilling left. She went to the nearest inn and handed to the inn-keeper a paper on which was Arthur's address. "Can you tell me the way to this place, please?"

"What do you want there?" he said.

"I want to see a gentleman who lives there," said Hetty.

"But no gentleman is living there. It's been shut up for two weeks. What gentleman is it you want? Perhaps I can tell you where to find him."

"It's Captain Donnithorne."

"Captain Donnithorne? A tall young officer in the Loamshire Regiment?"

"Oh, yes! You know him? Where is he?" said Hetty, excitedly.

"Many miles from here! The Loamshire Regiment went to Ireland two weeks ago."

This end to her search for Arthur was more than Hetty could bear in her weak state. She gave a cry and fell to the ground.

The inn-keeper's wife saw that Hetty was ill, so she put her to bed and took care of her.

Aids

Inn—hotel. *Shut up*—closed (बंद)। *Regiment*—पलटन।

III

Today our society abounds with persons who are mad after their own interest. In *Sarvodaya,* however, one has to be solicitous of other's interest. Man's nature will have to be changed. Values of life will have to be revalued. For, if the individual does not change even if exploitation is put out once, it will reappear afterwards. This is a high ideal no doubt, but is capable of being attained. That can be done by making a beginning somewhere.

Bhoodan is the process whereby we can reach this goal. The land problem is a problem that affects crores of people. Hence, the *Bhoodan* movement makes a direct appeal to the masses and would inevitably cast its influence on their approach and way of life.

Aids

Solicitous—desirous (इच्छुक, उत्सुक)। *Reappear afterwards*—reappear. यहाँ afterwards की जरूर नहीं, क्योंकि reappear में afterwards का अर्थ छिपा हुआ है। *Making a beginning*—beginning. *Goal*—aim (लक्ष्य)। *Crores of*—numerous, innumerable (असंख्य, अनगिनत, बहुत)। *Cast its influence*—influence (असर डालना)।

IV

All the great religous teachers of mankind have insisted on this: that men ought not to live for themselves alone. We ought not, they have said, to spend all our time and energy in getting just what we want for ourselves, power and money and importance in the world; we ought to serve something greater than ourselves, whether a god or a cause or our fellowmen. It is by serving this something greater that men will forget themselves and so achieve happiness. This or something like it is what the great religions have taught, and it is one of the most important of the things that civilization means. It is also the hardest to learn and practise; in fact, most people have found it much too hard.

Aids

Religious teachers of mankind—prophets, preachers. *Insisted*—emphasised (जोर देकर कहना)। *Ought*—should. *To live for themselves alone*—be selfish. *Achieve*—get (पाना)। *Much too hard*—difficult.

V

If today I have a quarrel with another man, I do not get beaten merely because I am physically weaker and he can knock me down. I go to law, and the law will decide as fairly as it can between the two of us. Thus, in disputes between man and man, right has taken the place of might. Moreover, the law protects me from robbery and violence. Nobody may come and break into my house, steal my goods, or run off with my children. Of course, there are burglars, but they are very rare, and the law punishes them whenever it catches them.

It is difficult for us to realise how much this safety means. Without safety those higher activities of mankind which make up civilization could not go on. The inventor could not invent, the scientist find out or the artist make beautiful things. Hence, order and safety, although they are not themselves civilization, are things without which civilization would be impossible. They are as necessary to our civilization as the air we breathe is to us; and we have grown so used to them that we do not notice them any more than we notice the air.

Aids

Knock down—beat down (मारकर गिरा देना)। *Disputes*—quarrels, fights (लड़ाई, झगड़ा)। *Might*—शारीरिक शक्ति। *Protects*—saves (रक्षा)। *Robbery*—dacoity (लूटपाट)। *Violence*—हिंसा। *Break into*—enter. *Run off with my children*—kidnap (अपहरण करना) my children. *Burglars*—thieves (चोर)। *Go on*—continue (आगे बढ़ना)। *Grown so used to*—habituated, accustomed (आदत पड़ना)। *Notice*—see (सूचित करना)।

VI

Educated women have to play the role of teachers. An educated lady can serve the country in the humble capacity of a teacher. The education of children depends mainly upon women. They can teach as well as amuse. They can do research work in art, literature, philosophy and science. We are fortunate in having very intelligent girls who are anxious to have training in foreign countries. They are being given scholarship by the Government of India and many of them have proceeded to western countries and have made their mark as educationists. Women can also render social service whenever there is flood, famine, earthquake or some natural calamity. It is also during war that they can be of utmost utility to their nation. In free India ladies are being given training in first aid, use of guns and rifles and some of them are getting training as drivers and pilots. The defence of the country is a matter of great importance to all and women should share the burden with men.

Aids

Play the role of—act as (काम करना)। *Made their mark*—distinguished (यश प्राप्त किया)। *Calamity*—misfortune (संकट)। *Of utmost utility*—useful. *Share the burden*—काम में भाग लेना। *Pilots*—वायुयान चालक।

VII

Human life consists of a succession of small events, each of which is comparatively unimportant and yet the happiness and success of every man depends upon the manner in which these small events are dealt with. Character is built upon little things—little things well and honourably transacted. The success of a man in business depends upon his attention to little things. The comfort of a household is the result of small things well-arranged. Good government can only be accomplished in the same way by well-regulated provisions for the doing of little things.

Accumulation of knowledge and experience of the most valuable kind are the result of little bits of knowledge and experience carefully treasured up. Those who learn nothing or accumulate nothing in life are set down as failures because, they have neglected little things. They may themselves consider that the world has gone against them but, in fact, they have been their own enemies. There has long been a popular belief in 'good luck', but, like many other popular notions, it is gradually giving way. The conviction is extending that diligence is the mother of good luck; in other words, that a man's success in life will be proportionate to his efforts, to his industry, to his attention to small things.

Aids

Transacted—done. *Household*—family (परिवार)। *Duly*—properly (उचित रूप से)। *Accomplished*—done, achieved. *Accumulation*—collection. *Treasured up*—gathered (जमा करना)। *Notion*—ideas (विचार)। *Conviction*—faith, belief. *Extending*—spreading. *Diligence*—labour. *Proportionate to*—according to. *Effors, Industry*—परिश्रम।

VIII

The problem that confronts most of us is whether the individual is merely the instrument of society or the aid of society. Are you and I as individuals to be used, directed, educated, controlled, shaped to a certain pattern by society and government or does society, the state, exist for the individual? Is the individual the end of society or is he merely a puppet to be taught, exploited, butchered as an instrument of war? That is the problem of the world—whether the individual is a mere instrument of society, a plaything of influences to be moulded or whether society exists for the individual.

How are you going to find this out? It is a serious problem, is it not? If the individual is merely an instrument of society, then society is much more important than the individual. If that is true, then we must give up individuality and work for society; our whole educational system must be entirely revolutionized and the individual turned into an instrument to be used and destroyed. But if society exists for the individual, then the function of society is not to make him conform to any pattern but to give him the feel, the urge of freedom. So, we have to find out which is false.

Aids

Confronts—faces (सामने, सम्मुख)। *End*—aim (लक्ष्य)। *Pattern*—model. *Puppet*—(कठपुतली)। *Moulded* —shaped. *Conform*—समान होना। *Urge*—inspiration (प्रेरणा)।

IX

Why is society crumbling, collapsing, as it surely is? One of the fundamental reasons is that the individual, you, has ceased to be creative. I will explain what I mean. You and I have become imitative; we are copying outwardly and inwardly. Outwardly, when learning a technique, when communicating with each other on the verbal level, naturally there must be some imitation, copy. I copy words. To become an engineer, I must learn the technique, then use the technique to build a bridge. There must be a certain amount of imitation, copying in outward technique, but when there is inward psychological imitation, surely we cease to be creative. Our education, our social structure, our so-called religious life, are all based on imitation; that is, I fit into a particular social or religious formula. I have ceased to be a real individual.

Aids

Crumbling—breaking (टुकड़ा होना, चूर-चूर होना)। *Collapsing*—falling (गिरना)। *Fundamental*—basic (बुनियादी)। *Ceased*—stopped. *Creative*—रचनात्मक। *Imitative*—अनुकरणशील। *Verbal level*—बातचीत का स्तर। *Structure*—frame.

X

One day, as she came into the room, where all the poor children were at work, my nurse sat down just over against me and after a while began to talk to me. "Thou foolish child", says she, "thou art always crying. Prithee, what dost thou cry for?" "Because they will take me away", say I, "and put me to service, and I can't work house-work." "Well, child", says she, "but though you can't work house-work, you will learn it in time', and they won't put you to hard things at first." "Yes, they will", say I, "and if I can't do it, they will beat me, and the maids will beat me to make me do great work, and I am but a little girl, and I can't do"; and then I cried again till I could not speak any more. This moved my good motherly nurse, so that she resolved I should not go to service yet; she bid me not to cry, and she would speak to Mr Mayor, and I should not go to service till I was bigger.

Well, this did not satisfy me, for to think of going to service at all was such a frightful thing to me, that if she had assured me I should not have gone till I was twenty years old, it would have been the same to me. When she saw I was not pacified yet, she began to be angry with me. "And what would you have?" says she, "Don't I tell you that you shall not go to service till you are bigger?" "Ay", says I, "but then I must go at last." "Why, what", says she, "is the girl mad? What! would you be a gentlewoman?" "Yes", say I, and cried heartily till I roared out again.

Aids

At work—working. *After a while*—after some time. *In time*—in course of time (समय आने पर, धीरे-धीरे)। *Maids*—maidservants. *Bid*—order. *Frightful*—fearful. *Pacified*—calm and quite (शांत)। *Must go*—must have to go. *Heartily*—bitterly. *Roared*—cried.

XI

The light has gone out of our lives and there is darkness everywhere and I do not quite know what to tell you and how to say it. Our beloved leader, Bapu as we call him, the father of our nation, is no more. Perhaps I am wrong to say that. Nevertheless, we will not see him again as we have seen him these many years. We will not run to him for advice and seek solace from him, and that is a terrible blow not to me only but to millions and millions in this country. And it is difficult to soften the blow by any advice that I or anyone else can give you.

The light has gone out, I said and yet I was wrong. For the light that shone in this country was no ordinary light. The light has illumined this country for these many years, will illumine this country for many more years, and a thousand years later that light will still be seen in the country, and the world will see it and it will give solace to innumerable hearts. For the light represented the living truth, and the eternal man was with us with his eternal truth reminding us of the right path, drawing us from error, taking the ancient country to freedom.

All this has happened. There is much more to do. There was so much for him to do. We could never think that he was unnecessary or that he had done his task. But now, particularly, when we are faced with so many difficulties, his not being with us is a blow most terrible to bear.

A mad man has put and end to his life.

Aids

No more—dead, *Solace*—consolation (धीरज)। *Illumine*—प्रकाश देना। *Eternal*—undying. *Blow*—चोट।

XII

A Californian girl of thirteen wrote in a letter : "I was really terribly sad to hear about Gandhi's death. I never knew I was interested in him but I found myself quite unhappy about the great man's death!"

In New York, a twelve-year-old girl had gone into the kitchen for breakfast. The radio was on and it brought the news of the shooting of Gandhi. There, in the kitchen, the girl, the maid and the gardener held a prayer meeting and prayed and wept. Just so, millions in all countries mourned Gandhi's death as a personal loss. They did not quite know why; they did not quite know what he stood for. But he was a good man and good men are rare.

"I know no other man of any time or indeed in recent history", wrote Sir Stafford Cripps, "who so forcefully and convincingly demonstrated the power of spirit over material things."

"Gandhi had demonstrated", Professor Albert Einstein asserted, "that a powerful human following can be assembled not only through the cunning game of the usual political manoeuvres and trickeries but through the cogent example of a morally superior conduct of life. In our time of utter moral decadence, he was the only statesman to stand for a higher human relationship in the political sphere."

Aids

Mourned—became sorrowful. *Spirit*—spiritual (आध्यात्मिक)। *Forcefully*—powerfully. *Asserted*—stated, *Manoeuvres*—clear plan. *Trickeries*—tricks. *Cogent*—convincing. *Utter*—total. *Decadence*—decay. *Statesman*—politician. *Sphere*—field.

XIII

The conditions under which democracy can flourish are difficult to define; but one thing is clear that democracy is always a slow growth, whereas dictators may rise to power and inaugurate a new regime with dramatic suddenness and success under suitable conditions. One great new force has appeared in the world since the Great War, the art of modern propaganda. It is invaluable to the dictator who can inculcate his creed day by day through the press, the cinema, the radio, to the whole body of the people and can suppress all counter propaganda. It is a terrible danger to democracy, since it tends to destroy the sound and commonsense judgement of the people which depends on constant access to facts and on honest public discussion based on those facts.

Then again the kindly and cooperative outlook which alone can make democracy a success depends on material conditions, on the economic security and welfare of the whole of the people; a starving man or a man in constant fear of unemployment cannot be expected to be a good citizen of democracy.

And lastly, war is utterly hostile to democracy. The horrors and passion of war inevitably produce a war mentality under which the method of democracy becomes impossible.

Aids

Flourish—prosper. *Inaugurate*—start. *Regime*—rule, administration (शासन)। *Invaluable*—very helpful. *Inculcate*—impress. *Creed*—principle (सिद्धांत)। *Counter*—opposite. *It tends to*—it has a tendency to. *Access*—reach, approach. *Hostile*—unhelpful, opposed. *Inevitably*—necessarily. *Mentality*—attitude.

XIV

The hand-spinning and weaving industries are extremely important in balancing our village economy. Therefore Mahatma Gandhi carried on a life-long crusade for the encouragement and growth of these industries. For many years all leaders and working members of the Indian National Congress have worn clothes prepared from cloth woven on the handloom from hand-spun yarn. The All India Spinners Association, started under Gandhiji's inspiration, has done excellent work in popularising *khaddar* or hand-woven cloth made from hand-spun yarn. It has also helped the handloom worker by supplying him with materials and with advice for the improvement of the quality of his product. More than a crore and a half yards of *khaddar* is produced in India every year. This cloth has been a great boon to many people during the recent shortage of millmade cloth.

Handmade cloth always costs more than millmade cloth. For this reason some people say that the industry should be allowed to die and cloth be produced in the mills. Those who see the benefits brought by the handloom industry to the villager say that it should be supported even by restricting the growth of mills. The Ministry in Chennai has decided that no new mills should be started in the province and that every encouragement should be given to handloom industry. These are extremely opposite views. One thing is clear, however, viz., that more than 60 lakhs of people earn their livelihood in their own homes with the help of the handloom industry. Until alternative work is found for this large number of people, encouragement must be given to the industry.

Aids

Crusade—holy fight. *Yarn*—सूत। *Boon*—blessing (वरदान)। *Restricting*—limiting (सीमित करना)। *Alternative*—some other work.

XV

Education, taken in its most extensive sense, is properly that which makes the man. One method of education, therefore, would only produce one kind of man; but the great excellence of human nature consists in the variety of which it is capable. Then instead of endeavouring, by unifom and fixed systems of education, to keep mankind always the same, let us give free scope to everything which may bid fair for introducing more variety among us. The various character of the Athenians was certainly preferable to the uniform character of the Spartans or to any uniform national character whatever. Uniformity is the characteristic of the brute creation. Among them every species of bird builds its nest with the same materials and in same form; the genius and disposition of one individual is that of all and it is only the education which men give them that raises any of them much above others. But it is the glory of human nature that the operations of reason, though variable and by no means infallible, are capable of infinite improvement. We come into the world worse provided than any of the brutes; but when their faculties are at a full stand and their enjoyments incapable of variety or increase, our intellectual powers are growing apace; we are perpetually deriving happiness from new sources, and even before we leave this world, are capable of tasting the felicity of angels.

Aids

Extensive—wide. *Excellence*—superiority. *Endeavouring*—trying. *Uniformity*—sameness. *Disposition*—स्वभाव। *Apace*—swiftly. *Perpetually*—constantly. *Felicity*—delight.

....

❐

Chapter XXV

COMPREHENSION

Comprehension का अर्थ होता है 'समझना'। किसी गद्यांश या पद्यांश को पढ़कर उसे समझना आवश्यक है, क्योंकि इसके बिना जीवन के किसी भी क्षेत्र में सफलता मिलना असंभव है। एक बात और। Comprehension के बिना आप precis, substance, explanation, critical appreciation आदि कुछ भी नहीं लिख सकते। इसका कारण यह है कि इन सबके लिए दिए गए पद्यांश या गद्यांश को ठीक से समझना पड़ता है। इसलिए आप Comprehension का अभ्यास अवश्य करें। इस अभ्यास के लिए इन बातों का ध्यान रखें—

I. MEANING II. LANGUAGE III. LENGTH

I. MEANING

Comprehension के लिए यह आवश्यक है कि आप दिए गए गद्यांश या पद्यांश का meaning (अर्थ) ठीक से समझें। इसलिए उसे दो-तीन बार पढ़ें और तब प्रश्न का उत्तर दें। प्रश्न की भाषा का पूरा ध्यान रखें और उसका अर्थ समझें। प्रश्न को समझना आवश्यक है, क्योंकि इसके बिना आपका उत्तर ठीक हो ही नहीं सकता। इसके लिए आप प्रश्न में प्रयुक्त what, how, where, when, who, why इत्यादि शब्दों का ध्यान रखें और सोचें कि प्रश्न क्या है। प्रश्न का उत्तर तो दिए हुए पद्यांश या गद्यांश में रहता ही है। उसे सावधानी से खोज निकालना है। यदि प्रश्न ही समझ में न आए, तो उत्तर कैसे दिया जा सकता है?

II. LANGUAGE

1. दिए हुए प्रश्न का उत्तर अपनी भाषा में लिखें। कुछ लोग दिए गए पद्यांश या गद्यांश के ही कुछ वाक्यों को चुनकर प्रश्न का उत्तर बना लेते हैं। यह उचित नहीं। उत्तर आप अपना वाक्य बनाकर दें।
2. उत्तर देने में व्याकरण के नियमों का पालन करना आवश्यक है। इसलिए वाक्य शुद्ध (correct) और पूरा (complete) होना चाहिए, बातचीत की भाषा में नहीं; जैसे—

   What is your name?

   आप ऐसा न कहें—Ram. आप पूरे वाक्य में उत्तर दें—My name is Ram.

   Comprehension में इस प्रकार के बहुत-से प्रश्न किए जाते हैं। आप उनका उत्तर पूरा वाक्य बनाकर दें, टेलिग्राम (telegram) की भाषा में नहीं।
3. उत्तर देने में आप उसी Tense और Person का प्रयोग करें जो प्रश्न में रहें। ऐसा नहीं करने पर उत्तर हास्यास्पद हो जाएगा।
4. उत्तर देने में Indirect Narration का प्रयोग करना चाहिए, क्योंकि यदि आप Inverted commas "......" के बीच में रखे गए वाक्यों को यों ही रख देंगे, तो इसका अर्थ यह होगा कि आपने कुछ समझा ही नहीं और इसलिए उन वाक्यों को यों ही रख दिया है।

5. भाषा सरल होनी चाहिए, अलंकृत नहीं। इसलिए गद्यांश या पद्यांश में जो अलंकार (Figures of Speech) रहें, उन्हें छोड़ दें और सारांश समझकर उसे अपनी भाषा में लिखें। इस प्रकार भाषा सरल हो जाएगी और मालूम पड़ेगा कि वह आपकी अपनी चीज है, चोरी का माल नहीं।

III. LENGTH

1. दिए हुए प्रश्न का उत्तर कितना बड़ा या छोटा हो, इसका कोई नियम नहीं। यह तो निर्भर है प्रश्न पर। किसी प्रश्न का उत्तर छोटा ही हो सकता है, वह बड़ा हो ही नहीं सकता। यदि आप उसे बड़ा बना देंगे, तो यह अनावश्यक (irrelevant) समझा जाएगा और इसलिए अंक (marks) कम मिलेंगे। Comprehension एक प्रकार की बुद्धि-परीक्षा (intelligence-test) है। इसलिए आपसे जितना पूछा जाए, उतना ही उत्तर दें। इस प्रकार आपका जवाब चुस्त और दुरुस्त होगा।
2. कभी-कभी ऐसा प्रश्न किया जाता है, जिसके कई उत्तर हो सकते हैं। यदि किसी गद्यांश या पद्यांश का शीर्षक (title) देने को कहा जाए, तो भिन्न-भिन्न प्रकार के उत्तर दिए जा सकते हैं। इसलिए वैसी अवस्था में आप अपना विचार तर्क (reasoning) के साथ रखें और उसका कारण बताएँ। इससे उत्तर कुछ बड़ा तो अवश्य होगा, पर साथ-साथ अच्छा भी।

EXERCISES WORKED OUT

1

Gandhiji always loved his people—Muslims as much as Hindus. Even when Pakistan was formed, he spoke for the Muslims of India, who were comparatively so few in number. Many Hindus thought that he favoured the Muslims too much. Nathuram Godse held misguided ideas of this kind. At a prayer meeting at Birla House in New Delhi, Godse shot Gandhiji on 30th January, 1948. The great Mahatma died with 'Hey Ram' on his lips. He was murdered, yet he was calm and peaceful even in death. It seemed as if he were sleeping.

Q. 1. Why was Gandhiji shot dead? 2. Where and when was he murdered?

3. How did he look after his murder?

Ans. 1. Gandhiji loved all men, both Hindus and Muslims. He loved the Indian Muslims even, after the formation of Pakistan. Many Hindus thought that he favoured the Muslims. Nathuram Godse held similar views. So, he shot Gandhiji dead.

2. Gandhiji was murdered on the 30th January, 1948. Godse shot him dead at a prayer meeting at Birla House in New Delhi.

3. The Mahatma looked peaceful and cheerful even after his murder. It appeared as if he were sleeping rather than dead. There was no sigh of sorrow or revenge on his face.

2

I

Fair daffodils, we weep to see
You haste away so soon;
As yet the early-rising sun
Has not attained his noon.

Stay, stay
Until the hasting day
Has rune
But to the evensong;
And, having pray'd together, we
Will go with you along.

II

We have short time to stay, as you;
We have as short a spring;
As quick a growth to meet decay,
As you, or anything.

III

We die
As your hours do, and dry
Away
Like to the summer's rain;
Or as the pearls of morning's dew
Ne'er to be found again.

Q. 1. Why does the poet weep to see the fair daffodils?

2. What does he think about man's life?

3. Explain the line: Like to the summer's rain.

Ans. 1. Generally, beautiful things make us happy, because we look at the beauty of things. But the poet here does not look at the beauty of the daffodils. His eyes are on the short life of the fair daffodils. Naturally, he is reminded of his own short life and also of the short life of others. So, he weeps to see the lovely daffodils.

2. Daffodils have a short spring. They grow and decay very quickly. Similar is the fate of human beings.

3. The poet in this line compares man's life to summer's rain. In summer the earth is very hot. So, when rain-drops fall, they disappear quickly. This is true of man's life as well. Life on this earth, therefore, is very much like rain in summer.

. . . .

EXERCISE

I. *Read the poems given below and answer the questions that follow.*

1

He prayeth well, who loveth well
Both man and bird and beast.
He prayeth best, who loveth best

All things both great and small;
For the dear God who loveth us,
He made and loveth all.

Q. 1. What is the best form of prayer?
2. Why should you love all things both great and small?
3. Suggest a suitable title.

Aids

Prayeth—prays (प्रार्थना करता है)। *Loveth*—loves (प्यार करता है)।

2

I

I lay in sorrow, deep distressed;
My grief a proud man heard;
His looks were cold, he gave me gold,
But not a kindly word.

II

My sorrow passed—I paid him back
The gold he gave to me;
Then stood erect and spake my thanks,
And blessed his charity.

III

I lay in want, in grief and pain;
A poor man passed my way;
He bound my head, he gave me bread,
He watched me night and day.

IV

How shall I pay him back again
For all he did to me?
Oh, gold is great, but greater far
Is heavenly sympathy!

Q. 1. Suggest a suitable title.
2. How did the proud man treat the poet when he (the poet) lay in sorrow?
3. What did the poet do when his sorrow passed away?
4. How did the poor man treat the poet when he (the poet) lay in grief and pain?
5. Which is greater—gold or sympathy? Give reasons.

Aids

Lay—पड़ा था। *Deep distressed*—बहुत कष्ट में। *Grief*—कष्ट। *Cold*—प्रेम और प्रसन्नतारहित। *Erect*—सीधा। *Spake*—spoke. *Spake my thanks*—thanked.

3

About Ben Adhem (may his tribe increase!)
Awoke one night from a deep dream of peace,
And saw, within the moonlight in his room,
Making it rich, and like a lily in bloom,
An angle writing in a book of gold.
Exceeding peace had made Ben Adhem bold,
And to the presence in the room he said,
"What writest thou?"—The vision rais'd its head,
And with a look made of all sweet accord,
Answered "The names of those who love the Lord."
"And is mine one?" said Abou. "Nay, not so,"
Replied the angel. Abou spoke more low,
But cheerly still; and said, "I pray thee, then,
Write me as one that loves his fellow-men."
The angel wrote, and vanished. The next night
It came again with a great wakening light,
And show'd the names whom love of God had blest.
And lo! Ben Adhem's name led all the rest.

Q. 1. Why should Ben Adhem's tribe increase?
2. What did Ben Adhem see when he awoke from a deep dream of peace?
3. What did he ask the angel and what did the angel reply?
4. Why did Ben Adhem's name top the list of the blessed?
5. Do you love the Lord, or your fellowmen, or your ownself, or all these at the same time, or none at all? Give reasons for your choice.

Aids

Tribe—race (जाति)। *Lily in bloom*—खिली हुई कुमुदिनी। *Exceeding*—बहुत। *Vanished*—disappeared (विलीन हो गया)। *Led all the rest*—सबसे ऊपर था।

4

My hear leaps up when I behold
A rainbow in the sky.
So was it when my life began;
So is it now I am a man,
So be it when I shall grow old,
Or let me die!
The Child is father of the Man;
And I could wish my days to be
Bound each to each by natural piety.

Q. 1. How does the poet feel when he sees a rainbow in the sky?

2. How did he feel when he saw it (rainbow) in his childhood?

3. What feelings does he wish to have towards it in his old age?

4. How do you feel when you see a rainbow?

Aids

Heart leaps up—हृदय आनंदविभोर हो उठता है। *Behold*—देखना। *Life began*—बचपन। *Man*—youngman. *So be it*—ऐसा ही हो। *Days to be*—आनेवाले दिन; भविष्य। *Piety*—पवित्रता।

II. *Read the passages given below and answer the questions that follow.*

1

Ram Mohan Roy was born at Radhanagar in the Hoogly district of Bengal on May 22nd 1772. His father, Ramkanta Roy, had settled at Radhanagar after giving up his post under Siraj-ud-daula, the Nawab of Bengal. He had been unjustly treated by the Nawab, and he also had some trouble about his lands. So, he became somewhat unattached to the world, and generally spent his time in prayer and thinking of God.

Ram Mohan's mother, Tarini Devi, was a very religious woman. She believed faithfully in the sound nature of the Hindu religion as it was then understood. Her great belief is shown by the fact that once she went for a pilgrimage to Puri on foot, without taking even a maidservant with her.

Q. 1. When and where was Ram Mohan Roy born?

2. Why did his father give up his post under Siraj-ud-daula?

3. Give a brief description of his mother.

4. How do you know that his mother had great belief in the Hindu religion?

Aids

Giving up—छोड़ना, त्यागना। *Pilgrimage*—तीर्थयात्रा।

2

Among the many scientists who helped to advance human knowledge, Jagadish Chandra Bose holds an important position. He was born in East Bengal, near Dacca, on November 30, 1858. His father was a Deputy Magistrate at Faridpur where Jagadish spent most of his childhood. He was a very inquisitive child, always asking questions. His father always tried to answer all his questions; he was never told not to ask them. He went to a Bengali school at the age of five, for his father wanted him to learn his own language and get to know his people before taking up English studies.

Jagadish Chandra wanted to go to England and complete his studies there. But there were many difficulties. His father had lost much of his money which he had spent on tea plantation. His mother's love for him was great; she could not think of parting with her only son for so long. It seemed that Jagdish Chandra's hopes would never be fulfilled. He felt sad and discouraged.

However, his mother found that he would not be happy unless he went to England. She made up her mind to bear the sorrow of separation. Now, the only thing was to get money. For such a mother, this was no difficult task either. She sold her jewellery and got the money. So, Jagadish was able to go to England.

1. Describe the early life of Jagadish Chandra Bose.
2. What were his difficulties when he wanted to go to England?
3. How were the difficulties solved?

Aids

Inquisitive—curious (इच्छुक, जिज्ञासु)। *Tea plantation*—चाय-बागान। *Made up her mind*—decided (तय किया)।

3

Portia: Do you admit the bond?

Antonio: I do.

Portia: Then the Jew must be merciful.

Shylock: Must I? Who can force me to show mercy? Tell me that.

Portia: Mercy is never forced. It comes naturally. We should all show mercy to one another.

Shylock: I will have nothing to do with mercy. I ask for justice.

Portia: But justice should always be softened by mercy.

Shylock: I know nothing of that. I must have what is due to me on my bond.

Portia: Is he (Antonio) not able to pay the money?

Bassanio: Yes. Here I offer it for him (Antonio) in the court. I am prepared to pay it ten times over.

Shylock: I will not have it.

Q. 1. How does Portia try to persuade Shylock (the jew) to show mercy?
2. What is Shylock's demand?
3. Which is greater—mercy or justice? Give reasons.

Aids

Softened—मुलायम किया हुआ, मिलाया हुआ। *Due*—बाकी। *Bond*—दस्तावेज।

4

Jumman had an old relation, a maternal aunt who had some property. This she transferred to him by a deed on the understanding that she would be well-looked after. So long as the deed remained unregistered none was so obliging to the old lady as her nephew, none so considerate to her. Her every wish was anticipated and cheerfully carried out. Jumman who used to wait dotingly on his old aunt now became supremely indifferent. His wife, Kariman, went even farther. She grudged even the little food that the old lady ate. No meal was now served to her without Kariman letting loose a barb or two dipped in gall or poison. The very bread that the aunt ate seemed to be seasoned with the meat of abuse. And this went on mounting.

Q. 1. How did Jumman treat his maternal aunt before her property was transferred to him by a deed?

2. How did he and his wife treat her after the deed was registered?

3. Suggest a suitable title.

Aids

Deed—दस्तावेज। *Obliging*—कृतज्ञ। *Considerate*—विवेकशील। *Anticipated*—पहले ही समझ लिया जाता था या अनुमान कर लिया जाता था। *Dotingly*—बहुत प्रेम से। *Wait on*—सेवा करना। *Supremely*—बहुत ही। *Indifferent*—उदासीन। *Grudged*—ईर्ष्या करती थी। *Barb*—तीर की नोक। *Dipped*—डुबाया हुआ। *Gall*—निर्दयता, कठोरता। *Seasoned*—मिलाया हुआ। *Mounting*—बढ़ता हुआ।

5

Arthur journeyed quickly from Ireland on receiving news of his grandfather's death. He was now Squire; and as he travelled towards his home, he thought of all he would have to do for the good of the estate and his tenants. Then he thought of the Poyser family and Hetty. He was at ease now about Hetty, for Mr Irwine's letter had told him of her coming marriage with Adam. He was glad of this pretty little Hetty! So, she had not cared for him half so much as he had cared for her! Well, he certainly was not in love with Hetty now! But he could feel that Hetty's husband had a special claim on him. He felt he could now offer Adam friendship again in spite of that painful memory. Well, here was Hayslope at last! And here was the dear old home! Arthur jumped from the carriage, ran up the steps and entered the house.

"Your letters are waiting for you, Sir", said his servant. Arthur found them on his table and on the top of the heap was one from Mr Irwine. Arthur took it up carelessly and read—

"I send this in a hurry, dear Arthur, because I had to go to Stoniton to perform the most painful duty. I will not add anything to the pain and sorrow that will now come upon you. I must just tell you the simple fact. Hetty Sorrel is in prison, and is awaiting punishment for killing her own child."

Q. 1. Why did Arthur journey quickly from Ireland?

2. What did he think as he travelled towards his home?

3. What were the contents of the letter from Mr Irwine?

Aids

Journeyed—travelled. *Tenants*—प्रजा। *At ease*—comfortable, at peace. *Memory*—याद। *Heap*—ढेर (collection).

....

❐

Chapter XXVI

EXPANSION

Expansion का अर्थ होता है—पल्लवन, अर्थात किसी भाव/विचार का विस्तार करना। इस प्रकार Expansion (पल्लवन) और Explanation (व्याख्या) में बहुत कुछ साम्य है क्योंकि ये दोनों ही भाव/विचार के विस्तृत रूप होते हैं। इस दृष्टि से Expansion (पल्लवन) का विपरीतार्थ है Pecis-writing (संक्षेपण), क्योंकि Expansion होता है बड़ा रूप, पर Precis-writing होता है संक्षिप्त या छोटा रूप।

Expansion के लिए इन बातों का ध्यान रखें—

1. दिए गए वाक्य का अर्थ ठीक से समझें। कभी-कभी छोटे-छोटे वाक्यों (विशेषकर प्रसिद्ध कथनों तथा कहावतों) में गूढ़ भाव कूट-कूटकर भरे रहते हैं। इसलिए दिए गए वाक्य का अर्थ सावधानी से समझने की कोशिश करनी चाहिए।
2. दिए गए वाक्य के भाव/विचार का विस्तार सटीक उदाहरण/वर्णन की सहायता से करें, पर दुहरावट के दोष से अवश्य बचें।
3. विस्तार करने का अर्थ होता है भिन्न-भिन्न दृष्टिकोणों से विचार करना, एक ही बात को बार-बार कहना नहीं। भाव/विचार का खंडन-मंडन या टीका-टिप्पणी न करें।
4. किसी बात का कितना विस्तार किया जाए? मेरे जानते भाव/विचार का विस्तार 15–20 पंक्तियों में किया जाना चाहिए। बहुत अधिक विस्तार कर देने से पल्लवन बन जाता है। व्याख्या (Explanation) और पल्लवन (Expansion) का आकार निबंध से तो छोटा होना ही चाहिए न!
5. अपनी भाषा का प्रयोग करें और व्याकरण के नियमों का ध्यान रखें।

अब Expansion के कुछ नमूने देखें—

1. Birds of A Feather Flock Together

Birds of the same sort live together. Crows live with crows. They can't live in the company of kites and vultures. This is true of insects and animals too. Ants live in company of ants, and dogs live with dogs. Dogs don't like to live with lions and tigers. So, it is with man as well. Good boys keep the company of good boys and bad boys keep the company of bad ones. Scholars like to live with scholars, and not with fools.

In this way, everyone selects the company of his choice. Our taste or like-mindedness decides this selection. Our likes and dislikes play an important role in the selection of our friends.

2. Peace Hath Her Victory No Less Renowned Than War

Which is greater—the victory of war or the victory of peace? A war wins a victory and soldiers and warriors are called conquerors. They are praised for their adventure, sacrifice and glorious conquest.

But victories of war are not lasting. Great conquerors appear and disappear like falling stars. On the contrary, the heroes of peace don't produce a class of victims. The victories of peace bring health and happiness, knowledge and wisdom. War conquers an enemy but peace conquers time and space and opens golden gates to human progress and prosperity. In this way, the victories of peace are more glorious than those of war.

3. Honesty is the Best Policy

Honesty is necessary in every walk of life. You cannot be a good businessman if you are not honest. You may cheat some people for some time and even all people for some time. But you cannot cheat all people for all times. A dishonest shopkeeper may earn a flood of wealth. But a flood, we know, does not last long. In public life, too, honesty is essential. You cannot become a great leader without honesty. A dishonest leader may get wealth and power. But he loses everything very soon. A dishonest leader is not a star. He is only a falling star.

4. Union (Unity) is Strength

What will happen if your fingers are cut off? Your hands will lose their strength. They will not work well. Human body is like a machine. It has hundreds of parts. All the parts work together and give strength to this machine. If even the smallest part goes wrong, this machine can't work. You are able to stand because your legs are united. If one leg is cut off, you will fall down. So, strength lies in unity and cooperation.

A society, too, cannot do without unity. Man is a social animal. He helps others, and others help him in turn. He has to depend on his friends and neighbours. If they are united, the society will be strong. Even birds and animals show a wonderful sense of unity. Ants are very small. But when they unite, they form a strong army. You cannot break a bundle of sticks. But how easily you break them one by one!

5. Waste Not, Want Not

We earn a lot and still we are not happy. Why so? We do not know the art of spending. We spend without any plan. We don't cut our coat according to the cloth. We beg and borrow and even steal to fulfil our wants. We spend a lot over drinking and gambling.

There is a huge waste on the occasion of marriage and other social functions. How foolishly food is wasted! We do not care to save small things. We forget that little drops of water make an ocean. The result is a tragic waste and a miserable life.

6. Sweet Are the Uses of Adversity

Suffering is bitter but the uses of suffering are sweet. The poet rightly says—

> The bud may have a bitter taste,
> But sweet will be the flower.

Adversity is a blessing in disguise. It is a nice training for our heart, mind and soul. The forces of character are brought to light. We pick up greater strength to face life even more bravely.

Suffering is a kind of trial, not a punishment. It comes only to test our merits. Suffering is like hot fire. Fire does not burn a piece of gold. It only purifies it. In the same way, suffering makes us stronger and wiser. It refines our character as fire refines gold.

....

EXERCISE

Expand the idea contained in one of the following.

1. All that glitters is not gold.
2. A stitch in time saves nine.
3. Rome was not built in a day.
4. Slow and steady wins the race.
5. Make hay while the sun shines.
6. To err is human, to forgive divine.
7. Charity begins at home.
8. A bad carpenter quarrels with his tools.
9. The crown and glory of life is character.
10. Example is better than precept.
11. God helps those who help themselves.
12. Look before you leap.

....

❒

A MODEL QUESTION PAPER

(A Question Bank)

1. *Fill in the blanks with* **a/an/the.** **4 marks**

(Questions based on the use of Articles)

1. That is …… HMT watch.
2. That is …… RTC bus.
3. Mohan is …… university student.
4. This is …… one-rupee note.
5. …… Taj Mahal is one of the wonders of the world.
6. He has sent our …… SOS to the government.
7. I have lodged …… FIR with the police.
8. …… Ganges is a sacred river of India.

Or

Add **a/an/the** *where necessary.*

1. Himalayas	2. paper	3. ink
4. butter	5. tobacco	6. milk
7. music	8. hour	9. lime
10. cement	11. Red Fort	12. by car
13. cheese	14. salt	15. sugar
16. grass	17. piece of	18. glass of
19. idea	20. nonsense	21. air
22. dirt	23. coffee	24. sky
25. poet	26. poem	27. poetry
28. rice	29. fish	30. sand

Or

Correct errors in these sentences.

1. We make a butter and cheese from a milk.
2. Window is made of a glass.
3. House is made of a stone and brick.
4. Chair is made of a wood.
5. He is writing letter in an ink.
6. Cigarette is made of a paper and tobacco.
7. Ring is made of a gold or a silver.

Or

Put into the singular.

1. Apple are sweet to eat.
2. Oranges grow on trees.
3. Cows are animals.
4. Eyes are blue or black.
5. Flies are insects.
6. Eggs are white.
7. They are MLAs.
8. We are NCC cadets.
9. They are Europeans.
10. They are university students.
11. These are useful books.
12. They are honest persons.

Or

Make correct sentences from this table.

A	B
This is a	LP School
Dr Sinha is an	Bible
I hit him on the	Kilo
That is an	new idea
He is reading the	MP
Wheat is sold by the	head

2. *Fill in the blanks with an appropriate preposition.* **4 marks**

(Questions based on Preposition)

1. She has been working …… morning.
2. He has lived here …… five years.
3. The baby fell …… a deep ditch.
4. Prizes were distributed …… all the boys.
5. This student is very quick …… figures.
6. That man was prevented …… speaking.
7. This boy is disqualified …… competing.
8. Lots of people have died …… cholera.
9. He went to Delhi …… air and I went …… train.
10. The property was divided …… the two sons.
11. Divide this apple …… four parts.
12. She is lying …… bed.
13. It is written …… pencil.

Or

Fill in the blanks with a preposition given in brackets.

1. That house was destroyed ...... fire. [by, with]
2. My house is within a mile ...... the market. [of, from]
3. The rich lady came here ...... a new red car. [in, by]
4. Engines are worked here ...... steam. [by, with]
5. There is a lonely little house ...... the river. [on, by]
6. It has been raining here ...... a week. [for, since]
7. She has been writing letters ...... 9 o'clock. [for, since]
8. He died ...... loss of blood. [of, from]
9. He is sitting ...... an armchair. [in, on]

Or

Correct errors in these sentences.

1. He has investigated into the case.
2. He has resigned from his post.
3. She has interest and passion for sports.
4. He always persists to do mischief.
5. You must refrain to harm others.
6. The boy is ill since a month.
7. This girl comes from a noble family.
8. Please see me between 5 pm to 6 pm.
9. He insisted me to go to Agra.
10. She is learning English since three years.

Or

Match the words under A and B to make meaningful sentences.

A	B
This window is	by 7 o'clock
She has been dancing	on horeseback
It smells	by her husband
We wash clothes	at painting
I will start	on grass
He is a tailor	a litre of petrol
She sat	of wine
A cow lives	made of glass
I bought	by trade
He travelled	since 9 o'clock
Wheat is sold by the	with soap

3. *Change these sentences into Interrogatives.* **4 marks**

(Questions based on the interchange of Assertives and Interrogatives)

1. She is making tea.
2. They are catching fish.
3. He went home by bus.
4. She didn't inform the police.
5. He always helps me.
6. The blind can't see.
7. What your father's name is.
8. Where you come from.
9. Why she is so happy.
10. How he cleans his teeth.
11. When he learns English.
12. Where she keeps money.
13. Human nature can't change.
14. We should love our mother.
15. We are sent to college to study.

Or

Correct these sentences.

1. Does he knows English?
2. Why you are so angry?
3. When he will come back?
4. Where you keep your books?
5. How you have came here?
6. What he wants to eat?
7. Didn't I warned you last week?
8. You are going to market?

4. *Change the voice of the following sentences.* **4 marks**

(Questions based on the change of Voice)

1. They say that Mohan is honest.
2. Someone stole my watch yesterday.
3. He satisfied everybody.
4. We elected him chairman.
5. She gave me a book.
6. Who gave you this pen?
7. Bring a glass of water.
8. I made them laugh.

9. People consider that he is wise.
10. He wants to be treated as a minister.
11. I saw her cross the road.
12. The Taj Mahal was built by Shahjehan.
13. Who was this poem written by?
14. I was shocked at his conduct.
15. Were you helped by Mohan?
16. She is loking after his baby.

Or

Supply correct forms of verbs given in brackets.

1. The bell is being (ring) now.
2. A new house has been (build) here.
3. Mahatma Gandhi can never be (forget).
4. Books are being (print) here.
5. She has been (give) a prize.
6. Pandit Nehru will always be (remember).
7. He was (appoint) a teacher.
8. The horse was made (drink).
9. He never (see) a sea.
10. I (see) him a month ago.

5. *Rewrite these sentences as directed.* **4 marks**

(Questions based on Time and Tense)

1. He will go to Mumbai next week. (use *Present Simple*)
2. She will buy a car next month. (use *Present Progressive*)
3. He will start a school next year. (use *going to*)
4. She played tennis in her youth. (use *used to*)
5. He leaves for home tomorrow. (use *Future Simple*)
6. The Prime Minister arrives tomorrow. (use *Present Progressive*)
7. He passed the examination last year. (use *Present Perfect*)
8. He is talking all the time. (use *Present Perfect Continuous*)

Or

Fill in the blanks with correct forms of verbs given in brackets.

1. The sun is ...... now. (rise)
2. The president ...... our college tomorrow. (visit)
3. The plane usually ...... here at 9 a.m. (land)
4. The train regularly ...... her at 4 p.m. (arrive)
5. A student ...... to school at 10 a.m. everyday. (go)

6. She ...... her examination last year. (take)
7. He is a vegetarian. He ...... fish. (eat)
8. He is a fisherman. He ...... fish everyday. (sell)
9. The baby is hungry. He ...... now. (cry)
10. Mohan ...... to me for over two months. (not write)
11. I ...... her since 1983. (not see)
12. Radha ...... to the picture on Sundays. (go)
13. He is not at home; he just ...... for Mumbai. (leave)
14. I already ...... the work. (finish)
15. I will wait here until she .... (return)
16. Never before I ...... such a lovely sight. (see)
17. No sooner the police ...... than he fled away. (reach)
18. It is time we ...... home. (return)
19. Hardly I ...... to bed when I had a dream. (go)
20. Use a candle in case electricity .... (fail)
21. Please come back before it ...... dark. (grow)
22. Students go to their class after the bell .... (ring)
23. Unless he works hard he ...... success. (get)
24. As I started in time I ...... the train. (catch)
25. Seven years have passed since I ...... here. (come)
26. She ...... in the kitchen since morning. (cook)
27. I ...... here since 1975. (live)
28. He ...... in this office for five years. (work)
29. I ...... my parents a month ago. (meet)
30. While I write books she ...... TV. (watch)
31. Doesn't he look as if he ...... a ghost? (be)
32. What is he doing now? He ...... fish. (catch)
33. What will you do after passing Bachelor Examination? I ...... a Competitive Examination. (sit for)
34. What are you doing these days? I ...... my examination. (prepare for)
35. What did she buy yesterday? She ...... a lot of toys. (buy)
36. If you touch electricity you ...... a shock. (receive)
37. Didn't he ...... sweets for you? (bring)
38. Doesn't your mother ...... you? (love)
39. She has been ...... all the time. (talk)
40. Where he ...... these days? (live)
41. When I ...... the door I opened the safe. (close)
42. Mohan ...... the work after Sohan began. (finish)

43. We saw him ...... the road. (cross)

44. Newton saw an apple .... (fall)

45. He got the house .... (build)

46. It is no use ...... now. (repent)

Or

Correct errors in these sentences.

1. He is leaving for home last week.
2. I have passed the examination last year.
3. The sun is sets in the west.
4. Never before I saw such a sight.
5. He is usually going to school at 10 o'clock.
6. The plane is normally taking off at 9 o'clock.
7. She is flying to London yesterday.
8. We have been learn English for five years.
9. She is going to buy a car last week.
10. I am going to the cinema on Sundays.
11. Take an umbrella in case it will rain.
12. You can't catch the bus if you will start late.
13. Don't get off a bus until it will stop.
14. I will return home before it will grow dark.
15. No sooner I reached the station that the train whistled off.
16. He made me to sing.
17. I heard her to whisper.
18. I saw her to cross the road.
19. He was made laugh.
20. She was let to go.
21. I can't help to laugh.
22. He avoids to see me.

Or

Put a tick (✓) by the right words.

1. We seldom $\frac{\text{go}}{\text{are going}}$ to college on holidays.
2. The teacher never $\frac{\text{sleeps}}{\text{is sleeping}}$ in the class.
3. He often $\frac{\text{catches}}{\text{is catching}}$ cold in winter.
4. The sun is $\frac{\text{rises}}{\text{rising}}$ now.

5. The Prime Minister arrives tomorrow / yesterday.
6. He has written me a letter last week / this morning.
7. He usually wakes / is waking up early in the morning.

Or

Match the words under A and B to make correct sentences.

A	B
He reached here	yesterday.
I have passed the examination	a month ago.
He will	leaves for home tomorrow.
She returned	next morning.
I saw him	this year.
Mr Sinha	sail for London next week.

Or

Distinguish between these pairs of sentences.

1. She lives in London.
2. She is living in London.
3. He comes from Madras.
4. He is coming from Madras.
5. She plays tennis.
6. She is playing tennis.
7. The sun rises in the east.
8. The sun is rising in the east.

6. *Join these sentences.* **3 marks**

(Questions based on Synthesis)

1. Is he ill? I don't know.
2. He is innocent. I know this.
3. Who is he? I can't say.
4. Where is she? I don't know.
5. When will he come? Tell me.
6. I am not rich. I wish to know him.
7. I do not know him. I wish to know him.
8. I didn't know him. I wished to know him.
9. He finished the work. Then he went out.
10. The bus stopped. Then I got off.
11. This diary is small. It can go into my pocket.
12. This diary is big. It can't go into my pocket.
13. We watched the children. They were playing.
14. The plane took off. We saw.

Combine these sentences as directed.

1. She is very poor. She can't buy a car. [use *so ...... that*]
2. He is very rich. He can buy a big house. [use *so ...... that*]
3. He was punished. He had stolen my pen. [use *for + gerund*]
4. She sings songs. She earns a lot of money. [use *by + gerund*]
5. He was very glad. He heard the news. [use *infinitive*]
6. He drew his sword. He rushed at the enemy. [use *participle*]
7. The mango fell. We saw. [use *infinitive without to*]
8. He is poor. He is happy. [use *though/although*]
9. Work hard. You will pass. [use *if/unless*]
10. Mohan is tall. Radha is tall. [use *as + adj. + as*]
11. Mohan is tall. Radha is very tall. [use *not as + adj. + is*]
12. He is rich. He is unhappy. [use *adj. + as*]
13. She didn't go to Agra. She didn't see the Taj. [use *if + past perfect*]

7. *Complete these sentences.*

(Questions based on Analysis—structures used in textbooks)

1. Although he is young ....
2. Though she is old ....
3. If I were an examiner ....
4. ...... because he was ill.
5. ...... since he came here.
6. ...... he would have seen the Red Fort.
7. ...... that he can't buy a car.
8. ...... in case electricity fails.
9. ...... you can't catch the bus.
10. ...... as if the path wouldn't end.

Or

Match the clauses under A and B to make meaningful sentences.

A	B
However hard you may try	that she fell ill.
I believe it	what you are doing now.
Note it down	shouldn't throw stones.
Rich as he is	since I saw him.
She worked so hard	you can't get success.
Please tell me	since you say so.
Those who live in glass houses	so that you may not forget it.
Five years have passed	he is not very happy.

8. *Fill in the blanks with a correct word.* **4 marks**

(Questions based on Subject and Verb)

1. There ...... a number of books in the library. [is, are]
2. There ...... still lots to do at home. [is, are]
3. Nothing but umbrellas ...... seen here. [is, are]
4. Neither of these roads ...... safe today. [is, are]
5. What he needs most ...... books. [is, are]
6. Our only guide ...... the stars. [was, were]
7. Each of them ...... finished the work. [has, have]
8. Neither he nor his parents ...... come. [has, have]
9. No boy and no girl ...... come today. [has, have]
10. The eyes of an elephant ...... very small. [is, are]
11. He as well as I ...... singing songs. [is. am]
12. She and I ...... walking together. [is, am, are]
13. She ...... not write to me any more. [need, needs]
14. If I ...... he, I would not do it. [was, were]
15. The jury ...... divided in their opinions. [was, were]
16. His knowledge of Indian languages ...... imperfect. [is, are]
17. The robber with all his associates ...... escaped. [has, have]
18. The colour of these shirts ...... blue. [is, are]
19. Both the bus and the train ...... unsafe these days. [is, are]
20. The bouquet of flowers ...... very lovely. [is, are]

Or

Correct errors in these sentences.

1. Can you see what appear to be a bird?
2. Many a men were injured.
3. The price of foodstuffs have gone up?
4. Lots of poison have been brought today.
5. The number of fools are increasing everyday.
6. Three tons of coal are enough for me.
7. The following is the new rates of taxation.
8. It is I who has always helped him.
9. It is one of the best men that has ever liked.
10. The poet and philosopher are dead now.
11. Each man and each woman are of the same view.
12. Bread and butter are a nice food.
13. The horse and carriage are waiting at the gate.

14. The thief as well as his sons were arrested.
15. The teacher with all his students have arrived now.
16. She, not less than you are responsible for this.
17. The thief, and not his sons, were arrested.
18. Neither she nor I is really guilty.
19. Either of these are unsafe.
20. Neither of the two boys are strong.
21. More books than one has been bought.
22. Many a man were killed in the accident.
23. Each of the students have homework to do.
24. They do not know to swim.
25. He has given his examination.
26. This is the best of the two pens.

Or

Match the words under A and B to make correct sentences.

A	B
He as well as I	are singing.
He, and not his sons	are weak.
Nothing but trees	have arrived today.
A part of the mangoes	has been prepared.
The wheels each	has been bought.
She and I	is listening to the radio.
The teeth of the baby	was found guilty.
A number of leaders	is seen everywhere.
Lots of food	are rotten.
More than one book	have fine spokes.

9. *Change the Direct Speech into the Indirect.* **4 marks**

(Questions based on Narration)

1. He told me, "Good morning. I am glad to see you."
2. She told me, "Are you sad? Why are you so sad?"
3. I told him, "Will you send me some money?"
4. He told me, "See me tomorrow, will you?"
5. I told her, "You are very rich, aren't you?"
6. He told me, "Please lend me your umbrella."
7. The teacher told us, "Don't write on desks and tables."
8. The doctor told me, "Take medicine on time."
9. The teacher told us, "Let no one come late."

10. The boy said, "Let it rain ever so hard, I will go out."
11. Radha told us, "Let us arrange a picnic tomorrow."
12. We all said, "How sweetly she sings!"
13. We all said, "What a nice place it is!"
14. He said, "What a fall, my friends!"
15. He said, "Nonsense!"
16. He told me, "Fool! Lier!"
17. She told me, "Happy Dipawali."
18. I told her, "Congratulations."
19. He told me, "Thank you very much."
20. He told me, "I must start at once."
21. I told her, "Shall I thread the needle?"
22. He told me, "Bravo! You have done well."

Or

Change the Indirect Speech into the Direct Speech.

1. I forbade him to write on walls.
2. He requested me to lend him my pen.
3. I told him to show me his homework.
4. He asked me whether I would help him.
5. I asked him not to smoke in my office.
6. He told me that he would leave for Delhi next day.
7. We all exclaimed with joy that we had won the match.
8. He asked me what my name was.
9. I asked her why she was so angry.
10. She advised me to take exercise daily.
11. He asked me where I was living.
12. He told me that it had been raining for a week.

Or

Correct errors in these sentences.

1. He forbade me not to smoke near a petrol pump.
2. I asked him that what you have been doing.
3. He told me that I will leave for Mumbai tomorrow.
4. He told the servant that bring a cup of tea.
5. She asked me that if I am in need of money.
6. I asked him that whether you have any money on you.
7. She told me that I have been looking since morning.

Or

Match the words under A and B to make correct sentences.

A	B
Mohan says	that she would buy a car.
He forbade me	not to touch a live wire.
She asked me	that we should live together.
I told them	if I could lend her my bicycle.
Radha told me	that he will take his exam. next week.
He asked me	to make a noise in the class.
He proposed	that I was glad to see them.

10. *Punctuate the following passage using capital letters where necessary.* **3 marks**

(Questions based on Punctuation)

what the matter ram asked mr prasad why are you crying is it that pain in your leg no sir said ram I have hurt my brother mohan and am sorry thats all right if you are sorry then go and tell him and shake hands he will love you again

Or

alas he is dead may he die what a lovely place it is what are you doing now

11. *Use the following Idioms/Phrases in sentences of your own.* **4 marks**

(Questions based on Idioms and Phrases)

1. apple of discord
2. bed of roses
3. blue blood
4. gala day
5. cold war
6. castle in the air
7. lion's share
8. maiden speech
9. open secret
10. snake in the grass
11. white elephant
12. wild goose chase
13. yellow journalism
14. swan song
15. utopian scheme
16. witch hunt
17. wool gathering
18. small fry

Or

1. at home in
2. attend to
3. break out
4. come upon
5. get rid of
6. face the music
7. keep out
8. keep on
9. look into
10. make up one's mind
11. pin one's hope/faith
12. turn out
13. steal a march
14. a rainy day

Match the words under A and B to make meaningful sentences.

A	B
This project seems to be	in the same coin
He was beaten	a red carpet welcome.
She was shedding	tooth and nail.
He was paid back	due to rash driving.
The Prime Minister was given	black and blue.
He opposed me	crocodile tears.
The accident was	a Penelope's web.

12. *Correct these sentences.* **6 marks**

(Questions based on common errors in the use of different Parts of Speech)

1. I like the poetries of Wordsworth.
2. The sceneries of Kashmir are charming.
3. All the furniture were burnt to ashes.
4. All your informations are wrong.
5. He has sold away his old machineries.
6. The gentries of the town were invited.
7. Dr Sinha is a man of words.
8. Indians have black hairs.
9. This house is made of bricks.
10. One must do his duties well.
11. Neither of the four sisters is married.
12. The mother was too glad to see her son.
13. I prevented him to drink in the office.
14. He prefers to die than to live in misery.
15. She reached the station after the train arrived.
16. Reading in the library, my dog began to bark.
17. Please don't mind me to come late.
18. If you will touch electricity you will receive a shock.
19. If she had gone to Delhi she will have seen the Red Fort.
20. Which is easier—Hindi, English or Sanskrit?
21. I went to market but didn't buy some sugar.
22. This box is five times heavier than that.
23. He is one of the tallest if not the tallest man.
24. Football is more popular than all games.
25. How is the patient now? He is comparatively better.
26. Work hard lest you shouldn't fail.

27. I, you and she are friends.
28. This is a most unique book.
29. He picked up a quarrel with me.
30. I couldn't catch up his words.
31. She is taller and better than me.
32. This pen is more inferior than that.
33. Not only I lost my book but also my bag.
34. All my family members are in Mumbai.
35. He bought a book for his son in three colours.
36. If he had not been poor, he will be very great.
37. If a tiger came here, all will flee away.

Or

Put a tick (✓) by the right words.

1. Mohan is more brave than $\frac{\text{wise}}{\text{wiser}}$.
2. She was $\frac{\text{kind enough}}{\text{enough kind}}$ to help me.
3. There are $\frac{\text{less}}{\text{fewer}}$ girls than boys here.
4. He seldom $\frac{\text{or ever}}{\text{or never}}$ tells lies.
5. He has neither a car $\frac{\text{or}}{\text{nor}}$ a scooter.
6. She has no pen $\frac{\text{or}}{\text{nor}}$ pencil.
7. Each of us $\frac{\text{has}}{\text{have}}$ $\frac{\text{his}}{\text{our}}$ own problems.
8. Newton saw an apple $\frac{\text{fall}}{\text{to fall}}$.
9. He had rather $\frac{\text{to die}}{\text{die}}$ than $\frac{\text{beg}}{\text{to beg}}$.
10. She had better $\frac{\text{rest}}{\text{to rest}}$ than $\frac{\text{work}}{\text{to work}}$.
11. He is enjoying full $\frac{\text{freeship}}{\text{free studentship}}$.
12. He has applied for $\frac{\text{lecturership}}{\text{lectureship}}$.

13. He is given free $\frac{\text{boarding}}{\text{board}}$ and lodging.

14. Unless you $\frac{\text{work hard}}{\text{don't work hard}}$, you can't pass.

15. What's your age? I am $\frac{\text{twenty}}{\text{twenty years old}}$.

13. (a) *Form nouns from these verbs/adjectives.* **16 marks**

(Questions based on Vocabulary)

1. add	2. accomplish	3. arrange
4. determine	5. disburse	6. examine
7. prepare	8. introspect	9. infatuate
10. suggest	11. speak	12. steal
13. indignant	14. impatient	15. immense
16. civil	17. contemptuous	18. empty
19. complex	20. rare	21. generous
22. scarce	23. humble	24. proper

Or

Rewrite these sentences as directed.

1. He looks like a sheep. [use *sheep* as an *adjective*]
2. He reads this book. [use *read* as a *noun*]
3. He has affection for me. [use *affection* as an *adjective*]
4. She admires me. [use *admire* as a *noun*]
5. This is a cowardly action. [use *cowardly* as a *noun*]
6. This river abounds in fish. [use *abound* as a *noun*]
7. When does the train arrive? [use *arrive* as a *noun*]
8. I will pay him Rs 100. [use *pay* as a *noun*]

(b) *Make sentences with the following pairs of words.*

1. lesson—lessen	2. duel—dual	3. council—counsel
4. nose—knows	5. mist—missed	6. place—plaice
7. cease—seize	8. border—boarder	9. advice—advise
10. wait—weight	11. stare—stair	12. story—storey
13. soldier—shoulder	14. principal—principle	15. check—cheque
16. coarse—course	17. alter—altar	18. access—excess
19. canvass—canvas	20. accept—except	21. berth—birth

(c) *Fill in the blanks with the opposites of the words in italics.*

1. The *entrance* is wide but ...... is narrow.
2. This post is *temporary* but that is ....

3. The *guilty* were punished but the …… were rewarded.
4. *Prosperity* unites but …… divides men.
5. I prefer *modern* history to …… history.
6. Ram is *kind* but Shyam is …… .
7. My income has *decreased* but expenditure has …… .
8. *Natural* behaviour is better than an …… one.
9. This piece of land is *fertile* but that is …… .
10. This train has *arrived* but that has …… .
11. India wants *peace* but other nations want …… .
12. The wife lives in *hope* but the husband is sinking into …… .
13. She is *smiling* but he is …… .
14. Glass is *transparent* but iron is …… .
15. He is an *optimist* but she is a …… .
16. I *agree* to this proposal but he …… .
17. This knife is *blunt* but that is …… .
18. She is *gentle* but he is …… .
19. We *won* the match but they …… .
20. This is very *vague* but that is …… .

Or

Which of the words given in brackets is opposite in meaning to the word italicised in each of these sentences?

1. I don't *remember* that story.
   [*know, deny, forget, agree*]
2. This sentence is *correct.*
   [*false, untrue, incorrect, good*]
3. You statement is *true.*
   [*good, bad, false, incorrect*]
4. This is a very *slow* train.
   [*quick, safe, fast, dull*]
5. She is very cruel.
   [*polite, kind, affectionate, just*]
6. This is a *sharp* knife.
   [*dull, rusty, blunt, costly*]
7. When does the train *arrive*?
   [*sail, take off, depart, reach*]
8. He doesn't have *many* pens.
   [*much, little, few, less*]

9. He has *lost* his bag.
   [*caught, found, brought, sold*]
10. The place is quite *safe.*
   [*bad, unsafe, unpleasant*]
11. She is very *beautiful.*
   [*unpleasant, cruel, ugly, indecent*]

Or

Fill in the blanks with a word given below.

1. The opposite of democracy is …… .
   (a) army (b) dictatorship (c) civil (d) imperialism
2. The opposite of rest is …… .
   (a) speed (b) motion (c) race (d)work
3. The opposite of virtue is …… .
   (a) voice (b) ice (c) vice (d) innocence
4. The opposite of junior is …… .
   (a) smaller (b) younger (c) senior (d) older
5. The opposite of nothing is …… .
   (a) something (b) anything (c) everything
6. The opposite of sane is …… .
   (a) bad (b) sad (c) mad (d) wise
7. The opposite of pride is …… .
   (a) nobility (b) humility (c) guilty (d) safety

Or

Add the right prefix to each of these words to make a word opposite in meaning.

1. regular 2. known 3. friendly
4. pleasure 5. religious 6. relevant
7. movable 8. legal 9. natural
10. rational 11. noble 12. kind
13. satisfactory 14. exhaustible 15. satisfied
16. decent 17. courtesy 18. convenient
19. competent 20. important

Or

Use the following prefixes/suffixes to form words.

Prefixes: im, in, ir, ig, un, de, dis, mis.

Suffixes: er, or, un, en, ed, est, ish, ship.

(d) *Give single words which mean the following.*

1. One who believes in fate.
2. One who attacks first.
3. One who lives on vegetables.
4. One whose wife is dead.
5. That which is not vague.
6. That which can't be avoided.
7. That which can't be known.
8. That which can't be believed.
9. That which can't be thought of.
10. That which can't be imagined.

Or

Match the words under A and B to make meaningful sentences.

A	B
One who walks in sleep is called	a somniloquist.
We keep our clothes in	illegible.
One who knows everything is	omnipotent.
One who talks in sleep is called	a somnambulist.
That which can't be read is	a wardrobe.
One who is all powerful is	omniscient.

Or

In the following sentences a number of choices to each sentence are given but only one of them is right. Write the one that is right.

1. A thermometer measures (a) light.
   (b) sound.
   (c) temperature.
2. Asthma is a (a) country.
   (b) fruit.
   (c) disease.
   (d) game.
3. Choloroform is a (a) tree.
   (b) bird.
   (c) food.
   (d) medicine.

4. Fertiliser is a kind of food for (a) cats.
(b) dogs.
(c) horses.
(d) plants.
5. Protein is a kind of (a) play.
(b) poem.
(c) story.
(d) food.
6. A telescope helps you (a) sing.
(b) laugh.
(c) dance.
(d) see.
7. A dentist (a) writes novels.
(b) teaches grammar.
(c) pulls out teeth.
(d) washes clothes.
8. We wear glasses (a) to play with.
(b) to see with.
(c) to write with.
(d) to walk with.
9. We go to church (a) to prey.
(b) to pray.
(c) to play.
(d) to drink.
10. A stenographer is (a) a photographer.
(b) a doctor.
(c) a lender.
(d) a clerk.
11. Bacteria (a) give milk.
(b) cause disease.
(c) cause poverty.
12. X-ray is a kind of (a) animal.
(b) bird.
(c) game.
(d) photograph.

13. We go to an editor for (a) food.
(b) clothes.
(c) medicines.
(d) news.

14. A person who mends shoes is (a) a carpenter.
(b) a cobbler.
(c) a sailor.

Or

Match the words under A with their meanings under B.

A	B
adversary	a common language over an area
titillate	one who hands on knowledge
solicitous	a set of rooms
wholesome	a hater of women
panegyric	a belt in the form of a ring
entourage	one who suffers for a noble cause
hatter	ruled by one's wife
lingua-franca	a opponent in a contest
misogynist	to excite pleasantly
torch-bearer	favourable to one's health
martyr	a circle of friends/attendants
henpecked	one who makes or sells hats
lifebuoy	a piece of writing in praise of
suite	anxious to help or serve

Or

Use the following words in sentences of your own.

1. faint-hearted	2. frivolous	3. giddiness
4. genuine	5. healer	6. intensive
7. inanimate	8. lagoon	9. legend
10. trifle	11. pellets	12. menu
13. musty	14. retaliate	15. quest
16. recess	17. conjure	18. clumsy

Or

Correct the spelling of these words.

1. fourty	2. nineth	3. untill	4. governer
5. athelet	6. altogather	7. agresor	8. massanger

9. violance	10. genious	11. vencher	12. suple
13. pinning	14. writting	15. plannet	16. piramyd
17. Tagor	18. expantion	19. gramer	20. introgative
21. Toolstoi	22. Aldus	23. Gardinar	24. Shelly
25. concel	26. lonly	27. sieze	28. shudering
29. prepair	30. persue	31. imense	32. presision

Or

Correct errors in these sentences.

1. He has gone to a fare.
2. She has not paid the train fair.
3. I am reading a storey now.
4. Please weight here a minute.
5. I want a glass of bear.
6. We wash clothes with shop.
7. The rain has seized now.
8. Which is the shortest root to the station?
9. I believe in plane living.
10. It is quiet impossible.

14. *Expand the idea contained in these sentences.* **10 marks**

(Questions based on Expansion)

1. A rolling stone gathers no moss.
2. Honesty is the best policy.
3. Sweet are the uses of adversity.
4. A bad carpenter quarrels with his tools.
5. Rome was not built in a day.
6. Where there is a will there is a way.
7. A stitch in time saves nine.
8. He that is down needs fear no fall.
9. Early to bed and early to rise
   Makes a man healthy, wealthy and wise.

15. *Read this passage carefully and answer the questions that follow.* **12 marks**

(Questions based on Comprehension)

Gandhiji always loved his people—Muslims as much as Hindus. Even when Pakistan was formed, he spoke for the Muslims of India who were comparatively so few in number. Many Hindus thought that he favoured the Muslims too much. Nathuram Godse held misguided ideas of this kind. At a prayer meeting at Birla House in New Delhi, Godse shot Gandhiji on 30th January, 1948. The great Mahatma died with 'Hey

Ram' on his lips. He was murdered, yet he was calm and peaceful even in death. It seemed as if he were sleeping.

I. Why was Gandhiji shot dead?

II. Where and when was he murdered?

III. How did he look after his death?

IV. Which of these statements are *right* and which are *wrong*?

(a) Gandhiji seldom loved his people.

(b) He didn't love Muslims as much as he loved Hindus.

(c) He loved Muslims and Hindus alike.

(d) He favoured the Muslims too much.

(d) Godse didn't hold misguided ideas.

V. Use **even** and **as if** in sentences of your own.

VI. Change the voice of—

(a) He was murdered. (b) Godse shot him dead.

❒